Restored America

Restored America

A TOUR GUIDE

The Preserved Towns, Villages
and Historic City Districts of
the United States and Canada

Alice Cromie

AMERICAN LEGACY PRESS
New York

To Barbara, Donna, Joan and Karel,
with love

Maps by Bill O'Brien
Copyright © 1979 by Alice Cromie

Originally published as *Restored Towns and Historic Districts of America*

This 1984 edition is published by American Legacy Press,
distributed by Crown Publishers, Inc., by arrangement with E.P. Dutton, Inc.

Manufactured in the United States of America

Library of Congress Cataloging in Publication Data

Cromie, Alice.
  Restored America.

  Previously published as: Restored towns and historic
districts of America. 1979.
    1. Historic sites—United States—Guide-books.
  2. Historic districts—United States—Guide-books.
  3. United States—Description and travel—1951-1980—
  Guide-books.   4. Architecture—United States—Guide-books.
  5. United States—History, Local.   I. Title.
  E159.C84   1984   917.3   83-22429
  ISBN: 0-517-426099

  h g f e d c b a

CONTENTS

MAPS

ACKNOWLEDGMENTS

Once again I would like to thank my husband, Bob Cromie, and my editor, Bill Doerflinger, a magician in more ways than one, without whom this book would not have been possible.

About 150 persons in North America and Hawaii aided immeasurably with valuable information, and it would be a pleasure to list them all if space allowed. Among those who must be thanked for help well beyond first aid or call of duty: the late Stanley Huffman Armstrong; my brother Frank Bertrand Hamilton; my long-and-usually-loud-suffering offspring, Mike, Rick, Barb, Jamie, and their mates; nine grandchildren who put up with having their three-hit ball games or baptisms or birthday parties missed; and many incomparable toilers in the fields of travel or history or both: Elmer C. Whiddon, Jr., Tyler Hardeman, Hugh DeSamper, Christianna Hills, Bill Chadwick, Agnes Conrad, Henry Bartels, G. Donald Adams, Dick Carlin, Sharon Eason, Dorothy Millikan, Sylvia McNair, Shirley Newman, Jim Luckey, Jenny Stacy, Bert Fireman, Harold Haney, Ray Scott, Bob Koebbe, Stewart Trisler, Len Barnes, Bill Burchardt, Don Russell, Richard Dunlop, Bern Keating, Ralph Newman, Al Reese, Jeanne McKown, Ginger Sisco, Augie Schultheis, John Davy, Earle G. Shettleworth, Jr., Lloyd Van Meter, Joice Veselka, William S. Wallace, John Weaver, Bill Worthen, Sheila Tryk, Tony Hillerman, Scottie King, Kay Nelms, Mary Jane Bremner, Bill Hensley, Patricia Kelly, Marian Paoliello, Edith Herman, Don Wick, Bob Elmore, Polly Mace Lewis, Lynne Babcock, Evelyn Echols, Jim Hoobler, Marty Sladek, Peter Rippe, Eugene Roark, Bob Kunz, Leonard Panaggio, Mrs. James J. W. Biggers, Jr., Mrs. J. Riley Gettys, Janet Fuhrman, John M. Franz, Michela Z. Hall, Dee Dickson, Marge Studer, Sam McKelvey, Jr., Steve Pisni, Norman Bermes, Jocelyn Dumont-Jerome, John MacBean, Betty Blake, Marion Culp, Ivan Sandrof, and a dozen others. And one loud hurrah for mapmaker Bill O'Brien!

INTRODUCTION

To the old American habit of tearing down historical and architectural landmarks to make room for more profitable banalities, under the guise of progress, many observers have attested. In 1831, for example, an editorial writer in the *New York Mirror* commented on the printed picture of a house that had been demolished:

"We present to our readers a correct and striking view of an ancient Dutch house, formerly familiarly known as Old Seventy-Six, and which was pulled down about three years ago, in compliance with that irreverence for antiquity which so grievously afflicts the people of this city, many of whom, we are credibly informed, demolish one house just for the pleasure of building another in its place."

And in *Harpers' Weekly* for January 19, 1861, a disgruntled citizen of New York wrote an editorial on "Old Houses":

"Somehow we seem resolved in this country that we will have no visible relics of the older epochs of our history. . . . when you saunter up the busy street, where you cannot find a footing upon the sidewalks, they are so crowded with carts and barrels and bales, and remember the quiet Dutch dwelling-houses and broad stoops that lined the street a hundred and fifty years ago, long before we had our Government and a President. . . . Alack! Alack! what is that foolish imitation of a white Greek temple that stares at you with new, columnar insolence?"

In 1965, in a foreword to *America's Historic Houses and Restorations* (New York: Hawthorn Books), Irving Haas understandably mourned:

"These are perilous times for the pitifully few historical landmarks remaining to us. In the countryside, as in towns and cities, historical buildings and sites are menaced today as never before. Each year our precious heritage of 'living history' falls victim to abuse, neglect and destruction. The enemies are poorly planned highway programs, exploding suburbs, urban blight, and the voracious demands for parking space. As one leading worker for preservation, Lewis Mumford, puts it, 'Our national flower may yet be the cement cloverleaf.' "

But in the second half of this century there has come a counter-movement. In less than two decades the picture has almost totally changed. There is a restoration and preservation boom in America today. More and more civic and history-minded persons are joining organizations, mainly nonprofit, or creating new societies to save our national heritage, and this effort is being made on national, state, city, and individual levels.

When my editor, William Doerflinger, and I first talked of preparing a guide to the major restorations and historic districts of the United States and Canada, he was thinking first in terms of the fine longstanding places such as Williamsburg, Greenfield Village, Sturbridge, Batsto, Storrowton, etc., and I, living in the Midwest and having spent much time in the far West lately, was thinking of the California restorations at Bakersfield, Monterey, San Diego, and Jacksonville Historic District, among others. When much of the information was compiled we found we had run at least 85,000 words too long for a book anyone could easily use. The National Register of Historic Places, which constituted a large but manageable volume in its 1973 edition, by its 1976 volume had acquired 961 pages, and heaven help the preservationist who drops it on his toe. The Register, for sale by the Superintendent of Documents, U.S. Government Printing Office, Washington, D.C. 20402, was prepared in the Office of Archeology and Historic Preservation and contains descriptions of all properties of sufficient historical significance to merit listing. These include areas of the National Park System, others listed in accordance with acts of Congress or Executive orders, designations as National Historic Landmarks by the Secretary of the Interior, and nominations from state and federal agencies. Additions are published in the Federal Register, a paperback listing also for sale by the U.S. Government Printing Office.

Authorized by the National Historic Preservation Act of 1966, the scope of the National Register was broadened to include properties of state and local as well as national importance, and it has grown from 1,500 properties in 1969, mostly National Historic Landmarks, to some 12,000 in June 1976. This includes more than 1,000 districts and many facets of American history: prehistoric sites, 18th-century missions and forts, 19th-century furnaces, canals, covered bridges, and government buildings, as well as a variety of dwellings from a barrio in San Antonio to the waterfront of Boston. There is now a system of State Historic Preservation Officers appointed by the governors of the states and territories and the mayor of the District of Columbia. The Historic Sites Act of 1935 also led to the establishment of HABS (the Historic American Buildings Survey), NHL (the National Historic Landmarks program) and the Historic American Engineering Record.

Many organizations issue helpful pamphlets for communities wanting to preserve their best heritage. The American Association for State and Local History, 1315 Eighth Ave., S., Nashville, Tennessee, 37203, has a fine list including such items as "Log Cabin Restoration," "Documenting Collections," "Historic Landscapes and Gardens," and so on.

The National Trust for Historic Preservation, chartered in 1949 to further the national policy of preserving for public benefit our heritage sites, maintains a number of fine buildings such as Woodrow Wilson House and Decatur House, Washington, D.C.; Chesterwood, Stockbridge, Massachusetts; Oatlands, Leesburg, Virginia; Woodlawn Plantation, and Pope-Leighey House, Mount Vernon, Virginia; Lyndhurst, Tarrytown, New York; Cliveden, Philadelphia, Pennsylvania; Shadows-on-the-Teche, New Iberia, Louisiana, and Drayton Hall, Charleston, South Carolina. It also publishes many fine books and pamphlets on restoration and preservation. A private, nonprofit group chartered by Congress, its headquarters are at 740–748 Jackson Place, N.W., Washington, D.C. 20006; phone (202) 638-5200. As merely one indication of the growth of new interest in heritage saving, the National Trust in 1974 had 50,000 members. In 1978 more than 121,000 individuals, organizations, and corporations made up the membership.

Another nonprofit group which dispenses good information on how to improve your local lands is the Small Towns Institute, P.O. Box 517, Ellensburg, Washington 98926. This organization publishes *Small Town*, a monthly newsjournal to bring new ideas and resources to citizens and businessmen in small communities across the nation. To illustrate briefly the kind of follow-up which has taken place, Albia, Iowa, a typical Iowa county seat with its main businesses surrounding the courthouse, has been sandblasted, painted, tuck-pointed, and grouted to a new beauty which it probably didn't have in its Victorian beginnings when local persons got interested in sprucing up the town. *Once Upon a Town,* a liberally illustrated booklet, has been published by the Albia Chamber of Commerce, 107 S. Clinton St., Albia, Iowa 52531, and also can be obtained from the Economic Development & Research Department of Iowa Southern Utilities. It was written by Robert W. Larson, a newspaperman and one of the many Albians who takes an extra interest in his town. The aid of the Iowa Development Commission and the Northern Natural Gas Co. was enlisted to complete the project begun by civic-minded individuals.

Restorations are not confined to wealthy estates, nor to any particular ethnic background. There is a Black Heritage Trail in Boston. A number of Indian villages are being restored, a notable example being Tsa-La-Gi, in the area of Tahlequah, Oklahoma, with others of growing interest. To mention examples is to run the danger of omitting others of equal importance.

This guide has tried to include all restorations that are sincerely done, whether large or small, and to exclude the honky-tonk. But American enterprise is hard to hold back. I remember with dismay standing in the lobby of a motel in Gettysburg a number of years ago and seeing a sign that told me I was at that moment astride the advance line of the Confederates on one of those sad days in July 1863. One hopes the popcorn, postcard, and pizza vendors can be held back from the historic and hallowed grounds. But visitors should be allowed to enter respectfully and see how America lived, wherever historical sites are properly maintained by organizations or individuals.

Unfortunately a guidebook is always out of date by the time it leaves the compiler's typewriter; the only sure thing is change. This is why we did not include admission prices and hours, unless they seemed reasonably steady and likely to remain so. In states where there is an abundance of historic sites, particularly all of those settled early and thickly, not all places of importance could be listed, but history-minded travelers will wander and discover the best of everywhere. In the 1960s, when I first began to write about history and travel, I was timid about approaching strangers for information. My husband, who had written *The Great Chicago Fire; Dillinger: A Short and Violent Life,* and other books based on research, told me I would soon find everyone wants to help someone "write a book." He said, "You'll soon find a lot of people absolutely insist on helping you." And this proved true: I stopped in a southern Ohio store to buy a pillow so I could nap in the back seat of the car. The clerk knew I was a stranger in town and couldn't contain her curiosity about why I had made, to her mind, an odd purchase and didn't want anything that was on sale that day. Recklessly I explained I was writing a book about the Civil War. Before I could say "Ulysses S. Grant save me," I was in the manager's office looking at his fine memorabilia of World War I when he had flown with Eddie Rickenbacker. He insisted on quitting work for the day and taking me to see where Dan Emmett lived when he composed "Dixie," and a dozen other places unknown to me but useful for the guide. But you don't have to write a book; just look interested wherever you are—someone will have great local stories to relate.

Because the larger cities have such fine bureaus of information for visitors, and the older restorations, such as Williamsburg, Greenfield Village, Sturbridge, although constantly changing and adding to their collections, also have excellent orientation programs and well-versed guides, we have tried to give a little more space to some of the lesser known restorations and those which are just getting started. Any area within the jurisdiction of our National Park Service has the best of interpretation and background ready for the visitor, in pamphlets and often in films or slide programs and guides. Wherever possible we have tried to avoid the obviously commercial, fake towns although many of these are a delight for children and adults in a holiday mood. For the preservationists, new buildings can blend with the old and the old can be happily adapted to present use. As Ada Louise Huxtable once wrote in the New York *Times:* "The best of the past deserves the best of the present, not make-believe muck." On rainy days you'll find real mud in some of the restored and reassembled towns, but not much muck, I hope.

David N. Poinsett, in an editorial for the National Trust for Historic Preservation, said that "preservation is mainly a state of mind, an attitude that says those who lived before have left us not only written history. . . . but also specific physical remains in the form of buildings, structures, objects and the sites where great events took place. . . . A true preservationist would no more destroy a particular building because it is not one's favorite style than smash a recording of Stravinsky because one liked Beethoven better."

"Nothing great was ever achieved without enthusiasm," Emerson wrote, and also: "Beauty will not come at the call of a legislature. . . . It will come, as always, unannounced, and spring up between the feet of brave and earnest men."

Luckily, there are plenty of earnest men and women full of enthusiasm for restoring the best of the past. Through their efforts, a wealth of beautiful and historic things, treasures we cannot afford to lose, have been preserved in cities, towns, and countrysides throughout North America. This book is designed to tell just where these treasures can be found, and what you will see when you visit them. It is a guide to a heritage restored.

—A.C.

New England States

Maine
New Hampshire
Vermont
Massachusetts
Rhode Island
Connecticut

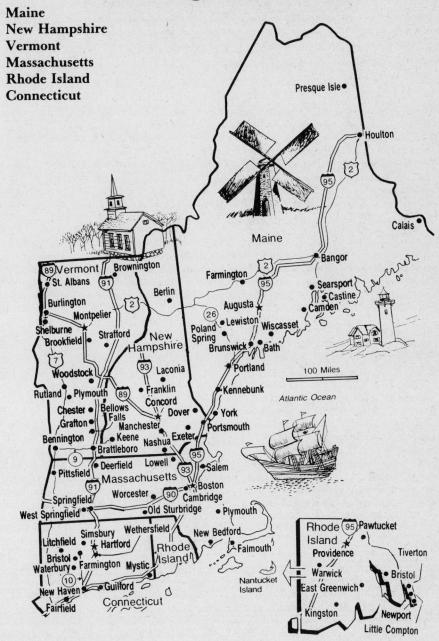

MAINE

Much good practical sense, and no little artistic skill as well, have of late been shown in our simplest country churches. Take, for example . . . St. Sylvia at Mt. Desert. It is thoroughly suited to its locality,—plain, unassuming, and rustic,—yet has sufficient dignity to be in keeping with its purpose. . . . Only to one point must we take objection. To shingle the entire outside was a natural and pleasing expedient; but to shingle the *inside* too—walls and pulpit and all—savors more perhaps of willful eccentricity than of artistic discretion.
—"Recent Architecture in America," by Mrs. Schuyler van Rensselaer, in *Century* magazine, New York, 1885

Along the now deserted wharves one stumbles upon suggestive relics of the days of ancient grandeur when the port of Castine was a famous depot for a thriving shipping trade, and when the sound of the ship-builders' mallet on the gnarled oak mingled with the "Yo, heave ho" of the sailor. These are all gone now, and the sleepy port, basking in the summer sun, seems a lotus-land, in which it is ever afternoon.
—*An Old Town With a History,* by Noah Brooks, New York, 1882

BANGOR, Penobscot County. I-95.

Broadway Historic District was primarily the residential area for wealthy Bangor citizens in the mid-19th century. The rich farmland and timber brought settlers after the War of 1812. The Bangor sawmills were busy and many fortunes were made. After the railroads took over most of the shipping by the lumber industry, paper became the main product. The district has been the focus of recent preservation endeavors. There is a large variety of upper-class residences, with Greek Revival predominating. Some of the finest existing Greek Revival mansions in America are in Bangor. Many were designed by local architects Charles G. Bryant and Benjamin S. Deane.

Individual listings on the National Register include **Bangor House,** 174 Main St., 1843, a five-story brick structure patterned after Boston's Tremont House. Ulysses S. Grant, Stephen A. Douglas, and Daniel Webster stayed here on occasion.

Blake House, 107 Court St., was built in 1858, with Calvin Ryder as architect. A bay was added in 1900.

Samuel Farrar House, 123 Court St., was designed by architect Richard Upjohn in 1836. The portico has Doric columns. An addition was made by Isaiah Rogers in 1846. Farrar was a leading merchant.

Godfrey-Kellogg House, 212 Kenduskeag Ave., built about 1847, is a good example of Gothic Revival and still has much of its original furniture.

Jonas-Cutting-Edward Kent House,

Winter quarters of Maine lumbermen. (Drawn by Reverend F. W. Hedge, 1851.)

48–50 Penobscot St., is two-storied with hipped roof and second-story iron balconies, built in 1837, a Greek Revival structure with two ground entrances so that it could be used as duplex law offices for Jonas Cutting and Edward Kent, who were partners. Kent later became governor.

Joseph W. Low House, 51 Highland St., designed by architect Harvey Graves and constructed by Fogg and Benson, builders, is two-story frame in Italian villa style. Joseph Low was a prominent businessman.

Zebulon Smith House, 55 Summer St., 1832, is two and a half stories, brick side walls with wooden front and rear walls, and is one of the two earliest-known examples of the Greek Revival style in Maine.

Isaac Farrar House (Symphony House), 166 Union St., 1842–44, is another fine example of Richard Upjohn's designs. It is brick, two and a half stories with hipped roof, two interior chimneys, stone Doric portico. Alterations were made by Isaac Merrill and architect Wilfred Mansur in the late 19th century. But originally it was Greek Revival, and one of Upjohn's first important commissions. Isaac Farrar was a lumberman, merchant, and banker. The house has been restored.

Upjohn, born in England, came to America in 1829 with his wife and small son. He joined a brother in New Bedford, Massachusetts, where he served as a draftsman for a local builder and taught drawing at night school. He moved to Boston to work for Alexander Parris and there designed the Isaac Farrar house and St. John's Church in Bangor. He was the founder of the American Institute of Architects. His book *Upjohn's Rural Architecture,* published in 1852, undoubtedly inspired other designers and builders.

St. John's Catholic Church, York St., built in 1855 (a troubled time when the Know-Nothings were opposed to the Catholic community), is Gothic Revival.

The **Wheelwright Block,** 34 Hammond St., is said to be the state's first commercial structure in Second Empire style. It was constructed in 1859, for a clothing firm, Wheelwright and Clark; Colonel Benjamin S. Deane was the architect. **Morse and Company Office Building,** Harlow St., 1895, is stone in eclectic style and was constructed in 1859. Morse was the main firm in town for nearly a century. (**Morse Bridge,** Valley Ave. over Kenduskeag Stream, built in 1882, is the longest covered bridge in the state.)

Grand Army Memorial Home, 159 Union St., Greek Revival built about 1840 with Upjohn as architect, was the residence of Thomas A. Hill, a leading merchant, and later the dwelling of Allen Gilman, Bangor's first mayor. It is now occupied by the Bangor Historical Society Museum.

The **Penobscot Expedition Site,** between Bangor and Brewer at the junction of the Penobscot and Kenduskeag Stream, is one of the most unusual on the National Register listings. This is a section of the Penobscot River containing some 15 to 25 warships from the Revolutionary War, sunk in an encounter of July 25, 1779. Most American military defeats are not commemorated, but the Yankees definitely lost this one: Dudley Saltonstall was in charge of the naval forces, General Solomon Lovell in command of land troops, and Colonel Paul Revere of the artillery. As history has it, Saltonstall was reluctant to attack the British ships on the western shore of the peninsula and this led to the destruction of the American fleet. If there is a military corner of heaven, perhaps Saltonstall and Confederate General James Longstreet, who was hesitant to attack at Second Bull Run (Manassas) and again at Gettysburg, have compared excuses by now.

Bangor has another unusual registered historic item: a **Standpipe,** Jackson St. It was designed by Ashley B. Tower in 1898 with a winding interior staircase between the steel standpipe and the round shingled structure, which encloses the area. The stairs lead to an observation deck, which has a conical roof, balustrades, and supporting columns. This was a popular observatory for viewing the town. The main use of a standpipe, of course, is to pump water high enough for pressure, as in more ordinary water-towers. (Louisville, Kentucky, has a water tower which resembles a Greek temple.)

Adams-Pickering Block, Main and Middle Sts., 1871, was designed by George W. Orff, and is brick with granite façade, four-storied with arched windows, bracketed cornice, dentil molding, and other trim. Only one corner pilaster remains of the original cast-iron ground floor. This is one of the few remaining High Victorian Italianate commercial structures in Bangor.

Besides these edifices on the National Register, the **Penobscot Heritage Museum of Living History,** in City Hall, 73 Harlow St., has local displays and is open weekdays except holidays. Free.

BATH, Sagadahoc County. I-95. US 1.

Bath Historic District takes in most of the 19th-century shipbuilding city. Dominant styles of architecture are Greek and Gothic Revival and Italianate, with a variety of others represented.

Bath Marine Museum, 963 Washington St., is housed in the 32-room Sewall Mansion, built about 1844. Harold M. Sewall was the first U.S. ambassador to the Republic of Hawaii. Five sites along the Kennebec River trace the local marine history. The **Winter Street Church,** built in 1843 by architect Anthony Coombs Raymond, was restored by the Sagadahoc Preservation Society. Part of the complex is the Percy & Small Shipyard, the only surviving U.S. builder of wooden ships, at 263 Washington St. The Apprenticeshop is turning out boats which actually are sold, although the sales income is only a third of what is needed to keep the place going. There sometimes are as many as 13 apprentices taking an 18-month course in reconstructions of traditional Maine workboats. There are a visitors' gallery and guides during the Museum season, usually end of May to late October, but check locally for exact dates. The *Seguin,* a tugboat, is part of the Marine Museum. Built in 1884 it operated out of Bath, towing sailing vessels and barges to points on the Kennebec River, and is now the oldest steam-powered tug in Maine.

U.S. Customhouse and Post Office, 25 Front St., was built in 1858, with Ammi B. Young the architect. Enlarged in 1912, it is Renaissance Revival, listed on the National Register.

Central Church, now the *Bath Performing Arts Center,* was built in the 1840s by Arthur Hilman. A board-and-batten Gothic-style structure, it has been called the "Chocolate Church," and has been restored.

BRUNSWICK, Cumberland County. I-95.

Federal St. Historic District is bounded roughly by Mason, Maine, College, and Federal Sts. *Lincoln St. Historic District* takes in Lincoln St. between Main and Union Sts.

Individual listings on the National Register:

Henry Boody House, Maine St.; *Richardson House (Captain George McManus House),* 11 Lincoln St., two-story brick built in 1857, for McManus, a master mariner; now the Pejepscot Historical Society Museum. *The Harriet Beecher Stowe House,* 63 Federal St., was erected in 1804, as an inn. *Uncle Tom's Cabin* was written here in 1851–52, and it seems as if Ms. Stowe was trying to get as far from the slave states as possible without leaving the country. The house, a National Historic Landmark, is now a restaurant. *Massachusetts Hall, Bowdoin College,* on campus, was built in 1802; the exterior has been restored. *First Parish Church,* 207 Maine St., built in 1845, with Richard Upjohn as architect, is Gothic Revival. *Harpswell Meetinghouse,* at Harpswell Center on St. 123, 9 miles S of Brunswick, is a typical New England meeting house, used as such from 1757 to 1759. It also has served as a church. Now it is again used for town meetings. NHL.

CAMDEN, Knox County. US 1.

Conway House Complex, Conway Rd., was built in the 1770s and enlarged in the early 1800s. Outbuildings include a barn and a blacksmith shop. The Mary Meeker Cramer Museum has costumes and other relics. Information Office, Town Landing, has maps for historic tours.

Norumbega, High St., built in the 1880s with Arthur Bates Jennings, architect, is a "random rubble, frame with shingling," three and a half stories, with an irregular outline, gabled roof, broken skyline with stone-stepped gable ends, and general Queen Anne style. It seems a good house for haunting, but is durable; it was built for Joseph B. Stearns, who got rich by inventing duplex telegraphy, a means of sending two messages over the same wire at once, which sounds as complicated as the house looks.

CASTINE, Hancock County. St. 175, on Penobscot Bay.

Castine Historic District takes in the peninsula town which was developed in the 18th and 19th centuries. There are frame Federal and Greek Revival houses from the mid-19th century and late-19th-century summer cottages. In the early 17th century the area was an outpost for the British, French, and Dutch. The British occupied the town in the War of 1812 and left, not by choice, in 1815. Castine became one of the richest small towns in New England.

On the National Register: *Cate House,* Court and Pleasant Sts., is an 1815 frame with clapboarding, gabled roof, and two interior chimneys; *John Perkins House,* Perkins St., built about 1765, has been moved and restored. It was one of the first houses in the settlement and survived the 1779 bombardment and British occupation during the Revolutionary and 1812 wars.

FARMINGTON, Franklin County. US 2.

Jacob Abbott House, St. 27, was built in 1819 by Benjamin Brainerd and was the home of Jacob Abbott, educator and author of children's books which were popular in his day and should be now. Abbott sent two of his characters, Rollo and Marco Paul, on travels in America and abroad and managed to be entertaining while instructing his young readers about geography and a little bit of everything else.

Much preservation and restoration are being carried on in the Farmington area, in addition to the Abbott House. The *Hiram Ramsdell House,* High and Perham Sts., is octagonal, two stories with a wooden hipped roof with octagonal cupola. The design may have come from Orson Squire Fowler's *A Home for All or the Octagon Mode of Building,* published in 1848. The *Nordica Homestead,* N of town on Holly Rd., off St. 27, 4, is 19th-century frame and clapboarding. It was the birthplace of Lillian Norton, an operatic soprano who was billed as Lillian Nordica, and has mementos of Miss Nordica's career. Open June to Labor Day.

Old Union Meetinghouse (Union Baptist Church), US 2, was built in 1826–27 by Benjamin Butler, a car-

penter-builder. The restoration of this building, a multidenominational church, was a Bicentennial project. Earle G. Shettleworth, Jr., director of the Maine Historic Preservation Commission, described the structure as a "rare Maine example of a church which is eighteenth century in form on the exterior, but was constructed in the 1820s and has Federal style details.... This handsome survival ... is a landmark at Farmington Falls. It commands its location and is a permanent memorial to all those denominations who made its creation possible."

Cutler Memorial Library, Academy and High Sts., built just after the turn of the century with William R. Miller as architect, is Neoclassical Revival design with Beaux-Arts elements (which should make it eclectic); *First Congregational Church,* Main St., George Coombs, architect, 1887–88, is Romanesque with some touches of other styles; and the *Free Will Baptist Meetinghouse,* Main St. (1835), also is worth a visit. All are on the National Register.

POLAND SPRING, *Androscoggin County. St. 26.*

Shaker Village, near St. 26, Sabbathday Lake vicinity, also in Cumberland County. There are 16 wooden buildings and structures, and a brick Central Dwelling House, on 1,700 acres, in this settlement which was a Shaker community from the late 18th century and was one of the last active Shaker communities. A village tour includes the old Shaker Meeting-House, from 1794; the Stone Building, once a community house; and the museum, which has Shaker furniture and crafts as well as agricultural displays. NHL.

PORTLAND, Cumberland County. I-95.

Spring St. Historic District and *Stroudwater Historic District* are both largely residential areas. In the former are a number of frame, brick, and stone 19th-century buildings, including several houses by Alexander Parris. The *Morse-Libby Mansion,* 109 Danforth St., was built in 1859–63. Henry Austin was architect. This was one of the first examples of Italianate architecture in the area. Ruggles Morse was a New Orleans hotel owner. NHL. The Stroudwater district comprises about 35 buildings from 1727 to the Civil War era.

The *Chamber of Commerce,* 142 Free St., has information on the many historic sites in this city, which was settled in 1632, served as the state capital from 1820 to 1832, and became an important shipping and trading center early in its history. Some 30 structures are listed on the National Register. The *Maine Historical Society,* adjoining the *Wadsworth-Longfellow House,* 487 Congress St., has displays and information on local history. The Longfellow home, built in 1785 by the poet's grandfather, has family furnishings and memorabilia.

SEARSPORT, Waldo County. US 1.

Penobscot Marine Museum, Church St., comprises the *Town Hall,* built in 1845; the *Captain Merithew House* of 1816, a two-story Federal building with collections of charts, navigational equipment, and paintings; the *Fowler-True-Ross House,* 1825, with displays of models and paintings; the *Nickels-Colcord-Duncan House,* built about 1880, which has rooms with special exhibits and a research library. The complex tells the history of local maritime activities in the 19th century. It is operated by the Penobscot Marine Museum.

WISCASSET, Lincoln County. US 1.

Wiscasset Historic District is a seaport area containing many brick and frame residences of the 18th and 19th centuries. Preservationists have been active here. The Lincoln County Cultural and Historical Association is one of the busiest in the state. Among fine old buildings on the National Register:

Nickels-Sortwell House, NE corner of Main and Federal Sts., 1807–8, is a restored Federal house which was constructed for William Nickels, a sea captain. NHL.

Captain George Scott House (Octagon House), Federal St., was built in 1855 for Scott, a shipmaster.

Red Brick School (Old Academy Building), Warren St., built in 1807, served until 1923 when the final bell rang. Now a museum.

U.S. Customhouse *(Old Customhouse) and Post Office,* Water St., from 1868–70. Alfred B. Mullett, architect, worked for the Treasury.

Jail and Museum, St. 218: the granite jail dates from 1809–11, the jailer's house from 1837. Museum in jailer's house.

YORK, York County. I-95.

York Historic District: three village areas along the York River are part of the district. There are many 17th- to 19th-century buildings which make up the settlement. The town of York has had to face the problem of being near to Boston and heavy tourist traffic, which was increased during the Bicentennial. To quote Christopher Glass, of Camden, who prepared an excellent booklet *Historic Preservation in Maine:* "Regulation of visual quality seems to go against the grain of traditional Maine independence, but in cases where outside pressures cannot be contained by the equally traditional forces of consensus and consideration, it is probably the only sure way of keeping the visual environment intact. . . . The inevitable pressure for growth places in jeopardy the very qualities which are attracting people."

While trying to keep Maine Down East, in other words, the Society for the Preservation of Historic Landmarks in York County has reopened the *Elizabeth Perkins House* after extensive restoration. It was built in 1691, added to in 1732 and 1898, and now belongs to the Society. It is at Sewell's Bridge on York River. The *Old Gaol,* 4 Lindsay Rd., built in 1720 and used until 1860, has a dungeon, and is the oldest stone building in Maine; it also is the oldest historic museum in the state, having been converted to this use in 1900 by the Old York Improvement Society. It is being restored. *Jefferd's Tavern,* also restored, was built before the Revolution.

The *York Village Information,* York St. and Lindsay Rd., has self-guiding tours of the area.

Note for dedicated history hunters: there are about 40 historic districts in Maine and others awaiting action by the National Park Service. For last-minute information, write to Maine Historic Preservation Commission, 242 State St., Augusta, 04333; or the State Planning Office, 184 State St., Augusta, 04333.

NEW HAMPSHIRE

It was but one story high, with a door in the middle, and a window on each side, and three windows at either end. It contained four rooms on the ground floor. . . . An addition in the rear answered the purpose of a kitchen. It had only one chimney, and this arose from the centre of the roof. . . . The framework was of heavy timber, the exterior clapboarded, and the ends pointed, differing in this respect from the gambrel roof. On the green in front of the house arose a large and graceful elm. . . . Many other trees of the same kind were scattered over the grounds, on which account the place received the appropriate name of "Elm Farm." Near one end of the house was a deep well, with a long, old-fashioned well sweep, to one extremity of which was attached a bucket, by means of which the clear, cool water was drawn up for the use of the family. . . .

In this house, on the 18th day of January, 1782, Daniel Webster was born.
—*The American Statesman,* by Rev. Joseph Banvard, Boston, 1853

If two New Hampshiremen aren't a match for the devil, we might as well give the country back to the Indians.
—"The Devil and Daniel Webster," by Stephen Vincent Benét, Boston, 1936

CONCORD, Merrimack County. I-89.

Concord Historic District, bounded by N. State St., Horse Shoe Pond, Boston and Maine Railroad tracks, Senator Styles Bridges Highway, and Church St. The city has been state capital since 1808. A trading post was here in 1660, but most settlers arrived in the early 1700s after a conflict about land claims had been settled. The first stagecoaches eventually used in the Old West came from Concord.

Old Post Office, N. State St., between Capitol and Park, was built in 1884–89, with James Riggs Hill as architect. It is a combination of Gothic and Richardson Roman- esque, of local granite and brick, and is listed in the National Register.

State House, 1816–19, Main St., is the oldest in the U.S., with the legislature still occupying its original chambers. (The capitols of Maryland and Massachusetts are older, but the legislatures have outgrown their original quarters.) Stuart J. Park used prison labor for the construction, and the original building cost $82,000; it has been remodeled and enlarged twice. The granite came from giant boulders on Rattlesnake Hill and is said to be more than 22,000 years old.

New Hampshire Historical Society and Museum, 30 Park St., has five period rooms among many exhibits of state history and rare documents.

The society was founded in Portsmouth in 1823, moved here in 1911.

Pierce Manse, 1 mile N at 14 Penacook St., was the home of President Franklin Pierce from 1838 to 1848. He was three when the family moved here. The house has both original and selected period pieces. Pierce is buried in *Old North Cemetery,* off N. State St. Benjamin Pierce, father of Franklin and eight other children, twice was governor of New Hampshire.

Shaker Village, 12 miles NE of Concord, in Canterbury, just W of St. 106, is a restoration of an 18th-century utopian community which was incorporated in 1792 and is one of the remaining Shaker colonies in New England (see also Poland Spring, Maine.) The Shaker movement was started by Ann Lee and a group of eight followers who came from England to settle in Niskayuna, New York, in 1774. There were 19 societies in America in the peak years of the colonization. This village was begun as a one-building museum in 1959 and is still growing. The restored buildings and museum are open May 24 through Oct. 15, Tuesday–Saturday. Guided tours are available.

DOVER, Strafford County, Spaulding Turnpike, is said to be the first permanent settlement in New Hampshire, founded in 1623, at Hilton Point.

Woodman Institute, on St. 16, at 182–192 Central Ave., is a three-building complex with exhibits. The *Dame Garrison House* was built in 1675, by William Damm and his son for protection against Indians; moved from original site. The *Hale House,* built in 1813, was the home of John Parker Hale, U.S. Senator. *Woodman House,* from 1818, was the home of John Williams, founder of the cotton industry in Dover.

The *William Hale House,* 5 Hale St., is a Federal-style mansion built in 1806. William Hale was host to the Marquis de Lafayette on his tour of the area, and to President Monroe. Open daily. Free.

EXETER, Rockingham County. St. 101.

Front St. Historic District, Front St. to the junction of Spring and Water Sts., includes 18th- to 20th-century buildings, the town square, churches, dwellings and commercial structures, Phillips Exeter Academy, and the site of the first Town House where the first state government was created. The town was founded in 1638 by John Wheelwright at the fall line of the Exeter River, with one main street winding along the waterfront and another leading to what is now Phillips Exeter Academy.

Ladd-Gilman House, also called the *Cincinnati House,* Governor's Lane and Water St., was bought by the Society of the Cincinnati in 1902 and restored by them. The dwelling is two and one-half stories high, L-shaped, with gabled roof and dormers. The original brick structure built by Nathaniel Ladd in 1721, and used as a jail, was enlarged and altered in 1752; later a rear ell was added. This was the home of Nicholas Gilman, Jr., delegate to the Constitutional Convention of 1787. The room that was used as the state treasury is on display. During the Revolution Colonel Nicholas Gilman was the first treasurer of New Hampshire. NHL.

Perry-Dudley House, 14 Front St., an early-19th-century frame, three stories, with fluted Doric columns, Federal style, has been the home of several generations of prominent local doctors, of one family.

Also on the National Register: *First Church (Congregational),* 21 Front St., was built by Ebenezer Clifford in 1801. It has been altered.

Gilman-Garrison House, 12 Water St., is an 18th-century house, built by Councilor John Gilman, expanded by his son in 1770. A portion of it is one of the oldest structures in the state. It was intended to provide adequate quarters for Royal Governor John Wentworth when in Exeter. The house has period furnishings and is open in summer.

Phillips Exeter Academy was incorporated in 1781 and was founded by John Phillips, who with his uncle, Samuel, also founded Phillips Academy in Andover, Massachusetts, in 1778. When the Academy opened, most of its first 56 students were admitted without charge. They had their first lessons at the *Wells-Kerr House,* on Tan Lane, and lived with townspeople, working for their room and board.

Nathaniel Gilman House, 46 Front St., was built about 1735 by Dr. Dudley Odlin. Colonel Nicholas Gilman bought the house in 1782. His son, Nathaniel, became state treasurer. Shortly after the turn of the 20th century the house was acquired and remodeled by Phillips Exeter Academy. It is the home of the Academy's principal.

Folsom Tavern, 21 Spring St., was built by Colonel Samuel Folsom on the site of his grandfather's house, in 1775. Revolutionary officers met here in November 1783 to form the Society of the Cincinnati. George Washington stopped here for a "collation" on the morning of November 4, 1789. The tavern was moved when Water St. was widened.

FRANKLIN, Merrimack County. US 3.

Daniel Webster Birthplace, 4 miles SW of town, then ½ mile W off St. 127. The two-room cabin has been furnished in period. It is owned and maintained by the Webster Birthplace Foundation. Guide service is provided in summer months. Webster, born on January 18, 1782, became one of the nation's outstanding orators and public servants. He was a Congressman, Senator, and twice Secretary of State. The great elm that shades the house was planted about 1765 by his father, Ebenezer Webster, and is referred to in the opening of this section.

PORTSMOUTH, Rockingham County. I-95.

Strawbery Banke Historic District, bounded by Court and Marcy Sts., and both sides of Hancock and Washington Sts. This fine restoration was one of the earliest major projects of renewal in New England, or indeed the nation. It has undoubtedly inspired other cities to clear away urban blight and replace it with handsome historic houses and buildings, to be used either for display and interpretation of the past, as shops and restaurants, or a combination.

In 1630 the first colonists found the banks of the Piscataqua River covered with strawberries and named their settlement for this happy circumstance. It was renamed Portsmouth in 1653. In 1957 residents, aware of the deteriorating historical landmarks, joined with the Urban Renewal Administration to preserve the buildings and other features of the early days. In seven years the nonprofit corporation of Strawbery Banke, Inc., had acquired 10 acres and 27 old houses, most of which are on their original sites. The work of restoration began in 1964 and is continuing.

The restoration is reached by following Strawbery Route markers, or from the Howard Johnson exit from the Portsmouth Traffic Circle at the junction of I-95, US 1 By-pass (Rt. 1-A) and St. 4, 16.

Captain John Clark House, on Jefferson St., was built about 1750 by William Farrow. The façade has Georgian detailing; otherwise it is a plain clapboard structure with a high-pitched roof and central chimney. The interior has painted dado paneling, Queen Anne pieces, and fine old pewter and ceramic displays.

The 1762 Chase house (left) and the Conant house (right), of about 1750–59, at Strawbery Banke, Portsmouth, New Hampshire. (Courtesy of Strawbery Banke, Inc.)

Clark, a packetmaster, bought the house from John Davenport, an innkeeper.

The **Chase House,** Court St., was built in 1762. It is clapboard, a classic New Hampshire colonial dwelling, with twin chimneys, quoined corners, and carved door frames. John Underwood, the builder, was a mariner, and the house had one other owner before Stephen Chase, the son of a minister, bought the place. Chase became a prosperous merchant; his counting house stood on Pier Wharf at the foot of State St. He was host to George Washington when the President toured the new country in 1789. Long after this illustrious occasion the house became a home for orphans and destitute children (1884). Still later Mrs. Thomas Bailey Aldrich, widow of the author and editor of *The Atlantic Monthly,* became the owner and lived here until she died in 1927. Restoration and furnishing were based on an inventory made at Stephen Chase's death in 1805.

Governor Goodwin Mansion, at the entrance on Dock Lane (Hancock St.), was built in 1811 and has been beautifully restored and furnished. The **Daniel Webster House,** at the other end of the block on Washington St., was built in 1783. The **Keyran Walsh House,** from 1796; the **Old State House,** 1758; **Pitt Tavern,** 1766, and the **Dunaway Store** are among the completed structures. There will be some 35 buildings in all. The Guild of Strawbery Banke has two gift shops open year round with unusual wares. One is in the **Kingsbury House,** 93 State St., which is also Guild headquarters and is one block W of the Restoration Area. The other gift shop is in the **Shapley-Gookin Houses,** built about 1770, at Court and Atkinson Sts., restored by the Guild. The Kingsbury House is a pink brick Georgian Colonial built about 1815.

The *Shapley Town House,* 454–456 Court Street, on the corner of Pitt (also Court) and Liberty Streets, contains the curatorial department. It was built about 1815 and is brick set in Flemish bond, three stories, with a low hipped roof and interior end chimneys. It comprises two attached identical houses treated as one. They were built after a fire in 1813 had burned much of the town. Captain Reuben Shapley was a wealthy mariner.

The *Jones House* on Newton Ave. will have archaeological exhibits from the area. For further information on the restorations write to Strawbery Banke, Inc., Box 300, Portsmouth, 03801, or call (603) 436-8010.

There are a number of restored houses in Portsmouth which are open to the public, but not part of the Strawbery Banke restoration:

Governor John Langdon Mansion, 143 Pleasant St., built in 1784, was the home of Langdon, who also was a U.S. Senator. The *Historic Information Center* is here. The house was called the handsomest in Portsmouth by George Washington when he was here several times in 1789. NHL.

Moffatt-Ladd House, 154 Market St., was the home of Captain Moffatt, who had a ship room on the second floor from which he could see his wharves and his ships. His office was in the low building next door. The mansion was built in 1763 in Georgian style and has an exceptionally fine stair hall, period furnishings, and a colonial garden. It was restored by the National Society of Colonial Dames in America in the State of New Hampshire. From 1768 to 1785 William Whipple, one of the signers of the Declaration of Independence, lived here. NHL.

Macpheadris-Warner House, 150 Daniel St., was built in 1716. It is Georgian brick, and probably had the first lightning rod in New Hampshire installed under the direction of Benjamin Franklin. Captain Archibald Macpheadris was a member of the King's Council. From 1748 to 1754 the house was the home of Governor Benning Wentworth. It is the oldest brick house in the city, a national historic landmark, and a house museum. The Warner part of the name came from Jonathan Warner, who wed Mary Macpheadris, Archibald's daughter. Warner family descendants lived in the house for two centuries. It is maintained by the Warner House Association.

Wentworth-Coolidge Mansion, Little Harbor Rd. off US 1A, was built toward the end of the 17th century. It is a rambling 2½ stories, with 42 rooms, one of which is a large paneled council chamber. Benning Wentworth, the first royal governor appointed by George II when New Hampshire became a separate province in 1741, lived here from the time of his appointment until 1766. Additions were made to the original structure because Wentworth liked to live well; he also shocked his friends and acquaintances when he married his young and beautiful housekeeper after his wife died. NHL.

Wentworth-Gardner House, 140 Mechanic St., was built in 1760 for Thomas Wentworth, younger brother of the last royal governor, John Wentworth. His mother had the house built as a gift for Thomas. It faces the river, has been restored, and is a National Historic Landmark and museum.

Governor John Wentworth House, 346 Pleasant St., was built in 1763 for the last royal governor. Wentworth left here on the run on June 13, 1775, when a mob threatened him. The interior stairway and the main parlor are in good repair, but a brick addition in 1927 did not help the exterior. The house is on the National Register.

John Paul Jones House, Middle

and State Sts., was built in 1758 and was the boardinghouse where Jones stayed while he supervised the construction of the *America.* The exterior has been restored, and the house is now headquarters and museum of the Portsmouth Historical Society. NHL.

Richard Jackson House, 76 Northwest St., was built about 1664 and was the home of a shipbuilder. The house, which possibly is the oldest surviving building in New Hampshire, was bought by the Society for the Preservation of New England Antiquities in 1927 and restored. It is now a house museum. NHL.

The Hill, Deer St., is a restoration of 14 houses, by a combined effort of the United States Department of Housing and Urban Development, the National Park Service, the Portsmouth Housing Authority, and private enterprise and local citizens. All buildings except one will be used for business establishments. They have been grouped to create a courtyard effect, with red-bricked sidewalks. Seven of the buildings, which are Georgian and Federal in style, were built before or during the Revolutionary War. Among houses on The Hill and the National Register: The *Jeremiah Hart House,* late-18th-century two-story frame; the *John Hart House,* mid-18th century, three-story, with Corinthian columns; the *Phoebe Hart House,* built 1808–10, two and a half stories with gabled roof, Federal style; the *Hart-Rice House,* mid-18th-century Georgian, moved and rehabilitated, two and a half stories with hipped roof and gabled dormers; the *Daniel Pinkham House,* 1813–15, three stories, built for Daniel and Isaac Pinkham. Isaac was a cabinet-maker who probably finished the interior. The *Henry Sherburne House (Richard Shortridge House),* 1766–70, now the Senior Citizen Center, open to the public; the Georgian two-story house was moved and rehabilitated; the *Simeon P. Smith House,* 1810–11, two and a half stories, is late Georgian, moved and rehabilitated; the *Whidden-Ward House,* 18th-century Georgian, moved and rehabilitated; and the *Samuel Beck House,* 18th-century, two and a half stories, with Georgian and Federal elements, moved and rehabilitated.

Other houses on the Register are the *James Neal House,* 74 Deer St., three-storied brick built in 1832; *Nutter-Rymes House,* 48 School St., 1809, built by James Nutter who was also an architect, with an unusual design of double urban Federal style; the *Benedict House (Thomas W. Penhallow House),* 30 Middle St., built about 1811, brick (Flemish bond), an outstanding town house of the era; the *Rundlet-May House,* 364 Middle St., built about 1807, an exceptional three-story Federal manse; and the *George Rogers House,* 76 Northwest St.

Portsmouth Athenaeum, 9 Market St., is Federal, built in 1804 by Bradbury Johnson, who was also the architect. The library has historical displays. *Portsmouth Public Library (Portsmouth Academy),* 8 Islington St., 1809, was built by James Nutter, local builder-architect, and was one of the first buildings put up for academic use in the area.

VERMONT

The afternoon of Wednesday, Oct. 19th, was cloudy, threatening rain, and the streets [of St. Albans] were particularly wet.... Immediately after the town clock had struck ... three, the banks were entered simultaneously by men [Confederates] with revolvers.... The banks were all situated upon Main Street, in a space not exceeding 45 rods.... At a short distance down Lake Street were the machine-shops and depot buildings of the rail-road, where hundreds of men were at work, who if made aware of what was doing, would have quickly disposed of the entire rebel party.... Some of the robbers now commenced the seizure of horses with which to effect an escape. Field's livery stable was first visited. Opposition to the appropriation of his horses being made by Mr. Field, a shot was instantly fired at him by Young [Confederate General Bennett Young], the ball passing through his hat....

Young frequently ordered his men to throw Greek fire upon the wooden buildings. This was a phosphoric compound in a liquid state. A bottle of it was thrown against the front of N. Atwood's store, but without much effect. The water closet of the American [hotel] ... burned until the next day; but as the wood-work was kept wet, it did no damage.

The robbers now began to move towards the north, and halted near the corner of Main and Bank streets. Bedard's shop was rifled of saddles, bridles and blankets. 7 horses were led out of Fuller's livery stable.... In front of Jaquez grocery-store, a horse was hitched belonging to a French-Canadian named Boivin. A robber had mounted the horse, but Boivin attacked him vigorously and pulled him off.... The raiders took the road to Sheldon.... They had intended to rob the bank at this place, but found it closed; and ... they contented themselves with stealing a horse from Col. Keith, and passed on to Canada....

—*Vermont Historical Gazeteer,* by L. L. Dutcher, ca. 1865,
reprinted St. Albans, 1968

Note: Vermont has 92 bridges listed on the National Register; most of them are covered bridges, some are railroad bridges. Railroads were important in Vermont until recent years. In **St. Johnsbury,** Caledonia County, there is **Railroad Street Historic District; Randolph,** Orange County, has **Depot Square Historic District.**

BELLOWS FALLS, Windham County. US 5.

Steamtown, U.S.A., 2 miles N of town on US 5, is not a restored village but is a collection of authentic railroad items in what was once a railroad center. There are locomotives, steam machinery from many countries, and exhibits relating to the history of steam machinery in the development of American industry. Also fire-fighting equipment. In summer and early fall there is a 26-mile steam train ride to Chester Depot, three times daily.

Adams Grist Mill, Mill St., was operating in 1831 and is still workable. A museum of early equipment is part of the display.

Vermont Country Store, 5 miles N on St. 103 in Rockingham, has an 1810 gristmill and an 1890s kitchen; it is high-tourist-trappery but worth a drop-in visit. Worth more time is the *Meeting-house,* which was built in 1787, restored in 1907, and is now a museum and a church in summer. The graveyard is a mecca for gravestone-rubbing enthusiasts.

BENNINGTON, Bennington County. US 7.

Old First Church, Monument Ave. in Old Bennington, was built in 1805—Lavius Fillmore was the architect—and has been restored. The *Burying Yard* adjacent to church has the graves of those who were killed in the Battle of Bennington in 1777—and poet Robert Frost. (Friend and foe are buried here, Hessians and Americans.) The church was actually organized in December 1762. The first meeting house looked rather like a barn and stood on the village green. It had a porch but no steeple. The present church was considered to be a nearly flawless example of Colonial architecture. It is supposed that the Bennington carpenters who designed it made their own alterations to drawings from Asher Benjamin's book *The Country Builder's Assistant,* which was much thumbed in small towns of the period. But the perfect church fell into imperfect hands. It was altered in 1832, again in 1865, and yet again in 1903. Now it is once more "the most beautiful old wooden church in America," or close to it.

Tourist Information Booth, at 507 Main St., has information on the many colonial homes of Old Ben-

nington and neighboring sites. *Bennington Museum,* W. Main in Old Bennington, has displays from the Revolutionary and Civil wars and an extensive collection of the much prized Bennington pottery.

Park-McCullough House, St. 67A in North Bennington, was built in 1864 with the gold gained by Trenor Park in the California gold rush. It has Victorian trimmings and furnishings. John G. McCullough served as governor of Vermont.

BROOKFIELD, Orange County. St. 14.

Brookfield Village Historic District comprises the 19th-century upland town bordering a main turnpike. There are a number of Greek Revival structures. Unfortunately for preservationists the 380 tarred wooden barrels of the one rare pontoon bridge are being replaced by styrofoam-filled containers!

BROWNINGTON, Orleans County. E of I-91, N of St. 58.

Brownington Village Historic District, Hinman and Brownington Center Rds., is a rural crossroads community with late-18th-century and 19th-century variations of Federal and Greek Revival structures. The natural setting looks like a stage-set for picturesqueness.

CALAIS, Washington County. St. 12.

Kent's Corner Historic District, Kent's Corner, is a 19th-century crossroads village. An 1837 tavern was a stagecoach stop. The mill has a timber wheelhouse and feeding and sawing equipment, and an iron flume.

CHESTER, Windsor County. St. 103.

Stone Village Historic District, both sides of highway, comprises a 19th-century town with 17 buildings, including dwellings, a church, a schoolhouse, and a tavern. *Jeffrey House,* North St., was built in 1797 by Jabez Sargent, Jr., son of the town's first settler.

GRAFTON, Windham County. St. 30.

Kidder Covered Bridge, SE of town, 1870s, is built like a parallelogram with a skew of 15 degrees from the perpendicular between its flanking tresses. It is frame with boards hung vertically; the roadway is 12 feet wide.

The Windham Foundation, Inc., 330 South St., Morristown, 05661— (802) 843-2211—has restored some 20 homes in Grafton and the *Old Tavern,* built in 1801. The Foundation modestly lays no claim to being "true restorers" because the interiors have been modernized (as in Fredericksburg, Texas, and many other places), but the exteriors have been restored or preserved, and John Franz, president of the Foundation, says: "We were fortunate Grafton, although not neglected, had not been spoiled [by modern stores, etc.]. . . . The net result has been a very attractive New England village still almost exactly as it was 100 years ago."

The *Village Store,* still in business, has its date in fresh white paint on its red walls: 1841. The *Old Tavern* seems to earn its claim of being "the most charming little inn in all New England" indoors as well as outside. The rooms are beautifully furnished in canopied beds, some with crocheted hangings. The tavern barn lounge is rustic, the pine dining room shining with furniture polished for a century, and both corner and open cupboards display pewter and other antiques.

PLYMOUTH, Windsor County. St. 100A.

Plymouth Historic District covers a valley area of about 21,500 acres with 15 early frame buildings; some of these are related to the life of Calvin Coolidge. The state board of historic sites maintains a hospitality center in the house where the President's mother, born Victoria Josephine Moor, lived. The birthplace house is being restored to its condition of July 4, 1872, when the future President was born. The homestead where Calvin Coolidge was sworn in as the 30th President in 1923 is maintained by the state. *The Wilder Barn,* opposite the *Wilder House,* now the *Hospitality Center,* is a *Farmer's Museum.* Across from the Coolidge home is the church that the future President attended as a boy. (*Plymouth Notch Cemetery,* where the Coolidges are buried, is S of town.)

ST. ALBANS, Franklin County. I-89.

Central Vermont Railroad Headquarters, a registered historic site, is the most completely intact 19th-century railroad complex in the state. There are 12 major structures in the complex. Bounded roughly by Federal, Catherine, Allen, Lower Welden, Houghton, and Pine Sts., it is headquarters of the state's major rail carrier, the first to provide rail and water connection from Boston and New England to the upper Midwest, where iron and grain production was a major business.

Houghton House, 86 S. Main, 1800, is Federal in style.

Main St. was where most of the action took place when the Confederates invaded the town in 1864. The village green where local citizens were rounded up as temporary prisoners looks much the same. The *Chamber of Commerce* has pamphlets and a map of the historic sites. On the centennial of the raid in 1964 a mock battle was held and a marker was dedicated at the Sheldon Village covered bridge which the raiders tried to burn in escaping, to delay pursuers. An interesting follow-up to the ill feelings and injuries of that famous event took place in Montreal in

Pictorial map of Shelburne Museum, Shelburne, Vermont. (Courtesy of Shelburne Museum)

July 1911, when four citizens from St. Albans paid their respects to General Bennett H. Young, the raid leader. The Montreal *Gazette* reported that "the quartet of Vermont citizens at once fired a volley of questions at the man who had been more talked about in their state than any one of its native sons."

SHELBURNE, Chittenden County. US 7.

Shelburne Museum, 1 mile S on US 7, is a 100-acre reconstruction which represents three centuries of American life in 35 buildings, carefully furnished in period style, and in outdoor displays of great value. The *Ticonderoga,* built in 1906, is a steel-hulled side-paddle-wheel vessel which has been preserved. NHL. Until 1963 it served as an excursion steamboat on Lake Champlain, and it is the only remaining vessel of its kind.

Shelburne Museum was founded in 1947 by the late Electra Havemeyer Webb, whose parents had also been collectors interested in Americana (and European art). Since her death the village has been operated

as a nonprofit charitable educational corporation.

The entrance is through a covered bridge, with a tollbooth and an information center. The *Railroad Station,* Victorian in style, has railroadiana, including a train shed, steam locomotive, wheel engine, and private car. There also is a freight building with many more exhibits. An open motor-drawn cart hauls visitors around on the graveled roads of the village, which has rose bushes, ponds, willows, and weathered barns and dwellings, brought from other parts of the state. There is something for everyone in the variety of displays. Children (and grownups) will enjoy the *Toy Shop* with its early mechanical items, music boxes, and other delightful collections. Women will enjoy the *Hat and Fragrance Unit,* with early bonnets and other items. There is even a *Live Bee Exhibit.* The museum is open daily 9 to 5, May 15 through October 15. Visitors under 16 must be accompanied by an adult. Maps of the area are provided at the entrance. Collections date from 1783 to present. For additional information: Rt. 7, 05482; (802) 985-3344.

STRAFFORD, Orange County. N of Secondary Rd. 132.

Strafford Village Historic District, Morrill Highway and Sharon Brook Rd., is a community of late-18th-century and 19th-century buildings. About 30 structures make up the town; most are frame, some Greek Revival in style. The 1779 *Meetinghouse* stands on a rise overlooking the village green.

WOODSTOCK, Windsor County. US 4.

Woodstock Village Historic District, along the Ottauquechee River, contains a great many carefully restored old homes from the early 19th century. The village green is boat-shaped. Four of the local churches have bells that were cast by the Paul Revere Works in Boston. The first one, which was hung in the Congregational Church in 1818, was guaranteed to last for "one full year."

MASSACHUSETTS

. . . no city has any right to be as crooked as Boston. It is a crookedness
without excuse, and without palliation. It is crooked in cold blood, and with
malice aforethought. It goes askew when it might just as easily go straight. It is
illogical, inconsequent, and incoherent. Nowhere leads to anywhere in particular. You start from any given point, and you are just as likely to come out at
one place as another. Of course, all this can but have an effect on the inhabitants. Straightforwardness becomes impossible where you are continually
pitching up against sharp points. People born and bred in angles, and blind
alleys, and cross-ways, cannot fail to have a knack at tergiversation and in-
trigue. Diplomatists should be chosen from Boston, or should at least take a
preparatory course of five years there, as soldiers do at West Point.

—*Country Living,* by Gail Hamilton, Boston, 1865

A SIGHT FROM BUNKER-HILL MONUMENT

. . . from the top of Bunker-Hill Monument . . . look out first to the north.
We notice, first, the singular peninsula of Nahant, with its long neck reaching
to Lynn, the city of shoes; and then we follow the coast across the mouth of the
Saugus River, along Revere or Chelsea Beach, to the little town of Winthrop.
To the left of the coast, we see the city of Chelsea spread out before us. The
towns of Malden, Everett, Melrose, and Saugus, with their numerous villages,
and the trains on the Eastern and the Boston and Maine Roads passing along
their swift but apparently snail-like course.

We turn now to the west, and here a glorious prospect opens before us. The
entire country is dotted with villages, crossed by railroads, watered by rivers,
made beautiful by being covered with pretty and comfortable
dwelling-houses. . . .

—*Strangers' New Guide Through Boston and Vicinity,* Boston, 1872

BOSTON, Suffolk County. I-93.

At present there are some 65 historic districts in Massachusetts, and
more are planned. In Boston there
are also 57 individual listings on the
National Register. These vary from
the *Ether Dome of Massachusetts
General Hospital* to the *Tremont St.
Subway;* or from *Quincy Market* to
the *U.S.S. Constitution (Old Ironsides)* at the Boston Naval Shipyard,
and all four are also National Historic Landmarks.

Poets from Longfellow to Robert
Lowell have written about Boston, as
have novelists, including Charles
Dickens, actors such as William Macready, Edwin Booth, and Fanny
Kemble, philosophers, versemakers,
social historians such as Cleveland
Amory; and nearly every serious traveler for the last three centuries who

stepped ashore at Boston harbor wrote about the city. Artists have painted it, sculptors sculpted, architects drawn inspiration from it. It comes as no surprise, therefore, that the Historic American Buildings Survey has photographed some 500 buildings in the state and listed 81 historic structures in Boston alone.

For specific information, maps, etc.: *Boston Visitors and Information Center,* Tremont and West Sts.: (617) 426-4984. *Boston and Massachusetts Information Desk,* State House, Beacon St. *The Greater Boston Chamber of Commerce,* 125 High St. *Greater Boston Convention and Tourist Bureau,* 9000 Boylston St. The *Freedom Trail* is a route marked with a red stripe. The *City Hall Hospitality Center,* Park and Tremont Sts., also has booklets.

Among historic districts: *Back Bay,* marshland in 1856, became fashionable when it was reclaimed and planned by Arthur Gilman, an English architect, who laid it out with squares and parks, and built houses which varied from Second Empire to Italian Renaissance. Gilman did not like the widespread use of Greek Revival in America. (*Boston City Hall,* School St., a Gilman and Gridley J. F. Bryant building, is Second Empire. Gilman was commissioned to design this structure during the Civil War, 1862–65, and to build the state capitol at Albany in 1867.) The district comprises brick and stone row houses, public buildings, and churches. *Trinity Church* was designed by H. H. Richardson; the *Boston Public Library* by McKim, Mead, and White.

Beacon Hill, on the Charles River, has Federal and Greek Revival structures, row houses, and the State House. The area was planned according to the designs of Charles Bulfinch in the years 1795 to 1808. Even a partial list of former residents

sounds like a celestial Who's Who: Charles Francis Adams, Edwin Booth, Francis Parkman, Bronson Alcott, William Prescott, Julia Ward Howe, John Singer Sargent, Ellery Sedgwick, Thomas Bailey Aldrich, Jenny Lind, Minnie Maddern Fiske, William Dean Howells, and Louisa May Alcott.

Blackstone Block has structures from the 17th century, amid winding lanes, alleys, and small-scale brick commercial buildings, in an area once the waterfront.

A relatively new and interesting tour is the *Black Heritage Trail;* a guidebook is available from the *Museum of Afro-American History* at 8 Smith Court. Guide service can be arranged. The *African Meeting House,* Smith Court, built in 1806 for a black congregation, has been restored, and is the start of the trail.

CAMBRIDGE, Middlesex County. I-95.

Cambridge Common Historic District, Garden, Waterhouse, Cambridge, and Peabody Sts., and Massachusetts Ave., surrounds the Common and contains a 1628 burying ground, homes, academic and religious structures in varying styles of the 18th and 19th centuries. In this historic area, which was common land set aside for grazing in 1631 and was the site of local elections in 1636, George Washington on July 3, 1775, took command of the Continental Army; less than two weeks later, 1,200 soldiers rallied here on their way to Breed's Hill and Bunker Hill. The site remained headquarters for the army during 1775–76. It later became a major trade route intersection and by the late 19th and early 20th century, a park. Renovated in the 1970s. NHL. Christ Church (see below) and the 1838 Gannett House, a Greek Revival structure, are notable buildings.

Christ Church, Garden St., was

built 1759–61, Peter Harrison, architect. Enlarged in 1857, it is a fine Georgian structure, frame with horizontal siding, one story with square entry tower. It was used as a barracks during the Revolution. Open daily. Free. NHL.

A *Heritage Walking Tour* begins at the Common. *Information Center* is in City Hall. Brochures, maps, and guided tours of Harvard University may also be obtained at the *Information Booth* in Harvard Square. Information is also available at the *Chamber of Commerce,* 69 Rogers St., near Harvard Square.

Among the many historic buildings, those presently listed on the National Register are: *Cooper-Frost-Austin House,* 21 Linnaean St., built about 1690, enlarged in 1720, two and a half stories, the oldest house in town. Inquire for hours open. Administered by the Society for the Preservation of New England Antiquities. *Longfellow National Historic Site,* 105 Brattle St., 1759, Georgian dwelling built for John Vassall by his father. It was part of Tory Row; used as headquarters by Washington, later the home of the poet Henry Wadsworth Longfellow, who came here in August 1837 to rent two second-floor rooms and stayed as a boarder for six years. When he married, his father-in-law bought the house as a wedding gift. The dwelling is also known as the *Longfellow-Craigie House.* Andrew Craigie acquired the house after the Revolutionary War and enlarged it. After his death, his widow took in Harvard men (and their wives), including Longfellow, as lodgers. There are gardens and a carriage house, with exhibits on the estate.

The *Margaret Fuller House,* 71 Cherry St., 1806–7, a three-story frame in Federal style. Here Sarah Margaret Fuller was born on May 23, 1810. The eldest of eight children, she studied Greek at 13, knew the leading authors and thinkers of her day, including Hawthorne, Emerson, and Greeley, and met them as equals. She married the Marquis Ossoli in Rome and was drowned returning home in a ship which was wrecked at Fire Island, N.Y. NHL.

Elmwood, 33 Elmwood Ave., 1766, was the home of James Russell Lowell. It was built by Lieutenant Governor Andrew Oliver in Georgian style, and was the home of Governor Elbridge Gerry, 1810–12; Lowell lived here from 1819 to 1891. NHL.

General William Brattle House, 42 Brattle St., was built about 1727 for a noted lawyer and politician. (HABS says it was built about 1735; NR says 1727.) The Georgian structure has had some alterations and reconstruction. Margaret Fuller lived here as a girl. Now used as adult education center.

Asa Gray House, 88 Garden St., 1810. A Federal dwelling altered and moved from its original site in Harvard Botanical Gardens, it was the home of Gray, one of the leading botanists of his time. NHL.

Oliver Hastings House, 101 Brattle St., 1844–45, is Greek Revival. Hastings was a Boston merchant. NHL.

Dexter Pratt House, 54 Brattle St., built by Torrey Hancock about 1811, has been altered but is still Federal in style and is the oldest remaining 19th-century dwelling in the area. Pratt was the "Village smith" of Longfellow's poem.

A number of other important houses are in the vicinity and listed either in HABS or the National Register. Many are part of Harvard University, including the following: *Memorial Hall,* Cambridge and Quincy Sts., 1870–78, built as a memorial for students killed in the Civil War. NHL. *Massachusetts Hall,* 1720, built as a dormitory. *Harvard Hall,* built in 1672, destroyed by fire in 1764 when there was also a smallpox epidemic, rebuilt in 1764 and enlarged. *Wadsworth Hall,* built in 1726 for Benjamin Wadsworth, first president of the college, also served General George Washington for a time in July 1775 and is now the Alumni Association headquarters. These Colonial structures are all still in use on campus.

DEERFIELD, Franklin County. US 5.

Old Deerfield Village Historic District comprises the 17th-century town, with some buildings from 1670. This was the northern outpost of the New England frontier and therefore in the line of fire for the French and Indian War. In 1667 the Pocumtuck Indians were paid fourpence an acre for 8,000 acres of wilderness in the Connecticut Valley. The first settlers arrived in 1669. Two fierce Indian raids, in September 1675 and September 1694, failed to wipe out the community. When Queen Anne's War began in 1702, Deerfield was hit again and more than half the residents were killed or taken prisoner before help finally arrived.

Deerfield Academy was established in 1797. *Memorial Hall,* 1797–98, on Memorial Road just off Old Deerfield St., is now a museum with Colonial and Indian artifacts, including a fine collection of pewter.

The *Information Center* is in *Hall Tavern,* Main St. *Historic Deerfield, Inc.* maintains 11 houses on a milelong street. In the 1940s, Henry N. Flynt and his wife, of Connecticut, took an interest in restoring the town. Flynt, an attorney and a trustee of the Academy, bought the old inn and restored and furnished it in period style. The Tavern, built about 1760, was moved from Charlemont, Massachusetts, in pieces and rebuilt here. A pewter shop is on the ground floor.

Among the restorations that have been handsomely refurbished are: the *Asa Stebbins House,* built in the 1790s, a two-story brick dwelling, with portraits by Gilbert Stuart and others, among its expensive furnishings. Some walls have hand-painted decorations, and the bedrooms are embellished with swag-type wallpaper. *Ashley House,* 1732, now restored, was the home of the Reverend Jonathan Ashley until 1780. He was a Loyalist and a militant Tory. The house has been returned to its original site, from which it was moved to be used as a tobacco barn. The fabrics and pewter are of special interest. The *Dwight-Barnard House,* built by Josiah Dwight in 1754 in Springfield, Massachusetts, was rebuilt at this site. The kitchen is spacious, with a fireplace and early equipment. There is also a doctor's office with period instruments.

The *Frary-Barnard House* is one of the few frame structures to have escaped the fires set in Indian raids. Samson Frary was not so lucky; he was killed. The main section dates from 1730.

The *Parker and Russell House,* 1814, has been returned to its original site. Isaac Parker was a silversmith; John Russell was his apprentice.

The *Sheldon-Hawks House,* 1743, was the home of George Sheldon, historian. Among the many family furnishings are Delft, Worcester, and Leeds china and fine fabrics.

The **Wells-Thorn House** has a central section built about 1717; the front portion was added later. Ebenezer Wells kept a tavern, farmed, and ran a business. The law office of Hezekiah Strong, on the second floor, has furnishings from the late 18th century.

Wilson Printing House, built in 1816, traveled five times before being returned to where it started. It was a print shop at the outset, later a grocery, then a cabinetmaker's shop.

Wright House, 1824, has a collection of antique furniture which includes some Samuel McIntire, Sheraton, and Duncan Phyfe pieces. Asa Stebbins, Jr., was the first resident. Wright was the next owner.

Indian House Memorial, Main St., has replicas of a 1698 home and an early-18th-century home, both with period furnishings.

FALMOUTH, Barnstable County. St. 28.

The Saconesseet Homestead and Ship's Bottom Roof House, on St. 28A in West Falmouth, is a fairly new restoration on 15 acres, which features a homestead built in 1678. The estate belonged to the Bowerman and Gifford families for about 300 years and is filled with Americana they collected and thriftily saved from 1670 to the present. Dairy and farm implements are on the grounds. Open early summer to late fall.

Falmouth Historical Society Museum, on the village green, in the 1790 Julia Wood House, has whaling items and other antiques. This was a sea captain's home. *Katherine Lee Bates House,* 16 Main St., was the birthplace of the author who wrote the poem that became "America the Beautiful." She was born here August 12, 1859; her father was pastor of the First Congregational Church.

LOWELL, Middlesex County. I-495.

City Hall Historic District, roughly bounded by Broadway, French, Colburn, and Kirk Sts. Known as the "Spindle City on the Merrimack," Lowell was the principal manufacturing center of the U.S. by 1840. Its location at the confluence of the Merrimack and Concord rivers provided inexpensive power for the mills. It was the nation's first planned industrial community and was bounded by the two rivers and two canals. Rows of mill complexes were constructed along the riverbanks, and a system of canals was developed. Ten of these cut the city into seven islands. The city thrived until the 20th century, when the use of electricity became widespread and decreased the need for water power.

Today the federal and state governments are planning an extensive restoration project here. The center of Lowell became a National Historical Park in the summer of 1978.

Lucy Larcom Park, on the Merrimack Canal in the City Hall Historic District, has a section of Boston and Lowell Railroad track, laid in 1835. This was New England's first steam railway.

The *Locks and Canals Historic District* is the second of five proposed districts. The *Urban National Cultural Park* will include the riverbanks and all of the Locks and Canals system and will extend throughout the area, linking existing state parks and other waterways.

A restored mill will be an interpretive center. Some corporation boardinghouses will be preserved, with an exhibition of how women millworkers lived, and other exhibits of 19th-century industry.

The *Greater Lowell Chamber of Commerce,* 176 Church St.: (617) 455-5633, has brochures on walking tours.

The *Downtown Walking Tour* begins at the *Merrimack Gatehouse,* built in 1848, Romantic/Romanesque. *City Hall,* on Merrimack St., was built in 1893. A national design competition was held to select the architects. The style derives from the work of Henry Hobson Richardson, who designed Boston's Trinity Church among other fine buildings; the winning architects were Merrill and Cutler. *Memorial Hall and City Library,* behind City Hall, was built in the same year, also to plans by the winner of a competition, Frederick Stickney. It, too, is in the Richardson style, and both buildings are of pink granite from New Hampshire quarries. There are gargoyles and grotesque masks in the window trim, which local wags say are members of the Building Commission.

Whistler House, 243 Worthen St., was built in 1824 for Paul Moody, a manager and vice-president of the Lowell Machine Shops. James McNeill Whistler was born here when his father, George Washington Whistler, was chief engineer of the Locks and Canals. The artist chose to say—not too seriously—that he was born in Baltimore.

On Shattuck and Merrimack Sts., *Old Town Hall,* built in 1830, was remodeled in 1893, from Federal to Classical Revival style. John Quincy Adams, Daniel Webster, Abraham Lincoln, and Henry Clay were among speakers here.

Behind Town Hall, to the left, is the *Lowell Institution for Savings,* organized in 1829, erected in 1845. It has been altered but still keeps some of its original Italianate style.

Generations of comedians who have joked about sarsaparilla and today's collectors of old trade cards should enjoy seeing the 1880s J. C. Ayer plant on Middle St. Dr. Ayer's Sarsaparilla could cure almost anything: it was 26 percent alcohol. Its *Almanac* was printed in English, French, Dutch, German, Norwegian, Spanish, Portuguese, and Chinese. Ayer was an eccentric philanthropist who invented the first machine for making pills and later became insane.

At Kirk and French Sts. is the 1830s *Linus Childs House.* In 1847 Abraham Lincoln was a guest of Childs, then agent of the Boott Mills. Kirk Boott was a town planner, architect, engineer, and agent of the first textile mill here. *St. Anne's Church,* on Merrimack and Kirk Sts., was built in 1825 by the Merrimack Manufacturing Company and intended as a nondenominational house of worship. In Early Gothic style, it was meant to resemble a parish church in Derby, England, for the pleasure of Kirk Boott's wife Anne. Boott was the architect. The church was supported by monthly tithes of 37½¢ deducted from the workers' salaries, but this didn't last long. Many workers pulled away to establish their own churches. The Episcopalians took over the building in 1844.

The *South End Walking Tour* begins at Merrimack Gatehouse. *St. Paul's Methodist Church,* Hurd and Warren Sts., had a touch of scandal in its earlier days: Reverend Avery was accused of adultery with a Miss Cornell, who later was strangled in Tiverton, Rhode Island. The minister was found not guilty, but his congregation tried to run him out of town on a rail. He escaped this treatment but was burned in effigy. The church was built in 1839, to replace an earlier one on Chapel Hill.

A clothing store and hairdressing studio currently occupy the corner of Central and Warren Sts., where *Frye's Tavern* once stood. Often Irish laborers in the 1820s who stopped at Frye's to refresh themselves after a walk from Charleston were met by Kirk Boott, who hired them to rebuild the Pawtucket Canal. This route, too, passes many commercial buildings of the 19th century. There is a bowling lane on Central St. with Gothic detail. This building was formerly the *Boston and Maine Railroad Terminal,* built in 1876.

The *Union House Hotel,* Green and Central Sts., was a tavern and inn in the 1820s. Its mansard roof was an 1870s afterthought. Benjamin Butler, the "beast of New Orleans" during the Civil War occupation of that city, stayed here in 1829 when he and his mother came to his father's funeral in Lowell.

The *Boston Fish Market,* Gorham St., was formerly the *Lowell House Hotel,* then the Appleton House, a stagecoach stop.

The *Eliot Presbyterian Church,* South Common, built between 1873 and 1880, was named for John Eliot, a character in Hawthorne's *The Scarlet Letter.* (As the unfortunate Reverend Avery might well have been.)

Hood's Sarsaparilla Plant is on Thorndike St. Hood's and Dr. Ayer's were both popular. Hood advertised a concentrated extract which used dandelion, mandrake, dock, pipsissewa, juniper berries, and other well-known and valuable remedies. Sales in mandrake may have fallen off in the 20th century, but extracts of juniper berry still are going strong. Hood was the first to use trading cards; Ayer was not far behind.

The old *County Jail,* of 1856, in Lombardy Romanesque style, cost $150,000. Architect J. H. Rand was a sash and blind manufacturer, which may explain the many windows, but not the towers that make this pile the sort of building you could expect to find in a medieval town with knights in armor clanking up the broad front steps. An outraged citizen once observed that if every one of its 102 cells was constantly occupied the average annual cost of each prisoner to the county would be 400 honest dollars: "Thus a scoundrel who with his family of six persons is fortunate enough to occupy a tenement whose annual rent is $50.00 finds when he is so fortunate as to get into this magnificent jail, that the County lavishes upon him alone an expense which if bestowed upon his large and suffering family, would enable them to live almost in luxury." Which is not an easy sentence to get in and out of, but the exasperated C. C. Chase was in no mood for the simple declarative statement. The jail, towers, high-flying flag, and all went out of business in 1926, and the building is now the YMCA.

The *Middlesex County Superior Court House,* Elm St., seems straight out of a Godey's book design. The rear part was built in 1850. Daniel Webster tried cases here. The back section is Romanesque; the front wing was added in Classical Revival style.

The *Mills and Canals Western Tour,* beginning at the Merrimack Canal Gatehouse, takes in only the western end of the system which comprises 5.5 miles of canals. In 1792 the Proprietors of the Locks & Canals on the Merrimack was formed by some Newburyport merchants and financiers to construct a canal around the Pawtucket Falls at East Chelmsford. Alexander Hamilton hoped that waterways would unite the new nation. For a decade timber and freight from New Hampshire to Newburyport came this route. In 1803 when the Middlesex Canal was opened the Pawtucket route was out of business.

This tour takes in an area once known as "Little Canada" because so many French-Canadians came to work in the local industries. The *Round House,* built in 1872 by "Gentleman Johnnie" Bowers, who made carriages and ran an amusement park, is Second Empire, with a central circular staircase and a cupola with Haley's Comet painted on its ceiling. The woodwork is mahogany and the fireplaces are of Italian marble; the cost was $30,000.

Spaulding House, on Pawtucket St., built about 1760 by Robert Hildreth, was a stop on the Underground Railroad in pre-Civil War days and is now owned and maintained by the DAR.

Many self-made tycoons lived on Pawtucket St., and their homes reflect their ambitions. Also on this tour is the *Lowell Museum,* housed in what was the *Suffolk Yard,* along with an operating textile firm. A long low building here is the *Counting House,* which was erected in 1831. Museum displays interpret the Industrial Revolution with paintings, photographs, and period rooms. The working cotton-manufacturing machinery is used to demonstrate how raw cotton is made into cloth.

NANTUCKET ISLAND,
Nantucket County.

Reached by ferry from Woods

Hole or Hyannis. Cars can be taken aboard if reservations are made (well in advance) through the Nantucket Steamship Authority, P.O. Box 284, Woods Hole, 02543, or call toll-free (212) 966-1929. From Woods Hole the trip takes about three hours; from Hyannis two hours.

Thomas Mayhew, a wealthy merchant in Watertown, was granted the rights to the island from the English Crown. He wanted it for grazing land for his sheep and cattle. He introduced Christianity to the Indians and soon after sold his lands and privileges to all but one-twentieth of the island for "Thirty Pounds in good Merchantable Pay and Two Beaver Hats, one for myself and one for my wife."

Nantucket Historic District comprises many buildings which were associated with the whaling industry. It has mansions, tree-lined winding lanes, and cobblestone streets. Houses are clapboard painted a crisp white, or brick, or weathered shingle. Some of the stones in Main St. were once ballast in ships from abroad. *Three Bricks,* 93, 95, and 97 Main, were three houses built by James Childs in 1838; Christopher Capen, master mason. Joseph Starbuck, oil merchant, deeded them to his sons. On Sunset Hill off W. Chester St., the *Jethro Coffin House,* 1686, is the oldest house on the island and has been restored. The *Nantucket Historical Association,* Old Town Bldg., Union St., has pamphlets and a walking tour, and maintains the Jethro Coffin House and the *Lightship Nantucket,* moored at Straight Wharf; the *Whaling Museum,* Broad St. near the Steamboat Authority Wharf, has massive whale skeletons, scrimshaw, etc.; the *Peter Folger Museum,* next door, is brick, and has Quaker memorabilia.

The *Old Windmill,* on Mill Rd., off Prospect St., was built of wood salvaged from wrecked vessels; *Hadwen House-Satler Memorial,* Main and Pleasant Sts., built in 1845, comprises two white-pillared Greek Revival mansions, opposite the "Three Bricks." William Hadwen, a whaling merchant who had been a silversmith when he came to the island, married one of the daughters of Joseph Starbuck and later formed a company with Nathaniel Barney, who married another Starbuck daughter. Hadwen & Barney was a leading firm, owning many whaling ships. The Hadwens were childless and adopted a niece for whom Hadwen built the house at 94 Main St. which matched his own. The niece, Amelia Swain, married George Wright; the house in early guidebooks is known as the *Wright Mansion.* After the Wrights moved to California, George Wright became the first representative California sent to the U.S. Congress. The architect for these structures was Frederick Brown Coleman, who based his plans on the Temple of the Winds. The houses are open in summer season and the winter holidays with hostesses to point out the valuable furnishings and the history of the buildings.

Also operated by the Nantucket Historical Association: *1800 House,* Mill St., off Pleasant, is restored with period furnishings and represents a typical dwelling of the whaling days; *Old Gaol,* Vestal St., was used from 1805 until the 1930s; *Old Fire Hose Cart House* is on Gardner St., off Main; *Nathaniel Macy House,* Walnut Lane and Liberty St., built before 1720, is furnished with antique items; *Folger-Franklin Seat & Memorial Boulder,* Madaket Rd., 1 mile from the W end of Main St., was the birthplace site of Benjamin Franklin's mother, Abia Folger.

Maria Mitchell Association, 1 Vestal St., the birthplace of the first American woman astronomer, is furnished as it was in 1818. There is an observatory adjacent to the house; a museum, at 7 Milk St., features nature exhibits; the library, across from the observatory, also provides lecturers on Monday evenings.

NEW BEDFORD, Bristol County. I-195, US 6.

New Bedford Historic District, bounded by Front, Elm, Acushnet (Ave.), and Commercial Sts., is a waterfront district, containing some 19 structures in several styles of Classical architecture. Settled in the mid-18th century, New Bedford grew into one of the most important whaling ports of the mid-19th century.

Old Dartmouth Historical Society and Whaling Museum, 18 Johnny Cake Hill, has a reproduction of an authentic whaling bark, replicas of craftsmen's shops, and many relics of whaling days.

Seaman's Bethel, 15 Johnny Cake Hill, frame with shingles, two stories, built 1832, rebuilt in 1867 with tower, is the chapel described by Herman Melville in the classic *Moby Dick*. The pulpit is shaped like a ship's prow:

"I stuffed a shirt or two into my old carpet-bag, tucked it under my arm, and started for Cape Horn and the Pacific. Quitting the good city of old Manhatto, I duly arrived in New Bedford. . . . it became a matter of concernment where I was to eat and sleep. . . . With halting steps I paced the streets, and passed the sign of 'The Crossed Harpoons'—but it looked too expensive and jolly there." And so on. Ishmael's adventures in New Bedford with Queequeg and others are timeless and should be required reading for anyone taking his "first daylight stroll through the streets of New Bedford," as did Ishmael.

Meanwhile many New Bedford citizens are actively restoring their city and waterfront. *WHALE (Waterfront Historic Area League),* 13 Centre St. (zip 02740), has a Preservation Design Service for the Waterfront Historic District, with line drawings, maps and old photographs, and a newsletter for members. The waterfront restoration does not interfere with modern business firms in the area or the famed New Bedford fishing fleet.

Chamber of Commerce, 1213 Purchase St.—(617) 999-5231—has information on the area. Also helpful are the *Office of Historic Preservation,* Room 13, City Hall, 133 William St. (zip 02740)—(617) 999-2931—and the *Bristol County Development Council,* P.O. Box 831, 154 Main St., Fall River, 02722; phone (617) 676-1026.

Among the many listings on the Historic American Buildings Survey: *Congregational (now First Unitarian) Church,* NW corner Union and Eighth Sts., was built in 1836–38; *Custom House,* SW corner Second and Williams Sts., built in 1834–37; *Friends Meetinghouse,* N side of Spring St. near Sixth, 1824, has two stories; *Harrison Building,* 23 Centre St., is granite rubble with brick façade, four stories, built about 1820, interior altered for warehouse use; *Institution for Savings,* Second and Williams, ashlar and brick with Greek Revival details, built 1853, became a machine shop in later years; *Merchants' and Mechanics' Banks Building,* 56–62 N. Water St., has two stories with an Ionic portico and was two banks in 1831–35, later altered; *Wamsutta Mill,* Acushnet Ave., was the first large textile mill designed for steam power and was begun in 1847.

PITTSFIELD, Berkshire County, US 20.

Hancock Shaker Village, 5 miles W on US 20, past intersection with St. 41, began in 1790 and lasted until 1960. The site covers a 1,000-acre tract in the Berkshire mountain valley. Massachusetts historian and author Ivan Sandrof, in *More*

Massachusetts Towns (Barre, 1965), writes that 12 years before Hancock was settled, Ann Lee, known as Mother Ann, came from England with a small band of followers to start the colony: "Mother Ann set up strictures on the Second Coming, a basic tenet, and added her own against war, bearing arms, taking of oaths, and marriage. The Shakers endured all but the last. . . ."

Some 18 buildings have been restored; many have been furnished with Shaker pieces. Among the structures on the HABS list: **Brethren's Shop,** S of US 20, just W of St. 41, frame with clapboarding, two stories, built in 1833. **Dairy and Weave Shop,** same area, frame with clapboarding, also first half of 19th century; **Main Dwelling,** brick, three and a half stories, 1830. **Meetinghouse,** N of US 20, W of St. 41, frame with clapboarding, one and a half stories with hipped roof, built 1792–93 by Moses Johnson at Shirley, where it was also a meeting house; moved here in 1962. Nearby is the **Ministry's Shop,** two-story frame with clapboarding, built before 1820. The **Round Stone Barn** is rubble masonry with frame and clapboarding, three stories, built 1826. Also the **Sisters Shop,** from the early 19th century; **Tan Shop,** 1835; **Trustees' Bldg.,** 19th century; and **Wash House Bldg.,** No. 4, brick, 19th century. The Shakers were peerless cooks, and today kitchen festivals and public "tastings" are held, and the gift shop sells recipe books. For information on events, call (413) 443-0188. The village is open from June 1 to November.

PLYMOUTH, Plymouth County. St. 44 and Plymouth Bay.

Plymouth Area Chamber of Commerce, 85 Samoset St., 02360, publishes an illustrated guide to the area, *Historic Plymouth; America's Home Town,* which gives hours sites are open, special events, emergency numbers, etc.

Visitor Center, N. Park Ave., has information on the many historic sites. With a whole lot of luck, there won't be chewing gum wrappers and aluminum rings from pop-top cans lying around Plymouth Rock when you visit it, on Water St. on the harbor.

The **Mayflower II** at State Pier is a 90-foot reproduction of the original bark and was sailed to America in 1957. Alan Villiers, the last of the great sailing captains and the author of many excellent books on the sea and his adventures, was in charge of this voyage and tried his best to sail without even a radio, thereby duplicating the original voyage totally, but was not allowed to keep this much to the authentic procedure. In every other way the voyage tried to follow the first one. For many visitors, the famous Rock is a major disappointment, with its often littered base and its "Grecian Temple" protection; honky-tonk also surrounds the **Mayflower II,** just as the social pretensions of all those who claimed descent from an original passenger have obscured the voyage itself. But no one can stand within the confines of the small ship and not be awed by the courage of those travelers in this risky bark on a perilous sea to an unknown land. It is to be hoped that someday a proper monument to the Pilgrims will be constructed.

Plimoth Plantation, 2 miles S on St. 2A, is a well-researched reconstruction by a nonprofit organization which re-creates life in the settlement as it might have looked in 1627. **Pilgrim Village** has guides and hostesses in period-style clothing carrying out the chores that would have been done in the 17th-century rural community. It is a Living Folk Museum, which is a fairly recent and entertaining way of presenting history and is becoming widespread.

The earliest Pilgrims are buried at **Cole's Hill,** S of Plymouth Rock. Most of the burials here were of those who failed to survive the dreadful first winter. **Burial Hill,** at the head of Town Square, has the grave of Governor William Bradford.

Plymouth buildings on the National Register include **Old County Courthouse,** Leyden and Market Sts., designed by Peter Oliver and built in 1747; **Pilgrim Hall,** 75 Court St., with Alexander Parrish as architect, dates from 1824–25; **Antiquarian House,** 126 Water St., from 1809; **Richard Sparrow House,** 42 Summer St., built in 1640, restored, has the only known intact 17th-century fireplace; **Harlow Old Fort House,** 119 Sandwich St., one of the oldest buildings in town, has been partially restored; it was built from timbers once part of a 1692 fort nearby. William Harlow, a Pilgrim leader, lived here. **Jabez Howland House,** 33 Sandwich St., was the home of the son of John Howland, one of the Mayflower Compact signers in November 1620. The house was built in 1667, enlarged in 1750.

SALEM, Essex County. St. 22, on Massachusetts Bay.

Salem has 7 historic districts: **Charter St., Chestnut St., Derby Waterfront, Essex Institute, House of Seven Gables, Salem Common,** and **Old Town Hall.** Among individual listings on the National Register are the **Nathaniel Bowditch House,** North St., the early-19th-century home of the scientist and navigator. NHL. **City Hall,** 93 Washington St., is from 1838. **Gardner-Pingree House,** 128 Essex St., was designed and built by Samuel McIntire, in 1804–5, for John Gardner, a local merchant. NHL. **Gedney and Cox Houses,** 19 and 21 High St., share one lot. The restored Gedney House was built about 1665; the Cox house dates from the second half of the 18th century. **Hamilton Hall,** 9 Cambridge St., is another fine structure designed and executed by Samuel McIntire, in 1806–7. NHL. The building was

named for Alexander Hamilton and has been the meeting place for town assemblies for nearly two centuries. **Peabody Museum,** 161 Essex St., built in 1825 to house the collection of the East India Marine Society, which was organized in 1799, is one of the nation's great museums. NHL. Guided tours may be arranged by appointment: (617) 745-1876. Open Monday through Saturday, 9 to 5; Sundays and holidays, 1 to 5. Closed Thanksgiving, Christmas, and New Year's Day. **Peirce-Nichols House,** 80 Federal St., is attributed to Samuel McIntire, architect; built in 1782, it is three stories with deck balustrade and authentic furnishings. NHL. **Joseph Story House,** 26 Winter St., is early 19th century. NHL. **John Ward House,** 132 Essex, dates back to 1684, restored with period furnishings. NHL.

The **Essex Institute,** 132 Essex, in front of the Ward House, contains, in the words of its charter, "the authentic memorials relating to the civil history of Essex County, Massachusetts, and of the eminent men who have resided within its limits from the first settlement through the 19th century." In addition to this the Institute, founded in 1848, maintains several historic houses, including the Ward, Gardner-Pingree, and Peirce-Nichols houses listed above; the **Crowninshield-Bentley House,** 126 Essex, built in 1727, relocated and restored by subscription; the **Assembly House,** 138 Federal St., built as a social hall in 1782 and remodeled in 1796 by Samuel McIntire as a residence for Jonathan Waldo.

The **City of Salem** and the **Chamber of Commerce** publish an illustrated guide to historic sites, listing those which are open and admission fees, with historic trail map. The trail is marked with a witch on a broomstick sign. Tours should begin at the *Chamber of Commerce,* Hawthorne Blvd. at Washington Square, as it follows many one-way streets.

Salem Maritime National Site has a visitor center in the *Custom House,* on Derby St., opposite the wharf. The 1819 building has been restored. *Derby Wharf* was the central point of Salem shipping, from 1760 to 1860. The *Scale House,* built in 1829, and the *Bonded Warehouse,* 1819, were part of the customs complex. The *Derby House,* Derby St., is Salem's oldest remaining brick dwelling. Captain Richard Derby built the wharf; it was used as a privateer base by his son Elias Hasket Derby during the Revolutionary War. Nathaniel Hawthorne worked as a surveyor of the Port of Salem from 1846 to 1849 at the custom house.

A 1908 *Visitor's Guide to Salem,* published by the Essex Institute, has this entry: "Giles Corey, who was pressed to death in 1692, lived on the site of 46 Boston street, before he removed to what is now West Peabody." Fortunately this ominous item had a follow-up on page 10. "The unpopular octogenarian, Giles Corey, who lived on a spot near the present railroad station at West Peabody, was greatly interested in the examinations [the witchcraft trials], but his wife Martha did not wish him to attend them and objected to his going." He went anyway and even testified against Martha, who was hanged shortly thereafter. Then Giles was arrested and refused to plead in his own behalf. So he was pressed to death by weights intended to make him speak out or die. He died. The guidebook adds: "This event has no parallel in American history."

The *Pioneers' Village,* in Forest River Park, E of junction of St. 1A and St. 129, is a reproduction of Salem in 1630; open daily until dusk. *Pickering Wharf Village,* P.O. Box 809, 01970—(617) 744-4080—is a new residential and commercial complex on a six-acre waterfront site, linking the downtown urban renewal district and historic Derby St. An open seaside walkway leads to the adjacent *National Parks Maritime Historic Site.* When the complex is completed, the entire South River waterfront will be a unit. One of the attractions already in operation is *Voyage of the India Star,* in continuous performance at the *Pickering Wharf Theatre.* The lobby has a diorama and maritime displays. For detailed information on the theater and other parts of the Wharf, call (617) 745-8694, or P.O. Box 809, Salem 01970.

STURBRIDGE, Worcester County. St. 131, off I-86.

Old Sturbridge Village, junction of I-86, US 20, St. 15, 30. A re-created New England country town and farm on a 200-acre site depict small-community life between 1790 and 1840. This was one of the first living-history re-creations. It began in the 1920s with two brothers, Albert B. Wells and J. Cheney Wells, who were collectors for the pleasure of it until their treasures grew to such proportions that they felt the need to find a use for them. Eventually the decision was made to set up a village where the Quinebaug River flows, to form ponds for the sawmills and gristmills. The village plan was made, and nearly 40 buildings were brought from other parts of New England. Today the village is a nonprofit educational institution embracing nearly the whole range of everyday life. A *Visitor Center* has orientation exhibits, a film, and other information. Staff members can advise how to organize your visit for special activities preferred. Three to six hours are recommended for a first visit.

The village celebrates its 33rd birthday in 1979. Its aim and its accomplishment have been to demonstrate in a great outdoor working museum how the common folks of the nation worked and played. The charming green is surrounded by fully furnished homes, stores, offices, church, and meeting house. Although everything seems perfect as it

The Farm, Old Sturbridge Village, Sturbridge, Massachusetts. (Courtesy of Old Sturbridge Village)

is, the administration is always trying to improve the reconstructions, and has weeded out anachronisms, such as stocks, or moved such areas as a formal herb garden, which would not have existed on the small town green. Changes occur constantly, so that those who have "seen" Old Sturbridge will find it new all over again. The village is open daily, year round, except Christmas and New Year's Day. For information on the many specific programs and monthly events, reservations, prices, etc., call (617) 347-3362; or write Secretary of Special Events, Old Sturbridge Village, Sturbridge, 01566.

The *Phoenix Mill,* a stone cotton factory built in 1823 in Connecticut, was added in 1977. It is used to manufacture shirting and sheeting while demonstrating the process of the old-time factory system. The reconstructed *Nichols-Colby Sawmill,* powered by a brook, is another addition.

Artifacts are explained by Old Sturbridge Village experts in costume who put the original objects or the reproductions to use in fitting surroundings. Pottery, blacksmithing, printing, coopering, and cabinetmaking are some of the skills demonstrated. Shoes, signs, and tinware are some of the products turned out in the old-time way. Everything from brooms to books, or from a carding mill to a law office, is here for the enlightenment of the visitor who wants to spend some pleasurable hours in the past.

WEST SPRINGFIELD, Hampden County. I-91.

Storrowton Village, 1511 Memorial Ave., W on St. 57, on the Exposition Grounds, is a reconstructed community. Old New England buildings were brought here to re-create a 19th-century village. The *Phillips House,* the oldest of the collection, came from Taunton, where it was erected in 1767 by Edward Phillips. The sills and beams are hand-hewn oak. Phillips sold the house to Dr. William McKinistry, who sold it to William Russell, who sold it to John Thurston, a Revolutionary soldier, in

The Schoolhouse, Storrowtown Village, West Springfield, Massachusetts. (Courtesy Eastern States Exposition)

1777. In 1785 William Seaver, adjutant brigade major of the Bristol County 3rd Regiment, took the house, but before the year was out he passed it on to Captain Thomas Foster, another soldier. Foster settled down until 1805 and left the house to his son Charles, who kept it until 1831 and then it went to David Brewer; in 1848 it came back to the Fosters; the new owner, Charles Foster, was a grandson of Captain Timothy Foster. Charles kept the house

for five years, and then it was bought by the Redferns, who were fairly steady. They kept it until December 1929. The *Phillips-McKinistry-Russell-Thurston-Seaver-Foster-Brewer-Foster-Redfern House* is not open to visitors. *C'est la vie.*

The *Schoolhouse,* from Whately, is one room with suitable furnishings including a barrel stove. It was built in 1810 with brick from the Whately pottery and brickyard.

The *Blacksmith Shop,* from Chesterfield, New Hampshire, dates from the mid-19th century. The *Gilbert Homestead,* from West Brookfield, was built in 1794. The *Atkinson Tavern,* built toward the end of the 18th century, came from Prescott. The 1822 *Town House* is from Southwick.

The *Eddy Law Office,* from Middleboro, was headquarters for Zachariah Eddy, who practiced law from 1806 until 1860. The *Potter Mansion* was built by Captain John Potter in N. Brookfield before and after the Revolutionary War. Except for the plastering, Potter did all the work, made all the nails, latches, and hinges, and carved all the elaborate ornamentation in wood.

RHODE ISLAND

But to the student of domestic architecture Newport is the most interesting of all our summer colonies. Its history is the longest. . . . Colonial houses are abundant, both on outlying estates and farms and in the old closely built portions of the town itself. Its newer portions show a characteristic instance of that way of village-planning which [is] . . . peculiarly American—wide streets of detached houses, each with its own small lawn and garden, and all overshadowed by thick-set and lofty trees. Here the architecture includes every post-colonial type: the plain, square, piazzaed box; the "vernacular" villa with "French roof" and jig-saw fringing and abnormal hues of paint; the pseudo "Queen Anne" cottage. . . . In its summer garments it is a pretty place indeed.

—*American Country Dwellings*, by Mrs. Schuyler van Rensselaer, New York, 1886

BRISTOL, Bristol County. St. 114.
Bristol Waterfront Historic District, harbor to the E side of Wood St., N to Washington St. and S to Walker Cove, was a busy port for trading vessels in its early days.
Bristol Customshouse and Post Office, 420–448 Hope St., was built in 1848; Ammi B. Young, the Treasury architect, designed the building in Renaissance Revival.
County Courthouse, High St., in 1816 was one of five courthouses in which the General Assembly met in rotation.
County Jail, 48 Court St., 1828, originally had quarters for the jailer, with cells on the second floor. A rear ell was added in 1859. The building was renovated in 1959. The *Bristol Historical & Preservation Society* has headquarters here, with a museum.
Benjamin Church House, 1014 Hope St., has Georgian Revival elements, and was designed by Howe and Church.

Longfield (Charles Dana Gibson House), 1200 Hope St., built in 1848, was the Gothic Revival home of the grandfather of the artist.
Joseph Reynolds House, 956 Hope, is a three-story building from 1698. A Colonial saltbox with Federal touches added. It served as headquarters for Lafayette when he came to Rhode Island in 1778, carrying on a campaign of the Revolutionary War.
Chamber of Commerce, in Town Hall, has maps and information on walking tours.
Coggeshall Farm, in Colt State Park, 2½ miles NW on St. 114, has a restored 18th-century farmhouse, blacksmith shop, and demonstrations of a working farm life.

EAST GREENWICH (and Warwick), Kent County. US 1.
East Greenwich Historic District includes many fine examples of early architecture from the 17th to 19th

34

centuries. The port became a rich fishing and shipbuilding center in the 1700s. Part of the district is in Warwick.

Also on the National Register: **Kent County Courthouse,** 127 Main St., early 19th century, with a hipped roof, balustraded deck, and clock tower with cupola.

General James Mitchell Varnum House, 57 Peirce St., 1773. Varnum was a Revolutionary War general, lawyer, and congressman. The beautiful Georgian dwelling, which overlooks Narragansett Bay, has been restored and has a museum. The 18th-century style gardens are maintained by the local Garden Club; the house, by the Varnum Continentals and the Continental Ladies.

Colonel Micah Whitmarsh House, 294 Main St., 1767–71, is brick with Georgian elements and was altered in the 1830s. Whitmarsh was also a Revolutionary War officer. **Windmill Cottage,** 144 Division St., is Federal with Italianate elements. The windmill dates from about 1790, the house from 1800, give or take a year. The poet Henry Wadsworth Longfellow bought the house for his friend Professor George Washington Greene in 1866. The windmill was purchased four years later and moved here. Longfellow used a second-story room as a study. (Also see Warwick for other sites in the area).

KINGSTON, Washington County. St. 108, 138.

Kingston Village Historic District contains 44 structures, most of which pre-date 1840. Among the earliest are the **John Moore House,** 1710, and the **Elisha Reynolds House,** 1739. Settlers came after the Pettaquamscutt Purchase in 1658.

Fayerweather House, St. 138, was the 1830s home of the village blacksmith, George Fayerweather, who was black. His descendants continued to run the shop, which is now a Craft Center. **Helme House,** 1319

Kingston Rd., was built about 1802 and now houses the Art Association. **Old Washington County Jail,** Kingstown Rd., 1856, has early cells and period rooms and changing exhibits showing South County life from the 17th to 20th centuries; maintained by the Pettaquamscutt Historical Society. All of the above are in the South Kingston area.

In North Kingston is the **Wickford Historic District,** roughly bounded by Tower Hill and Post Rds., N to Mill Cove and S to Lindley Ave. This is a small harbor village with a number of 18th-century dwellings, many of them clapboard mill houses with hooded center entrances and central chimneys. Also of interest and on the National Register are: **Old Narragansett Church (St. Paul's Episcopal),** 60 Church Lane, 1707, built on the meeting house plan, gallery added in 1723, moved from original site in 1800, and restored in the 1920s; the **Palmer-Northrup House,** 7919 Post Rd., dating from the 17th century; **Dr. William G. Shaw House,** 41 Brown St., 1803, a good example of early Federal style in Rhode Island; **Smith's Castle,** Post Rd., N of town, 1678, standing on the site of an early trading post. It has been restored and furnished with antiques.

Note: also in history-packed Washington County are the **Carolina Village Historic District,** at St. 91, 113; the **Historic Village of the Narragansetts in Charlestown,** bound by St. 2, 112, US 1, St. 91, and Kings Factory Rd.; and the **Hopkinton City Historic District,** St. 3, just W of I-95, once an important stop on the New London Turnpike in 1815. After the railroads came, the village again became a farming community. The **Old Harbor Historic District,** New Shoreham, comprises the east part of Block Island with piers, breakwaters, and early buidings including the **John Hooper House,** built early in the 18th century when this was a fishing and farming area. Later it became a resort and a number of late-19th-century structures remain. The **Wilcox Park Historic District,** Westerly, is bounded by Broad, Granite, and High Sts. and Grove Ave. including Elm St. The residential area surrounds a beautifully tended park; many architectural styles of the 18th century are represented. The **Wyoming Village Historic District,** Wyoming, St. 3, just W of I-95, has 59 buildings and sites; many are Greek Revival.

LITTLE COMPTON, Newport County. E of St. 77 on S. Commons Rd.

Little Compton Common Historic District comprises the triangular green and surrounding 17th- to 20th-century structures. The **Unitarian Congregational Church,** 1832, suffered changes in the Victorian era, but most of the area is still colonial. The monument to Elizabeth Pabodie, in the Commons burial ground, honors the first white girl born in New England. She was the daughter of John and Priscilla Alden. **Wilbur House,** Main Rd., began in the 17th century and was altered a number of times. Restored by the Little Compton Historical Society. Open summer weekends.

NEWPORT, Newport County. St. 138.

Newport Historic District is an 18th-century residential and commercial area, mostly concentrated near the waterfront and within the city limits of the 18th-century town. Many of the fine old buildings are Georgian, built by master carpenter Richard Munday and builder-architect Peter Harrison. There are mansions, row houses, and shops. The port was carrying on a brisk trade by 1618. **Bowen's Wharf,** off Thames St., has been restored even to its cobblestone streets. NHL.

Newport is one of those places where you couldn't throw a Frisbee or an old-fashioned paper dart without hitting something historic. Enough books on Newport alone have been published by writers, photographers, artists, historians, architects, and travel guiders to sink Rhode Island. The **Preservation Society of Newport County,** Washington Square, has annual tours of restored 18th-century houses, literature, and maps; it sells combination tickets to mansions which are open at times other than the tours. **Visitor Bureau,** 93 Thames, has maps for self-guiding tours and information on narrated bus tours and boat trips.

Newport Restoration Foundation, 39 Mill St., supports "Operation Clapboard," which encourages rehabilitation of old buildings. **Oldport Association,** 37 Touro, has a museum. **Newport Historical Society,** 82 Touro, founded in 1854, has a museum, also a junior museum. **Redwood Library and Athenaeum,** 50 Bellevue Ave., 1748, designed by Peter Harrison, is said to be the oldest library building in continuous use in the U.S. It has rare books and portraits. It was built for Abraham Redwood and others to be used as a meeting place for "gentlemen." The exterior is of "rusticated" wood, sanded and painted to resemble stone.

Bellevue Ave.–Casino Historic District, 170–230 Bellevue Ave., one-square-block commercial area, includes the Stick-style **Travers Block** of 1870–71, designed by Richard Morris Hunt; the Shingle-style **Newport Casino,** 1880–81, designed by McKim, Mead, and White; the **King Block,** in Jacobean Revival style (modified), by Perkins and Betton; and the **Andrian Building,** by Bruce Price, 1902–3, somewhat in the style of Louis Sullivan.

Brick Market, Thames St. and Washington Square, 1762–72, designed by Peter Harrison, now restored, is Georgian commercial architecture. NHL.

Clarke Street Meetinghouse, Clarke

St., built about 1735 by Cotton Palmer, has been remodeled twice. It was erected for the Second Congregational Society, with William Ellery and Henry Marchant among the early members. Ellery, born in Newport in 1727, was a founder of Rhode Island College, which became Brown University, a graduate of Harvard, a signer of the Declaration of Independence, and later chief justice of the Rhode Island Supreme Court, and a customs collector. Marchant, born in Martha's Vineyard in 1741, became state attorney general, accompanied Benjamin Franklin on a diplomatic mission to Scotland, served in the First Continental Congress, was a delegate to the Convention of 1787 which ratified the Constitution in 1790, and later a judge for the U.S. District Court in Rhode Island.

Common Burying Ground and Island Cemetery, Farewell and Warner Sts., contains 800 gravestones which are earlier than 1800. Ellery and Marchant (see above), Oliver Hazard Perry and his brother Matthew C. Perry are among those buried here.

Kay-Catherine St.–Old Beach R. Historic District, 17th to 20th century, has a variety of buildings including the Victorian eclectic "hypotenuse" style house built about 1870 by Richard Morris Hunt; the *Samuel Coleman House,* 414 Thames St., in Shingle style, by McKim, Mead, and White; the *Jewish Cemetery* (1677); and many costly residences used as summer homes by wealthy and famous persons, including the author Henry James, William B. Rogers, founder of MIT and a geologist, and the artist John LaFarge.

Old Colony House (Old Statehouse), Washington Square, 1779–1841, built by Richard Munday, architect, to house the General Assembly of the colony later served to accommodate the state legislature, was restored in 1932. It is brick Georgian and has a museum. NHL.

Perry Mill, 337 Thames, 1835, built by Alexander MacGregor, is one of four mills put up along the waterfront to aid the economy.

Shiloh Church (Trinity Schoolhouse), 25 School St., 1799, had adjoining parish hall and parsonage in 1844. Federal with Second Empire additions. A day school was operated on this site from 1742 to 1867.

Touro Synagogue National Historic Site, 85 Touro, built 1759–63, is considered the masterpiece of architect Peter Harrison. The interior has a gallery supported by 12 Ionic columns, and original furnishings, preserved and restored from 1822. It is the oldest synagogue in America. The congregation was established by Sephardic Jews in the 17th century, and the synagogue is still in use. Museum.

Trinity Church, Spring and Church, 1725–26, built by architect Richard Munday, enlarged in 1762, has a projecting square entrance tower with arcaded belfry, lantern, and an octagonal spire with a bishop's mitre weather vane pointing the Rhode Island wind direction since pre-Revolutionary days. Church restored in 1936. Open daily in summer.

United Congregational Church, Spring and Pelham, 1855–57, Joseph C. Wells, architect, has stained glass by John LaFarge. Romanesque Revival.

White Horse Tavern, 26 Marlborough St., 1670s, enlarged a century later, restored in the 1940s, is said to be the country's oldest tavern still pouring for customers.

Newport Steam Factory, 449 Thames, 1831, added to in 1865, is the most important surviving waterfront commercial structure of the 19th century.

Ochre Point-Cliffs Historic District is bounded more or less by the coastline N to Memorial Blvd., S to Sheep Point Cove, and to Bellevue Ave. *Ocean Drive Historic District* unsurprisingly follows Ocean Drive. NHL. Individual dwellings on the National Register include:

Charles H. Baldwin House, Bellevue Ave., opposite Perry St.; 1877–78, Potter and Robinson architects. Queen Anne and Shingle style, built as a summer home for Commodore Baldwin.

Isaac Bell House (Edna Villa), 70 Perry St., 1882–83, McKim, Mead, and White. An outstanding example of Shingle style.

The Breakers, Ochre Point Ave., one of the most-photographed houses in America, was built 1893–95; Richard Morris Hunt, architect. Second Renaissance Revival, it was the home of Cornelius Vanderbilt II. Museum.

Chateau-sur-Mer, Bellevue Ave., built in 1852, Seth Bradford, architect. Remodeled in the 1870s by Richard Morris Hunt, who put in America's first French ballroom. There is a toy museum.

Sherman Clark House, 279 Thames, 18th-century frame, stuccoed, with shingling in the rear.

Commandant's Residence, Quarters Number One, Fort Adams, Harrison Ave. (1872–73), George C. Mason and Son, architects. Second Empire with Stick style elements. President Eisenhower used the dwelling for a summer home in 1958 and 1960.

Dr. Charles Cotton House, 5 Cotton's Court, early-18th-century frame and clapboard, was the home of Cotton, a surgeon on the U.S.S. *Constitution* (Old Ironsides).

William King Covell III House, 72 Washington (1870). William Ralph Emerson and Carl Fehmer, architects. Museum.

The Elms, Bellevue Ave. (1899–1901), Horace Trumbauer, Philadelphia architect, was modeled to some extent after a French château. The mansion was a "summer" home for E. J. Berwind, Philadelphia coal merchant. Sunken garden designed by Jacques Greber, who was French.

Levi H. Gale House, 89 Touro (1833–35), Russell Warren, architect, moved in 1925, is an example of Federal and Greek Revival blending.

John Griswold House, 76 Bellevue (1863–64), Richard Morris Hunt, architect, is in Stick style.

Hunter House, 54 Washington, built about 1748, for Deputy Governor Jonathan Nichols, Jr. Museum includes a special exhibition of the famous Townsend-Goddard furniture, silverware, art. This was headquarters of French Admiral de Ternay during the Revolutionary War. NHL.

Edward King House, Aquidneck Park, Spring St. Richard Upjohn was the architect in 1845–47. This example of Italian villa was published in A. J. Downing's book, *The Architecture of Country Houses,* which influenced many builders.

Kingscote, Bellevue Ave. and Bowery St., also designed by Upjohn. The house was built in 1839–41, as a summer home for George Noble Jones of Georgia. During the Civil War it was acquired by William Henry King. Additions were made in the 1880s by McKim, Mead, and White. Museum.

Lucas-Johnston House, 40 Division St., built about 1721. Enlarged in the next century and has been restored. It was the home of Colonial Attorney General Augustus Johnston. In 1765 when he was stamp distributor, Johnston was forced to sign a pledge to refrain from carrying out his duties; later a mob attacked his home. He became a Loyalist, and his house was confiscated. It later was acquired by Commodore Oliver Hazard Perry.

Francis Malbone House, 392 Thames St., built by Peter Harrison for Malbone, a merchant and slave trader in 1744. There are many subterranean passages that seem fitting for a slave trader who may not have been above smuggling. A small building on the property is thought to have been a British Treasury during the Revolutionary War.

Marble House, Bellevue Ave., Richard Morris Hunt, architect, for house built in 1888–92, another of the most-photographed dwellings in America. There is a one-story pagoda near the water. It is all Beaux-Arts Classicism and plain rich. A Gilded Age survivor. Museum.

Captain John Mawdsley House, 228 Spring St., 17th- and 18th-century frame, with clapboarding. The residence was divided into apartments in the 1920s. The original structure is attributed to Jireh Bull; it was expanded by Mawdsley, a wealthy merchant. Sometimes listed as the *Bull-Mawdsley House.*

Joseph Rogers House, 37 Touro St., built about 1790, three stories, frame and clapboarding. Rogers was an early merchant.

Rosecliff, Bellevue Ave., built in 1902, another Gilded Age mansion, with McKim, Mead, and White, architects. Also known as the *Hermann Oelrichs House; J. Edgar Monroe House,* it is a Gilded Age spectacular summer home. Museum.

(Note: Although McKim, Mead, and White sound like a pharmaceutical house, they were New York architects in business together from 1879 to 1909. Charles Follen McKim, William Rutherford Mead, and Stanford White were the largest and best-known firm in the country, and one, White, became even better known—or if not exactly *better,* more widely known—when he was murdered in June 1906 at Madison Square Garden by Harry Thaw, who later was adjudged insane.)

William Watts Sherman House, 2 Shepard Ave., designed by world-famous H. H. Richardson, built in 1875–76, was later enlarged by McKim, Mead, and White. Service wing added in 1905. Queen Anne. NHL.

Ezra Stiles House, 14 Clarke St., built in 1756, as a parsonage. Stiles was a colonial leader as a minister, educator, and scientist.

John Tillinghast House, 142 Mill St., dates from 1760, with remodeling in the 19th century.

Vernon House, 46 Clarke St., 1758 frame, built by Rhode Island Supreme Court Justice Metcalf Bowler, then the home of merchant and shipowner William Vernon. The French general Rochambeau stayed here in 1780–81. Museum. NHL.

Wanton-Lyman-Hazard House, 17 Broadway, built about 1695, was damaged during the 1765 Stamp Act riots when the stamp master lived here. Restored. NHL.

Samuel Whitehorne House, 414 Thames St. Built about 1800–10, for Captain Samuel Whitehorne, Jr., a wealthy merchant, is Federal. It never was completed because he was bankrupted by shipping losses, and it was sold at auction in 1844. Fine interior with many rare Newport antiques in Goddard and Townsend crafts. Summer kitchen in authentic Pilgrim style and a garden of the Federal period with early varieties of plants.

Also of historical interest is the **Prescott Farm,** W. Main Rd. near Union St. The group of restored buildings includes a **Windmill,** built about 1812, and operating today, producing five to six bushels of corn per hour. Cornmeal is sold at the **Country Store,** formerly the **Earle-Hick House,** built about 1715 in Portsmouth where it served John Earle as the ferry-master's home. **General Prescott's Guardhouse,** built about 1730, has a museum and Pilgrim furnishings and was used by the general's troops during the Revolution when it was next door to the **Prescott (Nichols-Overing) House,** of the 1730s. Mrs. Henry Overing was having an affair with General Richard Prescott, commander of British forces in Rhode Island, who was captured here, not by Prescott but by Colonel William Barton in July 1777. The Newport Restoration Foundation maintains the farm and the Whitehorne House.

Beechwood, Bellevue Ave., was the summer palace of the Queen of Society, "Mrs. Astor," a name that the lady felt needed no introduction in her era, although there were three Mrs. William Astors. According to society's biographer (and mortician, his detractors would say) Cleveland Amory, the Astors were first Astorga, then Ashdor. The family founder John Jacob Astor was a butcher's son who left the hams and blood sausage of his native Germany to make his fortune in America. He arrived in 1782, age 20, with $25 in cash and seven flutes. He soon began to play a pretty tune financially; by 1835 he was the richest man in New York and was founding a dynasty. "The" Mrs. Astor came in the third generation of the famous family: Caroline Webster Schermerhorn, daughter of a Dutch ship-chandler, who liked to wear a diamond tiara and a diamond stomacher, and who insisted that her husband William Backhouse Astor drop his offensive middle name. When William Waldorf Astor's wife in the late 1880s came to live next door in Newport she too insisted on having her mail addressed simply as "Mrs. Astor." Pity the postman. Beechwood was remodeled in 1893, gaining the largest ballroom in town. Restored, in ten acres of fine trees, the home is open daily.

"Belcourt Castle," Bellevue Ave, 1891, was built for Oliver Hazard Perry Belmont, whose wife was Alva Smith, the former Mrs. William K. Vanderbilt and mother of Consuelo, later Duchess of Marlborough. The house has an eclectic collection of antiques, stained glass from 32 countries, and a Royal Coronation coach. There are costumed guides. The *Children's Museum* has an unusually fine collection of toys and furniture.

PAWTUCKET, Providence County. US 1A. I-95.

Old Slater Mill Historic Site. From I-95 heading S take exit 29; heading N take exit 28. Roosevelt Ave. The mill was built in 1793 by Samuel Slater, William Almy, and Smith Brown to produce machine-spun cotton yarn and was the first American factory to use water-powered machines for yarn production. There are three buildings on the site, the mill itself, the *Sylvanus Brown House,* built in 1758, and the *Oziel Wilkinson Mill* of 1810. Guides are on duty in the area. Hand spinning and weaving are demonstrated.

Daggett House, in Slater Park, Armistice Blvd. off US 1A, was built in 1685 and has period furnishings. *Trinity Church,* 50 Main St., was built about mid-19th century, with Samuel J. Ladd, architect.

PROVIDENCE. Providence County. US 1.

The *Greater Providence Chamber of Commerce,* 10 Dorrance St., has maps and information on the many historic sites of Providence.

Broadway-Armory Historic District, a suburban area, has 19th-century structures, mostly Greek Revival or Victorian, including the Stick-style *J. B. Arnold House* and the eclectic *George W. Prentice House.*

College Hill Historic District, bounded by Olney St., Cohan Blvd., Hope St., and the Providence and Moshassuck rivers, a chiefly residential area within the original 17th-century settlement bounds. There are some 300 structures from the 18th and early 19th centuries in the district. This may be the greatest concentration of intact early buildings anywhere in the U.S. NHL.

Hope-Power-Cooke Sts. Historic District, roughly bounded by Angell,

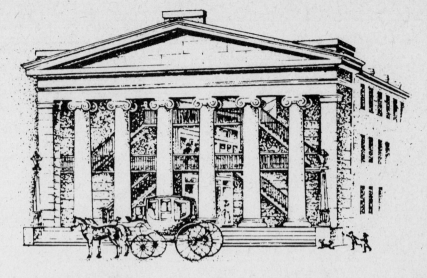

The Arcade, Providence, Rhode Island. (Courtesy Arcade Association)

Governor, Williams, and Brook Sts. Among the notable Renaissance Revival houses here are the *Robert Lippitt House,* built 1854, by Thomas Alexander Tefft; Italianate *Henry Lippitt House,* about 1863, by Henry Childs; *Esther Baker House,* of 1882, by Stone and Carpenter in Queen Anne style. There are a number of Victorian houses in the district.

Stimson Ave. Historic District, both sides of Stimson and Diman Place between Angell on the S, Hope on the W, and a stone wall on the N. Among the many fashionable early homes are the *Amos Beckwith House,* built about the beginning of the Civil War, by Alpheus C. Morse; the *Joseph E. Fletcher House,* by Stone, Carpenter, and Willson, in 1890.

Market Square, Main St. and the river, is the area where townspeople tossed tea into a fire in 1775. *Market House* was built in 1773–75, with Joseph Brown, architect. French troops were quartered here during the Revolution. Restored in 1940.

The *First Baptist Meeting House,* 75 N. Main, was built in 1775, Georgian style. NHL.

The *Arcade Building,* from Westminster through to Wybosset St., 1827–28, is the only survivor of its type. James C. Bucklin, Jr., and Russell Warren were the architects.

Old State House, 150 Benefit St., held the General Assembly in 1762–1900. Independence was declared here two months before the Declaration was signed in Philadelphia.

John Brown House, 52 Power St. at Benefit, has been handsomely restored by the Rhode Island Historical Society, which has headquarters here. John Quincy Adams once called it "the most magnificent and elegant mansion that I have ever seen on this continent." Joseph Brown was the builder and architect in 1786–88. It is three-story brick with sandstone trim and a low balustraded hipped roof, four large interior end chimneys, Doric entrance. Original paint colors and French wallpapers have been duplicated. Brown was a China trade merchant, slave trader, privateer, and patriot. NHL. Tours by trained guides take about an hour.

This area, on Benefit St. and vicinity in the College Hill district, has been restored from near-slums in the 1950s. It is known as the Mile of History. Sites along the walk are the *William G. Angell House,* 30 Benefit (1869), Italianate Victorian; *Joseph Jenckes House,* 34 Benefit (1779–91), pre-Revolutionary; *Samuel Staples House,* 75 Benefit (1825–28), Federal; *John Reynolds House,* 88 Benefit (1783–84), early Federal; *Sullivan Dorr House,* 109 Benefit (1801), Federal; *Old State House* (see separate listing above); *Brick School House,* 24 Meeting St. (1768), Georgian, one of the first free schools in the U.S., now headquarters of the *Providence Preservation Society; John Carter's Shakespeare's Head,* 21 Meeting (1772), home of the first newspaper in Providence; *Truman Beckwith House,* 42 College St. (1821), Federal; *Athenaeum,* 251 Benefit (1839), Greek Revival; *Athenaeum Row,* 257–267 Benefit, also known as the Brown and Ives Block, built about 1845, upper-middle-class housing for several families; *Stephen Hopkins House,* 10 Hopkins St., 1707, expanded ca. 1742; now a museum; *Thomas Poynton Ives Houses,* 270–276 Benefit (1814–19); *General Ambrose Burnside House,* 314 Benefit (1866); *John Brown House* (see separate listing above); *Joseph Nightingale House,* 357 Benefit (1792); *Thomas F. Hoppin House,* 383 Benefit (1853), Renaissance Revival, Alpheus C. Morse, architect; *Barker Playhouse,* 400 Benefit (1840), originally St. Stephens Church.

Roger Williams National Memorial, N. Main St., honors the man who arrived in the summer of 1636 with a small band of followers and settled the area. They came by canoe, landed near a hill at the junction of two minor streams, the Mooshasuc and the Woonasquatucket, and found a fine spring on shore. Williams made friends with Canonicus, chief of the Narragansetts, and was given land, with a deed of sale signed by the Indian. The colony sheltered people of all religious faiths and those who were denied public expression elsewhere. *Roger Williams Park* is a historic district and includes the 1773 Betsy Williams cottage. Betsy, a descendant of Roger Williams, was the first to donate land for a public park in Providence.

TIVERTON, Newport County. St. 77.

Tiverton Four Corners Historic Site, St. 77, has buildings from colonial days. Many homes belonged to whalers and those active in the China trade. *Chase-Cory House,* Main Rd., built about 1730, now the Tiverton Historical Society headquarters, is open May–October on Sunday afternoons.

Soule-Seabury House, built about 1760, by Abner Sowle (Soule), blacksmith, soldier, and whaleman, and a descendant of George Soule, who came to America on the Mayflower; later this was the home of Abner's son, Cornelius, who was in the China trade and who traveled to the Pacific Northwest in command of John Jacob Astor's ship, *Beaver;* his story is in Washington Irving's *Astoria.* The gracious Georgian house is open May–October.

WARWICK, Kent County, S of St. 117 on secondary road.

Pawtuxet Village Historic District, bounded roughly by Pawtuxet and Providence rivers and Post Rd. (also in Providence County), covers the 17th–20th century seaside town. It offers buildings of many styles, including the 1690s *Captain Crandall House,* the 1800s Federal *Christopher Rhodes House,* 25 Post Rd., and the Italianate style (1799) *Colonel Ephraim Bowen House.* The village of Pawtuxet was settled by Samuel Gorton in 1638 and became part of

Warwick in 1647. It was a seaport stop on the Old Post Rd. Local merchants engaged in African slave trade as well as importing West Indies sugar and molasses which they exchanged for New England rum. Colonists here took part in the destruction of the British customs schooner *Gaspée* in 1772, an event often called the first blow of the Revolution. By the 19th century Pawtuxet was a summer resort.

John Waterman Arnold House, 11 Roger Williams Ave., late 18th century, a typical farm house, has been restored. Museum and headquarters of the Warwick Historical Society. Open year round.

Forge Farm, 40 Forge Rd., 1684, with 18th-century additions, was built by James Greene; birthplace of Nathanael Greene, a major-general in the Revolution. There are a number of 17th–19th-century outbuildings and a cemetery.

Greene-Bowen House, 698 Buttonwoods Ave., built about 1750, with typical Rhode Island "stone-ender" construction. Fones Greene was a farmer.

Pontiac Mills, Knight St., 1863, is a 38-building complex. The four-story brick mill building has a central projecting tower and Romanesque Revival elements.

Among other structures are an Italianate gatehouse of the 1870s, a Second Empire company store, 1866, and buildings of stuccoed and scored rubble with brick trim, in typical early New England mill and village style.

CONNECTICUT

Connecticut is pleasant, with wooded hills and a beautiful river; plenteous with tobacco and cheese; fruitful of merchants, missionaries, sailors, peddlers, and singlewomen. . . . The brisk little democratic State has turned its brains upon its machinery. Not a snug valley, with a few drops of water at the bottom of it, but rattles with the manufacture of notions, great and small—axes and pistols, carriages and clocks, tin pans and toys, hats, garters, combs, buttons, and pins.

— *The Pleiades of Connecticut,* by F. Sheldon, Boston, 1865

There is an old stone house in Guilford, Con., which is believed to be one of the oldest houses now standing in the United States. This building was erected by the company who first settled the town, about the year 1640. . . . The stone of which the building is constructed was brought on hand-barrows, from a ledge some considerable distance from the place where the house stands. The cement used in building the walls is said now to be harder than the stone itself. The walls were plastered fifteen or twenty years since. This house was used by the first settlers as a kind of fort, for some time, to defend themselves against the hostile savages. The first marriage which took place in this town was solemnized in this building. The supper which was provided for the occasion consisted of pork and peas.

— *Indian Battles,* by Rev. Henry White, New York, 1859

FAIRFIELD, Fairfield County. I-95.
Fairfield Historic District, Old Post Rd. to Turney Rd., takes in some 75 buildings in various styles ranging from pre-Revolutionary to Victorian. The earliest houses are those that survived the burning by the British in 1779. This was the first center of the English settlement and the town retains a portion of its original four squares.

Fairfield Historical Society, 636 Old Post Rd., opposite the Town Hall, has antique dolls, kitchenware, and other early items. Open weekdays. Free.

Ogden House, 1520 Bronson Rd., built about 1700, has been handsomely restored to its Colonial state, and furnished with priceless period items.

Southport Historic District is an area on the edge of Fairfield founded in 1639 as a farming community. It became a shipping and commercial center until the railroad came in 1849. There are more than 150 structures of various styles, Federal, Greek Revival, Second Empire, etc.; most were built after the burning of Fairfield in 1779.

Another historic district in Fairfield County is *Greenfield Hill,* on secondary roads, W of St. 136, and slightly NW of Fairfield. The old town has 13 pre-Revolutionary buildings, a windmill, and other structures of the 18th and 19th centuries. The Congregational Church, 1855, and a saltbox house built in 1751 are worth a visit.

FARMINGTON, Hartford County. St. 10.

Farmington Historic District comprises a residential district of fine houses dating back to the 17th century. There are 115 pre-1835 buildings with early colonial examples of Georgian, Federal and Greek Revival architecture. Farmington was settled in 1640 and became a successful trading center for the area to the north and west.

Stanley-Whitman House, 37 High St., was built about 1660, a rear section was added about 1700, and it was partially restored in 1934. It now has been fully restored and houses a museum with many 17th-, 18th-, and 19th-century exhibits, and there is a carriage shed with an old sleigh and a collection of early farm tools. The old-fashioned garden is bright in summer with a wide variety of herbs and blooms. NHL.

First Church of Christ, Congregational, 75 Main St., was built in 1771.

Hill-Stead Museum, Farmington Ave., Mountain Rd., is in a fine 1901 mansion designed by Stanford White. Numerous artifacts from an earlier day, fine Impressionist paintings, and precious art objects are here as when the house was occupied by former Ambassador and Mrs. John W. Riddle.

GUILFORD, New Haven County. I-95. St. 77, 146.

Guilford Historic Town Center, bounded by West River, I-95, East Creek, and Long Island Sound. The town, settled in 1639, was named for Guildford in Surrey, England, and will be found with this spelling on a number of early maps. But if the town fathers had kept to the *original* name, there would have been even

worse typesetter's problems: Menunkatucket. The village green is considered one of the most beautiful in New England, and there are many 18th-century homes in the vicinity.

Whitfield House, Old Whitfield St., was built in 1639 of stone with a steeply gabled roof, large exterior end chimneys, and small gabled dormers. The house was altered several times, and has been restored. It was the home of the Reverend Henry Whitfield, a town founder, who used it for many public functions. The house is believed to be the earliest stone structure of its sort in New England. Now a museum with a variety of 17th-century items among the displays, and an herb garden.

Hyland-Wildman House, 84 Boston St., a block E of the green, was built in 1660 for George Hyland. A lean-to was added early in the 18th century by Ebenezer Parmelee, who made the first town clock in America for the Guilford church steeple. The clock is now displayed at Whitfield House Museum. The house is furnished in Pilgrim style.

Leete House, SW of town off St. 146, was the home of Pelatiah Leete, one of the town founders, about 1710. The two-and-a-half-story frame was added to in later years, and has been restored.

Thomas Griswold House, 161 Boston St., is a classic 18th-century saltbox, now restored as a house museum. Built in 1735, it was occupied by members of the Griswold family in 1958. Rare early farm equipment, and a blacksmith shop, are in a barn museum on the grounds.

Chamber of Commerce, 669 Boston Rd.—(203) 453-9677—has information on other historic sites and events of historical interest in Guilford.

HARTFORD, Hartford County. I-91.

The capital since 1662, Hartford has numerous fine museums and his-

toric sites. See first the **Convention &
Visitors Bureau,** 1 Civic Center
Plaza, 06103, for information and
maps.

Old State House, 800 Main St., is a
Charles Bulfinch design and served
as state capitol, 1796–1878, then as
city hall. Restored offices and historical displays. Open Tuesday through
Saturday, except holidays. NHL.
Bulfinch was a well-born Bostonian
and a 1781 Harvard graduate, who
began as an amateur architect in financial stress because of bad management of his fortune. Eventually
his version of the Adam style dominated local architecture in the Federal period. He either completed or
totally planned many other outstanding buildings: the Massachusetts State House, the Capitol at
Washington, the Maine State Capitol, and a number of churches and
private dwellings.

Armsmear, 80 Wethersfield St.
(1855), was the home of Samuel Colt,
revolver inventor. NHL. Not open at
present, but the Colt collection is on
display at the **State Library,** opposite
the Capitol, open daily except Sundays and holidays.

Nook Farm, 351 Farmington Ave.,
has the Mark Twain House, which
he built in 1873–74, with a porch like
a steamboat, and where he wrote *Tom
Sawyer, Huckleberry Finn,* and other
classics. The **Harriet Beecher Stowe
House,** 73 Forest, restored 1871, the
house where she lived from 1873
until her death in 1896, has memorabilia. Among them is a photograph
showing a smiling Mrs. Stowe in the
kitchen (a place most authors avoid if
possible, except for the Julia Childs
of this world). Mrs. Stowe had times
when she felt church mouse poor, but
by 1873 she had the proceeds of one
of the world's best sellers, *Uncle Tom's
Cabin,* and probably could afford the
fancy dress she wears in the picture,
with no apron and no flour smudges,
beside a table laden with bread, bis-
cuits, muffins, and other pastries.

The house, however, is much plainer
than the cluttered Twain manse.

Butler-McCook House, 396 Main
(1872), has a carriage house museum
at the rear. Period furnishings in the
house. Open May 15 to October 15,
daily. **Amos Bull House,** 59 Prospect
St. (1788), was built by Bull, who
had a store and a school here. Moved
and restored. Now a museum. **Noah
Webster House,** 227 S. Main, in West
Hartford, early 18th century, with
memorabilia. Open Thursdays.

LITCHFIELD, Litchfield County.
US 202.

Litchfield Historic District roughly
takes in both sides of North and
South Sts., between Gallows Lane
and Prospect St. The residential district comprises fifteen 18th-century
structures, three early-19th-century
residences, and some later 19th-cen-
tury buildings, which are mostly
Georgian. NHL.

**Tapping Reeve House and Law
School,** South St. (1772, house; 1784,
school). The charming white frame
law school with its brick walks and
circular gardens looks like a Hollywood set but is America's first law
school not associated with a university or college. It was opened here by
Tapping Reeve. Among its best-
known graduates were Aaron Burr,
Reeve's brother-in-law, and John C.
Calhoun; in all, among its 18th- and
19th-century graduates were two
Vice-Presidents, three Supreme
Court justices, six cabinet members,
14 governors, and 130 members of
Congress. The restored house, two-
story frame with central and end
chimneys, has period furnishings.
House, office, and gardens are administered by the Litchfield Historical Society.

Oliver Wolcott House, South St.,
was built in 1753 and has been restored. Oliver Wolcott was a state
governor, a delegate to the Continental Congress, and a signer of the Declaration of Independence. NHL.

Litchfield Historical Museum, on the green, has many fine exhibits, including a restored colonial kitchen. A tour of old homes takes place the second Saturday of July. There is also a restored church on the green. Write: Chamber of Commerce of Northwest Connecticut, Litchfield Division, 40 Main St., Torrington, 06790.

MYSTIC, New London County. I-95.

Mystic Seaport, Greenmanville Ave., St. 27, 1 mile S of I-95. An excellent maritime museum provides living history of land and sea and recreates the era of the sailing ships. Seaport St. is a cobblestoned path back to adventure for young and old. Shops and lofts are staffed by craftsmen who demonstrate the old seaside trades and shipbuilding and whaling industries of the 19th century. This splendid outdoor museum on the east bank of Mystic River is supported by the Marine Historical Association which is made up of international members—persons who love the sea and its history. The area occupies 40 acres and was once a shipbuilding site.

At anchor is the *Charles W. Morgan,* the only survivor of a great fleet of American whalers. It was built in 1841 and went whaling for 80 years. It is a National Historic Landmark and is open to the public.

Mystic Seaport, founded in 1929, grew from a small collection of memorabilia to a museum that is known around the world and visited by thousands of starry-eyed adults, as well as children, and is most fittingly named. There is something mystical about the great sailing ships which touches almost everyone. The museum is open daily, year round, except Christmas and New Year's Day.

Shipbuilding began on the Mystic River in the 17th century. After the War of 1812, there were sealing voyages to the far South Atlantic; later shipbuilding and whaling became

Mystic Seaport, Mystic, Connecticut. (Courtesy of the Seaport)

important. During the gold rush period clipper ships were launched in the Mystic River, but in the Civil War, Mystic built 56 transports and some steamships, and later sailing yachts. In World War II the yards of Mystic produced small craft needed by the Navy and Coast Guard.

Visitors entering from the South Parking Lot find the *Museum Store* on their left, and the first formal exhibit on the left is the *Thames Keel,* in the Henry B. duPont Preservation Shipyard, open for touring. On the right is the *L. A. Dunton,* a Gloucester fishing schooner.

Entering from the North Parking Lot, you will find the *Seamen's Inne* restaurant on the right. On the left the *G. W. Blunt White Library.* This is not an exhibit area but is open daily except Sunday, free, for reference and research. It contains more than 250,000 manuscripts on the maritime history of the U.S. Beyond the North Gate, the first formal exhibits are the full-rigged ship *Ben-*

jamin F. Packard, and the *North Boat Shed,* with a collection of small craft.

Also on display are the *Regina M.,* a schooner built in Perry, Maine, in 1900; the *Nellie,* an oyster sloop built in Smithtown, Long Island, in the 1890s, and used for oyster dredging under sail along the Connecticut shore and Great South Bay, Long Island; *Robie Ames Salmon Fishing Shack, Thomas Oyster Shop, Block Island Life-Saving Station,* built in 1874, one of the last of many stations that reached from Maine to Hatteras, the *Noyes Building,* with a fisheries exhibit, the *Australia,* a 77-foot schooner, and the *Joseph Conrad,* a training ship now, which sailed under three flags after its construction in Copenhagen in 1882. Captain Alan Villiers, who brought the *Mayflower II* to America, took the *Joseph Conrad* on a 58,000-mile two-year voyage around the world.

Other outstanding exhibits are the *N. G. Fish Ship Chandlery* and the *Charles Mallory Sail Loft,* moved here by barge in 1951 (Mallory was a sailmaker from 1816 to the 1860s); the *William White Rigging Loft,* the *James D. Driggs Shipsmith Shop,* and many, many more buildings and ships. Just don't plan a short stop.

SIMSBURY, Hartford County. St. 309, 10.

Massacoh Plantation-Simsbury Historic Center, 800 Hopmeadow St. Furnished buildings and exhibits present 17th-, 18th-, and 19th-century history. There are many old tools and much agricultural equipment, a meeting house, an icehouse, craft demonstrations, and farm relics. The complex is open from May to October.

WETHERSFIELD, Hartford County. I-91, Marsh St. exit.

Old Wethersfield Historic District, bounded by Hartford, railroad tracks, 1-91, and Rocky Hill, contains about 1,200 structures. Many early homes were built by sea captains who settled on land acquired from the Massachusetts Bay Colony, an area which became a transportation center on the Connecticut River until 1700. The village green is a historic spot which played an important role in pre–Revolutionary War activities.

Buttolph-Williams House, 249 Broad St., was built in 1692 and has been restored; contains what is considered to be one of the most authentically furnished kitchens of its period. NHL.

The *Joseph Webb House,* 211 Main St., built in 1752. George Washington and Comte de Rochambeau, commander of the French Army in America, here planned the campaign against Cornwallis which led to victory. NHL.

The *Silas Deane House,* 203 Main St., was built in 1764 for Deane, a lawyer, merchant, and politician. NHL.

The *Isaac Stevens House,* 213 Main, dates from 1778–89 and was the home of our first commissioner to France. There is a combination ticket for the Webb, Deane, and Stevens houses, all of which have been handsomely furnished in period.

Old Academy Museum, 150 Main, is headquarters for the Wethersfield Historical Society. The building, a 1692 warehouse, built for the West Indies trade, is being restored as a maritime museum.

First Church of Christ, Main and Marsh Sts., was built in the 18th century, has been restored, and is the third to occupy this corner. The church was established in 1635.

Middle Atlantic States

New York
New Jersey
Pennsylvania
Delaware
Maryland
District of Columbia

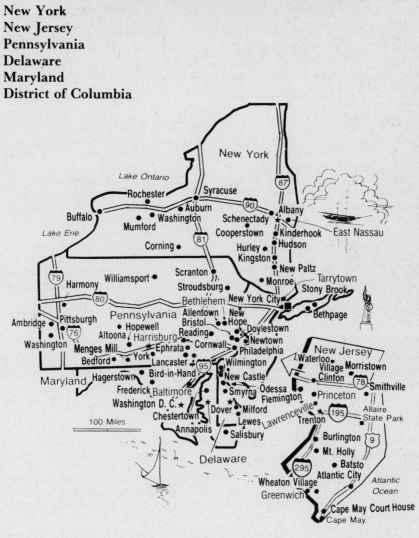

NEW YORK

No man is felt in Wall Street more than Commodore Vanderbilt, yet he is seldom seen there. All of his business is done in his office, . . . a plain brick residence in Fourth Street, near Broadway. . . . Here we see a table, a few chairs, and a desk, at which a solitary clerk of middle age is standing at work.

The walls are bare, with the exception of a few pictures of those steamships which originated the title of "Commodore." This is the antechamber, and a pair of folding doors screen the king. . . . At length you are permitted to enter. . . . you behold an office as plain in appearance as the one just described. It contains a few armchairs and a long business-table, thrown flush before you, on the opposite side of which sits a large man, with his face fronting you. . . . He smiles in a pleasant and whole-souled manner, and in a moment puts you at ease. . . . we know a man who would rather give five dollars to sit and look at Commodore Vanderbilt for an hour than to see any other sight in this city.

—Anonymous author quoted in *Great Fortunes, and How They Were Made,* by James D. McCabe, Jr., Cincinnati, 1871

ALBANY, Albany County. I-90.

Pastures Historic District, bounded by Madison Ave., Green, South Ferry, and S. Pearl Sts., is a 19th-century commercial and residential area with many brick row houses with stone trim. This was once a Dutch farming area.

Washington Park Historic District takes in the 90-acre park and surrounding residential area. The site was chosen by the elite of the late 19th century. Many outstanding residences remain.

Onesquethaw Valley Historic District, about 10 miles SW of Albany off St. 43, has some 25 dwellings with farm outbuildings of the 18th and 19th centuries. The site of a prehistoric Indian community, it was settled by Dutch colonists who remained pro-British during the Revolution.

The *Area Chamber of Commerce,* 510 Broadway, 12207 has information on the many historic sites of the capital city. The *Historic Albany Foundation,* 191 Elm St., (518) 463-0622, conducts guided tours on ten days' notice and sells a walking tour guide for a small fee.

AUBURN, Cayuga County. US 20, in the Finger Lakes region.

Owasco Stockaded Indian Village, St. 38A, Emerson Park, is on the site of the original Indian settlement. The village is a reconstruction designed to show the history and crafts of the Owasco culture. Two long houses, craft centers, and an exhibition lodge are on display, with demonstrations of skills and arts. The village is operated by the Cayuga Museum of History and Art. Guided tours.

Also in town: The *William Henry Seward Home,* 33 South St. (St. 34), was built in 1816–17. Seward served in Lincoln's cabinet and was one of the targets of the assassins on the night of April 14, 1865, but survived his wounds. His efforts to purchase Alaska in 1867 when he was Secretary of State under Andrew Johnson were labeled "Seward's Folly." The house has Lincoln, Civil War, and Seward family memorabilia. NHL. The *Harriet Tubman Home for the Aged,* 180–182 South St., built sometime before 1850, has been restored. Miss Tubman, a former slave, helped many others to escape to Canada in the years of the Underground Railroad. The house is operated by the AME Zion Church. Museum. NHL.

BETHPAGE, Nassau County, on Long Island. Reached via Long Island Expressway, exit 48, or Northern State Parkway, exit 39.

Old Bethpage Village Restoration, 1 mile S of exit 48, on Round Swamp Rd., Rt. 110. This rural village has been authentically re-created on 200 acres, with buildings moved from other parts of Long Island. Tours begin at the *Reception Center* with an interpretive film. There are about 24 structures at present, all carefully restored. Visitors can watch, in season, sheep shearing, harvesting, threshing. Candle- and soapmaking, dressmaking, blacksmithing, needlepoint, and cooking over an open hearth are year-round activities. A proper visit takes about three hours. Walking shoes are advised. There is a cafeteria and a picnic area. Open year round except for Thanksgiving, Christmas, and New Year's Day.

COOPERSTOWN, Otsego County. St. 28.

Lippitt Homestead, Farmer's Museum, and Village Crossroads, St. 80. A farmhouse, smithy, tavern, printing shop, and church represent a rural village of 1785–1860. The "Cardiff Giant," a 10-foot statue which the gullible of 1869 were led to believe was a prehistoric man, is on the grounds. The *Fenimore House,* also on St. 80, contains James Fenimore Cooper memorabilia, a fine collection of American folk art, and a Hall of Masks. It is now *Central Headquarters* of the *New York State Historical Association.*

Also in town: *Busch Woodlands and Museum,* St. 89, a nature trail and many 19th-century exhibits; *Carriage and Harness Museum,* on Elk St.; *Indian Museum,* 1 Pioneer St., with dioramas and exhibits depicting the daily life of New York State Indians; and, of course, the *National Baseball Hall of Fame,* on Main St.

Otsego County Courthouse, 193 Main St., 1880, is brick in High Victorian Gothic, designed by Archimedes Russell. In continuous use as a courthouse, it is listed on the National Register.

CORNING, Steuben County. St. 17, W of Elmira.

Market Street Restoration is a project that has brought back the turn-of-the-century look with tree-lined brick sidewalks, restored storefronts, and handcrafted signs. The area is listed on the National Register. Also in town: the *Corning Glass Center,* dedicated to the art, history (some 3,500 years), and science of glassmaking, has a museum, a Hall of Science and Industry, and a gallery where visitors can watch workmen fashion Steuben glass. Rockwell-Corning Museum has the largest collection of Old West relics in the Old East. Paintings, sculpture, weapons, and Indian artifacts are on display.

Chamber of Commerce, 42 East Market St., has brochures and information for the area.

EAST NASSAU, Rensselaer County. St. 66.

Eastfield Village is a collection of

18 structures with shops, dwellings, and outbuildings, from 1787–1840. The village has recently begun summer workshops on historical American trades, with instruction on tinsmithing, housewrighting, calligraphy, stone carving, heirloom textile making, and early food preparation. For information write Eastfield Village, Box 145 R.S., East Nassau, N.Y. 12062.

HUDSON, Columbia County. St. 66, 9G.

Front Street–Parade Hill–Lower Warren St. Historic District: The area was first called Claverack Landing and was established toward the end of the 18th century as a commercial venture by a group from New England; therefore it differs considerably from the Dutch-settled towns of the area. On the bluff above the river are a number of business structures from the 18th century.

Olana, St. 9G, is a 35-room Persian-Moorish mansion, built in 1872 by the artist Frederic Edwin Church. The house, operated by the state, has Victorian gardens. NHL. Also in Hudson is the *American Museum of Fire-Fighting,* Harry Howard Ave., with exhibits dating back to the early 18th century. A *Shaker Museum* is 18 miles NE on St. 66, then E on County 13, Shaker Museum Rd. (W of Old Chatham). The complex includes 35 rooms with Shaker exhibits. The celibate religious group, which established settlements in several areas of the U.S., came here in the late 18th century.

HURLEY, Ulster County. St. 209, exit 19, New York State Thruway.

Hurley Historic District, Hurley St., Hurley Mountain Rd., and Schoonmaker Lane, was named Nieuw Dorp in 1661 by the Dutch and Huguenot families. *Main St. Hurley* has ten stone houses of Dutch architecture, some in their original state and lived in by Dutch descendants of the first settlers. The *Jan Van Deusen House,* the *Elmendorf House* (also known as *Half Moon Tavern*), *Polly Crispell Cottage,* the *Guard House* (also known as the *Spy House*), the *Bevier Home,* and the *Crispell House* are part of this section.

Hurley Patentee Manor combines a 17th-century Dutch cottage and an 18th-century English country mansion, and is the only restored Old Stone House that is open to the public from June 30 to Labor Day. The *Jan Van Deusen House* was the capitol for one month in 1777; it was built in 1723 and is open by appointment.

Sojourner Truth, the black evangelist, was born here. The town was a stop on the Underground Railroad in the 1850s.

The *Reformed Church and Parsonage,* at the end of Main St., also are historic buildings. The church was built in 1853, replacing an earlier structure built in 1801. The parsonage, originally the home of the Crispells, was built in 1790.

KINDERHOOK, Columbia County. St. 9H.

Lindenwald, E of town on St. 9H, was the home of Martin Van Buren, eighth President of the United States, after he served in Washington until his death in 1862. The house was built in 1797. It is brick, originally Georgian; it was enlarged by Richard Upjohn for Van Buren after he came here in 1840. It has been restored and is a National Historic Landmark, also HABS.

Luycas Van Alen House, St. 9H, about 2 miles S of US 9. A Dutch Colonial brick, built in 1737, with additions to 1750, has been restored by the Columbia County Historical Society, which also maintains Lindenwald. A National Historic Landmark, also HABS.

Martin Van Buren was born in Kinderhook in 1782 and is buried here.

KINGSTON, Ulster County. St. 28.

Clinton Ave. Historic District includes all of Clinton Ave. between Westbrook Lane and N. Front St., plus some of Fair St., in an area laid out as a Dutch village in the mid-17th century. A stockade was built around the town in 1654 under the direction of Peter Stuyvesant; the streets still follow the original pattern.

The *Senate House State Historic Site,* 312 Fair St., dates from 1676. The first New York State Senate met here the following year. The original building was burned in 1777 except for stone walls, and has been restored. Furnishings are 18th century in style. There is a boxwood garden of 18th-century design and a *Stockade Children's Museum,* which is a see-and-also-touch historical museum.

Old Dutch Church and Cemetery, on Main St. between Wall and Fair Sts. The church was established in 1661 under Dominie Blom, who had gone back to Holland to get his license of ordination. It was a wooden structure and was burned by the Indians in 1663. A stone church was completed in 1680. A brick building came next, in 1832. This was used as a church for 20 years, then as a Civil War armory. Later St. Joseph's Catholic Church replaced the armory and it still stands on the SE corner of Wall and Main Sts. The first governor of New York, George Clinton, is buried in the old cemetery, which dates from 1661.

Walking tours leave the Senate House and take in more than 20 homes of the 17th and 18th centuries, also, in the stockaded area, buildings from Stuyvesant's day. The tours take place on the third Thursday of the month, May through September.

MONROE, Orange County. St. 6, 17; 4 miles W of the New York State Thruway exit 16 at Harriman (an hour's drive from the George Washington Bridge).

Old Museum Village of Smith's Clove, lately known as *Museum Village in Orange County,* 1¼ miles W of town on St. 17M. About 40 buildings surround a village green and re-create the atmosphere of 19th-century America in rural New York. An information center near the entrance has marked maps for a self-guiding tour. Along the way are a dress emporium, blacksmith's shop, wagon-maker's shop, cobbler, tinsmith, one-room schoolhouse, carriage house, harnessmaker's shop, a general store, printer's shop, firehouse with hand and steam pumpers, a weaver's shop, a log cabin moved from near West Point, an apothecary with plenty of placebos and patent medicines of the 1800s, a pottery, a Quaker meeting house, barbershop, broommaker's shop, cooper's, cider mill, and assorted exhibitions of tools, artifacts, and natural history. This is a nonprofit educational institution.

MUMFORD, Monroe County. St. 36, N of Caledonia. About 20 miles SW of Rochester.

Genesee Country Village, Flint Hill Rd. (George St.), 1 mile W of town. This restoration of some 35 buildings to form a village representative of rural western New York of the early 19th century has been directed by architectural historian Stuart B. Bolger. The structures on the 125-acre site have been carefully selected and furnished to fit the original use.

A tour begins at the entrance, Genesee Country Village offices, and *Flint Hill* store, on a circular drive which is S of Flint Hill Rd. and E of the parking area. Going back a short distance N after leaving the entrance, the first stop is the *Gallery of Sporting Art,* which features the John H. Wehle collection. There are eight gallery areas in the connecting barn-like structures, covering subjects ranging from the Old West to Africa. The tour road leads past a carriage museum and a tollhouse, built about 1850 in Lima, to the *Altay Store,* from the mid-19th century. The store was moved here from the small village of Finger Lakes. The last shopper went home in 1899 and the store was closed for 70 years. Now it is "back in business" with a full inventory of goods based upon the store's itemized records, which were found in the attic.

Another store in the village is a *Boot and Shoemaker's Shop,* built about 1820 in East Avon, for a lawyer who reportedly vanished with his portfolio, although his horse came back on a day long ago. After the second story was added to the building the shoemaker moved in. There are also the *Levi Rugg Blacksmith Shop,* from Elba, built about 1830; *Thompson's Trading Post,* from Peru, 1806–1840s; a print shop, cooper shop, brewhouse, drugstore; widow's shop, from Roseboom, for millinery and dressmaking; tinsmith shop, and a trading post from about 1806.

The *Ward-Hovey House* is the first dwelling passed on the route. It is a cottage from Stone Church, built about 1832 and renovated in the 1840s. At present it houses offices and is not open to the public. *Livingston Manor* was built in Rochester in 1830. A number of additions were made. During the Civil War the building became a fashionable girls' school, Livingston Park Seminary, but it has been restored to its elegance as a town house. The *Foster-Tufts House* was the home of Charles Foster and his family in 1836 in Pavilion. The legend is that when the Fosters and their four sons and four daughters arrived in Pavilion two of the kids rode in the potash kettle. The *Peck-Jones (or Phelps) Farmhouse* is a frame structure from the 1820s. The *Morgan-O'Day House (Amherst Humphrey)* was a one-and-one-half-story frame built on the Genesee turnpike in 1799. The *McKay House* comes from Caledonia,

where John McKay moved in 1803. He operated a gristmill and dabbled successfully in real estate. He built this home about 1814. The *MacArthur House,* from the York vicinity, was a cordwainer's home, dating from 1831. (Cordwainer is a fancy way of saying leatherworker. The term came from Cordovan, a fine Spanish leather.) *Kieffer's Place,* 1814, is a two-story log house from Rush.

There are three churches in the village: the *Quaker Meeting-House,* from the Wheatland area, built about 1854; *Brooks Grove Church and Parsonage,* dating from 1844; and *St. Feehan's Catholic Church,* built in 1854 in Chili, New York.

There are a doctor's, lawyer's, and insurance man's office, but not an Indian chief's. A little red schoolhouse, built in the 1800s, once served a rural community near Avon, a town that briefly caught the jaundiced eye of Mrs. Trollope in her book, *The Domestic Manners of the Americans* (1836).

An inn, a female seminary, a brewery, and the post office are among other sites in the growing settlement. The railroad is part of the picture, and visitors can visit a depot which once served passengers in Caledonia. Appropriately dressed villagers carry on the usual crafts and old-time chores of pioneer life. The village is open daily from May 15 through October 16.

NEW PALTZ, Ulster County. St. 32S.

Huguenot St. Historic District, a National Historic Landmark, also HABS, comprises five stone houses along Huguenot dating from the 17th and 18th centuries. The *Jean Hasbrouck House* of 1712 and the *Abraham Hasbrouck House* of 1717 have changed very little over the centuries. The *Daniel de Bois House* from 1775 and the *Bevier House,* late 17th century, have been altered considerably. The *Freer House* is from the early 18th century. The Huguenot Historical Society maintains the houses. Tours leave 6 Brodhead Ave. A *Stone House Festival* is held annually on the first Saturday in August, with tours of historic sites and other events, including a reenactment of the signing of the treaty between the Huguenots and the Indians.

NEW YORK, New York County.

"The Big Apple," as everyone from show business to the Convention & Visitors Bureau calls it, can be sliced every whichway, and has been and will be. For now, a listing of historic districts and some of the not-to-be-missed landmarks. The Parks Department has begun a program of self-guided walking tours through the historic neighborhoods. For information on this and other sites consult the New York Convention & Visitors Bureau, 90 East 42nd St., New York, 10017; call (212) 687-1300. The Bureau also has a handy pamphlet listing landmarks, maps, guides, and calendars of events.

Midtown Area

Chelsea, bounded roughly by West 22nd and West 20th Sts., Tenth Ave., and points midway between Ninth and Eighth Aves. This district goes back to 1750, when Captain Thomas Clarke, the grandfather of Clement Clarke Moore, who wrote the immortal " 'Twas the Night Before Christmas," bought property along the Hudson River to be used for his summer home and named it for the London suburb of Chelsea (now a busy part of London). Clarke's main residence was at the corner of Charlton and MacDougal Sts. in Greenwich Village.

The oldest house in the district is at 404 West 20th St. It was built in 1829–30 but has suffered many alterations of its original Federal style.

The *Gramercy Park District* is roughly bounded by Park Ave. South, Third Ave., East 18th and 21st Sts. It was developed in 1831 by Samuel B. Ruggles, who bought the Crommeshie marshes. The area is due east of Chelsea, also in midtown. It was high fashion when it began and it is high fashion today. Gramercy evolved from "Krom Moerasje," Dutch for "little crooked stream," to Crommesshie and Crommeshie. Ruggles drained the swamp and put in a park and locked up the whole works with an 8-foot fence and gate. Only the owners or tenants of buildings around the park itself have keys. Walkers can look through the palings.

Sniffen Court, East 36th St., between Lexington and Third Aves., comprises ten former stables for the houses on Murray Hill in the 1860s, facing a common alley. In the 1920s they were converted into town houses, a studio, and a very small theater.

Turtle Bay Gardens, between East 48th and 49th Sts., Second and Third Aves. In 1919–20 ten back-to-back 1860 brownstones were altered and their yards combined into a common garden. They are Italianate in style. Brownstone is actually brick construction covered with 4 to 6 inches of brownstone, an easily worked form of sandstone. Brownstone became very popular with builders and was quarried in mass quantities in Connecticut and New Jersey in the 19th century.

Downtown Area

Greenwich Village, roughly bounded by St. Luke's Place, Washington Square South, University Place, West 13th and Washington Sts. The historic district takes in 65 irregular blocks which do not fit the city's grid for the good reason that by the time the plan was agreed upon, the area was too built up for change. Epidemics of cholera, yellow fever, and smallpox in the late 18th and early 19th centuries had sent most of the residents of lower Manhattan into the country areas in such numbers that when the Commissioners' Plan of 1811 was adopted, the Greenwich Village streets were already settled. The Village keeps on changing in life styles, but many rows of Federal, Greek Revival, and Victorian houses remain.

The narrowest house in the city, at 75½ Bedford St., is 9½ feet wide. Edna St. Vincent Millay lived here in the 1920s, when she was a slim young poet with plenty of other poets in love with her. Next door, at the corner of Commerce and Bedford, is the oldest house in the Village. It dates from 1799.

The *St. Mark's District,* between Second and Third Aves., East 11th and Stuyvesant Sts., was partly developed by a great-grandson of Peter Stuyvesant, whose farm or "Bouwerie" it was. The foundations of what is believed to have been Stuyvesant's house were uncovered in 1854 when the cellar was excavated for the building now at 129 East Tenth St. The *Stuyvesant-Fish House,* 21 Stuyvesant St., is a National Historic Landmark. It was built by a great-grandson of Governor Peter Stuyvesant in 1803 as a wedding gift for his daughter Elizabeth. Her groom, Nicholas Fish, had been a major in the Revolutionary War at 18, perhaps the youngest major ever in the U.S. Army. Lafayette was entertained in the house during his famous tour of 1824. Hamilton Fish, who was born here, became governor of New York. Many original items have been preserved in the interior, but the outside has been considerably altered.

St. Mark's-in-the-Bowery Church, Second Ave. at 10th St., was built in 1799. The steeple was added in 1828 and the portico in 1854. It is a combination of architectural styles. The site was originally that of Peter Stuyvesant's "Bouwerie," where he con-tinued to live even after 1664, when the English took possession of the colony. Stuyvesant was buried here in 1672. A lot of later Stuyvesants also are buried in the churchyard. Shortly before this book went to press the church was severely damaged by fire.

MacDougal-Sullivan Gardens, between West Houston and Bleecker Sts. The Greek Revival houses, built between 1844 and 1860 on the Nicholas Low estate, were remodeled in 1926 and share a garden.

The *Soho Cast-Iron District,* bounded by Canal St., Broadway, Howard, Crosby, East and West Houston Sts., and West Broadway, contains the largest remaining group of cast-iron structures in the world, in a range of styles which were favored in the latter half of the 19th century. In the past few years many buildings have been converted into studios and galleries by artists who appreciate the loft space. The *Haughwout Building,* 488–492 Broadway, built in 1857, with John P. Gaynor as architect, is of prefabricated cast-iron construction of the type first developed by James Bogardus. It had the first passenger elevator service in a commercial building and is an individual building landmark.

The *Charlton-King-Vandam District,* bounded roughly by Varick and MacDougal Sts., has some of the finest Federal and Greek Revival houses in town; the earliest are from the 1820s. Washington had headquarters here during part of the Revolutionary War in what was Richmond Hill, a mansion built for a British officer before the war. It was used by John Adams, when he was Vice-President and the capital was in New York. Later Aaron Burr bought the house, but was not able to enjoy it after the duel with Alexander Hamilton in 1804 in which Hamilton was killed. Burr left town and John Jacob Astor took over, developing the area according to the plan Burr had made.

In a 19th-century book on money-makers of the day (*Great Fortunes, and How They Were Made; or the Struggles and Triumphs of Our Self-Made Men*), James McCabe wrote of John Jacob Astor:

"In his purchases of land Mr. Astor was very fortunate. He pursued a regular system in making them. . . . As a rule he bought his lands in what was then the suburb of the city, and which few besides himself expected to see built up during their lifetime. His sagacity and foresight have been more than justified by the course of events. . . . When Mr. Astor bought Richmond Hill, the estate of Aaron Burr, he gave one thousand dollars an acre for the hundred and sixty acres. Twelve years later, the land was valued at fifteen hundred dollars per lot.

"In 1810, he sold a lot near Wall Street for eight thousand dollars. The price was so low that a purchaser for cash was found at once, and this gentleman, after the sale, expressed his surprise that Mr. Astor should ask only eight thousand for a lot which in a few years would sell for twelve thousand.

" 'That is true,' said Mr. Astor, 'but see what I intend doing with these eight thousand dollars. I shall buy eighty lots above Canal Street, and by the time your one lot is worth twelve thousand dollars, my eighty lots will be worth eighty thousand dollars.' "

East Side, above 59th St.

Henderson Place, opening off East End Ave. between East 86th and 87th Sts., comprises 24 small town houses which were built in the early 1880s in Queen Anne style. John C. Henderson was a furrier and hatter—that is, he made fur hats—and

Gracie Mansion, New York.

he wanted this area to have dwellings for "persons of moderate means," though whether or not they could afford his wares as well as the row houses is not clear. The architectural firm of Lamb & Rich built 32 houses in two years. Twenty-four remain. The eight which were lost to a high-rise apartment house are deeply mourned by those who treasured the cul-de-sac as it used to be.

Treadwell Farm, East 61st and 62nd Sts. between Second and Third Aves. Here are two blocks of brownstones from the 19th century on tree-lined streets. The land was once Adam Treadwell's 24-acre farm.

Gracie Mansion, official residence of New York's mayors, a handsome edifice in Colonial style, can be seen at East End Avenue and 88th St., though it is not open to visitors. The date of its building is uncertain: it is believed that is may have been built before 1765 and rebuilt after the Revolution by its first known owner, Jacob Walton, who later sold it to Archibald Gracie. Or Walton may have built the home after the Revolution. Both he and Gracie were merchants.

West Side, above 59th St.

Jumel Terrace, bounded roughly by West 162nd and West 160th Sts., Edgecomb and St. Nicholas Aves. The district has about 50 row houses and one apartment house, erected between 1882 and 1909. The ***Morris-Jumel Mansion,*** 160th St. and Edgecomb Ave., was built in 1765 and is the major surviving landmark of the Battle of Harlem Heights, September 1776. Washington had headquarters here in the fall of 1775 after the Battle of Long Island. The house had been the home of Lieutenant Colonel Roger Morris, a Loyalist, and was

The Morris-Jumel Mansion, New York. (New York Public Library Picture Collection)

confiscated and sold after the war. Stephen Jumel, who bought the house in 1810, restored it in Federal style. It has been renovated and refurnished in recent years. It is a National Historic Landmark; also HABS. Anyone who became a Burr watcher after Gore Vidal's best-selling novel based on Aaron Burr's adventures will be interested to see the house where Burr was married, when he was almost 80, to the widow of Stephen Jumel, Madame Betsy Bowen Jumel, from Providence, whose son—George Washington Bowen, no less—was illegitimate. The wedding took place in the small parlor to the left of the main hall on the ground floor. The couple was divorced in a few months and Burr died soon after.

The home of the man Burr killed—Alexander Hamilton—was *The Grange,* on Convent Ave. N of 141st St. It was designed by John McComb, Jr., in 1801. Philip Hamilton, a son, was killed in a duel before the house was finished. Hamilton lived in it less than two years before his dueling date with Aaron Burr. The house was moved to its present site in 1889; the move was a short one—about 100 yards. The house had been given to St. Luke's Episcopal Church. The National Park Service now owns the historic building and is restoring it.

St. Nicholas, West 138th and 139th Sts., between Seventh and Eighth Aves., comprises four rows of town houses built in the early 1890s.

Mount Morris Park, between West 119th and West 124th Sts., Mount Morris Park West, and Lenox Ave. The district includes fine town houses and notable churches. In the neighboring area is onetime Mount Morris Park, which was renamed Marcus Garvey Memorial Park in 1973, to honor one of the first black nationalist leaders. In 1776 it was the site of a fort defended by Washington's forces but captured by the British. Garvey, who came to the States from Jamaica in the British West Indies, preached of black unity and a return to Africa for the Negro race. His weekly newspaper, *The Negro World,* was as eloquent as Garvey in spreading the word that black was beautiful. He died in 1940 after an eventful life which included a sentence to a five-year prison term in Atlanta (for using the mails to defraud), and a presidential pardon granted by Calvin Coolidge.

The *Central Park West–76th St. District* comprises Central Park West between West 75th St. and West 77th St., including both sides of West 76th St. The buildings date from 1887 to 1889, with some of the structures influenced by the World's Columbian Exposition of 1893. There are varying architectural styles, but the general design, scale, and setbacks are similar enough for conformity.

The *Riverside–West 105th St. District* occupies an L-shaped area along West 105th St., Riverside Drive, and part of the south side of 106th St. It is a turn-of-the-century residential area with the elegance of French Beaux-Arts style.

In Brooklyn:

Boerum Hill, bounded roughly by Wyckoff, Nevins, Pacific, and Hoyt Sts., is a 19th-century residential area.

Brooklyn Heights bounded roughly by Fulton, Henry, Clinton, and Court Sts., Atlantic Ave., and the Esplanade, has brownstone houses and churches of varying 19th-century styles. The Italianate *Plymouth Church* on Orange St. was built in 1849. The famous Henry Ward Beecher, brother of Harriet Beecher Stowe, was the pastor there from 1847 to 1887. NHL.

Carroll Gardens, bounded by President, Carroll, Smith, and Hoyt Sts., includes more than 158 buildings from the second half of the 19th century.

Cobble Hill is bounded roughly by Atlantic Ave., Hicks, Degraw, and Court Sts. It is a 20-block area of well-preserved ironwork and houses in the Gothic, Romanesque Revival, and Queen Anne styles, which were built for low- and moderate-income families.

Stuyvesant Heights, an L-shaped district between Chauncey and Macon Sts., from Stuyvesant to Tompkins Ave., was developed between 1870 and the first two decades of this century. Some houses, however, date from the Civil War period.

Park Slope is roughly bounded by Prospect Park, Flatbush Ave., Park Place, Sixth, Seventh, and Eighth Aves. The district contains more than 1,900 structures built between the Civil War and World War I. The *Montauk Club,* designed by Francis H. Kimball, completed in 1891, is a rarity, one of few survivors of the many onetime private clubs of upper-crust Brooklyn.

In Queens:

Hunter's Point, 45th Ave. between 21st and 23rd Sts., has a variety of late-19th-century favorite styles in row houses built from 1870 to 1890, but the late Italianate rows are dominant.

Bowne House, 37–01 Bowne St., was built for John Bowne in 1661. Bowne was tried, and acquitted, for holding Quaker meetings here, an ordeal which helped to ensure the freedom of worship in America. The main body of the house has been added to over the years. Some furnishings are original. The house is operated by the Bowne House Historical Society.

King Mansion, 150 St. and Jamaica Ave., was built in 1730. After 1805 Rufus King, a delegate to the Constitutional Convention, a U.S. Senator, and minister to Great Britain, lived here, as did his son, John Alsop King, governor of New York in the 1850s. The house was expanded

in the 18th century and again after the Kings bought it. It is a house museum operated by the King Manor Association.

In the Bronx:

Mott Haven, Alexander Ave. between East 137th and 141st Sts., has post–Civil War row houses and other buildings, including one of the earliest branch libraries to be established in the borough named for Jonas Bronck, a Dane who bought 500 acres from the Dutch in 1679. This was once the hunting ground of the Mohicans, and George Washington slept here.

The Van Cortlandt House, Broadway and 242nd St., Georgian-style of the mid-18th century, has been restored and is maintained by the National Society of Colonial Dames in the State of New York. Olaf Van Cortlandt, of Wyck, Holland, arrived in Nieuw Amsterdam in the same year that Peter Minuit, who had bought Manhattan Island, perished at sea. One of Olaf's sons, Stephanus, in 1677, became the first native-born mayor of New York (then British) and built his home at Croton-on-Hudson (where it has been restored by the Rockefellers). Olaf's grandson Frederick Van Cortlandt began this house in 1748, but died within a year from when the cornerstone was laid. His son James inherited the almost-finished house in August 1749. In September 1776, Augustus, James's brother, brought valuable city records and hid them for safety in the family burial vault on a hill north of the house. The tin box container is on view today. There were plenty of skirmishes in the area during the Revolutionary War. Washington dined and spent the night here in 1781 and again in 1783.

Poe Cottage, 2640 Grand Concourse and E. Kingsbridge Rd., was built in 1816. Edgar Allan Poe lived here from 1846 to 1849 with his wife, who was ailing, and her mother, Mrs.

Schermerhorn Row, Fulton Street, called by many the finest example of Federal architecture in New York. Erected in 1811, these buildings are being restored as part of the South Street Seaport Museum. (William Doerflinger Photo)

Clemm. Mrs. Poe died of tuberculosis during their first winter in the cottage. Poe wrote "Annabel Lee," "Ulalume," and other works while here. The house is operated by the N.Y.C. Department of Parks and is open to the public. Guided tours.

The *Valentine-Varian House,* 3266 Bainbridge Ave. at East 208th St., is pre-Revolutionary Georgian, built of fieldstone, by Isaac Valentine. It was captured by the Hessians in 1776 and served as their headquarters. Isaac Varian, mayor of New York, lived here later. The house has been moved from its original site. It is now the Museum of Bronx History.

The *Bartow-Pell Mansion,* Shore Rd., Pelham Bay Park, built about 1842, was restored in 1914. The grounds were landscaped by the International Garden Club. House and gardens are open to the public. At *Wave Hill,* 665 West 252nd St., only

the gardens are open. This Federal-style building, from 1820–30, with 20th-century additions, has been the residence of Mark Twain, Theodore Roosevelt, and Arturo Toscanini. It is now a Center for Environmental Studies.

There are individual landmarks all through Manhattan and the other boroughs and plenty of literature available at the Convention & Visitors Bureau for any kind of sightseeing tour your time allows. A major restoration in progress is the *South St. Seaport Museum,* an entire area along South St. at Fulton St.; an indoor-outdoor museum, it will have the appearance of the great days of the sailing ships when it is finished. There are now a restored printing shop and three piers of historic ships for visiting. Among the vessels which can be seen there are the *Alexander Hamil-*

County Clerk's and Surrogate's Office, Stephens House, and Third County Court House, Richmondtown, Staten Island, New York. (The Staten Island Historical Society)

ton, the last of the Hudson River Day Line sidewheelers, a fishing schooner from Gloucester, the original Ambrose Lightship, and the full-rigged ship *Peking,* veteran of many voyages around Cape Horn. There will be a variety of others.

In Richmond (Staten Island):

Richmondtown, in almost the exact geographical center of Staten Island, is a restoration of an American village, and can be reached by the world-famous Staten Island ferry and bus from the St. George ferry terminal. The ferry costs 25¢ round trip; you also get a splendid view of the harbor, Governor's Island, and the Statue of Liberty. Staten Island can also be reached via the Verazzano Bridge from Brooklyn and several bridges from New Jersey.

Richmondtown was the local seat of government from 1729 until 1920, when the county seat was moved to St. George. It was originally called Coccles Town, probably from the large amount of oyster and clam

shells from Fresh Kills nearby. The Staten Island Historical Society bought the first building and restored it in 1939. This was the *Voorlezer House,* the home of a schoolteacher, built in 1696, and believed to be the oldest elementary school building still standing in the U.S. The **Second Court House** and the **Treasure House,** on adjoining sites, were purchased next. Treasure House, built by Samuel Grosset, a tanner, in 1700, got its name from a happening of a century ago when a former owner, Patrick Highland, found hidden in its walls about $7,000 in gold, which may have been tucked away during the Revolution. The Second Court House was lost in a fire in 1944.

In 1952 the New York City Department of Parks and the Borough of Richmond officials became interested in the restoration project. Former Park Commissioner Robert Moses was successful in having the other property needed for the project acquired by the City and assigned to the Department of Parks. Other groups have taken an interest, and funds received have been used to move and restore the *Lake-Tysen House,* a Dutch Colonial farmhouse built about 1740 at New Dorp; the *Britton Cottage,* also from New Dorp, of the period 1670–1750; and the *Grocery Store,* built about 1850 at El-tingville, now used as a print shop.

About 30 buildings are being re-built with great care for authenticity.

Among other landmark buildings are the *Basketmaker's Shop,* from about 1810; the *Bennett House,* about 1837, a two-story dwelling of Greek Revival style; the *Boehm-Frost House,* a clapboard with brick end chimneys, of the 18th century.

There is a reconstructed sawmill of 1820 and a *Third Court House,* this one built in 1837. The *First Court House, Gaol and County House* will cost an estimated $477,000 to complete.

Some existing streets within the boundaries have been closed to mod-ern traffic; others will be closed as restoration progresses. Peripheral highways give access to parking fields and visitors' entrance.

Museums and other buildings are open to the public from July 1–Labor Day on following schedule: Tuesday–Friday, 10 A.M.–5 P.M.; Sat-urday, noon–5 p.m.; Sunday, 2–5 P.M. Closed Monday.

During the rest of the year, the museum only is open to the public on the following schedule: Tuesday–Sat-urday, 10 A.M.–5 P.M.; Sunday, 2–5 P.M. During these months the other buildings are open only to school groups, by appointment, on the same schedule.

SCHENECTADY, Schenectady County. I-90.

The Historic Stockade Area, down-town area. The first proprietors built a stockade around their village estab-lished at the angle of the Mohawk River and Binnie Kill. Nearly all original structures of the 1661 settle-ment were burned during the French and Indian conflict in 1690. Some buildings date back to the early part of the 18th century. The settlers were mostly from Holland and built their houses close to the streets on deep narrow lots. The dwellings had stoops and high Dutch gables. A walking tour can be self-guided, or a 1½-hour trip with guide starts from the YWCA, 44 Washington Ave., daily. Reservations necessary. The *Schenectady County Historical So-ciety,* 32 Washington Ave., has a bro-chure with map and a listing of houses and other historical buildings. Several blocks of the colonial homes are marked with the name of the original owner and the date of con-struction. A *Walkabout,* which tours several houses in the Historic Stock-ade, is held annually in late September.

Starting a walking tour at the His-torical Society, the visitor not only can pick up a marked map but can also see historical exhibits pertaining to the area.

Jacob Vrooman House, 3–5 Wash-ington Ave., was built in 1835 next to the tollkeeper's house of the old Washington Ave. bridge, on the site of an earlier house destroyed in the fire of 1819.

Governor Yates House, 17 Front St., built by merchant Tobias Ten Eyck in 1760. The architect, Samuel Fuller, also designed St. George's Church. A third story was added in the 19th century. James Ellice, an Indian trader, was the second owner of the house. His widow married Jo-seph C. Yates, the first mayor of the town and governor from 1823 to 1825. His law office was in the added west wing. The Marquis de La-fayette, who seems to have made a stopover in the most elegant houses of the young America, was a guest here on his tour of 1825.

The *Jeremiah DeGraaf House,* 25–27 Front St., built by DeGraaf as one house but later divided, as was the Vrooman House, dates from about 1790.

Hendrick Brouwer House, 14 North Church St., was the home of a fur trader. The house goes back to the first years of the 18th century.

Johannes Teller House, 121 Front St., built about 1740 and handsomely restored.

Abraham Yates House, 109 Union St., was built about 1700. It is the only example of Dutch urban style in the Stockade area.

Among other not-to-be-missed buildings: *Old Public Market,* Front and Ferry Sts., from 1795; *St. George's Episcopal Church* (1759), 23 North Ferry; *Old County Courthouse,* 108 Union St., was built in 1833; *Union College,* between Union and Nott Sts., was the first New York State Board of Regents–chartered institute of higher learning, with the first planned college campus in the U.S. The college was organized in 1795; the Union buildings were designed by Joseph Jacques Ramee, famous for landscape architecture, in 1813. North and South College, used as residence halls today, were the only two structures actually erected according to Ramee's plan. A later architect, Edward Tuckerman Potter, 50 years later finished the project in the then popular Romantic Venetian Gothic style—sometimes called eclectic. Sometimes called a mishmash.

STONY BROOK, Suffolk County on Long Island. St. 25A.

The *Museums at Stony Brook,* on St. 25A, include a *Carriage House Museum,* early print shop, a restored 1818 schoolhouse, a harnessmaker's shop, and a blacksmith shop, all on the south side of the village green. On the north end of the green is the *Suffolk Museum;* among its exhibits are a cobbler's shop, general store, and toy shop. A 1750 gristmill and millhouse are on display.

TARRYTOWN, Westchester County. US 9.

Sleepy Hollow Restorations include three historic houses: *Van Cortlandt Manor,* in Croton-on-Hudson, *Philipsburg Manor,* off St. 9, North Tarrytown, and *Sunnyside,* W. Sunnyside Lane, off St. 9. For information: (914) 631-8200. Washington Irving's home, Sunnyside, has many of his belongings and is open daily except major holidays as are the other restorations. Philipsburg Manor was a trading center in the 1680s; the main house has period furnishings. There is also an operating gristmill on the 20-acre estate. Van Cortlandt Manor was saved from demolition by John D. Rockefeller, Jr., who also bought 175 acres of the original estate of which about 80 percent is marsh and riverbed. All three restored homes are handsomely furnished, with selections based on extensive research and care in reconstruction.

[At last count there were 80 historic districts in New York, not counting the national historic sites, eg., *Theodore Roosevelt Inaugural Site,* on Delaware Ave., in Buffalo, or the *Sailors' Snug Harbor National Register District,* Richmond Terrace, New Brighton, Staten Island. Obviously space did not allow a total listing here.]

NEW JERSEY

May 31st [1749]. We sailed up the river with fair wind and weather. *Sturgeons* leaped often a fathom into the air. We saw them continuing this exercise all day, till we came to *Trenton*. . . . We saw some small houses near the shore, in the woods; and, now and then, a good house built of stone. The river now decreased visibly in breadth. About three o'clock this afternoon we passed *Burlington*. . . . The houses were chiefly built of stone, though they stood far distant from each other. The town has a good situation, since ships of considerable burden can sail close up to it. . . . The house of the governor at *Burlington* is but a small one: it is built of stone, close by the river side, and is the first building in the town as you come from *Philadelphia*.
—*Travels into North America* by Peter Kalm, London, 1770–71.

ALLAIRE STATE PARK, Monmouth County. SE of Farmingdale, St. 524.

Historic Howell Works, a bog ironworks, stood on the site of an 18th-century sawmill and was first known as Monmouth Furnace; Benjamin B. Howell leased the works in 1821. In 1822 James P. Allaire bought the foundry and built a model village for his 500 employees. Allaire had a brass and an iron foundry in New York and was a highly successful man who built engines and boilers; he cast the brass air chambers for Robert Fulton's *Clermont,* the first steamboat to navigate the Hudson River between New York City and Albany (1807); he was associated with many important vessels and undertakings of his day, including making the pipes for Manhattan's first waterworks. For 24 years he kept the town named for him busily employed, but eventually it became the "Deserted Village of Allaire." Since 1941 the area has belonged to the state and is now a 1,405-acre state park.

The brick beehive furnace stack is all that remains of the ironworks, but several shops survive from the early 19th century. Craft demonstrations are given in season. The post office is in the first brick building, put up in 1827, and also used as the foreman's cottage. There is a visitor center in the only building left from what was a row of workers' houses. Christ Church, 1831, enlarged later, has the steeple at the rear because the front of the building would not support the bell which was cast at the Howell forge. Nearby, the Pine Creek Railroad provides narrow-gauge steam rides for a small fee. Open in spring and summer daily, weekends in winter season. Inquire locally for hours or write Allaire State Park, Route 524, Allaire, 07727.

BATSTO, Burlington County. County Rd. 542, NE of Hammonton.

Historic Batsto in the Wharton State Forest is a restored village which originally developed around the Batsto Iron Works, founded in 1766. The furnaces supplied muni-

65

tions for the Revolutionary War and the War of 1812 and other iron products until 1848; later the community produced window glass. Batsto glass also was used for the old gas streetlamps in New York, Philadelphia, and other cities.

The restoration of the village was begun in 1954. Guided tours take visitors through or past some 27 sites, including the mansion, furnished with antiques, which stands on a hill, workers' houses across the Mullica River, a gristmill, sawmill, blacksmith and wheelwright shop, and general store which includes a post office still in use.

Buildings are shown only by guided tour; there is a fee which is used toward development of the restoration area. Write Visitors Center, Batsto, R.D., Hammonton, 08215, for hours, rates, appointments, or a brochure, *The Batsto Story,* which gives not only the history of the place but explains that the odd word stems from *baatsstoo,* which meant "steam bath" to the Scandinavians and Dutch and "bathing places" to the American Indians.

BURLINGTON, Burlington County. US 130.

Burlington Historic District on the Delaware River takes in varied structures in the town, settled in 1678, which became a busy port in the 18th century.

James Lawrence House, 459 High St., restored, was the 1781 birthplace of naval hero Captain Lawrence, who is credited with first saying "Don't give up the ship" (he was fatally injured during a sea fight in the War of 1812). The house is a state historic site. In New Jersey these are listed in local phone books under the heading Department of Environmental Protection—Lawrence House, etc. Hours vary; check before visiting.

James Fenimore Cooper House, 457 High St., was the birthplace of the author who created the unforgettable Deerslayer and many other characters once known to every schoolchild. Cooper lived here only one year, but the house has many historical exhibits. The Burlington County Historical Society, housed here, has booklets for walking tours of the town, which has several early-18th-century structures. The Cooper House is usually open by appointment, or Sunday afternoons; check locally for hours.

CAPE MAY, Cape May County. US 9, tip of peninsula.

Cape May Historic District comprises the early resort town with some 600 structures from the second half of the 19th century to the early 20th. The area was settled by the Dutch in the 17th century and became a famous watering place when steamboat traffic on the Delaware River was at a peak.

Cornelius Jacobsen Mey, a Dutch captain, brought the propitiously named *Glad Tidings* around the cape in 1620, and noted that the climate seemed like home. The Dutch gained a foothold here and tried to make a profit on whaling, but later arrivals from New England were more successful in the dangerous endeavor which William Penn called "whalery."

Regular steamboat service to Philadelphia began in 1819, and soon the summers were packed with visitors from nearby cities and the South. Two Presidents and a future one were among the many famous visitors to enjoy the balmy cape: Franklin Pierce, James Buchanan, and Abraham Lincoln (in 1849) with his wife Mary. Today's "Victorian Village," built with a $3 million federal urban renewal grant, has horse-drawn trolleys for sight seeing past the rich Victorian architecture.

CAPE MAY COURT HOUSE, Cape May County. US 9. W of Garden State Pkwy. exit 10A.

Chamber of Commerce, Crest

Haven Rd. and Garden State Pkwy., has information on the numerous Victorian resort hotels and dwellings which have been restored.

Cape May Court House, US 9 in midtown, built in 1850 for slightly more than $6,000, including a 333-pound bell, is a handsome building which now houses a historical museum. Closed Sundays and holidays.

CLINTON, Hunterdon County. I-78.

Clinton Historical Museum Village, 56 Main St., has a mill with a working water wheel and several early shops, displays of 19th-century crafts and industries and farm tools. The Old Red Mill on the Raritan River was built in 1763, enlarged in 1820. Once a gristmill, it later produced lime and linseed oil. Open daily, April to November, with weekday hours 1 to 5 P.M.; weekends noon to 6 P.M.

FLEMINGTON, Hunterdon County. County 523 just S of St. 31.

Liberty Village, 2 Church St., adjacent to Turntable Junction Village (a shopping and residential area), is a re-created 18th- and 19th-century town with craft demonstrations given by costumed workers. The *Swan Museum of the American Revolution* is here. Open daily except major holidays.

GREENWICH, Cumberland County. St. 49.

Greenwich Historic District, Main St. from Cohansey River N to Othello, covers most of the oldest of old S. Jersey towns (1684) and should be seen on foot. *Cumberland County Historical Society* in the *Nicholas Gibbon House,* Main St., a 1730 merchant's dwelling with period rooms, has information on self-guiding tours and also provides guides from April to October. There are about a dozen colonial buildings in the old town, including the 18th century *Quaker*

Meeting House; the *Mark Reeve House,* built about 1686; *Harding House,* about 1734; *Dr. Holme's House; Pirate House,* 1734; *Richard Wood Mansion,* built about 1795; and the *Schoolhouse,* c. 1810. The post office and general store are on Main St.

LAWRENCEVILLE, Mercer County. US 206.

Lawrenceville Township Historic District covers the town and vicinity, which have a number of 18th- and 19th-century structures. The residential main street has Georgian homes. The Lawrenceville School buildings were designed by Peabody and Stearns and the campus was landscaped by Frederick Law Olmsted.

MORRISTOWN, Morris County. US 202, 287.

Acorn Hall, 68 Morris Ave., Italianate clapboard mansion, three stories with fourth-story tower, was built in 1853 for Dr. John Schermerhorn, a physician; architect unknown. After his wife's death Dr. Schermerhorn decided to move his practice to New York. In 1857 he sold the house with all its furnishings, to Augustus Crane. Descendants of Crane lived in the house until 1971, when Mary Crane Hone, a great-granddaughter of Augustus Crane, gave the mansion and its contents to the Morris County Historical Society, which now maintains it. The mid-Victorian furnishings are just as they have always been. Open Thursdays, 11 A.M. to 3 P.M.; Sundays, 1:30 P.M. to 4 P.M.; and by appointment. Admission $1.00; students 50¢. (201) 267-6435.

Morristown National Historic Park, administered by the National Park Service, preserves buildings and encampment areas occupied by George Washington and his army during the critical winters of 1777 and 1779–80. On Morris Ave., not far from the center of town, is *Washing-*

ton's Headquarters, the Jacob Ford mansion, with separate *Historical Museum* also on the grounds. The three-story, 13-room Georgian mansion was Morristown's finest when completed in 1774 for Jacob Ford, Jr., prosperous farmer and owner of iron mines and a powder mill. During the months from December 1, 1779, until late June, 1780, when Washington lived here, the house was a busy command center as staff officers came and went to confer with the commander-in-chief on the many problems facing the Continental forces encamped that winter in the Jockey Hollow area, SW of Morristown. Washington received the Marquis de Lafayette here in the spring of 1780. The mansion has contemporaneous furnishings. The museum offers historical exhibits, a research library, and historical film and slide showings.

The *Jockey Hollow Encampment Area* can be reached by driving about three miles from Morristown via US 202 (Mt. Kemble Ave.), or US 287, and right on Tempe Wick Rd.; or from town via Western Ave. Here some 13,000 troops lived and drilled that winter of 1779–80, quartered in drafty log huts they built in the deep snow. Reconstructed huts, a log field hospital, and a *Visitor Center* with exhibits and a historical film, recall the hardships suffered by officers and men as Washington managed to hold his army together despite freezing weather, scanty rations, and severe supply shortages of every kind.

Also in the Encampment Area is the *Wick Farm,* consisting of a well-preserved eighteenth-century farmhouse with period furnishings and, in summer, an interesting old-style produce and herb garden. This was General Arthur St. Clair's headquarters in 1779–80.

Park roads open 9 A.M. to sunset; Visitor Center, Wick Farm, and Washington's Headquarters buildings open 9 A.M to 5 P.M. All park buildings closed Thanksgiving Day, December 25, and January 1. Small admission fee at Washington's Headquarters.

Speedwell Village—The Factory, 333 Speedwell Ave., is an 1837–38 ironworks now developed to show how America lived after the Revolutionary War when great things were happening in industry and agriculture. The Village preserves a part of the Stephen Vail Homestead Farm. The Vail family developed machine production and steam-powered transportation and aided Samuel F. B. Morse with the development of the telegraph.

The Whippany River runs through a natural gorge here; a dam powered a forge in the 18th century before Stephen Vail and his partners built the ironworks. Vail took over the foundry in 1815. In 1818 the *Speedwell Iron Works* made the engine and several parts for the *S. S. Savannah,* the first vessel to cross the Atlantic with the aid of steam. Vail bought land on the north side of the river and built a mill in 1829 which was rented out for cotton weaving. He later became a judge.

Vail's oldest son, Alfred was studying for the ministry in 1832 when S. F. B. Morse was first working on plans for an electromagnet to record signals over long distances. Morse was professor of fine arts at New York University, where Vail was a student. When Alfred saw a demonstration of Morse's instruments he felt that the inventor could use technical as well as financial help and soon became a partner in the ambitious enterprise.

Early in January 1838, in the factory on the Homestead Farm, the judge sent a message by telegraph, "A patient waiter is no loser." The first public demonstration was given soon after, and the second floor of the factory was jammed with an audience. Even city slickers from Newark had come to gape at the sight of Morse and Vail discussing, via 2 miles of wire, the fact that railroad cars had arrived with 350 passengers. By now Morse, Vail, and a third partner, Leonard D. Gale, had their laboratory set up on the second floor of the factory while the first floor remained a gristmill.

After demonstrations in major eastern cities, and after Alfred had made another set of instruments which recorded dots and lines, using the "Morse" code, Congress finally appropriated money for an experimental telegraph line to be run between Washington and Baltimore. Morse sent the now famous message "What hath God wrought?" to his assistant Alfred Vail in 1844. When Morristown citizens organized to save the site, they acquired, with some original furnishings, the Vail House, the farm buildings, and the factory which was damaged by fire in 1908. Other historic houses of the community which were about to be demolished were moved here and the factory has been restored to its 1838 condition. NHL.

Open April 1 to November 1, Thursday through Saturdays, 10 to 4; Sundays, 2 to 5; small admission fee.

MOUNT HOLLY, Burlington County. County 537, 541.

For two months in 1779 Mount Holly was the state capital. The town was founded by the Quakers in 1676, but most remaining historic buildings date from the 18th century. The *Courthouse,* High St. (1796), is Georgian Colonial. Buildings on either side date from 1807. *Burlington County Prison,* 128 High (1811), was designed by Robert Mills and is now a museum. Guided tour. *Mill Street Hotel,* 67 Mill St., has the brick walls of the original building of the 1720s which was *Three Tun Tavern.*

John Woolman Memorial, 99 Branch St. Woolman once owned the land on which this house was built in 1783. Period furnishings, open daily.

He was a persuasive abolitionist of the 18th century, and a religious leader. He traveled widely in behalf of the Friends and trying to abolish slavery. Woolman had a tailor shop early in his career but became so devoted to his beliefs he gave up most worldly endeavors and even his horse. He died of smallpox while on a walking trip in England in 1772. The *Old Schoolhouse,* 35 Brainard St., where he taught, and *Peachfield,* Burr Rd., his home in 1725, have been authentically furnished by Society of Colonial Dames of America. Open May to October one day a week or by appointment: call (609) 267-9682 for both buildings.

PRINCETON, Mercer County. US 206.

Princeton Historic District covers an odd-shaped area from Lovers Lane to Olden St. between Lytle St. and Haslet Ave. *Princeton University,* founded in Elizabeth in 1746, came here in 1756; visitor information available in *Stanhope Hall. Morven,* 55 Stockton St., now the Governor's residence, was used by Cornwallis when the British held the town in 1776. It was the home of Richard Stockton, signer of the Declaration of Independence. NHL.

Westland, 15 Hodge Rd., 1854, was the Italianate home of President Grover Cleveland from 1897 to 1908, after his second term in office. NHL.

Joseph Henry House, on campus, is brick, built in 1837 in Greek Revival style. It was the home of Henry, the scientist who developed the electromagnet and a prototype telegraph, and who was the first secretary of the Smithsonian Institution.

Maybury Hill (Joseph Hewes Birthplace and Boyhood Home), 346 Snowden Lane, built about 1730, later altered, has a large stone barn among its outbuildings. Hewes signed the Declaration of Independence for North Carolina. NHL.

Nassau Hall, on campus, 1754–56,

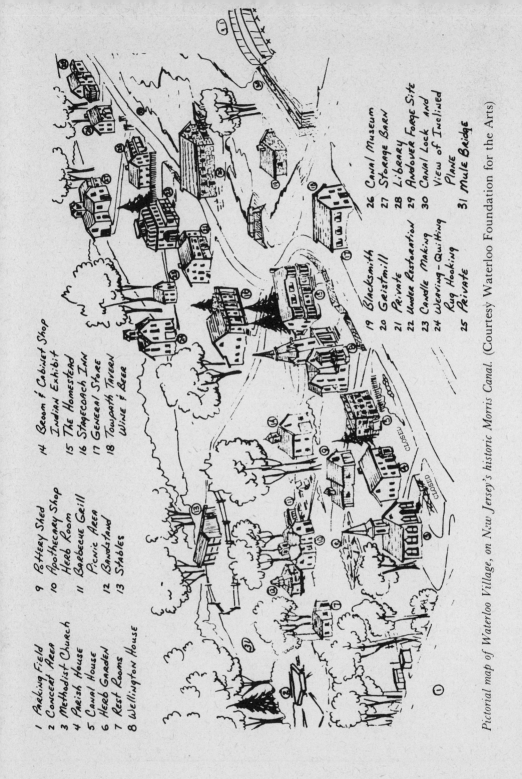

Pictorial map of Waterloo Village, on New Jersey's historic Morris Canal. (Courtesy Waterloo Foundation for the Arts)

was built by Robert Smith, who was also the architect; rebuilt by Benjamin H. Latrobe after a fire in 1804. It was again rebuilt, and a cupola added, by John Notman after a fire in 1855. It remains Georgian. Nassau Hall was the first important college building of the area and it set the pattern for many others. It was used as a hospital and barracks during the Revolution and as a meeting-place for the Continental Congress. NHL.

President's House (MacLean House), Nassau St., 1756, built by Robert Smith, with later additions. John Witherspoon, president of the University, delegate to the Second Continental Congress, and a signer of the Declaration, lived here in 1768–79. NHL.

SMITHVILLE, Atlantic County. US 9, County 561A.

Historic Towne of Smithville is a restoration built around the 1781 Smithville Inn, formerly a stagecoach stop. Some 30 structures have been moved to this site to make up the community of 18th-century structures and crafts. There are dwellings, shops, Hosea Joslin's tiny chapel from May's Landing, and a gristmill from Sharptown among the exhibits. Open daily.

WATERLOO VILLAGE, Sussex County. On Morris Canal, 4 miles NW of the junction of US 46, 206, near Stanhope.

Early in this century the Newark *Sunday Call* printed an unbeatable description of Waterloo: "Along the Musconetcong River, in the narrow valley between the Allamuchy and Schooley's Mountain Ranges, lies the little village of Waterloo. . . . The

mountains close by on either side, the river playing tag, as it were, with the Morris Canal, the canal basin at the foot of the inclined plane, the raceways feeding the old mill, various brooks dashing foam over stony beds, the lake with its indented shores and island—all these, thrown together in an irregular, picturesque confusion, form a scene, which, from whatever point of view observed, is the delight of artists and camera fiends alike, or those who love the beauties of nature."

The old stone buildings are still on their sites of the 1700s. Frame Victorian houses and the church are from the 19th century. The church has been in use since it was built in 1859. The whole village, bought by Percival H. E. Leach and Louis D. Gualandi, has been restored and refurnished with fitting antiques. Among exhibits (which may be seen on weekends by horse-drawn carriage) are the church, a canal house, the Wellington House, the Stagecoach Inn, a gristmill, general store, and smithy. Fees are used by the Waterloo Village Restoration for maintenance and expansion. Open daily except Mondays, all year round, from 10 A.M. to 6 P.M. Methodist church services are held every Sunday; visitors welcome.

WHEATON VILLAGE, Cumberland County. In Millville, St. 47, 49.

The restoration of a typical southern New Jersey glass-blowing town will have about 60 buildings when completed. At present there are a general store, shops, a glass factory with demonstrations of glass blowing, and a glass museum of the late 19th century. Open daily; hours vary.

PENNSYLVANIA

The trolley ride to Willow Grove is of itself an extremely interesting experience. Open cars may be taken on Thirteenth Street, or Eighth Street, or elsewhere, and these, beyond Columbia Avenue, run along North Broad Street, showing many of the beauties of that new and wealthy part of the city. Gradually, the city is left behind, and the cars run along the old turnpike, which becomes more and more rural and inviting. Grand trees shade the ancient highway. . . . Fine country-seats, some of them going back to colonial times, border the road, and here and there quaint old stone houses abut upon it, and speak of the peaceful and prosperous past.
— *Handy Guide to Philadelphia and Environs,* Chicago, 1910

Almost all the houses hereabouts were built either of stone or bricks: but those of stone were more numerous. Germantown, which is about two English miles long, had no other houses, and the country houses thereabouts were all built of stone. But there are several varieties of that stone which is commonly made use of in building. Sometimes it consisted of a black or grey glimmer, running in undulated veins, the spaces between their bendings filled up with a grey, loose, small-grained limestone, which was easily friable. . . . When therefore a person intended to build a house, he inquired where the best stone could be met with. It is to be found on cornfields and meadows. . . . It must be observed, that when the people build with this stone, they take care to turn the flat side of it outwards.
— *Travels into North America,* by Peter Kalm, London, 1770–71

AMBRIDGE, Beaver County. St. 65, near I-79 and the Pennsylvania Turnpike.

Old Economy Village, NW edge of town near the Ohio River, is the third and last home of the Harmony Society, a band of hardy German immigrants whose first home in the U.S. was Harmony, Pennsylvania, established in 1804. Their second community, in New Harmony, Indiana, was set up in 1815. They moved to Ambridge in 1825. They were led here by George Rapp, a vinedresser and weaver, who was considered a prophet and called "Father" Rapp.

On the 3,000-acre tract, Rapp's 25-room *Great House,* 1825, is one attraction. Others are the *Feast Hall,* where community dinners were served, housing the museum, printing press, and an adult school; the *Feast Kitchen,* where meals for 800 could be prepared; several shops, including a cabinetmaker's, tailor's, barber's, apothecary's, and cobbler's; a doctor's office and wine cellar. The church, 1831, has the original pews and a clock with only one hand that tolls the time from the steeple. The *Langenbacher House* is a typical dwelling, less grand than Father

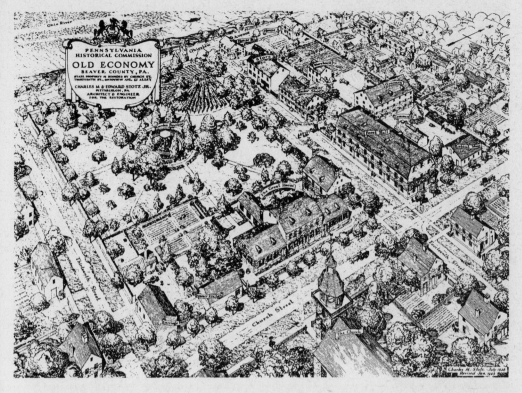

Old Economy Village, Ambridge, Pennsylvania. (Courtesy Harmonie Associates, Inc.)

Rapp's. Information is available from the Beaver County Tourist Promotion Agency, Courthouse, Beaver, Pa. 15009, or the Pennsylvania Historical and Museum Commission, Ambridge, (412) 266-4500. Hours vary slightly with the season, but the village is open daily.

BEDFORD, Bedford County. US 220.

Bedford Historic Village, US 220-Bus., 2 miles N, is a 72-acre tract which presents living history of the time of the Revolution. The village is entered across the restored Claycomb covered bridge, which is 141 years old. Authentic log structures have been moved here from other parts of the county and restored to their original period with proper furnishings.

Craftsmen and artisans demonstrate old-time skills of lacemaking, weaving, spinning, leatherwork, candle dipping, woodworking, tinsmithing, glass blowing, and ropemaking. Homemade goods are on sale. An operating farm is part of the complex, which is still growing.

BETHLEHEM, Northampton County. I-78.

Historic Bethlehem, Ohio Rd. and Main St., is an 18th-century commercial area being restored. There are waterworks of 1762, with an 18-foot wooden water wheel, a tannery of 1761, a 1764 springhouse with early agriculture tools on display. Guided tours of the restored area include *Goundie House,* built in 1810, 501 Main, in Federal-style brick.

Goundie was a brewer and town leader. Some rooms have period furnishings.

Bethlehem Historic District is in Lehigh County as well as Northampton. Bounded by Main, Nevada, and E. Broad Sts. and the Lehigh River, it covers the downtown 18th- to 19th-century area. There are many structures of a variety of styles, numerous limestone buildings from the early settlement made in 1741 by Moravian immigrants. The community had civic planners earlier than many American settlements.

The **Bethlehem Convention and Visitors Bureau,** 11 W. Market, has a film and tours of the historic district: (215) 867-3788.

BIRD-IN-HAND, Lancaster County. St. 340.

Amish Village, 1 mile W on St. 340, then 3 miles S on St. 896, has both original and reconstructed buildings which include the inevitable blacksmith shop, schoolhouse, smokehouse. There are guided tours, buggy tours as well.

BRISTOL, Bucks County. US 13.

Historic Fallsington, 4 Yardley Ave., in Fallsington, 5 miles N off US 13. A restoration of 17th- and 18th-century buildings includes the **Gillingham Store,** which houses the **Information Center; Stage Coach Tavern, Burges-Lippincott House,** and **Moon-Williamson House** are all open. There are self-guiding tours or guided tours. Audiovisual presentation. Open March 15 to November 15.

Fallsington Historic District, S of US 1, E of New Tyburn Rd., is late 17th to 20th century with residential stone, frame, and brick structures, mostly in Colonial and Federal style. Originally this Quaker community was known as "Crewcorne." Meeting-house Square was at the junction of five roads.

Fallsington Day is an annual 18th-century fair, and old homes are open and there are craft demonstrations. Second Saturday in October.

CORNWALL, Lebanon County. St. 419, N of turnpike.

Cornwall Furnace, on Old US 322, 2 miles E of junction with St. 72. In the complex is the well-preserved sandstone foundry with the large square stone furnace which was in operation from 1742 to 1883. **Miners Village,** from 1754, is still occupied. The two-family houses were built in the 1860s. Museum in charcoal house has dioramas on the furnace history and operations. NHL.

Historic Schaefferstown, 6 miles E of town at the junction of St. 419, 501, 897. The village square has authentic stone and log buildings. There is an 18th-century farm which was established by Swiss-German immigrants. The stone barn is one of the best-built in the area. The first waterworks in the U.S. were here in 1750 and are still used. There is a museum of local history and artifacts in the **Thomas R. Brendle Memorial Library.** A **Folklore and Craft Festival** is held the last weekend in July; a **Cooking and Horse Plowing Festival,** early in September, and a **Harvest Fair** late in September.

DOYLESTOWN, Bucks County. St. 611.

Mercer Museum, Pine and Ashland, is a complex with a log cabin from the late 18th century, moved to this site in 1911, a brick Georgian Revival house of 1904, later enlarged, built by Dr. Henry Chapman Mercer to house an extensive collection of tools, farm and other early machinery and implements, and assorted artifacts of young America. Mercer was an archaeologist and potter. His home, **Fonthill,** E. Court St., has decorative tiles and memorabilia. There are guided tours. The **Moravian Pottery and Tile Works,** E. Court and Swamp Rd., has been restored as a museum. Guided tours. *Mercer Mile* is a route connecting the three buildings, which resemble concrete castles. Mercer worried about fire and used reinforced concrete, with tile roofs.

Bucks County Historical-Tourist Commission, One Oxford Valley, Suite 410, Langhorne, 19047, has information on the historic sites of the county and a descriptive map of 13 covered bridges.

Fountain House, State and Main Sts., a stone and stucco house from 1758, enlarged in 1830, has two side sections added in 1849, a mansard roof put up in 1876. The whole works was restored in 1971. It is the oldest Doylestown tavern and also was the first post office in town as well as the community social center.

James-Lorah House (Judge Chapman House), 132 N. Main, was built in the 1830s, enlarged in the 1840s. Chapman, a state senator and U.S. Congressman, was the father of Dr. Henry Chapman Mercer. Museum.

EPHRATA, Lancaster County. US 322, 222.

Ephrata Cloister, 632 W. Main, is a complex of restored buildings including the *Saal* (community house) and *Saron* (Sister's House), which are large log and frame structures, the *Almonry* (bakehouse), *Beissel's log house,* the *1837 Academy,* and several other dwellings. The religious community was founded in 1732 by Conrad Beissel, a German Pietist mystic. Members wore white habits and were celibates in a brotherhood or sisterhood group or belonged to a married order. Self-denial was stressed, as in other religious communities, and the buildings seem to reflect the same sort of society formed by the Shakers, but the latter had no married members. Also, the recluses here were even harder on themselves than the Shakers in some ways. They had wooden benches for beds and wooden blocks for pillows.

The colonists turned out beautifully hand-illuminated books and religious music. After the Revolutionary War the settlement, which had a population of 300, diminished, but members were living here until the mid-1920s. NHL. *Ephrata Museum,* 249 Main St., in a Victorian mansion, has period displays.

HARMONY, Butler County. I-79, St. 288.

Harmony Historic District covers the community founded in 1805, the first of three settlements of the Harmony Society, led by George Rapp. (See New Harmony Indiana, and Old Economy Village, Pennsylvania.) The *Frederick Rapp House* has Georgian elements. The two-story church is brick, and there are a number of brick structures remaining, around a central square. Most have late Georgian details. *Harmony Museum,* Main and Mercer Sts., is in a building which was constructed in 1809. Among displays is a 1650 tower clock with a single hand, brought from Germany. In 1807 the Harmonists adopted celibacy, a practice which soon thinned their ranks and led ultimately to their extinction. The town of Harmony was put up for sale in June 1814. A year later Abraham Ziegler, a Mennonite, paid $100,000 for the village of empty houses. The cemetery, with its revolving stone gate, saw some 100 burials but contains only one headstone, that of Johann Rapp, George's son.

Even earlier the site of the restored town had been a crossing point of Indian trails. George Washington "slept here" in 1783 and in his journal refers to the locality as Murderingtown. NHL.

HOPEWELL, Berks County. Off Pennsylvania Turnpike, Morgantown interchange.

Hopewell Village National Historic Site: Visitor Center has a museum and an audiovisual program on the

Buildings at Hopewell, Pennsylvania's old iron-smelting village. (U.S. National Park Service)

restored iron furnace and village founded in 1770 by ironmaster Mark Bird, and its role played in the colonies and the Revolutionary War. A self-guiding tour takes in many buildings of the furnace operation, tenant houses, the ironmaster's home, and the company store and office. The structures are restored stone and reconstructed frame. Voices of workers talking about their jobs are played in various buildings, to simulate reality.

LANCASTER, Lancaster County. US 30.

A *Downtown Visitors Center* has recently been opened by the Pennsylvania Dutch Visitors Bureau in the Brunswick Mall, Chestnut St. In addition to brochures, maps, and information on city and county, it will handle scheduling for the *Historic Lancaster Walking Tour,* although tour headquarters remain at 15 W. King St. Costumed guides conduct the two-hour walk daily except Monday.

Visitors Information Center, US 30, E of town near Hempstead Rd., has an orientation film, exhibits, and maps. There are many tours avail-

able, and none should be rushed through.

On the National Register: *Old City Hall,* Penn Square, built in 1797, brick with Flemish bond, restored in 1924. *Central Market,* William Henry Place, was built in 1889, with Richardson Romanesque elements. *Ellicott House,* 123 N. Prince, was built about 1780 by Gottlieb Schner. In the early 19th century it was the home of Andrew Ellicott, first U. S. surveyor-general, who redrew plans for Washington, D.C., laid out a number of Pennsylvania towns, and taught at West Point.

Old Main, Goethean Hall, and Diagnothian Hall are on the campus of Franklin and Marshall College. *General Edward Hand House (Rock Ford),* 881 Rock Ford Rd., 1793 Georgian home where Washington was once a guest, was owned by Hand, a doctor and a member of the Continental Congress.

Fulton Opera House, 12–14 N. Prince St., Italianate, 1852, was built on a former jail foundation, Samuel Sloane as architect. It was named for inventor Robert Fulton. NHL. *Hans Herr House,* 1851 Hans Herr Drive, 1719, of uncoursed sandstone, is the oldest Mennonite meeting place in the U.S.

Wheatland, James Buchanan House, 1120 Marietta Ave., built in 1828, became the home of the 15th President of the United States. Buchanan, to date, has been the only bachelor President. Banker William Jenkins built "The Wheatlands," as it was first known, for his country home. The wheat fields are long gone. A Philadelphia lawyer bought the house from Jenkins. Buchanan purchased the property in 1848. The brick mansion was 1½ miles out of town when he moved in with his niece, Harriet Lane, who later served as hostess in the White House. Harriet was more successful at making friends than the President in the arduous days before the actual outbreak of the Civil War. Many of the furnishings were here in Buchanan's day. NHL.

Pennsylvania Farm Museum of Landis Valley, 2451 Kissel Hill Rd., is about 3 miles N of town off St. 272. There are four early homes, craftshops, with demonstrations, a large collection of early farm machinery, weapons, seven Conestoga wagons (which may be the largest concentration outside of Disneyland), and thousands of artifacts on display. Henry and George Landis began the massive collection in 1900. *Harvest Days* are the first weekend in October; *Craft Days* are held the third weekend in June.

Mennonite Information Center, 2209 Mill Stream Rd., about 5 miles E of town on St. 462, US 30. An orientation program on the Mennonite and Amish communities is provided. Guided tours are arranged; open daily except Sunday, Thanksgiving, and Christmas: call (717) 299-0954.

Amish Farm and House, 6 miles E of town via St. 462, US 30, has a talk on the "Plain People" and a guided tour of the early-19th-century stone buildings, which have been furnished

in early Amish style. There are water wheels, a windmill, hand-dug well, early vehicles, farm animals, and growing crops. Another **Amish Homestead** is 3 miles E of town on St. 462, on a 71-acre farm; guided tour of 18th-century house.

Mill Bridge Craft Village, 7 miles E off US 30 in Soundersburg, has an operating gristmill from 1738, covered bridge, craft demonstrations, the smithy, and other village necessities. The settlement developed on land granted by William Penn to John Herr, grandson of Hans Herr, whose home may be seen in Lancaster.

Rock Ford, 3 miles S of Lancaster on Rock Ford Rd. off S. Duke St. at Williamson Park, was the home of General Edward Hand, Revolutionary War commander, a member of the Continental Congress, and a physician. He was born in Ireland. From 1791 to 1801 he was federal inspector of revenue. The homesite also has the **Rock Ford-Kauffman Museum,** a collection of rifles and other early artifacts. Hand was a member of the Lancaster County Associators, a group of colonial riflemen, in 1776.

MENGES MILL, York County. St. 116.

Colonial Valley, 6 miles NE of town off St. 116, is a village complex with a 1783 farmhouse, gristmill, general store, blacksmith shop, a sawmill, and other shops. A vast collection of colonial tools is on display.

NEW HOPE, Bucks County. US 202.

This old town on the Delaware River was once called Coryell's Ferry; later it was named for the New Hope Mills, established by Benjamin Parry in 1790.

Chapman House, S of town off St. 232 on Eagle Rd., was built in 1745. It is two and a half stories, stone, and was owned by Dr. John Chapman, a local politician. The house served as headquarters of General Henry Knox and Captain of Artillery Alexander Hamilton, before the Battle of Trenton. Knox actually became a brigadier general as a result of his performance in the battle.

Old Delaware Canal, built by the Lehigh Coal & Navigation Co., is at the S end of town, where mule-drawn barge rides are available (New St.).

New Hope & Ivyland Railroad, 32 W. Bridge St., has 14-mile round-trip steam train rides in Victorian-style coaches. Hours vary with seasons.

Old Franklin Print Shop, 40 S Main, provides demonstrations on a Washington Hand Press from 1860.

Parry Mansion, and Barn, on S. Main, are open to the public; the barn is owned by the New Hope Historical Society and is operated as a commercial art gallery. The house was built in 1784 and has been restored.

New Hope Town Hall was built in 1790; the *Logan Inn,* on Cannon Square, has been serving since 1732. *Coryell's Ferry* operates between New Hope and Lambertville every half hour, from May until fall.

Washington Crossing State Park, is 7 miles S of St. 32. The park is in two sections, covering the site where the general and 2,400 soldiers crossed the Delaware in a heavy snowstorm on Christmas night, 1776. On Bowman's Hill the *Thompson-Neely House,* of 1701, has period furnishings. There are a gristmill and an observation tower. In the Washington Crossing section, headquarters are in the Taylor House, on St. 532, built in 1812. *Old Ferry House* here is from 1757 and is being restored. *Memorial Building,* near the Point of Embarkation, has the famous Emanuel Leutze painting of the scene. A third part of the park is in New Jersey.

NEWTOWN, Bucks County. St. 413.

Forty colonial buildings have been preserved. A free brochure, with a complete walking tour, is available at

Independence Square, Philadelphia. Ink sketch from an early photograph. (From Edward M. Riley, *Independence National Historic Park,* courtesy of U.S. National Park Service)

the Enterprise Building. The *Brick Hotel* was built in 1764; the *Newtown Presbyterian Church* in 1769, on the site of an earlier structure; *Court Inn,* Court St., now headquarters of the Newtown Historic Association, was once a tavern, built in 1733.

The *Hicks House,* 122 Penn St., was the home of colonial artist Edward Hicks. *Temperance House,* 5 S. State, was built in 1772. *Bird-in-Hand House,* 1690, is the oldest frame building in Pennsylvania and was used as an army supply depot during the Revolutionary War. Edward Hicks painted the Franklin advice: "A bird in the hand is worth two in the bush."

Makefield Meeting, NE of town at Mt. Eyre Rd. and Dolington Rd., was the site of monthly meetings in the 18th century, and the center of the township social gatherings. The meeting house was built in 1752. The schoolmaster's house dates from 1787; both houses are stone, stuccoed.

PHILADELPHIA, Philadelphia County. I-95.

Independence National Historical Park, bounded by Walnut, 6th, Chestnut, and 2nd Sts. *Independence Hall,* 1732–56, is the heart of the district, which also includes *Old City*

Hall, 1789–91; *Congress Hall,* 1787–89, which was built as the County Courthouse and was used by the Federal Congress, from 1790 to 1800; *First and Second U.S. Banks,* the *Philadelphia Exchange, Franklin Court, Liberty Bell Pavilion,* etc. *Visitor Center,* 3rd and Chestnut. *American Philosophical Society Hall,* 1785–89, built by Samuel Vaughan (NHL); *Carpenters' Hall,* 320 Chestnut St., housed the First Continental Congress, museum, NHL; *Christ Church,* 22–26 N. 2nd St., 1727–44; *Deshler-Morris House,* 5442 Germantown Ave., 1772; *Gloria Dei (Old Swedes') Church,* Swanson St. between Christian and Water Sts., built 1698–1700; and *Mikveh Israel Cemetery,* NW corner of Spruce and Darien Sts., all are administered by the National Park Service. The best and latest information is available at the National Park Information centers.

The *Historic Square Mile* begins at the Visitors Center, 3rd and Chestnut, where there is a fully detailed map.

The *Philadelphia Convention & Visitors Bureau Tourist Center,* 1525 J. F. Kennedy Blvd., also has maps, literature, information, and a film: (215) 864-1976. There are many sightseeing bus tours, boat tours, specialized walking and audiotaped tours; phone the above number for list.

Clinton St. Historic District, bounded by 9th, 11th, Pine, and Cypress Sts., is a two-block district with tree-lined streets and brick row houses of the 1835 to 1850 period.

Colonial Germantown Historic District, Germantown Ave. between Windrim Ave. and Upsal Ave., comprises about 50 structures of the 18th and early 19th centuries. The area was founded by immigrants from the Netherlands in 1683 who were seeking religious freedom. NHL.

Clarkson-Watson House, 5275 Ave., is a museum featuring colonial costumes: Thomas Jefferson spent the summer of 1793 here, when he was Secretary of State. The residence was later used as the Bank of Germantown.

Cliveden, 6401 Germantown Ave., was a Georgian home in the 1760s for jurist Benjamin Chew. The Battle of Germantown was fought here in 1777. The home has Chippendale and Federal furnishings. Daily tours. NHL.

Coyningham-Hacker House, 5214 Germantown Ave., is the main museum of the Germantown Historical Society; rooms have 17th-, 18th-, and 19th-century furnishings.

Mennonite Church, 6121 Germantown Ave., was a log cabin in the first years of the colony; now has a museum, a bookstore, and a media presentation on the history of the area. *Mennonite Meeting-place,* of 1770, is at No. 6119.

Grumblethorpe (Wister's Big House), 5267 Germantown Ave., built in 1744 by John Wister, a rich merchant. It is fieldstone, restored by the Philadelphia Society for the Preservation of Landmarks, furnished in the 18th-century style, with a colonial garden.

Howell House, 5218 Germantown Ave., contains a needlework museum. It is a good example of row housing in the area.

Loudoun, 4650 Germantown Ave., built by Thomas Armat in 1801; this house has an official ghost, listed on the U.S. Department of Commerce guide to special attractions No. 10. It is the "spirit" of a small boy called Little Willie, who was William Armat Loudoun.

Stenton Mansion, 18th and Courtland Sts., was the home of James Logan, William Penn's secretary, who later became chief justice of the state. Both Washington and British General William Howe used the house as headquarters during the changing times of the Revolutionary War. The house tour includes a restored barn from the 18th century. NHL.

Upsala, 6430 Germantown Ave., built in 1795–98 in Federal style, is a museum house.

Beggarstown School, 6669 Germantown Ave., built about 1740, restored in 1915, is typical of early German parish schools.

John Johnson House, 6306 Germantown Ave., built in 1768, with a façade of rubble, ashlar, was a center of the Battle of Germantown. Museum.

Michael Billmeyer House, 6505–06 Germantown, 18th-century home of a printer and publisher, has a museum.

Elfreth's Alley Historic District, between 2nd and Front Sts., comprising 33 buildings with façades flush to the street, is the oldest continuously inhabited street in town. NHL. The cobblestones which Benjamin Franklin may have trod on still are here. The area was first Gilbert's Alley, then Preston's Alley, then Jeremiah Elfreth's, a blacksmith who inherited two properties on the street from a couple of his five wives. The dwellings date from 1713 to 1811. No. 126 is a museum with period furnishings.

Fairmount Park on the Schuylkill River and Wissahickon Creek from Spring Garden St. to Northwestern Ave. More than 8,000 acres; includes many fine structures from the 18th to the 20th century. This is said to be the largest landscaped city park in the world.

A **Fairmount Park Trolley-Bus** takes visitors on an old-fashioned ride with 29 stops on the 90-minute scenic loop. The ride begins at the Tourist Center, open daily except Christmas, but passengers may board at any stop. The **Historic Houses of Fairmount Park** are owned by the City of Philadelphia and maintained by the Fairmount Park Commission, in cooperation with some other civic organizations. **Ohio House,** an exhibition building at the 1876 Centennial Exposition, is now the **Fairmount Park Information Center.** Free parking, daily 10 A.M. to 4 P.M. The trolley bus runs at 15-minute intervals from 9:30 to 4:45.

Among the historic tour houses open 10 to 5, 6 days weekly, with guides:

Lemon Hill was originally owned by Robert Morris, signer of the Declaration of Independence, who owned 350 acres on the banks of the Schuylkill and built his farm and greenhouses in July 1770. He was sent to debtors' prison in 1798. "The Hills," as the house was named then, was sold to Henry Pratt, who developed the gardens and lemon trees and built this house in 1800. The dwelling has been restored by the city, and furnished by the Colonial Dames of America, who maintain it. Closed Fridays.

Hatfield House, moved from another site, was a farmhouse in 1769; restored and furnished with authentic Federal Empire pieces, it is now the finest Greek Revival dwelling in the park. Closed Wednesdays.

Mount Pleasant, built in 1761–62 by a Scots sea captain, John Macpherson, is a model of Georgian architecture. When John Adams dined here he called it the "most elegant seat in Pennsylvania." (He didn't go so far as to include Massachusetts, where the Adams home, 135 Adams St., Quincy, is a national historic site.) Mt. Pleasant has had a fascinating history. Benedict Arnold bought it as a bride's gift for Peggy Shippen, but he was convicted of treason before the newlyweds could occupy it. Ironically Jonathan Williams, first superintendent of West Point, was a later owner. The Philadelphia Museum of Art maintains the house and furnished it in the style of the 1760s. (The Art Museum also decorated Hatfield.) Closed Wednesdays.

Woodford, which has a museum of colonial furniture, and *Strawberry Mansion,* once a dairy farm, are closed Mondays. *Cedar Grove* and *Sweetbriar,* also handsomely restored and furnished homes, are closed Tuesdays. *Solitude,* built by John Penn, the grandson of William Penn, in 1785; and *Letitia St. House,* which may have been built by William himself, and once stood near the riverfront, now a house museum; both are are closed Thursdays.

Old City Historic District includes parts of Washington Square East Development Area and Franklin Square East Development Area, a 75-acre urban district which was part of the original 1682 plan. There are many outstanding buildings in the district, with 18th- to 20th-century styles of architecture. William Strickland, James Windrim, Stephen Button, and John McArthur, Jr., are among the architects whose works are represented.

Society Hill Historic District, bounded on the N by Walnut St., on the S by Lombard St., on the E by pier line of the Delaware River, and by 8th St. on the W. There are some 575 structures from the 18th and 19th centuries in the district. Much of the area is being restored. The original portion of town laid out in 1682 by Thomas Holme, surveyor for William Penn, is within the district. NHL.

South Front St. Historic District (Southwark) is a continuous block of Flemish bond brick houses from the 18th century. District starts at 700 Front, takes in W side of Bainbridge to Kenilworth.

Because Philadelphia is so history-oriented, there is free and excellent literature available all over town. The city also has provided a Cultural Loop Bus—which was thought up by the clever minds at the *Philadelphia Convention and Visitors Bureau* and is operated by the *Southeastern Penn-*

sylvania Transportation Authority; it includes 19 discount rides to various attractions and links more than 24 historic and cultural sites from Independence Hall to Fairmount Park. A family of four, for example, could save $28 in admission fees. Tickets are good for the entire day; riders can get on and off as they please. *Black History Strolls* are on Sunday afternoons; phone (215) 923-4136 for details.

READING, Berks County. US 422, 222.

Old Dry Road Farm, near Blue Marsh, is an experiment of the sort that is becoming nationwide: a non-profit organization, formed by representatives from the Berks County Historical Society, is restoring a 260-acre historic farmstead near Blue Marsh Lake. Their aim is to represent the living history of an early Berks county rural home and lands. Students can participate in splitting logs, planning gardens, drying herbs, preserving foods, and carrying on other early-day chores. A group of log structures from the area that were in danger of being flooded will be relocated here. Among them are a homestead with barn, springhouse, smokehouse, and other outbuildings. Architects from the Pennsylvania Log House Society are supervising the reconstruction and restoration at the Farm. Others of the community who have volunteered to help are the Art Council, the Preservation Trust, Horizon Center, and individuals interested in preserving the past. For details inquire at the *Historical Society of Berks County,* 940 Centre Ave., Reading, 19601.

STROUDSBURG, Monroe County. US 209.

Quiet Valley Living Historical Farm, 3½ miles SW on US 209 Business Route, then 1½ miles S. An 18th-century log house with a kitchen added in 1892 and nine other original or reconstructed buildings are on display, with demonstrations of colonial farm skills. Guided tours.

WASHINGTON, Chester County. St. 18.

Meadowcroft Village, 19 miles NW via St. 18, 50, in Avella, has 30 structures from the 18th and 19th centuries which have been moved to this site and are furnished in period. There is a trapper's cabin as well as the general store, log dwellings, carriage barn, etc.

LeMoyne House, 49 E. Maiden St. in Washington, was built in 1812 and is now a museum.

David Bradford House, 175 S. Main, has been restored. It was built in 1788. Bradford was a leader of the "Whisky Rebellion," a revolt against a tax imposed by the new federal government.

YORK, York County. US 30.

This historic city was the first capital of the U.S. (from September 30, 1777 to June 27, 1778, when the British held Philadelphia). *Visitors and Tourist Bureau,* 13 E. Market St., has information and free parking during walking tours. The *Museum of the Historical Society of York County,* 250 E. Market, has an outdoor living-history area that is a village square. *Bonham House,* at 152 E. Market, is maintained by the Historical Society as a house museum, from the 1870s. *Billmeyer House,* on E. Market, Italianate, was built in 1860 for Charles Billmeyer, a leading industrialist. *Cooke's House (Thomas Paine House),* 438–440 Cordorus St., was built in 1761; according to local legend Paine stayed here when the Congress met at York late in 1777 to June 1778.

Gates House, and Golden Plough Tavern, 157–159 W. Market St., date from 1751 and 1741 (the tavern). General Horatio Gates stayed in the house after the victory at Saratoga. Museum.

DELAWARE

We embarked at six in the morning, and at twelve reached the Chesapeake and Delaware canal; we then quitted the steamboat and walked two or three hundred yards to the canal, where we got on board a pretty little decked boat, sheltered by a neat awning, and drawn by four horses. This canal cuts across the state of Delaware, and connects the Chesapeake and Delaware rivers; it has been a work of great expense, though the distance is not more than thirteen miles; for a part of this distance the cutting has been very deep, and the banks are in many parts thatched, to prevent their crumbling. At the point where the cutting is deepest, a light bridge is thrown across, which, from its great height, forms a striking object to the travellers passing below it. Every boat that passes this canal pays a toll of twenty dollars.
—*Domestic Manners of the Americans,* by Frances M. Trollope, London, 1836.

DOVER, Kent County. US 13, St. 8.

William Penn made plans for the village green, which was finally laid out in 1717. Here the Continental Regiment was mustered in 1776; a celebration followed the reading of the Declaration of Independence and George III's portrait was burned. In 1800 a sadder crowd heard John Vining deliver a eulogy on the death of George Washington.

Gracious old dwellings and the *Old State House* embellish the green. The latter was built in 1722 and rebuilt in 1787–92. It has been restored, with the courtroom and governor's offices on the first floor and the House and Senate chambers on the second.

Bureau of Travel Development, 45 the Green, has a map for the *Heritage Trail,* with 27 historical sites detailed. During *Old Dover Days* in May many of the structures are open. Write "Friends of Old Dover," Box 44, 19901. Also write *Chamber of Commerce,* Box 576, 19901, for information on tours and historical sites.

Delaware State Museum, Meeting House Square, Governor's Ave., is housed in four buildings, two of which are from the 18th and 19th centuries. Displays follow Delaware life from the early 17th century to the present. Open daily except Mondays and holidays.

John Dickinson Mansion, 5 miles SE of town and 3 miles E of US 13 on Kitts Hummock Rd., built by Samuel Dickinson, ca. 1740, was the boyhood home of John Dickinson, called the "Penman of the Revolution," as the author of the Articles of Confederation. Dickinson also lived here when he became chief executive of the state. Restored. NHL. House and outbuildings are open most days, but check locally, as they are open on Monday only if a holiday falls on that day.

McDowell-Collins Country Store House, 408 S. State St., is now a mercantile museum. In 1718 the site was privately owned, and it still varies little from the 1768 Plan of Dover.

Wesley McDowell bought the place in 1824. A Mr. Collins operated a store here in the late 19th century. Antique toys and mercantile goods on display. It is now headquarters of *Dover Heritage Trail, Inc.;* open weekdays.

Octagonal Schoolhouse, St. 9, is a restored 1836 school, furnished with early texts, relics, and desks arranged in two circles. The historical site is administered by the Delaware Historical Society. Open weekends; group tours by appointment.

Governor's House, King's Highway (ca. 1790), was an Underground Railway station in antebellum days, when it was known as "Woodburn." The house is Georgian, furnished with exceptionally fine antiques and is open Tuesday afternoons from 2 to 4:40 P.M.

LEWES, Sussex County. St. 18.

Zwaanendael Museum, Kings Highway and Savannah Rd. Modeled after the Town Hall of Hoorn, Holland, the museum is a memorial to the Dutch founders of Lewes, in 1631. Tours are available. Open daily except Monday and holidays.

Several restored structures are maintained by the Lewes Historical Society: *Cannonball House,* named during the War of 1812; the *Burton-Ingram House; Thompson Country Store,* where crafts and home-canned goods can be purchased; *Marine Museum,* Front and Bank Sts., has displays covering the history of the fishing and mercantile port. Inquire *Chamber of Commerce* for hours: (302) 645-8073.

NEW CASTLE, New Castle County. US 13.

The oldest town in the Delaware Valley was settled by the Dutch in 1651. The *Historic District* takes in the *Strand,* still a cobbled street along the river. A three-square-block area has houses from the 17th through 19th centuries. Many public buildings have associations with the great days of the colonists and the celebrities of that time. Take note that George Washington danced at a wedding at the *Amstel House* (1730) in case, as history hunters, you begin to think all he ever did was fight a war, be a President, or sleep overnight somewhere. The restored house has colonial furnishings and a display of dolls and clothing.

Peter Stuyvesant planned the town to be the seat of the New Netherlands government on the Delaware River. Some of the houses, which face each other rather than the street, are from 1679. On *New Castle Day* in May, several historic homes are open. Write *Mayor & Council of New Castle,* 19720, for a list of annual events and special festivals, also for a handsomely illustrated brochure with map and details on the many structures of interest, including an 1832 ticket office which served the New-Castle–Frenchtown Railroad, whose famous steam locomotive *Delaware* pulled coaches often filled with notables in antebellum days. The *Old Town Hall* (1823) had an arch connecting Delaware St. with *Market Place,* which was used as a market from the 1680s; in 1730 an ordinance forbade the sale of any food except fish, milk, and bread anywhere else in town but here on Wednesdays and Saturdays. *Old Court House,* Delaware St. between 2nd and 3rd, built about 1732, was later enlarged. It served as the capitol of the Assembly of the Three Lower Counties, then as state capitol until 1777; a museum, the mayor's office, and small shops are now in the building. NHL. *Stonum,* 9th and Washington Sts., begun in 1730s, finished in 1850, was the home of George Read, a signer of the Declaration of Independence, Senator, and Chief Justice of the Delaware Supreme Court. NHL.

ODESSA, New Castle County. St. 3.

Odessa Historic District, bounded

roughly by the Appoquinimink Creek, High, 4th, and Main Sts., takes in 23 buildings in a four-block area from the 18th and 19th centuries. Five 18th-century houses have been restored.

Corbit-Sharp House, Main and 2nd Sts. (1772–74), a fine Georgian structure with a Chinese lattice roof deck, was built by the gifted Robert May for William Corbit, a Quaker who operated a tannery. H. Rodney Sharp bought and restored the house, furnishing it with antiques, in the 1930s. He later gave it to the Winterthur Museum. Open daily except Mondays and major holidays. NHL.

Next door is the *Wilson-Warner House,* also administered by the Winterthur Museum, with the same hours. This two-story Georgian dwelling was built about 1789 as an addition to a 1740 house.

Among the many historic structures in town are the *John Janvier Stable,* built in 1791 by a master cabinetmaker; the *Brick Hotel* (1822); the *Davis Store* (1824); the *Cyrus Polk House,* Italianate from 1853. Write *Historic Odessa,* Rt. 13, zip 19730, for information and hours open.

SMYRNA, Kent County. US 13, St. 9.

Dutch Creek Village, off highway 13, N of town, has *The Lindens,* a 1765 miller's home; open daily; *Allee House,* on Dutch Neck Rd., on St. 9, E of town, at Bombay Hook, built by a Huguenot about 1753 with excellent workmanship inside and out. Open weekends. Groups by appointment.

WILMINGTON, New Castle County. I-95.

While experienced walkers could easily cover the entire state—it is 96 miles long and 35 miles from east to west at its widest point, 9 miles at its narrowest—the many historic houses of Wilmington are too scattered for normal strollers.

The *Henry Francis du Pont Winterthur Museum,* 6 miles NW of town, on St. 52, has more than 100 period rooms representing American home fashions from 1640 to 1840. The building was named by its first owner, James Antoine Bidermann, a Paris banker's son, who came to the United States in 1814 with letters of introduction from the Marquis de Lafayette, one of the most popular Frenchmen to the Americans of the early 19th century. Bidermann traveled beyond Delaware, but not for long and probably not farther than the Mississippi River. In 1816 he married the granddaughter of Pierre Samuel du Pont de Nemours, who had come to America from France in 1799. Bidermann bought land from his father-in-law and built Winterthur, named for a Swiss city where his ancestors had lived. The house of 1839 was brick and stucco, with a flat roof. Bidermann's son inherited the house and sold the estate of 445 acres to his uncle, Henry du Pont, who bought adjoining farms to increase the holdings. Henry's son, Henry A., added considerably to the house in 1876 and again in 1889 and improved the grounds. His son, Henry Francis du Pont, on inheriting the mansion, enlarged it further and began to install rooms from old houses along the eastern seaboard. He also began to collect woodwork, furnishings, and fittings. After some two decades of gathering the items for each room, du Pont gave the house and its collection to the Winterthur Museum.

The Main Museum is open by appointment for half-day tours. The South Wing is open without appointment; check locally for times.

Hagley Museum, off St. 52, 141, is the site of the original Du Pont Powder Mills on the Brandywine. By the Revolution the mills were known throughout the colonies. In 1817 the first U.S. papermaking machine was installed here. The Museum preserves and interprets the industrial site. On the 185 acres are millraces, granite powder mills, a wooden water wheel, and many exhibits. Open-air jitneys carry visitors along the mill-races on a 3-mile trip. *Eleutherian Mills,* the 1803 residence of E. I. du Pont, and the adjacent *First Office* are also open to the public, daily except Mondays and major holidays. NHL. Write Hagley Museum, Greenville, Wilmington: (302) 658-2401.

Brandywine Village Historic District, bounded roughly by Tatnall, 22nd, and Mabel Sts., Vandever Ave., and Brandywine Creek, was an agricultural and milling center after Captain Jacob Vandever received the first land patent in 1669. Market St. was part of the old toll road between Philadelphia and Wilmington and was lined with houses built of local granite. Six still remain. *Old Town Hall,* 512 Market, has had many distinguished visitors including the peripatetic Lafayette in 1824. Restored by the Historical Society of Delaware. Open daily except Mondays and holidays. A nearby area, *Willingtown Square* and *Market Street Mall,* has been developed recently. The Victorian-style *Opera House* still stands on the mall and is in use. It opened in 1873. Four 18th-century homes have been moved to Willingtown Square and fully restored.

Fort Christina (1638) commemorates the site of the first permanent European settlement in Delaware by the Swedes. The historic park is at the foot of 7th St. with a typical early log cabin on display. Open daily except Mondays and holidays.

MARYLAND

The city [Baltimore] is about two miles in extent from east to west, and one and a half from north to south, and most of the streets are straight and at right angles. The favorite promenade is in Baltimore street, the principal avenue, which is two miles long; and the west part is the favorite residence of the wealthier citizens. The principal public buildings are the city-hall in Holliday street, the courthouse at the corner of Washington and Monument streets, the state penitentiary, above one hundred churches, eleven banks, seven markets, eight insurance offices, two theatres, the circus, the museum, and the savings bank. . . .

The first settler was a man named Gorsuch. . . . Among those who settled soon after him in this vicinity was Charles Carroll, whose estate, on the high ground behind Baltimore, still bears his name. . . . The original purchase of Carroll included some of the most eligible parts of the present city of Baltimore, which, at an early day, were sold by Charles and Daniel Carroll, at prices now surprisingly low, viz., sixty acres at forty shillings an acre, payment being made in tobacco at one penny per pound.

—Sears' Pictorial Description of the United States, by Robert Sears,
New York, 1855

ANNAPOLIS, Anne Arundel County. I-301, 50.

Colonial Annapolis Historic District takes in the city as surveyed in 1695, with about 120 buildings from the 18th century. NHL. Walking tours conducted by *Historic Annapolis, Inc.,* leave the Old Treasury Building, State Circle, and are held daily from mid-June to Labor Day, other times by appointment. Special tours can be arranged here—(301) 267-8149—and a free self-guiding tour is available, *A Walk in Old Annapolis,* four pages with map. The full tour takes about two hours and covers more than 3 miles.

Maryland State House, on State Circle, was built in 1772–79, with additions later, and is the oldest state capitol still in use. It was the seat of the Continental Congress, and here George Washington resigned his commission. Guide service. NHL.

Among the many outstanding historical homes and restorations: *Chase-Lloyd House,* 22 Maryland Ave., begun in 1769 for Samuel Chase, a signer of the Declaration, completed in 1774 by Edward Lloyd IV, a planter; the three-story Georgian mansion has many distinctions. No other three-story house was built in town before the Revolutionary War. Chase was a 28-year-old lawyer but, as the son of a minister, had no inherited wealth, and when he ran out of money he sold the unfinished house to Lloyd, who was one of the richest tobacco planters in the colonies and owned Wye House, in Talbot County. While supervising the completion of this building, Lloyd often came from his plantation in a large barge, rowed by liveried slaves and with all flags flying. Lloyd was defeated when he ran for governor, but served in the Continental Congress. One of his six daughters married Francis Scott Key here in 1802. In 1897 the house was willed to the Protestant Episcopal Church as a home for destitute women. The upper floors are still used for this purpose; the first floor is open to the public. NHL.

Hammond-Harwood House, Maryland Ave. and King George St., was built about 1774; William Buckland, architect, was also a gifted joiner and woodcarver, and the house is considered his masterpiece. Matthias Hammond, the first owner, was a great patriot; his law office was here. NHL.

Brice House, 42 East St., probably was designed by William Buckland. Built in 1766–73, restored in the 1950s with great care, the house is of particular interest to architectural students. No major alterations were made. The building was constructed of oversize brick on a fieldstone foundation, with 35 rooms, each with distinguishing touches, and 90-foot chimneys which dominate a steep-pitched roof. John Brice, a merchant and planter, died in the year construction was begun; the house was finished by his son James. NHL.

Peggy Stewart House, 207 Hanover St. (1761–64), is also brick. More pre-Revolutionary brick buildings are preserved in Annapolis than in any other town in the U.S. Anthony Stewart was a merchant forced by angry patriots to burn his ship, the *Peggy Stewart,* because he had paid the tea tax on its cargo. From 1783 for four years this was the home of Thomas Stone, who served in the Continental Congress and signed the Declaration, was elected to the Constitutional Congress but declined because of illness and died that year, 1787.

Paca House (Carvel Hall Hotel), 192 Prince George St. (1763–65), was the home of William Paca, lawyer, governor, and a signer of the Declaration. The mansion and gardens have been beautifully restored. St. Clair Wright, of Historic Annapolis, in *Antiques* magazine for January 1977, tells the encouraging story of how the gardens were rescued. The Paca garden, covering some 2 acres originally, was described as the most elegant in town by an early traveler, but in the 19th century was covered by landfill and later a hotel, parking lot, and even a bus station. Archaeologists directed by D. Bruce Powell of the National Park Service dug through tons of debris and earth and found remains of the original garden. Enough of the old wall was uncovered so that the contours of the garden could be restored. A number of agencies and experts were involved in the project and as Wright sums up: "The restoration of the garden has been an exhilarating experience for those concerned. The extraordinary discovery of a long-buried eighteenth-century garden has added an unexpected dimension to preservation in Annapolis. In this prosaic era when the value of gardens as solitary places for quiet enjoyment is often forgotten the city has regained a resource of exceptional value." NHL.

Whitehall, off St. Margaret's Rd., was built about 1765 for bachelor Governor Horatio Sharpe. The handsome Georgian mansion was the first colonial dwelling with temple-type portico and sits majestically on a beautifully landscaped lawn. NHL.

Shiplap House, 18 Pinkney St., was condemned to demolition in 1957, but a year later was bought by Historic Annapolis; now restored, with the aid of architectural findings in the 1723 will of Edward Smith, innkeeper and sawyer, which described the building and its furnishings, the house is headquarters for the association.

Also among the many restorations of major interest are *Artisan's House,* 43 Pinkney, from the 1770s; *Franklin Law Office,* 17 State Circle, about 1850; *Reynold's Tavern,* 1747, built on land leased by St. Anne's Church to William Reynolds, who made hats as well as served as tavernkeeper and named the inn "The Hat in Hand." (The building has been acquired recently by the National Trust for Historic Preservation and probably will be open to the public as a museum.)

A Visitor Information Booth at City Dock has maps and information for self-guiding tours. October is Heritage Month, when many special events are held.

BALTIMORE, Independent City. I-83.

Baltimore has a number of historic districts: *Dickeyville,* Forest Park Ave., in the Gwynn's Falls area, was the first community restoration project and is a rare example of a prosperous mill town from the 19th century which has remained an entity. The *Druid Hill Park District* covers 746 acres, laid out in 1860 by Howard Daniels; *Maryland House* was built in 1876 for the Centennial Fair in Philadelphia. *Federal Hill,* an area bounded by Covington, Hughes, Charles, and Hamburg Sts., has several hundred early structures which are mostly row houses, brick with marble trim. *Fells Point,* at the harbor, and bounded by Aliceanna, Wolfe, and Dallas Sts., was a shop and residential area for seamen, sailmakers, and other merchants in the 18th and 19th centuries. William Fell, a Quaker, had settled here sometime before 1763. The *U.S.S. Frigate Constellation* was built here in 1797 as were many ships used in the War of 1812. The *Constellation* is now a National Navy Historical Shrine and has been restored. Pier 1, Pratt St. NHL.

The *Baltimore Area Convention & Visitors Council,* 102–104 St. Paul St., 21202—(301) 727-5688—has a Visitors Center with maps and information on historic sites and events. Information is also available from the *Chamber of Commerce of Metropolitan Baltimore,* 22 Light St., 21202; *Maryland House and Garden Pilgrimage* takes in more than 100 homes and gardens; for information write 600 W. Chesapeake Ave., 21204. A tour book is available for $1; the pilgrimage takes place the first two weeks in May, and covers the entire state.

CHESTERTOWN, Kent County. St. 213, 20. US 301.

The historic district takes in some 50 Georgian and Federal dwellings of the 18th century. A number of Georgian brick town houses were built after 1750. The port developed into a major tobacco and wheat shipping center on the eastern shore until much of the trade went to Baltimore in the 1800s. The *Town Square* still has a cast-iron fountain, old lamps, and old-style storefronts. A walking tour of this area along the Chester River will lead you past handsome brick and frame mansions, many with Victorian trellises or Italianate cupolas. The wealthiest merchants lived on Water St. *Washington College,* the only college associated with George Washington himself, was chartered in 1782. The *Hynson-Ringgold House,* at Front and Cannon Sts., has a rear section dating from 1735; the front was built in 1771, designed by William Buckland. Now the home of the college president.

The *Customs House,* Front and High Sts., built in the 1730s, was the hub of trade with the British West Indies. Near here in May 1774, angry patriots went on board the brigantine *William Geddes* and threw tea into the river.

Widehall, 101 Water St. (1769), is a brick mansion which has been restored, after early changes which imposed Victorian trim and blocked a view of the river. Thomas Smythe, owner, was a merchant and shipbuilder; he was said to be the richest man in Kent County. He took an active interest in politics and became the first head of Maryland's revolutionary provisional government. In 1782 he gave much of his money and his efforts to Washington College, serving as its first treasurer.

Denton House, 107 Water St., dates from the 1780s. Georgian brick. Fine old houses at 103, 109, 110, 115, and 201 on Water St. were also homes of 18th-century merchants.

Nicholson-Deringer House, 111 Maple, was built in 1777 by Captain John Nicholson, a Continental navy officer.

Moore-Geddes House, 101 Church Alley, was once the home of William Geddes, customs collector involved in the Chesterton Tea Party. Now headquarters of the *Kent County Historical Society,* which has information on sites and markers. There are many preserved and restored structures in the area; some are best reached by car, others by walking. One of the most unusual houses is at 532 High St., called the *"Rock of Ages" House,* built of stone which is said to have been brought across the Atlantic as ship's ballast by Captain Palmer, who erected the dwelling. Candlelight tours are held irregularly; inquire locally.

FREDERICK, Frederick County. US 40, 15.

Chamber of Commerce of Frederick County, which has the Charter Number 1 of the Chamber of Commerce U.S., has published a Star Spangled Trail walking tour of historic Frederick. The stars are numbered, and there are 23 in all. Park in the municipal lot on S. Court St. (tour cannot be made by auto because of many one-way streets). On leaving lot, turn left, cross W. Patrick to Star Stop No. 1, *All Saints Parish House* (1813), designed by Henry McCleery, continue N to W. Church St. and *Court House Square,* which is surrounded by 18th- and 19th-century dwellings and law offices and was where the first official repudiation of the Stamp Act took place in November 1765.

Turning left on W. Church, you will pass *All Saints Episcopal,* designed by Richard Upjohn, and used as a hospital after the Battle of Antietam in the Civil War.

Star 7 marks *Trinity Chapel (Evangelical Reformed),* begun in 1763 by German settlers. In the second church on the opposite side of the street General Stonewall Jackson is said to have napped during a sermon in 1862.

One-half block N on Market St. at *Frederick City Hall,* on July 9, 1864, General Jubal A. Early of the Confederacy demanded and got $200,000 on a threat of burning the town. Three days before, Early got $20,000 from Hagerstown.

Star 12 marks the *Historical Society Home,* 24 E. Church, built about 1830, once the home of John Loats, later the Loats Orphanage, now houses the historical society and museum. Star 13, looking down Middle Alley, is the house at *101 W. Patrick,* said to be built by John Thomas Schley, and thought to be the oldest house in town, but not yet restored. Star 14, rear of Visitation Academy, marks a row of early homes recently restored for use as classrooms.

In *St. John's Roman Catholic Church Cemetery* is the grave of Roger Brooke Taney (on Third St., Star 17); *Taney's Home* and the *Francis Scott Key Museum* (Star 19) are at 123 Bentz St. The house, built in 1799, was the residence of Taney from 1801 to 1823. Chief Justice Taney was appointed to the high court by President Andrew Jackson; he administered the oath of office to

Van Buren, Harrison, Polk, Taylor, Pierce, Buchanan, and Abraham Lincoln, but is remembered now for his decision in the Dred Scott case. He argued that Negroes could not bring suit in a federal court. Taney's wife, Anne, was a sister of Francis Scott Key, who often visited this house.

Star 20 marks the famous *Barbara Fritchie House,* 154 W. Patrick, a restoration of the home of Barbara and John Casper Fritchie, a glovemaker. Barbara may actually have waved a flag at Jackson's troops but not quite the way John Greenleaf Whittier put it. Jackson went down Mill and Bentz streets and rejoined his men some distance from this house. The museum is worth visiting, in any case.

Star 23 marks the grave of Francis Scott Key in *Mt. Olivet Cemetery,* Market St. Here the flag flies day and night. Barbara Fritchie and more than 400 Confederates, killed in the Battles of Antietam and Monocacy, are also buried here.

Governor Thomas Johnson House, next to Thomas Johnson High School, Market St., at the opposite end of town from the cemetery, is to become a tourist and information center.

DISTRICT OF COLUMBIA

Here is Washington.... Take the worst parts of the ... straggling outskirts of Paris, where the houses are smallest, preserving all their oddities, but especially the small shops and dwellings.... Burn the whole down; build it up again in wood and plaster; widen it a little; throw in part of St. John's Wood; put green blinds outside all the private houses, with a red curtain and a white one in every window; plough up all the roads; plant a great deal of coarse turf in every place where it ought *not* to be; erect three handsome buildings in stone and marble, anywhere, but the more entirely out of everybody's way the better; call one the Post Office, one the Patent Office, and one the Treasury; make it scorching hot in the morning, and freezing cold in the afternoon, with an occasional tornado of wind and dust, leave a brick-field without the bricks, in all central places where a street may naturally be expected; and that's Washington.

—*American Notes,* by Charles Dickens, London, 1850

The prices of labor and material are such as to enable one to buy the ground and put up a very handsome three-story house, having all the modern improvements, for $5,000. If one feels like it, and feels his purse can stand it, he can go to the Riggs House, for instance, deposit one dollar and fifty cents, and eat to his heart's content from a bill of fare equal to any hotel in any city in the country.

—Editorial in the Washington *Post*, December 24, 1878

National Visitor Center, 50 Massachusetts Ave., N.E., was inaugurated on our Bicentennial birthday, July 4, 1976, and already has hosted far more than a million visitors. The Center, under the jurisdiction of the National Park Service, provides free touring and travel assistance to all, by phone (202) 523-5319, or write to the above (zip: 20002). The Center hands out a warm welcome to the nation's capital along with information; there is an 80-screen slide show, motion pictures, a bookstore, gift shop, displays, restaurant, and special facilities including a post office, Traveler's Aid, USO information, multilingual assistance, and aid for the handicapped. Exhibits in the Gallery change frequently, showing historical scenes.

In the Discover America Hall of States are nine different regional counters to provide information on specific areas in the states, territories, and possessions. The Center is located in the former Union Station and is a remarkable adaptation of a historic structure to present needs. The building was designed by Daniel H. Burnham, completed in 1907. NHL.

Washington Area Convention and Visitors Association, 1129-20th St., N.W.—(202) 857-5500—has much information on the many historical sites of the city and surroundings. Their attitude is a friendly one: "You and every other American own a big hunk of Washington. So, you can expect free admission to your federal properties. This is a city where the best things are free, where a dime can buy you a storybook vacation and history book education rolled into one. The dime? That's to pay for your elevator ride to the top of the Washington Monument. But the 898 steps make the dime ride the best bargain in town. Your children ride free." Brochures with easy-to-read maps describe and locate everything from the African Art museum to the Zoological Park.

For recorded schedules of events dial **National Archives,** 523-3000; **Smithsonian Institution Museums,** 737-8811; **Convention & Visitors Bureau,** 737-8866. Persons planning to visit the city are urged to phone ahead to verify hours of operation, as they are subject to change without notice. Many facilities are available to handicapped persons; others are available by advance arrangement.

One of the many booklets available from the association is a "Group Tour Planner," which lists what's new, popular group attractions, accommodations, rates, special events for groups, sightseeing companies, travel agencies, etc.

Among historic houses open to the public:

Decatur House, 748 Jackson Place, N.W. (1818–19), Benjamin H. Latrobe, architect for the three-story brick Federal home built for Stephen Decatur, naval hero. The house was later occupied by Henry Clay and Martin Van Buren. NHL.

Frederick Douglass Memorial Home, 1411 W St., S.E., built about 1855, was the home of the man who escaped from slavery to become a famous author, editor, and diplomat. Douglass lived here from 1877 to 1899.

The Octagon, 1799 New York Ave., N.W. (1798–1800), William Thornton, architect. The three-story brick town house was built for Colonel John Tayloe, who lived in Mount Airy, Virginia; President Madison stayed here after the White House was burned by the British in 1814. The Treaty of Ghent was ratified here. Since 1898 the American Institute of Architects has had headquarters here. Museum. NHL. Make advance arrangements for touring.

Old Stone House, 3051 M St., N.W. (1765), is thought to be the oldest pre–Revolutionary War building in the district. Shown by advance arrangement.

Petersen House, 516 10th St., N.W., a three-story brick town house owned by William Petersen, where Lincoln was taken after being shot at Ford's Theatre, and where he died in April 1865, is part of the **Ford's Theatre National Historic Site.** Open daily. Ford's Theatre was restored in the 1960s.

White House, 1600 Pennsylvania Ave., N.W., is open Tuesday through Saturday, 10 A.M. to noon. June through August, to 2 P.M. Closed some holidays. Facilities for the handicapped are available.

Georgetown was a tobacco port in the early part of the 18th century, settled by Scottish merchant importers. The area soon grew prosperous; many wealthy citizens built handsome brick homes. With the coming of steam navigation and railroads, other towns grew more important commercially. In 1871 the town lost its charter and was joined with Washington County as part of the District of Columbia. In the 1930s restoration began as Washingtonians sought the old houses, bringing them back to fine condition. Fine restau-

John Wilkes Booth leaps to the stage of Ford's Theatre, Washington, D.C., after shooting President Lincoln. The playhouse has been restored. (Courtesy Ford's Theatre)

rants and shops were developed, and the town named in honor of King George II was again a desirable place to live. *Georgetown Historic District* comprises a variety of structures in the town laid out in 1751 which became both a social and diplomatic center during the early 19th century. Now a National Historic Landmark. A walking tour, "Rambling Thru Georgetown," is one of a series available for 50¢ each or $1.50 for four (Annapolis, Capitol, Alexandria), 3039 Albemarle St., Washington,

20008, or 710 Warren Drive, Annapolis, Md., 21403.

Comfortable shoes are strongly urged for walking on the bricks and cobblestones of Georgetown. Among historic sites:

The *Old Stone House,* 3051 M St., N.W., the oldest existing house in Georgetown, built about 1765, for Christopher Layman, a cabinetmaker who used the ground floor for his business. After his death, Cassandra Chew, a successful businesswoman, acquired the house. Open daily except holidays, with guides in colonial dress. Free, but group and school tours should make an appointment.

Thomas Sim Lee Corner, 30th and M Sts., N.W., 1790s home of Lee, who was twice elected governor of Maryland and was a friend and adviser of George Washington. The building was saved in 1951 by Georgetown residents who restored it and rented out the space.

Duvall Foundry, 1050 30th St., N.W. (1856), was an important source of the Union strength in the Civil War. Located near the Chesapeake and Ohio Canal, the foundry also had access to rail and land transportation, and here William Duvall forged the tools and implements much needed. After the war blast furnaces elsewhere took most of the business and the building became a veterinary hospital, stable, stonecutter's shop, and studios for artists. In 1976 the foundry was renovated, after careful research, and now serves as a restaurant and part of a shopping and office complex.

First Mayor's House, 3118 M St., N.W. (1758); Robert Peter from Scotland was a rich tobacco merchant and landowner and became first mayor. His son, Thomas Peter, married a granddaughter of Martha Washington.

Grace Episcopal Church, 1041 Wisconsin Ave., N.W., began in 1855 when a small frame building was built on "Brickyard Hill" below the Canal. The present church of stone was built in 1867 for $25,000. It was a mission church for seamen from the sailing ships which docked in the Potomac and for bargemen on the Canal. In later years its membership dwindled to two elderly parishioners. In the 1970s the parish subsidized ministry to the street kids, who called the church "Amazing Grace" and filled it with life again.

The **Old Dodge Warehouse,** 1000 Wisconsin Ave., N.W., from about 1800, has been restored and is considered one of the outstanding buildings on the waterfront. Ebenazer Dodge and his younger brother Francis were wealthy shipping merchants in trade with the West Indies. After Francis died in 1851, his two sons carried on for a few years but went bankrupt in 1857.

Bank of Columbia, 3212 M St., N.W. (1796), had George Washington as stockholder and director. It became a firehouse in 1883, and later served other functions. It is to be restored as a firehouse with horses and a fire dog.

Dumbarton Oaks, 3101 R St., N.W. The central section was built in 1801 by William H. Dorsey, first judge of the Orphans Court. Owners since then have included John C. Calhoun, who lived here while he was Vice-President, cabinet member, and Senator. The house was remodeled a number of times. In 1920 the Honorable and Mrs. Robert Woods Bliss acquired the house and land, restored it, and gave it the present name. The gardens are outstanding. In 1940 Dumbarton Oaks was donated to Harvard University. A museum was added in 1963. The house is open daily except Mondays and holidays, 2 to 5 P.M.

Dumbarton House, 2715 Q St., N.W., not be confused with Dumbarton Oaks, is a Georgian mansion built in the late 18th century by George Beall, son of Ninian Beall, who owned Rock of Dumbarton, one of the original tracts surveyed in 1752 as part of Georgetown. The mansion, moved to this site from the end of Q St., has been restored and furnished in period by the National Society of Colonial Dames of America, who have headquarters here. Open daily from 9 A.M. to noon, except Sundays and holidays. Closed July and August.

Southeast States

Virginia
North Carolina
South Carolina
Georgia
Florida

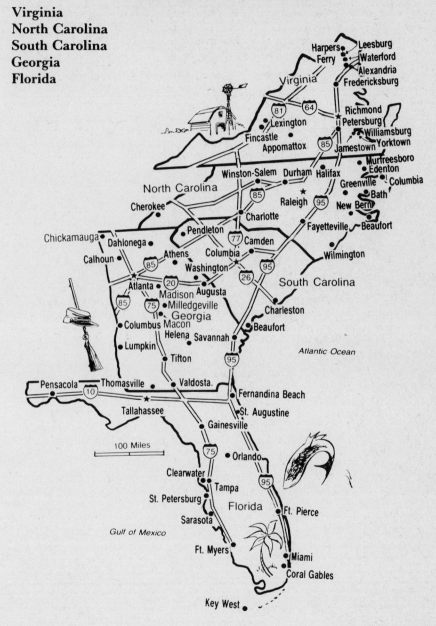

Harpers Ferry
Leesburg
Waterford
Alexandria
Fredericksburg
Virginia
81
64
Richmond
Lexington
Petersburg
Fincastle
85
Williamsburg
Appomattox
Jamestown
Yorktown
Murfreesboro
Winston-Salem
Durham
Halifax
Edenton
North Carolina
Greenville
Columbia
Cherokee
85
Raleigh
95
Bath
New Bern
Charlotte
Chickamauga
Pendleton
Fayetteville
Beaufort
Dahlonega
77
Camden
Wilmington
Calhoun
Athens
Columbia
85
Washington
95
Atlanta
20
26
South Carolina
85
Madison
Augusta
75
Milledgeville
Georgia
Columbus
Macon
Charleston
Helena
Savannah
Beaufort
Lumpkin
Tifton
Atlantic Ocean
95
Pensacola
Thomasville
Valdosta
10
Fernandina Beach
Tallahassee
St. Augustine
Gainesville
100 Miles
75
Orlando
Clearwater
Tampa
95
St. Petersburg
Florida
Sarasota
Ft. Pierce
Gulf of Mexico
Ft. Myers
Miami
Coral Gables
Key West

VIRGINIA

Situated on the James river, at the head of navigation, in Henrico county, 120 miles from the open sea and about 90 miles from Hampton Roads, is the county seat, and also the capital of the State of Virginia. . . . The city is remarkably healthy and exempt from malarial and climatic diseases. . . .

Being built upon several hills, nature provides ample drainage. Copious rains wash the streets as clean as if they had been swept and scrubbed by the hand of man. Nevertheless, sewers are constructed in the principal streets, after the latest and most approved plans.

The origin of the city is succinctly given in the following few lines from the "Westover Manuscripts," written by Col. William Byrd of Westover, in 1733, by whom it was founded:

"Sept. 19, 1733.—When we got home we laid the foundation of two large cities, one at Shacco's, to be called Richmond, and the other at the falls of Appomattox river, to be named Petersburg. These Maj. Mayo offered to lay out into lots without fee or reward. The truth of it is, these two places being the uppermost landing of James and Appomattox rivers, are naturally intended for marts where the traffic of the outer inhabitants must centre. . . ."
—*Richmond, Va. A Guide,* by Daniel Murphy, Richmond, 1881

In the early settlement of Virginia, when the adventurers were principally unmarried men, it was deemed necessary to export such women as could be prevailed upon to quit England, as wives to the planters. A letter accompanying a shipment of these matrimonial exiles, dated London, August 12, 1621 . . . is as follows:

"We send you a ship, one widow, and eleven maids, for wives for the people of Virginia; there hath been especial care had in the choice of them. . . .

"In case they cannot be presently married, we desire that they may be put with several householders that have wives till they can be provided with husbands. There are nearly fifty more that are shortly to come, and are sent by our Honorable Lord and Treasurer, the Earl of Southampton, and certain worthy gentlemen, who, taking into their consideration that the plantation can never flourish till families are planted, and the respect of wives and children for their people on the soil, therefore having given this fair beginning; for the reimbursing of whose charges, it is ordered that every man that marries them, give one hundred and twenty pounds of the best tobacco for each."
—*The Visitor, and Lady's Parlor Magazine,* New York, 1840

ALEXANDRIA, Independent City. I-495, exit 1-N to Rt. 1 N.

Alexandria Historic District is a large concentration of late-18th- and early-19th-century structures in a town which was formally authorized in 1748, with George Washington as one of the original surveyors. This was the principal upstate seaport and trading area until the Civil War. During the war the town was heavily fortified, partially because of its proximity to the capital, and was spared invasion. Many fine old structures, therefore, remain. NHL.

Ramsay House Visitor Center, 221 King St.—(703) 549-0205—has a beautifully illustrated booklet with map for self-guiding tours, and excellent color photographs of ten sites. There is an annual *Tour of Homes in Old Alexandria,* 1210 Burtonwood Court, Alexandria, 22307—(703) 768-4499—which benefits the Alexandria Hospital. Tourists are requested not to wear heels that could damage old floors and rugs. Tickets available at any of the homes on the tour, some of which are open at other times of year, also at the Ramsay House tourist center, or St. Paul's Episcopal Church, 228 South Pitt.

The take-anytime tour begins at the **Ramsay House,** built in 1724 as the home of the city's first postmaster, William Ramsay. Free parking passes available to visitors from outside the city. A 13-minute color film is shown. Open 10 A.M. to 5 daily.

Stabler-Leadbetter Apothecary Shop, 107 S. Fairfax, has early pharmacy items, hand-blown glass containers, and original furnishings. In a brochure published during the Civil War Centennial, this is said to be the place where Robert E. Lee received orders delivered by Jeb Stuart to command the group of marines sent to Harpers Ferry to stop the John Brown raid. And it was here that—according to legend—he learned Virginia had seceded. It was stated that he found out by reading the Alexandria *Gazette,* founded in 1784, the oldest daily newspaper in the country. Why Lee used to hang out at the drugstore is never added to the stories, but Mrs. Lee was an invalid, and so was their daughter, Mildred, which could have been an explanation. However, like a lot of good

stories it probably didn't happen. According to Lee's finest biographers, and he has had many, he was working in his study at Arlington when Jeb Stuart came with the orders. And no one in Lee's position would have to hear about secession from a newspaper. The shop is still worth a visit, just for the collection of medical ware. And Lee *would* have been in and out on many occasions.

Carlyle House, 122 N. Fairfax, is considered Alexandria's "grandest" home. It was built in 1752 by John Carlyle, one of the original incorporators of the town.

Gadsby's Tavern, 134 N. Royal St., consists of two buildings from 1752 and 1792. The earlier one was a Coffee House, two-story brick. The 1792 City Hotel was brick, three and a half stories, Georgian. The original tavern was enlarged by John Wise in 1792 and named when John Gadsby leased both buildings under single management in 1794. Many patriots met here in perilous times; this was headquarters for George Washington during the French and Indian War, a meeting place of the 1785 conference which agreed to send an invitation to all the colonies to attend a commercial convention in Annapolis in 1786, a convention which instituted plans for the Constitutional Convention of 1787.

The restoration of this most historic site has been meticulously researched and executed. Colonial meals again are served in the same dining room where George Washington had a meal in 1799. Gadsby's had fallen on hard times in the 19th century when it was a hotel, and was used by Civil War troops who seldom cared what their heels or weapons did to floors, furniture, or walls. It became a rooming house, a brothel, a saloon, tenements, and a thrift shop. The Metropolitan Museum of Art bought the ballroom, some of the furnishings, including the original front door, and mantels from the first floor. The door is back and so is the taproom mantel; the ballroom here is a duplicate. The original is in the American Wing at the Metropolitan. The building deteriorated further and was nearly condemned but survived until saved by the resurgence of interest in matters colonial and restorations, both private and public. Now resplendent with paint and polish and fine furnishings, the tavern again is in business. Curator William Adam, an Alexandrian, found an 1802 inventory drawn up by Gadsby and preserved in the Fairfax County Courthouse, which he used in recreating the interiors as authentically as possible. NHL.

Gentry Row and Captain's Row, 200 block of Prince St., are houses dating from the 18th and early 19th centuries. Many were the homes of sea captains.

Atheneum, 201 Prince St., began as a banking house in the mid-19th century. It is now the gallery of the Northern Virginia Fine Arts Association.

Old Presbyterian Meeting House, 321 S. Fairfax, was built in 1774 and served as a gathering place for patriots.

Friendship Fire Company, 107 S. Alfred St., was organized in August 1774 as a volunteer corps. Museum.

Christ Church, Cameron and N. Washington, dates from the 1760s or early 1770s. George Washington's pew is preserved. Robert E. Lee was confirmed here. NHL.

Lee's Boyhood Home, 607 Oronoco St., was the last home of Henry, known as Light-Horse Harry, Lee, father of Robert E. Lee. Henry Lee was governor of Virginia, a Congressman, and military officer in the Virginia Cavalry. He was a major in charge of Lee's Legion, which surprised the British at Paulus Hook in 1779, and for this he was awarded the gold medal by the Continental Congress. He continued to serve his country in various offices until 1801. His for-

tunes changed in the early 19th century and he was twice imprisoned for debt. Later he spent years in the West Indies hoping to regain his health. He died in 1818. His widow, Ann Carter Lee, had not been able to help her impoverished husband because her father had put her inheritance in trust. The family first lived at 611 Cameron St., but this house is not open to the public. They remained at the Oronoco St. house during Robert's boyhood years, until he went to West Point in June 1825. In 1824 when Lafayette came back to tour America he had not forgotten Henry Lee, the brilliant cavalryman, and paid a call on Mrs. Lee here on the morning of October 14, 1824. About the same time, a Quaker, James Hallowell, newly married, came to open a boys' school in the house adjoining the Lees. Robert entered the school in February 1825 and remained in attendance until he left for West Point. The charges were $10 a quarter.

Fendall-Lee House, 429 N. Washington, built about 1785 by Philip Fendall, was the home of several Lees. "Light-Horse Harry" Lee wrote the farewell address from the citizens of Alexandria to George Washington when the latter left Mount Vernon to become President. Daily guided tours. (The Lees and the Carters—his mother's family—were leading citizens in peace and war and were scattered all over the Old Dominion.) On the National Register:

The Lyceum, 201 S. Washington, built about 1837, Greek Revival, has been restored. The society for scholarly activities was founded by Benjamin Hallowell.

Bank of Alexandria, 133 N. Fairfax, 1807, served the state's first chartered bank. Brick, with Federal elements.

In the vicinity and open to the public:

Arlington House, in Arlington National Military Cemetery, 5 miles N

Mount Vernon. (Drawing by staff member Gloria Matthews. Courtesy Office of Comprehensive Planning, Fairfax County, Virginia)

via George Washington Memorial Parkway, was built between 1802 and 1817 by George Washington Parke Custis, who was Martha Washington's grandson. It became the home of Robert E. Lee when he married Mary Ann Randolph Custis in her family home in 1831. She was the daughter of G. W. P. Custis.

Mount Vernon is 9 miles S via George Washington Memorial Parkway, and few tourists need to be told whose house this was. Washington lived here from 1754 until his death in 1799.

Woodlawn Plantation was given by George Washington to Nellie Custis, Martha's granddaughter, and her husband, Major Lawrence Lewis, George's nephew. Furnished in colonial period, gardens restored; 3 miles W of Mount Vernon.

Gunston Hall, built in the second half of the 18th century, was the home of George Mason, who wrote the Fairfax Resolves, which led in time to the Bill of Rights. Luxurious furnishings and gardens with boxwood more than two centuries old. 19 miles S on George Washington Parkway and US 1.

Pohick Church, built between 1769 and 1773, was under the direction of a committee which included George Washington and George Mason.

Pews were removed during the Civil War when the church was used as a stable. Now restored.

Sully Plantation, 1794, the home of Richard Bland Lee, younger brother of Henry Lee, is handsomely furnished, and the plantation grounds also have a schoolhouse, warehouse, and wine cellar. On St. 28, Sully Rd., 5 miles S of Dulles Airport, or ½ mile N of US 50 on St. 28. Open daily except Sunday.

APPOMATTOX, Appomattox County. US 460, St. 24.

Appomattox Court House National Historic Park, 3 miles NE of town on St. 24. The 970-acre park includes reconstructions of buildings which were here when Robert E. Lee surrendered his Confederate troops to Ulysses S. Grant, Union commander, on April 9, 1865.

A *Visitor Center* with an orientation audiovisual program and literature giving the history of the war's end is in the reconstructed *Court House. McLean House,* reconstructed on the original site, has some of its original furnishings. There are other period buildings and shops.

A controversy still exists about the circumstance that some of the officers present took away furniture as souvenirs of the surrender. Some items have been returned; some are at the

Gunston Hall. (Drawing by staff member Gloria Matthews. Courtesy Office of Comprehensive Planning, Fairfax County, Virginia)

Smithsonian and the Chicago Historical Society. Others, real and fake,
are in private collections. A staunch
supporter of the Lost Cause in the
present century was the late Henry
Bass of Oklahoma, who served on the
Civil War Centennial Commission
for his state, and on the Chisholm
Trail memorial committee. Bass was
dedicated to American history, so
when he saw a cabinetmaker's ad he
ordered an exact duplicate of the
table on which Lee signed the surrender. He was most happy with the
piece when it was delivered to his
Enid, Oklahoma, home. Sometime
later he happened to restudy the famous L. M. D. Guilaume painting of
the historic scene and was struck with
horror: "There sat Grant with his fat
legs tucked under *my* table!" said
Bass. "Lee barely had a hand on it. I
should have gone for the chair." The
chair, unless it has been returned to
the McLean House, is in the Smithsonian. National Park Service personnel are on duty at McLean House
and elsewhere in the village to interpret the sites.

FINCASTLE, Botetourt County. US
220.
Fincastle Historic District comprises several buildings of the 18th
and 19th century with a variety of
styles, including Greek and Gothic
Revival and Victorian. In 1818
Thomas Jefferson designed plans for
a county courthouse. William Clark
came here after the incomparable
Lewis and Clark Expedition to marry
Judith Hancock, and from here
many emigrants set out for the west
to find their fortunes.

The first *Court House* was built of
logs in 1770. The second one, begun
in 1818 on the same site, was brick
with a dome in the center, following
Jefferson's plans, and the present
Court House, erected in 1847–48,
was copied from Jefferson's plans. In
the vaults of the clerk's office in the
building are the grants to General

George Washington and Thomas
Jefferson for land now a part of West
Virginia and Kentucky. Also the
marriage records of William Clark
and Judith Hancock.
Hayth Hotel is on the site of an
1820 tavern, operated by one William Craft. In 1878 W. B. Hayth
converted the building here to a 30-
bed hotel, to which people flocked
from as far away as Galveston and
New Orleans, to try the mineral
springs waters in the summer. In
1882 Hayth expanded his holdings
by buying the Western Hotel and
using it as an annex. By 1894 the
main hotel had been enlarged to accommodate 100 guests.
The *Presbyterian Church* is a land
grant from the British to Israel
Christian. The building pre-dates
1770 and was first used by the
Church of England. Presbyterians
took over after the Revolution. The
structure was renovated in 1840.
Some burials in the churchyard are
from 1795.
St. Mark's Episcopal Church was
begun in 1837. The *Baptist Church*
was organized in August 1831 by
Absalom Dempsey, with 15 members, who probably all were slaves.
One wooden building was destroyed
by high winds. The second was
burned out. The third and present
building of brick was erected in the
late 19th century.

FREDERICKSBURG, Independent
City; some neighboring sites in Spot-
sylvania County. US 1. I-95.
Fredericksburg Historic District
covers the original downtown area of
the town which was chartered in
1727. In 1748 a ferry was established
across the Rappahannock River and
the city prospered as a busy trading
center.
Fredericksburg Visitor Center, 706
Caroline St. Free parking passes for
the metered zone, an audiovisual
presentation here in a city-owned
center, literature and maps for self-

guiding tours of a town which calls itself the "Hub of Historyland," and that's more truth than poetry, as the saying goes.

Among the many historic sites: *Fredericksburg Museum,* 623 Caroline, in "The Chimneys," built in the 1770s; *Hugh Mercer Apothecary Shop,* restored to its original appearance in the 18th century, 1020 Caroline; *Historic Stoner's Store,* 1202 Prince Edward St., has Americana going back to the 18th century and more than 13,000 antique items in the collection; *Kenmore,* 1201 Washington, the home and gardens of Colonel Field Lewis and his wife, Betty Washington Lewis, the only sister of George Washington. She was a bride when she came here in 1752. NHL. *Rising Sun Tavern,* 1306 Caroline, built about 1760 by Charles Washington, George's brother. A popular meeting place for patriots. NHL. *James Monroe Museum,* 908 Charles, home and law office of President Monroe at the beginning of his career in 1786; the desk on which he signed the Monroe Doctrine is here. *Mary Washington House,* 1200 Charles, was a home George gave his mother in September 1772 after he had the house remodeled; Mrs. Washington moved from Ferry Farm, and remained here until her death in August 1789. Some of the boxwood in the garden was planted by Mary Washington. *Masonic Lodge No. 4,* 803 Princess Anne St. George Washington was a member in 1752. General Lafayette was given honorary membership on his visit in 1824.

Ferry Farm, 2 miles E across the river on St. 3, was the site where the famous legend of the chopped-down cherry tree began.

JAMESTOWN, James City County. St. 31, Colonial Parkway.

Jamestown National Historic Site, Jamestown Island. Little remains of the 1607 English settlement, which was the first permanent foothold the British held in America. The church tower from the 17th century structure remains, also a 1907 memorial church on the site of an earlier church. There are a number of foundations from early times and the remains of a Confederate fort. This was the leading town in the area and the colonial capital until 1700. Museum. Maintained by the Association for the Preservation of Virginia Antiquities.

Colonial National Historical Park (also in York County) includes the Jamestown site and Yorktown, as well as the Yorktown Battlefield where Cornwallis surrendered to General Washington in 1781.

Glasshouse and Island Drive. A reconstructed glasshouse is maintained by the National Park Service at the site where colonists first tried to manufacture glass in 1608. Costumed glassblowers are on duty year round. There is a five-mile drive through 1,500 acres of wooded land and marsh on the island which will give the imaginative some idea of what the New World looked like to the weary travelers arriving in 1607. Enormous oil paintings along the route aid those who don't want to rely on their imaginations or schoolbook memories to picture the early colonists: tobacco farmers, lumber workers, silk producers, and plain farmers. *Festival Park,* near the glasshouse, has reconstructions of the three ships, *Susan Constant, Godspeed,* and *Discovery,* which brought the colonists. A Visitor Center has a 15-minute orientation film. From here a walkway leads to the church tower of 1639, on the site of the first legislative assembly.

LEESBURG, Loudoun County. St. 7, St. 9, US 15.

Leesburg Historic District comprises the area of the original town centered at US 15 and St. 9, which was established in 1758. The settlement was named for Francis Lightfoot Lee, a landowner and later one of the signers of the Declaration of Independence. When Washington was burned by the British during the War of 1812, President Madison and his cabinet fled to Leesburg with 22 wagonloads of priceless documents including the Declaration, the Articles of Confederation, and Constitution, Congressional records, and George Washington's correspondence.

The *Loudon County Chamber of Commerce,* 16 W. Loudoun St., has a walking tour brochure, written by Melvin Lee Steadman, Jr., also giving the history of the town, with a numbered map, covering 33 sites.

Oatlands Historic District, S of town off US 15, covers the plantation acreage and *Oatlands,* the mansion home of George Carter; *Mountain Gap School,* built about 1827, the county's last one-room school; and the *Church of Our Saviour,* built from the 1870s. Also the ruins of a mill complex. The "big house" was built about 1800, with the two-story Corinthian entrance portico added in 1826. Carter designed and built his home.

LEXINGTON, Rockbridge County. US 11, 60. I-80, I-64.

Visitor Center, 107 E. Washington St., has brochures for two self-guiding walking tours and other literature. Guide service is available without charge by prearrangement. Write to the above at Lexington, 24450, or phone (703) 463-3777.

Stonewall Jackson House, 8 E. Washington, the only house he owned, has Jackson memorabilia. He lived here while teaching at VMI in the late 1850s. Thomas J. Jackson hadn't yet earned his nickname in those days. He and Mary Anna Morrison were newlyweds when they arrived here. When he left town on April 21, 1861, to join the Confederate Army in Richmond, it was for the last time. Over the years, the old house became a hospital, with wings

and a new façade added. In 1954, when the Stonewall Jackson Memorial bought the building and began to furnish it as a house museum, it was a sad-looking and somehow depressing memorial to Jackson. I recall seeing it soon after visiting his comparatively luxurious headquarters in Winchester and thought (but only in passing) it was just as well he never went home again. (His accidental killing was also a hard blow to the Confederacy. Arguments go on about what would have happened if he had lived.) Happily the Historic Lexington Foundation has now acquired the building and begun a complete restoration of both the house and the garden which Jackson loved to work in. It would have astonished the Jacksons to know that $250,000 would be spent in restoring their one-time home to its original lovely appearance.

Among the many historic sites: *Lee-Jackson House,* on the Washington and Lee campus, built in 1842 for Henry Ruffner, president of then Washington College. Thomas J. (later Stonewall) Jackson married Elinor Junkin, daughter of college president George Junkin in this house in 1856, and they lived in the east wing. When his wife died and he remarried in July 1857, he bought the other house listed above. General Lee lived here 1865 to 1868. It is now a faculty residence.

The *Washington and Lee President's House* was designed by Robert E. and built while he served as president. Mrs. Lee and her wheelchair were often to be seen on the large veranda which surrounds the house. The stable behind the building was erected to house Traveler, Lee's famous horse.

PETERSBURG, Independent City. I-95, US 1.

Historic Petersburg Information Center, 400 E. Washington, has hostesses on duty daily from 9 A.M. to 5

P.M. except Christmas and New Year's Day. Free literature, maps, and information.

Among highlights:

Old Blandford Church and Cemetery, on Crater Rd. (US 301, 460). There are 14 Tiffany windows given by the Confederate states when the church became a shrine in 1901. The building was erected in 1735; some of the burials are from 1702. About 30,000 Confederate soldiers are interred here. British General William Phillips was secretly buried behind the church. There is a monument to him.

There will be no more listings here for this city. Check at the Information Center for any site you've read about and want to see. Petersburg once had one of the finest museums anywhere—an antebellum mansion packed with weird and interesting items, including one of Sherman's supply wagons in the basement—though how it ever got there is still a wonder, as William Tecumseh Sherman didn't cut his path this way. There was a complete set of Yankee dental equipment—and a piano played by a local young woman who was accompanied by Sidney Lanier playing the flute; there were bullets which had collided in midair and fused, and a revolving cannon and other rare displays. But no more. Another site connected with the great siege of Petersburg has become a parking lot within the last decade. The Bicentennial, probably, is responsible for the Visitor Center with its hostesses and new brochures. But it seems a pity that in one of the most important cities of historic Virginia, what's strongly touted is a cigarette factory tour.

RICHMOND, Independent City. I-95.

Richmond Information Center, 6th St. at the Coliseum, (804) 770-2051, has maps and literature on city tours and on the vicinity, which is equally rich in historic sites. Open daily 9 A.M. to 6 P.M.

The *White House of the Confederacy,* 1201 E. Clay St., was the residence of Jefferson and Varina Davis when he was President of the Confederate states; for many years it housed the *Museum of the Confederacy,* which now has moved to new quarters close by, and the White House is being restored to its appearance in the 1860s.

St. John's Church Historic District (Church Hill) is a residential section of fine homes which is being restored by the Historic Richmond Foundation, with headquarters in the *Elmira Shelton House,* 2407 E. Grace St. Some houses are open on special tours. This area was known to the colonists as Indian Town Hill, later called Richmond Hill, and has been Church Hill since the construction of St. John's in 1741. In this church Patrick Henry made his stirring "Give me liberty or give me death" speech in 1775. *Bellevue School,* 23rd to 24th on Grace St., is on the site of the home of Elizabeth Van Lew, who helped northern soldiers held at Libby Prison escape through a tunnel from her house. After the war Grant appointed her postmistress of Richmond. She was despised by patriotic southern women. The *Hardgrove House,* 2300 E. Grace, was built in 1849 in Greek Revival style. In its servants' house, John Jasper, a black minister, lived while he worked at Hardgrove's tobacco factory. This house also has been restored. *Adam Craig House,* 1812 E. Grace, was the home of Jane Craig, who was the inspiration of Edgar Allan Poe's poem "To Helen." *Oldest Masonic Hall,* between 18th and 19th on Franklin, has been in continuous use since 1785. *Adams House,* 2501 E. Grace, built in 1809; restored.

Monument Avenue Historic District, bounded by Grace and Birch Sts., Park Ave., and Roseneath Rd., is a residential section along a lovely avenue with monuments honoring Confederates. Robert E. Lee statue at Allen Ave. is an equestrian bronze by Jean Antoine Mercie, who thought that Lee's noble brow should not be hidden by a hat and therefore created the first U.S. equestrian monument with the rider bareheaded.

The many fine public buildings in Richmond should not be missed. The *Valentine Museum* and the *Museum of the Confederacy* are exceptionally endowed with rare artifacts, manuscripts, and art. There are a number of fine old churches, historic parks, homes lived in by Lee, John Marshall, Edgar Allan Poe, and other famous names of the American past, and even the cemeteries are worth a visit.

The *Greater Richmond Chamber of Commerce,* 616 E. Franklin, has maps for self-guilding city tours, brochures, and information on industrial and James River plantation tours. *Historic Garden Week in Virginia* is an annual event in April when private homes and gardens in many parts of the state are open to the public; inquire at 12 E. Franklin St., Richmond, 23219.

WATERFORD, Loudoun County. St. 662, NE of Leesburg.

Waterford Restoration creates again the Quaker village of the 1700s. Amos Janney, who once had been a surveyor for Lord Fairfax, built a house near the banks of Kittocktin Creek in 1733. Six years later he built a mill just across the stream from today's mill which is now a craftshop. Next he put up a house for the miller, then a smithy and a log house, and the whole works was known as Milltown. Then came Thomas Moore, from Waterford, Ireland, who had the name changed to honor his birthplace.

In 1804 Edward Dorsey built a house halfway up a local hill, and *Dorsey House* is still standing. The

town tavern came into existence when a row of houses on the north side of what is now Main St. were joined together about 1800. The town council also used the place for meetings after the settlement was incorporated in 1810. A woolen factory and a bank were built. By 1834 the town was prosperous, with some 70 houses, a tannery, a chair factory, and a population reaching 400. The Mutual Fire Insurance Company came in 1849 and has remained.

The *Waterford Foundation* has been restoring the village. An arts and crafts exhibits fair and annual homes tour always are held the first full three-day weekend in October. The *Waterford Mill* and the *Country Store* sell handcrafted articles during the fair; home-cooked lunches are served, but accommodations must be found in nearby towns. For information write the foundation at Waterford, 22190.

WILLIAMSBURG, Independent City. US 60.

If restorations were jewels this would be the Kohinoor and the Star of India combined. It somehow remains enchanting even though a million visitors now tramp through it yearly and have been arriving, in increasing numbers, ever since the museum village of Colonial Williamsburg opened in the 1920s.

Williamsburg Historic District is a 173-acre area containing more than 490 structures which have been restored or reconstructed to their 18th-century appearance. NHL. Williamsburg, settled in 1633 as Middle Plantation, served as the Virginia capital from 1699 to 1780. The *College of William and Mary,* established in 1693, is the second oldest in the United States.

Bruton Parish Church, Duke of Gloucester St., was built in 1712–15, with the steeple added in 1769. It was restored in 1905 and 1939. Spotswood, who was the Royal Governor,

Bruton Parish Church, Colonial Williamsburg, Virginia. (Courtesy Colonial Williamsburg Foundation)

designed the building; it served as the court church of Virginia for a number of years. NHL.

It was the Rev. W. A. R. Goodwin, rector of this church, who in 1926 talked to John D. Rockefeller, Jr., about preserving the city's historic buildings. Rockefeller established a nonprofit corporation, now the **Colonial Williamsburg Foundation,** and gave about $100 million to purchase and restore property. There are 88 original 18th- and early 19th-century buildings within or near the historic area, 90 acres of gardens and greens, and nearly 85 percent of 18th-century Williamsburg has been preserved. The maintenance crew includes more than 300 carpenters, painters, laborers, mechanics, and custodians, as well as more than 85 gardeners and landscape experts.

In the more than 225 exhibition rooms of the Historic Area are some 505 persons in costume to serve as guides and interpreters. Another 350 employees do not meet the public daily but are essential to the operation: curators, architects, historians, archaeologists, draftsmen, seamstresses, accountants, etc. About 1,850 employees keep the hotels, restaurants, and shops humming.

Something seasonal is happening year round in addition to the exhibitions. An annual Garden Symposium is held in spring; special days are celebrated with music, pageantry, and dramatic presentations. There are candlelight concerts, 18th-century plays enacted, and more than 40 activities in all are available on varying daily schedules. There are new ticket options for touring Williamsburg's historic houses, public buildings, and craft shops. The admissions policy now permits unlimited access to exhibition buildings and craftshops except for the Governor's Palace, which requires a separate admission. Tickets will be offered for a one-, two-, or three-day period and will have a visible tag to make entry easier into exhibition areas. Visitors arriving after 3 P.M. will have a reduced price.

Information Center, open 8:30 A.M. to 8 P.M. Information on side trips is available. An orientation film is shown daily from 9:15 to 5:15.

Bus service is provided from the Information Center to the Historic Area on a 15-minute schedule which begins at 9 A.M. daily, ending at 6

The Governor's Palace, Colonial Williamsburg, Virginia. (Courtesy Colonial Williamsburg Foundation)

P.M. One of the special activities is "Carriage and Waggon Rides" through the Historic Area from the Courthouse of 1770, daily 9:30 to 3:40. Special two-hour walking orientation tours are available and recommended for first-time visitors. Also children's tours are given on a seasonal basis.

Individual listings on the National Register:

Peyton Randolph House, Nicholson and New England Sts., built about 1715, in three stages; the east section was connected to the older part of the house by Sir John Randolph, or his son, Peyton, about 1724. Most of the original paneling remains; handsomely restored. NHL.

James Semple House, Frances St. between Blair and Waller Sts., built ca. 1772-78, restored. NHL.

Wren Building, College of William and Mary, on the campus, 1695-1716, design attributed to Sir Christopher Wren. The building was burned and rebuilt three times, restored 1928-31 and 1978. It is one of the oldest academic structures in the U.S. NHL.

Wythe House, W side of the Palace Green, built about 1755, Richard Taliaferro, architect. (A Taliaferro from Virginia says the name is pronounced Tolliver—whether this covers architects is anybody's guess.) NHL.

Carter's Grove Plantation, in James City County, 8 miles SE of Williamsburg on US 60, is a 20-room mansion in Georgian style, built about 1755, restored in 1928-36. George Washington, Thomas Jefferson, and many other bigwigs of the colonies and the Revolutionary period were guests here.

YORKTOWN, York County. US 17.

Visitor Center, end of Colonial Parkway, has literature, maps for self-guiding tours, and an audiovisual program.

Swan Tavern, Main and Ballard Sts., is a reconstruction of the old tavern, kitchen, smokehouse, and stable built in the early 18th century and blown up in the Civil War.

Grace Church, Church St., was built in 1848 in Greek Revival style, later additions. *York County Courthouse,* across from the Swan Tavern, has records from 1633.

NORTH CAROLINA

Not many years ago, a miner from the Lehigh region of Pennsylvania, tired of strikes and half-pay, put his wife, children and household goods into a wagon, and set off through the Blue Ridge district of Virginia. The family had little else than bread and water to live upon. They found a high, cool table-land in North Carolina, where the soil was rich to blackness, the water good, and the climate equable. They bought a farm at fifty cents an acre, and camped down in the unbroken forest. The mountaineers helped them to raise a log-house. The next year, an energetic New Yorker bought the adjoining section. They have long had their broad fields, fruit, and comfortable homes; and a little log schoolhouse and church, and a post-office, which they were instrumental in erecting, have become the focus of civilization for that mountain country.

—"Home and Society," by R. H. D., printed in *The Century Magazine,* New York, 1883

BATH, Beaufort County. US 264, St. 92.

Bath Historic District bounded by Bath Creek, St. 92, and King St. The town was incorporated in 1705, and in 1715 designated a port of entry for the colony. Main (Water) St. ran the length of the town. In the 18th century when Washington became a more important port the county courthouse was moved there. This must have been hard on the citizens of Bath, but present residents enjoy the relatively undisturbed charm of its fine old buildings. A *Visitors' Center,* on St. 92, has a film on the history of Bath which is shown on request. The historic site is administered by the State Department of Archives and History in cooperation with the Historic Bath Commission. Groups planning tours should write to Historic Bath, Bath, 27808.

St. Thomas Church, on Craven St., is the state's oldest existing church building in the state's oldest town.

(The first church was St. Paul's near Edenton, a wooden structure which was destroyed.) The building was begun in 1734, and finished about 1740. All of the interior wood trimming was made locally of Carolina pine. A sawmill had been in business since 1731. About 60 early parishioners were buried beneath the brick pavement of the floor, to keep the Indians from finding out whites were mortal, according to an early history of the church, but it seems unlikely the hardy pioneers would ever underestimate the intelligence of the Indians. Beyond doubt, however, the candelabra on the altar were the gift of King George II and the original bell was a gift from Queen Anne in 1710. It is now housed in a small tower near the church. A large Bible, published in England in 1703, is kept in a glass case and was used fictionally by Edna Ferber in her novel *Show Boat,* along with the rest of St. Thomas Church, all moved for the purposes of Miss Ferber's plot to Tennessee. The building has been restored.

Glebe House, the home of John F. Tompkins, publisher of the *Farmers' Journal,* in the mid-19th century, is now the Community Library. Glebe House was built in 1750, with Parson Alexander Stewart as the first occupant. It is said to be the only house ever built for a preacher by the Church in the whole colony.

Palmer-Marsh House, on the E side of Main St., was built about 1744 by Captain Michael Coutanch, from the Isle of Jersey. In 1764 it was bought by Captain Robert Palmer, a member of the Governor's Council and the surveyor general of the colony. In 1782 Jonathan and Daniel G. Marsh, who were brothers, bought the place. The General Assembly met here in 1744, 1752. The house has been restored and furnished in period. A National Historic Landmark; also HABS.

Buzzard Hotel, S of the Palmer-Marsh House on the E side of Main St., was an inn built about 1740 and named for its builder and operator, whose first name seems to have been lost from the record. The building has been remodeled. Visitors can note the stepped chimney, but the house is a private dwelling at present.

Bonner House, on the NE corner of Main and Front Sts., is believed to have been built about 1825. Joseph Bonner acquired the place in 1830. It has been restored by the Oscar F. Smith Memorial Foundation. Listed on the National Register.

BEAUFORT, Carteret County. US 21.

Beaufort Historic District comprises the quaint seaport town founded in 1709. It is surrounded on three sides by water and was once the center of the colony's whaling industry. Historical marker in town points out the location of a whale fishery 6 miles SE at Shackleford Banks.

Among houses listed on the National Register:

The *Joseph Bell House,* on Turner St., was built in 1767 by Bell, who was a plantation owner, legislator, and sheriff. It is West Indies style and has been restored and furnished with 18th-century pieces. The 1820 home of Josiah Bell, grandson of Colonel Joseph Bell, is nearby and being restored at present.

The *Alphonso Whaling Museum* on Front St. has relics of the busy days of the whaling industry. *Hampton Mariners Museum,* 120 Turner St., has mounted fish, seashells, and other exhibits.

Also in town: the *Old Jail* and the *Old Burying Ground,* in which one dead English seaman is reportedly buried standing up, at his own request. The land was deeded to the town in 1731; the earliest date on a marker is 1756, though earlier ones may have been eroded. In the north corner of the cemetery, graves are facing east so the occupants will be facing the sun on that Great Getting-Up Morning. The *Beaufort Historical Association,* 138 Turner St., has information on the more than 125 homes which are over a century old and even has maps for a self-guiding tour of the Burying Ground.

CHEROKEE, Swain County. US 19, US 441.

Oconaluftee Indian Village, ½ mile N on US 441, next door to the Mountainside Theatre, is a replica of an Indian village of the 18th century. There are a seven-sided council house, a typical Cherokee home, a botanical garden, craft demonstrations, and guided tours, led by Indians in native costume. The village is maintained by the nonprofit Cherokee Historical Association, which also sponsors the Museum of the Cherokee Indian and an outdoor drama, *Unto These Hills,* at the Mountainside Theatre. Descendants of the Cherokees on whose lives Kermit Hunter based his drama often enact the principal roles. The *Museum of the Cherokee Indian* is on US 441 at the information center, with displays, and lectures on Cherokee customs and history.

Oconaluftee Museum, 3 miles N on US 441 at Smokemont Ranger Station in Great Smoky Mountains National Park, is a restored farmstead with reconstructed buildings, including a blacksmith shop, which re-create how the white pioneers lived in this area.

EDENTON, Chowan County. US 17. On Albemarle Sound.

Edenton Historic District covers the land which was once called Queen Anne's Town until it was incorporated in 1727. Founded in 1658, it was the site of the first permanent colonial settlement in North Carolina. The *Chowan County Courthouse,* on E. King St., was built in 1767, replacing an earlier one completed in 1719. It is two-story, late Georgian in a T-shape plan with a one-story semicircular apse at the center rear. Some of the building was altered in the 19th century. NHL. The Courthouse faces the green which once had stocks, racks, and a pillory.

Cupola House, 408 S. Broad St., is a two-story frame combining forms of the 17th and 18th centuries in architecture, a rare example of a southern house which has the Jacobean second-story overhang usually associated with New England. The octagonal cupola was used for sighting ships at sea. The original paneling of the two main rooms on the first floor was sold in 1918, but the house has been carefully restored. It is furnished in period and operated by the Cupola House Library and Museum. (Anyone determined to see the original paneling will find it on display in the Brooklyn Museum, New York.) NHL.

On the National Register:
James Iredell House, 107 E. Church St., was built about 1776 for Iredell, a member of the North Carolina Provincial Congress, a state attorney general, and associate justice of the U.S. Supreme Court. Later his son James, Jr., lived here. Junior was governor, 1827–28. After additions in the 19th century, the house served as St. Paul's rectory for a time. The D.A.R. saved the building in 1949 and opened it as a state historic site. There are several outbuildings, a garden, and a plantation schoolhouse.

Thomas and Penelope Barker House, S. Broad St., was moved from another location; it was the home of a woman who knew her own mind and spoke it, managing to persuade 51 of her townswomen to join her in protesting the tax against tea in October 1774. The site of the protest is marked on the west side of the village green by a large bronze teapot sitting on a cannon. Mrs. Barker's defiance was despite her husband's serving as London agent for the colony for the last ten years before the Revolution. The building, put up in the 1780s and later enlarged, is now headquarters for historic Edenton, with a Visitor Center and Museum. Tours are available here.

St. Paul's Episcopal Church, Broad and Church Sts., was begun in 1736, partially destroyed by fire in this century, but restored. The Courtyard is of historical importance, too. The graves of three proprietary governors, Henderson Walker, Thomas Pollock, and Charles Eden, were moved here from plantation burying grounds in the late 19th century. The vestry in 1725 complained to London that they had no ornaments and that the books sent to Bath should have come to them. On June 19, 1776, the vestry signed "The Test," a set of patriotic resolutions protesting some British practices. This was a full fifteen days before the Declaration of Independence was signed by the Continental Congress. Not surprisingly, Joseph Hewes, one of the signers, was a member of St. Paul's outspoken vestry.

During the Civil War the bell was given to the southern cause and became part of the four cannon of the Edenton Bell Battery. Here, as in Bath, burials were made beneath the brick floor, but this practice ended and the floor is now wooden.

Among early rectors of St. Paul's was Daniel Earl, who was here from 1759 to 1778 and was not allowed to hold services during the Revolution because, reportedly, he "combined fiery Revolutionary activities with adherence to the Church of England." He was a fox hunter, planter, and fisherman, and is said to have arrived one morning to find a note tacked to the church door:

> A half-built church,
> A broken-down steeple,
> A herring-catching parson,
> And a damn set of people.

Among other historic houses on the National Register: *Albania,* US 17 W of junction with St. 32; *Wessington House,* 120 W. King St.; *Hayes Plantation,* E. Water St., a National Historic Landmark, *Mulberry Hill,* SE of town; *Shelton Plantation House,* off St. 32; and *Pembroke Hall,* W. King St. Ask locally.

The Chamber of Commerce, 116 E. King St., has a tour map for Edenton. Several houses are not open to the public except on special occasions. For information, call (919) 482-3400.

FAYETTEVILLE, Cumberland County. I-95.

Heritage Square, 225 Dick St., is a restoration project which began in 1966 when the Woman's Club bought property of historic value in the heart of the old town. *Sandford House,* first of the three structures in the restoration, is now used as the Woman's Club. The house dates from 1800 and is Georgian in style.

The *Oval Ballroom* was built about 1830 on Gillespie St., one block away from its present site, by Robert Halliday for his daughter's wedding. It has been restored. The *Baker-Haigh-Nimocks House* is also called "The House with the Spiral Stair." Tradition says the stairway was built by sailors who wintered here, about 1804. The grounds are landscaped with brick walkways and walled gardens. The complex is listed on the National Register.

Old Market House, in midtown, on Market Square, was built in 1838 on the site of Convention Hall, where the state's constitution was drafted and the legislature met. The earlier building was destroyed by fire in 1831. The *Chamber of Commerce* now has offices here. A National Historic Landmark, also HABS.

First Presbyterian Church, Bow and Ann St., was built in 1816 in Classic Colonial style. NHL. On the National Register.

Also on the Register: *Liberty Row,* N side of the first block of Person St., bounded by Market Square and Liberty Point; *Belden-Horne House,* 233 Green St.; *Cool Spring Place (Cool Spring Tavern),* 119 N. Cool Spring St., also called the *McKethan Home* (the Tavern was open for business in September 1789); *Kyle House,* 234 Green St.; *Mansard Roof House,* 214 Mason St.; *Sedberry-Holmes House,* 232 Person St.; and the *St. John's Episcopal Church,* on Green St.

HALIFAX, Halifax County. US 301.

Halifax Historic District takes in the town, which was founded in 1757, helped establish a major route from Virginia because of its position on the river, and soon became an important political, social, and commercial center. Many buildings of colonial times have been restored and furnished by the Historical Halifax Restoration Association. The *Constitution House,* in which the first state constitution was drafted in 1776, has been moved from its original site and restored by the Daughters of the American Revolution. *Owens House* is a restored and furnished pre-Revolutionary frame with gabled ends and a gambrel roof, once the home of George W. Owen.

The *Colonial Jail* was built in 1764 and actually used until 1913. It is a rectangular two-story brick with ground plantings. The *Clerk's Office* is next door, built in 1832 to replace an office of 1784 which was a printer's and was used for the publication of the Halifax *Journal.*

The *Old Cemetery* is across the road, but the *Colonial Church* which stood here is long gone. There are a number of tombstones with 18th-century dates in the graveyard.

The *Magazine Spring* was developed by Tuscarora Indians and later by the Halifax residents. On the National Register: *William R. Davie House,* Norman St., built about 1783; *Eagle Tavern,* Main St., a popular spot in the politically minded town; reputedly Lafayette stopped here in 1825; *Sally-Billy House,* St. Andrews St. Both Eagle Tavern and the Tap Room, a smaller saloon, built in the 18th century or possibly 1810, are being restored.

MURFREESBORO, Hertford County. US 258.

Murfreesboro Historic District, roughly bounded by Broad, 4th, Vance, and Winder Sts. The Murfreesboro Historical Association has been restoring many old houses of the area, which was visited in the 16th century by John White of Roanoke Island.

An expedition came from Jamestown, Virginia, in the 17th century. The Indian tribes here were mainly Nottoways, Meherrins, and Chowanokes, and many of their village locations and artifacts have been found. By 1740 the site was known as Murfree's Landing. William Murfree donated 97 acres for the town in the

mid-18th century and his son, Colonel Hardy Murfree, a hero of the Revolutionary War, moved in 1803 to Tennessee, founding another Murfreesboro there. William Hill Brown, locally known as "the first American novelist," died here in 1793. Dr. Walter Reed spent some of his boyhood here and came back to marry a local girl. Richard John Gatling, who invented the Gatling gun, was born on a plantation in the countryside nearby.

The Murfreesboro Adaptive Restoration Program, founded in 1967, combines local, state, and federal support to preserve and restore the old riverport and King's Landing. Historic Murfreesboro is considered a leader in adaptive restoration and visitors and supporters of the program are welcome. For information write the Association, P.O. Box 3, Murfreesboro, N.C., 27855; (919) 398-4886. The Association also has information on the award-winning publication *Renaissance in Carolina 1971–1976,* which has more than 250 photographs of the town's early buildings in its 212 pages.

Chowan College, on Jones Drive, was the earliest Baptist women's school in North Carolina; it was founded in 1848 as the Chowan Baptist Female Institute and remained open during the Civil War and Reconstruction as many other schools did not. *The Columns,* built in 1852, housed a chapel, classrooms, offices, and dormitory. It is brick Greek Revival, three stories, with a low hip roof and an octagonal belvedere. The portico on the north side has eight fluted Doric columns which originally supported two galleries. It has been renovated and is on the National Register.

Among other National Register buildings: *Freeman House* (*Hertford Academy*), 200 E. Broad St., was built in 1810. It is two-story brick, with a hipped roof, and decorative details which include an intricate band of fretwork and pierced dentils. From 1848 to 1852 the Baptist Female Institute met here before moving to The Columns.

Melrose, 100 East Broad St., is a restored two-story, gable-roofed plantation of the early 19th century, and was the home of William Hardy Murfree.

Myrick House, 402 Broad St., is a Federal town house, not a common architectural style for North Carolina. It is two-story brick, with a hip roof, built in the early 19th century, and has been restored.

William Rea Store, on E. Williams St., was built about 1790. Rea was a Bostonian who traded between here and New England. With his four brothers he outfitted ships and helped establish the town as an export center of the Roanoke Valley. A wing was added to the main building about 1803. There is a museum in the restored store.

Roberts-Vaughan House, 130 E. Main St., was built as a two-story frame dwelling in the 19th century and is now Greek Revival—the central portico having been added later. It is restored and has four dependencies.

The *John Wheeler House,* 403 E. Broad St., is two-story with a gabled roof, brick laid in Flemish bond, as are most of the brick dwellings of the early-19th-century period in Murfreesboro. Wheeler was postmaster and a trustee of the Murfreesboro and Hertford academies. His son John was the first U.S. minister to Nicaragua. Another son, Samuel, founded the Murfreesboro *Citizen,* and both lived here. The house was given to the Historical Association in 1969.

NEW BERN, Craven County. US 70, 17.

New Bern Historic District is roughly bounded by the Neuse and Trent Rivers and Queen St. in a town founded in 1710 by Baron Christopher de Graffenried, who had received a grant of 10,000 acres from Queen Anne of Great Britain. The colonists were mostly Swiss and German. New Bern served as the provincial capital for several years. The first provincial congresses met here in 1774 and 1775.

The New Bern-Craven County Chamber of Commerce, 211 Broad St., has a helpful booklet which gives the story of New Bern from 1710 to 1960, and maps for a self-guiding tour of the old city. Write Drawer C, New Bern, 28560; (919) 637-3111.

Christ Church, Middle and Pollock St., 1873, has silver communion service, a Bible, and a prayer book that were gifts from King George II in 1752.

Firemen's Museum, 420 Broad St., has 19th-century equipment on display. The department, chartered in 1845, is believed to be the oldest continuously active volunteer fire department in the U.S. The engine called the Atlantic Steamer dates from 1879 and the Button Steamer from 1884.

First Presbyterian Church, New St. near Middle St., was built in 1819–22, after a Christopher Wren design, and was used as a hospital in Civil War times.

Also in the downtown area: *Wade House,* 214 Tryon Palace Dr., an early 19th-century Federal house, remodeled in the 1880s with a mansard roof, cast iron roof cresting, and a hitching post. *Harvey Mansion,* nearby at 218, is Federal, built about 1810 by Harvey, a shipowner and merchant, to serve as dwelling, office, and storage for his mercantile business. The Adamesque Federal woodwork in the residence is excellent; the house has been restored by the City Urban Renewal Commission. *Isaac Taylor House,* 228 Craven, 1792, had a counting house on the first floor and contains fine woodwork. Taylor was a merchant, shipowner, and planter. *Judge William Gaston's Of-*

fice, Craven between Pollock and Broad Sts, was the law office of a state jurist; it was moved here from its original location near the Gaston House (see below). It was built in 1792 and has fine interior woodwork. During the Civil War the 48th Massachusetts headquartered here. The *Baxter Clock,* 323 Pollock St., made by the Seth Thomas Co. about 1920, is now such a rare item it is listed on the National Register. The *Attmore-Oliver House,* 513 Broad St., begun about 1790 by Samuel Chapman, a merchant, was a cottage; in 1834 the Greek Revival porch and cast iron balconies were added to the front. The dwelling has been restored and furnished by the New Bern Historical Society. The *First Baptist Church,* Middle St. at Church Alley, was built in the 1840s in Gothic Revival design by Thomas and Son of New York.

Tryon Palace Restoration, 613 Pollock St., S end of George St.: the John Wright Stanly House and the Stevenson House are part of the restoration complex. Tryon Palace, designed by John Hawks of England, served as the capitol and residence of the governor of the colony from 1770–94. During the Revolution it was the capitol of the independent state. The main building burned in 1798. The Palace has been handsomely restored and reconstructed and furnished with 18th-century antiques. The gardens are also 18th century in design. There are guided tours by hostesses in costume. The *Stanly House,* at 307 George St., an 1870s Georgian mansion, has been restored and furnished as it was in the days when George Washington and Nathanael Greene were guests. (This house can boast that Washington actually slept here two nights.) Stanly was a shipowner, merchant, and patriot during the war. The gardens are typical of those which surrounded the town houses of the period. The *Stevenson House,* 611

Pollock St., Federal, was built about 1805 on one of the Palace lots which were sold after the fire of 1798. The widow's walk is typical of a seaport town here as in New England. The house was bought by the Tryon Palace Commission in 1957, carefully restored and furnished in Federal and Empire era styles, and opened to the public in 1966. The houses and gardens of the complex have won various awards for excellence. The gardens may be entered without charge during the day from Pollock St. behind the Reception Center-Auditorium-Gift Shop building.

Also in the Tryon Palace area: *Jones House,* 231 Eden St., built about 1818 in Federal style, is now used as a guest house for the Palace Commission. Confederate spy Emeline Pigott was held here during the northern occupation of New Bern. A number of private early houses in the area have been restored. The *Major John Daves House,* 313 George St., a late 18th-century Georgian coastal cottage, was the home of the Revolutionary patriot. A mulberry tree at the rear may be a relic of the silk industry attempted by Baron Christopher de Graffenried. Open.

Among other notable buildings of the 67 listed on the self-guiding tours are several fine early churches and private homes and several former dwellings adapted for commercial use with preservation of their best features. *New Bern Academy Complex,* New and Hancock Sts., dates from 1764. *New St. Building,* 1806, has original Federal woodwork. *Bell Building,* 1884–85, faces Hancock St.

Gaston House, 421 Craven, restored late-18th-century Georgian home, was built by architect-builder and Revolutionary patriot James Coor. The talented Judge William Gaston, orator, lawyer, member of Congress, associate justice of the State Supreme Court, bought the house in 1818.

Slover-Bradham House, 201 Johnson St., is brick in Renaissance Revival style, built 1846–48 by Charles Slover, a merchant. General Ambrose Burnside picked this house as his headquarters when his troops occupied the town during the Civil War. In 1908 the house was bought by C. D. Bradham who had got rich with a beverage he called "Brad's Drink," now known as Pepsi-Cola. Alas, the house is private.

In the rear garden of 520 E. Front St. is a magnificent cypress tree, one of 20 in the Hall of Fame of American Trees.

Coor-Bishop House, 501 E. Front St., built about 1767 by James Coor. George Pollock, a later owner, had President James Monroe and Vice-President John C. Calhoun and his wife as his guests.

New Bern has more than three dozen listings on the National Register and is clearly worth a lingering visit. You may not want to miss the *Cedar Grove Cemetery,* bounded by Queen, George, Cypress, Howard, and Metcalf Sts., which opened in 1854. The weeping arch entrance (of coquina, which holds moisture and consequently tends to drip) is the thing to be wary of and sidestep. If water drips on a visitor, legend says, that person is the next to be buried here. Judge William Gaston is interred here with his law desk and chair.

RALEIGH, Wake County. I-85.
Oakwood Historic District is bounded roughly by N. Boundary, Person, Jones, and Linden Sts., and Oakwood Cemetery.

The *Chamber of Commerce,* 411 S. Salisbury, has information on walking and auto tours of the historic areas.

The *State Capitol* was completed in 1840. Andrew Johnson, who followed Lincoln into the presidency, was born in Raleigh. His little birthplace, built in 1795, has been moved

to Pullen Park, adjoining the campus of the North Carolina State College, and has been restored; furnished in period.

The *Joel Lane House,* 728 W. Hargett St., was built about 1771. The state assembly met here during the Revolutionary War. Owned by the Colonial Dames, it has been restored and carefully furnished in period. Joel, Jesse, and James Lane came to Raleigh and built their house before the courthouse and jail were constructed smack-dab in front of their place in 1771. Joel Lane then built a tavern and helped to erect a log church. The settlement was called Wake Courthouse for Mary Wake, wife of William Tryon, the royal governor.

Department of Archives and History, Box 1881, Raleigh, 27602, has a list of the county historical societies or individuals "able and willing" to help visitors interested in history with local information and in architecture and restoration. There are more than 100 counties in the state. In Raleigh there are many private houses on the National Register. With the Chamber of Commerce map, visitors can drive past to admire the many 17th- and 18th-century structures still handsomely maintained. Walking tour maps are also available.

Christ Episcopal Church, 120 E. Edenton St., was designed by Richard Upjohn, completed in 1849. Open daily.

Mordecai House, Mordecai Sq., Mimosa St., 1785–1826, has been restored. Many furnishings are original. Tours in season. Free.

WILMINGTON, New Hanover County. US 74, 76.
Wilmington Historic District: the town was incorporated in 1739 at the junction of two branches of the Cape Fear River and therefore prospered quickly. The historic district takes in

the old residential section and public buildings from the 18th century through the 19th century.

City Hall–Thalian Hall, 100 N. 3rd St., was built in 1858. The final performance was in 1928, but still hanging in place is the curtain which rose on the opening night in 1858. The civic part of the building has an oil painting in the lobby, a replica of *My Mother;* Whistler's mother, Anna Mathilda McNeill Whistler, was born in Wilmington.

The *Chamber of Commerce,* 4th and Princess Sts., has maps for self-guiding auto tours of historic Wilmington and the Cape Fear Trail. P.O. Drawer 330; (919) 762-2611.

Burgwin-Wright House, 224 Market St., dates from 1771. Cornwallis had his headquarters here in 1781. Now headquarters for the North Carolina Society of Colonial Dames of America. A legend says that a tunnel led from here to the river. The basement rooms served as a prison, and the original floor still has musket scars. The colonial kitchen has been reconstructed. *St. James Church,* across the street, was used by the British as a stable. The present church was built in 1839 with materials from the church of 1751.

Latimer House, 126 S. Third St., was built in 1852. Classic Revival in style, it is a double house, with servants' quarters in the rear. Furnished in period.

Oakdale Cemetery, N on 15th St. from Market, is not to be missed by tombstone readers. A host of individualists are resting here: one gentleman buried with his dog; the last man killed in a political duel; a young lady seated in a chair and enclosed in a cask of rum; Henry Baker, the man who designed the Lincoln Memorial; and Mrs. Rose O'Neal Greenhow, Confederate spy, who got secret Union plans to Beauregard to help the Confederates win at First Manassas (Bull Run). She was placed under house arrest in 1861 but was sent back south in 1862. A year later she ran the blockade to England and France, representing the Confederacy. She wrote a book about her imprisonment, but while coming back to North Carolina she fell overboard off the coast near Wilmington and was drowned.

WINSTON-SALEM, Forsyth County. US 52, I-40.

Old Salem Historic District comprises the Salem College campus and the area near Salem square. This is a restoration of a planned community which the Moravians settled in 1766. Many original structures have been restored and furnished with both original and period pieces. Early crafts are demonstrated. Tours start at the *Reception Center,* on Old Salem Rd. A number of buildings are open as shops or for exhibition purposes; others are private dwellings or offices.

The *John Vogler House,* facing the square, 1819, was the home of a silversmith, and his place of business. It has been restored.

Market-Fire House Museum, on the square, is a reconstruction on the original site of the Market-Fire House of 1803.

Miksch Tobacco Shop, on S. Main St., was opened in 1771 to sell the North Carolina weed and also served as the residence of Matthew Miksch. *Salem Tavern,* 800 S. Main St., had George Washington as a guest in 1791. NHL. *Single Brothers' House,* S. Main and Academy Sts., 1769 and 1786, half-timbered construction, German style, is the oldest major building still standing in the Moravian area. It is two-story with a full basement and two attics. Teenage boys learned their crafts in the nine shops on the ground floor and in the basement, while they were earning their own way as journeymen. The upper floor served as a dormitory for unmarried master craftsmen, journeymen, and apprentices. NHL.

Winkler Bakery, 52 S. Main St., built in 1800, has been restored. It is used for demonstrations and as a shop.

Home Moravian Church, on the square, erected in 1800, is still in use. Visitors are welcome.

Wachovia Museum, S. Main and E. Academy St., built in 1794 as a boys' school, has been restored.

Over 30 buildings have been restored, reconstructed, or renovated since 1949 when the project began. The interiors are authentic, even to the exact colors of paints.

Historic Bethabara, 2147 Bethabara Rd., is the site of the first Moravian settlement in North Carolina in 1753. A number of restored and reconstructed buildings are open to the public. Fifteen men chosen for their special skills left the Moravian settlement in Pennsylvania to begin a new life here. Arriving on a cold November day in 1753 they spent the night in an abandoned log cabin which became home for eleven of the men, who stayed to begin building the town which they named Bethabara,

meaning "House of Passage." In three years, word had spread that here was a place to find fine craftsmanship and medical treatment. The original settlers then built Salem, a short distance away, and most residents moved to the new town. In 1762, when a Philadelphia botanist stopped here, he found rare herbs and wild flowers in the medical gardens. A nature trail is marked today.

After the main move to Salem most buildings were allowed to deteriorate or were torn down or moved. In the early 19th century, a farmer filled in the open cellars left behind and the settlement was buried. Archaeological research was begun in 1964–66. Many valuable artifacts, mainly pottery, have been found. The 1788 church and meeting house has been restored, as has the 1782 *Krause-Butner Potter's House.* A museum is located in what was the brewer's home. Exhibits pertain to the historical background of the settlement and feature the pottery made by Gottfried Aust, master potter, and his apprentices. Admission free. Open from Easter through November.

SOUTH CAROLINA

My house, you say, is in a very ruinous condition. And this in spite of my lares; those beautiful & elegant plaster headed household Gods, who could have been posted on the outward Wall, for no other purpose, but that of affording protection. I hope it will not be inconsistent with the plan to be formed by you, and Dr. Drayton, to have them dismissed, the old bricks rubbed from the top of the House to the bottom, & the Interstices new pointed. My intention is to have a Piazza in each front, & an Area sunk; to give light to the offices under the House.
 —Letter written May 30, 1783, by Ralph Izard of South Carolina
to his architect Arthur Middleton

My upright piano is my most cherished possession, companion, and friend, and I am always nervous over the perils of its four-mile drive from plantation to summer house.

A small mattress is put in the plantation wagon—I have no spring wagon—and on that the piano is put and steadied by two men while it is slowly driven out. It always takes eight men, as they are not accustomed to lifting, and they make a great ado over it. Just as the piano was lifted out of the wagon up the rather high steps on to the piazza at the pineland [house], they set it down at the head of the steps, and gave it a great push to roll it toward the sitting room door. There came a tremendous crash. The piazza had fallen in on the side toward the house. Fortunately there were no men in front of the piano; they were all behind. I had two heavy planks brought and put as a bridge from the place where the piano rested into the door, and as soon as they got the front rollers on the plank all danger was over, but for a time it looked as if there must be a terrible smashup. I sent one of the men under the house to see what had caused the crash. He reported it was the giving way of one of the blocks, which was so rotten it had crumbled away. "Why, Bonaparte, I sent you to examine the foundation of this house and see if any repairs were needed, and you said it was all in order." Bonaparte only murmured apologetically that he was too busy to see about such small matters.
 —*A Woman Rice Planter,* by Patience Pennington, edited by Cornelius O.
Cathey, Harvard University Press, 1961 (from a 1903 diary)

BEAUFORT Beaufort County. US 21, on the Beaufort River.

The first Europeans to see the area were the Spanish in 1521. The French arrived in 1562, and Jean Ribaut declared there was "no fayrer or fytter place than Porte Royall." In 1684 a group of Scots led by Lord Cardross settled on the east side of Port Royal island. They were Cove-

119

nanters, a religious lot, but they armed the Yemassee Indians and set them to fight the Spaniards, who nearly wiped out the settlement in retaliation. In 1710 the town was laid out and named for Henry, Duke of Beaufort, one of the proprietors. Five years later the Yemassees went on the warpath again and burned most of the settlement. Matters settled down relatively, except for hurricanes, pirates, yellow fever, smallpox, and some harrassment by British ships during the War of 1812. Otherwise all went well until the Civil War, when the Federal forces easily occupied the town—all but one white citizen had fled.

Charles Stockell explains the existence of the many fine homes in town: "Beaufort grew wealthy prior to the Revolution because of the rice and indigo grown in this area. There was a handsome bounty of 7 shillings a pound on indigo, and many profited from this. After the Revolution, Sea Island cotton was developed locally. . . . The homes in Beaufort were for the most part the summer homes of the planters who had large plantations 20–30 miles away. Because of this and because the Secessionist movement began here, the Yankeees made Beaufort a primary objective for capture and repression. . . . this area was a Yankee headquarters and hospital base and was spared. . . . After the war Beaufort was ruined economically and the white population largely left. The old homes could not be torn down and replaced because no one had any money. New furniture could not be purchased, so the old was preserved. All that was a blessing, too, because it is still here. . . ."

The *Historic District* is bounded by Boundary, Hamar, and Bladen Sts. and the Beaufort River, but there are outlying homes of historic importance, too. The *Historic Beaufort Foundation* has arranged three walking tours and a driving tour for the fine old structures, some of which have been restored as house museums.

The early settlers built houses of clapboard and tabby, which was a cementlike mixture of oyster shells, sand, and the lime obtained by burning oyster shells. The "Beaufort style," which developed as the community prospered, used elements of Georgian and Colonial architecture, along with Greek Revival and Spanish elements suited for the tropics.

Beaufort-styled houses were freestanding on large lots and built to take every advantage of the southeasterly breeze. A 20th-century observer, James Henry Rice, Jr., in writing of the Carolina coast, said: "Beaufort has been termed the most beautiful town on the Atlantic—true enough, except that it is not on the Atlantic but on the Beaufort River. The panorama of its harbor is one of the sights of North America. Were it in California or Florida it would be as well known as the Riviera."

The waterfront is now being restored with parks, pavilion, amphitheater, shops, and landscaping at a cost of more than $4.5 million.

George Elliott House, 1001 Bay St., was built about 1840, later a veranda was added. One of Beaufort's wealthiest men, Dr. W. J. Jenkins, who bought the house before the war, left valuable books and furniture when he quit town hastily in 1861 as the Union forces approached. He was able to retrieve many of his possessions at Hilton Head after the war and brought them home by barge, but in 1866 the government sold his house for taxes. It is now restored as a house museum.

Trescot House, 1011 Bay, was brought by boat from Barnwell Island by Congressman William Elliott. The English correspondent William Howard Russell, who reported his travels in America just before the war and during the opening stages of the conflict, visited the home when it was on Barnwell Island in April 1861. He arrived at night: "... groping along through a thick shrubbery for a short space, I came out on a garden and enclosure, in the midst of which the white outlines of a house were visible. Lights in the drawing-room—a lady to receive and welcome us—a snug library—tea, and to bed: but not without more talk about the Southern Confederacy, in which Mrs. Trescot explained how easily she could feed an army, from her experience in feeding her Negroes." The house was reerected on Bay St. exactly as it was on Barnwell Island.

William Elliott House, "The Anchorage," 1103 Bay, built before the American Revolution, was used as a hospital during the Civil War and known as the "Mission House." Remodeled in the 1900s, and recently threatened by demolition, it was saved by the Historic Beaufort Foundation.

John A. Cuthbert House, 1203 Bay (ca. 1810), has an interesting legend: Reputedly the house was first located near an unhealthy pond, and the family—after much illness and deaths—had it sawed in half and moved to this site. It was occupied during the war and appears in the diary of Henry Hitchcock, on Sherman's staff. As Sherman marched north from Savannah, he quartered for a day in this "fine large double house on Bay Street, fronting the sea, with a handsome yard, evergreens, etc., in front." Union Brigadier General Rufus Saxton had bought the house, Hitchcock relates, "at one of the U.S. tax sales, and I was told gave $1000 for it. These tax sales—for U.S. direct taxes—are simply a means of confiscation in fee simple...."

Thomas Fuller House, "Tabby Manse," 1211 Bay (1786), still has its original eight rooms, with three paneled in heart pine and cypress. Planter Thomas Fuller married Elizabeth Middleton in the same year

"Tabby Manse," Beaufort, South Carolina. Drawing by George Bauman. (Afterglow Studios)

the house was built. Richard Fuller, one of their seven children, became a Baptist minister and built the Baptist Church in Beaufort and the Brick Church on St. Helena Island.

At 1301 Bay is a pre–Revolutionary War plantation house, relocated by Dr. Benjamin Rhett in mid-19th century. The front door has its original lock; a large wooden bar in iron brackets is inside the door. William Ritchie, a foot soldier from Connecticut, stayed after the Civil War and built the house at 1307 Bay in the 1880s.

John Joyner Smith House, 400 Wilmington St. (ca. 1811), was occupied during part of the Civil War by General Isaac Stevens, who was killed the following year at Chantilly, ending a promising career. The house also was used for a time as a hospital.

The restored **Edward Barnwell House,** 1405 Bay St., a frame structure with an imposing portico and unusually attractive chimneys, was beautifully balanced architecturally when it was built in 1785, but later suffered a strange division. Builder Edward Barnwell, a great-grandson of Indian fighter "Tuscarora" Barnwell, fathered 17 children. Two of the sons who inherited the house built a wooden "spite wall," dividing the building from cellar to attic, and lived on opposite sides. When the house was occupied during the Civil War, federal officers knocked down one of the chimneys to erect a platform from which to signal the navy anchored downriver.

St. Helena's Episcopal Church, 501 Church St., built in 1724, has bricks which came to Beaufort as ballast on English ships.

Bythewood House, 711 Prince St., was the 18th-century home of British merchant Daniel Hingston Bythewood, who owned ships that sailed between the British Isles and the Carolinas. The house, built for his bride Elizabeth Taylor, who persuaded him to give up trade to become a missionary, has original floors, paneling, and hand-carved mantels.

Robert Smalls House, (Henry McKee House), 511 Prince St., has the two-story portico of the Beaufort style, 12-foot ceilings, and 18-paned windows. Smalls was born a slave in a cabin behind the big house, which he bought during the tax sales with funds he received for delivering the Confederate ship *Planter* to the Union Navy. He became a U.S. Congressman in 1865 and is buried in the churchyard of the *Tabernacle Baptist Church.*

Milton Maxcy House got the popular name of "Secession House" because Robert Barnwell Rhett is believed to have drawn up a draft of the Ordinance of Secession in the east room of the house. This Beaufort-style dwelling at 1113 Craven St. was built about 1813. Maxcy founded a boys' school, and sold the building to Edmund Rhett, a brother of the secessionist. Keeping Rhetts and Barnwells straight is a full-time matter. Robert Barnwell Rhett was a U.S. Congressman and later Senator (1851). He became known as a Fireeater in the years just before the war. He served in the Confederate Congress during the conflict. The house

was used as a hospital for a time, and basement walls still have names and drawings made by wounded Union men.

William Fickling House, 1109 Craven, from the early 1800s, was a boys' school taught by Fickling and later owned by a Rhett. John Joyner, grandfather of the John Joyner Smith of Wilmington St., owned a house at 1009 Craven. To add to the confusion, Thomas Rhett lived here before the war. He was one of 17 Smith children who changed their names to honor an ancestor, William Rhett, fearing the family name had died out.

"Woodbine Cottage," at 308 Charles St., like the John A. Cuthbert house, was bought by General Rufus Saxton in 1864 at a U.S. Tax Commission Sale. Saxton was in Beaufort as the first head of the Freedman's Bureau. He seems to have liberated houses from southern ownership at a nice profit for himself, but this was a practice fully approved by his northern peers.

Lucius Cuthbert House, 915 Port Republic St., is Beaufort style from the 1820s, originally one room deep. During the war the house was used as a bakery instead of a hospital. Its owners had fled to Aiken, South Carolina, and never came back.

In the business district, the pre–Revolutionary War building at 920 Bay was once the home of a beautiful daughter of the Murry family who was known as the "Belle of Beaufort." The building has a Classic Revival façade. Parson Weems and John Wesley were among the persons who stayed at the original *John Cross Tavern* at 807–813 Bay; now restored.

John Mark Verdier House, or "Lafayette House," 801 Bay, is 1790s Adam-style. Verdier was a merchant whose ships carried rice, indigo, and Sea Island cotton to England, returning with the best of British goods to enhance the life style of the luckier

Beaufort citizens. The Marquis de Lafayette delayed a welcoming committee here, arriving after dark from Edisto Island, and leaving at midnight for Savannah. Although he never slept here, as Washington might have done, for the benefit of future plaque writters, he apparently was so charming that the house has borne his name ever since. The house has been handsomely restored recently by the Historic Beaufort Foundation with a matching grant from the National Park Service, to re-create the look of the gala time when Lafayette stepped ashore and a sleepy bunch of townspeople came wide awake to greet him with torches and cheers.

Thomas Hepworth House, 214 New St. (ca. 1717), is the oldest dwelling in town. Hepworth was chief justice of the colony. There are piercings in the tabby foundation to hold muskets to be used in case of Yemassee Indian attack, still a likely threat when the house was new. Supposedly a shot fired from a British gunboat during the Revolutionary War went through this house, just missing the owner's wife but killing a luckless horse in front of a church a considerable distance beyond. The Order of the Eastern Star is said to have begun here when a mischievous young woman hiding in a closet heard the secrets of a Masonic meeting. She was caught eavesdropping in a closet and for penalty was made charter member of the new order. Take your pick of stories.

George Stoney House, 500 Port Republic St. (ca. 1830), survived a hurricane in 1898, but the piano on the first floor was set afloat in tidal waters that invaded the house.

Philip Martin Angelo House, 601 Port Republic St. (ca. 1759), stands on land granted to Francis La Basseur in 1717. It was sold at one of the Civil War tax sales in 1863 for $100.

The **Arsenal,** 713 Craven St., built in 1795 on the site of the first court-house, rebuilt in 1852, had its problems during the Civil War when its books were shipped north to be sold. Salmon P. Chase, of Lincoln's cabinet, stopped the sale and had the books sent to the Smithsonian Institution until "the authority of the Union should be re-established in South Carolina." Before the books went south again, many had been destroyed by a Smithsonian fire in 1868. In 1940 Congress finally passed a bill to reimburse Beaufort some $10,000 for their lost library.

Joseph Johnson House, known as "The Castle," 411 Craven St. (ca. 1850), is Greek Revival, with four huge octagonal chimneys and six large octagonal columns supporting double porticos. During the war the house served as a hospital and the building at the back as a morgue.

Another wartime hospital was the **Henry Farmer House,** 412 East St., from the early 1800s. John Bythewood's daughter and her husband, John Bell, lived at 315 Federal St. in antebellum days. In 1863 a former slave bought the house, signing the deed with an "X." The house has been restored.

William Fripp House, "Tidewater," 302 Federal St. (1830), was one of nine homes owned by the wealthy Fripp, a scholar and traveler who was known as "Good Billy Fripp," despite the fact that he owned 313 slaves. This house, too, was sold for taxes after the war.

James Rhett House, 303 Federal, was begun by the optimistic Rhett in 1884 when he was 23, but he ran out of money and the place was called "Rhett's Folly." It is a lovely structure today with a high ground floor, with Beaufort-style arches, wide verandas, and 13-foot ceilings on both floors.

James Robert Verdier House, "Marshlands," 501 Pinckney St., was built about 1814. The U.S. Sanitary Commission had headquarters here during the Union occupation of the town. A Civil War novel, *Sea Island Lady,* by Francis Griswold, had a heroine named Emily who lived at Marshlands.

Paul Hamilton House, "The Oaks," 100 Laurens St., still embellished by the live oaks for which it was named, was built in 1856 by Colonel Hamilton, grandson of Paul Hamilton, Secretary of the Navy under President Madison. The Hamiltons left town when the war came and the house was occupied. When the family returned in a wagon drawn by mules, they reoccupied the house only when the rent was paid by a relative. The house was bought by a George Holmes, a northerner, for Colonel Hamilton when it came up for auction in 1865. On the night following the sale the Hamilton daughter, who had vowed never to shake hands with a Yankee, managed to touch palms with Mr. Holmes.

Edgar Fripp House, "Tidalholm," 1 Laurens St., built in the mid-19th century by a planter from St. Helena's island. It was owned by his brother James when the war began. James returned when the house was being sold for taxes and is said to have watched the proceedings with tears in his eyes. A Frenchman, who had been staying in Beaufort, bought the house, presented it to Fripp, saluted him with a Gallic kiss on both cheeks, and departed.

Hext House, "Riverview," 207 Hancock St., could well bring a tear to the viewer's eye today. It sold in 1864 for $640, and again the U.S. Tax Commission was the seller. The gracious dwelling was once the home of Elizabeth Hext, who at 15 married William Sams of Wadmala Island, a grandson of "Tuscarora" Barnwell, the Indian fighter. In 1783 Sams bought Datha Island, where he and Elizabeth raised a large family and where they are now buried. Elizabeth and her children lived here after her husband died in 1798.

Reverend Henry Ledbetter House,
411 Washington St. (ca. 1805), is an excellent example of Beaufort style, in a river setting with many unusual plantings on the grounds.

Elizabeth Barnwell Gough House, 705 Washington St. (ca. 1789), is a tabby building covered with cement stucco. For those who are trying to follow the Barnwell-Rhett connections, Elizabeth was a granddaughter of "Tuscarora" Barnwell. She married against her family's wishes after the family had sent her to England when she was 20, to forget Richard Gough. Gough followed her and the wedding took place in London in May 1772. The Goughs lived at Goose Creek, where their only child Mariana was born in 1773. After a quarrel Elizabeth took her daughter and returned to Beaufort to live in this house which her family built for her. Mariana (sometimes spelled Marianna) married James Harvey Smith and had six sons who changed their names to Rhett. One of these former Smiths was Robert Barnwell Rhett.

The **Beaufort Chamber of Commerce,** 1006 Bay St., has tour and other information.

CAMDEN, Kershaw County. US 1, 521.

Historic Camden is immediately S of the original townsite. This oldest existing inland town in the state began with orders in 1730 from King George II, who specified that a township be located "on the River Water." Fredericksburg Township was laid out in 1733–34. By 1758 it was known as Pine Tree Hill and Joseph Kershaw came from Charleston to open a store overlooking Pine Tree Creek. He added sawmills and gristmills in in the 1760s. The settlement was named for Charles Pratt (Lord Camden) in 1768.

Most of the early houses were log. Then Joseph Kershaw built a mansion, later known as the Cornwallis House. The **Camden Historical Com-**

mission is carrying on archaeology in the area and reconstructing foundations.

Cunningham House, Wateree St., houses a craftshop with many locally made goods, tour headquarters, and administrative offices. The 1840s house, given to the foundation by the Nicholas Gaffos family, was originally located at Market and DeKalb Sts. The original owner, Mrs. Joseph Cunningham, never lived in it. The *Dogtrot* is a replica; a 10-minute slide show is provided.

The *Craven House,* 816 Mill St., was built in 1789. Craven, an accountant and a bachelor, was left an annuity in Joseph Kershaw's will. Otherwise mystery surrounds him and his one-room house; the last heard of him was in a land title suit in 1817 when he was described as John Craven, "a lunatic." The restored house is furnished with reproduction pieces appropriate to the post-Revolutionary period. Small as the dwelling is, it had a ghost in the 1950s, and a stained ax in the kitchen wall plus a flintlock rifle beneath the barn door. These seem to be associated with a subsequent owner named Henry Cantey, who died young and unexpectedly, sometime before 1842.

The 1800 *Bradley House* is a log dwelling with a sandstone chimney. The log *Drakeford House* was built ca. 1812. Both are now museum houses.

The *Greater Kershaw County Chamber of Commerce,* 700 West DeKalb St., has a booklet and a map for an auto tour of more than 60 historic places here.

Six Confederate generals were born in Camden. The town became a warehouse for the Confederacy, and a hospital and refugee center, during the Civil War. Sherman's troops burned most of the town in February 1865. It is an area as fascinating to readers of Mary Boykin Chesnut's *A Diary from Dixie* as Tara is to Margaret Mitchell fans. Mrs. Chesnut was the wife of James Chesnut, Jr., who served in the U.S. Senate, then became a member of the secession convention and later was an aide to Beauregard and to Jefferson Davis. She brilliantly describes the life of the Confederacy from many of its vantage points, especially, during the early days, at Montgomery and then at Richmond. She never was too content in Camden when all the activity was going on elsewhere, but Mulberry Plantation was her husband's boyhood home. James Chesnut, Sr., also owned plantations named Sandy Hill, Sarsfield, Cool Spring, Knight's Hill, and the Hermitage, all in the Camden area, before the war.

One of the many vivid, if acerbic, descriptions of Mrs. Chesnut's life and times deals with an afternoon at Mulberry, in December 1861, when she writes: "From my window high (I sit here in the library alone a great deal), I see carriages approach. Colonel Chesnut drives a pair of thoroughbreds, beauties, mahogany bays with shining coats and arching necks. It is a pleasure to see Scip drive them up. Tiptop and Princess are their names. Mrs. Chesnut [Mary's mother-in-law] has her carriage horses and a huge family coach for herself, which she never uses. The young ladies have a barouche and their own riding horses. We have a pair, for my carriage; and my husband has several saddle horses. There are always families of the children or grandchildren of the house visiting here, with carriage and horses, nurses and children. [Mary Boykin Chesnut, however, was childless and apparently happily so.] The house is crammed from garret to cellar without intermission. As I sit here writing, I see half a dozen carriages under the shade of the trees, coachmen on their boxes, talking, laughing. Some are 'hookling,' as they call it. They have a bone hook something like a crochet needle, and they hook themselves woolen gloves. Some are reading hymn books or pretending to do so. The small footmen are playing marbles under the trees. A pleasant, empty, easy-going life, if one's heart is at ease."

CHARLESTON, Charleston
County. I-26.

In 1680 the settlement here began as a city-state and was known as Charles Towne. It grew to become the most prosperous city south of Philadelphia, despite plenty of trouble with the French, Spanish, Indians, pirates, and epidemics. The first royal governor arrived in 1730. The Stamp Tax of 1765 aroused the citizens, who refused to allow the stamps to go on sale and sent delegates to a New York convention to join with other colonies in rebelling against the act. The city was captured and occupied by the British in 1780, but peace returned with only minor disturbances until the Civil War began with the firing on Fort Sumter in Charleston harbor, in April 1861. The *Charleston Historic District* has many national landmarks within its boundaries. Today Charleston is like London for historic sightseers. It would take days, or weeks, to see it all. Luckily there are many tours available.

The *Chamber of Commerce,* Lockwood Drive at Municipal Marina, is the oldest city commercial organization in the U.S., organized in 1773. The building was once a rice mill. Brochures for walking or driving tours are available, with maps. Private guides can be hired. There is a *Visitor Center* at 85 Calhoun St., also with tour information. The *Historic Charleston Foundation,* 51 Meeting St., is in the historic *Nathaniel Russell House.* The free-flying staircase which reaches to the third floor without touching the walls is one of the many fine features of the house, which was the home of a northerner, Nathaniel Russell, son of a Rhode Is-

land chief justice, who became "The King of the Yankees" and was president of the Charleston New England Society. One of the projects of the Foundation is the Ansonborough Rehabilitation effort to restore a once prosperous historic district, now in slum condition. More than 135 antebellum houses of architectural value are to be revitalized.

Charles Town Tours, with tapes of walking, driving, or biking tours for rent, are available not only at the Historic Charleston Foundation but at several hotels. Write Box 118, Charleston, 29402, or call (803) 577-2400, or 722-3269.

Gray Line Tours begin at the historical Francis Marion Hotel, King and Calhoun St. Box 219, Charleston, 29402, or (803) 722-4444.

Charleston Carriage Company, 96 Market St., has horse-drawn tours of Old Charleston daily from 10 A.M. until sunset: (803) 722-3269.

Festival of Houses under the direction of the Historic Charleston Foundation is held from mid-March to mid-April; 65 homes are open. There is a fee and advance reservations are recommended.

Among outstanding buildings open most of the year:

Heyward-Washington House, 87 Church St., 1770, was the lodging place rented for President George Washington when he was a guest of the city in 1791. It is a three-story double house, built by Daniel Heyward, a prosperous rice planter. His son Thomas Heyward, Jr., was a delegate to the Continental Congress, a signer of the Declaration of Independence, and a curator of the Charleston Museum, which now owns the house. The kitchen and carriage house are in the courtyard behind the main house. There is also a formal 18th-century garden.

Dock Street Theatre, Planters Hotel, 135 Church St., is a reconstructed theater. The original building in 1736 was the first erected solely for use as a playhouse. The hotel was built around the theater site after 1809.

There are a number of churches not to be missed, including *St. Philip's* (1838), at 144 Church St., with a steeple that was fired upon by the Union Navy; *Huguenot Church,* of 1845, at 138 Church St., the third to be built at this site; and *St. Michael's* (1752) at Meeting and Broad Sts. The four-faced clock in St. Michael's tower has been telling time since 1764. *St. Mary's,* 93 Hasell St., between King and Meeting Sts., was built in 1838. The *Unitarian Church,* 8 Archdale St., was erected in 1772 and may have been used as a stable for British horses in the Revolutionary period; restored in 1962. *Kahal Kadosh Beth Elohim,* 90 Hasell St., was founded in 1749; the 1840 building is the second-oldest synagogue building in America. *St. John's Lutheran Church,* Archdale and Clifford Sts., built in 1817, has a restored interior.

Joseph Manigault House, 350 Meeting St., is an 1803 Adam-style building. Gabriel Manigault, brother of Joseph, who designed the house, was a merchant, rice planter, and amateur architect, had collected a fine library on architecture and was in a sense the first Charleston architect when he made the plans which were used for this house.

Boone Hall Plantation, 7 miles N on Long Point Rd. in Mount Pleasant, is a 738-acre estate. The mansion was renovated in 1935. Of historical interest only and far less pleasant to view than the Avenue of Oaks is the "slave street," which has nine original houses built for the house servants. The field slaves lived in small cottages elsewhere on the plantation. There were about 1,000 field hands.

Middleton Place, 15 miles N on St. 61, built in 1755, is now a house museum, with America's oldest landscaped gardens; the first plantings were in 1741. NHL. Henry Middleton, president of the First Continental Congress, began the gardens with the help of an English landscape architect and about 100 workmen. His son, Arthur, a signer of the Declaration of Independence, inherited his father's interest in the gardens. The Middleton Oak is thought to be about 1,000 years old. The stable yards, old rice mill, the springhouse, and ruins of the original Henry Middleton home, which was burned in the Civil War, are on view. The restored south wing of the early house is now a private residence. A section of tabby wall has been preserved. The plantation office is now a gift shop and the plantation kitchen is a restaurant.

COLUMBIA, Richland County. I-26, US 378.

The first General Assembly met here in January 1790. Washington was a visitor the following year. In December 1860 the Ordinance of Secession was drawn up at the First Baptist Church. In February 1865, General W. T. Sherman occupied the city, and on February 18 a disastrous fire swept the town. Except for the unfinished State House and the French consulate, no antebellum buildings were still standing on Main St. By some accounts, 84 blocks and nearly 1,400 buildings were destroyed.

Columbia Historic District I is bounded by Laurel, Gadsden, Calhoun, and Park Sts.; the area is known as *Arsenal Hill,* with the *Governor's Mansion,* 800 Richland St., as focal point. The house, built in 1855, extensively renovated in the 1960s, was originally intended for officers' quarters for the Arsenal Academy and was the only important Academy building to survive the 1865 fire; it became the governor's house in 1868. There is a 30-minute guided tour. Also within the district are:

The *Lace House,* 803 Richland St., opposite the Governor's Mansion, was built in 1854. The name comes from the elaborate ornamental cast-iron trimmings on the two-story veranda and the fencing, a photographer's delight.

Caldwell-Hampton-Boylston House, 829 Richland St. a three-story Greek Revival, was built in the 1820s.

Columbia Historic District II, Taylor, Blanding, Marion, Sumter, Richland, Calhoun, Bull, Pickens, and Henderson Sts. **Robert Mills House** and park, 1616 Blanding St., houses the Historic Columbia Foundation. Robert Mills was the designer for most of the historic houses in this old residential section. He designed the building but did not live here.

An excellent description of Columbia in the 1820s written for the Historic Columbia Foundation tells of the live oak and pride-of-India trees being planted along unpaved streets which were dusty in dry weather and muddy the rest of the time. The streets were named for Revolutionary generals: Continental generals west of Assembly, which was intended to be the main north–south thoroughfare, and South Carolina militia generals east of Assembly, "with Laurens and Roberts thrown in as deserving heroes of lesser rank." Four stage lines were in business, leaving from Gervais St., opposite the State House, for Charleston, Augusta, and Camden three times a week, and once a week to Greenville, where the coaches connected with another line which crossed the Alleghenies to Knoxville, Tennessee. A ferry operated across the river until a bridge was built at the foot of Gervais in 1827.

The Robert Mills House was built in 1823 for Ainsley Hall, an Englishman who became a Columbia merchant. A few years earlier Hall had built the house across the street (the **Hampton-Preston Mansion**) and was living there only a short time when Wade Hampton I persuaded him to sell the house with its furnishings for his third wife, Mary Cantey Hampton. Ainsley Hall promised his own wife Sarah a finer house on the four acres across the street and commissioned Robert Mills to design the new home. Hall died before the house was finished and his widow sold it to the Columbia Theological Seminary; it was never used as a residence, but is now restored as a house museum, furnished in keeping with the period to reflect an Englishman's home in Columbia as it might have been. Robert Mills, appointed by President Andrew Jackson to be the first federal architect, retained the federal position under seven administrations.

Hampton-Preston House, 1615 Blanding St., has been restored and contains many original furnishings. For 50 years the house was occupied by members of the illustrious Hampton family. Wade Hampton I was a Virginian by birth who was reluctant to fight against the British in the Revolutionary War but who became a general in the War of 1812. Two wives died fairly young, but his third wife, Mary Cantey, outlived the general by 30 years and occupied this house until her death in 1863. Their daughter Caroline, who inherited the house, married John Preston, a wealthy Virginian. Their daughter Sarah Buchanan Campbell Preston was known as "Buck" and is one of the many fascinating young women written about by the perceptive Mrs. Mary Boykin Chesnut in *A Diary from Dixie.* At one time during the war years, when James Chesnut was away and his diarist wife was staying with the Prestons here, she wrote of a dinner party:

"General Hampton and Blanton Duncan were there also; the latter a thoroughly free-and-easy Western man, handsome and clever; more audacious than either, perhaps. He pointed to Buck—Sally Buchanan Campbell Preston. 'What's that girl laughing at?' Poor child, how

The Hampton-Preston Mansion, Columbia, South Carolina. (Historic Columbia Foundation)

amazed she looked. He bade them 'not despair; all the nice young men would not be killed in the war; there would be a few left.'" Buck was courted by General John Bell Hood, and some friends said she was throwing her life away to marry a maimed man (he had lost his right leg at Chickamauga, and had a crippled left arm from the Battle of Gettysburg), but others said, "She will love him fourfold for his honorable wounds." When President Jefferson Davis visited Columbia in October 1864, he spoke well of Hood, and Mrs. Chesnut duly noted: "While Jeff Davis stood up for her General, Buck said she would kiss him for that, and she did, he all the while smoothing her down the back from the shoulders as if she were a ruffled dove." The romance ended, however. Buck went abroad to forget the war in August of 1865. Hood married in 1868, in New Orleans, had 11 children in ten years, and died, with his wife and eldest daughter, of yellow fever in 1878.

When Sherman occupied the city this house served as headquarters, and was not burned. A group of Ursuline Sisters moved in to use the dwelling as a temporary convent.

Now restored to the look of the 1850s, it is operated by the Historic Columbia Foundation.

Woodrow Wilson Boyhood Home, 1705 Hampton St., restored as of the 1870s, contains original furnishings. The 1872 building is Tuscan Villa style. Operated by the Historic Columbia Foundation.

Chesnut Cottage, 1718 Hampton St., built before the Civil War, is a small Neoclassical house, adapted for southern living. Confederate General James Chesnut and his wife Mary lived here intermittently in the Civil War years.

Greater Columbia Chamber of Commerce, 1308 Laurel, has an information center. There are a number of houses on the National Register and many historic gardens in the area.

PENDLETON, Anderson County. US 76, 123.

Pendleton Historic District, Anderson, Oconee, and Pickens counties, was Cherokee Indian country until the American Revolution. The town of Pendleton was the county seat of the Pendleton District in the early 19th century. Situated at the crossroads of the Cherokee Trading Path into the low country of the Carolinas and the Catawba Path to Virginia, the town, which had been laid out in 1790, developed into a center of activity for the area. The **Historical and Recreational Commission Headquarters** are in the **Hunter's Store,** 125 E. Queen St. There are brochures, tape tours for walking or driving, and a craftshop.

Ashtabula Plantation, St. 88, built ca. 1830, has been restored, and is operated by the Foundation for Historic Preservation. Furnishings are of the early 19th century to midcentury.

Fort Hill, on Clemson University campus, was the home of Vice-President John C. Calhoun from 1825 until 1850, and the home of his son-in-law, Thomas Green Clemson, from 1872 until 1888. Clemson deeded the house to the state for an agricultural college. It has been restored by the United Daughters of the Confederacy and Clemson University. Family possessions are among the furnishings.

Hanover House, also on the campus, was moved from Berkeley County in the low country, where it was built in 1716, and restored as an 18th-century house museum at Clemson University in 1941, by the Spartanburg Committee of the National Society of Colonial Dames. It was once the home of a French Huguenot, Paul St. Julien.

Caldwell-Johnson-Morris House, Manning and Morris Sts. (1850), has been restored and is operated by Anderson Heritage. One of its owners was Dr. William B. Johnson, chancellor of the Johnson Female Academy and the first president of the Southern Baptist Convention.

The *Pickens County Art and History Museum,* Johnson and Pendleton Sts., was once the county jail. *Hagood Corn Mill,* US 178, an 1825 mill with an overshot wheel, is restored, with water-ground meal for sale.

In Pendleton, fronting on the village green, the *Pendleton Farmers Society Hall* was intended for a courthouse in 1826, but the district was divided that year and the farmers' society completed the hall; it is the oldest of its kind in America. *St. Paul's Episcopal Church,* 1822, still has original furnishings. Among the graves in the churchyard are those of

Mrs. John C. Calhoun, Thomas Green Clemson, Francis Burt, first governor of Nebraska, and General Barnard E. Bee, a veteran of the Mexican War who made the famous statement at the Battle of Bull Run (First Manassas) that Jackson's brigade was standing like a stone wall. Bee was mortally wounded and died the next day.

Woodburn, about 1½ miles W at the end of Woodburn Rd., was the 19th-century summer home of Charles Cotesworth Pinckney. It has a two-story veranda across the front. Pinckney was a lieutenant governor of the state.

Stumphouse Tunnel Park, St. 28, 5 miles N of Walhalla in Oconee County, is only one of the many curious sites maintained by the Pendleton District Historical and Recreational Commission. If the name stumps you, it comes from a tunnel for the Stumphouse railroad, which was begun in 1853 but never finished.

Old Stone Church, US 76, between Pendleton and Clemson, was begun in 1797, completed in 1802. The Episcopal Church sent the Reverend Rodolphus Dickinson of Massachusetts to Pendleton to lead the congregation. The official name was Hopewell, but it was always known as the Old Stone Church or Stone Meeting House. The fieldstone building was put up by John Rusk, a Revolutionary veteran. It has now been restored.

GEORGIA

St. Simon's Island, Sunday, March 17th, 1839.... Art never devised more perfect combinations of form and color than these wild woods present, with their gigantic growths of evergreen oak, their thickets of myrtle and magnolia, their fantastic undergrowth of spiked palmetto, and their hanging draperies of jessamine.... I inhabit a house where the staircase is open to the roof, and the roof... presents... the seamy side of the tiles, or rather wooden shingles, with which the house is covered.... Every door in the house is fastened with wooden latches and pack-thread, the identical device of Red Riding-hood antiquity....
— *Records of Later Life,* by Frances Ann Kemble, New York, 1882

Savannah, December 25, 1864.... I am at this moment in an elegant chamber of the house of a gentleman named Green. This house is elegant and splendidly furnished with pictures and statuary. My bed room has a bath and dressing room attached which look out of proportion to my poor baggage.
— *Home Letters of General Sherman,* New York, 1909

ATHENS, Clarke County. US 29, 78.

Chamber of Commerce, 155 E. Washington St., offers a number of walking tours of the town which grew from a settlement in 1800 at Cedar Shoals where an old Cherokee trail crossed the Oconee River. The *Athens-Clarke Heritage Foundation,* 280 E. Dougherty St. in the *Church-Waddel-Brumby House* of the 1820s, has a welcome center and conducts annual tours. The house has been restored and furnished in period.

Dearing Street Historic District is roughly bounded by Broad and Baxter Sts. and Milledge Ave., and includes Finley St. and Henderson Ave.

Wilkins House, 387 S. Milledge, built in 1860 by Alfred L. Dearing, later owned by Professor Leon Charbonier, has been remodeled and is on the National Register. *A. P. Dearing House,* 338 S. Milledge, 1856, has white Doric columns around three sides and is considered one of the classic Greek Revival houses in America. Many fine homes on Milledge Ave. have been restored but are occupied by sororities and fraternities.

Cobb-Erwin House, 126 Dearing, was begun in 1828 by Addison Cobb for his sister, who had just married William H. Jackson, son of Governor James Jackson. In 1832, Malthus Ward, professor of natural history and curator of the University Garden, bought the house and created a fine garden on the adjoining hillside with rare specimens which included ginkgo trees, which still are standing. Ward enlarged the house, probably in the 1850s.

Lucy Cobb Institute Campus, 200

131

N. Milledge Ave., is a two-building complex. The brick stuccoed three-story institute building of 1858 has a gabled center section, flanked by wings, and a full-width, 100-foot veranda with cast iron railing. The *Seney-Stovall Chapel* dates from 1882. The girl students were asked to write to leading philanthropists to request funds for a chapel. Miss Nellie G. Stovall wrote the gift-winning letter to George Seney of New York.

General Howell Cobb House, 698 Pope St., was built in 1835. Howell Cobb brought his bride, Mary Ann Lamar, here. Cobb, a statesman, earned many honors in his career: he was speaker of the 31st Congress, governor of Georgia in 1851–53, a Secretary of the Treasury under Buchanan, president of the Confederate Congress in 1861, and became a major general. He was a lawyer and a planter after the war.

Cobb-Bucknell House, 425 Hill St., mid-19th-century Greek Revival, was the second Athens home of General Howell Cobb.

Moss-Side, 479 Cobb St., 1838, was the birthplace of William Lorenzo Moss, one of two men who simultaneously discovered the technique for typing blood. The Moss family moved here in 1861.

Sledge-Cobb House, 749 Cobb St., built about 1860, has interior walls of solid brick and a cast-iron veranda. James A. Sledge edited the *Southern Banner.* Mrs. Lamar Cobb, first president of the Ladies Garden Club, lived here later.

E. K. Lumpkin House, 973 Prince, begun in 1858 by General Robert Taylor and finished by Richard S. Taylor, has lacy ironwork on the front veranda and has been restored. The world's first garden club was organized in the front parlor by Mary Bryan Thomas Lumpkin and 12 friends.

Taylor-Grady House, 634 Prince Ave., was built in 1839 by General Robert Taylor, who didn't live to finish the Lumpkin house. Thirteen Doric columns on three sides of the house are said to represent the thirteen original colonies bound by the Union as the columns are by the handsome iron railing. Henry Woodfin Grady, journalist and orator, edited the Atlanta *Constitution* in the 1880s. The Henry Grady School of Journalism at the university is named for him. The house, restored by the Athens Junior Assembly, has been furnished in period; now owned by the city. NHL.

The *University President's House,* 570 Prince Ave., built in 1857–58 by John Thomas Grant, a Virginian, is Greek Revival with 14 Corinthian columns around three sides. Doric columns across the back face a 9-acre garden. In 1869 the house was owned by Benjamin H. Hill, a Georgia statesman who became a U.S. Congressman and Senator. Hill was graduated first in his class from the university in 1844. He was a unionist, but when secession came he did not want division at home and voted with his fellow southerners. He served in the Confederate Senate during the war. In 1872 he actually supported Horace Greeley for the presidency. He served in the U. S. Senate from 1877 until his death in 1882. The gardens have been restored.

Old North Campus Historic District begins at the Arch on Broad St. at the foot of College Ave. *Demosthenian Hall* was completed in 1824. The Greek Revival–style *Chapel* was built at a cost of $15,000 in 1832. *New College* was first built in 1822–23, burned in 1830, and rebuilt in 1832. *Old College* dates from 1801–5 and was the first permanent building on campus. It is patterned after Connecticut Hall at Yale. (Early presidents of the university were from Yale.)

In the long-gone days, planters' sons and other privileged students used to bring their body servants with them. Little cells were made for their sleeping quarters by partitioning off the main sleeping rooms. Alexander H. Stephens and Crawford W. Long were roommates here in 1832—a plaque on the north side of the building indicates which room they occupied. Stephens was the son of a merchant's clerk, but a benefactor helped him to attend Franklin College (which became the University of Georgia), and he was graduated first in his class. He became a U.S. Representative, and was a Union delegate to the Georgia secession convention, but he signed the Ordinance and became Vice-President of the Confederacy in February 1861. A number of years after the war he again served in the U.S. House and in 1882–83 became governor of Georgia. The building is now used by the administration; the office of the university president is here.

Founder's Memorial Gardens, Lumpkin St., on campus, the Garden Club of Georgia headquarters, was built in 1857 for a university professor. The original kitchen and smokehouse still stand. The house has been retored and furnished in period. The formal garden is surrounded by a serpentine brick wall.

Governor Wilson Lumpkin House, Cedar St., South Campus, was against the current trend in 1842 when the governor decided to build his home to resemble an old millhouse at Cedar Shoals instead of a classic mansion. He was a Virginian who came to Georgia with his father and studied law, after a common school education. In 1823 President Monroe appointed him to mark the boundary between Georgia and Florida, and in 1835 General Jackson appointed him a commissioner under the Cherokee treaty. He was also a U.S. Senator. The house, high on a hill overlooking the Oconee River, has a matchless view of the town. Lumpkin's daughter, Martha Atalanta Lumpkin Compton, had the same city named for her twice. Atlanta (with the *a* dropped) was first called Marthasville.

ATLANTA, Fulton County. US 41, 278.

Chamber of Commerce, 1300 Commerce Bldg., and *Convention & Visitors Bureau,* 229 Peachtree St., have information on auto and walking tours. On the grounds of the *Atlanta Historical Society,* 3099 Andres Drive, N.W., is the restored *Tullie Smith House,* an 1840 farmhouse with a slave cabin and other outbuildings and gardens; open daily except January and holidays.

Stone Mountain Park, 16 miles E on US 78, has a restored antebellum plantation complex, with period furnishings.

Martin Luther King Jr. Historic District, bounded by Irwin, Randolph, Edgewood, Jackson, and Auburn Aves., is a commercial and residential area which includes the birthplace and gravesite of Rev. Dr. King, assassinated Civil Rights leader and Nobel Prize winner. Many shotgun-row houses are typical of those rented to blacks in the early 20th century. A Center for Social Change is planned for the area.

Inman Park, a suburban residential area on the National Register, has houses of the 1890–1910 period and is an area undergoing restoration; other active areas of restoration are the *West End, Midtown,* and *Ansley Park.* West End has antebellum to High Victorian homes. It grew up around the White Hall Tavern, once a stagecoach stop long before the city of Atlanta was founded. The richest part of town in the 1880s, it fell on shabby days, but since 1966 more than 1,000 buildings have been restored and parks have been constructed. Peeples St. has brick sidewalks, gas lamps, and well-tended houses and lawns. *Wren's Nest,* 1050 Gordon St., S.W., was the 19th-century home of Joel Chandler

Harris, a journalist and author of the Uncle Remus tales. NHL.

Inman Park was developed as an English garden suburb but became a slum section and has lately been restored by individuals. There is an annual spring tour of houses. Midtown was developed in the early part of this century. Lately the Midtown Association has been formed to bring back the area with newly-planted trees and landscaping, newly-painted houses, and polished hardware.

CALHOUN, Gordon County. US 41, just W of I-75.

New Echota, 3 miles NE on St. 225, was capital of the Cherokee Nation in 1825–28. Among the authentically furnished buildings is a reconstructed printing office with a handpress like the one first used for the *Cherokee Phoenix,* the first newspaper in Indian language. The shop also turned out handbills, a Moravian hymnal, and parts of the Bible translated into Cherokee. Also on the 220-acre tract are a reconstructed Supreme Court Building, the Vann Tavern, moved a short distance from where it was erected in 1805, the Worcester House (1827), and a museum-orientation center.

When gold was discovered in the region, the Cherokees were forced to move. It was a sad time in American history, but New Echota, where the Trail of Tears began, is a memorial to a proud and talented Cherokee Nation.

The village is open daily except Mondays and major holidays.

CHICKAMAUGA, Walker County. US 27.

Gordon-Lee House, Cover Rd., is a beautifully restored antebellum mansion, built in 1847 by James Gordon in Greek Revival style, with giant Doric columns. It furnishes an impressive view at the end of the oak-lined drive which is no longer used by any but foot traffic. The house was used as a hospital during the Civil War. General William Rosecrans, in the fall of 1863, ordered the Gordons to leave the main house, which he then occupied. James Garfield, later to become president, was stationed here as the General's Chief of Staff. The library became an operating room. When the fortunes of war temporarily turned, the Confederates retook the house and returned it to the Gordons. The house is now on the National Register. Tours are held from June through Labor Day. Closed on Mondays.

The village of Chickamauga has undergone a change as well. During postwar years James Lee, head of a land company, patriotically laid out the streets with names of generals who had fought here. The town itself was known as Crawfish Spring. Hard times came and the village declined. In the 1970s the local garden club began to restore the railroad station and soon local merchants were following their lead. The look now is of the 1890s, and is handsomely maintained. The *Longstreet's Charge Restaurant* now overlooks historic Crawfish Springs and serves superb southern-style cooking.

Nine buildings and sites have been nominated for the National Register. The First General Store, the Presbyterian Church, and the Depot are among the historic structures.

COLUMBUS, Muscogee County. US 80, 280, 27.

Columbus Historic District, between 8th, 4th, 3rd, and the river, has much restoration and preservation work going on. There are brick streets, fine old trees, and more than 600 structures ranging from Greek Revival and Gothic Revival to cottages. This part of town was surveyed in 1828. *Georgia Welcome Center,* on US 27, US 280, has tour information. *Heritage Tours,* conducted by the Junior League, leave here twice weekly.

700 Broadway, Columbus, Georgia. (Historic Columbus Foundation)

Among the historic buildings on tour: *Springer Opera House,* 103 10th St., established in 1871 by Francis J. Springer, had many famous entertainers on its boards: Edwin Booth, Joseph Jefferson, Oscar Wilde, George M. Cohan, and many more. Vacant after 1959, it was in danger of demolition but was saved by public action and reopened in 1965. A second phase of restoration completed in 1976 included an enlarged Museum Room.

Walkers-Peters-Langdon House, 716 Broadway, now headquarters of the Historic Columbus Foundation, is considered the oldest standing dwelling in town. It was built in 1838 on Lot 138, on the original town survey made by Edward Lloyd Thomas, and sold for $105 to landowner Virgil Walker, whose plantation is still in Harris County. The house has period furnishings and outbuildings moved from other early homes, to make up—with the gardens—the typical surroundings of a town house.

Rankin House, 1440 2nd Ave., was begun before the Civil War, completed afterward. James Rankin was a planter and merchant who came to Georgia from Scotland. The house is French Empire with wrought-iron trim. The first floor has been restored

as a house museum of the 1850–70s by the Junior League.

Pemberton House, 11 7th St., owned by the Historic Columbus Foundation, was occupied by Dr. John Styth Pemberton from 1855 to 1860. Styth originated the Coca-Cola formula. His kitchen-apothecary shop is adjoining and also open to the public. *Illges House,* 1428 2nd Ave. (ca. 1850), is southern Greek Revival, with six Corinthian columns and flying balcony, wrought-iron trim. *Wynnwood,* 1846 Buena Vista Rd. (1834), has wings added in 1868. Century-old boxwood in the formal garden forms the outline of a butterfly.

Tours for all of the above leave the Welcome Center Wednesdays 10 A.M., Sundays 3 P.M. and take two hours by bus. Fees vary.

Chamber of Commerce, 1344 13th Ave., 31902. (404-327-1566), has self-guiding tour maps (also available at the Welcome Center).

Inquire at the *Historic Columbus Foundation,* 716 Broadway, 31906 (see Walkers-Peters-Langdon entry above) for an excellent booklet, *Historic Preservation in Columbus, Georgia,* which was prepared for the Bicentennial and has a complete list of historic houses and many photographs, histories, and descriptions. Mrs. James J. W. Biggers, Jr., executive director of the Foundation, was chairman of the committee responsible for the publication. Call (404) 322-0756. Or write Box 5312.

Hamilton-on-the-Square, 25 miles N of town on US 27, is an authentically restored village town square, with museums, country stores, antique shops, etc.

DAHLONEGA, Lumpkin County. St. 60.

Gold Hills of Dahlonega, St. 60 just ½ mile S of the town square, is a recreated gold rush town where visitors can pan for gold (or pan out). *Courthouse Gold Museum,* on the square, has relics from the rush which began in 1828. Ten years later a branch of the U. S. Mint was here, and more than $6 million in Georgia gold was coined in the next 23 years. The museum is owned and operated by the Department of Natural Resources. Hours vary with season; always closed Mondays.

LUMPKIN, Stewart County. US 280, 27.

Westville, S of town at US 27 and St. 27, a re-created rural village of the 1850s with authentic buildings moved to the site, restored, furnished, and period, is a living-history center. Working craftsmen demonstrate old trades such as brickmaking and basketmaking, even accomplishments such as guitar-picking. Open daily except major holidays.

Bedingfield Inn, on the town square, is a restored and furnished 1835 stagecoach inn. Guided tours. Open daily June to Labor Day. Also on the grounds is a hand-hewn log dogtrot house.

MACON, Bibb County. US 80.

Macon Historic District contains many commercial, civic, and residential structures in the heart of the original town area. *Greek Revival City Hall,* Cotton Ave. at Poplar St., was built in 1836 and served as state capitol briefly in 1864–65. The College Hill section has Greek Revival mansions, some Victorian houses, and Tatnall Square Park. The grid plan of 1823 was prepared by James Bibb.

Chamber of Commerce, 640 1st St., and the *Tourist Center,* 15 miles N on I-75, have self-guiding maps or will arrange tours for a fee. There are some 47 listings of historical structures or sites that are on the National Register. A map would be useful, indeed essential, for the serious history hunter.

Among highlights: *Johnston-Hay House,* 934 Georgia Ave., a 24-room Italian Renaissance house packed with rare furnishings. There are 19 marble mantels and a secret room in the dwelling, which was buit in the 1850s. Scarce, these days, is the kind of ceiling plasterwork found in the high ceilings, and also rare is the 50-foot ballroom with a skylight. The owner was superstitious and left the house unfinished, as he believed he would die if the last nail were driven. He left one piece of iron fencing unhung and possibly gave St. Peter an argument when he arrived at the Pearly Gates despite his precautions. Hours vary; inquire locally.

Cannon Ball House, 856 Mulberry St., 1853, was the home of Judge Asa Holt. The Greek Revival house was hit by a cannonball during the battle of Dunlap Hill in 1864. Museum.

Grand Opera House, Academy of Music, 651 Mulberry St., 1884, has a brick seven-story front, a five-story rear section, and an auditorium with about 2,500 seats, balconies, boxes, and an enormous stage, all with gilt trim and ornate fixings. It suffered a change when a new office building was constructed there in 1905, but has been restored to its 1884 elegance.

Sidney Lanier Cottage, 935 High St., built about 1840, in Gothic Revival style, was the poet's birthplace. Open, but inquire locally for hours.

MADISON, Morgan County. US 129, 441, 278.

Madison Historic District comprises a village of fine Greek Revival and Victorian homes of the 19th century, and was a center for cotton planters. The *Nathan Bennett House,* Dixie Ave., was built in 1850 with Italianate elements. An argument that arose when the owner's husband lost the house during a poker game contributed to the change of state laws, permitting women to own property. *Bonar Hall,* Dixie Ave., 1832, was built for John Byne Walker, a wealthy cotton planter. *Presbyterian Church,* S. Main, early

1800s, has Tiffany windows and a silver Communion service which was stolen during the Civil War and returned later. *Casulon Plantation* (inquire locally for directions), was a 10,000 acre site with a manor house and, now with 16 acres, is being restored and open to the public. Lecture tours are arranged through the Morgan County Historical Society. The *Chamber of Commerce* has a map for a walking tour. To inquire in advance: zip 30650.

MILLEDGEVILLE, Baldwin County. US 441.

Milledgeville Historic District covers the town planned in 1803 as state capital and includes a beautiful residential area with Greek Revival dwellings and a Gothic Revival gateway and reconstructed statehouse. Some business structures in the district are Italianate and Georgian Revival. *Old State Capitol (Georgia Military College),* Greene St., is a reconstruction of the 1807 building destroyed by fire in 1941. The former *Governor's Mansion,* 120 S. Clark St., 1838, is now occupied by the president of Georgia College. Period furnishings. Guided tours, except Mondays. Atkinson Hall, on the college campus, is Neoclassical Revival in style and dates from 1896.

SAVANNAH, Chatham County. I-16.

Savannah Historic District, bounded by E. Broad St., West Broad St., Gaston St., and the Savannah River, is one of America's best areas for walking tours. James Oglethorpe's plan for Savannah was something new for the 18th-century colonies, and much of it has been retained, along with many structures put up from 1816 to 1822 from the plans of English architect William Jay. There are 20 parks and squares in the historic section. The district, about 2½ square miles, is the nation's largest urban registered National Historic Landmark. A main feature is the overall restoration of the riverfront, with cobblestone streets and old cotton warehouses now occupied by shops, restaurants, and pubs.

Savannah Visitors Center and *Chamber of Commerce,* 301 W. Broad St., P. O. Box 530, 31402—(912) 233-3067, or 233-6651—are in the former Central of Georgia Railroad Station (1860), elegantly restored, with hostesses, an orientation slide program, and plenty of information about tours. The Visitors Center is open daily except Christmas. NHL.

The historic city, founded by James Oglethorpe and 120 settlers in February 1733, may be seen on foot, by bike, auto, guided bus or tram, self-guiding or with cassettes for driving, walking, and bicycling. For information on *Tours on Tape,* write 17 Price St., 31401; or call (912) 234-9992. *Historic Savannah Foundation Tours,* Box 1733; call 233-3597. *Savannah Scenic Tours, Inc.,* 1113 Winston Ave.; call 355-4296. *Georgia Week,* with many open-house tours, begins about February 12; *Homes and Gardens Tours,* co-sponsored by the *Christ Episcopal Church* and *Historic Savannah Foundation,* has daylight and candlelight tours of more than 20 historic dwellings, museums, or gardens in late March and early April. Write *Tour Headquarters,* 18 Abercorn St., 31401.

A sentimental first stop for anyone might be the *Oglethorpe Bench* on Bay St., half a block E of City Hall, where the settlers pitched their tents on February 12, 1733, after the voyage from Gravesend, England.

Among the beautiful squares: *Johnson Square,* Bull St. between Bay and Congress, is the first which formed the pattern of Oglethorpe's innovative plan and was named for Robert Johnson, governor of South Carolina, who was helpful to the colonists. In early days the church, the house for strangers, the public bake oven, and stores surrounded the area.

The Riverfront Plaza, Savannah, Georgia. (Savannah Area Convention and Visitors Bureau)

Revolutionary hero Nathanael Greene is buried here. **Wright Square,** Bull St. between York and State, named for the last colonial governor, Sir James Wright, has a boulder which honors Tomo-chi-chi, the Yamacraw Indian chief who was friendly to Oglethorpe and the colonists and is buried here. **Chippewa Square,** Bull St. between Perry and Hull, has a Daniel Chester French statue of Oglethorpe.

The **Andrew Low House,** 329 Abercorn St., was built by Low, a cotton merchant whose son William married Juliette Gordon, later a founder of the Girl Scouts of America. The house, built about 1848, is stuccoed brick with ironwork railings on the front and side balconies. There is a brick-walled garden in the rear. William Makepeace Thackeray was a guest here on two lecture tours to America in the 1850s. General Robert E. Lee also was a guest, in April 1870.

In March of 1853, when Thackeray was in Savannah to speak to the Literary Society of Young Men, he complained about his hotel quarters and was invited to stay with Andrew Low. In a letter home he wrote he had the best two nights' sleep he'd had for "many a long day." He added, "Mr. Andrew Low is my host here, and we have struck up a kindness because he has 2 daughters in Europe: whom he goes to see every year. He is a widower. . . . I enjoyed the quiet all yesterday inexpressibly, lolling about the house all day, reading, smoking, yawning. It is the first quiet day I have had in the States. . . . I read in the papers of snow twelve inches thick falling in New England, here all windows open, peach trees in most lubly blossom; leaves coming out, fish salad for dinner . . . a friendly pretty little place; and Mr. Low my host has made me . . . as comfortable as mortal man could be—in such hot weather." Now houses the National Society of the Colonial Dames of America in the State of Georgia.

The **Davenport House,** 324 E. State St. on Columbia Square, built in the early 19th century, is a fine example of late Georgian style, with an elliptical stairway and handsome ironwork. Isaiah Davenport, its owner, was a leading builder. Headquarters of the Historic Savannah Foundation are here.

Owens-Thomas House, 124 Abercorn St., was designed by William Jay. In 1825 General Lafayette was a guest here. The house is Regency in style. The basement was that of a house which was built here in the mid-18th century. The kitchen has been restored. There is a formal garden in the rear. NHL.

Juliette Gordon Low House, 10 Oglethorpe Ave. E., being a corner house, is also listed as 142 Bull St. It is a restored Regency house, reputedly designed by William Jay, built in 1818–21, and was the birthplace of Mrs. Low. Many family possessions are among the furnishings. NHL. The old stable has been converted into lodgings for visiting Girl Scouts. The ***Girl Scout National Center*** is here. When Juliette Low was a girl she could sometimes strike sparks faster than a Boy Scout could do with his two sticks of dry wood. When General Oliver Otis Howard was visiting the house in 1865 after the city had fallen to Sherman's forces, Juliette is supposed to have looked at his empty sleeve (he lost his right arm at Seven Pines) and snapped: "I shouldn't wonder if my papa *did it!* He has shot lots of Yankees." General Sherman was a guest here several times. Juliette's mother was Nellie Kinzie Gordon, of Chicago, but was pro-Confederate and did her best to help southerners.

Green-Meldrim House, 14 West Macon St., built in 1852, was Sherman's headquarters in December 1864. It was not a happy time for him despite the victory for the Union. While he was here he learned that his seventh child, a son he had never seen, had died of pneumonia. He spent a lonely New Year's Eve writing home from this house. It is now the Parish House of St. John's Church. NHL.

The ***Olde Pink House,*** 23 Abercorn St., built in 1771, housed the state's first bank in 1812. The Georgian-style structure now contains a restaurant.

Telfair Academy of Arts and Sciences, W. State and Barnard Sts., was built before 1820 by William Jay. NHL.

William Scarbrough House, 41 W. Broad St., built by William Jay in 1818–19, remodeled sometime before the midcentury, was restored in 1969. It is English Regency; Scarbrough was a wealthy merchant.

Factors' Walk, along the river bluff on Bay St., was the meeting place for the cotton merchants in the 19th century. The cobblestone streets were made from stone used as ballast in ships from abroad. Antique street-lamps still are in use.

The riverfront has a new look as centuries-old warehouses and shipping offices have been refurbished in a $7 million project to restore the area where James Edward Oglethorpe and his colonists first arrived. When completed, this will be the largest urban-designed Historic Landmark District in America (until some other city comes up with a larger one).

THOMASVILLE, Thomas County. US 84.

Thomasville Historic District covers the section bounded by North Blvd., Loomis, Hansell, and Oak Sts. The town, established as the county seat in 1826, became a fashionable wintering place after the Civil War. Six major resort hotels had been built by 1888. ***Thomasville Landmarks, Inc.,*** is preserving the Victorian architecture and is even saving the brick paving. The group, organized as a nonprofit educational venture, has saved some major historic structures, encouraged restoration and renovation in the whole area, and a number of places are now individually listed on the National Register; also all of S. Hansell St. has been preserved.

The annual historic tour takes in 24 points of interest. For information write Thomasville Landmarks, Inc., P.O. Box 1285, 31792; or phone (912) 226-6016.

The most historic road in the county is ***Old Coffee Rd.,*** which opened in 1823 as a postal and travel route from the Ocmulgee River through Barwick and Thomasville to the Florida state line.

Pine Tree Blvd., which is one of America's oldest beltways, between US 84 W and US 319, encircles the town and passes by the largest stand of virgin long-leaf pine in the world on the Greenwood property. The *Lapham Patterson House (Scarborough House)*, 626 N. Dawson, built about 1885, is a rambling Queen Anne structure, NHL; it has been restored and is maintained by the state. Open Tuesday through Saturday from 9 A.M. to 5 P.M., and Sunday from 2 to 5:30. Free. *Thomas County Courthouse*, N. Broad St., has been restored, in part, to its original 1858 appearance, after it had been considerably altered in the Victorian era. *Bryan-Davis House*, 312 N. Broad, built about 1833, is believed to be the first two-story home in town. *Hanna-McKinley House*, Smith Ave. near Pine Tree Blvd., built in 1883, was where Mark Hanna, Ohio politician, brought William McKinley as a presidential candidate to meet Republican leaders in 1895. *Ephraim G. Ponder House*, 324 N. Dawson, built in the 1850s with Greek Revival elements, belonged to a slave trader. In 1869 the house was acquired by Young's Female College and served as the main building until the school closed in 1914. *Dr. David Brandon House*, 329 N. Broad, built about 1851, is mostly Second Empire, a style it acquired in the 1870s when additions were made. *Burch-Mitchell House*, 737 Remington Ave., is from 1856, with Greek Revival elements. *Augustine Hansell House*, 429 S. Hansell, was designed by John Wind, architect, in the early 1850s. Wind also designed the courthouse. *Park Front*, 711 S. Hansell, 1891, is Neoclassical. *Wright House*, 415 Fletcher St., is 1854 Greek Revival. Arthur Wright was a banker, alderman, and mayor.

Greenwood Plantation, (inquire locally for directions), and *Millpond Plantation*, S of town on Pine Tree Blvd., are recent additions to the National Register.

TIFTON, Tift County. I-75.

Georgia Agrirama, at the intersec-

tion of I-75 and 8th St., is a restoration of more than 25 buildings from the 19th century. The village newspaper is printed on an 1885 press. Craftsmen demonstrate old skills including milling, the distilling of turpentine from pine gum, and farming jobs. There is a chapel used for service on Sundays, a steam-powered cotton gin, and a working farm on the 70-acre complex.

WASHINGTON, Wilkes County. US 78, 378.

The *East Robert Toombs Historic District* takes in E. Robert Toombs Ave. between Alexander and Grove; the *West Robert Toombs Historic District* is an area between Allison St., Rt. 44, and Lexington Ave.

The *Barnett-Slaton House,* 308 E. Robert Toombs Ave., built in 1835–36, has been enlarged and restored. It has 13 doors and may have needed all of them in the many perilous times in Washington, when great and small persons of the Confederacy sped through town on their way to safety or to capture. The *Washington-Wilkes Historical Museum* is here. Albert Gallatin Semmes, later an associate justice of the Supreme Court of Florida, built the house. He was a cousin of Admiral Raphael Semmes of the Confederate Navy, and sold the property in 1835 to a Mrs. Mary Sneed for $4,500. In 1857 Samuel Barnett, a lawyer and author, and Georgia's first railroad commissioner, bought the place and enlarged it. The restoration and operation of the house have been the work of the Georgia Historical Commission. The museum is rich with Confederate relics as well as other items from both Indian and Reconstruction days.

The Robert Toombs for whom the streets are named was born in Washington on July 2, 1810, studied law at the University of Virginia, and was elected to Congress in 1845. He was a captain in the Creek War of 1836 and a Senator in the famous 33rd Congress, from which he resigned in February 1861. As a member of the Georgia secession convention, he was chosen a delegate to the Montgomery Convention, where he tried to win the presidency of the new confederation. Losing to Jefferson Davis, he accepted the office of Secretary of State and helped to shape the Constitution. He lasted in office only a short while. By summer he had joined the state militia and was soon in command of a brigade in Virginia. He was an impulsive man in battle as in peacetime. When General D. H. Hill, his commanding officer, reprimanded him for his performance at Malvern Hill, Toombs challenged Hill to a duel, but the war kept them both too busy for private fights. After being slightly wounded at Antietam, Toombs demanded a promotion which was not granted and he resigned. Back in Georgia, he became inspector general of the state militia. When the war was over he heard that a warrant was out for his arrest as a traitor to the Union, so he fled first to Cuba and then to London. Toward the end of the 1860s he came back to Washington and resumed his law practice.

One of the most interesting records of the Civil War is *The War-Time Journal of a Georgia Girl,* by Eliza Francis Andrews. Readers who can overlook her extremely limited view of human rights, blacks, and Yankees of any color will find a rich description of wartime Washington. So many of "Fanny's" friends were the people whose houses can be visited today. The Andrews family home, which became virtually an inn for refugeeing friends and strangers, was called Haywood. It was on the west side of town about 200 yards from the road leading into Washington, but it has vanished and there are only oak trees remaining from the Andrews time.

Robert Toombs House, 216 E. Rob-

ert Toombs Ave., not open to the public, built in 1794 by Dr. Joel Abbott, from Connecticut, is white frame with a Doric colonnade, and a high basement in the southern style, set in beautiful lawns with magnificent old trees.

Ficklen House, also known as **Holly Court,** 301 S. Alexander St. (ca. 1825), has been handsomely restored. In 1851, Dr. Fielding Ficklen remodeled the dwelling. There are high mantels, deep windows, and a carved mahogany stairway. In May 1865, Mrs. Jefferson Davis and her children were guests here when everyone in town was trying to find out where her husband was (as was the federal government). Fanny Andrews writes: ". . . Mrs. Davis. . . . is being entertained at Dr. Ficklen's. Nobody knows where the President is, but I hope he is far west of this by now. All sorts of ridiculous rumors are afloat concerning him; one, that he passed through town yesterday hid in a box marked 'specie'. . . . Mrs. Davis herself says that she has no idea where he is, which is the only wise thing for her to say. The poor woman is in a deplorable condition—no home, no money, and her husband a fugitive. She says she sold her plate in Richmond, and in the stampede from that place, the money, all but fifty dollars, was left behind."

Mary Willis Library, E. Liberty and S. Jefferson St., was founded in 1888 by Dr. Francis T. Willis in memory of his daughter, who died in a fall suffered when she was sleepwalking. Georgia's first free library, the red-brick building is late Victorian, with a cupola and stained-glass windows. Mary Willis is remembered in stained glass; Robert Toombs and Alexander H. Stephens in steel engravings. Fanny Andrews writes of the perilous times when leading Confederates were to be arrested by the Union officials: "The Yankees began favoring Gen. Toombs with their attentions today [May 11, 1865]. He and Gov. Brown and Mr. Stephens have been permitted to remain so long unmolested that people were beginning to wonder what it could mean. To-day, however, news came of the arrest of Brown and Stephens, and an attempt was made to take Mr. Toombs. An extra train came in about noon. . . . The general was in his sitting-room when the Yankees were seen entering his front gate. He divined their purpose and made his escape through the back door as they were entering the front, and I suppose he is safely concealed now in some country house. The intruders proceeded to search the dwelling, looking between mattresses and under bureaus, as if a man of Gen. Toombs's size could be hid like a paper doll!"

Tupper-Barnett House, W. Robert Toombs and Allison St., is a two-story 19th-century frame dwelling with imposing Doric columns and porch encircling the building, and sweeping double entrance steps above the high basement, which was used for business rooms, a common practice for planters. The fan-lighted doorways on both stories are unusually beautiful. Fanny Andrews writes of harrowing times for the Tuppers: "Miss Kate Tupper is at her brother's completely broken in health, spirit and fortune. She was in Anderson [S.C.] during the horrors committed there, and . . . all her jewelry was taken except a gold thimble which happened to be overlooked. . . . Old Mrs. Tupper, one of the handsomest and best-preserved old ladies of my acquaintance, turned perfectly gray in five days. . . ."

The Cedars, 201 Sims St., is a 20-room mansion Italianate in style. The oldest part was built by Anthony Poulain, a French immigrant whose son was the Marquis de Lafayette's physician. Francis Colley lived here from 1838 to 1859, and the house has remained in the family to the present. The furnishings are Victorian. Descriptive marker at front tells the story of this house. There are many such markers in town.

Barnett-Edwards House, St. 47, Spring St., restored, was the home of Samuel Barnett, one of the first railroad commissioners in the U.S. He established a small school in the side yard to teach the children of the area. Woodrow Wilson was here as a boy when his father came from Augusta to preach.

Berry-Hay-Pope House, W. Robert Toombs Ave., has a fine widow's walk above the Greek Revival mansion. The older part of the house was built with material from Washington's first Masonic Temple. On the plaster in a closet is the date 1818. The grounds have formal gardens and a beautiful stand of trees. The Yankee soldiers appreciated the trees even in 1865. The Andrews diary notes: ". . . some one knocked at my door and said: 'The Yankees have come, and are camped in Will Pope's grove.' "

Dugas House, E of Poplar Drive near Grove St., was built about 1800 by Louis Dugas, a French refugee from Santo Domingo. Dr. Louis Alexander Dugas, physician and surgeon, who founded the Medical College of Georgia, was born here. The house has an unusual false front with portico and four imposing columns that make the building look as if it had been put up for a movie. The wisteria on a trellis in the grounds is quite real and beautiful.

Gilbert-Alexander House, 117 Alexander Drive, was first built in 1808 by William and Felix Gilbert from Connecticut with hand-blown windowpanes and walls three bricks thick, still remaining. General Porter Alexander was co-founder with Major Albert Myers of the U.S. Signal Corps. He was an instructor at West Point when he resigned to join the Confederacy and became a brigadier general, chief of ordnance, and chief of artillery in Longstreet's Corps. The main house is Federal; outbuildings include the original kitchen, smokehouse, and carriage house.

Peacewood, 120 Tignall Rd., built about 1790, on a land grant made to George Walter, a signer of the Declaration of Independence, was expanded in the early 19th century. The original smokehouse, wellhouse, and dovecote remain. The overseer's cabin has been converted to a guesthouse. A giant tulip tree beside the house was planted in pioneer days and has grown so large it takes six people to reach around it.

Campbell-Jordan House, The Colonnade, 208 Liberty St., was originally built about 1808 in Federal style. About 1841 it was remodeled with Greek Revival elements so that it has a Federal interior, Greek Revival exterior. Two houses were united to make this mansion.

The *Presbyterian Church,* 206 E. Robert Toombs Ave., was the only Presbyterian meeting house built in Washington. It dates from 1825. Woodrow Wilson's father often was a visiting preacher.

The *Chamber of Commerce,* on the courthouse square, has a brochure with a marked map to 76 points of interest. Most of the houses have descriptive plaques in front. Biennially a tour of homes is sponsored by the Woman's Club and the Kiwanis; about 10 or 12 buildings are open. There are 27 sites within walking distance of the courthouse. This city of firsts was the first to be incorporated in the name of George Washington, 1780. The first successful cotton gin was finished and set up in the county by Eli Whitney. His workshop, which dates from 1795, is on St. 47 in an area of historic structures including the *George Otis–Holiday House,* S from US 378 on a paved road, about 10 miles from Washington. This building is on land granted to the Holiday family by the King of England. The house dates from 1848. Another first for Washington was Sarah Hillhouse's becoming the first woman newspaper editor in the U.S. She edited the Washington *Monitor* in 1804. Her home is just across E. Robert Toombs Ave. from the Presbyterian Church.

Less lucky but also a first was Polly Barkley, hanged in 1806, from a poplar which is long gone, but the site is marked. There are many conflicting stories about the event and Mrs. Barkley's name is often spelled Barclay, but all stories agree that her husband John was shot to death, and she was convicted of murder. Some say her body was cut down, and she was pronounced dead, but revived and lived to old age. (But no grave has been located.) The site is on W. Robert Toombs Ave., across from the Morris House, which was the Planter's Hotel in the 1850s.

The *Callaway Plantation,* US 78, across from the airport, is a restored area with a working plantation-complex. The oldest building is probably the hewn-log kitchen, which may have been an early settler's home in the 1780s. It is furnished with many early domestic and agricultural artifacts and furniture. The house is Federal style, two-story, with 1790s furnishings. The red-brick Greek Revival house was built in 1869. A smokehouse and a cemetery are also on the property, which is administered by the Wilkes County Historical Foundation.

FLORIDA

It is (as all who are acquainted with the outline of the United States will allow), a singularly-formed peninsula. Mr. Seagrove alleges that it is a sand-bank; but Mr. Williams supposes it to be a calcareous fragment of the Appalachian mountain, clothed with some sterile sand-banks, some rich, variegated clay-banks, and some beautiful coralines.

> —*Sears' Pictorial Description of the United States,* by Robert Sears,
> New York, 1855

Perhaps the most important quality of Florida architecture is its understandability to laymen. This affinity between architecture and people is often lost in the sheer abstract nature of much contemporary architecture. . . . As disenchantment with the Modern Movement grows, Florida's creative eclectic treasures may serve as the basis for a new architecture—thus adding another impelling reason for their preservation.

> —"Preservation in Florida," by Harold W. Kemp,
> in *Historic Preservation,* 1978

CORAL GABLES, Dade County. US 1.

The City of Coral Gables Preservation Board, City Hall, 405 Biltmore Way, P.O. Drawer 34-1549 (zip 33134)—(305) 446-0881—is involved in a $3 million restoration complex. *Coral Gables House,* formerly known as Coral Gables Plantation, then Merrick Manor, 907 Coral Way, the home of the founder of the city, is being returned to its original splendor. George Merrick was a developer who with his father, Solomon Merrick, operated the largest grapefruit shipping company in the Southeast. The elder Merrick was a minister of the Congregational Church in Massachusetts when he decided to grow fruit instead of shoveling snow. His 12-year-old son George accompanied him on a scouting trip to Florida, where he bought the 160-acre Greg-

ory Homestead for $1,100 in July 1899. The rest of the family moved south; Mrs. Merrick made the small frame Gregory cabin livable, and the fruit and vegetable business prospered. By 1916 the plantation covered 3,000 acres. The Merricks continued to add to their riches until the crash ended the stock market and land booms; then Mrs. Merrick and her daughter Ethel added five bathrooms, changed the name to Merrick Manor, and took in boarders. It remained a boarding house for many years.

FERNANDINA BEACH, Nassau County. On the Atlantic Ocean, via St. A1A, E of I-95.

Fernandina Beach Historic District takes in some 30 blocks of the old town. The gingerbread architecture, the scent of magnolias in season, the

144

live oaks draped with Spanish moss, and the beautiful old mansions set in green estates make this the kind of place Scarlett O'Hara might have emigrated to after Rhett closed the door in her face. Fernandina has saluted eight flags: French, Spanish, British, Patriots, Green Cross of Florida, Mexican, Confederate, and American. In the mid-19th century it was an active seaport. When the Atlantic terminus of the first cross-state railroad for Florida was built here, the town was a busy transfer place for rail and ship passengers and freight. *Bailey House,* 7th and Ash Sts., *Fairbanks House,* 227 S. 7th St., and *Lewis House (or Tabby House),* also at 7th and Ash, are listed individually on the National Register. *The Palace,* on Center St., claims to be Florida's oldest saloon; built in 1878, it is still serving.

KEY WEST, Monroe County. US 1. *Key West Historic District* is on the Gulf. Florida became a part of U.S. territory in 1821 when Key West was still owned by Juan Pablo Salas, who had received it as a gift from the King of Spain. Before the year was out, however, Salas sold it to John Simonton, an American. Two years later a U.S. naval station was established here, and the city was incorporated in 1828. Most of the buildings are of the Bahamas style, intended to resist high winds, with wide porches having slender square columns. The high-pitched roofs were designed to catch rainwater for cisterns. After the fire of 1886, brick was used in some construction work. Most earlier houses are frame.

The *Old Island Restoration Foundation,* P.O. Box 689, Key West, 33040, has a brochure with a map and information for walking or auto tours. *Old Island Days,* an annual event with house and garden tours as well as other attractions, organized by the Foundation, is held for six weeks beginning the first weekend in February. *"Pelican Path,"* a self-guiding tour, begins at *Hospitality House,* Foundation headquarters, on Old Mallory Square.

Old Post Office and Customshouse, Front St., made of red brick, was used as a custom house until 1896. Commodore David Porter's headquarters were on this site in 1824. When carpenters went ashore to work on the navy yard that Porter had laid out the year before, squads of men had to be put to work chopping underbrush and filling in mosquito swamps. Porter moved his family ashore in May. Soon after they were settled he caught yellow fever. A few days later the only doctor at Thompson's Island, as Key West was called, also caught the fever. Mrs. Porter, a true navy wife and mother (her son David Dixon Porter became a Union admiral), nursed her husband through the worst of the fever and kept it from spreading to her children (including young David). As soon as the Commodore could sit up, she moved him and the rest of the family back on shipboard and ordered the captain to take them to Washington.

Audubon House, Whitehead and Greene Sts., was a temporary home for John James Audubon in 1832, when he was the guest of Captain John H. Geiger, a salvager and master pilot for the navy. The house, built about 1830, has been restored. While Audubon was here he painted *The Birds of the Keys.*

Ernest Hemingway House, 907 Whitehead, was the home of Asa Tift, from New Orleans. It reflects the Louisiana style of wrought-iron balconies and shutters, but is basically Spanish of native stone with a flat roof. When the Hemingways lived here from 1931 to 1940, they added the pool house in the rear, with a study on the second floor, where he wrote many of his novels while here with Pauline, his second wife. The garden has a variety of

The Audubon House, Key West, Florida. (Courtesy Old Island Federation, Inc.)

trees and plants from other parts of the world collected by Hemingway. NHL.

Eduardo H. Gato House, 1209 Virginia St., is listed on the National Register and on the Historic American Buildings Survey, as is the **Dr. Joseph Y. Porter House,** 429 Caroline St.

Among houses on the Pelican Path is **The Oldest House,** now a museum, said to have been built in the 1820s and moved to Duval St. in 1832. Its unusual three dormer windows are graduated in size. An early owner and possibly the builder, Richard Cussons, came from Nassau about 1828, and seems to have been a carpenter, grocer, and auctioneer. William Wall, an Englishman who bought the house for $750 in 1838, was a wrecker, merchant, and builder

of the large warehouse in **Old Mallory Square,** now the **Community Center.**

Captain George Carey House, Caroline St. near Whitehead, has a Pirate's Well where buccaneers are said to have gathered. **Captain Philip Cosgrove House,** Whitehead N of Eaton St., is more than 120 years old; Cosgrove commanded the first rescue ship to reach the victims of the battleship *Maine.* **Old Montgomery Place,** Angela near Simonton, is one of the oldest houses in town; built about 1827, it has had no structural changes; the garden has a fine collection of tropical plants. The **Bahama House (1),** Eaton and Margaret Sts., was the home of the island's best shipbuilder, John Bartlum. In 1847 Bartlum and his friend Richard Roberts of Green Turtle Key in the Bahamas dismantled their homes and floated them here. Bartlum reportedly built the only clipper made with mahogany timbers, the *Stephen R. Mallory,* in 1851. This was one of the largest ever to be built in Florida. Next door is **Bahama House (2),** once the home of Richard Roberts.

There are 32 sites on the Pelican Path.

A **Conch Tour Train,** depots at 303 Front St. and at 3850 North Roosevelt Blvd., offers a 1½-hour tour with narration. **Old Town Trolley,** Old Mallory Square, also has 1½-hour tours of the city.

PENSACOLA, Escambia County. US 98.

Pensacola Historic District, bounded by Chase St., 9th Ave., Pensacola Bay, and Palafox St. NHL. Settled in the 18th century, Pensacola served as the capital of West Florida during the British occupation, and the last Spanish period (1781–1821). Residences are a mixture of styles: Greek Revival, Victorian, and Gulf Coast or Creole.

The **Pensacola/Escambia Development Commission,** 803 N. Palafox St., has an excellent brochure with marked map for both auto and walking tours of the historic areas.

Seville Square, E. Government and S. Alcaniz Sts., is a historic English and Spanish park. The **Walking Tour** is sponsored by the **Historic Pensacola Preservation Board.** Brochures are also available at the **Pensacola Historical Museum,** 405 S. Adams St., at Zaragoza St., in **Old Christ Church,** which was used by federal soldiers as a barracks and hospital during the Civil War. Guided tours. Construction was begun in 1830, making this the oldest church in West Florida. Construction is of local brick and hand-hewn heart-of-pine beams. The church was extended in 1879.

Among dwellings on the walking tour: **Dorothy Walton House,** 221 E. Zaragoza St., was the home of the widow of George Walton, a signer of the Declaration of Independence from Georgia. The house has been moved from its original site, and restored by the Preservation Board.

Moreno Cottage, 221 E. Zaragoza, built in 1879 by Don Francisco Moreno as a honeymoon home for his daughter Perle (one of his 27 children) when she married a man named O. H. Smith, is owned by the Preservation Board.

Dorr House, 311 S. Adams, built six years after the war, is an example of the modified Classical Revival architecture of the 1870s.

Lavalle House, 203 E. Church, ca. 1810. Charles Lavalle, builder and merchant, also a brick mason, constructed this one-and-one-half-story dwelling in Gulf Coast style. It is elevated on brick piers and has brick noggings in all the walls, thought to be Lavalle's own handiwork. Restored in 1974 by the Preservation Board.

Moreno-Anderson House, 300 E. Government St., built 1859–68, for Theodore Moreno, son of Don Francisco Moreno, in two-story Gulf Coast style. William E. Anderson, who bought the house in 1873 and lived here until 1898, was twice mayor of Pensacola.

Gray House, 314 S. Alcaniz St., built in the 1880s, is supposed to have a ghost whose footsteps can be heard in the hall. The Historic Pensacola Preservation Board, or perhaps the Development Commission, should get this spirit listed with the U.S. Department of Commerce, which has a *Traveler's Guide to Special Attractions No. 10* called "The Supernatural; Haunted Houses and Legendary Ghosts," with ghosts from Maine to Louisiana to California. (Louisiana and Virginia have ten each, at present, leading the field by a shade.)

Lee House, 420 S. Alcaniz St., built

in 1866 for William Franklin Lee, an engineer and Confederate officer, who had lost an arm in the Battle of Chancellorsville. While he was surveyor and land developer, he named Lee St. for his family and Lloyd St. for his wife's. (Many streets and other places in the South are named for Robert E. Lee. There was also a William Henry Fitzhugh Lee, called "Rooney," who was the general's second son and who also served in the war.) The Historic Pensacola Preservation Board bought the house, moved it to this site, and restored it to be used as their office.

Barkley House, 410 S. Florida Blanca St., ca. 1815, is believed to be the oldest masonry building in town. Barkley was a prosperous local merchant.

Axelson House, 314 and 318 S. Florida Blanca St., built late 19th century, of French West Indian design, was restored in 1974, retaining hand-hewn floor joists and handmade brick with oystershell mortar.

In the **Seville District** are:

Hispanic Building, Zaragoza and Tarragona Sts. The local mapmakers and tour listers seemed to be totally pixyish about whether to spell the street Zaragoza, Zarragossa, or Zarogossa, but Zaragoza came from the Spanish city where Napoleon was repulsed in the Peninsula War of the early 1800s. The north section of the building was constructed about 1877 and used as a warehouse. Ten years later the south addition was built, now the main gallery of the **West Florida Museum of History.**

Transportation Building, S across Zaragoza, was built at the turn of the century and now houses the **Historic Pensacola Preservation Board's Transportation Museum,** with early vehicles, fire equipment, and an early railroad station waiting room. Both museums are open daily and free.

Site of the Tivoli Complex, Barracks and Zaragoza St.: the Spanish governor's old residence was the site for the Tivoli High House, built by three Frenchmen in 1805. In 1843 when the busy Don Francisco Moreno bought the property, the house became a boarding place called Hotel Paree. Morenos still owned the building when Union officers billeted here in the Civil War, and *they* called it the Spanish Barracks. This structure and the Moreno home next door were torn down in the history-careless 1930s. But the Preservation Board in cooperation with the American Revolution Bicentennial Commission of Florida reconstructed Tivoli High House for the Bicentennial Trail. The **Tivoli Dance Hall** was built in 1805 by the same three Frenchmen: Juan Baptiste Cazenave, Pedro Bardenave, and René Chandiveneau. It was an octagonal building used for dancing, cockfights, and theater.

Piney Woods Sawmill, Barracks and Main Sts., was bought by the Preservation Board and moved to this site where a sawmill stood in the 19th century. It is the first exhibit in a complex which will feature the industrial history and development of West Florida.

St. Michael's Cemetery, Alcaniz and Garden Sts.: Don Juan Ventura Morales, Spanish intendent, gave the title to this land to the Catholic settlers in 1807 for use as a burial ground. St. Michael's deeded the land to the city in 1964, and the Preservation Board now administers the historic area. Special flags fly over the graves of Dorothy Walton, widow of George Walton, who signed the Declaration of Independence, and Stephen R. Mallory, secretary of the Confederate Navy, whose family came to Key West from Trinidad in 1820. In 1838, Mallory married Angela Moreno. Mallory was taken prisoner at LaGrange, Georgia, in May 1865. After his release from prison in March 1866 he practiced law in Pensacola and lived here until his death in November 1873.

There are 43 sites in the combined auto and walking tour of historic Pensacola, and then there is the **North Hill Preservation District,** N of Garden St. (business district) between Pace Blvd. and Palafox (US 29). This is an area of homes built during the prosperous lumber days of the 1870s and 1920s. It is being preserved and developed.

ST. AUGUSTINE, St. Johns County. I-95.

St. Augustine Historic District, central area, where Pedro Menéndez de Avilés founded a military base in September 1565, was just a collection of huts thatched with palm, but it was the only permanent European settlement in what became the United States and is therefore the oldest continuously occupied city in the nation. After a fire set by English troops in the early 18th century, stone dwellings were erected. There are 31 original residences in the historic district with aboveground portions earlier than 1821.

Visitor Information Center, 10 Castillo Drive, near City Gate, has a 15-minute color film and a visitor's guide. Sightseeing trains leave from 3 Cordova St. for a one-hour narrated tour with stopover privileges. Horse-drawn carriage tours are provided by the St. Augustine Transfer Company: (904) 829-8218.

The **Old Gate,** built in 1808, leads onto a narrow street that runs the length of the early city. It was the *Calle Real* until the British took over, and it became St. George St. in 1763. Many buildings have been restored; some are reconstructed on their original sites. The most popular building material, because of its availability, was coquina, a shell-rock which is tough but porous. This was usually covered with plaster to keep out dampness. Many dwellings have patios and little gardens protected by high walls with gates opening onto the street.

In 1959 the state began to restore much of the original townsite to its 18th-century look. Among structures open to the public:

Ribera House, 22 St. George St., early-18th-century Spanish dwelling, has been reconstructed and furnished in period.

Gallegos House, 21 St. George St., an early period tabby house with a walled garden. Reconstructed. Demonstrations of colonial life as living history have been held here—as elsewhere—by Flagler College students in summer. This widespread practice seems to be as informative and entertaining to the participants as to the sightseers. The girls work in primitive kitchens, spin wool thread, boil soap, etc. Boys make their own fishnets and even build their own fishing dugouts. (On the Lincoln Heritage Trail in Kentucky young people are actually farming as the Hanks family once did.)

Salcedo House, 42 St. George St., a reconstructed Spanish house, with a separate kitchen in rear, which now operates as a bakery, and an ancient well. Candymaking can be watched. The second story was added by the British after they acquired Florida in 1763.

De Mesa House (Old Spanish Inn), 43 St. George St., was built in the early 18th century and has been partially restored.

Avero House, 39 St. George, is on the National Register.

Arrivas House, 46 St. George, one of a complex of homes belonging to the Avero family, built about 1720. Headquarters for the Historic St. Augustine Preservation Board. The De Mesa House is part of the complex. There are demonstrations of candlemaking, weaving, etc.

Rodriguez-Avero House (Museum of Yesterday's Toys), 52 St. George, is an early-18th-century building which has been altered over the years. National Register and HABS.

Marin-Hassett House, 97 St.

George, now the Pan-American Building, is reconstructed, with changing exhibits of Latin-American art and culture.

Spanish Military Hospital, 8 Aviles St., is a replica of a colonial hospital and pharmacy. The **Florida Medical Museum** is on the second floor.

Llambias House, 31 St. Francis, is late 18th century with coquina walls, plaster-covered and whitewashed. The kitchen is a reconstruction. National Register.

Gonzalez-Alvarez House, 14 St. Francis, is a National Historic Landmark. The actual date of construction of this "oldest house" has not been determined, but it was between 1703 and 1727, probably in 1723 when Tomas Gonzalez Hernandez was married. It had one story with coquina walls and tabby floors. Later owners added a second story and a two-story tier of six rooms at the rear. Restoration was completed in 1960. There is a museum in the **Tovar House** next door, which was built before 1763.

Ximenez-Fatio House, 20 Aviles, is on the National Register. It was built in 1798 and houses a museum operated by the Florida Society of Colonial Dames of America.

Dr. Peck House (Old Spanish Treasury), 143 St. George, was built after 1702 when fire destroyed the original house at this site which had belonged to the Spanish royal treasurer. Dr. Silas Peck bought the place in 1837 and added the frame second story. Furnished with 19th-century items, the restored building also houses a treasury room of old coins and other Spanish treasures. Operated by the St. Augustine Woman's Exchange.

Old Wooden Schoolhouse, 14 St. George, is believed to be the oldest school building in the U.S. It was a residence and also a schoolhouse long before the Civil War. It probably was built before the 18th century, in the first Spanish period.

Also in town are the oldest Catholic parish, first mission to the Indians established by the Spanish, the Castillo de San Marcos, the northernmost outpost of the Spanish Empire; and so it goes. Almost everything is just about the oldest of its sort in the U.S. except perhaps the tourists, and some of them may well qualify. This is a fine area for nonstrenuous sightseeing. As is also:

ST. PETERSBURG, Pinellas County. St. 19.

Chamber of Commerce, 4th St. and 3rd Ave. S., has a self-guiding tour map and brochures. The **U.S. Post Office,** SW corner of 1st Ave. N. and 4th St., is on the National Register. So is the **John C. Williams House (Manhattan Hotel),** 444 5th St. S., and the **Don CeSar Hotel,** 3400 Gulf Blvd. The Don CeSar has been handsomely restored.

The **Haas Museum Village Complex,** 3511 Second Ave. S., has the **Lowe House,** 3527 Second Ave. S., one of the oldest homes in Pinellas County, built about 1850 of board-and-batten structure. Its original site was in Anona. Captain John Lowe built it for his bride. The materials are cypress and pine. It has been furnished in period. **Grace S. Turner House,** 3501 Second Ave. S., has antique furnishings and early St. Petersburg relics. It is a typical Florida bungalow. The **Haas Museum** is in the former home of Edna Haas; among exhibits are shells, minerals, an old-time barbershop, and blacksmith's shop. A banyan tree at the smithy may be 90 years old. It measures 62 feet in circumference.

TALLAHASSEE, Leon County. US 319.

Tallahassee Historic District, Zones I and II, Calhoun St. between Georgia and Tennessee Sts., and E. Park Ave. between Gadsden and Calhoun Sts. Tallahassee was selected as the site for the seat of the government two years after the territory became a part of the U.S. Andrew Jackson was the first territorial governor. The *State Capitol,* S. Monroe St., sits on the highest hill in town and is imposing with columned porticos and large dome. The central part was completed in 1845.

The Columns (Benjamin Chaires House), 100 N. Duval St., moved from the corner of Adams St. and Park Ave. Chaires was an architect and builder; this three-story brick Greek Revival–style dwelling was erected about 1830 as his residence. It has been restored, furnished with antiques, and serves as the office of the Chamber of Commerce. A tour map and information on the area may be obtained here.

The Grove, Adams and 1st Ave., was built for the bride of Gov. Richard Keith Call. Begun in 1825.

Goodwood (Old Groom Mansion), 1500 Miccosukee Rd., from the 1830s, was built by George Anderson, architect. The mansion has been altered several times and there are numerous outbuildings. The estate once had its own racetrack in addition to the formal gardens.

Bellevue, SW of the town off St. 371, a 19th-century house, moved and restored, was the home of Catjerine Murat, widow of Archille Murat, nephew of Napoleon. Museum.

TAMPA, Hillsborough County. I-4.

Ybor City Historic District, about 2 square miles between Nebraska Ave., 22nd St., Columbus Drive, and E. Broadway. This district has a Cuban, Spanish, and Italian population. Ybor City was founded in 1886 by Vicente Martinez Ybor, a Cuban cigarmaker who was in business in Key West. He moved his plant here at the invitation of the Tampa city government. Three enormous brick buildings preserve an aroma from the days of rolling cigars by hand, then the biggest industry in the Tampa area. Original wooden interiors, grillwork, and hand-blown glass windows have been preserved.

There are Spanish malls, plazas, arcades, old casinos, sidewalk coffee shops, and even the traditional old men playing dominoes. Historical markers describe each landmark along the walking tour which begins at the *Cradle of Cuban Liberty—El Liceo Cubano,* at the SW corner of 7th Ave. and 13th St., a social center used by Jose Marti to organize Cuban freedom fighters in 1891.

La Casa de Pedroso, SE corner of 8th Ave. and 13th St., is the site of the home of Paulina Pedroso, an outstanding woman patriot who aided Marti after an attempt on his life. The *Parque Jose Marti* honors both of these patriots.

There are 22 historical sites on the tour. *The Tourist Information Center at the Chamber of Commerce,* 801 E. Kennedy Blvd., has brochures, maps, and details of a 27-mile bike route around town: (813) 229-9221. Maps and information on Ybor City may also be obtained at Trend Publications, on the third floor of the Stemmery Building, or P.O. Box 2350, Tampa, 33601; call (813) 247-5411.

Midwest States

**Ohio
Indiana
Illinois**

OHIO

We visited one farm which . . . was a partial clearing in the very heart of the forest. The house was built on the side of a hill, so steep that a high ladder was necessary to enter the front door, while the back one opened against the hillside. . . . The house was built of logs, and consisted of two rooms, besides a little shanty or lean-to, that was used as a kitchen. Both rooms were comfortably furnished with good beds, drawers, &c. The farmer's wife. . . . told me that they spun and wove all the cotton and woolen garments of the family, and knit all the stockings; her husband, though not a shoemaker by trade, made all the shoes. She manufactured all the soap and candles they used, and prepared her sugar from the sugar-trees on their farm. All she wanted with money, she said, was to buy coffee, tea, and whiskey, and she could "get enough any day by sending a batch of butter and chicken to market."
—*Domestic Manners of the Americans,* by Frances M. Trollope, 1836

How rapid has been the advance of this western county. In 1803, deer-skin at the value of forty cents, per pound, were a legal tender; and if offered instead of money, could not be refused—even by a lawyer. Not fifty years ago, the woods which towered where Cincinnati is now built, resounded only to the cry of the wild animals of the forest, or the rifle of the Shawnee Indian: now Cincinnati . . . is a beautiful, well-built, clean town. . . . The streets have a row of trees on each side, near the curb-stone; and most of the houses have a small frontage, filled with luxuriant shrubs. . . . I was told a singular fact, which will prove how rapidly the value of land rises in this country as it becomes peopled. Fifty-six years ago, the major part of the land upon which the city of Cincinnati stands, and which is now worth many millions of dollars, was *swapped away* by the owner of it for a pony!! The man who made this unfortunate bargain is now alive, and living in or near Cincinnati.
—*Diary in America,* by Captain Frederick Marryat, 1839

ARCHBOLD, Fulton County. St. 66, S of I-80, 90.

Sauder Museum, Farm & Craft Village, E of intersection of St. 66 and St. 2. The 15-acre complex has a Homestead area, a craft village, a museum, and a restaurant and bakery in a restored barn. This part of Ohio had to be settled by individualists who were willing to cope with the Black Swamp, low, wet, and covered with hardwood forests to be cleared. The farmers also had to dig ditches for draining the swamps, which today are rich farmlands. The pioneers were mostly Mennonites from central Europe. In 1835 farmers with grain for milling had to back-pack it as they walked to Maumee to the mill. There was no road for carts and oxen.

Roaming wild wolves are said to

have made the journey a lively one. The grandfather of Eric Sauder, founder of the museum, frightened off wolves with kitchen matches on his way back from the Maumee mill.

The Homestead is a restored Victorian farmhouse from 1860, with a summer kitchen, smokehouse, barn, and other outbuildings. In the village are a farm shop for toolmaking, a cabinet shop, potter, barber, blacksmith, and leathermaker, a flour mill, general store, log schoolhouse, log cabin, and St. Mark's Lutheran Church, built in 1880 as a school. The log cabin was built in 1847 on the first road in the settlement. The schoolhouse is a replica. Outlying buildings include broom, weaving, furniture, and glass shops. An 1890 schoolhouse, a 1901 doctor's office, and a depot which once served on the Wabash line at Elmira also are on display.

BATH, Summit County. St. 21.

The *Hale Farm and Village,* 2686 Oak Hill Rd., near the conjunction of I-271, 77, and the Ohio Turnpike. The Western Reserve was a large section of land W of Pennsylvania reserved by Connecticut in 1786 when it gave up other western holdings to the federal government. In 1800 the land became Ohio territory. In 1810 Jonathan Hale, a Connecticut farmer, came to the Cuyahoga Valley and found the land he had bought occupied by a squatter with a log cabin and several cleared acres. Hale paid off the squatter and lived in the cabin for several years. The brick house standing today was completed enough for occupancy in 1826. Hale had started a small lime-burning business in 1819, so he and his sons built the large farmhouse of bricks, not the usual building material for the area. Mrs. Mercy Hale died in 1829, probably before the splendid home was quite finished. Hale married a widow with three children, had three more of his own,

The Hale House, Hale Farm and Village, Bath, Ohio. (Ohio Office of Travel and Tourism)

and used all of the rooms. The house has been altered several times.

In 1956, by the will of Miss Clara Bell Ritchie, a great-granddaughter, the house was given to the Western Reserve Historical Society for a museum, and the farm to be worked as in the early days "to the end that the greatest number of persons may be informed as to the history and culture of the Western Reserve."

One impressed visitor wrote, "The stamina and strength of the pioneer-settler are baked into the red bricks of the Hale Homestead."

The farm is on the W side of Oak Hill Rd., with about 140 acres. The village lies on the E side. All buildings except the carriage shed are original, moved from other parts of the Western Reserve.

The *Benjamin Wade Law Office,* built in Streetsboro in 1825, belonged to a man who might have been President. Wade was president *pro tempore* of the United States Senate when Vice-President Andrew Johnson became President after Lincoln had been assassinated. If Johnson had been impeached, Benjamin Wade would have been President, as next in line. He used this law office from 1850 to 1870.

The *Bordner Land Office* was built in 1830 in North Bloomfield. The *Goldsmith House,* 1826, was built in Willoughby. Jonathan Goldsmith was one of the outstanding builders of the Lake Erie area. The *Jagger House,* a Greek Revival, built in 1845, in Bath, was the home of carriagemaker Clement Jagger. The *Saltbox House,* 1830, comes from West Richfield. The *Stow House* is from 1850. The *Meetinghouse,* 1851, served as the First Baptist Church in Streetsboro, then as a Methodist church. The *Log Schoolhouse,* from about 1816, was used as a farm home, then a church, and finally a school. The *Log Barn,* housing the Franklin Glassworks, came from Kent and was built in 1824. There are blacksmiths, woodworkers, potters, and glass blowers among the craftsmen demonstrating their trades as carried on more than a century ago. Costumed hostesses explain the various buildings and their furnishings. The *Farm* is stocked from ducks to horses. From May with its sheep shearing to December with an old-fashioned Christmas, there are many special events.

BERLIN, Holmes County. St. 39.

Guided tours of Ohio's Amish country begin in this area. The *Amish Farm,* on St. 39 between Berlin and Walnut Creek, has a slide presentation on Amish life, and farm buildings, house, buggy shop, and a buggy ride around the farm. In summer months hayride tours can be taken, from the Berlin House, a restaurant, at the corner of St. 39 and St. 62 in Berlin. Stops are made at an authentic Amish home and a cheese factory. The wagons, however, are pulled by tractors, not horses. There are many fine restaurants serving Amish cooking in the area. In nearby Walnut Creek is *Der Candlemaker,*

where children can make their own candles and get a certificate to prove it. There are many cabinet and buggy shops near Berlin operated by skilled craftsmen. Civil War buffs will remember the Holmes County Rebellion and Fort Fizzle; this was near Glenmont. Copperheads stoned a federal recruiting agent in protest against the war and other citizens formed a mob in sympathy, but everyone went home when 400 troops arrived to see what was going on.

BURTON, Geauga County. St. 87.

Geauga is an Iroquois word, probably a corruption of Cuyahoga, meaning "stream," or possibly "raccoon."

Century Village and Pioneer Museum, 14653 Park St., sponsored by the Geauga County Historical Society, comprises 11 restored buildings. The village period is that of the decade before the Civil War, although the first settlers of Burton came in the early part of the 19th century. It is fitting that apple butter, maple syrup, and sweet cider are products of this county in the Western Reserve which was once a part of New England.

Eleazer Hickox Home, a brick dwelling which fronts on the village green, was built in 1838 and is furnished with antiques. *Boughton House,* built in 1834, has been restored and furnished with period pieces of the Western Reserve style. The *Law House,* built by Merritt Nettleton in 1817, has been restored. There are also a country store, a cabinet shop, and a red barn brought from Newbury and erected here by Amish carpenters. Among annual attractions are the apple-butter festival and Village Ox-roast in October. There are art shows and craft shows in summer; pancake dinners during maple syrup season (early spring), and a butter-churn festival in June which includes the making of ice cream and chocolate milk. No season is safe for weight watchers in Burton.

CINCINNATI, Hamilton County. I-70.

Sharon Woods Village: From Cincinnati take I-275 to Sharonville exit; go S on St. 42 about 1 mile to Sharonville. A group of 19th-century buildings has been moved to this site and reconstructed in a village pattern, furnished and open to the public, with guides on duty. The nonprofit Miami Purchase Association operates the village. *Elk Lick House* is a Gothic farmhouse of the 1850s which came from Clermont County along with the original outbuildings and was restored to the original appearance. *Winton Place Station* served the Baltimore & Ohio railroad at Clifton and Spring Grove Aves. in suburban Cincinnati, where it was known as the Chester Park depot. It has been restored. *John M. Hayner House* is a Greek Revival–style farmhouse. The barn complex at the rear of the house is one of the oldest from Clermont County. *Dr. Henry Archer Langdon Office* is restored to its appearance in Civil War days and has medical and pharmaceutical equipment used in that period. Dr. Langdon practiced in Cincinnati in the 1860s. *Vorhes House* is a two-story brick which was moved from Cornell Rd., Sharonville, and dates from the mid-19th century.

John Hauck House, 812 Dayton St., in Cincinnati's West End, also has been restored by the Miami Purchase Association. The preservation society's name was taken from the original million-acre land grant which covered an area between the Little and the Great Miami rivers north of the Ohio. The two-storied town house, the home of a prosperous German brewer, has been furnished in the late-19th-century period. Hauck lived here from 1881 until his death in 1896. A two-block area of Dayton St. has been listed on the National Register. Walking tour brochures are available.

COLUMBUS, Franklin County. I-70.

German Village, S. Third St. at Livingston Ave. A turn S off I-70 on High St. leads to the entrance. A map of the village is available for 25¢ at the Village Society, 624 S. Third St. A *Haus und Garten Tour* on the last Sunday in June visits ten houses and five gardens. Each September there is a *Candlelight Tour* of patios and gardens. The area was settled by Germans between 1840 and 1860. Many early brick houses have been restored. The German Village Society also provides speakers for local and out-of-town engagements.

A narration with slides at the *German Village Meeting Haus,* 138 E. Columbus St., can be the start of a walking or chartered bus tour. For group tour details: (614) 221-8888.

The typical German settlement of the mid-19th century had brick walks and streets, low iron fences, grape arbors, and small wine houses, all immaculate. The first houses were usually one-and-one-half-story brick with gray slate roofs; toward the end of the century two-story houses with pitched hip roofs were built, tall but narrow. The *Reiner's Backerei* (bakery) and other shops and restaurants are old-style German, too. The *Lindenhof,* on the corner of Beck and Mohawk Sts., was a posh saloon, then became a flower shop and a honky-tonk and is now a fine restaurant with a German chef. *Schmidt's Sausage Haus* was once a livery stable. The *Old World Bazaar,* housed in a former streetcar barn, on City Park, has ten small shops. Next door is the *1814 Shop,* which has much beautifully knitted, crocheted, or hand-sewn "fancywork," made by the talented senior citizens.

Ohio Village, on the grounds of the *Ohio Historical Center,* I-71 and 17th Ave., is a complex of 14 buildings which are replicas of those which would have made up a typical Ohio county seat in the years before the Civil War. Eventually there will be about 60 buildings on the 10-acre site.

In the village are the *Town Hall,* the *American House Hotel,* general store, drugstore, print shop, gun shop, market, tin shop, watch and clock shop, millinery story, a museum, blacksmith shop, glass and china shop, lawyer's office, weaving, cabinet, and shoe and harness shops. There are also a doctor's home and office, a pumphouse, garden, and church.

So far as is possible the atmosphere and look is that of the 1840s, but the dirt roads have been chemically treated so that they do not get too muddy even in a downpour. The boardwalks, however, are splintery, and shoes are advised.

Costumed guides talk of the 1800s as if they'd lived in that period. Craftsmen demonstrate early skills, including tinsmithing, saddlemaking, and shoemaking. One of the latest buildings added to the village is a working bank, with an 1850 safe and other early furnishings, which handles accounts for village employees.

COSHOCTON, Coshocton County. US 36.

Roscoe Village Restoration, St. 16, on the W side of town. Canal days and the old towpaths are by now a romantic concept for most Americans, as fully entrenched as the riproaring Old West, with the work and dreary times forgotten. Well, why not? Restorations offer the best of the past without its pests and usually without its extremes of heat or cold. Daniel R. Porter, of the Ohio Historical Society, once pointed out in a speech to the Coshocton County Archaeological and Historical Society, "Old Roscoe can never be recaptured in every respect. I doubt if anyone would want to, but like the tavern candlelight which used to be reflected in the canal water, the town's architectural and historical essence of old is beginning to shine.... Once again a canalboat may be afloat and the village bustling with activity. But it will be a prosperity founded upon a different type of commercial transaction. The meek but wallet-bulging tourist will replace the brawling packet crews and their heterogeneous passengers....

"In the wildest dreams of Roscoe's founders and leading citizens in 1841, there could have been no thought that more than a century later their architecture, their tavern menus, their very way of life would be preserved for appreciation by quite a different type of visitor and resident."

Many novels and children's tales have used the adventuresome canals as background. Anyone lucky enough to lay hands on Jacob Abbott's old books for children will enjoy Marco Paul on the Erie Canal. Marco was a bright little fellow who made his travels in company with a know-it-all adult who explained everything from time to time, interrupting the story but enlightening young readers of the 1850s.

Happily for modern Marcos, the old village has been restored and the *Monticello II* now travels along a 1-mile restored section of the old Grand Canal (the Ohio-Erie) and carries more than 100 sightseers, if not emigrants. The speed is ¾ mile per hour. (The first *Monticello* arrived on a day of enormous excitement in August 1830.)

New Englander James Calder came to Coshocton in 1811, but his business failed in 1816, and he laid out a town on a tract he owned across the Muskingum River, which he called Caldersburgh. In 1831, how-

Roscoe Village Restoration, Coshocton, Ohio. (Courtesy Roscoe Village Foundation)

ever, a canal engineer, Leander Ransom, and Noah Swayne, a lawyer, became the proprietors of the land Calder had owned and named the settlement Roscoe, for an antislavery English poet, William Roscoe. Roscoe's boom days began when the 309-mile canal was built. The **Township Hall** has a slide show, displays, and information.

The **Williams House,** built in the 1830s, has been restored. One of its residents, Dr. Maro Johnson, enlarged the building in 1841. Charlie Williams was a tavernkeeper.

Other structures along Whitewoman St. include shops; the Old Warehouse, now a restaurant; and the former home of the first tollkeeper, Jacob Welch, who lived here in the 1840s. This is now a handsome museum, but in 1968, when restoration was begun, the ramshackle old building seemed to lean a little drunkenly against the warehouse for support. For many years "Tinker" Dobson was the village blacksmith. His tools are on display in the blacksmith barn. There are horse-drawn wagons for a round trip to the Triple Locks, where canal boats were lowered from the Walhonding Feeder Canal into Roscoe Basin. The sandstone locks are well preserved.

Visitors should stop at the Cosh-octon National Bank to see the Canal Days Mural in the lobby. It depicts a fine day in Roscoe in the 1850s and was the last work to be completed by muralist Dean Cornwell, who died in 1960.

DEFIANCE, Defiance County. US 24.

Au Glaize Village, on Krouse Rd., S of US 24, 3 miles SW of town. This re-created village was begun by the Defiance County Historical Society in 1966 to depict a rural town of the late 19th century. On the 40-acre tract are an operating cider mill, a cane mill, a doctor's office, St. John's Lutheran Church, a school, railroad station, lockkeeper's house, blacksmith shop, and the Black Swamp cabin, which is part of the Black Swamp farm. More buildings are planned. Among these will be a sawmill and a broom factory. Two museums are in operation. There is a length of canal, a rifle range, and a pioneer cemetery, which may sound like a jumble of historical items, but they are neatly arranged for touring and for special events that range from harvest days to Civil War skirmishes. Village personnel are in costume. The Johnny Appleseed Festival is one of the year's highlights, but some city kids may think riding in a cart pulled by harnessed pigs is a bigger event.

NEW PHILADELPHIA, Tuscarawas County. I-77.

Schoenbrunn Village, St. 800, 416, US 250 (I-77, New Philadelphia exit 14), about 3 miles SE of town.

The Moravian-Indian settlement of 1772 has been reconstructed by the Ohio Historical Society and is a state memorial. The site was acquired in 1923; the first cabin was completed in 1927 and two more structures were finished the following year. There are now 19 structures, a cemetery, and 2½ acres of planted fields. The Church of the United Brethren, or Moravians, wanted to remain neutral in all conflicts. They made a fine start when they laid out a village here in the early 1770s, after being invited to the area by the chief of the Delaware Indians. David Zeisberger, John Heckewelder, and John Ettwein had brought some 228 converted Indians from Pennsylvania. The town was named for the "beautiful spring," and was laid out in T, or cross, shape. The schoolhouse was completed in 1773 and a meeting house was begun. The village was caught between the British and American forces when the Revolutionary War broke out. Both Indians and whites were mistrustful to hostile in regard to the Moravians and their Christian Indians. By 1777 the band had to move on, still searching for religious freedom and peace.

The village has guides in mid-18th-century costume who demonstrate the old-time activities. The first church and school in the Ohio territory and the cabins are on their original foundations and furnished with 18th-century artifacts.

VERMILION, Erie County. US 6, St. 2, on Lake Erie.

Harbor Town-1837, Liberty Ave. (US 6) between Main and Grand Sts. This section of the city has been restored and remodeled to re-create the 1830s when the town was founded and became a shipbuilding center as well as a home port for many lake captains. The *Chamber of Commerce Reception Center,* in Exchange Park, N of Liberty Ave., has brochures for a self-guiding tour of the many old homes. Among recently restored buildings are the *Harbour Store,* 5542 Liberty Ave., believed to be the oldest building still standing; the *Ship's Galley* and the *Captain's Chair,* also on Liberty. The Captain's Chair has been a barbershop for more than a century. The *Sail Loft,* on Main St. paralleling the river, has been made over as offices for the Friends of Harbour Town, and others, and also contains a French restaurant.

Vermilion got its name from the river, which was so named for the color of the soil along its banks. The area, known as the Firelands, had no permanent settlers before 1808. The Eries and the Iroquois roamed the land until the mid-17th century, when the Iroquois nearly wiped out the Erie Indians. Apparently for good reasons this was known as Sufferer's Land when Connecticut held title in 1805. Early settlers found it easier to reach by lake than overland. In 1841 the federal government took an interest in the harbor, dredged the river, and built piers. Vermilion was to become a thriving port. The first known settler was William Haddy, who built his log house at the mouth of the river on the west bank in 1808. Ten years later Peter Cuddebach built a frame house. William Austin built a house of stone in 1821. Horatio Perry was the first local builder to use bricks made in the local kiln. Austin had the first hotel, but the Maudelton became the best-known and is being restored as the Harbour Town Inn.

WAYNESVILLE, Warren County. US 42, 17 miles off I-71, midway between Xenia and Lebanon.

Caesar's Creek Pioneer Village, N of Wellman on Clarksville Rd., is a reconstructed town in the making. One way to reach the site is to go via St. 73 into Harveysburg, then S on a back road, Oregonia Rd. But this misses Wellman, which used to be Henpeck and is about 12 miles SE of Waynesville. The *Levi Lukens House* was built in 1807 after Lukens bought 1,000 acres along Caesar's Creek. When the U.S. Corps of Engineers was building a dam on Caesar's Creek to prevent downstream flooding on the Little Miami, they found a number of old log houses. A pioneer village association was formed, and volunteers have been at work putting the settlement together. A barn belonging to pioneer Lukens has been fully restored. There are to be a working farm, a chestnut-log smokehouse, and a number of other buildings. The *Caesar's Creek Friends Meeting House* was moved from another area and restored. Village-made crafts will be on sale at the general store, once the Harris house in Paintersville. A "saddlebag" log cabin, one of the latest acquisitions, is among the oldest constructions in the village; it was once the home of Amos Hawkins.

ZOAR, Tuscarawas County. N of Dover, off St. 800 on St. 212, 3 miles from I-77, Bolivar-Zoar exit.

The village was founded in 1817 by German members of the Society of Separatists who were seeking religious freedom. Their communal society was based on economic necessity but became one of the most successful communities of its time. The Society disbanded in 1898, dividing all property equally. The Ohio Historical Society has restored and reconstructed the buildings on their original foundations.

Through Quaker friends the Separatists were able to purchase a 5,500-acre tract here. Leader of the group, Joseph Baumeler, and others erected the first houses and planted the first crops. When the Panic of 1819 brought hardship, the new settlement decided to pool their holdings and work for the common good. By 1834 they were not only debt-free, they had a surplus. Under Baumeler the community prospered, but after his death in August 1853, the best of times were over and the community failed to find another leader of his quality. From all accounts it wouldn't be easy to find his like even now. He was a remarkable person. In the old days when Hollywood filmmakers used to cast a Gary Cooper or a Charlton Heston into every historic leader's role, they would have gone really wide of the mark if there had been a film based on the life of Joseph Baumeler. He had a limp, an oversized head, and different-sized eyes; but no physical handicaps held him back. He could serve as teacher, doctor, weaver, musician, pastor, and business agent almost equally well, it seems. He was not only selfless in aiding his people but was also a gifted orator. His home and office were in *Number One House.*

The *Garden House,* restored in 1970, overlooks a longtime famous garden which was symbolic of the New Jerusalem as described in the Revelation of John in the Bible. The Separatists grew exotic blooms in their greenhouse and supplied cuttings to many Ohioans in the 19th century. Even in 1837 a traveler wrote of the "extensive variety of plants and fruits" contained in the greenhouse. The city folks of Cleveland used to send their best plants to spend the winter at Zoar's greenhouse. Among other buildings are the wagon and blacksmith shops, tin shop, bakery, and the Bimeler Museum (the family name was altered to Bimeler). Peter Bimeler, grandson of Joseph, was the community miller but was multitalented, too, and built a pipe organ which he played in the flour mill.

Costumed guides are on duty in each house to relate the history of the settlement. The Zoar Hotel, built in the 1830s, and later a "white elephant," was bought a few years ago by a family from Pennsylvania who restored it, using old historical society records and photographs as guidelines. The German steamed black pudding, reportedly a favorite with President McKinley, is back on the menu of the fine restaurant now in operation. The Bert Reis family, now owners, have apparently scotched a popular rumor that McKinley once kept his mistress here. The Cadogan Hotel in London, with its Lily Langtry bar and other associations, would have told any British equivalent of Bert Reis to keep his mouth shut. Hotels where kings brought their favorite women are tourist meccas. On the other hand, in view of the current spate of confessional memoirs about American Presidents, there will soon be too many rendezvous spots on record to keep them all restored.

INDIANA

Oftimes in riding through the West,
A stranger finds a "Hoosher's nest," . . .
The "Hoosher" meets him at the door,
Their salutations soon are o'er. . . .
The stranger stoops to enter in,
The entrance closing with a pin,
And manifests a strong desire,
To seat him by the log-heap fire,
Where half a dozen "Hoosheroons,"
With mush and milk, tin cups and spoons,
White heads, bare feet, and dirty faces,
Seem much inclined to keep their places
But madam, anxious to display
Her rough and undisputed sway,
Her offspring to the ladder leads,
And cuffs the youngsters to their beds.

Invited shortly to partake
Of venison, milk, and jonny-cake,
The stranger makes a hearty meal,
While round his anxious glances steal.
One side is lined with divers garments,
The other spread with skins of varments,
Dried pumpkin over head is strung,
And venison ham in plenty hung;
Two rifles placed above the door,
Three dogs are stretched upon the floor.—
—"The Hoosheroons," from the *Cherokee Intelligencer,* 1855

H. ABDILL

Would respectfully inform his friends that he will manufacture for sale all kinds of
Copper, Tin, and Sheet-Iron Ware, in all its various branches.
He solicits the attention of dealers, to his stock of wares, intending to offer them at all times an assortment complete, as well as perfect in its workman-ship.—He intends his ware shall be equal to any in the west, and to offer it upon as reasonable terms as it can be purchased in Louisville or any other western market.
All kinds of job work attended to, with neatness and despatch.
House-Gutters made and put up in good order, and on reasonable terms.
Feathers, old pewter and copper taken in exchange for wares.
—*Western Sun and General Advertiser,* Vincennes, Saturday, March 20, 1841

CENTERVILLE, Wayne County. US 40.

Centerville Historic District, bounded by 3rd and South Sts. and Willow Grove Rd. and the corporation line. A 19th-century town with many early two-story brick buildings, some row houses, Greek Revival and Italianate styles among the more than 100 historic structures. Centerville was one of the first chartered towns on the Old National Road; several early stage stops remain.

Wagonwrights practiced their trade in this busy place on the western road. The *Lantz-Mulligan-Boyd House,* 214 W. Main, has been restored, and the Wagon Shop now displays antiques for sale.

Morton Home, 111 S. Morton Ave., is being restored. An 1845 Greek Revival house, once the home of Indiana's Civil War Governor Oliver P. Morton. Morton served in the U.S. Senate after the war. His first term began in 1867; he was reelected and died in office in 1877.

Mansion House Hotel, 214 E. Main, was a popular stop for stagecoach travelers on the Old National Road. An 1840 Federal-style structure, it is now being restored by the Historic Centerville corporation, also renovating other old buildings of the area.

Jacob Julian House, 116 E. Plum, built in 1857, has fine trim indoors and out—in the latter case, cast iron.

Rawson Vaile House, 111 W. Walnut, is an 1840s Greek Revival cottage, now housing antiques. Vaile was an early educator.

COLUMBUS, Bartholomew County. I-65.

Visitors Center, 506 Fifth St., open daily 9 A.M. to 5 P.M.; Sundays from noon until 5 P.M. In a 19th-century building which is a renovated private dwelling, the Center has architectural exhibits, slide shows, and an art gallery. With the help of the Cummins Engine Foundation, the city has

The modern North Christian Church, designed by Eero Saarinen, is an example of the contemporary architecture that blends the new with the old at Columbus, Indiana. (Drawing from an Indiana series. Reprinted by special permission from the artist, Kanwal Prakash Singh, Indianapolis)

instituted a program of historic preservation and contemporary architecture, blending the new with the old. Leading architects have been commissioned since 1942 to carry out the project. The Center provides information concerning bus tours and walking tours which take the visitor past many historic and new designs. Sites range from a Henry Moore sculpture to a Victorian courthouse.

CONNERSVILLE, Fayette County. St. 44.

Canal House, 111 E. 4th St., was built in 1842 as a clearing house for the Whitewater Valley Canal Company, and is now being restored by the *Historic Connersville* corporation. Four Doric columns support a portico with balcony, Greek Revival, two stories, painted brick. (Note: the **Whitewater Canal State Memorial** is on US 52 W of **Brookville,** open all year. When the Whitewater Valley was the gateway to Indiana, the **Metamora Canal Lock and Mill** was the transportation center. There are a reconstructed shed aqueduct, several period buildings, and a working water wheel at the mill; in season, canal boat rides are provided.)

First Ward Hose House, 214 W. 7th St., built in 1870; the structure has been restored by the Historic Connersville corporation. It is brick with arched double doorways and was used for hose storage by the early fire company.

Elmhurst, W of Old Whitewater Canal Rt., S of town off St. 121, built in 1831 and known as Old Elm Farm, was the home of Caleb Smith, Secretary of the Interior in Lincoln's cabinet; then of James N. Huston, U.S. Treasurer under Benjamin Harrison, and later of Samuel W. Parker, once president of the Whitewater Canal Co. Now owned by the Masonic Lodge; open by appointment.

Whitewater Valley Railroad, St. 121 S of town, takes visitors on a tour of the wooded river valley behind an old steam locomotive. It is the largest scenic standard-gauge railway in the world and reaches areas not accessible by car.

CORYDON, Harrison County. US 460, St. 135.

Corydon Historic District, 19th-century town planned by Harvey Heth in 1808, became the county seat that year, then served as territorial capital of Indiana from 1813 to 1825. It was the first state capital when Indiana was admitted to the Union in December 1816. The **Corydon Capitol** still stands on the Court House Square, at 200 N. Capitol Ave., and is a state memorial. Built about 1810, it has been restored and furnished in period.

Posey House, Walnut and Oak Sts., built in 1817 a year after Corydon became capital of the new state, was the home of Colonel Thomas Lloyd Posey, son of a territorial governor. It houses a museum operated by the DAR.

There were lively times during the Civil War when Confederate General John H. Morgan and his raiders in July 1863 invaded the town, which was defended gallantly but unsuccessfully by a home guard team who were badly outnumbered and inexperienced. They were taken captive while the raiders held the village.

EVANSVILLE, Vanderburgh County. US 460.

Old Vanderburgh County Courthouse, entire block bounded by Vine, 4th, Court, and 5th Sts. Built in 1888-91, with Henry Wolters as architect. The three-story stone structure is in Greek Cross shape, with all sorts of "elements," as architectural lingo goes. Indeed, to quote the National Register, the courthouse has "hipped roof sections; central dome on round base with projecting Ionic sections dividing those with round arched openings, volutes over columned sections, clockfaces over windows and beneath segmental pediments, open cupola surmounting dome; projecting bowed corner bays, elaborate classical elements include swag and wreath reliefs, fancy Ionic columns and pilasters, circular windows inside scrollwork, and denticulated cornices supporting roof balustrades, Beaux-Arts, Classicism and Neo-Classical Revival." In short, a building worth going miles out of your way to see. It served as county seat for 78 years. The wonder is that wreckers' balls didn't hit it from all four directions in "modern" times past. It is said to have been modeled after Germany's Württemberg Castle.

Reitz Home, 224 S.E. 1st St., is three-story brick built in 1872 for

John Augustus Reitz, pioneer lumber king and philanthropist. Second Empire, with gold leaf cornices, painted ceilings, and other embellishments, it is being restored.

Evansville Post Office, 100 block, N.W. 2nd St., built in 1876–79, with Alfred B. Mullett as architect, is High Victorian Gothic in rock-faced limestone, two and one-half stories. Mullett was the architect for the U.S. Treasury.

Sheriff's House, 4th St. between Vine and Court Sts., is two and one-half stories, stone, Romantic eclectic, the residence of the county sheriff from 1891 until 1969.

Willard Library, 21 1st Ave., was built in 1883–84; James Reid was architect. A two-story brick in High Victorian Gothic style with interior cast-iron columns.

Convention-Visitors Bureau, 329 Main St., has information on local historic sites with brochures for self-guiding walking tours. On Riverside Drive and First St. between Walnut and Chandler are 22 residences, two chapels, and a carriage house. Many have been restored to their original appearance, but are not open to the public.

MADISON, Jefferson County. US 421.

Madison Historic District comprises the 19th-century Ohio River town with many early buildings of Federal, Italianate, Greek Revival, and Second Empire style. Incorporated in 1823, the town became the pork-packing center of the world.

Chamber of Commerce, Vaughn and Mulberry Sts., has a walking tour brochure which takes in more than 60 residences, most of which have been handsomely restored. The tour includes a stroll along the riverbank.

J. F. D. Lanier Mansion, W. 1st St., was built in 1840, architect Francis Costigan, in Classic Revival style. The house, open to the public with period furnishings, grounds overlooking the river, and a columned front portico overlooking both, is a state memorial, dedicated to Lanier, who twice placed his own fortune at the disposal of Indiana. During the Civil War he advanced $1 million as an unsecured loan for equipment much needed by the Union.

Shrewsbury House, 301 W. 1st St., built in the early 1800s, has a free-standing three-story spiral staircase. Francis Costigan was architect. The house is of brick with yellow-poplar trim and ironwork wrought locally by pioneer craftsmen. There are 12 rooms and 13 fireplaces in the building, which is said to have cost $50,000 when it was constructed. The drawing room still has its original paint, and Louis Philippe chandeliers from France.

Sullivan House, 304 W. 2nd St., built in 1818 for Judge Jeremiah Sullivan, has been restored by the Historic Madison corporation; the paint in each room matches the original. It is brick, Federal style, with poplar and ash interior woodwork. Many of Sullivan's personal possessions are on display. He was a state supreme court judge from 1836 to 1846. Note that all doors and mantels are handmade and varying in design.

Talbott-Hyatt Pioneer Garden, 1st and 2nd at Poplar Sts., is an 1820s garden, with spice bushes and a potting shed which has been rebuilt on its original location. The **Hyatt House,** 301 W. 2nd, was built about 1819.

Dr. William Hutchings Office and Hospital, 120 W. 3rd St., built in 1845, has one of the most complete exhibits of midcentury medical equipment in mid-America. The hospital on the second floor comprises two bedrooms, furnished appropriately with original items, including handwoven blankets.

Jefferson County Court House; Old Jail, Main and Jefferson, has been modified inside for additional floor space, but the original section is the oldest intact jail in Indiana. The imposing two-story stone and brick, partially stuccoed, building was erected in 1848–50. A kitchen wing was added in 1859. The brick forepart of the Greek Revival structure contains the sheriff's office. There are two-tiered jail cells surrounded by open vaulted space. The dome houses a bell which weighs more than 3,000 pounds and a clock installed by Israel Fowler, a local clockmaker.

Jefferson County Museum, Elm St., has many items pertaining to early steamboat days. The *Bright House,* 312 W. 3rd, was built on a lot which had been bought from the federal government by John Paul in 1821 and was resold four times before Jesse D. Bright acquired it in 1837. Bright, a lawyer, became a U.S. Senator (1845–62). The house has been restored.

Historic Madison's Auditorium, 101 E. 3rd St., built in 1835, E. J. Peck, architect, is the town's first and oldest public building, Greek Revival, now owned by *Historic Madison, Inc.,* and open to the public for meetings, art exhibits, etc.

The Colonial Inn, Elm and 2nd Sts., built by James F. D. Lanier and used as the family residence while the present Lanier mansion was being constructed, became an inn, serving the area for nearly a century. Now a residence.

Costigan House, W. 3rd St., was constructed by architect Francis Costigan for his own use in 1849. Land was expensive; Costigan had learned his trade in Baltimore, where lots were narrow, and he built a handsome two-story brick Greek Revival house on grounds barely 22 feet wide. The double stairs have a push gate at the top. The Costigan knack and inclination for finely molded woodwork has been carried out in his own home. The 30-foot living room (narrow but long) has twin fireplaces.

There are many churches and a number of public buildings in Madison from the 19th century which are well worth a visit. In 1870 there were many iron foundries in town; consequently verandas have lacy wrought-iron columns and trim, and the excellent and long-lasting work is also to be found in fences, gates, and balconies. One example is the balcony of the *John T. Windle Building,* at 306 W. Main, which has a lyre pattern. *Christ Episcopal Church,* 506 Mulberry, is a reproduction of English Gothic, designed after St. John's of Louisville, in 1847–48, of handmade brick. The heavy roof timbers are secured by wooden pins, the door locks are handmade, and possibly even more unusual is a plaque to General William Tecumseh Sherman's quartermaster on the March to the Sea, Colonel M. C. Garber, a name that was anathema to Georgia. And not too popular in southern Indiana.

NEW HARMONY, Posey County. US 460.

New Harmony Historic District, Main St., between Granary and Church, is a National Historic Landmark. There are more than 35 restored buildings, with work continuing. In 1970 the town had fewer than 1,000 residents, some of these at poverty level and about one-third at retirement age; now the whole town seems busily employed, including elder citizens who contribute vastly to the pleasant scenery and lore. Janet Blaffer, a Texas heiress whose father founded the Humble Oil Company, married Kenneth Dale Owen, a descendant of Robert Owen, who was most important to the history of New Harmony. When Mrs. Owen took an interest in the onetime colony she sought the very able help of Ralph Schwarz, an architectural historian and noted urban planner, to bring New Harmony to its best potential in any century. With his able assistant, Loretta Glenn, in behalf of Mrs. Owen,

Schwarz bought the lands needed for the new-old look of New Harmony. As Mrs. Glenn pointed out, "We were concerned not with just one house here and there but with the look of the whole street or the area beyond it." When Historic New Harmony had enough options on property, the master plan of restoration went into production. Since then more land and buildings have been acquired, the Lilly Endowment and others have advanced or invested funds to carry on the plan, and it seems to be working for both visitors and residents, not all of whom were delighted to be in the midst of change, and some of whom were quite naturally suspicious that eastern experts and spenders would fly out some night as fast as they came in. This has not happened, and Ralph Schwarz says it will not.

In 1814 Father George Rapp led a group of Harmonie Society members to this part of Indiana to settle. They were dissenters from the Lutheran Church, from Württemberg, Germany, and had previously set up a colony in Pennsylvania. They were celibates not only for self-denial but because they believed Christ was coming again soon and children were not needed for what was left of this world. Meanwhile they worked to raise funds to take their whole community to Jerusalem to await the Second Coming. With most of their energies devoted to work, they soon had 2,000 acres under cultivation, large vineyards and orchards, granary, distillery, sawmills, and other conveniences. Rapp decided markets were too far away, and he was worried that some of his human flock might stray from the straight and narrow spiritual path, so in 1824 he sold the town for $150,000 to Robert Owen, a Welsh-born industrialist and social reformer, who had a utopian experiment in mind.

William Maclure, a follower of Owen's thinking, was a Scotsman from Philadelphia who brought a boatload of scholars and scientists to settle in New Harmony. The idea was to set up an "empire of good sense," but the individualists fell to quarreling among themselves and Owen left in two years, though others stayed on.

The state memorial preserves five structures of the early colony. Today there is also a Roofless Church (North St. between Main and West) which has in its center a fine piece of sculpture by the late Jacques Lipchitz (once my part-time neighbor in Camaiore, Italy), who was both enormously talented and innovative, but it *is* mildly startling to find his bronze Madonna under what looks to be a half-inflated, or deflated, wooden shingle parachute, designed by Philip Johnson, "down home in Indiana." Less surprising is the late Paul Tillich's memorial in Tillich Park, where his ashes are interred. The great theologian often visited New Harmony. The most disturbing is the *Atheneum,* a new Visitor Center and theater being completed on the edge of town which was designed by Richard Meier of New York. Some call it an "exciting example of future building construction"; others admire its Corbusierian elements of angles, corners, and pipe balustrades. I would call it New Disharmony. If it floated you would expect Ethel Merman to be belting out a 1930s ballad from its top deck, and William Gaxton to be tap-dancing down the ramps. Which is not a kind remark to make about a building that cost at least $1.5 million and has a seat capacity of 1,000 in its outdoor theater, in addition to a rare book room, visitor orientation facilities, and convention and meeting rooms.

Tours start at the *Visitor Center,* North and Arthur Sts. Among the state memorial sites are the *Fauntleroy House,* 411 West St., built in 1815 by the Harmonists, enlarged by Robert Fauntleroy in 1840. Here the

Minerva Society, said to be the first U.S. women's club, was organized in 1859. The house has been restored. *Dormitory Number Two,* from the 1820s, was used as a residence for singles; later it was a Pestalozzian School (a system of education). It has education and printing exhibits. The *Opera House,* last of the communal dormitories used by the Harmonists, was later a ballroom for the Owenists, then a boardinghouse. In the 1850s it again served for theatrical purposes. By the 20th century it was an auto repair garage, but has been restored as a theater. The *Labyrinth,* a 19th-century shrubbery maze with a small temple, and the *Harmonist Cemetery,* with unmarked graves and some Indian burial mounds, are also part of the state memorial. The Harmonists believed in equality in death as in life; there are no imposing headstones.

Also to be toured are the log houses on West St. which have been reerected to create a streetscape of 1814-19. There is a rope walk where rope was dried, stretched, and twisted. The *Workingmen's Institute,* Tavern and West Sts., was one of America's first public libraries.

David Lentz House, 324 North St., is a restored family dwelling with period furnishings and Harmonist items supplied by the Colonial Dames of America. It was built about 1820. The *George Kepler House,* Tavern St., dates from the 1820s and has been restored, with a geology museum. *Owen House,* Brewery and Tavern Sts., restored from 1830, has decorative arts on display. *John Beal House,* Church and Brewery, of wattle and daub construction, from the 1820s, was later the home of Charles W. Slater, printer and publisher, and houses a printing museum.

Solomon Wolf House, on the corner of Brewery and Granary Sts., was a Harmonist brick dwelling of 1823. Moved from its original site, it houses an electronic scale model of the community in 1824. A *Cooper Shop* and *Theater Barn* next to Thrall's Opera House are old and new. The Second Harmonist Cooper Shop was built about 1819. The barn, from 1975, was built with traditional techniques. These provide scene and costume shops for the New Harmony Theatre Company. There is a gallery for visitors to watch scenery building. Amish carpenters raised the barn in one day with old-time vigor and enthusiasm.

All of this is just a beginning for the ever fascinating new-old village. There's a granary not to be missed, and the *"Golden Rain" Tree,* planted from seed imported from the Orient. It blossoms in mid-June, as you will learn probably within an hour of arriving in town. If it's not June you'll be advised not to miss the spectacular event next year. The *Barrett Gate House,* 500 North St. at Main, the oldest house in town (1815), has been restored and is not open to the public but well worth strolling past. There are the *New Harmony Inn;* the *Red Geranium Restaurant;* the *Shadblow Restaurant,* which is built around a shadblow tree; and in the business section, the *Mumford Emporium,* painted turquoise and red, gingerbread trimmed, which looks like a prize-winning stage setting. There are even a distillery shed from the 1820s and a brick hop house from the 1830s.

NOBLESVILLE, Hamilton County. St. 32.

Conner Prairie Pioneer Settlement, 6 miles N of Allisonville Rd. exit of I-465; 116th St.-Fishers exit off I-69 W to Allisonville Rd. (1 mile), then N 2 miles. There are 16 buildings, including a brick mansion built in 1823 by William Conner, the first settler in the area. A tour begins at the orientation building, then leads to the *Nichols' Home and Barn,* the *Conner House and Barn, Mrs. Conner's Loom House,* a *Springhouse, Still House,*

Alex Fenton Home, an "itinerant's cabin" (minus wanderer), a blacksmith shop, another family dwelling, kiln, pottery, more houses including *Dr. Campbell's Home,* settlement schools, and *The Inn.*

In case of rain, tour continues. The settlement is open from the first Tuesday in April through the first Sunday in November, closed Mondays.

William Conner set up a trading post on the White River in 1802 when Delaware Indians lived in the area. Conner had been born in a Delaware-Moravian settlement in Ohio and knew the language and culture of the tribe, who trusted him and traded with him.

He married Mekinges, daughter of Chief Anderson, and continued to trade in furs while his family grew to include six children. Conner occasionally left others to mind the store while he scouted for William Henry Harrison or aided him by serving as an interpreter at Indian councils. Two-thirds of the state lands were owned by Indians when Indiana was admitted to the Union in 1816. Two years later a treaty was signed releasing their lands and they were compelled to move west across the Mississippi. In 1820, when a large group of Delawares packed up to leave Conner's "prairie," Mrs. Conner and their six children went with them.

Conner remarried and when his fur trade declined he stocked his post with supplies needed by new settlers and soon replaced his log house with a brick mansion overlooking the one-time prairieland which he had planted with grain. His brick house was the first dwelling in the area known as the New Purchase and was used as first post office as well as a handy place to hold circuit court sessions. Conner and his new wife produced seven children while they lived here, and three more after they moved to Noblesville, where Conner

had founded and platted the county seat in 1823. Conner served in the state house of representatives for three terms and was locally active in civic affairs. He died in Noblesville in 1855.

More than a century after Conner had moved away, Eli Lilly discovered the mansion and began renovation, after researching the history of the building and area. Several log buildings from other parts of the area were moved here and restoration continued. The museum and grounds were given to Earlham College in 1964. In 1973 the guides began their effective "first-person" way of telling the settlers' story. This type of presentation, in which the costumed personnel act and speak only as they would if they were the original inhabitants of the area, and never lapse into answering questions about modern happenings our ancestors would not have known of, is a challenge to many visitors, particularly those who know history well and try to trick the beautifully trained and alert "inhabitants" into speaking of affairs that happened after their "time." This is also being used in some historical areas of our national parks and is both entertaining and informative, particularly in small presentations. It works well here, and at the *Lincoln Living Historical Farm,* at *Lincoln Boyhood Memorial,* in southern Indiana on the *Lincoln Heritage Trail* (I-64), but would not fit all restorations.

NORTH WEBSTER, Kosciusko County. St. 13.

Clarksville Restoration, on St. 13, is a reconstructed log-cabin village with a covered bridge, general store, shops, a farmhouse which has been furnished and has demonstrations of living history, a smokehouse, blacksmith shop, barn, and buggy shop. The little settlement was planned with schoolchildren in mind. Special tours are arranged through Box 283, North Webster, 46555; phone (219)

834-4111. Children can ride the Puffer Belly Railroad to see a covered bridge spanning the old Erie Canal, animals in the barn, people weaving, spinning, etc.

RICHMOND, Wayne County. US 40.

Old Richmond Historic District, roughly bounded by the C. & O. Railroad, 11th, South A, and South E Sts., takes in the original plat laid out in 1816, and includes many structures which served the Quaker community, including blacks who arrived here by way of the Underground Railway. The *Richmond Renewal Area,* a fine example of civic planning, with a four-block downtown Promenade, has renewed the oldest section of the city. Central Park has inviting benches and shady trees, and the safety while lingering that is long gone from the famous Central Park.

Hicksite Friends Meetinghouse, 1150 North A St., an 1864 building, houses the Wayne County Historical Society Museum. There are a cobbler's shop, general store, apothecary shop, pioneer kitchen, etc., among the displays. Ask here about the historic sites of the area, including the *Levi Coffin House* at nearby Fountain City, on US 27N and Mill St. Coffin was a famous agent on the underground Railroad, the only "railway" line in America no one could regret seeing abandoned as unnecessary.

ROCKPORT, Spencer County. St. 45.

Lincoln Pioneer Village, in City Park on Seminary St., is a collection of some 18 log buildings, including replicas of the Lincoln Homestead and the Old Pigeon Primitive Baptist Church. The village re-creates the look of a town Lincoln might have lived in or visited. A stockade surrounds the settlement. A museum has a variety of pioneer items.

Note: For the many who would like to follow the Lincoln family through Kentucky, Indiana, and Illinois, there is a well-established *Lincoln Heritage Trail* which begins in Louisville and ends in Springfield, Illinois. To do the trip justice, plan for a week of stops along the way. In any season but winter, it is a leisurely and enlightening experience with many unexpected delights of historical interest in the many little towns and countryside the Lincolns touched in their life journey. For details, write the *Lincoln Heritage Trail Foundation,* 702 Bloomington Rd., Champaign, Il. 61820, or call (217) 352-1968. They will help plan a whole itinerary or any part of the trip your time allows. At this writing Rockport is not on the trail, but *New Harmony,* which has no particular Lincoln associations except for its location, is a bonus overnight stop.

SPRING MILL STATE PARK, Lawrence County. St. 60.

Spring Mill Village is an authentic restoration, considered one of the best community rebuildings in the country. It was settled about 1816. Today's Main St. has the appearance of mid-19th century, with village shops and dwellings; a reconstructed sawmill and an operating water-powered gristmill are part of the complex. Among structures are a tavern, cobbler's shop, distillery, a milliner's, bootshop, post office, pharmacist's dispensary, and a pottery. The park, which comprises 1,200 acres, is open all year. Richard Lieber, a former state conservationist, who was responsible for the restoration, said, "You come back from the top of the hill 200 feet and you go back 100 years."

VINCENNES, Knox County. US 41.

Vincennes Historic District takes in the old Indian settlement, three fort sites, and the old French town which became territorial capital. There are early college buildings, commercial structures, and residences in the district. The *Territorial Capitol of Former Indiana Territory,* listed on the National Register, is bounded by Harrison, 1st, Scott, and Park Sts. The early-19th-century two-story frame building has been moved several times. It served as headquarters for the territorial governor and housed the general assembly for 13 years following the beginning of the territory in 1800.

Harrison Home (Grouseland), 3 W. Scott St., has been restored, handsomely furnished, and is open to the public, which must mind its p's and q's, as the saying used to be, because the hostesses are tart-tongued ladies who do not want anyone to wander, even in attention, from their spiel and route for seeing the rooms. Grouseland was the home of William Henry Harrison from 1804 to 1812 when he was territorial governor. Harrison met the great Indian leader Tecumseh (for whom William T. Sherman was named) here, and in 1811 began the campaign that ended with the Battle of Tippecanoe. Harrison was our 9th President. The house has many mementoes of Harrison and of Tecumseh. NHL.

Old State Bank, N. 2nd St., was built in 1838 by John Moore, and was the only bank west of the Alleghenies to survive the 1837 panic. Two stories in brick and stucco, Greek Revival style.

Old Cathedral Complex, 207 Church St. The cathedral was built about 1830 on the site of a 1732 cathedral. The library building contains a papal manuscript from 1319, and a land grant signed by President Martin Van Buren, Thomas Jefferson's survey work, and parish records from 1749. An early settlers' burial ground is part of the complex.

Elihu Stout Print Shop, Scott and Park Sts., is a replica of the original two-story frame building which housed the first newspaper in Indiana Territory, the Indiana *Gazette.*

Log Cabin Tourist Center, W. 1st St. at College Ave., has brochures on the many historic sites of old Vincennes and arrangements for tours of Vincennes University, which was founded in 1806 and has a 42-acre campus on the Wabash River. The *Mariah Creek Baptist Church* on campus was founded in 1809 with a militantly antislavery group that denied membership to slaveholders. Original pews, pulpit, and other furnishings are still here.

Note: The *George Rogers Clark Memorial* is well worth visiting but is being omitted from this guide along with most chiefly military sites.

ILLINOIS

Chicagoans pointed with pride to majestic structures of brick and "Athens marble" which graced the blocks in the center of town. (Actually the Athens was in Illinois, and the marble was medium-grade limestone, but the effect was unquestionably impressive.) The most up-to-date buildings were beginning to use cast-iron plates and columns in their facades, a new fashion imported from the effete East. But these were by no means typical. . . .

It was even common to use wood in disguise. Most church steeples were built with a wooden framework, covered with tin or copper sheathing, and often shaped and painted to resemble the stone they were not. Even decorated cornices on the finest marble buildings were usually "sculptured" in this way. . . . Aside from the fact that it was readily available in what then seemed like inexhaustible supply, wood also had the virtue of lightness, compared to the brick, stone, iron and steel it imitated, and was far easier to work with. But because of the great amount of impermanent construction, and the swiftness of growth and change, the city looked like a stage which was never quite set, and whose scenery was constantly being shifted.
—*The Great Chicago Fire,* by Robert Cromie, New York, 1958

BISHOP HILL, Henry County. St. 82, N of US 34.

Utopian-minded colonists from Sweden, led by Eric Janson, walked 160 miles from Chicago across the prairies to settle here in 1846, but nearly 100 died the first winter, when most of the group lived in caves. In the spring more immigrants came from the homeland; then by hard work and dedication the colony prospered for more than a decade.

The town has been restored. *Old Colony Church,* the first permanent structure, has a number of small rooms on the ground floor which were occupied by families who shared the communal dining room. The second story was for church meetings. Olof Krans paintings on exhibit show Bishop Hill life as it was long ago. The *Steeple Building,* from 1854, still fails to tell the time with its one-hand clock. Guides relate that the minute hand was lost during the busy days of construction and never replaced by the settlers, who were too industrious to care what time it was. The *Bjorklund Hotel,* once a stage stop, is being restored. An old country school still is used for special occasions. During summer months crafts are demonstrated in the shops, including weaving, candle dipping, and smithing. Guided tours are available on weekends from April to October. A fall festival celebrates Swedish agricultural days, *Jordbrukdagarna.*

The murder of the leader, Janson (sometimes spelled Jansson or Johnson), in 1850, by John Root, who was trying to persuade his wife to leave the commune, was a serious blow to the colonists, who had already been hit by cholera in 1849. The story is complicated by the varying reports of participants and witnesses, but Janson was 42 years old in the spring of 1850 when he preached what proved to be a farewell sermon to his people; the next day at Cambridge, Illinois, he went to circuit court to defend several suits brought against the colony and was shot and killed instantly by Root, during the noon recess. John Root, a well-born Swedish immigrant who had served with the American Army in the Mexican War, had been trying to remove his wife from Bishop Hill for some time. She had once gone to live with him in Chicago but returned to Bishop Hill. The community was harassed by rowdy gangs for months before the death of Janson and the arrest of Root. The trial was postponed for two years; Root was sentenced to serve two years in Alton Penitentiary and was pardoned a year later.

By the opening of the Civil War the peaceful colony with its skillful artisans and hard-working farmers was abandoned and collective ownership was ended with the division of property. About 13 of the original 16 buildings have been kept in use. The colonists were especially gifted in linen weaving and the manufacture of woodenware, from utensils to wagons. In addition to the church, homes, and shops, in their best times they also ran a large flax machine, two sawmills, a gristmill, and a steam-flouring mill.

CHICAGO, Cook County. I-90.

Chicago Convention & Tourism Bureau, 332 S. Michigan Ave—(312) 922-3530—has a "Vacation Kit," listing attractions and events. The *Visitors Bureau,* Chicago Association of Commerce & Industry, 130 S. Michigan, 60603, has maps and local information. The newly restored landmark survivor of the great Chicago fire, the *Water Tower,* N. Michi-

The Water Tower, Chicago. (Chicago Convention & Tourism Bureau, Inc.)

gan and Chicago Aves., is now a public information center for the bureau, open daily.

Chicago on Foot, by Ira J. Bach, is an excellent book on walking tours of Chicago's architecture.

Glessner House, 1800 S. Prairie Ave., built in 1886, Henry Hobson Richardson, architect, has been restored by the *Chicago School of Architecture Foundation.* Bus, bike, and walking tours are planned and conducted by the group: (312) 326-1393. *The Prairie Ave. Historic District,* on either side of 18th St., includes Glessner House and three other fine early homes from what was considered "Millionaire's Row" in the 1800s. A once best-selling novel, *Prairie Avenue,* by the late Arthur Meeker makes vivid use of this background. The area is being restored to its gaslit days with cobblestone streets and handsomely furnished dwellings. Glessner House has 35 rooms and a collection of Frank Lloyd Wright furniture. Guided tours three days weekly. *Kimball House,* 1801 S. Prairie, built in 1890, resembles a French château; *Coleman House,* 1811 S. Prairie, dates from the mid-1880s, with Richardsonian influences; the *Keith House* (about 1870), 1900 S. Prairie, has a mansard roof and was lucky enough, along with the other mansions of this section, to be south of the great fire of 1871. The *Clarke House,* built about 1837, is to be moved here.

Pullman Historic District, on the far south side near Lake Calumet, from 111th to 115th Sts., and from Cottage Grove E to the railroad tracks near Langley, was once a model company town for the Pullman Palace Car Company. Moran's *Dictionary of Chicago,* in 1909, called Pullman "the most beautiful little city on the face of the earth. Its great manufacturing plants are surrounded by broad and sinuous drives, walks, lawns, miniature lakes, fountains, etc., that give it the appearance of a park. . . . The Arcade, an immense building, in which are all the shops or stores, a bank, a library, a theater, etc.; the Market House, in which all meats and vegetables are sold; the hotel and all the residences, are built principally of pressed brick, showing Gothic, Swiss and other styles of architecture. . . ."

George M. Pullman, Chicago railroad industrialist, built the town for his employees in 1880. Nine years later it became part of Chicago.

The town, designed by Solon S. Beman and Nathan F. Barrett, occupied about 300 acres of the 4,000 owned by the company. By 1885 there were some 1,400 dwellings in addition to commercial buildings and by the 1890s, 11,800 residents. Rents for the row houses were reasonable, averaging about $14 per month, which was about a quarter of the average wage. Pullman hoped to avoid strikes and absenteeism by creating a pleasant place to live with parks, playing fields, church, and places of entertainment available for all. A general depression in 1892 and a strike in 1894 led eventually to Pullman's having to cut wages and then to sell all of the nonindustrial company properties.

Over the years the *Arcade, Market Hall,* and leading structures were greatly damaged or destroyed by fire or demolition, but recently the *Historic Pullman Foundation* has been restoring the area, now a National Landmark District. The *Historic Pullman Center,* formerly a Masonic Lodge, has been renovated and is used as a community center. *Market Hall* is being reconditioned to be used again. The *Hotel Florence,* named for Pullman's daughter, is being handsomely restored. It was built in 1881.

Greenstone Church, on the corner of 112th St. and St. Lawrence Ave., was designed by Solon Beman, and dedicated in December 1882. Its stained-glass windows and crystalline, serpentine rock façade, beneath the impressive steeple, look much as they did when the opening ceremonies took place, although the church is now the Pullman Methodist.

The *Pullman Stables,* at E. 112th and S. Cottage Grove, once housed all the horses of residents and visitors, and a volunteer fire company.

Pullman's Utopian dream, with commercial touches, ended, but one of the achievements that must have pleased the inventor the year before his death was the town's being voted world's most perfect, at the Prague International Hygienic and Pharmaceutical Exposition, in 1896. During the Pullman strike of 1894 Mark Hanna said to someone who had praised Pullman: "Oh, hell! . . . Go and live in Pullman and find out how much Pullman gets sellin' city water and gas to those poor fools!" Pullman left an estate $17,400,000, and his

Hotel Florence, Pullman, Illinois. (Courtesy Historic Pullman Foundation)

family buried him with extra care, putting the coffin in asphalt and steel rails, warding against any depredations that might be made by disgruntled former employees.

GALENA, Jo Daviess County. US 20.

Chamber of Commerce, 124 N. Main St., 61036—(815) 777-0203. Information is available here. There are more than 100 mansions and cottages built in the 1800s, now restored, furnished with antiques of the area, and open twice a year for tours. The *Historical Society* has an open house in June; the *Guild of the First Presbyterian Church* sponsors a September tour.

Old Market House State Memorial, on Water St. at the river between Hill and Perry Sts., built 1845–46, was the public market in the town's richest days. Exhibits detail architectural history of the area.

Vinegar Hill Historic Lead Mine & Museum, 6 miles N on St. 84, has guided tours. Early mining methods and tools are displayed.

Dowling House, N. Main and Diagonal Sts., built about 1826, has

been restored and furnished as a trading post and dwelling, with guided tours. The stone building is thought to be one of the oldest in town.

The *U. S. Grant Home,* 511 Bouthillier St., built in 1857, is brick and handsomely furnished. NHL. It was given by the town to Grant and his family in 1865 in recognition of his outstanding Civil War services. He lived here until 1867, when he became Secretary of War, and again after the world tour he took following his presidency. The Grants came back early in 1880 and stayed here for a short time until they moved to New York. In 1904 the house was deeded to Galena by Frederick Dent Grant, son of the President; a number of family possessions are on display. Grant's pre–Civil War home is at 121 High, just E of St. Matthew Lutheran Church. In his *Memoirs* the future general and President wrote of recruiting day in Galena in March 1861: "After the speaking was over, volunteers were called for. . . . I declined the captaincy before the balloting, but announced that I would aid the company in every way I could, and would be found in the service in some position if there should be a war. I never went into our leather-store after that meeting to put up a package or do other business.

"The ladies of Galena were quite as patriotic as the men. They could not enlist, but they conceived the idea of sending their first company to the field uniformed. They came to me to get a description of the United States uniform for infantry; subscribed and bought the material; procured tailors to cut out the garments, and the ladies made them up. In a few days the company was in uniform and ready to report at the State capital for assignment."

Old General Store, 227 S. Main, a reproduction, carries the kind of stock the ladies must have looked for in 1861. All merchandise is genuine but not for sale.

I Remember Mama Antique Doll & Toy Museum, 117 N. Main, has over 2,000 antique dolls and toys on exhibit. Open daily.

Lolly's Toy & Doll Museum, 225 Magazine St., has a fine collection of antique miniatures, toys, and dolls. Open daily. (There is an admission charge to both toy museums.)

"Orrin-Smith Guest Suite," 600 Park Ave., built in 1852 by a riverboat captain, has French and Italian styles. Open June to October.

"When Grandpa Was a Boy" Museum, 204 N. Main St., has six scenes of early American holidays. Open daily April through December.

Turney House, 612 Spring St., built about 1835, is the restored stone home of Galena's first lawyer, John Turney. His office and living quarters are furnished and on display, from May to November. Guided tours.

The *Belvedere House,* 1008 Park Ave., built in 1857 by J. Russell Jones, a steamship owner and ambassador to Belgium, has 22 furnished rooms restored to the grandeur of the mid-19th century. Open daily June through December.

The *Maxeiner House,* 104 S. Bench St., is now called "Little Salem." The frame house, built in 1838, has wooden pegs fastening oak and black walnut timbers. Philip Maxeiner was a tailor and is said to have had his shop in this house and to have made Grant's uniform. Period furnishings.

The *Galena Historical Society,* 211½ Bench St., maintains a large museum in its headquarters, which also houses the Galena Community Center. *Old Firehouse No. 1* is another project maintained by the group. The museum has an almost overwhelming variety of items, partially because the families of many war veterans who had served under General Grant sent souvenirs to the Galena collection. One of its features is Thomas Nast's life-size painting of Lee's surrender to Grant at Appomattox. General John A. Rawlins and General Ely S. Parker, also from Galena, are depicted as they stood at that historic moment.

John A. Rawlins, a Galena lawyer at the outbreak of war, became chief of staff under Grant, a major general, and Secretary of War in Grant's cabinet. His home was at 517 Hill St. Charles A. Dana, as a war correspondent, complained that Rawlins "bossed everything" at Grant's headquarters at Vicksburg. Rawlins also kept a careful eye on Grant's drinking and tried to shield him from reporters.

Ely S. Parker, a full-blooded Seneca Indian and a construction engineer, in 1858 was in charge of the building of the custom house on Green St., later the post office. Parker wanted to be a lawyer but was refused admission to the bar because he was not a citizen. After his graduation from Rensselaer as an engineer he became acquainted with Ulysses Grant, who was then a clerk in his father's leather store. Parker became a brigadier general and military secretary for Grant and was appointed Commissioner of Indian Affairs after the war.

William R. Rowley, who became a Union general, lived at 515 Hill, next door to Rawlins; the houses were neat, look-alike, one-and-a-half-story frame structures. Rowley was provost marshall on Grant's staff, but ill health forced his early retirement from service.

John E. Smith Home, 807 S. Bench, built in the 1850s. Smith ran a jewelry and silversmith shop; he became a major general on Grant's staff during the war.

Galena's other generals were Augustus L. Chetlain, John C. Smith, John O. Duer, and Jaspar E. Maltby. Elihu B. Washburne, a lawyer, diplomat, and Congressman, was a great influence in Grant's life. Born in Livermore, Maine, educated at Harvard, he settled in Galena in 1840, nominated Henry Clay for President at the Whig convention in 1844, and was considerably luckier later when he sponsored Grant, first as brigadier general and then as lieutenant general. Washburne served in Congress for many years, was Secretary of State in Grant's cabinet, then minister to France. It was on the lawn of his Colonial residence at 908 Third St., near Decatur (US 20), that Grant first drilled his recruits in 1861.

Dr. Edward Kittoe Home, 105 High, was the dwelling of Lieutenant Colonel Kittoe, a surgeon and medical director of the Army of Tennessee, on Grant's staff.

Jo Daviess County Court House, 312 N. Bench St., was built in 1839: Captain U. S. Grant attended a mass meeting here in April 1861 when Lincoln called for 75,000 volunteers to save the Union. Grant was 38 and making a modest living in his father's leather store, which stood at 120 S. Main. In a letter written to his father, Jesse Root Grant, April 21, he revealed his modesty as well as his feelings: "Having been educated for such an emergency, at the expense of the Government, I feel that it has upon me superior claims, such claims as no ordinary motives of self-interest can surmount. I do not wish to act hastily or unadvisedly in the matter, and as there are more than enough to respond to the first call of the President, I have not yet offered myself. I have promised and am giving all the assistance I can in organizing the Company whose services have been accepted from this place. I have promised further to go with them to the state Capital and if I can be of service to the Governer [sic] in organizing his state troops to do so. What I ask now is your approval of the course I am taking, or advice in the matter."

De Soto House, Main and Green Sts., had a grand opening as the "largest hotel in the West," in April 1855. The 240 rooms were ready for hundreds of guests arriving daily by river, stage, and railroad. In 1856 Lincoln spoke from a balcony, now gone. Grant had headquarters here in his 1868 and 1872 presidential campaigns. In 1880 two unused upper stories were removed; 70 rooms remained for the declining trade.

Galena Gazette & Advertiser, founded in 1834, second-oldest newspaper in Illinois, 210 N. Main St., has old presses and other exhibits.

Stockade and Underground Refuge, 208 Perry St., at Main, are Black Hawk war sites. Amos Farrar, a fur trader, came to town in 1823. His log cabin is part of the original stockade built for defense in the war in the spring of 1832. An Indian museum and frontier post office are part of the displays. Open daily from May to November.

Grace Episcopal Church, Hill and Prospect Sts., 1847, is English Gothic, remodeled by William LeBaron Jenney, often called the "father of the skyscraper."

First Methodist Church, 125 S. Bench, founded in 1829, has a pew marked for the Grant family.

During the *June Open House,* sponsored by the Historical Society, five handsomely restored homes are visited; other attractions include a lamplight tour of the Grant home and *Spring Skills from the Hills* at the *Old Market House.*

NAUVOO, Hancock County. St. 96.

Nauvoo Restoration, Inc., Visitor Center, Young and Partridge Sts. A historical film, free guide service to restored buildings, and literature on sites are available.

Times and Seasons Building, Kimball & Main, held the offices of the Mormon newspaper and the post office. *Heber C. Kimball House,* Munson and Partridge, has been handsomely refurbished. Kimball was one of the 12 apostles who served Joseph Smith. *Wilford Woodruff House,* Durphy and Hotchkiss Sts.: Woodruff was an apostle, missionary, and the fourth president of the church. *Brigham Young House,* Kimball and Granger: Young, who succeeded Smith, lived here in the 1840s. In 1841 he was the leading fiscal officer of the Mormon Church in Nauvoo. He campaigned for Smith's candidacy for President of the U.S. in 1844; after the death of Smith and the burning of Mormon homes, Young directed the migration west. As of now, 12 Mormon Nauvoo homes have been reconstructed and appropriately furnished and are hosted by Mormon volunteers. There will be some 40 structures when the project is completed. Local hopes are to make Nauvoo the Williamsburg of the West.

Joseph Smith Historic Center, Main and Water Sts., has a 45-minute tour with a slide presentation, a visit to the graves of Joseph Smith, his wife Emma, and his brother Hyrum. Also the *Joseph Smith Homestead,* 1803, the town's oldest structure, and the *Smith Mansion,* 1843, where Smith lived for about one year. Both homes have period furnishings.

The *Webb Blacksmith and Wagon Shop* is a replica. Two large forges, copies of the original, have bellows from Utah, and original anvils which were taken west long ago, but have been returned.

Old Carthage Jail, 307 Walnut St., in Carthage, 10 miles S on St. 96, then 14 miles E on US 136, is where Joseph and Hyrum Smith died. The building has been restored; a *Visitor Center* has slides, exhibits, and brochures.

Ritter House, in *Nauvoo State Park,* S of town on St. 96, has been restored. It has a typical wine cellar and vineyard, also a museum. A "sunstone" from the Nauvoo Temple is also in the park.

Nauvoo Temple Site, Temple Square, has been excavated. The temple, begun in 1841, was trimmed with stone cuttings of the sun, moon, and stars as seen in a vision of the Apostle John. One of the three sunstones is in Quincy, Illinois, and one in the Smithsonian. A number of moonstones have been found but only one starstone. The temple was destroyed by a fire, set by an arsonist in 1848, then leveled by a tornado in 1850. Some stones from the ruins were used in the construction of other buildings, including the one which now houses the *Information Center of Nauvoo Restoration, Inc.* This was put up by French Icarians in the mid-19th century.

The Icarians, led by Etienne Cabet, came to Nauvoo in the late 1840s, after the Mormons had gone, and tried a Utopian communal way of living for a number of years before moving on. German Roman Catholics, the next to arrive in the community, planted the grapevines and began the wine industry which still is carried on.

Among the many historical structures in town is the *Jonathan Browning House,* Main St. near Kimball, where the father of John Moses Browning (who invented the automatic rifle) was a wagonmaker, gunsmith, and blacksmith.

Visitors are advised to see the orientation films and brochures before touring the beautiful old river city. There is a tendency to think of the Mormon movement as a westward one, but Joseph Smith, the prophet who was both a temporal and a spiritual leader, received his first vision in New York in 1820; he published the Book of Mormon in 1830, took his community to Kirtland, Ohio, then moved on to Jackson County, Missouri. In 1838 the Missouri governor issued an extermination order against the Mormons and they fled to Illinois and the Iowa territory in 1838-39. Smith was in prison in Liberty, Missouri, from November 1838 until April 1839, when he was being transferred to Boone County for retrial, and escaped, managing to join his people at Quincy, Illinois. Nauvoo was then the largest city in Illinois (the census for 1845 listed 11,052 residents), and here the Mormons thought they had found an ideal and safe place to live.

There was trouble both within and outside of the church. Joseph and Hyrum Smith were assassinated by a mob while awaiting trial in the Carthage jail in June 1844. The trial concerned the destruction of an anti-Mormon newspaper. More troubles followed and led to a Mormon "war" in September 1846. When the Mormons surrendered, some scattered to parts of Illinois, others went west. One group became the Reorganized Church of Latter-day Saints, under Joseph Smith III, with headquarters at Independence, Missouri (which see). This group still owns some of the Nauvoo land, including the Smith structures.

NEW SALEM, Menard County. St. 97.

Lincoln's New Salem State Park, 2 miles S of Petersburg, 20 miles NW of Springfield, is one of the most important stops on the *Lincoln Heritage Trail.* There are 26 reconstructed buildings in the village which re-creates the town where Lincoln lived in 1831-37. The only original building is the *Onstot Cooper Shop,* but all have been carefully constructed after detailed research into family archives and early maps. Anyone who has visited New Salem over the years will be astonished at the way in which time, so to say, has been reversed, and the newer New Salem becomes the more it resembles the old Salem of Lincoln's time.

In 1889 when William H. Herndon, Lincoln's law partner, went back to see the New Salem he had known as a thriving village he found: "Not a building, scarcely a stone, is left to mark the place where it once stood. To reach it now the traveler must ascend a bluff a hundred feet above the general level of the surrounding country. The brow of the ridge, two hundred and fifty feet broad where it overlooks the river, widens gradually as it extends westwardly to the forest and ultimately to broad pastures. Skirting the base of the bluff is the Sangamon River. . . . The hills are bearded with timber—oak, hickory, walnut, ash, and elm. . . . In the days of land offices and stagecoaches it was a sprightly village with a busy market. . . . singularly enough, contemporaneous with the departure of Lincoln from its midst it went into a rapid decline. A few crumbling stones here and there are all that attest its former existence."

New Salem declined in 1839 (just two years after Lincoln left for Springfield to practice law), when the county seat was established at Petersburg.

In 1906 William Randolph Hearst, who was lecturing at the Old Salem Chautauqua, bought the townsite and gave it in trust to the Chautauqua Association. A Lincoln League was formed in 1917 to begin research and create interest in the site. With the approval of Hearst the land was transferred to the state and soon became a state park. Visitors from all parts of the country came in growing numbers; in 1931 the state appropriated $50,000 for park improvements, and the cornerstone for the first of the reconstructions, the *Berry-Lincoln Store,* was laid in 1932. The *Onstot Cooper Shop,* built in 1835, had been moved to Petersburg in 1840, and returned to New Salem in 1922 by the *Old Salem Lincoln League.* It was here Lincoln studied by the firelight provided by cooper's shavings.

Timber dwellings, plus the *Rutledge Tavern,* shops, stores, industries, and a school where church services were held, have been reproduced faithfully and furnished in 1830s style. Some items were actually used by the residents here. The landscaping has historical authenticity: redhaw, Osage orange hedges, wild crab, wild plum, witch hazel, wild blackberry, wild gooseberry, and other plants, shrubs, and trees bloom in season. There are herb gardens at the homes of New Salem's two doctors. The park is closed only when bad weather makes the tour impossible. Access to facilities is by foot only. There is now a post office in the *Berry-Lincoln* store where all mail deposited bears the cancellation "Lincoln's New Salem."

Abraham Lincoln: His Story in His Own Words, edited by Ralph Geoffrey Newman, Lincoln scholar (New York: Doubleday, 1975), quotes the young Lincoln: "I stopped indefinitely, and, for the first time, as it were by myself, at New Salem. This was in July, 1831. Here I rapidly made acquaintances and friends. In less than a year Offutt's business was failing—had almost failed—when the Black Hawk war of 1832 broke out. I joined a volunteer company, and to my own surprise, was elected captain of it—a success which gave me more pleasure than any I have had since."

Most New Salem visitors of any age are interested in the Ann Rutledge story. Newman says: "For a brief time Lincoln did board at the tavern [Rutledge's], and in the tiny village of only one hundred souls, Ann Rutledge and Abraham Lincoln would certainly have been friends. But the facts in this story do not support the romantic rumor. The facts are that this pretty twenty-two-year-old, blue-eyed girl was engaged to be married to John McNamar [McNeil], the partner of Samuel Hill, New Salem's leading merchant. He had returned east for a visit to New York where his family lived, and his lengthy absence began to cause some gossip. In the summer of 1835, at the Rutledge farm on Sand Ridge, seven miles north of New Salem, Ann contracted a disease—probably typhoid fever—and died after a short illness. It was not until almost thirty years later, that some hint of this supposed romance came to light. After Lincoln's death in 1865, his law partner, William H. Herndon, helped to circulate the story."

An *Information Center,* near the parking area, has brochures and maps for touring the village. Groups larger than 25 must have permission from the park ranger to be admitted to any Illinois state park or conservation area, and pets must be on a leash. For details, write Ranger, Lincoln's New Salem, 62659; phone (217) 632-7953.

An addition to the park, which Lincoln would have enjoyed, is *The Great American People Show,* an outdoor drama, presented from late

June through August, although dates may change. The theater in **Kelso Hollow,** just beyond the restored village, is well designed to fit the rustic background and yet accommodate modern players. *Your Obedient Servant, A. Lincoln* is a documentary-drama with music, chronicling the life of Lincoln, with dialogue based on authentic reports, letters, accounts, and songs of Lincoln's time. It is to be hoped that continuing public support will keep this worthwhile project a permanent part of the Lincoln experience.

SPRINGFIELD, Sangamon County. US 66, 36.

Convention & Tourism Commission, 500 E. Capitol Ave., has maps for the Lincoln Trail and a walking tour of Lincoln sites in town.

Lincoln Home, NE corner of Eighth and Jackson Sts., is now part of a four-block area, owned and maintained by the National Park Service, which has been restored or preserved to resemble its original condition when the Lincoln family lived here in the only home they ever owned, 1844–61. There are uneven and slippery boardwalks and steep, narrow staircases; visitors are advised to step carefully while discovering how life was more than a century ago.

A fine orientation program is presented in the new **Visitors Center,** which should be seen before visiting the Lincoln house. A number of Lincoln sites are within walking distance. The restored **Lincoln-Herndon Law Offices** at 6th and Adams are across from the **Old State Capitol,** which is one of the showplaces of Springfield, splendidly restored and furnished as it was in Lincoln's time. NHL. Brochures with detailed accounts of Abraham Lincoln and his life in Springfield are available at the many sites associated with him. Among the most important of these,

in addition to the above, are the **Lincoln Marriage Home & Museum,** 406 S. 8th St., a replica of the 1836 home of Ninian Edwards, Mary Todd's brother-in-law, where the Lincolns met and were married. Mary Lincoln died here in 1882. The **Lincoln Depot Museum,** 10th and Monroe Sts., is the site where Lincoln gave his farewell address to Springfield when he left for the White House, February 11, 1861.

WOODSTOCK, McHenry County. US 14.

Orson Welles was moved to eloquence when he saw Woodstock. A poster of the historic **Opera House,** 119 Van Buren, built in 1889–90, quotes the actor: "Like a wax-flower tree under a bell of glass, in the paisley and gingham county of McHenry is Woodstock, grand capital of mid-Victorianism in the Midwest. Tower-

Woodstock Opera House, Woodstock, Illinois. (Drawing by James E. Pearson. Courtesy City of Woodstock)

ing over a Square full of Civil War monuments, a bandstand, and a spring house . . . is a very rustic and rusticated thing: a real, old honest-to-horse hair Opera House."

Actually *City Park* sports only one Civil War monument, erected by the Woodstock Women's Relief Corps, but the rest of the description is accurate. The Opera House has been fully restored to its days of glory, and Welles himself is among the famous who have appeared on its stage. With stenciled walls and ceilings, stained-glass windows, gaslights, and ornate Victorian door trim and banisters, the building is worth nearly as much attention as the performances given. Jane Addams, Eugene Debs, and Count Leo Tolstoy spoke from its stage. In the mid-20th century a group called the Woodstock Players, including Paul Newman, Betsy Palmer, Tom Bosley, Geraldine Page, Shelley Berman, and Lois Nettleton gave 16 shows a season here.

Old McHenry County Courthouse, City Square, was built in 1857–58, with John Van Osdel, Chicago's first architect, making it a Greek cross shape. In 1887 a two-story brick jail was added next door. Now restored, the courthouse and jail house shops and restaurants. Eugene Debs, labor leader and humanitarian, was the most famous prisoner. He was jailed here in 1895, having taken a part in the Pullman strike, and later said he made his plans for founding the American Socialist party while locked up in Woodstock.

A handsome brochure, illustrated by James E. Pearson, offers a walking tour of the town's landmarks and period houses. Inquire at City of Woodstock offices, P. O. Box 190, 121 W. Calhoun; phone (815) 338-4300. The Woodstock Landmark Commission has marked many local sites with descriptive historical plaques.

One of the most decorative of the landmarks is the 1873 *Spring House* in Woodstock Square, which was built over a mineral spring. The present structure is a reconstruction, which was completed and dedicated during the Bicentennial.

Appalachian Mountain Region

West Virginia
Kentucky
Tennessee

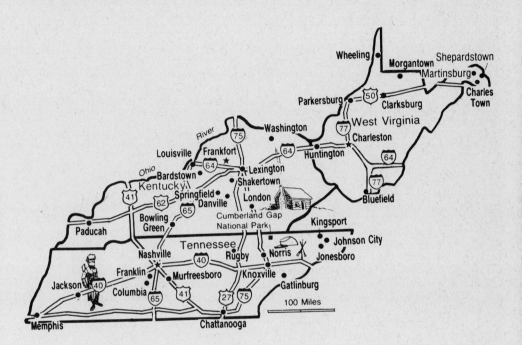

WEST VIRGINIA

Wheeling is in the state of Virginia, and appears to be a flourishing town. It is the point at which most travellers from the west leave the Ohio, to take the stages which travel the mountain road to the Atlantic cities.

It has many manufactories, among others, one for blowing and cutting glass, which we visited. We were told by the workmen that the articles finished there were equal to any in the world; but my eyes refused their assent. The cutting was very good, though by no means equal to what we see in daily use in London. . . .

Wheeling has little of beauty to distinguish it, except the ever lovely Ohio. . . . and a fine bold hill, which rises immediately behind the town. This hill, as well as every other in the neighbourhood, is bored for coal. Their mines are all horizontal. The coal burns well, but with a very black and dirty cinder.
—*Domestic Manners of the Americans,* by Frances M. Trollope, London, 1836

Clay Court House is a place of six or eight houses and is the County Seat of Clay County. The whole populace knew of our arrival. We should have passed by the town without knowing of its existence had not some boys in swimming told us of a settlement. I went up to the only store in the town to buy some eggs, butter, soap, candles and crackers but the store did not deal in any of these articles. A crowd of men and boys gathered around me in wonderment at the flies fastened to my hat. No one of them had ever seen a fly before or heard of taking fish by such a lure.
—*West Virginia Trek 1879; from the Diary of Albert P. Tallman,* edited by Robert W. Hazlett, Charleston, 1977

CHARLES TOWN, Jefferson County. US 340.

Jefferson County Courthouse, corner of N. George and E. Washington Sts., was built in the 19th century in Greek Revival style. It has been enlarged and restored. It was the site of John Brown's trial for treason in 1859.

Jefferson County Museum, N. Samuel and E. Washington Sts., houses John Brown memorabilia.

Charles Washington Hall, N. George and W. Washington Sts., was a post office in 1896 when the first rural free delivery mail route was inaugurated from here.

Zion Episcopal Church, E. Congress between S. Mildred and S. Church Sts., was built in 1852. Many Revolutionary War and Confederate soldiers and about 75 members of the Washington family are buried in the church cemetery.

Claymont Court, Summit Point Rd., S of town off US 340, is an 1820 mansion with wide two-story verandas and spacious lawns. It was built by Bushrod Corbin Washington, a grand-nephew of George Washington and a member of the Virginia House of Delegates and General Assembly. The house was later owned by Frank Stockton, author of the classic *The Lady or the Tiger?* and many other stories. Stockton lived here until his death in 1902.

Happy Retreat, S of town off St. 9, an 18th- to 19th-century dwelling which was the home of Charles Washington, founder of Charles Town and brother of George Washington, who was often a visitor here. Judge Isaac R. Douglas bought the house in 1837 and finished construction. Colonel Charles and Mrs. Washington are buried on the grounds.

Piedmont, 2 miles W off St. 51, was built about 1780 and is brick with Flemish bond. It is one of the best examples of Georgian design in West Virginia. Built by Robert Worthington in the 1730s, one stone wing was known as Quarry Bank. Dr. John Briscoe built the main house, using bricks that had been brought from England and Holland as ballast.

Harewood, 3 miles W off St. 51, was built 1768–70, with John Ariss (sometimes spelled Arise) thought to be the architect-builder. It is two stories of fieldstone with hipped roof, built for Samuel Washington, brother of George and Charles. James Madison and Dolley Payne Todd were married here. The mantel is said to have been a gift from Lafayette. The house has been handsomely restored. Colonel Washington's office and a family graveyard are on the grounds.

Cedar Lawn, W off St. (VA) 51, was built in 1825, two-story brick, with hipped and gabled roof, Federal style. It was built for John Thornton Augustine Washington, a great-nephew of George Washington.

Richwood Hall, W off St. 51, an early-19th-century brick with Flemish bond, with Federal touches, was

here when Confederate General Jubal Early's men stayed overnight during the Battle of Cameron's Depot.

A *House and Garden Tour* takes place in Martinsburg, Shepherdstown, and Charles Town (as well as Harpers Ferry) the last weekend in April. Call (304) 876-2242; write Tour, Box 24, Charles Town, 25414.

HARPERS FERRY, Jefferson County. US 340.

Harpers Ferry National Historical Park, at the confluence of the Shenandoah and Potomac rivers, also extends into Maryland, and comprises the original town center and surrounding area, with numerous structures restored and park service buildings.

In October 1859, the raid led by abolitionist John Brown, with 18 men and a wagonload of supplies, attempting to take the U. S. Armory at the Ferry, brought the whole country's attention to this little river-carved gateway in the mountains, and it has been a controversial subject in history ever since. Today there are those who think Brown was an inspired leader, others who think he was mad, and correspondingly courageous or foolhardy.

Whatever the case, the townspeople fought back, help came from Charles Town and eventually from Washington, and some soon-to-be-famous names were among those present on that Sunday night of October 16, or on December 2 when Brown was hanged at Charles Town. Robert E. Lee and J. E. B. Stuart came to the rescue at Harpers Ferry, with 90 marines. Thomas J. Jackson, who had not yet earned his soubriquet of Stonewall, was at the hanging. Ironically, Heyward Shepherd, free black baggagemaster at the train depot, was the first person killed and is remembered chiefly here where displays, restorations, and literature tell the whole grim story.

The *Visitor Center,* in *Stagecoach Inn,* built in 1826–34, Shenandoah Ave., is open 8 to 8 in summer, with earlier closing hours in winter. There is literature available, a slide program, and guided tours can be arranged. The *Master Armorer's House,* S side of Shenandoah St., near Market, has been restored and offers a museum. The *Harper House and Garden,* 1775–82, was the home of the town founder; restored, with period furnishings. On Marmion Row behind the Harper House are four restored homes from the early 19th century. *Lockwood House,* near Jefferson Rock, was built in 1848, and served as a classroom building for Storer College in the 1860s; lately it has been a training center for National Park personnel. The Park Service Design Center, a $1.2 million brick and concrete center, brings together previously scattered interpretive functions such as audiovisual, museum, and environmental planning and publications projects. It overlooks the Shenandoah River from Camp Hill. This is a showcase for interpretive devices being developed for use in historic national parks.

Harpers Ferry is on the annual tour which includes Charles Town, Shepherdstown, and Martinsburg, in late April. See Charles Town also for details. The tour varies somewhat over the years, but it usually includes the several Washington homes in Charles Town and historic public buildings there. In Shepherdstown, the *Public Library,* at Main and King St., which was a market house with open stalls from 1800 to 1855, is now a tour headquarters and the home of the Woman's Club, with guidebooks and hostesses on hand. The *John B. Shepherd Farm* is on Shepherd Grade, 2½ miles N of town. The house was built by the great-grandson of Captain Thomas Shepherd, town founder, just before the Civil War, and was not completed until 1867.

In Martinsburg, county seat of Berkeley, the first city plan was made by Adam Stephen, who had 130 acres in 1778, the year in which the charter was granted. He decided that each purchaser of a lot was "to build a dwelling house at least twenty feet by sixteen feet wide, with a brick or stone chimney, to be finished in two years." Stephen, a Scotsman who had studied medicine and had a practice in Fredericksburg in the 1740s, raised a company from near Winchester and served as its captain in the French and Indian War, rising to the rank of lieutenant colonel by war's end. He became a major general in the Revolutionary War and is buried on S. Queen St. just S of the entrance of "Boydville," home of General Elisha Boyd, dating from about 1800.

General Boyd designed his house in Georgian style and planned the gardens enclosed by a brick wall. On the front lawn is his law office. It has a large fireplace, high ceilings, and an upstairs room, used by Boyd and also by his son-in-law Charles James Faulkner I, minister to France, 1860–61, and Charles James Faulkner II, U.S. Senator, 1887–99. During the Civil War, an officer of the 1st New York Cavalry in command of Union troops here was ordered to burn the house. He issued orders for Mrs. Faulkner to vacate the house, but she appealed to President Lincoln (presumably by telegraph), for his return message read: "The property of Charles James Faulkner is exempt from the order of General David Hunter for the burning of residences of three prominent citizens of Shenandoah Valley in retaliation for the burning of Governor Bradford's house in Maryland by the Confederate forces." Signed: Abraham Lincoln. The house has been restored.

The **Stephen House,** off E St. John, was given to the city and has been restored as a memorial.

Altair, on St. 45, 2 miles E of Martinsburg, was built in three periods, with the oldest part a log structure which was standing when the property was bought in 1847 by Henry Shepherd Van Metre. George Whitson added the brick portions of the house. He also built the Parish House of the Episcopal Church in Martinsburg, part of the Catholic Church, the Reform Church, and the Lutheran Church.

Huxley Hall, on Old Mill Rd., W of Martinsburg, is stone and brick, facing Tuscarora Creek with a fine lawn running down to the banks of the stream. Captain John Kerney built the original stone section in 1782. He served in the Revolutionary War and later served as a county court judge. In 1806 David Killmer, from Pennsylvania, bought the house and built the brick addition.

KENTUCKY

Early in the year 1780 three hundred "large family boats" arrived at the Falls of the Ohio [near Louisville]. . . . The prospect of possessing a four-hundred acre farm by merely occupying it, and the privilege of exchanging a basketful of almost worthless continental currency for an unlimited estate at the nominal value of forty cents per acre, were irresistible to thousands of land-loving Virginians and Carolinians. . . . Stealing a horse was punished more swiftly and with more feeling than homicide. . . . Sloth was the worst of weaknesses. The man who did not do a man's share where work was to be done was christened "Lazy Lawrence," and that was the end of him socially.

They dressed in the skins of wild beasts killed by themselves, and in linen stuffs woven by themselves. They hardly knew the use of iron except in their firearms and knives. Their food consisted almost exclusively of game, fish, and roughly ground corn-meal. Their exchanges were made by barter; many a child grew up without ever seeing a piece of money. . . . Large families lived in log huts, put together with wooden pegs. . . . An early schoolmaster says that the first place where he went to board was the house of one Lucas, consisting of a single room, sixteen feet square, and tenanted by Mr. and Mrs. Lucas, ten children, three dogs, two cats, and himself.

—*Lincoln as Pioneer*, by John G. Nicolay and John Hay, 1886

BARDSTOWN, Nelson County. US 62, 150.

Chamber of Commerce, Court Square, has an Information Center with free tickets for a ride on a Tourmobile which leaves the center four times daily, in summer months (except Sundays), passing many historic structures. The tour ends at a historic distillery.

The second-oldest Kentucky city still has the gracious look of an early time. Even by daylight you can be transported back to the 18th century by hostesses in crisply pressed costumes, speaking in soft tones, who escort you through the tastefully furnished rooms of *Federal Hill*, US 150, a brick Flemish-bond mansion of 1795. The home reflects the life of a well-read, well-traveled family who knew the celebrities of their day, including Henry Clay and Aaron Burr. Judge John Rowan, Jr., was a U.S. Congressman and Senator, a state chief justice, and a U.S. commissioner to Mexico. He built the first part of the house on the 1,300-acre plantation owned by his father. It was enlarged in 1818. In the spacious grounds are a garden, a replica of the old springhouse which was Rowan's law office, and the family cemetery. Open daily; hours change with the season. The site is now a state park.

Old Talbott Tavern, Court Square (1770), was a busy place at the end of the stage line from Philadelphia and Virginia late in the 18th century. Andrew Jackson, Henry Clay, William Henry Harrison, Stephen Foster, and other notables were guests. It is the oldest continuously operating tavern west of the Alleghenies.

St. Joseph Proto Cathedral, W. Stephen Foster Ave. (1816–19), is the oldest Catholic cathedral west of the Alleghenies and is thought to be the second-oldest in the country. Its fine art pieces were given by King Louis Philippe of France, who was in Bardstown during part of his exile. *Spalding Hall,* N. 5th St., was the main building of St. Joseph's College in 1839. Now houses the Bardstown-Nelson County Museum, which has an eclectic collection including memorabilia of Pope John XXIII, Lincoln papers, Indian relics, Stephen Foster items, John Fitch papers concerning the first steamboat and a replica of the boat, Trappist monks' tools, Civil War relics, William Quantrill's sash, Jesse James's hat, Louis Philippe's candlesticks, etc.

Wickland, US 62, just E of town, was built in 1813–17 by Charles A. Wickliffe from designs by John Marshall Brown and John Rogers. Wickliffe, his son, and grandson all became governors and lived in the house, giving it the nickname of "Home of Three Governors." Excellent period furnishings. Open daily except major holidays.

The *Chamber of Commerce* also has maps for short or long walking tours of the historic town. Among highlights: *Gertrude H. Smith Home,* 212 E. Stephen Foster, Georgian brick with 18 rooms, built in the early 19th century by Colonel Ben Doom, used as a hospital during the Civil War. *B. B. Sisco House,* next door to the E, built by Colonel Doom in 1814 with John Rogers as architect. Just beyond these houses turn left on N. First for one block to an old cobblestone path, from the early 19th century, which was uncovered and restored not very long ago so that children could have a tree-shaded path into the past. The *Old Inn,* 105 E. Stephen Foster, 1814, became the post office in the 1840s and is a fine example of Georgian style. The *Old Nelson County Jail,* on W. Stephen Foster (1797), has 2-foot-thick walls with iron rings to which prisoners were chained. *One-Room Log School,* near the jail, is a reconstruction, a DAR Bicentennial project, representing the type of early schools of the area. Open weekdays in summer.

CUMBERLAND GAP NATIONAL HISTORICAL PARK, Bell County. Just S of Middleboro on US 25E.

In 1750 Dr. Thomas Walker, who was surveying a land grant, came upon the Indian Warrior's Path through the mountains. Daniel Boone led 30 men through the break in the mountains in 1775, blazing what became the Wilderness Road. US 25E now takes this route, and there is a superb 20,170-acre park extending into three states, with a *Visitor Center-Museum,* near the Middleboro entrance, open daily with historical exhibits.

Hensley Settlement, on Ridge Trail, is a reconstructed mountain village; open daily except Christmas.

DANVILLE, Boyle County. US 150, 27.

Constitution Square Historic District, Main and Walnut, 1st and 2nd Sts., is an authentic reproduction which preserves the site where the first state constitution was framed and adopted, 1792. The post office is original. Jail, pillory, log courthouse, and meeting house are replicas. Buildings are open daily.

McDowell House and Apothecary Shop, 125–127 S. 2nd St., are authentic restorations of the buildings where in 1809 Dr. Ephraim McDowell, a pioneer surgeon, performed an abdominal operation without anesthesia for the patient (or himself—as the elbow-bending surgeons of old Westerns frequently did). Museum. Maintained by the Kentucky Medical Association; hours vary. NHL.

Boyle County Courthouse, Main and 4th Sts., 1862, has been altered several times. The brick, two-story building with octagonal cupola was used as a hospital following the Battle of Perryville.

William Whitley House State Shrine, 19 miles SE just off US 150, is one of the first brick houses beyond the Alleghenies, built by Colonel Whitley about 1788; a popular stopping place on the Wilderness Road, furnished in late-18th- to early-19th-century styles. Open daily; hours vary with season.

FRANKFORT, Franklin County. I-64.

The town was established by the Virginia legislature on a 100-acre land grant in 1786 given to General James Wilkinson for his services during the Revolutionary War. Lexington and Louisville both hoped to become state capital, but Frankfort was the compromise choice in 1792. The railroad came in 1835, followed by industry—lumber, distilleries, and livestock. The Confederates tried to take over in the Civil War. Troops of E. Kirby Smith's command occupied Frankfort early in September 1862, but state officials had already fled to Louisville and Kirby Smith was in Lexington. When Richard Hawes was inaugurated as Confederate governor on October 4, General Braxton Bragg was present, but no one lingered long. Within four days the Confederate invasion of Kentucky was over. The limestone springs continued to flow and bourbon was king.

Old Capitol Restoration, St. Clair and Broadway: the 1827–30 building was beautifully restored and furnished, 1972–75. The marble was quarried in Kentucky. Gideon Shryock was the architect; this was his first major work, and he used the opportunity to introduce Greek Revival style in Kentucky. It was the first of thirteen Greek Revival state capitols in America. NHL. **Museum of Kentucky History** in the annex has Indian, Civil War, statehood, and early explorations exhibits and a log cabin. Open daily; hours vary on weekends; closed Easter and Christmas.

Liberty Hall, 218 Wilkinson St., built about 1796 by John Brown, who was first to represent Kentucky in the U.S. Senate and was a friend of five Presidents. The house has not one but three ghosts in sometime residence. Some of the architecture reflects designs by Thomas Jefferson. The two-and-a-half-story brick Flemish-bond mansion is an outstanding example of Federal style. James Madison, Andrew Jackson, General Lafayette, Aaron Burr, and Zachary Taylor have been entertained here. Now maintained by the National Society of Colonial Dames of America.

Liberty Hall and other fine houses are within Frankfort's **Corner in Celebrities Historic District,** a residential area with varying styles of 18th- and 19th-century architecture. The **Orlando Brown House,** 202 Wilkinson (1835), is Greek Revival designed by Gideon Shryock for the son of John Brown of Liberty Hall. Furnished with many fine Brown family antiques. Both houses are open daily except Monday and major holidays.

Old Governor's Mansion, 420 High St. (1797–98), was the official residence of early governors; now the lieutenant governor's home, with the first floor maintained as a public shrine. Louis Philippe and Lafayette of France visited here, as have a number of U.S. Presidents. Restored, with Georgian and Federal period furnishings. Open weekdays and by appointment.

Chamber of Commerce, 71 Fountain Place, has maps and brochures for self-guiding tours. A walking tour passes nearly 40 historic buildings within easy strolling distance.

Among historic sites is the *John Bibb House,* 411 Wapping St., a brick residence with sharply pointed dormers and gingerbread trim reminiscent of Hansel and Gretel style. The 20-room Gothic Revival structure is on the site of an earlier home built by Britisher John Instone, who came to make boats for General James Wilkinson and found the Kentucky River reminded him of the Thames at Wapping–Old Stairs. In a greenhouse, now gone, John Bibb developed the lettuce which bears his name.

LEXINGTON, Fayette County. US 60, 162.

Gratz Park Historic District is a residential area near to the center of the city with houses bordering a city park. *Hopemont,* the John Wesley Hunt house of 1814, 201 N. Mill St., became the home of John Hunt Morgan, Confederate general and raider, who was J. W. Hunt's grandson. Now a museum, the house is owned by and used as headquarters for the Blue Grass Trust for Historic Preservation. Guided tours for the ground floor. Nobel Prize winner Dr. Thomas H. Morgan, nephew of the general, was born here in 1866.

Mount Hope faces Gratz Park. Built about 1819, it was acquired in 1824 by Benjamin Gratz, who came to Kentucky from Philadelphia. His descendants still own the handsome brick Flemish-bond house built by fine Kentucky craftsmen. The *Thomas Bodley House,* across the park from the Hunt-Morgan place, was the home of Bodley, a War of 1812 veteran. A porch and portico were added just before the Civil War. *First Presbyterian Church,* 174 N. Mill, only a short distance from Hopemont, dates from 1872, Cincinnatus Shryock, architect. Nearby is the *Henry Clay Law Office,* 176 N. Mill, an 1803 brick Flemish-bond structure, which has been restored. It is one of two buildings remaining in town which were built as professional offices. Clay used it until 1810.

Mary Todd Lincoln House, 574 W. Main St., has been recently restored to its appearance when she lived here in the 1830s, with a number of items which belonged to her, all given to the restoration by her great-grandson, Robert Todd Lincoln Beckwith. The Kentucky Mansions Preservations Foundation restored the house over a period of nearly ten years with extensive renovation to the 20 rooms, once the home of Robert Todd. It was built as an inn in 1803–6 and was the largest house in town when Todd bought it. Abraham Lincoln visited it several times before he became President and observed slavery in action from here. Hours are subject to change; inquire locally. This is one of the many stops on the *Lincoln Heritage Trail.*

Ashland, E. Main and Sycamore Rd., was the home of the great statesman Henry Clay from 1811 until his death in 1852. The design has been attributed to Benjamin Latrobe, a Yorkshireman who was responsible for many fine buildings of early America. (His first U.S. work was the Virginia State Penitentiary, 1797–98.) The grounds of Ashland were planned by L'Enfant, designer of Washington, D.C. Open daily from 9:30 to 4:30, small admission.

Chamber of Commerce, 421 N. Broadway—(606) 253-1230—has maps and brochures for historic homes and museums open to the public. Among these, *Waveland,* on Higbee Mill Pike, 5 miles S of town, Greek Revival, 1847, has been restored with period furnishings as the *Kentucky Life Museum,* with workshops and slave quarters as part of the exhibit.

LONDON, Laurel County. US 25.

Levi Jackson Wilderness Road State Park, 2 miles S on US 25, comprises 815 acres deeded to the state by the descendants of pioneer Jackson as a historical shrine to the early

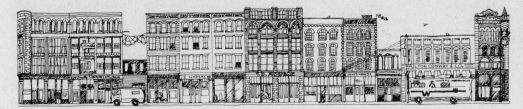

Eight-hundred block, West Main Street, Louisville, Kentucky. (Drawing by Louis Johnson, Jr. Copyright © 1977, by Preservation Alliance of Louisville and Jefferson Counties, Inc. Reproduced by permission)

Kentuckians who made their homes in the wilderness. Boone's Trace and the Wilderness Road cut through the area. *Mountain Life Museum* has rustic cabins, split-rail fences, and a number of outbuildings with pioneer tools, Indian relics, a prairie schooner, etc. *McHargue's Mill* of 1812 has been reconstructed.

LOUISVILLE, Jefferson County. I-64.

The *Louisville Visitors Bureau,* Founders Square, 40202—(502) 583-3377—is a lively and friendly bunch who have brochures, maps, and the answers to any questions about their city, as well as narrated bus tours which depart from their office. They also maintain an information center at the airport. Even if horses and tobacco are a major concern, your historic interests are welcomed.

The *Preservation Alliance of Louisville and Jefferson County,* 712 W. Main St., is a nonprofit organization to preserve landmarks and publishes a Preservation Press booklet recording the latest gains or losses in the long struggle. Other community groups also are helpful in trying to save old-time Louisville or to restore it.

Old Louisville, as such, is mostly an area of Victorian mansions built during the prosperity that followed the Civil War. The *West Main St. Historic District* contains some of the finest cast-iron fronts left in America. An Alliance publication, illustrated

by Louis Johnson, Jr., gives the history of the area and provides a step-by-step tour of several blocks. The street was not paved until 1813 and then only from 3rd to 6th Aves. Fires, floods, and a tornado restructured some of the buildings. Brick replaced logs; then came cast iron and plate glass. In the mid-1880s trolley cars began to rattle down the now fully paved thoroughfare. Then many Louisvillians moved to newer parts of town. Only recently has it all been revitalized. Among highlights: No. 131 was designed by Henry Whitestone for the Louisville, Cincinnati & Lexington Railroad; built in 1877 on the site of the first Galt House. Louisville brochures refer to the fact that Charles Dickens was a guest in the first Galt House which stood on the corner of 2nd and Main and burned in 1865. Civil War fans will remember that William T. Sherman also favored the Galt House and during a conference here gave others the impression that he had lost his mind, that he was overestimating the strength of the Confederate Army, was subject to unreasonable fears, and should be taken out of command. The report, published in the Cincinnati *Commercial,* did considerable harm to Sherman's career, but not for long. Unfortunately there is only a marker today for the building which saw much excitement in the heavy traffic of wartime, as officers and reporters gathered, drank, quarreled, carried on the business of the war in a decorous manner, or in some cases had their last great flings before moving south to battle.

At No. 107–109 the 1905 *J. T. S. Brown* distillery had Frank James among employees. No. 300 was built in 1890 for the *Kentucky National Bank* for $100,000, with Richardson Romanesque style. Decorative carvings embellish the limestone. *Southern National Bank,* No. 320, built in 1837, Gideon Shryock, architect, has Greek and Egyptian Revival elements. NHL. Now provides a lobby for the Actors Theatre.

The *Schulten Building,* No. 530, recently restored, has lavish stonework. In the 600 block are many fine old buildings and possibly the most ornamental manhole covers in America. Nos. 726–730, the *Hart Block,* is called the "Queen Bee" of cast-iron buildings. The pieces were made at the Merz Architectural Iron Works in 1884 for the Hart Hardware Co. No. 800 was the *Pickett Tobacco Warehouse* for more than 70 years; built in mid-19th century, it is one of the oldest of Main Street structures. Nos. 731–737, *Carter Dry Goods,* 1878, was the first department store in town. Now occupied by the *Museum of Natural History & Science,* it has red sandstone columns and cast-iron trim from the Snead & Bibb Iron Works.

Butchertown on Beargrass was a suburb in 1840 when Story Ave., leading to Main St., was the Frankfort Pike, paralleling Beargrass Creek part of the way. Neglected for years, the area is now being revitalized. *Linden Hill,* 1607 Frankfort, the oldest house, dates from the early 18th century; built by Colonel Frederick Geiger as his country home. The butchering trade was dominated by German immigrants; droves of cattle and hogs were sent along the pike to meet a demand for salt pork, and special inns were set up for drovers. Today's *Bakery Square* occupies the site where Butchertown breweries once flourished. Thomas A. Edison, as a young telegrapher for Western Union, boarded at 729 E. Washington. When one of his experiments ruined the boss's office rug, he was fired. The neighborhood association has bought the building and plans to restore it. A Spring Festival each May has art displays and historic homes open to the public.

Highlights of a general walking tour of historic Louisville include the *Jefferson County Courthouse,* 527 W. Jefferson St., begun in 1838, Gideon Shryock, architect; *City Hall,* 6th and Jefferson (1873), Italianate, with carved pigs, cows, and horses over the windows; *The Belle of Louisville,* the last authentic sternwheeler in the U.S., docked at the restored wharf near the Plaza, runs daily except Mondays.

Two important outlying restorations: *Locust Grove,* 561 Blankenbaker Lane (6 miles NE on River Rd., then 1 mile SW), was begun by Major William Croghan and his wife, Lucy Clark, in 1808. Lucy's brother, George Rogers Clark, came to live here in 1809. In 1961 restoration began for the house and its furnishings. The mansion stands on 55 of the original 693 acres, with a formal garden. Among illustrious visitors have been James and Dolley Madison, Aaron Burr, John James Audubon, Cassius Clay, James Monroe, Andrew Jackson, and Zachary Taylor. The house and outbuildings are open daily except for major holidays.

Farmington, 3033 Bardstown Rd., 6 miles SE on US 31E, is another historic house open to the public. The Federal 14-room mansion was built, from plans made by Thomas Jefferson, in 1808–10 by John and Lucy Speed on a 1,500-acre tract, now 14 acres. The original land was given to Captain James Speed in 1785 for Revolutionary War services. Among documents here is a deed to the land signed by Governor Patrick Henry of Virginia, and there is a letter to Joshua Speed, son of Judge Speed, by his friend Abraham Lincoln, who visited in 1841. The house was neglected for many years but has been restored by the Historic Homes Foundation. Guided tours. Closed only on three major holidays.

SHAKERTOWN at Pleasant Hill, Mercer County. US 68.

Visitor Orientation Center and ticket booth are on the entrance road. Exhibits, literature, and maps are available in the 1815 *Carpenter's Shop,* used as a blacksmith and wagon shop until 1843 and later, after rebuilding, as a broom factory. The colony began in 1805, settled by a religious group named the United Society of Believers in Christ's Second Appearing, called Shakers by those who saw their devotional dancing. Celibacy was only one of their tenets, which also included confession of sins, separation from the world, and communal property, but it was the principle which caused the most curiosity and mockery. The local settlement lasted for a century. The last member at Pleasant Hill died in 1923. The village has been authentically restored by a nonprofit educational corporation and once again welcomes visitors with plain but delicious cooking and gentle hospitality. Crafts are demonstrated during the summer and at special winter events. Shaker furniture and handmade goods are for sale in the village. Dining and room reservations can be made by writing Shakertown at Pleasant Hill, Inc., Rt. 4, Harrodsburg, 40330, or calling (606) 734-5411. Reservations are advisable and should be made well in advance. Rates vary; available on request.

The west end of the village was restored to house various programs, conferences, lectures, and executive seminars. The *Conference Building* is the old *West Family Wash House* but has audiovisual equipment instead of tubs and clotheslines. In the tourist area tidy buildings sit well apart on the bluegrass fields where hand-stacked rock fences keep out the "wilderness" of the 20th century. The spacious look is also enhanced by the radius of farmland which surrounds the village. Some 27 buildings have been restored on the more than 2,000 acres of the compound. Hostesses with Shaker dress and manner greet visitors and point out architectural or historical facets, or demonstrate the old-time crafts of weaving, broom- and basketmaking, cabinetwork, soap- and candlemaking, wool dyeing, and quilting.

Lodging is in restored structures throughout the village. Sixty-one original rooms are furnished authentically as "retiring rooms," though founding Mother Ann Lee is not at hand to separate the sexes as in the old days when flour was sometimes sprinkled on floors to catch any footprints of would-be minglers. Probably any determined suitor brought flour, instead of flowers, to cover up his tracks when headed for romance.

Among the many buildings on display are the *Farm Deacon's Shop,* the first permanent structure, put up for the minister and a center family and made into a tavern for travelers in 1817; *Old Yellow Frame Shop,* built about 1812; *Old Stone Shop,* 1811, a residence, then a workshop, later a medical and dentist office; *West Family Sisters' Shop,* 1844, where corn-shuck mattresses were made, as well as carpeting, and herbs were packaged; *Drying House,* about 1840, for apples; *Carpenter's Shop,* 1815; *Tanyard Brick Shop,* 1823, and a spring.

SPRINGFIELD, Washington County. St. 528.

Lincoln Homestead State Park, 5 miles N of town on St. 528, has a replica of the cabin built in 1782 by Abraham Lincoln, Sr., the President's grandfather. Thomas Lincoln lived here until he was 25; several pieces of furniture he made are among the furnishings. In the compound framed by split-rail fences are also the **Berry House,** which was the home of Lincoln's mother, Nancy Hanks, when she was being courted by Thomas Lincoln; a replica of the blacksmith and carpenter shop where Thomas worked, and many relics on display. The logs are more than a century old. Open daily, May to Labor Day.

WASHINGTON, Mason County. US 68.

Old Washington, 3½ miles S of Maysville on US 68, founded in 1784, was the original county seat and the second-largest town in Kentucky with 119 cabins. *Paxton Inn,* Main St., built about 1810, is furnished in period, open May through Labor Day. There are more than 30 buildings in the preserved district. *Albert S. Johnston Home,* 1780s, is where the Confederate general who was killed in action at Shiloh during the Civil War was born in 1803. A nonprofit community fund, with federal help, has been restoring the town. A number of historic houses on Main St. are becoming antique stores and craftshops. A walking tour includes the *Simon Kenton House,* once the home of the great Indian fighter who scouted for Daniel Boone; row houses, and *Broderick's Tavern* of 1794. The state department of information wryly advises that reservations are suggested for staying overnight at the Tavern, "now offering overnight lodgings and meals. . . . as there is only one room available for guests"—(606) 759-7934.

Old Washington, Inc.—(606) 759-7431—has information on special events and guided tours, and publishes an illustrated historic guide and walking tour map. Harriet Beecher (Stowe) before her marriage visited Washington in 1833 and saw a slave auction which she wrote about in *Uncle Tom's Cabin.* The *Colonel Marshall Key House,* on Main St., E of S. Court, built in 1807, was the home of the colonel and his wife Harriet and their six children. It was here Harriet Beecher visited her pupil Elizabeth Key.

There are 35 sites on the tour, with seven historic buildings open to the public.

TENNESSEE

March 26th. [1849]—Rose in good time to see the city—all towns are cities here—of *Memphis;* like all the rest of these spick-and-span new places, industry and energy observable everywhere. White wood houses, large hotels, &c. . . . Walked on upper-deck, pleased with the pink blossoms of the red-bud, profusely growing in some of the woods. . . . Walked, watching the passing steam-boats. . . . The flat-boats, which are from 70 to 100 feet long, and 17 to 25 feet in width, are broken up for lumber at New Orleans, the good passage to which is about seventeen days. Saw the log-huts standing in the water, quite insulated, children, women &c., within. . . . Watched in the morning the flocks of wild geese flying in their letter or figure form.
—*Macready's Reminiscences, and Selections from His Diaries and Letters,*
London, 1875

Nashville.—This town, the capital of the state, stands at the head of steam navigation, on the left bank of the Cumberland river, one hundred and twenty miles from its junction with the Ohio. Near it are three lofty bluffs. The situation is fine, the climate healthful and inviting, and the town has been rapid in its growth.

One of the most striking of the public buildings is the markethouse, which is one of the finest in the western country. There are 13 churches, a lunatic asylum, the state penitentiary, three banks, a lyceum, and many handsome houses. The population in 1850 was eighteen thousand.
—*Sears' Pictorial Description of the United States,* by Robert Sears,
New York, 1855

CHATTANOOGA, Hamilton County. I-24, I-59.

Chattanooga at present has no historic district, as such, and no walking tours; this is because its history, while plentiful, is scattered. The best place to check is the ***Convention & Visitors Bureau,*** 399 McCallie Ave.—(615) 266-5617—which has information and maps for self-guiding tours, recommendation for guided tours by bus, boat, or train. The ***Carolenda Tours*** may be unique in the U.S. or the world. Carol (Mrs. William) Hobbs started the city's first commercial bus tours with a friend named Brenda (thus Carolenda) Chisholm, who later moved to Delaware, but Carol Hobbs is still going strong and singing *a capella* on request by her passengers. Ms. Hobbs is a contralto soloist at the First Christian Church, and has also done Little Theater musicals. It is a rare experience to be busing on the steep and curving roadway of Lookout Mountain where the Union forces once toiled upward in the hard-fought campaign of November 1863, and hear a lilting voice advising you to

"Climb every mountain, ford every stream," etc. When she isn't singing, Ms. Hobbs is giving accurate historical information on her hometown and its rich, if sometimes bloody, past. Carolenda Tours are at 4711 Tarpon Trail, Chattanooga, 37416—(615) 892-8018. Your bus or theirs.

Tennessee Valley Railroad Museum, 2202 N. Chamberlain Ave., offers a living history experience for railroad buffs or anyone interested in the 19th century. The museum itself is worth a visit, but the chief attraction is the train ride. Four round-trip excursions are operated each year from here to such points of interest as Huntsville, Gadsden, Crossville, Knoxville, Atlanta, or other stops on the Southern Railway. There are open-window coaches as well as air-conditioned cars, and dining-car service. Sundays, from April through October, the Museum is open to the public and 3-mile, 45-minute round trips, usually behind a steam engine, are available. The route goes through a tunnel in Missionary Ridge.

Cravens House, on Lookout Mountain, is the oldest surviving structure in the historic mountain area. It was the home of Robert Cravens, built in 1855, served as headquarters for both Confederate and Union generals during the Civil War, has been restored, and is accurately furnished; administered by the National Park Service.

Chattanooga's old *Southern Railroad Terminal* at 1434 Market St. has been made into a Hilton Inn. The station has the highest freestanding brick arch in the world and was built in 1906-8, Don Barber, architect. The adaptive use of the building as part of a hotel and shopping complex is worth seeing for anyone interested in restoration and commercial renovation.

There are many Civil War sites and scattered historical houses in the Chattanooga area. The *Chamber of Commerce,* 819 Broad St.—(615) 267-2121—also has information and maps of the greater Chattanooga area. *Hunter Museum of Art, Houston Antique Museum,* 201 High St., and the restored *Gordon-Lee House,* of 1847, in historic Chickamauga, Georgia, are recommended stops. Although Chickamauga is in a neighboring state it is easily reached by visitors to Chattanooga.

COLUMBIA, Maury County. US 31, 43.

(Although the information doesn't seem to fit directly, this was once the greatest street mule-market in the world.)

James K. Polk Ancestral Home, 301 W. 7th St., built in 1816 by Samuel Polk, the father of the 11th President, handmade bricks. Most appealingly furnished.

The *Athenaeum Rectory,* 808 Athenaeum Place, is the last building remaining from the female school which once stood here. It is an unusual building with Moorish design. Nathan Vaught was the builder in 1838. More than 10,000 girls were graduated from this school in the 19th century. The house is maintained by the Association for the Preservation of Tennessee Antiquities (APTA), which keeps up 14 historic sites covering every period of Tennessee history.

Also on the National Register in the Columbia vicinity:

Blythewood, Trotwood and Hatcher, built about 1856–60, Italianate, the home of Thomas Keesee, a coachmaker from Richmond. Keesee wasn't yet 20 years old when he came from Richmond, Virginia, to ply his trade here.

Mayes-Hutton House, 306 W. 6th St., built of brick in the 1850s with Greek Revival and Italianate elements, with an impressive Corinthian portico. This was the home of Samuel Mayes, who not only built a lasting mansion but had perfectly patterned formal gardens on his estate, covering nearly 5 acres in all. The gardens are gone, but a legend lingers that there was a mysterious tunnel running underground from the house to the bluffs of Duck River.

Beechlawn, S of town on US 31, built in the 1850s, a brick Greek Revival, the home of Major A. W. Warfield, became headquarters for both the Confederates and the Federals during the Civil War. Much of the woodwork and flooring is original; outbuildings include an icehouse, log smokehouse, and an 1820 log cabin in which the family lived while the main house was being constructed. At one time or another during the conflict, Union General John Schofield, General J. B. Hood, and the great cavalry leader of the Confederacy, Nathan Bedford Forrest, were here. Indeed Hood and Forrest had a violent argument in the library. After Hood was defeated at Nashville, Forrest came back to Beechlawn to oversee the retreat of the Confederates from Middle Tennessee. The day after the sad affair took place, Schofield and 40,000 Union men came back. They cleaned out the pantry and smokehouse, and later Schofield intervened to see that Major Warfield got a safe passage home.

Cherry Glen, SW of town off US 43, is an 1810 frame house with clapboarding. Wings were added in 1858. The usually reserved National Register mentions that it is an "example of local piano-box style." And adds that there are Italianate decorative elements. This is a one-story building worth going out of one's way to admire. Author Reid Smith, in *Majestic Middle Tennessee* writes that Lucius Polk built the first part of the structure before 1810 and probably lived in it while he was building Hamilton Place nearby. In 1858 the house was bought by Colonel Fount Wade, a son-in-law of Gideon Pillow, who was a general in the Mexican and Civil wars and one of two Confederate officers to escape from Fort Donelson.

A log cabin with a massive chimney, dating back to the time of the first settlers, stands at the rear of Cherry Glen.

Clifton Place, SW of Columbia on Mt. Pleasant Highway, was built for Gideon Pillow in 1838–39, by Nathan Vaught, and is a handsome Greek Revival structure. The mansion, with 12 rooms and two large halls, was completed within a year. The stone was quarried on the premises, the bricks were slave-made on the land, and even the wild cherry used for doors, molding, and mantels came from the estate's trees. During the war the gracious home was pillaged several times by Federals who knew that it belonged to Pillow.

Hamilton Place, Mt. Pleasant Pike, W of town off US 43, was built in 1832, probably by Nathan Vaught. It is brick, Flemish bond, with a Doric and Ionic two-story pedimented portico. The one-story wings, a later addition, in Georgian and Greek Revival style, were built for Lucius Polk, once of Cherry Glen. Polk married Mary Jane Eastin, in the White House, with President Jackson in attendance. Mary Jane was a niece of Rachel Jackson. Among visitors to the house was James Knox Polk, a cousin of Lucius, who would become President of the U.S. Another visitor was Leonidas Polk, Lucius's brother, who became the fighting bishop-general of the Confederacy.

Rattle and Snap, Andrew Jackson Highway, St. 43, was built about 1845 with a ten-column portico, and all the best of Greek Revival trimmings. Built for George Knox Polk, whose father, Colonel William Polk, is said to have played a game of "beans" with the governor of North Carolina and won a deed for 5,468 acres in Maury County. William Polk's sons—Lucius, Leonidas, Rufus, and George—all prospered; and George kept the original name of the property when he built this mansion on his portion of his father's estate.

St. John's Episcopal Church, W of town on US 43, was built in 1839–42, one-story brick in Gothic Revival style. The Polk family erected it for themselves and their slaves.

FRANKLIN, Williamson County. US 31.

Franklin Historic District takes in the heart of the old town, around Main St. and 3rd Ave. There are many fine structures from the 19th century.

Visitor Information Center, on the Public Square, has brochures for walking or driving tours, maps, etc.

Carter House, 1140 Columbia Ave., on US 31, was built in 1830 for merchant Fountain Branch Carter. He was also a surveyor and farmer. It served as command post for the Union forces during the Battle of Franklin late in 1864. The house is open to the public; museum.

Carter's Court, across the street, is a complex with 23 shops, cobblestone streets, and the look of early America in storefronts.

A guide for a walking tour of the area, published by the Williamson County Historical Society, in cooperation with the Franklin Chamber of Commerce and the Mid-Cumberland Council of Governments and Development District, is available from the Chamber of Commerce, and probably at the Visitor Center. It takes in 29 sites, including the **Williamson County Courthouse** (1858), with Greek Revival elements; **St. Paul's Episcopal Church,** 510 Main St. (1831–34), the oldest Episcopal church in the state, used as a hospital during the Civil War; **St. Philips Catholic Church** (1871), with bricks made and burned on the site. The **Hiram Masonic Lodge,** S. 2nd Ave. (1823), was the scene of the negotiation and signing of the Treaty of Franklin in 1830, which provided for the removal of the Chickasaw In-

dians from their homelands to beyond the Mississippi. NHL. President Andrew Jackson, Secretary of War John Henry Eaton, and General John Coffey were among those present. Peggy O'Neill Eaton, it is said, had an organ moved to the porch so that she could entertain the group. Margaret (Peggy) O'Neill Eaton, daughter of an innkeeper, was never accepted by Washington society; Eaton was forced to resign from his post in Jackson's cabinet. Major Eaton became governor of Florida Territory after his resignation, and later minister to Spain.

The **Rainey-Lawrence House,** 244 1st Ave., built in 1839 by mechanic and merchant Robert Rainey, is brick Greek Revival. It is not on the tour.

The **Heritage Foundation of Franklin and Williamson Counties**—(615) 790-0378—has an annual Heritage Spring Tour of Homes, in May. Some of the houses open during this event are modern; one is noted for its Tennessee Walking Horses. **Twenty-Three Trees,** on Wilson Pike, was built in 1812, and **Valley View Farm** was built about 1880; the tollgate on Wilson Pike and the first Brentwood Post Office were located on the property. **Walnut Winds** dates from the 1840s and was built by Solomon Oden, who came to the area from Maryland. The house was of blue poplar, cut into lumber by a whipsaw. All the timber was oversized and the braces were strongly pegged. During the Civil War Confederates often met here secretly. It has been restored and furnished with family heirlooms. **Crockett-Knox House,** built between 1796 and 1810, was a two-story log home on land deeded to Andrew Crockett for his services in the Revolutionary War. He was a gunsmith and farmer. In 1840 a new wing was added and a fine two-story columned entrance. It has been restored recently. **Meadowview** on the Lewisburg Pike is Federal, with oak and chinquapin trees that are more than two centuries old. Many of the furnishings were brought from Virginia by oxcart by James and Priscilla Ragsdale Buford, who bought more than 3,000 acres for 17¢ an acre on Columbia Pike 7 miles from Franklin. *Mooreland,* built in 1838, was a land grant to General Robert Irvin for his Revolutionary War services. The woodwork is bird's-eye maple, adzed by slaves.

GATLINBURG, Sevier County. US 441.

The mountain town has become a handicraft center. Mountain women skillfully spin yarn from wool they have carded themselves, weave, make baskets and brooms; men make furniture, including "sittin' chairs" without nails, screws, or glue, but sittable for a century. And visitors are welcome to observe the artisans at work.

Pigeon Forge, 6 miles N on US 441, is a restored mountain village where visitors can watch potters at work with local clay; an old mill, stone-grinding with water power, from the 19th century is still working; other mountain crafts are displayed.

Headquarters for the *Great Smoky Mountains National Park* are here, and will soon distribute a much-needed comprehensive map of the region. The 512,000-acre park is one of the nation's most popular. More than 1,300 species of flowering plants grow in these mountains. The *Sugarlands Visitor Center* is in the Tennessee part of the park, which also can be reached from North Carolina at Oconaluftee. Park personnel give lectures, lead guided walks, motor caravans, etc. Auto-tape tours, self-guiding, are also available. The center is S of town on US 441. *Roaring Fork Historic District* is also S of town, off St. 73.

Within the park, on the National Register, are the *Alex Cole Cabin,* 5 miles S of Gatlinburg off US 441;

King-Walker Place, W of town off St. 73; *Little Greenbrier School and Church,* about 9 miles W of town off St. 73; *Tyson McCarter Place,* 10 miles E of town on St. 73; *Messer Barn,* near Greenbrier Cove; *John Ownby Cabin,* 3 miles S of town off St. 73.

Cade's Cove is in the west section of the park. There is an 11-mile loop road which runs past open fields and log houses, church, blacksmith shop, smokehouse, and the Cable Mill, where a miller grinds corn. *Becky Cable's Store* is open for business. An information center interprets the history of the Cove.

JOHNSON CITY, Washington County. US 11E, 19W.

Tipton-Haynes Living Historical Farm, S edge of town on US 19W. The house was built by a spring which Indians, hunters, and early travelers had used, and where Daniel Boone had a hunting camp. Captain James Tipton built his two-story house here in the 18th century, with an entrance porch added later. Tipton led a fight against a group which wanted to establish the independent state of Franklin.

The adjacent law office was added by Landon Carter Haynes, who became a member of the Confederate Senate. It has been restored.

Rocky Mount Historic Shrine, at Piney Flats, 5 miles NE of Johnson City on US 11E. Rocky Mount was built by William Cobb in 1770; a two-story log house, it was a stopping place for soldiers en route to Sycamore Shoals, a gathering place for the Battle of King's Mountain in the Revolutionary War, in 1780. A decade later William Blount, governor of the Territory of the United States South of the River Ohio, chose Rocky Mount as his headquarters. For 18 months this was the first recognized government west of the Alleghenies.

The house became a favorite stopping place for stagecoach travelers from Baltimore to the Southwest and served as a post office until 1847. Now restored, it is the oldest original territorial capital still standing. A brick museum has many artifacts of the Tennessee frontier.

JONESBORO, Washington County, US 11E, 411.

Jonesboro was chartered in January of 1779 as Jonesborough; the shorter spelling was adopted in the 1870s. The county was the first named for George Washington. The town was named for Willie Jones of Halifax, North Carolina, a wealthy man who remained a friend of mountain people.

Jonesboro Historic District, the oldest town in the state, contains 152 religious, public, commercial, and residential structures of the 18th and 19th centuries. The town was established in 1779 and was the meeting place of a constitutional convention and early legislative sessions for the proposed state of Franklin. The *Robert May House,* Federal-style with an Italianate porch, and the Gothic Revival *Irwin House* are outstanding, among others in a town which retains the look of early times.

Christopher Taylor House, Main St., was built about 1776, two-story log construction, with stone exterior end chimney; it was the home of Taylor, a delegate to the convention for the state of Franklin. Moved and restored.

Devault Tavern, W on Leesburg Rd., is a large brick building from 1821. Outbuildings include log slave quarters and a brick springhouse. In town *Sisters Row* was built about 1820 by Samuel Jackson for his three daughters. The long brick building on Main St. is actually three houses.

Mansion House was an inn in the 1850s; now a residence. The *Dosser House* was built in 1887 by James Dosser as a wedding gift for his daughter Mary Dosser and Isaac

Reeves, and is a large red brick Italianate villa with a tower, wood brackets, a bay window in the front, and arched windows; nearly a textbook example of the "Tuscan villa" as interpreted by American builders; the *Hoss House* on Main St. was built in the 1830s by William Gammon, later owned by J. M. Hoss; there was once a bank in the basement which has a walk-in door because the building is on a rise, making the rear portion three stories. The *Methodist Church,* on Main, is a beautiful building of brick, Greek Revival with columned portico, built in the 1840s. The spire is not as old as the building, but there are seats for slaves in a gallery in the back of the sanctuary, which are original. The *Presbyterian Church,* on Main St., was also built in the 1840s, has a slave gallery, is Greek Revival with a full-front portico and six columns, also has original pews and pulpit. The *Chester Inn,* built in 1797, on the Great Stage Route from Washington, is the oldest building in town. The porch was added in the 1870s. Andrew Jackson, James Polk, and Andrew Johnson are said to have been guests here. The building now houses the library and apartments.

KINGSPORT, Sullivan County. US 11 W.

Netherlands Inn Complex, on the banks of Holston River, is the site of a river port that served travelers on the Great State Road from Baltimore and Washington to the Southwest. It has been restored, with other restorations planned. There are dwellings, public buildings, and the *Boatyard Historic District* with a wharf and warehouse. The *Netherland Inn* was built between 1802 and 1818. The Netherland Inn Association with the help of state aid has been in charge of restorations. Richard Netherland ran the inn and added and remodeled a number of outbuildings.

Church Circle District, in the center of town, along Sullivan St., comprises two small parks with surrounding buildings.

Clinchfield Railroad Station, 101 E. Main, was built in 1905. Eclectic, it served the South and Western Railroad.

Johnson House, 1322 Watauga Ave., built in 1915–17, has Doric columns and a Chinese Chippendale rail on the roof.

Mount Ida, 1010–1012 Sevier Terrace, from 1884. A two-story log house, built sometime in the 1790s, with Colonial and Federal touches, it was moved from its original site in 1884 to make way for the brick structure. A stone chimney was replaced with a brick one. Outbuildings include a barn and wellhouse. Victorian eclectic. The two houses show the development of building in Kingsport. The log structure was the home of David Ross, who established a furnace and forge; the brick was for David Sevier, farmer and financier.

Old Kingsport Presbyterian Church, Stone Drive and Afton, dates from the mid-19th century. Moved from original site, but the oldest church in town, it replaced an original log Presbyterian church.

Preston Farm (Exchange Place), 4812 Orebank Rd., is from the early 19th century. It is being restored. The house was built for John Gaines, who operated a store and stage stop as well as farmed. Bought by John Preston in 1845.

Other National Register houses in the area: **Roseland,** S of town on Shipp St., built about 1825, for Jonathan Bachman, father of ten children, four of whom grew up to be leading Presbyterian ministers; **Pearson Brick House,** E of town, Shipley Ferry Rd., early 19th century; **Spring Place,** NW of town on W. Carter's Valley Rd., off US 23, hewn log construction, from the early 19th century, the home of the Reverend Samuel Patton. **Wills-Dickey-Stone House,** NW of town off US 23 on W. Carter's Valley, 18th century, of limestone rubble, the only stone house remaining in the county; **Yancey's Tavern,** E of town on St. 126, dates from the 1780s. It was an important stop on the Island Rd., which was the first main thoroughfare in Tennessee. Not on the Register at present but open to the public is **Allendale,** 5 miles W on US 11W, from the 1850s, lavishly furnished.

MEMPHIS, Shelby County. On the Mississippi River. I-40.

Beale Street Historic District, Beale St. from Main to 4th, where the Blues were born. Includes the Palace and Daisy theaters, the Hole-in-the-Wall Saloon, and Pee-Wee's Saloon, headquarters of W. C. Handy, who wrote "Memphis Blues," the first published tune of this now classic genre. Handy also wrote the "St. Louis Blues" and "Beale Street Blues." NHL.

Victorian Village District, Adams and Jefferson Sts., is a downtown residential section with many dwellings built between 1840 and 1890. **Lee and Fontaine Houses of the James Lee Memorial,** 680–690 Adams Ave., are two dwellings with a carriage house between. Fontaine House, 1870, was built by Amos Woodruff, who founded the Memphis and Charleston Railroad; later the house was bought by Noland Fontaine. Lee House is a mid-19th-century mansion with Victorian remodeling in 1873. The houses were later owned by the daughter of James Lee, who founded the Lee Steamboat Line. Both houses have towers with a view of the river. A block of Adams has been restored, with hostesses on duty at the Fontaine and Mallory-Neely houses.

The **Mallory-Neely House,** 652 Adams, is a 25-room mansion, with stucco over brick, built between 1849 and 1861. The second floor was added in 1883. James Columbus Neely, a cotton factor, restyled the house in the 1890s, adding a third floor and extending the tower. *Annesdale,* on Lamar Ave., built in 1850, has a wing added in 1900. The Italianate house was named for the wife of Colonel Robert Bogardus Snowden, who bought it after the Civil War. Lamar Ave. was once Pigeon Roost Rd., a stage route.

Magevney House, 198 Adams, was built about 1836 and is the oldest surviving house in town. Eugene Magevney was an Irish-born Roman Catholic pioneer teacher; the first Catholic mass in Memphis was said here, and the first wedding and baptism were held here.

MURFREESBORO, Rutherford County. US 41, 70S.

Cannonsburgh, a re-created 19th-century village, opened in 1977 to depict pioneer life in this area. Murfreesboro was once called Cannonsburgh, for John Cannon, who became governor. There are 12 reconstructed or restored buildings, including an operating gristmill, general store, church, and museum. The *Leeman House* is an early log structure which was a private home until recently. It was moved here with its outbuildings, a carriage house, smokehouse, and ash hopper and fully restored. The country store was built in 1899, with its own post office, and it carries the kind of merchandise that would have been available in the 19th century. The Haynes cotton gin still has the original machinery. On display, also, is the last bale of cotton ginned in Middle Tennessee. The gristmill has two enormous millstones to grind meal, which will be available in small packets for souvenirs. The museum is still being assembled. There is to be a church with stained-glass windows; also, a schoolhouse, print shop, sorghum mill, and arts and crafts buildings.

Write Chamber of Commerce, Box 64, Murfreesboro, 37130, (615) 893-6565.

NASHVILLE, Davidson County. I-40, I-65.

This is the capital city, with many historic sites and buildings, public, religious, commercial, and residential, but they are not concentrated in one area. See the *Nashville Area Chamber of Commerce,* 161 4th Ave. N., 372191; phone (615) 259-3900, for maps, brochures, and self-guiding tours. The *Historical Commission of Metropolitan Nashville & Davidson County,* Stahlman Bldg., Room 329, has walking tours and other information; and literature on historical sites is available at most hotels.

The *Hermitage,* which was Andrew Jackson's home, is not far (12 miles E on US 70); *Tulip Grove,* another fine antebellum mansion, is near the Hermitage. *Belle Meade,* about 7 miles SW, is open to the public on Harding Rd., US 70 S.; it once was the mansion house for a 5,300-acre plantation. *Travellers' Rest Historic House,* on Farrell Pkwy., 6 miles S off US 31 (Franklin Rd.), dates from 1799. It was the home of Judge John Overton. Guides tell the history of the house. Among guests have been Andrew Jackson, Lafayette, Sam Houston, Nathan Bedford Forrest, and John B. Hood, and part of the Battle of Nashville was fought in the peach orchard in December 1864.

Other notable houses on the National Register:

Belmont, Belmont Blvd., built in 1850 on 180 acres with formal gardens, marble fountains, fine statuary, and five ornate cast-iron summer-houses by Colonel J. A. S. Acklen and his wife Adelicia after a 19-month honeymoon abroad. Belmont had its own greenhouses and a watering system ahead of its time. It even had a private zoo and an art gallery, so it's small wonder that the

The Belle Meade Mansion, Nashville, Tennessee. (Courtesy of John E. Hilbolt)

mistress of all this splendor became acquainted with the Empress Eugenie of France, also said to be a good spender and patron of the hunt.

Belair, 2250 Lebanon Rd., was begun in the 1830s by John Harding for his daughter and expanded by William Nichols. Federal with Greek Revival elements. Harding, who owned Belle Meade, gave 1,000 acres to Elizabeth and her husband, Joseph Clay. Clay died before Belair was completed. William and Julia Lytle Nichol of Virginia were the next owners. The house was finished in 1838, with a double-decked Greek Revival entrance and wide verandas.

Two Rivers, 3130 McGavock Pike, was built in 1859 for David H. McGavock. His wife Willie was a

daughter of John Harding of Belle Meade. Now maintained by the City of Nashville.

NORRIS, Anderson County. US 441.

Museum of Appalachia, SW on St. 61, has restored cabins, blacksmith shop, harnessmaker's shop, cooper's, broom and rope factory, a mule-powered molasses mill, and other buildings depicting typical pioneer life. Open from mid-February until mid-November.

RUGBY, Morgan County, St. 52.

Rugby Colony, St. 52, extends into Scott County. The rural district of the 1880s consists of 17 buildings remaining from more than 60 original structures.

Thomas Hughes, British writer and reformer who had founded the Working Men's College in London, wanted this community to be based on manual labor and a cooperative economic system. Hughes was the author of *Tom Brown's School Days,* a best seller in its time. His idealistic endeavors to provide homes and jobs for young Englishmen failed financially within three years. There had been a disastrous fire and a typhoid epidemic. *Kingston Lisle,* Hughes's home, is now a museum. *Christ Episcopal Church* has an 1849 rosewood organ, made in England. Arsonists recently destroyed the just-restored Board of Aid Building.

Gulf States

Alabama
Mississippi
Louisiana

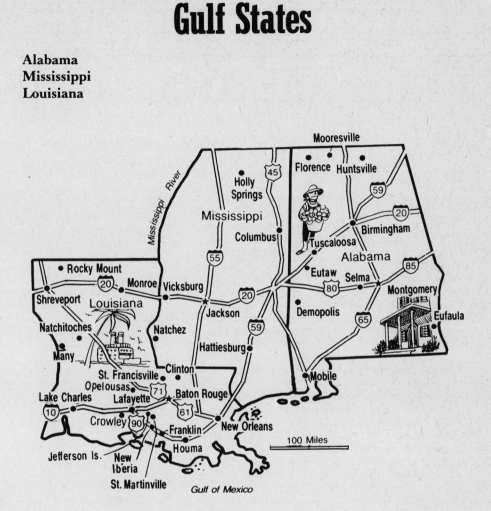

Mississippi River

Mooresville

Florence Huntsville

Holly Springs 45

59

Mississippi

20

Columbus

Tuscaloosa Birmingham

Alabama

Rocky Mount 55

Eutaw Selma

Monroe Vicksburg 20 80

Shreveport Louisiana Jackson Montgomery

Natchitoches Natchez 59 65

Demopolis Eufaula

Many Hattiesburg

Clinton

St. Francisville Mobile

Opelousas 71

Lake Charles Baton Rouge

Lafayette

10 61

Crowley 90

Franklin New Orleans

Houma 100 Miles

Jefferson Is. New Iberia

St. Martinville Gulf of Mexico

ALABAMA

The log-houses on their best estates consist of a room at either end, with a passage between (but seldom enclosed with doors) through which a loaded team could be driven, and the enclosed rooms would generally afford a tolerably distinct view of the opposite scenery through the *unchuncked* double walls. . . . The best houses are sometimes painted, and the chimneys are well laid up in brick and mortar, while those attached to the poorest are more frequently made of mud and sticks, and the surrounding buildings are limited to a rough hovel or two, about as closely housed in, as a field under a well-laid worm fence.

—Sears' Pictorial Description of the United States,
by Robert Sears, New York, 1855

There being no railraod connection between Tuscaloosa and Huntsville . . . we made the journey from the capital in a big four-wheeled stage-coach. The stretch of country . . . was then a rugged place of rocks and boulders over which our vehicle pitched perilously. Stone Mountain reached, we were obliged to descend and pick our way on foot, the roughness of the road making the passage of the coach a very dangerous one. . . .
We arrived in Huntsville on the evening of the second day of our journey. Our driver . . . touched up the spirited horses as we crossed the Public Square and blew a bugle blast as we wheeled round the corner; when, fairly dashing down Clinton Street, he pulled up in masterly style in front of "Clay Castle." It was wide and low and spacious, as were all the affluent homes of that day, and now was ablaze with candles to welcome the travellers. All along the street friendly hands and kerchiefs had waved a welcome. . . .
A Belle of the Fifties, by Mrs. Clement-Clay, Jr., New York, 1905

When the National Register of Historic Places was compiled in 1968, Alabama had only ten landmarks listed among some 800 for the nation, but now has more than 200 individual listings and nearly 30 historic districts. For a complete list write **Alabama Historical Commission,** 715 Monroe St., Montgomery, 36130; phone (205) 832-6621. The pamphlet is free; other publications on Alabama architecture and history are offered by AHC at varying prices. Some are available at a newly opened **Welcome Center** on I-65 N of Athens.

DEMOPOLIS, Marengo County. US 43, 30. St. 13.
In the summer of 1817 a hardy group of French exiles tried to beat back the wilderness and establish olive groves and grapevines. These refugees from Napoleon's army and court had been given four townships

on the bluff of the Tombigbee River near its confluence with the Black Warrior River. But the ambitious Association of French Emigrants for the Cultivation of the Vine and the Olive failed to make a living, dispersed, and drifted off to Mobile and New Orleans or back to France.

Bluff Hall, 405 N. Commissioners Ave. (1832), Greek Revival built for Francis Strother Lyon, lawyer, U.S. and Confederate Congressman, now restored as a house museum by the Marengo County Historical Society. The slave-built mansion stands on the white bluffs where the French landed. Inquire locally for hours.

Gaineswood, 805 S. Cedar, begun 1842, designed by its first owner, Nathan Bryan Whitfield, state legislator, is Greek Revival; now restored as a house museum. The mirrored ballroom, music room, galleried bedroom, and terraced grounds with statuary and a temple are among the many distinctions of this fine antebellum mansion. There may also be a beautiful pianist, the ghost of a housekeeper who died young but still is said to play tinkly tunes on a longgone piano in the Corinthian drawing room. Operated by the Alabama Dept. of Conservation, usually open except Mondays and major holidays.

Confederate Park, in midtown, was laid out when the village was planned; the bandstand is turn-of-the-century. *Lyon Hall,* 102 S. Main, from 1853, is Greek Revival with Gulf Coast adaptations. *Glover Mausoleum,* Riverside Cemetery, an 1856 Greek Revival "house for the dead" is even listed in the Historic American Buildings Survey (HABS). The wrought-iron, pre-1880 *Half-Chance Bridge,* between Linden and Dayton across Chickasaw Bogue, is worth seeing for its name alone, but is no longer in use even for those willing to take half a chance.

EUFAULA, Barbour County. US 82, 431.

Shorter Mansion, Eufaula, Alabama. (Courtesy Eufaula Heritage Association)

Sheppard Cottage, 504 E. Barbour St. (1837), the oldest known house in town, a raised southern adaptation of a Cape Cod style, of clapboard with wooden pegs and hand-worked laths, now houses the **Chamber of Commerce,** which has information on self-guiding walking tours.

Shorter Mansion, 340 N. Eufaula Ave., is an ornate Classic Greek Revival house, now headquarters for the **Eufaula Historical Museum** and the **April Pilgrimage.** The central part of the house dates back to the mid-19th century. When cotton planter Eli Sims Shorter II enlarged and rebuilt the house in 1906 it cost about $100,000. In 1965 it was sold at auction for $33,000 to a group who organized the Eufaula Heritage Association and obtained a state grant to refurbish the place as a culture center and house museum. Many of its fine antiques have been loaned or given by Eufaulians. Open daily.

Fendall Hall, 917 W. Barbour St. (1854), constructed by Edward Brown Young, who also built the first toll bridge across the Chattahoochee River. The pine timber was cut from his property, dressed at his sawmill, and seasoned for three years before used in construction. The first floor is put together with pegs. One of the finest Italianate houses in Alabama, Fendall Hall also has a cupola and widow's walk with a view of the lake and town. It is next door to the Cato House, and has been restored by the Alabama Historical Commission.

Cato House, 823 W. Barbour, was the 1858 home of ardent secessionist L. L. Cato, a good friend of William Lowndes Yancey, leader of the so-called Southern Fire-eaters, eager to leave the Union. A gala celebration took place here when Alabama seceded.

Welborn House, Livingston Ave. (1847), is Greek Revival, built for Dr. Thomas L. Welborn; restored and occupied by the *Eufaula Arts Council.*

The Tavern, 105 Riverside Dr. (1836), was the first permanent building in town, which was then called Irwinton, a trading post on the river. The name, honoring an early settler, was changed to avoid confusion with Irwinton, Georgia. Eufaula was a Creek Indian tribe. The tavern, once an inn for steamboat passengers, also has been a dwelling, an Episcopal church, and was used as a hospital during the Civil War. The two-story full-length veranda has square columns on the ground floor, round columns and a balustrade on the second.

McNab Bank Building, Broad St., an Italian Renaissance Revival structure from mid-19th century, has a cast-iron façade on the ground floor; iron shutters on first-floor windows can be pulled down and locked.

Lore Historic District, bounded by Eufaula Ave., Browder, Livingston, and Barbour Sts., has some 75 structures of varying styles. When the area was laid out, with Front St. along the river bluff commanding a fine view, and center parkways for other thoroughfares, Livingston, Orange, Randolph, and Eufaula Sts. were planned to spell LORE to honor

Seth Lore, town promoter. Several houses in town are on the National Register; inquire at the Chamber of Commerce—some may be open during Pilgrimage. (Note: For the many fanciers of octagonal houses, Alabama's sole remaining one is at 103 N. Midway in Clayton, 19 miles W on St. 30.)

EUTAW, Greene County. US 11, just off I-20, 59.

Coleman-Banks House, 430 Springfield Rd., built about 1847, is Greek Revival with four large fluted Ionic columns embellishing a full front veranda. The original smokehouse and kitchen are on the grounds. Restored, open to the public, by the Greene County Historical Society.

First Presbyterian Church, Main St. and Wilson Ave., is Carpenter Greek Revival, built in 1851. *Greene County Courthouse,* on the square, is the last Greek Revival public structure built in Alabama; completed in 1869. Also on the square are the 1824 and 1856 grand jury building and probate office.

Kirkwood, 111 Kirkwood Drive, is an impressive 1860 mansion with Ionic columns lining two sides, iron balconies, four tall chimneys, and a cupola. The heavy doors are framed with Austrian glass.

FLORENCE, Lauderdale County. I-72, 17.

W. C. Handy Home, 620 W. College St., restored birthplace of composer Handy, has been moved to this site, with a museum adjacent, operated by the Florence Historical Board. The piano on which the musician composed "St. Louis Blues" is among displays.

Pope's Tavern, Seminary St. and Hermitage Drive, was a stage stop in 1811. Andrew Jackson was among many famous guests. The building was used as a hospital during the Civil War. Operated by the Florence

Pope's Tavern, Florence, Alabama. (Drawing by Emily Priestly, courtesy Florence Historical Board)

Historical Board; hours and fees are the same as for the Handy Home; check locally.

Karsner-Carroll House, 303 N. Pine (1825), has been restored. Smokehouse. Florence Housing Authority has offices here. Inquire locally for hours open; the house is also known as the **Karsner-Kennedy House.**

Patton House, Sweetwater and Florence Blvds., was begun in 1828 by General John Brahan. His son-in-law, Governor Robert M. Patton, lived here later.

Sannoner Historic District includes N. Pine and N. Court from Tuscaloosa Ave. to the University of North Alabama.

Walnut Street Historic District, N. Walnut between Hermitage and Tuscaloosa.

Wesleyan Hall (Wesleyan University), Morrison Ave., is one of the few remaining Greek Revival buildings in Tennessee Valley. Built in 1855.

Larimore House, Mars Hill Rd., was built in 1870 by Theophilus Brown Larimore as a residence and part of a complex of school buildings. It has served almost continuously as a school building.

Rogers Hall, Court St., is Greek Revival, built 1854–55, by John Ballinger. It was the home of George Washington Foster, a planter, and later of Emmett O'Neal, governor from 1910 until 1915. Lately it has served as social center on the University of North Alabama campus.

HUNTSVILLE, Madison County. I-231, 72.

The name was changed to Twickenham, for the home of Alexander Pope, one of planter Leroy Pope's favorite poets, but was changed back to honor early settler John Hunt as the War of 1812 approached and English names lost favor.

Twickenham Historic District is Alabama's largest. There are 159 buildings in an area bounded by Clinton and Hermitage Aves. and Madison and California Sts.

Clemens House, Church St. and

Clinton Ave., W., a two-story brick built in the 1830s, was the residence of Jeremiah Clemens, who maintained friendship with some leading Confederates although he was antisecessionist and a peace advocate. It is now the offices of City Utilities.

Steele-Fowler House, 808 Maysville Rd., a Greek Revival home built by architect George Steele in 1840 for his own use, is graced by an elliptical staircase with cherry handrail and balustrades. One of the many gala affairs held in the spacious rooms was a celebration of James K. Polk's election to the presidency.

Pope-Spraggins House, Adams Ave. and McClung St., was built by pioneer Colonel Leroy Pope before 1820. Later the house was the residence of Leroy Pope Walker, Confederate Secretary of War. When Federal troops occupied the town during the Civil War they thoroughly searched a number of homes, hoping to catch the Confederate officer. One elderly woman, seeing the soldiers looking into a cut-glass decanter, snapped: "You don't expect to find General Walker in that brandy bottle, do you?"

Howard Weeden House, Green and Gates Sts., was the birthplace of Miss Howard Weeden, a writer and artist, and has been bought by the Twickenham Historic Preservation District for restoration as a house museum. There are also archaeological excavations in the grounds. The building is said to have been started by Dr. H. H. Chambers in 1819. Chambers, a surgeon under Andrew Jackson in the Indian wars, later served as U.S. Senator from Alabama. William Weeden, who bought the building in 1832, finished construction. Federal troops were housed here during the Civil War.

MOBILE, Mobile County. I-10, US 43. On Mobile Bay.

Church Street East Historic District, downtown area along Government and Church, between Bayou and Water Sts. This largest and most heterogeneous of three historic districts comprises some 70 structures varying from residential, single-family, to commercial—hotels, shops, museums, restaurants, etc. The streets are lighted by imported gas lamps; some are shaded by centuries-old live oaks.

A riding and walking tour, planned by the *Mobile Historic Development Commission,* takes in 66 historic sites. Self-guiding brochure available at headquarters or P.O. Box 1827. Among highlights:

City Hall, 111 S. Royal St., completed in 1857. Live fish were sold on the ground floor when the building was a marketplace. It served as an armory during the Civil War. When the building was renovated in the 1930s the original style was preserved; brick covered with stucco, Italianate. NHL.

Kirkbride House (Fort Conde-Charlotte House), 104 Theatre St., was restored by the Historic Mobile Preservation Society and is now owned by the National Society of Colonial Dames of Alabama. Part of the walls, from the period when the building was used as the city's first jail (1822–24), have been saved. The house may also have served as the first courthouse.

Dr. Henry LeVert Office, 153 Government, is listed in the 1859 City Directory. The house where the beautiful Madame LeVert held salons is now a parking lot. Octavia LeVert seems to have dazzled everyone: Mrs. Clement Clay, Jr., who wrote of social and political life in the 1850s, described her as moving like a bird on the wing when she danced. Washington Irving found her a rare bird indeed, saying only one of her sort was "born in the course of an empire." A portrait of her by Thomas Sully hangs at Oakleigh.

Phoenix Fire Company, 203 S. Claiborne, was organized in the mid-

19th century. The station built in
1859 was bought by the city, moved
to this site, and restored in 1964. Now
a fire station museum.

Hamilton House, 407 Church, was
built in 1859 as a town house for
Thomas Hamilton, a prominent lawyer. At 401 Church a handsome antebellum mansion has been restored
as a gift and antique shop.

William Frolichstein and Isaac
Goldsmith, who were brothers-in-law
and business partners, built twin
houses in 1862. These structures at
357–359 Church were joined in 1965
to make an inn. At 350 Church, the
1854–55 home of William Carter
now houses the Junior League.

Waring Buildings, 110 and 108 S.
Claiborne, are oddities. The 110 address was a lodge apart from the
main dwelling and called the
"Texas" because Texas had been
apart from the U.S. It was occupied
by the sons of the family. No. 108 was
occupied by the Waring servants,
about 1856; it is one of few such
quarters preserved in Mobile.

Portier House, 307 Conti, a Creole
cottage built about 1833–34, was a
residence for the first Roman Catholic bishop of Mobile and founder of
Spring Hill College, Michael Portier.
Later Father Abram Ryan, called the
Poet Priest of the Confederacy, lived
here.

Bernstein-Bush House, 355 Government St., built in 1872 in Italianate
style, was bought by the city for use
as a unit of the Museum of the City
of Mobile.

Martin Horst House (Moongate),
407 Conti, was built in 1867 for
Horst, an early mayor who had arrived in town as an immigrant from
Germany. The building was bought
by the city when it was in danger of
being demolished; since then it has
been sold and privately restored.

Spear House, 453 Conti, is one of
the few remaining dwellings built
before 1838.

**Government Street Presbyterian
Church,** 300 Government, built in
1836, was designed by J. Gallier and
C. Dankin. It is the oldest church
building in Mobile and an outstanding Greek Revival structure.

Barton Academy, 504 Government
St., also designed by Gallier and
Dankin, was built in 1836, and by
1852 became the first public school in
Alabama. Early students paid a
small tuition if they could afford to
do so. The handsome building is particularly striking at night when it is
floodlighted. At 503 Government, the
William Hallett House was the Italianate home of a cotton broker, built
in 1859. Its flagstone walk is one of
the few remaining in Mobile. An
Italianate town house at 501 Government was the home of Jacob Pollock,
a leading merchant in 1876.

Gilmore House, 751 Government,
Italianate, completed in 1864, now
serves as headquarters for the National Junior Miss Pageant—a circumstance which surely would have
surprised builder George Gilmore.

Semmes House, 802 Government,
was built about 1859, bought in 1871
by the grateful citizens of Mobile,
and presented to Confederate naval
hero Raphael Semmes. It is now the
property of the First Baptist Church.
The dashing and literate admiral,
who wrote two fine accounts of his
adventures on land and sea, died in
Mobile in August 1877.

De Tonti Square Historic District,
western downtown section, has some
53 structures from the 19th century
in a nine-block section. This was the
fashionable residential section in the
1860s. The riding and walking tour
of the Mobile Historic Development
Commission takes in 48 sites.

A few highlights: Twin houses at
157–159 N. Conception, in Federal
style, were built by Cornelius Robinson about 1852, restored in 1963. At
156 St. Anthony, the 1857 Italianate
home of F. V. Cluis, a descendant of
the Vine and Olive colony of exiles
from Napoleon's army and court who

founded Demopolis; at 201 N. Conception, another 1857 home belonged to Thomas St. John, who gave
up his last dollar for the Lost Cause.
The house was bought from his heirs
for restoration in 1968. The onetime
wine cellar is now a law library. At
205 N. Conception is the Greek Revival cottage which was once the
home of Gustavus Beal (1836). Later
Charles Batre, of Bordeaux, who
came to Demopolis with the Napo-
leonic exiles, lived here. Restored for
offices in 1965.

The *Revault House,* 254 N. Conception, built in 1856 by Alexander
Revault, commission merchant and
cotton factor, and the *Foote House,*
255 N. Conception, build in mid-
19th century for Charles Foote, grocer, have cast-iron trimmings.

Nearby at 256 N. Conception is
the 1840s town house of Charles
Stuart, editor of the *Merchants and
Planters Journal.* He is buried in the
Church Street Graveyard, Scott and
Government Sts. The burial ground
was opened in 1819 and closed to
burials but not to visitors in 1899.

303 and 305 N. Conception is a
double Federal house built in the
1840s by Ludolf Parmly, a dentist.
When he grew prosperous he built
the town house at 307 in 1852. It has
a remarkable "Egyptian" door.

Richards House, 256 N. Joachim, is
an 1860 Italianate mansion, the
home of Charles G. Richards, with
the "Four Seasons" represented in
ironwork. The ironwork fence is as
lovely as the veranda. The house
served as the headquarters of the
Ideal Cement Co. in the practical
1940s; luckily the company gave the
building to the city and it is now a
house museum operated by the six
Mobile Chapters of the DAR, who
have restored and furnished it.

Not far away, at 261 N. Joachim,
the 1860 home of *Thomas Temple
Armstrong Lyon,* a cotton factor, was
restored as offices in 1958.

Price Williams House, 250 St.

Anthony, is a town house built in
1853. Williams came from Virginia
to become a leading merchant and
president of the Board of Trade.
Later this was the home of Colonel
Jones M. Withers, West Pointer and
a veteran of the Creek, Mexican, and
Civil wars, who also served as mayor
for two terms. During the Battle of
Mobile Bay in 1864 the third floor
was used as headquarters by Confederate Admiral Franklin Buchanan.
He was a Marylander who came
back to Mobile in 1869 and became
secretary of the Life Insurance Co. of
America, but he returned to Talbot
County, Maryland, where he died in
1874. When the city fell to the Federal forces in 1864, Union General
Slaughter commandeered this house.

Oakleigh Garden Historic District
has some 125 residential structures
from the 19th century. A walking
and riding tour is available from the
Development Commission, with
marked map and 41 sites. Government St. became fashionable about
the turn of the century, as did Georgia Ave.

Oakleigh, 350 Oakleigh Place, has
been elaborately furnished as a house
museum and is a fine Greek Revival
raised T-shaped dwelling. When constructed in 1833–38, it was a mile
from town, the home of James
Roper, a local businessman.

Washington Square was given to
the city in 1850 by Archibald W.
Gordon to be used as a promenade. It
had wide wooden walks with hedges
enclosed with a picket fence to keep
stray cattle or horses out. A city ordinance forbade anyone from piling up
bricks or lumber or hanging out
clothes to dry in the square. A pump
and a gazebo were provided for
thirsty, and concert-loving, patrons.
The *Fairy Tree,* a giant large oak
often written about in children's
stories, stands at the corner of Palmetto and Chatham.

Repalje House, 1005 Government,
Greek Revival from 1865, home of

cotton broker George Repalje, has several hundred thousand jumbo bricks in the building, which was designed by George Woodward Cox. The 29-room residence has been restored as dwelling and office.

Georgia Cottage, 2564 Springhill Ave., a mixture of Creole and Greek Revival of 1845, was the home of Augusta Evans Wilson. In 1868, Miss Augusta Jane Evans married a widower older than her father and gave up her career as a writer. (Eventually she penned seven novels.) Then a publisher sent her a check for $25,000 as advance against any novel she might write, and her husband, L. M. Wilson, found he could tolerate her scribblings after all.

Carlen House, High School Dr., on an 1804 Spanish land grant Sts., is an 1840 Creole-style cottage, furnished in period and open daily except Mondays and major holidays.

Historic Mobile Tours take place in the second half of March. Inquire *Chamber of Commerce,* P.O. Box 2187, 36601; phone (205) 433-6951.

Azalea Trail Festival is a marked route of some 35 miles, with guides available. Inquire *Jaycee Tourist Information Center,* 1209 Government St., Monday through Friday; maps and details for self-guiding tour of historic sites.

MONTGOMERY, Montgomery County. I-65, 85.

First White House of the Confederacy, 644 Washington Ave. (1825), was used by Jeffferson Davis and his family, March to May 1861, when the capital was moved to Richmond for nearly the duration of the war. (In its last days the government was on the run; see Washington, Georgia, etc.) The building, which is now a Confederate shrine and house museum, restored by architect Nicholas H. Holmes, Jr., has been moved from its original location at Bibb, Moulton, and Lee Sts.

Ordeman-Shaw Historic District, bounded by McDonough, Randolph, Decatur, and Madison, is a restoration complex which re-creates the look of a southern town during the economic boom before the Civil War. Headquarters for the Landmarks of Montgomery, Inc., are here. The *Visitors Center* has information on the area. The *Ordeman-Shaw House,* begun in 1842, was completed by architect and civil engineer Charles Ordeman in 1852. He also built the *Campbell Cottage,* slave quarters and laundry buildings. *DeWolf-Cooper Cottage* houses the *Chamber of Commerce,* which has information on local historic sites and a film.

Murphy House, 22 Bibb St., is a restored 1851 Greek Revival dwelling, once the home of a cotton merchant, now housing the Montgomery Water Board. The double parlor, which also served as a ballroom, has been restored with period furnishings.

Perry St. Historic District comprises 19 structures from the 1820s to 1848 with a number of Greek Revival and Federal-style buildings.

Rice-Semple-Haardt House, 725 Monroe St. (1850s); was first occupied by a state supreme court justice; restored in 1974, now a museum and offices of the *Alabama Historical Commission.*

Alabama State Capitol, Goat Hill, E end of Dexter Ave. (1851), is where the Ordinance of Secession was passed in 1861 and Jefferson Davis was inaugurated. On the main portico is the six-pointed bronze star marking the spot where he stood while Howell Cobb administered the oath of office. NHL. Open daily except holidays.

Teague House, 468 S. Perry, an 1848 Greek Revival mansion, occupied by Wilson's Raiders in 1865. Open weekdays. *Edgewood (Thomas House),* 3175 Thomas Ave., is the oldest residence in the city; dates from 1821.

Yancey Law Office, Washington and Perry Sts. (1850s), was used by

William Lowndes Yancey, a secessionist leader; the building still contains law offices.

Winter Building, 2 Dexter Ave.
(1841–43), held the Southern Telegraph offices where the message to
General P. G. T. Beauregard, giving
him permission to open fire on Fort
Sumter, was sent by Leroy Pope
Walker, Confederate Secretary of
War. First floor has been altered for
shops.

MOORESVILLE, Limestone
County. Alternate 72, St. 20, E of
Decatur.

The historic district encompasses
about 29 square miles. Most houses
are white frame with picket fences.
There are 14 antebellum structures,
including two churches. The post office still uses the original wooden call
boxes.

SELMA, Dallas County. US 80, St. 22.

John Tyler Morgan House, 719
Tremont, an 1859 Greek Revival
structure, was the home of the Confederate general, now occupied by
the **Selma-Dallas County Preservation
Society.** Readers occasionally confuse
this Confederate general who served
in the cavalry under General Forrest
with General John Hunt Morgan, a
cavalry leader and raider from Kentucky (although he was born in
Huntsville, Alabama). John Tyler
Morgan commanded a brigade in the
cavalry corps during the Atlanta
campaign. After the war he served in
the U.S. Senate.

Sturdivant Hall, 713 Mabry St., is
an outstanding structure built in
1856. Architect Thomas Helm Lee
was a cousin of Robert E. Lee. The
house has been completely restored.
Outbuildings, including kitchen with
slave quarters above, smokehouse,
and carriage house are original.

Historic and Civic Building, 109
Union St., Greek Revival from the
1840s, has been restored. It has
served as a Masonic institute, courthouse, military institute, and
hospital.

Water Ave. Historic District, six
blocks between Franklin and Lauderdale Sts., is one of the few antebellum riverfront streets in the
Southeast. There are 21 structures in
the district.

Note: **Cahaba,** 11 miles SW of
town off St. 22, is the site of Alabama's first permanent capital; privately owned but accessible to the
public. There are plans to build a
replica of the original state house.

TUSCALOOSA, Tuscaloosa Coun-
ty. US 82, 43.

The town was named for the Creek
Indian Chief Tuskalusa, who was
host to Hernando De Soto and his
followers in 1540, but later fought
with the Spaniards disastrously.
Nearly all the Indians were killed
and the victors were in bad shape,
without supplies and with most of
their number badly wounded. Tuscaloosa was the state capital from
1826 to 1846. Much of the city was
destroyed during the Civil War.

Druid City Historic District,
roughly bounded by 16th Ave., 21st
St., Queen City Park, and 15th St.,
has 48 structures, the earliest from
1820.

Collier-Overby Home, 9th St. and
21st Ave., restored Federal–Greek
Revival house of the 1820s, was once
the home of Governor H. W. Collier.

Battle-Friedman Home, 1010
Greensboro Ave., 1835 Federal–
Greek Revival house, has been handsomely restored and serves as a Civic
and Cultural Center. It was once the
home of Senator Clement C. Clay,
author of *A Belle of the Fifties,* and his
wife.

Friedman Library, 1305 Greensboro Ave., mid-19th-century Italianate house, was known as
Cherokee, the home of Robert Je-
mison, antisecessionist; now county
library.

Guild-Verner House, 1904 University Ave. (1822), Georgian style, is thought to be the oldest brick residence in the county and is being restored as an arts center.

Gorgas-Manly Historic District, University of Alabama campus, comprises eight institutional structures from 1829 to 1888. William Nichols was architect for the **President's Mansion,** 1841, still used by the university president. Nichols also planned the campus; the 1886 **Clark Hall,** with brick pointed arched tracery windows, is flanked by **Manly Hall** and **Garland Hall** in similar style. **Old Observatory,** N of University Blvd. (1844), is one of four buildings to survive the Federal invasion of the campus. The 1929 **Gorgas House** was named for General Josiah Gorgas, Confederate chief of ordinance, also president of the university, whose son Dr. William Gorgas helped conquer yellow fever.

Old Tavern, University Blvd., an inn in the 1820s, later used by Governor John Gayle and the legislature; restored by the Tuscaloosa County Preservation Society as a museum.

Searcy House, 2606 8th St., an 1830s two-story frame with two-story portico, was the home of Henry Minor, a state supreme court justice, and Dr. James T. Searcy, head of the state mental hospital (Bryce's), now acquired by the Tuscaloosa County Preservation Society for restoration.

Tuscaloosa Heritage Week takes place in April; write the **Tuscaloosa County Preservation Society,** Box 1665, 34501, for details on this and on the several other famous houses of the area which may be seen by driving past. The **Chamber of Commerce,** 513 Lauderdale St., has information and maps for an auto tour of the city. Take note of **Christ Episcopal Church** (1840), the **Mayfield Mansion** (1820), the **Washington Moody House** (1820), and **Whigham House,** a sprawling Italianate manse.

MISSISSIPPI

March, 1840.

2. Rolled logs with 6 hands in new ground; finished plowing in oats; Gilbert breaking out baulks in corn field; women rolling and beating down cotton stalks; Jacob sick; Amy commenced work this day; rain about midday. The spring has every appearance of having opened; forest trees budding out; cotton up where good seed thrown out; planted peas in garden this day. . . .

3. Gardening this day; planted peas, onions, radishes, spinach, leeks, lettuce and pepper grass; garden not in fine condition, too busy at other things; 14 lambs, very small and poor; cattle look badly, hogs look well.

4. Jacob laying off corn rows; Gilbert breaking out baulks; Ned and Viney hauling cotton seed; fellows chopping; women and children burning brush; a beautiful spring day; we weighed this day the listed sow pig, weight 58 lbs. . . .

6. . . . Winter has gone and spring is marching on, hailed with exultation by the chorists of the air, and met at every step with flowers. . . .

8. Sunday; left for Jackson and Brandon; postponed till Monday to eat a piece of fat turkey.

—*Diary of a Mississippi Planter,* edited by Prof. Franklin L. Riley,
Oxford, Mississippi, 1909

When we moved to the plantation we lived on the big road on the west side of it, in the settlements already built, during the first part of 1856. While we built on the east side of Matubba Creek a nice six-room, chinked and plastered log-house, with a row of frame "Shanghai," servants' houses, cribs, stables, etc. . . .

Between a quarter and a half-mile southwest of our new home, in the woods, was a circular Indian mound, twelve or fifteen feet high. At the base of this mound we made a brick kiln for plantation use, and used the mound itself, which was very rich, for a turnip-patch. In plowing over the mound many arrow heads and Indian relics were turned up within a few inches of the surface. I wonder what was done in it!

—*Antebellum Times in Monroe County,* by R. C. Beckett,
Oxford, Mississippi, 1910

COLUMBUS, Lowndes County. St. 69, 82E.

Chamber of Commerce, 318 7th St. N., has information on pilgrimages, when many of the more than 100 mansions of the area can be visited, or for a walk or drive-past tour; some are open all year, some by appointment. Columbus was an important stopover on the old Military Road, which dates back to about 1817, and became a showplace for cotton planters and their homes. First on the driving tour:

Lee House (*Blewett-Harrison-Lee House*), next door to the Chamber of Commerce, was the home of General Stephen D. Lee. As aide-de-camp to General P. G. T. Beauregard, Lee was in at the beginning of the Civil War and was sent to demand the surrender of Fort Sumter. By 1864 he was a lieutenant general in the Confederate Army. He was severely wounded in the retreat from Nashville, but served in the North Carolina campaign until war's end. He was arrested with other Confederate leaders, paroled within a month, and moved to Columbus, where he became a planter. He served in the state senate in 1878, became a college president, and headed the Vicksburg National Park Association and the United Confederate Veterans. He died, much respected and honored, in 1908. The house was built about 1847 by Major Thomas G. Blewett, grandfather of Mrs. Lee, and later was the home of James T. Harrison before it passed to Stephen Dill Lee. It has been restored. The first floor is to be used for social functions, including wedding receptions. The second floor has Lee memorabilia.

One block N on the right, at 416 7th St. N., is *Camellia Place,* built in 1847, Greek Revival style, with its original red painted roof. The traditional captain's walk is inside the cupola, which is not so traditional. There is a mahogany spiral staircase, unsupported above the first floor. *Themerlaine,* across the street on the right, at 510 7th St. N., was built in 1844; Greek Revival with some Gothic touches. It is a strikingly beautiful house with raised first floor, imposing verandas; indoors, cross halls have Venetian glass sidelights, elaborate plasterwork, and marble mantels.

Going N two blocks on 7th St., *Rosewood Manor,* on the left, was built in 1838. It stands on a hill, as do many houses in town, because low places were considered fever spots.

The mansion was built for a Yankee, so the local story goes, who said the vapors were unhealthy and went north again. The vapors for a Yankee around here got much more unhealthy a decade later, and kept on worsening.

Half a block farther, on the right, is *Leighcrest,* built in 1841, with lovely old gardens. The house is to be restored.

Hickory Sticks, 1206 7th, almost incredibly began as a log cabin in the 1820s and was remodeled in the 1840s. It was the residence of Robert Hayden, first mayor of Columbus. It was owned at one time by Stephen Dill Lee, who gave *Lee Park* to the city. Keep to the left through Lee Park, turn right to *Magnolia Hill,* built in 1835, of hand-hewn logs with random pine flooring. It still has many hand-blown glass windows. Two blocks past Magnolia Hill is *Military Road;* turn right. This is the famous old road which was begun five years after the War of 1812 and finished in 1821. It was called Jackson's Military Road, for Andrew Jackson. Going right on Military Road to 5th Ave. N., turn right. On the left is the *Cumberland Presbyterian Church,* built in 1840. Its rectory was built by Major Blewett for his daughter, who married lawyer Harrison, and their daughter Regina married General Stephen Dill Lee here. The construction is handmade brick. Turn right on 9th St.

Temple Heights, 515 9th, is a beautifully placed Greek Revival home which looks impressive on its high rise of ground, with ancient trees framing it. There are 14 Doric columns embellishing three sides of the 1837 structure. It has four stories with two rooms and a hall on each floor.

Turn left onto 6th Ave. N. *Wisteria Place,* 524 8th St. In season, even with no number, you would know Wisteria Place by the blooms which hang heavy before its fine portico. The mansion was built in 1854, Old South style, with many fine antebellum furnishings. Across the street, **Beckrome** is a New England–style cottage, built in 1832 by the first principal of Franklin Academy. The house had no two doors or windows the same size; they were made to fit whatever holes the carpenters cut. Some doors are 40 inches wide—probably to fit a hole cut after a long lunch.

Franklin Square, Franklin Academy, the Courthouse, and **Lawyers' Row** are all in the downtown section and very old. Many offices are being restored in Lawyers' Row. **St. Paul's Episcopal Church,** on 2nd Ave. S., was completed in 1858 and has a Tiffany window. Tennessee Williams was born in the rectory (built 1876–80) when his grandfather was pastor.

Twelve Gables, 220 3rd St., built in 1838, has been completely restored. A historical marker gives the history of the house. Turn right here onto 3rd Ave. S. for **Errolton,** an 1840s mansion, with twin double parlors that have twin pier mirrors, which reflect chandeliers endlessly. The glass, and marble mantels, came from Italy. The exterior lacy trim uniting the six columns is particularly attractive in the verdant setting of trees and flowering shrubs.

Thomas Pratt House is a raised cottage from 1833, at 519 2nd St. **Riverview,** 514 2nd St., was built in 1847 of handmade bricks weighing nearly 12 pounds each, twice the size of today's bricks. A spiral stairway soars unsupported from the first floor to the fourth-floor observatory. There are twin parlors with 14-foot ceilings embellished with ornamental plaster. The cupola has floor-to-ceiling stained-glass windows and a captain's walk.

In the middle of the next block on the left is **Lehmquen,** built in 1838, a raised cottage of typical Old South construction made from virgin timbers and with landscaped gardens.

Across the street, **The Colonnade,** 620 2nd St. S., built in 1860, has an asymmetrical front door which is unusually high in an otherwise typical Greek Revival mansion with six two-story columns supporting the full front veranda. The upright framework of the house is held together with wooden pegs. The original outdoor kitchen is a guesthouse.

South of this house, on the right, is **White Arches,** 122 7th Ave. S. Built in 1857, it combines Greek and Gothic Revival elements with an octagonal tower, and Italianate round arches and cast-iron balcony rails. This may sound terrible, but it looks not too bad, though it would never win any architectural prize, except maybe an E for effort.

Amzi Love House, 306 7th St., is Italianate, built in 1848, and has been occupied by five generations of the family. The furnishings are original with family memorabilia on display. The original kitchen has been attached to the house. The old smokehouse, well, and woodhouse still stand.

Max Andrews House, 403 9th St., was built during the 1840s, of board-and-batten construction. It was a school at first, later became a stage-coach stop, and is now a residence.

Two blocks E is the **Mississippi University for Women,** founded in 1884, the oldest state-supported school for women in the U.S.

Kenneth Gatchell House, 1411 2nd Ave. S., was built in 1829 of handmade brick and cypress and was used as a prison during the Civil War, at which time the French doors on the front were bricked over and small windows cut in the façade.

Shadowlawn, 1024 2nd Ave. S., dates from 1860, an outstanding antebellum mansion with the white columns, wide veranda, balconied upper hall, and the same attractive

Gothic trim between columns which distinguishes Errolton.

Snowdoun, 906 3rd Ave. N., was built in 1854 for Governor James Whitfield. Jefferson Davis was a guest during his campaign for the U.S. Senate. It has rectangular rooms opening into octagonal halls and a spiral stairway.

Taynore, 806 3rd Ave. N., was built by Henry Taylor in 1854 and once served as parsonage for Thomas Cox Teasdale, a Baptist minister who was a friend of both Abraham Lincoln and Jefferson Davis. The plank floors are original. Furnishings are of the Empire and Victorian periods. The house has a fine display of cut glass.

Waverly, 10 miles NW via US 45, St. 50, near West Point, is a restored antebellum plantation mansion. The plantation is also being restored, with plans for a small village and steamboat ride. The house has twin circular self-supporting stairways and a 65-foot-high octagonal observation cupola.

The pilgrimage to most of the above homes, with costumed guides, takes place in late March and early April. For details write **Historic Columbus,** Box 1016, Columbus, 39701; phone (601) 328-4491, or 327-3448.

HOLLY SPRINGS, Marshall County. US 78.

Holly Springs Garden Club has headquarters in **Montrose,** an 1858 Classic Revival brick mansion which was built by Alfred Brooks as a wedding present for his daughter. A wide brick walkway edged with boxwood leads to the door. Ask here for information on houses open to the public and on the annual three-day pilgrimage; (601) 252-3368. The house tour usually takes place late in April. Mrs. Maxine Elgin, of Holly Springs, has slides of pilgrimage houses, available for programs. During the pilgrimage

a guide in each of the five churches tells the history of the building.

Among mansions on the tour are **Cedarhurst,**1857; **White Pillars,** 1838; **Herndon,** 1839; **Walter Place,** 1850s; **The Magnolias,** 1850s; **Mimosas,** 1836; **Heritage,** mid-19th century; **Grey Gables,** antebellum; **Mosswood,** antebellum; **Arlie Wood, Cuffawa,** and the **McCarroll Place.** Inasmuch as Holly Springites do not prefer to publish addresses, for whatever reason, it is suggested that visitors try to catch the Garden Club "at home" at Montrose and ask for details.

Walter Place, at 331 W. Chulahoma Ave., was used by General and Mrs. Grant during the occupation of the town in 1862. If Grant could find it, so can you. Mrs. Grant, an unflappable sort, is said to have awaited her husband in this house when Confederate General Van Dorn captured the town. She asked him to protect the privacy of her bedroom and thus saved her husband's papers. Earl Van Dorn did not honor the privacy of another bedroom later on and was killed by a jealous husband. The large Greek Revival mansion has two battlemented octagonal towers flanking the portico, which has four Corinthian columns. Colonel Harvey C. Walter built the house. Dr. Anne Walter Fearn, who became a surgeon, was born here. The house has remained in the Walter family into the 20th century.

JACKSON, Hinds County. I-55.

Chamber of Commerce, 208 Lamar Life Bldg., 317 E. Capitol St., has literature on local historic sites and on the annual pilgrimage. The town was burned by Sherman in 1863, but some antebellum homes remain, including the **Governor's Mansion,** Capitol & N. Congress Sts., which is on the tour. **City Hall** is also antebellum, 203 S. President St. The **Old State Capitol,** 100 N. State St., as well as the present capitol, on Mississippi

St., are on the National Register. So are the **Capitol Green; Central Fire Station,** S. President St.; **Edwards Hotel,** Capitol and Mill Sts.; **Manship House,** 412 E. Fortification St.; **Millsaps-Buie House,** 628 N. State St.; **The Oaks (Boyd House),** 823 N. Jefferson; and **Smith Park Architectural District,** roughly bounded by N. West and N. Congress Sts. between Capitol St. and State Capitol.

Old State Capitol, now restored, houses a fine state historical museum; the State Department of Archives and History is on the grounds. Note that Fortification St. got its name because it was the line of defense for the Confederates. It runs east and west through the northern part of town and extended west between Raymond and Clinton roads. Fortifications crossed the lawn of the Manship House (see above); a fire bell on the lawn was the only bell in town which was not melted down to be used for ammunition during the war.

NATCHEZ, Adams County. US 61.

Natchez Pilgrimage is probably the best-known tourist pilgrimage in America. It is held from March 6 through April 4, sponsored by the Pilgrimage Garden Club and the Natchez Garden Club. For information write Natchez Pilgrimage, P.O. Box 347, or P.O. Box 537, Natchez, 39120. **Pilgrimage Headquarters** are in the Gay 90s Bldg. on Stanton Hall grounds, Commerce St. between Monroe and High Sts. The **Natchez Garden Club** will be found in Connelly's Tavern. And the **Natchez-Adams Chamber of Commerce,** which has a fine map for self-guiding tours and a complete list of historic homes, is at 300 N. Commerce St. There are six different tours, some afternoon, some morning; tickets are sold only at Pilgrimage Headquarters. Rates for students. To make the complete pilgrimage takes three full days.

Among the number of houses on the National Register are:

Arlington, Main St., early 19th century, brick, attributed to John Hampton White. NHL.

Auburn, Duncan Park, built 1812. Levi Weeks, designer and builder. NHL.

Baynton (John) House, 821 Main St., from the 1830s.

Commercial Bank and Banker's House, 206 Main St. and 107 Canal St., marble façade on bank. The two buildings have been incorporated as one, with the main banking room used as a Christian Science church. NHL.

D'Evereux, D'Evereux Drive, about 1840. Henry Clay was a guest here. Greek Revival, built for William S. Elliot, an insurance company president. Union soldiers once camped on the lawn.

Dunleith, 84 Homochitto St., built ca. 1855 by C. C. Dahlgren on the site of Routhlands, built by his father-in-law in the late 18th century. (John Dahlgren was a Union admiral; Ulric Dahlgren a Union colonel—both were much better known and are not to be confused with this Dahlgren, later a Confederate officer.)

Hope Farm, 147 Homochitto St. (1774–89), once the home of the Spanish governor.

House on Ellicott's Hill, N. Canal and Jefferson Sts., built about 1800. Restored. One of the first buildings erected after the Spanish laid out the town. NHL.

Johnson (William) House, 210 State St.

King's Tavern, 611 Jefferson St., built about 1789. Oldest building in Natchez, it was operated as a public house and as a mail and stagecoach stop.

Melrose, Melrose Ave., built in 1845. Greek Revival. NHL.

Monmouth, E. Franklin and Melrose Ave., from the 1820s, was the home of John Anthony Quitman, military governor of Mexico City after it was conquered in the Mexican War.

Monteigne, Liberty Rd. (1854–55), home of William Thompson Martin, Confederate general, who had organized the Adams County Cavalry when Mississippi seceded. He became a personal aide to General Robert E. Lee and later commanded the District of Northwest Mississippi. After the war he practiced law and was active in politics. He was postmaster in 1905 and president of the Natchez, Jackson and Columbus Railroad. He died in Natchez in 1910.

Natchez Bluffs and Under-the-Hill Historic District, bounded by the Mississippi River, Broadway, and S. Canal St., is the site of an early French settlement in the first part of the 18th century, with the original Natchez landing and town square included in the district. This frontier post became notorious for illegal activity in the 18th century and later. Even in early romantic fiction it was the place where rich young scoundrels went to act up.

Oakland, 9 Oakhurst Drive.

Stanton Hall, High St. (see Natchez Pilgrimage, above). NHL.

The Elms, 215 Pine St.

In Natchez vicinity: *Fair Oaks* is S of town on US 61. *Longwood (Nutt's Folly),* 1½ miles SE, was built 1860–62 (Samuel Sloan was architect), for Dr. Haller Nutt, a planter. It was never finished. It is High Victorian, Italianate with octagonal elements and Far Eastern touches, and is supposed to have a ghost. NHL. *Mistletoe,* NE of town on St. 554, was built in 1807.

LOUISIANA

Scarcely had the low, clay chimneys of a few woodsmen's cabins sent up, through a single change of season, their lonely smoke-wreaths among the silent willow jungles of the Mississippi, when Bienville began boldly to advocate the removal of the capital to this so-called "New Orleans." But, even while he spoke, the place suffered a total inundation. Yet he continued to hold it as a trading post of the Mississippi Company, and, by the close of 1720, began again, in colonial council, to urge it as the proper place for the seat of government. . . .

A hundred frail palisade huts, some rude shelters of larger size to serve as church, hospital, government house, and company's warehouses, a few vessels at anchor in the muddy river, a population of three hundred, mostly men—such was the dreary hunter's camp. . . . [where] Bienville set up his headquarters; and where this was but just done when, in September, a tornado whisked away church, hospital, and thirty dwellings, prostrated the crops, and, in particular, destroyed the rice.

—*Who Are the Creoles?* by George W. Cable, New York, 1883

The dwellings on the Coast are generally frame, of one story in height, but there are many constructed with tolerable elegance. The sugar houses, on either side of the river, at intervals considerably distant, were easily distinguished by the vast columns of smoke which they sent up into the air. Within thirty or forty miles of the city there are but a few of the *petits habitants,* the lands being engrossed by the wealthy planters.

—*Views of Louisiana,* by Henry Marie Brackenridge, Pittsburgh, 1814

BATON ROUGE, East Baton Rouge Parish. I-10.

Baton Rouge Convention & Visitors Bureau, P.O. Box 3202, Old State Capitol, 70821, phone (504) 383-1825, has brochures and maps for the area as well as the city. The *Louisiana Tourist Development Commission,* Box 44291, Capitol Station, 70804, (504) 389-5981, also has information, including routes and hours for plantations scattered all over the state.

Riverside and Beauregard Town: In 1971 the Riverside Area was the part of town bounded by the river, the Capitol Lake, and I-110 loop to the new Mississippi River Bridge. Within the Riverside Area are two historic districts: Beauregard Town and Spanish Town. The restorations and renovations of the old business section and the residential areas are worth studying by preservationists. Subdistricts within Beauregard Town are the *Riverside Centroplex,* the civic center area; *Catfish Town,* the warehouse district; and the residential areas both N and S of Government St. Commercial Strip.

224

Within the residential section are homes converted to office use. The city planning commission, which hopes to keep Beauregard Town as a living folk museum, describes the townscape as "divided by narrow roads climbing up and down the unusually hilly terrain ... the narrow houses on small narrow urban lots combine their character with the mature landscape to blend into an exciting, small scaled, intimate old town character."

Trees have been saved wherever possible. Retaining walls have been built to keep the hilly aspect of the area. As the commission points out, this is "quite different from the 'leveled' subdivisions that prevail today. The street/walk scale in Beauregard Town is one connected with the luxuries of open-public space of a bygone era. . . . Sidewalks exist along every street. . . . making for a very social-walking community. There is a liberal amount of green lawn between the walk and the curb which serves as a planting space for trees including an abundance of crape myrtles."

Among historic places: **Old State Capitol,** North Blvd. and River Rd., built in mid-19th century, had James Harrison Dakin for architect; the building was burned during the Civil War, rebuilt, and a fourth story added in 1880–82, Visitor's Information Desk on the first floor. NHL. **Yazoo & Mississippi Valley Railroad Station,** same area, has been adapted to house the Louisiana Arts & Science Center. **Old Louisiana Governor's Mansion,** St. Charles St. and North Blvd., will not seem old to many visitors, but it is historic. The Neoclassical structure was first occupied by Huey Long and has been restored as a house museum. Huey Long patterned the building after the White House, saying that he wanted "to get in practice." The **Bailey House,** 900 North Blvd., built about 1840, is now headquarters

from the Foundation for Historical Louisiana, Inc.

There are about 40 historic places to see; get a map from any of the offices listed in this section.

Spanish Town, in the parish of East Baton Rouge, is an older neighborhood bisected by Spanish Town Rd. In 1805 Don Carlos de Grand Pre, governor of West Florida, drew up the plans for the site "out of cannon shot" of the fort on the river bluff. It was to be settled by Spanish colonists from Galvez Town. But by 1819 the English and French had moved in. In 1828 yellow fever wiped out many of the Spanish settlers who were still here. In 1832, Asiatic cholera struck in epidemic proportions. In 1930, when the new state capitol was being constructed, bulldozers invaded the old burial ground, scooping up human bones and mummy-shaped cast-iron caskets of the Spanish colonists. These were reburied secretly in a large concrete vault because grave-robbers might understandably search for the fortune in swords, jewelry, and other treasures buried with the Spaniards.

There are many architectural gems on the streets of Spanish Town. **Charlet House,** built about 1821, is probably the earliest remaining building. Also known as the **Pino-Charlet House,** 721 North, it is a cottage built by Antonio Pino. The **Stewart-Dougherty House,** 741 North, dates from 1848, built by master brickmason Nelson Potts; it was occupied by Union troops later and used as a hospital. **Potts House,** 831 North, from the 1840s, has antique furnishings.

The **LSU Rural Life Museum,** on the LSU Burden Research Plantation, Essen Lane, just S of I-10, is an outdoor complex of 19th-century rural-life buildings. The buildings are arranged in typical plantation style, with furnished workers' (a euphemism understandably preferred by the university) cabins, overseer's house, blacksmith shop, sugarhouse, barn, kitchen, schoolhouse, commissary, and church.

Steele Burden and his family brought buildings and artifacts to the 5-acre site from other parts of Louisiana and elsewhere. Some of the structures once served on the Welham Plantation in St. James Parish in the early 19th century. The blacksmith shop and sugarhouse are replicas. Free, but open only by appointment. Call (504) 766-8241. Open Monday through Friday.

Magnolia Mound Plantation House, 2161 Nicholson Drive, 1790, has been extensively restored with well-selected furnishings. There are guided tours. The Overseer's House is being restored and other buildings fitting the plantation will be acquired and restored. Indigo and later sugar were grown on the plantation.

CLINTON, East Feliciana Parish, St. 19.

East Feliciana Parish Courthouse, 1839–40, in the square, was designed by J. S. Savage and is one of the state's oldest buildings still used for its original purpose. Greek Revival with a two-story Doric portico, octagonal cupola with dome.

Lawyers' Row, St. Helena, Woodville, Liberty, and Bank Sts., was erected in 1840–60; J. S. Savage was the architect for these buildings also. The Greek Revival complex has a Doric colonnade and some iron balustraded balconies. Open except Sundays. NHL.

Marston House, Bank St., 1837, was the bank and home of banker and planter Henry Marston. Greek Revival, restored. Open daily except holidays. *Silliman College,* Bank St., 1852–67, had building interrupted by the Civil War. A private school now but visitors are welcome. *Brame-Bennett House,* 227 S. Baton Rouge St., built about 1839, side wings added later, is a fine example of Greek Revival temple form.

CROWLEY, Acadia Parish, off I-10, on US 90.

Chamber of Commerce has information on the historic town which became the rice capital of America in the late 19th century. Call (318) 783-3051.

The *Blue Rose Museum,* 5 miles SW, more than a century old, is Acadian style, moved from its original site and restored. Cypress, with original pegged construction, handmade bricks, and mud-and-moss walls. Closed January, February, and holidays.

FRANKLIN, St. Mary Parish. St. 87.

The town was founded in 1808 and had the first bank in southern Louisiana, outside of New Orleans. Main Street is called the "Oak Arcade." Antebellum mansions and cottages line the tree-shaded streets. The *Franklin Tour of Homes* is usually a March event; check locally.

Oaklawn Manor, on Irish Bend of the Bayou Teche, 3 miles off US 90, is a restored Greek Colonial mansion with oaks said to have been growing when Columbus sighted America. Builder Alexander Porter was Irish, a founder of the state, later a U.S. Senator, and founder of the Whig Party in Louisiana. Cedar Walk on the grounds is a double row of cedars from Tennessee; the gardens were landscaped by a French architect. Open daily; special rates for schoolchildren or adults in groups. Write Oaklawn Manor, Irish Bend, Franklin, 70538, (318) 828-0236.

Frances Plantation, use 90E, 4 miles E of town, built about 1820, with handmade brick and cypress lumber, wooden pegs, and square nails. It is one of the oldest homes on Bayou Teche. The lower floor is of herringbone brick design. Furnished with antiques, the home is open daily except Sunday and Monday, all year. There is a gift shop.

Albania Plantation House, US 90,

just E of Jeanerette, 12 miles W of Franklin, was begun in 1837, completed 1842. The mansion features an unsupported spiral stairway. The Doll Room has a rare collection of children's treasures, Open daily; for hours call (318) 276-4816.

Grevemberg House, in City Park on Sterling Rd., 1853, has Corinthian columns and a balcony with a balustrade of wooden spindles. Open daily.

HOUMA, Terrebonne Parish, US 90, St. 311.

Southdown Plantation, 1 mile SW on St. 311. The 1858–62 Greek Revival home with Queen Anne elements was built by William J. Minor, a wealthy sugar cane producer who developed the local sugar industry.

JEFFERSON ISLAND, Iberia Parish.

Ask at *Acadian Regional Tourist Information Center,* junction of US 90 and St. 14, for information and directions. The home, *Bob Acres Plantation,* named for the famous character played by actor Joseph Jefferson III, is not open to the public at all times, but is on the National Register, and there is a museum. The home was built in 1870. Jefferson, whose ancestors were famous comedians and actors also (though none grew as famous and wealthy as Joe III, who played Rip Van Winkle for decades to rapturous audiences), chose this location in his later years, or what would be later years for most men of his day. (He had other homes as well.) The kindly and multi-talented man lived until 1905. He had made his debut at age four in 1833. The *Live Oak Gardens* are 20 acres of tropical plants with fountains, pools, woodland paths, and flowers that bloom all year, as did Jefferson himself when he became the leading comedian of his day; he also painted and was a great friend of President Grover Cleveland, who visited him here. They were fishing pals as well. The house, which is encircled by the gardens, is sometimes called Moorish neo-Gothic, with southern touches, an eclectic design, fitting a great comedian. The gardens are open daily including holidays.

LAFAYETTE, St. Landry Parish. US 90, 167.

Lafayette is in the heart of what is called Acadiana. The *Evangeline Economic and Development District & Acadiana Planning and Development District,* P.O. Box 3322, Lafayette, 70501, published a splendid illustrated map which lists scores of historic sites in the Acadiana Area (it may not still be available but it's worth a try). Antebellum buildings include the *Old Bayou Hotel,* 1300 Pinhook Rd., once the Acadian Inn, during steamboat days, built about 1820, now beautifully restored; *Acadian Ante-Bellum Home (Mouton, or Mudd, Home),* 338 N. Sterling, which has the mud-and-moss construction for the lower floor, upper floors cypress with cypress pegs, was taken over as Union headquarters by General N. P. (sometimes called Nothing Positive, by his own men) Banks, during the Civil War.

Acadian Village, 1½ miles from US 167S. off Ridge Road, S of Lafayette, is a relocated and restored bayou town. There are a village store, blacksmith shop, chapel, and dwellings typical of the early bayou country settled by the Acadians from Nova Scotia about 1755. Mud and moss were used between posts in a type of construction known as *bousillage entre poteaux.* Tropical gardens adjacent to the village have brick walkways and rustic bridges. Open year round except for major holidays.

Lafayette Parish Convention & Visitors Bureau and the Chamber of Commerce, 804 E. St. Mary Blvd., and the *Tourist Information Center,* Pinhook and University, have infor-

The Village Chapel, Acadian Village, S of Lafayette, Louisiana. (Drawing by Floyd Sonnier, Cajun artist, Lafayette, Louisiana)

mation on tours, houses open, festivals, etc.

MANY, Sabine County. US 171.

Fisher, S of Many on US 171, is a picturesque old sawmill village, once a company town, founded in 1899 and built with loving care. There were a three-story office building, a commissary with a false front, an opera house, a barbershop (which later became the post office and library), and a large dwelling for Oliver Williams Fisher. Lately the *Fisher Heritage Foundation* has acquired most of the town, including the old Kansas City Southern depot, and has made this a "sawmill town" representing the best of the lumbering times in western Louisiana.

NATCHITOCHES, Natchitoches (pronounced NAK-uh-tush) Parish, St. 167.

Natchitoches Historic District is

believed to be the oldest permanent settlement in Louisiana. "Old Town" has a variety of architectural styles. The French came in 1714; later the Spanish were here (after 1763). When the river shifted, the town lost its river trade, 1825–50.

Cherokee, SE of town on Cane River Rd., from the 1830s, is one of the typical early plantation houses, reflecting the French colonial days in the area.

Chamber of Commerce, Dept. C.T., 781 Front St., 71457, has both enthusiasm for developing the area again and information on what's to be seen now.

NEW IBERIA, Iberia Parish. US 90.

Acadiana Regional Tourist Information Center, at the junction of US 90 and 14, has information on the history-rich area. The building is an 1880 plantation cabin. *Shadows-on-the-Teche* is—deservedly—one of the best-known plantation mansions in the South. Built in the 1830s by David Weeks, a sugar magnate, it is a six-pillared brick Greek Revival dwelling, which was left to deteriorate after the Civil War, but was restored by the National Trust for Historic Preservation. Open daily except Christmas. *Loreauville Heritage Museum Village,* on St. 86 and Bayou Teche, has buildings spanning three centuries on a 1-acre site. Open daily, dawn to dusk.

NEW ORLEANS, Orleans Parish. I-59.

Visitor Information Center, 334 Royal St., opens daily and has excellent brochures for walking or driving tours of this historic city. Also every restaurant of any size, every hotel or tourist site, is well stocked with pamphlets and maps. Most of the city is worth a lingering look. Start and stop almost anywhere and start again the next day. The *Vieux Carré Historic District* is bounded by the Mississippi River, Rampart and Canal Sts., and

The New Orleans levee was busy in 1875. (From *The American West,* by Lucius
Beebe and Charles Clegg)

Esplanada Ave. The **Garden District,**
filled with Greek Revival and other
antebellum homes, is bounded by
Carondelet, Josephine, and Magazine Sts. and Louisiana Ave. NHL.

Lower Garden District, roughly
bounded by Mississippi Ave., Phillips St., St. Charles Ave., and US 90,
Annunciation St., and Race St., is an
urban 19th-century area with many
residential and commercial buildings
still keeping their 19th-century appearance.

The **Greater New Orleans Tourist
and Convention Commission,** which
runs the visitor center at 334 Rue
Royale, even tells you what to wear
and what kind of weather to expect.
Don't fail to check with them—they
also are bilingual. Keep in mind that,
as Mississippian, author, historian,
and travel writer Herb Phillips says:
"Only a Mississippi gambler would
start out for New Orleans without
room reservations—even when
there's no Mardi Gras, Sugar Bowl,

Super Bowl, or similar town-packing extravaganza going on." There are claims that **Mardi Gras,** Shrove Tuesday, the day before Ash Wednesday, which takes place annually in February and has been called the greatest free show on earth, began as early as 1699 in Iberville. By 1857, the street pageants had added the now historic Krewe of Comus. Rex, King of Carnival, first appeared in 1872. The pageantry is historical, but ever changing. For details, write the Convention Commission listed above (zip 70130).

Restorations are in progress all over the city. The **Jackson Square Mall** was a major project. The **Vieux Carré Commission** keeps a careful eye on their historic district, regulating all construction, demolition, and modification in the area. New business must conform to existing architecture.

Among the most recent restorations is that of the **Old U.S. Mint,** 420 Esplanade Ave., built in 1835–38, William Strickland, architect. It is Greek Revival, America's oldest mint on its original location. NHL. This was the first major branch of the U.S. Mint. The Louisiana State Museum is in charge of the project, which is scheduled for completion in 1980. The New Orleans Jazz Museum and the Jazz Hall of Fame will be among the new uses for the building. There will also be exhibitions on minting, shops, restaurant, and display areas.

One of the most interesting of the many house museums in the city is the Italianate town house built in 1857–60 at 1132 Royal St., which was designed by architect James Gallier, Jr., for himself and his family. Gallier, Sr., was an Irishman, also an architect, who moved to New Orleans from New York and built the **Second Municipality Hall,** now called **Gallier Hall,** 545 St. Charles. NHL. Gallier, Jr., also built the French Opera House which burned in 1919. His former home has been restored to

the 1860s period and is part of a complex with a garden courtyard. Two movies are shown to visitors; one of these shows the construction of the ornate frieze in the parlor and other plaster cornices; the other shows how the wrought ironwork on the front of the house was made. Archaeology was used to learn how to furnish the house. The earth of the courtyard was sifted by hand and articles retrieved from long-buried trash piles to discover china patterns, wine bottles, etc., once the family possessions. The supplier's ledger book for the original decorating listed 145 rolls of wallpaper and three rolls of bordering. Samples were found—and reproduced. The doghouse, woodshed, and servants' outdoor toilet have all been reconstructed.

National Historic Landmark buildings or areas in New Orleans also include: **The Cabildo,** Jackson Square, 1795, seat of the Spanish government at the turn of the 18th century, and the site of the transfer of the Louisiana Territory from France to the U.S.; **George Washington Cable House,** 1313 8th St., 1874, eclectic, home of the writer whose works were very popular in the 19th century; **James H. Dillard House,** 571 Audubon St., mid-19th-century home of an educator who resigned from Tulane University to help rural southern black schools and teachers; the **Garden District,** residential area with many styles of the 19th century; **Nicholas Girod House,** 500 Chartres St., brick stuccoed home in French Colonial style, built in 1814 for Girod, who was mayor 1812–15; **Hermann-Grima House,** 818–820 St. Louis St., built about 1831, Federal and Greek Revival; **Jackson Square (Place d'Armes),** public park laid out in 1720—statue of Andrew Jackson and flagpole mark the first raising of the American flag over Louisiana Territory; **Lafitte's Blacksmith Shop,** 941 Bourbon St., late-

18th-century home of Jean and Pierre Lafitte, privateers and smugglers; *Madam John's Legacy,* 632 Dumaine St. (1788), believed to be the oldest house in the Mississippi Valley, now owned by the Louisiana State Museum, restored in the 1970s for more than $400,000; *Old Ursuline Convent,* 1114 Chartres St. (1748–52), extensively remodeled; *The Presbytère,* 713 Chartres, built about 1791–1813, designed as rectory for St. Louis Cathedral but served as courthouse, a museum since 1911; *St. Mary's Assumption Church,* 2039 Constance St., 1858, built for a German congregation; *St. Patrick's Church,* 724 Camp St. (1837–41), Charles and James Dakin, architects, with interior designed by James Gallier, and the U.S. Mint (see above) and the Vieux Carré District, the 85-block French Quarter, laid out on gridiron plan in 1721 as one of the first planned cities in America. Most buildings postdate the 1794 fire.

OPELOUSAS, St. Landry Parish. US 190.

The village was founded as a trading post by the French in the mid-18th century. *Acadian Information Center,* US 167, also accessible from US 190, has brochures, etc., on the area and the *Bayou Ramble Tour of Homes,* usually a March happening. *Jim Bowie Museum,* 153 W. Landry St., is small, but so was the Bowie knife. Memorabilia of the soldier/inventor from Georgia, who was killed at the Alamo. *Magnolia Ridge,* N on St. 182 to Washington, just off St. 103 NW, is an 1830 plantation, open daily by appointment. *Washington,* originally called Church Landing, is a historic settlement which had its gala days in the steamboat era (1830–1900). It was once the second largest port in the state. Many fine old homes still stand and restoration has begun on many of them. *Ringrose Plantation House,* Prud-

homme Circle, off Prudhomme Lane, was built about 1770 by Michael Prudhomme and is typical of French architecture in Louisiana. The *Opelousas Pink,* a tree which blooms in February and March, is one of the largest camellia trees in the country. *Estorge House,* Market and Bloch Sts., built by Pierre Labyche in Greek Revival style in the 1830s, has many original furnishings. The reception rooms have *trompe l'oeil* ceilings. *Governor's Mansion,* Grolee and Liberty Sts., was the home of Lieutenant Governor Homere Mouton and his bride when Opelousas was the state capital during the Civil War. It is Greek Revival with Italian marble mantels, silver hardware, and fine woodwork. *Comeau House,* Liberty and Bellevue Sts., built in 1853 by Dr. James Ray, a Kentuckian, has ancient live oaks for shade. *Grand Coteau,* off US 167, is one of the old towns on the Bayou Ramble and has fine alleys of pine and oak trees and two schools where young Creole "bluebloods" were educated in the 19th century. *Academy of the Sacred Heart,* 1821, and *St. Charles College,* 1818, are both on grounds beautifully landscaped with sweet olive, camellias, azaleas, and other plantings.

ROCKY MOUNT, Bossier Parish. St. 3, 160, NE of Shreveport.

The town was known as the "birthplace of secession." At a barbecue held when news came that Lincoln was elected President, the citizens decided to vote for secession and to organize a militia. It is believed to have been the first town in the South to take this action.

A number of old buildings are being restored, including one which may be the oldest dogtrot house in Louisiana, the *Jim Hughes House.* The popular dogtrot construction meant that the rooms were divided by an open breezeway through the center. The home has many valuable pioneer relics and is open Saturday and Sunday afternoons during summer months.

ST. FRANCISVILLE, East Feliciana Parish. US 61.

Rosedown Plantation and Gardens, US 61, is an extensive restoration of a fine antebellum home and its setting. It was built in 1835 by a planter wealthy enough to go to Europe to select its furnishings. Open most days; inquire locally for hours, or ask at the many information centers in the state. There are a great many plantations which have been restored in the East and West Feliciana parishes, and elsewhere in Louisiana. *Asphodel Plantation,* S of Jackson on St. 74, is another restoration of an early-19th-century dwelling, a Greek Revival cottage. *Audubon Pilgrimages* are held annually in March; the 1978 one took in historic Oakley, Propinquity, The Oaks, Beechwood, Wildwood, Rosedown, and Afton Villa Gardens. The *Historical Society Museum,* housed in a restored Old Hardware Store, has miniature rooms among its displays and serves as pilgrimage headquarters. Many of its exhibits pertain to Audubon's life in the parish and with the West Feliciana Railroad, America's oldest standard-gauge line, it is believed. For additional information on this rich area: *West Feliciana Historical Society,* P.O. Box 338, St. Francisville, 70775; phone (504) 635-6330.

John James Audubon, naturalist and painter, probably had no idea that almost every place he visited would become a historic site. He was hired as a tutor at Oakley, where he was supposed to teach the daughters of the mansion part of the time and have the remainder of the day for roaming the woods and painting. He painted 32 of his bird series while here and was paid $60 a month and

room and board for himself and his 13-year-old assistant, John Mason. He moved on, but his wife came to teach here and he returned; in all he painted 82 subjects in *The Birds of America* in this parish. He liked the whole place: "The rich magnolias covered with fragrant blossoms, the holly, the beech, the tall yellow poplar, the hilly ground, and even the red clay, all excited my admiration. . . ."

ST. MARTINVILLE, St. Martinville Parish. St. 92.

Longfellow-Evangeline State Park, St. 31, N of town, has a 1765 house said to have been that of Louis Arceneaux, whose romance with Emmeline Labiche and subsequent marriage to another girl inspired Longfellow's poem "Evangeline"; *Acadian House* is now a museum. NHL.

St. Martin de Tours Catholic Church, 133 S. Main, 1838, has a baptismal font and other items which were gifts from Louis XVI and Marie Antoinette.

There are many interesting structures in the quiet town. The *Court House* with four Ionic columns was built in 1853 by slave labor and has records from 1760. The Post Office, built in 1876 of red cypress, has been restored by the federal government for preservation of its architecture. It was the home of Eugène Duchamp de Chastagnier originally.

SHREVEPORT, Caddo Parish. I-20.

U.S. Post Office and Courthouse, Marshall and Texas Sts., recently added to the National Register, is Italian Renaissance, built in 1912. The *Chamber of Commerce,* Crockett and McNeil Sts., has a fine illustrated brochure for several walking tours of the area. In the old days as many as 25 steamboats were docked at the levee, now Commerce St.

Lake States

Michigan
Wisconsin
Minnesota

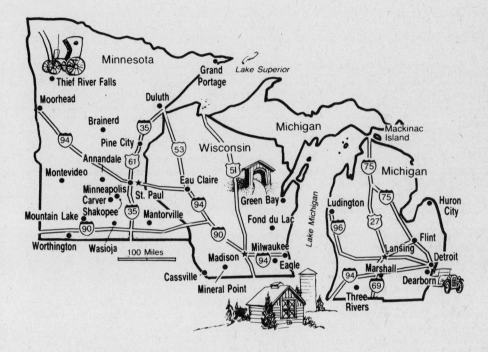

MICHIGAN

"My advice to the women of America," wrote William Allen White, "is to raise more hell and fewer dahlias!"

Michigan women have been doing both ever since Mme. Cadillac stepped onto the shore of "du troit" back in 1701. . . .

. . . a town called Stephenson in Michigan's Upper Peninsula was rocked like a cradle by four women who gave up tending dahlias for a brief time. In 1930 the lumbering town was in bad shape, rubbish stayed on Main Street, the winter snows were never plowed away and buildings were rickety. So Grace Sanders, Mary Lanthier, Lillian Paine and Dorothy Nelson decided to run for City Council. And they won. Grace was named mayor, the first woman village president in Michigan, and under her leadership the council bought some land for $50 at the outskirts of town for a municipal dump, the rubbish was cleaned off Main Street, a park was built, complete with a white fence, bandstand, and permanent Christmas tree, the old jail was torn down, the ancient dance hall was disposed of and the Music Hall was rebuilt into a community center.

—"No More Dahlias?" by Fran Harris, from *Michigan Living*, Dearborn, 1978

DEARBORN, Wayne County. I-75.

Greenfield Village and Henry Ford Museum, Michigan Ave., Village Rd., Southfield Expressway, and Oakland Blvd., is the nation's largest indoor-outdoor museum complex, on 240 acres with some 100 historic structures in the village; the museum comprises 14 acres under one roof. Henry Ford said, "When we are through, we shall have reproduced American life as lived." This is true; the complex has enlightened as well as entertained generations of visitors, and is continuing to be refreshed and expanded even as it celebrates its 50th anniversary during the summer of 1979.

The village founded by Ford in 1929 preserves early American treasures in buildings which have been moved from all parts of the country and restored to their appearance of the 17th to 19th centuries. The *Visitor Center* is in the *Gatehouse,* where guided tours begin; passengers leave from the Main St. Station of the Greenfield Village Railroad for a narrated 2-mile trip behind two old steam locomotives, the *Mason No. 1* and the *Torch Lake.*

Areas include the world of *Henry Ford and His Contemporaries;* the *Thomas Alva Edison Menlo Park Compound; Homes of Our Ancestors,* with demonstrations of their daily life from the 1640s to the late 19th century; *Suwanee Park,* with a steamboat which circles the lagoon around a wooded island on which a merry-go-round is a popular feature; the *Village Green,* with commercial buildings, church, and courthouse; the *Village Crafts Center,* with crafts-

The Edison Lab, Greenfield Village and Henry Ford Museum, Dearborn, Michigan.

men's home workshops; and *Industrial America,* with displays of the Industrial Revolution. The 8-acre *Hall of Technology* has been completely redone for the celebration of the 50th anniversary, also the 100th anniversary of Edison's invention of the incandescent light.

The *Henry Ford Museum* has exceptionally fine collections relating to America's development. Four main areas are *Henry Ford Personal History Room,* with letters, documents, photographs, and the steam engine Ford operated as a young engineer, his first engine, first automobile, and first Model T; *Fine Arts Galleries; Mechanical Arts Hall,* an 8-acre display with locomotives, steam engines, early vehicles, and farm equipment; *Street of Early American Shops,* with some 20 stores.

The museum and village are open in summer Monday through Friday, 9 to 6; winter months to 5 P.M.; weekends and holidays to 6 P.M.; closed Thanksgiving, Christmas, and New Year's Day.

FLINT, Genesee County. I-75

Historical Crossroads Village, Bray Rd., 6 miles NE of town, is a recreated community of the 1869–70 period. Restored or reconstructed buildings include the *Atlas Grist Mill,* built on the Atlas Mill Pond in the 19th century; it will be in operation again here. *Dr. Julius Barbour's Office* is a replica of a Bristol, Indiana, building used by the doctor. *Buzzell House* was built in 1854 by John Buzzell, and was set for demolition to make way for a highway improvement when the Historical Crossroads Village was organized and received it as the first building moved to the site.

Clayton Township Hall was built in 1878, at a cost of $500. *Cohoctah Church,* a Gothic Revival frame building, has been restored; it served a small community in north Livingston County. It will be used for nondenominational services and weddings. *Davison Depot* was built about 1900; it originally served the Grand Trunk and Western Railroad.

There are other houses, a township hall, a sawmill, school, bank, cider mill, carriage barn, and a village park in the neatly laid-out and well-landscaped village. There are plans to add about 25 structures in the next 12 years. Open daily Memorial Day to Labor Day, weekends, April 9 to May 28.

HURON CITY, Huron County. US 25.

Pioneer Huron City preserves the lumber era buildings of 1850–90. There are nine original buildings with authentic furnishings. Costumed guides are on duty in July and August, when the historic area is open daily. The town was built by Langdon Hubbard in the middle of the 19th century. Hubbard had a sawmill and extensive timber holdings. Forest fires destroyed the settlement in 1871 and 1881, but Hubbard rebuilt both times. Three of the buildings on Main St. are on their original foundations. Four have been moved to this site. There are among the buildings the *Langdon Hubbard General Store, Community House Inn,* and *Huron City Church,* where William Lyon Phelps used to attract an audience for his summertime sermons for 40 years. The brick museum preserves much of his summer library.

Michigan's poet laureate, Edgar A. Guest, was a golfing friend of Professor Phelps. In 1936, Guest wrote about the church that there was "none holier," because services began at 3 P.M., thus, of course, permitting him to golf before attending service.

Lucky for Guest the service didn't start at 11:30; but what golfer could be indoors on a summer morning?

The *Travel Bureau,* Michigan Department of Commerce, Lansing, 48913, phone (517) 373-0670, has information on all state areas of historic interest and hours open. A number of communities are adding to existing sites:

Holland, US 31, the long-popular Dutch Village, is planning a windmill, in addition to the 100-year-old *Working Water Mill,* and other improvements.

Grand Rapids, I-96, has a *"Gaslight Village"* in the *Grand Rapids Public Museum,* 54 Jefferson Ave. S.E.

Fayette, S of US 2, on Big Bay De Noc, began in 1867 on the southern end of the Garden Peninsula and isn't even listed on most maps but is busy with restorations. A Chippewa Indian chief found the rocks there were "bright and shiny." They were a high-grade iron ore, and the Jackson Mine company soon developed. In 1883 a fire destroyed the furnaces. Now the remains have been stabilized and other buildings are being restored, including the hotel and the Opera House. From the hotel porch you can look out over Snail Shell Harbor, which sounds worth going the distance for. Fayette is fairly near Escanaba.

LUDINGTON, Mason County. US 10, 31.

Pioneer Village, S. Lakeshore Drive, 5 miles S of town. The *Mason County Courthouse* of the 1800s has been restored on its original site. There is a broom factory, fire barn, blacksmith shop, school, post office, and two museums.

MACKINAC ISLAND, Mackinac County. Off I-75, in St. Martin Bay.

The island keeps the look and ways of the 19th century. No cars are allowed; transportation is by foot, horse, carriage, or bike.

Mackinac Island State Park Visitor Center, Huron St., has information and guidebooks with the history of the area and what's to be seen. Open from mid-June to Labor Day, daily 9 to 5.

The *Grand Hotel,* built in 1887, Mason and Rice, architects, is five stories with a full-length three-story veranda and rounded end pavilions, enlarged twice. The island had been a resort since 1840, but when John Oliver Plank, the leading resort operator, opened the Grand Hotel in the summer of 1887 "everyone" came. President Grover Cleveland sent his regrets, but Midwest society, merchants, packing and beer families came in force. The Adolph Busch family came from St. Louis, the Uihleins (also a beer baronage) from Milwaukee, the Swifts, Armours, Cudahys, Pullmans, and Marshall Fields from Chicago, and Mrs. Potter Palmer arrived with three hackney teams, saddle horses, a tallyho, carriage, and a party of friends, although Potter Palmer stayed in Chicago, perhaps to mind the Palmer House. The Whitneys, Algers, and Newberrys came from Detroit; Charles Warren Fairbanks (later Vice-President under Theodore Roosevelt), from Indianapolis, and Chauncey B. Depew, soon to become a U.S. Senator, was the toastmaster at the dedicatory dinner.

Geary House, Market St., was built about 1844 for Mathew Geary, who was active in government service.

Mission Church, Huron St., built in 1830, is the oldest church building in Michigan. It has a New England look.

Mission House, Huron St., was built in 1825 as a school, run by the Reverend William Montague Ferry for the American Board of Commissioners for Foreign Missions. It closed in 1837 and served as a hotel until the 1960s.

Stuart House, Market St., built in 1817, was the agency house of the American Fur Company, altered in 1871, restored in 1941, 1965. This was one of four structures of the original company formed by John Jacob Astor. Robert Stuart was the head of the operation. It now displays early fur-trade relics.

Benjamin Blacksmith Shop, Market St., is a replica.

MARSHALL, Calhoun County. I-69.

Honolulu House Museum, 107 N. Kalamazoo, was built in 1860 by the former U.S. consul to the then Sandwich Islands (Hawaii). It has period furnishings and is open to the public. The headquarters of the Marshall Historical Society are here, with a list of the many 19th-century buildings in town. The Society also maintains the *Capitol Hill School,* built in 1860, a Gothic Revival two-room schoolhouse, and the *Governor's Mansion,* Greek Revival, built in 1839, when there was hope that Marshall would be selected as the site of the state capital.

The annual *Historic Home Tour,* sponsored by the Historical Society, P. O. Box 15, Marshall, 49068, takes in the above buildings, six private homes, the newly restored *National House Inn,* built in 1835, and an Arts & Crafts Show. A Grand Parade is held in September.

The *American Museum* of Magic, 107 E. Michigan, is housed in a century-old building, lovingly restored by the owners and museum operators, Robert and Elaine Lund. The museum has more than 250,000 items, one of the world's largest collections of conjuring memorabilia, posters, apparatus, and books. The building has cast-iron trimmings, gingerbread cornices, arched windows, and ceilings 12 to 14 feet high.

Marshall was always a pleasant, well-kept town; now with its restorations it is a delightful place to see 19th-century America.

THREE RIVERS, St. Joseph County. St. 60.

Jones, 10 miles W off St. 60, a restored community, from the late 19th century to the early 20th century, falls about halfway between a recreation center and a real restoration. Some of the buildings are on their original site: a bank, general store, and restaurant. Other shops have been added and restored to the 1890s up to 1930s period (plenty of tourists, including me, will have a slightly hostile feeling about the 1930s being considered fair ground for historic sites). In any case, the farm buildings are restored and have unrestored domesticated animals within. Craftsmen's shops feature continuous demonstrations. Call (616) 244-5804 for further information.

WISCONSIN

As soon as they [Menominee Indians] disembarked, their first care was to go and cut long flexible poles, which they planted in the ground in a circular form. These they bent at the height of five or six feet, and fastened them together above, two by two, leaving at the top an orifice about three feet in diameter for the smoke to pass out. Then they fastened their mats all around on these poles, with bark cords, saving only one narrow passage between two poles, where one of the mats, fastened at its upper edge alone, performed the office of a door. Two forked sticks stuck in the ground held up the cross-bar which was to support the kettle. The fire was lighted, the baggage placed around within the cabin, and in less time than it takes to write this, their house was constructed, and behold, our Indians were *at home!* . . .

Once they have their poles, ten minutes is enough to complete a structure, which will sometimes lodge them all winter. Anywhere that he finds wood and water, an Indian is at home. The mats which cover these cabins, as well as form their beds, are made of rushes fastened together with cords of basswood bark. These they roll up and take with them whenever they change their domicile.

—From a manuscript on the Menominee Indians in 1838, by Gustave deNeveu; Wisconsin Historical Society, Madison, 1911

The Norwegians wisely built their houses beside some little brook or river and understood how to select a good soil. They came thither as old and accustomed agriculturists and knew how to make use of the ground. They help one another in their labor, live frugally, and ask for no pleasures. The land seems to me, on all hands, to be rich and has an idyllic beauty. Mountains there are none; only swelling hills crowned with pinewood. About seven hundred Norwegian colonists have settled in this neighbourhood, all upon small farms, and often at a great distance from one another. . . . The number of Norwegian immigrants at this time in Wisconsin is considered to be from thirty to forty thousand.

—*Homes of the New World; Impressions of America,* by Fredrika Bremer, Stockholm, 1853

CASSVILLE, Waukesha County. St. 133, 81.

Stonefield Village, in Nelson Dewey State Park, is a re-creation and restoration project of the State Historical Society and the Department of Natural Resources which includes the restored home of Nelson Dewey, Wisconsin's first governor, and the **State Farm Museum.** Horse-drawn carriages take visitors on a tour of the charming 1890 town, where a cov-

Stonefield Village, Cassville, Wisconsin. (State Historical Society of Wisconsin)

ered bridge leads to the village green. Artisans demonstrate the old skills, blacksmithing, printing, etc., and crafts are displayed. Among the sites, a livery stable, firehouse, bank, and a jewelers-clock store, which can't be missed, since L. Cornelius's giant watch shows eighteen past eight as it hangs on his shop veranda. A *Visitor's Center* has an orientation program.

The *Dewey House* is furnished in the period of the former governor's best days. In 1887, the 73-year-old man went to Madison expecting to take part in a welcome for President Grover Cleveland, but when he arrived at party headquarters, this elder statesman who had been a lifelong Democrat was not recognized and was totally ignored. He went home before anyone found out who the "old man" really was; apologies flew, but Dewey never went back to the capital. He had been elected when he was 35, and was also a success at law and business and married to the daughter of a territorial chief justice, but he died in poverty in a rented room at the Denniston Hotel in Cassville, a building he once owned.

Although most of Stonefield is replica, the buildings have been carefully researched. A farmhouse was built from plans published in 1901 by the U.S. Department of Agriculture. (In 1901 it would have cost about $1,100. In 1973 it cost $24,749.) The bee house and equipment were donated by Wisconsin Honey Producers; the building is patterned after an 1890s honey house. The Covered Bridge is a one-third-size replica of the last 19th-century one in the state and was finished according to original drawings, filed in the Library of Congress.

From the Broom Factory to Undertaking and Furniture Parlor, this is a complete town, or nearly. What's missing? Only a cemetery. Nobody dies in a made-up town, which must be why the mortician also "sells" furniture.

EAGLE, Waukesha County. St. 67.
Old World Wisconsin, St. 67, is a handsomely and carefully executed museum village on 576 acres of land in the Kettle Moraine forest. The project is owned and operated by the State Historical Society, an ambitious and persevering lot who were

organized in 1846, two years before Wisconsin became a state. They also operate six other historic sites: **Old Wade House,** a stagecoach inn at Greenbush on St. 23, midway between Sheboygan and Fond du Lac; **Villa Louis,** an 1843 frontier mansion rebuilt in 1870, on the Mississippi at Prairie du Chien; the **Circus World Museum,** 426 Water St., Baraboo; **Madeline Island,** near Bayfield, an early fur trade area; **Stonefield Village** (see above), and **Pendarvis** (see **Mineral Point**).

A **Visitors Center** is the place to begin, for the developing museum has a number of houses already in operation and many more planned or partially finished. Original buildings put up by the 19th-century immigrants and settlers of Wisconsin are being arranged and furnished to show the heritage and changing life styles of more than 50 nationalities. The completion will take about another decade. The master plan is for some 20 ethnic settings, mostly farm-

steads, and a rural village. Old World Wisconsin is open daily May through October, 9 to 5, no tickets sold after 4 P.M. Visitors can walk on well-marked trails—some 3 miles in all—to see all the attractions, or the trip in horse-drawn vehicles takes in some 7 miles. A *minimum* of three hours should be allowed per visit. Provisions for handicapped will be provided if arrangements are made in advance. This is true of most major museum villages in the U.S. and is a growing concern which builders with foresight are keeping in mind for new or restored areas.

Wisconsin hopes to make this an enduring restoration as authentic as Williamsburg, Sturbridge, Shelburne, Greenfield Village, and the other major museum villages of America. (Word of mouth is already a p.r. person's dream, and I wish I had a greenback for every time I've heard "Have you seen Old World Wisconsin?") Some 24 buildings now are open; among these are a Finnish

Turck-Schottler House, Old World Wisconsin, Eagle, Wisconsin. (State Historical Society of Wisconsin)

farmstead with farmhouse, barns, granary, horse stable, outhouse, and sauna. Costumed guides display the small but charmingly furnished interior of the farmhouse, built in Bayfield County at the turn of the century by Heikki Ketola, and decorated with the aid of someone who had seen the original. Luck has been with the hard-working teams of researchers and furnishings-hunters, in decorating a log house built in 1846, Emilie Tari, curator of artifacts, had the aid of a researcher who went through ancient court records and found an 1871 probate list which itemized the possessions of Anders Kvaale, a Norwegian immigrant, who had settled in Dunkirk Township, Dane County, and died in 1869. Kvaale's old home, a log house he built in 1846, is now part of Old World Wisconsin and its furnishings will be accurate. Ms. Tari, who had begun to select basic items for the house, had guessed accurately, as the list proved. Then with the probate information she circulated a want list for other items "and over the winter acquired furniture, implements, and artifacts to create the pleasantly cluttered pioneer house the visitor can see today." The biggest surprise was finding that Kvaale had ten chairs, which was unusual for a pioneer in 1865, since they must have been expensive even in the 19th century. The persevering curator at last count had acquired eight of them.

Eventually there will be about 100 buildings, furnished in proper period style.

FOND DU LAC, Fond du Lac County. US 41.

Historic Galloway House and Village, 336 Old Pioneer Rd. The 30-room former home of Edwin H. Galloway, which he bought from an early settler in 1868, and which was remodeled into an Italianate villa with Victorian touches in 1880, was donated to the Fond du Lac County Historical Society in 1954, by Galloway's grandson, Edwin P. Galloway.

They have taken excellent care of it and have added many artifacts. The carriage house has early vehicles. An original log cabin has been reassembled and furnished. The wooded and pleasantly arranged complex which forms a village with the look of the late 1800s has a century-old church, toy shop, print shop, general store, photographer's gallery, a pharmacy, doctor's office, one-room schoolhouse, gristmill with an overshot waterwheel, and depot with a caboose. The reception house has supplies typical of the period and features a display of candymaking equipment, from a local pioneer candymaker. The museum and village have been restored and are maintained by the Society on a nonprofit voluntary basis. It is open May 1 through September, from 1 to 4 P.M., daily except Mondays. Guides are available.

Also in town is the *Octagon House,* 276 Linden St., built about 1856. It is based on the style made popular by Orson Fowler in his *A Home for All,* which was a best seller of its sort in the 19th century.

Note: *Wade House,* a restored inn maintained by the State Historical Society, along with the *Jung Carriage Museum* and a blacksmith shop adjoining the house, will be found in *Wade House State Park,* on St. 23 between Fond du Lac and Sheboygan (6 miles W of Plymouth).

MINERAL POINT, Iowa County. US 151.

Mineral Point Historic District comprises an area within the 1837 boundaries of Mineral Point with about 40 historic sites and buildings, including stone cottages which were the homes of Cornish miners. The area was settled in 1827 after ore deposits were found. Many unemployed miners came from Cornwall,

England, and this became the leading lead-mining community in the Wisconsin Territory. It was the county seat and the site of the first U.S. land office. The first territorial governor, Henry Dodge, was inaugurated here. Some zinc mining developed, but the town declined by the middle of the 19th century.

Pendarvis Restorations are a group of Cornish miners' homes which were built in the early 19th century when this was a leading lead-mining region. The miners usually had an expert knowledge of stonecutting and masonry which they used to build limestone houses very like the ones they had left behind. More than 30 of these dwellings were built in a ravine along a street that was popularly known as Shake-Rag-Under-the-Hill. The women supposedly shook rags from the doorway to signal the men in the nearby mines that it was suppertime. Most of the houses fell into ruin and were demolished, but in 1935 Robert Neal and Edgar Hellum bought a one-story cottage which they called *Pendarvis* after a Cornish village and restored as a restaurant. They later restored a number of others and furnished them with period items and lead-mining artifacts. *Polperro,* built in 1828, a three-story stone and log house, has a fine end chimney and—unexpectedly —a birdbath. *Tamblyn's Row* is an interesting example of row housing which contains a kiddlywink or pub, another Cornish import. It is three structures, built at different times but contiguous. The State Historical Society has owned the site and maintained it since 1971. It is open from May through October, from 9 to 5 daily. For further information, Pendarvis, 114 Shake-Rag St., Mineral Point, 53565; phone (608) 987-2122.

MINNESOTA

The months or moons of the Sioux have different names from those of the Cypowais [Chippewas]: it is proper therefore to take distinct notice of both. We will first mention those of the Sioux, beginning with the first moon.

March	the moon of bad eyes
April	the moon of game
May	the moon of nests
June	the moon of strawberries
July	the moon of cherries
August	the moon of buffaloes
September	the moon of oats
October	the second moon of oats
November	the moon of the roebuck
December	the moon of the budding of the roebuck's horns
January	the moon of valour
February	the moon of wild-cats

The Cypowais months are as follow:

June	the moon of strawberries
July	the moon of blue fruits
August	the moon of yellow leaves
September	the moon of falling leaves
October	the moon of migratory game
November	the moon of snow
December	the moon of the Little Spirit
January	the moon of the Great Spirit
February	the moon of the coming of eagles
March	the moon of hardened snow
April	the moon of snow-shoes
May	the moon of flowers.

The Indians have no division of the week. They reckon the days only by sleepings.

> —From a letter written by J. C. Beltrami, from Fort St. Peter, on the Upper Mississippi, June 28, 1823

St. Paul, Minnesota, October 25, 1850. . . . The city is thronged with Indians. . . . I was extremely curious to see the inside of one of those tepees or wigwams . . . and as we chanced to see, soon after entering the Indian territory, four very respectable Indian huts, I hastened to visit them. . . . The Indians filled their pipes; the flames flickered merrily; the kettle boiled; the women, half reclining or sitting carelessly by the firelight, ate or looked at me. And I—looked at them. . . . I thought that the wigwam of an Indian was a better and a happier world than that of the drawing-room. There they sat at their ease, without stays or the anxiety to charm, without constraint or effort, those daughters of the forest. . . . Their world might be monotonous, but in comparison it was calm and fresh within the narrow wigwam, while without there was free space and the rustling forest open to them with all its fresh winds and odors. Ah!

—*America of the Fifties,* by Fredrika Bremer, New York, 1924

ANNANDALE, Wright County. St. 24, 55, NW of Minneapolis.

Minnesota Pioneer Park has a pioneer town with a town hall, furniture store, blacksmith shop, barbershop, an 1886 post office, law office, harness and buggy shop, a caboose without a train, but of 1886 vintage, a depot, an 1886 church, a smokehouse, a log cabin from 1894, a turn-of-the-century house, and even a mortuary; also a museum in a barn and a nature trail.

The nature trail is well worth a visit in the springtime, following the welcoming brochure which points out dangers as well as attractions. Dr. Freeman Weiss, former director of the American Type Culture Collection for the Department of Agriculture in Washington, now lives nearby and has furnished the field of daffodils which would have pleased the poet Wordsworth, who—if anyone has forgot—"wandered lonely as a cloud / That floats on high o'er vales and hills / When all at once I saw a crowd, / A host, of golden daffodils." About the time or not too long after these buildings were new, most schoolchildren had to memorize those lines. The great days of rhyming poetry seem to be as long gone as the harness and buggy shop. But to get on down the trail, you will pass a deer enclosure. Look to your left at an elm which to date has escaped blight. If cut down and sawed into boards, it would produce 6,000 board feet, about enough for a small two-bedroom home, and probably more than enough for a new-fangled A-frame. There are trembling aspen, basswood, ash, ironwood, and hard maple as well as elm trees along the way. The inner bark of prickly ash is like cinnamon in flavor and was used to relieve toothaches.

The hard maple trees, more than 100 years old, could each produce up to 50 quarts of sap each spring from which a quart of maple syrup could be drawn. At the junction of the trail with the old road, the guide sheet kindly warns that you will find a lot of poison ivy. "Few are susceptible to poison ivy, except if they get in the smoke while it's burning, or if the juice is rubbed directly on the skin." Also to be seen are the remnants of a beaver dam, an area of wild deer and turkey, and a dispenser for feeding corn to not-so-wild Little, one of the deer.

BRAINERD, Crow Wing County. US 210.

The town possibly was named for Ann Eliza Brainerd Smith, wife of the president of the Northern Pacific Railway, who was made a lieutenant colonel during the Civil War for "gallant and efficient service," according to an early history, but this is Paul Bunyan land and legends grow easily.

Lumbertown, U.S.A., 4 miles N on St. 371, 8 miles W on County 77, Pine Beach Rd., a commercial enterprise which re-creates the 1870 lumber days. Thirty buildings line old-time streets, with boardwalks, a cigar store Indian, and a buckboard wagon with a fake horse going no-

The Old Church, Carver-on-the-Minnesota, Minnesota.

where, but the rhubarb sauce, the walleyed pike, or chicken iron-skillet-fried are real in the family-style dining room.

CARVER, Carver County. On the river and St. 93, just S of US 212, SW of Minneapolis.

Carver-on-the-Minnesota has been restored with all buildings on their original sites. The *Old Church* (1913) serves as headquarters, with interpretive programs and guided tours. The *Temperance Hotel,* from 1856, is a two-story frame with a porch across the entire front, the oldest building in the settlement. The *Carver Cottage,* of brick and stone, was built in 1865; *Springside,* a two-story frame, in 1867. *Hilldale,* a two-story brick building with a veranda across the front, dates from 1871; another brick dwelling, *Dikeside,* from 1873. The *General Store,* with a false front, and *The Gables,* a rambling two-story frame structure with a handsome veranda, are from 1895.

The town was named for Jonathan Carver, who camped here in the winter of 1766–67 and had an up-and-down career which ended rather tragically. He was born in Weymouth, Massachusetts, in 1710, where he grew up, married, and carried on a normal life as a member of the town council and a shoemaker. When trouble arose with the Indians in 1757, Carver joined the local militia and had a number of adventures and near-escapes which gave him a taste for something more exciting than town life. He set out to explore the Upper Mississippi area in the fall of 1766. He actually traveled 200 miles into the interior by way of the Minnesota River and then continued on foot into Sioux territory. When he returned to the East he tried to sell his story to a publisher, but had no luck. He sailed to England, and his book finally appeared in London as *Travels through the Interior Parts of North America in the Years 1766, 1767, and 1768.* A ghost writer had badly rewritten Carver's own accounts of the Minnesota Territory and its Indians, but the book became a best seller. More editions were printed, but Carver was accused of plagiarism, since parts of the altered book had been copied from other authors. He died in poverty and disgrace. Some of his detractors tried to prove that he had never visited the Sioux at all. In all, about 40 editions of the bungled book were published. As for the town of Carver, its busy days as a transportation center on the river came to an end in 1875, when the railroad became more important than shipping. The village is now being restored by a nonprofit corporation, and the Carver name is back on the map, so to say.

GRAND PORTAGE NATIONAL MONUMENT, Cook County. US 61, about 38 miles NE of Grand Marais.

A 9-mile portage route which connects the Great Lakes with the network of waterways in the interior probably was discovered in 1731 by a European explorer, La Verendrye. Until the French and Indian War most voyageurs used this route, landing their large lake canoes on the shore of Lake Superior and redistributing their trading goods to be carried to the Pigeon River and by smaller canoes thereafter.

The most active period was from 1783 to 1803, when the North West Company was in business. Every summer, brigades brought their goods from Montreal and met trappers and traders here for exchange. The company held its annual meeting at the same time. The reconstructed stockaded lake post, which was built under the direction of the Bureau of Indian Affairs, Department of the Interior, contains a *Great Hall,* a *Gatehouse,* a *Fur Press,* a *Canoe Warehouse,* and other buildings. The portage route runs through the Chippewa Reservation. Before the monument was established in 1960, conferences were held with the Minnesota Chippewa Tribal Council and the Grand Portage Band of the Chippewa Tribe. Additional restoration work is being carried on. National Park personnel are on hand in summer months.

MANTORVILLE, Dodge County. St. 57.

Mantorville Historic District covers the entire town. The *Hubbell House* on Main St. was built in 1857 and once served as a stagecoach stop. There are framed land grants signed by Lincoln on the restaurant wall. The post office was a saloon in 1896. The *Dodge County Courthouse,* the oldest working courthouse in Minnesota, was completed in 1871. The *Edmond Beatty House,* on Main St., was built in 1867. Beatty was owner of a furniture store which is now tour information center (Suzy's Shoppe and Gallery) on Main St., a building

which housed a lodge and a district court before it became a furniture store. *Restoration House,* on the E side of Main, was built in 1856 and used as the county office building; restored by the Mantorville Restoration Association, (507) 635-5132.

The *Opera House* seems to be the newest building in town. It was erected in 1918, and now is air-conditioned for summer theater patrons.

Among other old dwellings are the *Teunis Slingerland House* and the *Cordenio Severance Home,* which also has a carriage house. The Slingerland who built the house on 5th and Clay Sts. in the 1890s was the son of "the wealthiest man in Dodge County," who owned about 10,000 acres in 1884. Slingerland gave a park to the city. It is about a half block W of the house and has a stone-arch entrance. E. C. Severance, whose house is on 4th St., was a state senator. His son Cordenio became an attorney and president of the American Bar Association. The *L. M. Blanch House,* on 5th St., is just W of a landmark, the *Cottonwood Tree,* the largest tree in the county because three trunks were chained together years ago. Arnold Blanch, who grew up here, founded a New York art school with Adolph Dehn and Grant Wood. Several other houses are being restored.

The *First Congregational Church,* on Walnut St., missed being the Methodist Church by a twist of fate. The foundation was laid by Methodists in 1858, then work stopped because of hard times. The Methodists set to work again in 1860, but the Congregationalists finished the building and have owned it since 1875.

St. Margaret's Catholic Church, Sixth and Clay, was built as a church in 1862 but also used as a residence, hotel, and newspaper office before its dedication in 1910.

St. John's Episcopal Church, on Main near 6th, built in 1869, now is the *Dodge County Historical Society*

Museum. Also called *Hilltop Church.*

More than 200 gaslights were installed in 1965 as part of the restoration project. A one-room schoolhouse has been restored on the grounds of the Historical Society. An interesting and fairly unusual (if not indeed unique) example of adapting old structures to modern purposes has been making six craftshops out of the old coalbins behind the Hubbell House. The Zumbro River behind the dam has been dredged so that canoeists and paddle-boaters can enjoy the waters around Goat Island.

MONTEVIDEO, Chippewa County. US 59.

Chippewa City Pioneer Village, at the junction of US 59 and St. 7, was built and has been maintained by the *Chippewa County Historical Society.* The town, laid out around a square, began with a rural school building, donated by a district organized in 1869. The present building dates from 1911, when it replaced the original, which was destroyed by a tornado. It is furnished in old-time style. The church, built in 1882 by Norwegian Lutherans, has original pews and organ. Another rural school was remodeled to serve as the Chippewa Bank. Among other structures are a log cabin, corncrib, farmhouse, blacksmith shop, rooming house, barbershop, harness shop, general store, millinery and dress shop, fuel and ice company, trading post and fur company, log barn, fire hall, law office, and print shop. Most buildings and furnishings have been donated and a number have been remodeled to fit the village plan. The harness shop was once a granary. The general store was a school building which was later intended for a café to open for business when the railroad came. The railroad went elsewhere.

This pleasant village reflects the interest of the townspeople and the ingenuity of the Historical Society members who have restored the area.

Fittingly, it won a state tourism award in 1972.

MOUNTAIN LAKE, Cottonwood County. St. 30, 60.

Heritage House Village, on a 22-acre tract, depicts the Mennonite way of life in the 19th century. Many Mennonites came to the area from southern Russia, where they had fled from Holland, Germany, and Austria because of their objections to military service. When Russia also made service mandatory, they came to Minnesota. The chapel was once a hired man's house; it has been remodeled and furnished. Services are sometimes held. The first building in the village was the old depot, which was bought from the Burlington Northern for $1. There is a farmhouse with the barn adjoining, moved from the countryside nearby where they were built about 1884. The original family came from Pordenau, Russia, and have contributed to the furnishings of the farmhouse. The general store was moved from Darfur, 14 miles away, and is suitably furnished. There are also a schoolhouse, machine shed, and barbershop. The current interest in heritage is so great that nearly 2,000 visitors showed up on opening day in this not-yet-finished and fairly remote restoration. At Windom, which is not far west of Mountain Lake, is a reconstructed *Hidatsa Indian Village.*

PINE CITY, Pine County. I-35.

Connor's North West Company Fur Post, off I-35 at Pine City exit, on County 7. Traders representing the British North West Company landed on the banks of the Snake River and set up a post for the winter of 1804–5 for trading with the Chippewa Indians of the area. The post has been authentically reconstructed and stocked with the furnishings and trading goods which might have been found here in the early 19th century. Guides dressed as voyageurs demonstrate the day-by-day activities of a frontier post. The post was reconstructed and is maintained by the Minnesota Historical Society, an organization that was formed before Minnesota became a state.

SHAKOPEE, Scott County. US 169.
Murphy's Landing, just S of town, is a Minnesota Valley Restoration Project. A living outdoor museum, still being expanded, the restoration reflects the period of 1840–90. There are an 1850 farm, an 1880 farm, an 1890s river village, an Indian area, and nature areas. There will be some 40 buildings when the project is completed.

THIEF RIVER FALLS, Pennington County. US 59.
Pennington Pioneer Village, on St. 32, S edge of town, was dedicated in 1976; it has a church, school, depot, blacksmith shop, barbershop, general store and post office, two log cabin homes with period furnishings, and a museum. This is a continuing project of the Pennington County Historical Society.

WASIOJA, Dodge County. 1 mile N of Mantorville on St. 57, then 3 miles W on County 16.
There are about 75 residents now, though once the village was thriving, with a fine seminary and much optimism. But the location of the county seat went to Mantorville, and the railroad by-passed the town, too. The ruins of the Seminary, which burned in 1905, still stand. There is a school, a church, a Civil War recruiting station in an 1855 bank, and an 1860 house which has been restored. The Doig family were master stonecutters from Scotland. Thomas Doig had worked on the statue of Lord Nelson which still stands in Trafalgar Square, London. The Doigs built this house and the Seminary and school, all in 1860. The town is listed on the National Register.

WORTHINGTON, Nobles County. I-90 exit at St. 60.
Pioneer Village, S of I-90 and W of fairgrounds, was planned to re-create a settlement and its environs of the 19th century. Among the more than 30 structures are a schoolhouse, depot, jail, doctor's office, prairie house, barbershop, church, general store, cream station, lawyer's office, harness and shoe repair store, farmhouse and outbuildings, and even a doghouse. The village was built and is maintained by the Nobles County Historical Society.
In Worthington, the *LaPachek House,* 320 Thirteenth St., built in the 1870s, an imposing structure with an exceptionally intriguing wrought-iron fence, has been given to the Historical Society and may open to the public in the near future. An excellent museum operated by the society is at 4th Ave. and 12th St.

Plains States

Iowa
Nebraska
Missouri
Kansas
Arkansas

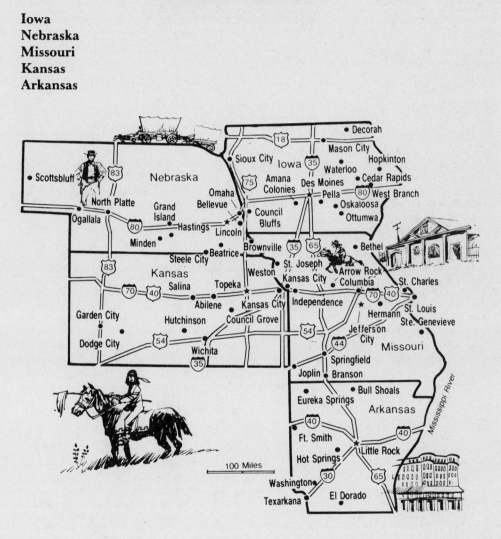

IOWA

The town of Du Buque is handsomly situated on the West bank of the Mississippi river. . . . There are already surveyed, thirty-five blocks, which are sub-divided into two hundred and eighty town lots, all of which are occupied by houses and gardens. The village contains about one thousand inhabitants, and two hundred and fifty buildings of different descriptions; among which are fifteen dry good stores, and one methodist meeting house. A large Catholic church is now building, and preparation is making for building a Presbyterian church.
— *Du Buque Visitor,* Du Buque Lead Mines, Wisconsin Territory, 1836

An assortment of Franklin, Ten plate, Seven plate, Box and Parlor Stoves. All of the above Stoves were cast . . . from *pig* metal, and are not only better constructed than *all* other Stoves in the western market, but admit of a finer polish, being smoother and of superior finish.
The subscriber assures the public there is no humbuggery about his Stoves, being neither Yankee Notions, or any other kind of *notions,* but simply *Resor's Improved Stoves,* the best and cheapest in market. . . .
P.S. Just received a fresh supply of Resor's Cooking, Parlor, Franklin, Box and Ten Plate stoves, which will be sold very low for cash, wheat or pork.
WANTED at the Hawk-Eye Office, Fire Wood, Pork, Potatoes, Corn, Oats and other country produce, in payment of Subscription.
LOOK HERE!!—I am now in want of Pork or cash, all those who know themselves to be indebted to me either by note or book account, will oblige me by paying what they owe me in cash or pork, one or the other I must have. J. S. David.
— *Hawk Eye,* Burlington, Iowa, December 7, 1843

AMANA COLONIES, Iowa County. US 6, St. 149
The area, composed of villages founded by a religious society in 1855, is a National Historic Landmark. The two-story brick, stone, and frame buildings are large, plain, and meant to serve communal gatherings and life style. The Amana Society was one of the most successful of several Utopian communities in early America and was reorganized as a joint stock company in 1932.

Visitors must leave the Little Amana "sample" structures near I-80 and go to the real villages, N of I-80. The village of Amana was settled in 1855 by emigrants from Germany who first settled in New York, then moved on to Iowa. Between 1855 and 1862, five more villages—East, West, High, Upper South, and Lower South Amana—were established. The town of Homestead was acquired so that the colony could have access to a railroad. The colony was

252

incorporated in 1859 as the Amana Society.

"Amana" came from the biblical Song of Solomon 4:8: "Come with me from Lebanon, my spouse, with me from Lebanon: look from the top of Amana. . . ." The community bought 25,000 acres from the government and added another 1,000, which they farmed, with each member of the group—of German, Swiss, and Alsatian ancestry—handing down his skills. Farms, woolen mills, meat smoking plants, a furniture factory, wineries, and community kitchens were established and still function, although the "Great Change" of 1932 separated church and state and the members of the community, no longer being directed solely by the elders of the church, adopted a system of free enterprise.

All villages can be toured by bus or by car; group tours available year round by appointment: P.O. Box 121, Amana, 52203; phone (319) 622-3269. Information is also available at the Amana Holiday Inn and the Colony House Motel on I-80, where buses leave at 8 A.M. and 12:30 P.M., or from the Old Homestead Inn and the Die Heimat Motor Hotel in Homestead, at 8:15 A.M. and 12:45 P.M., or the Colony Inn Restaurant in Amana, 8:30 A.M. and 1:00 P.M.

West Amana, off St. 220, has a store, post office, the Schanz Furniture Refinishing Store, and Ye Olde Broom and Basket Shop.

South Amana, US 6 and St. 220, has a general store, winery, post office, marketplace, and horse barn museum, which not only has old-time tools but features Henry Moore's *Amana and Americana in Miniature.* Moore (not the English artist) is a talented retired farmer and a perfectionist whose miniatures are among the most delightful anywhere in America. He built his first barn in 1968, scaled 1 inch to the foot, and now has included even Lin-

coln's New Salem in the historically accurate displays.

Upper South Amana, St. 220, S of US 6, features the Amana Society Bakery.

High Amana, about 1 mile E of West Amana and just N of St. 220, has an old-fashioned general store and gift shop with many Amana products for display and sale. The interior has remained the same for more than a century.

Middle Amana, St. 220, has the Kraus–Old Style Colony Winery, Hahn's Hearth Oven Bakery, a Community Kitchen, Cooper Shop, Hearth Oven Museum, a print shop, a general store, and other gift shops.

Amana, at the junction of St. 220 and 149, is the central part of the community, with the main office, bank, shops, wineries, inns, sawmill, woolen mill, an airport, and a fine museum of Amana history, where excellent pamphlets and illustrated booklets on Amana's past can be purchased.

The *Museum of Amana History Complex,* in a pleasantly roomy corner of town with grape arbors and gardens, is a good place to begin a visit. The *Noe House,* built in 1864 for a doctor's home and office, is now a museum. *Amana Village Schoolhouse,* used 1870–1955, has old school furnishings. The *Washhouse* and the *Woodshed* were outbuildings for the Noes; they now display early tools and laundry equipment.

East Amana, off St. 220, has no commercial establishments.

Homestead, US 6, has shops, winery, restaurants, inns, and the *Amana Helm Museum* in a house more than a century old.

DECORAH, Winneshiek County. US 52.

Vesterheim, Norwegian-American Museum, W. Water St., is housed in three historic buildings with a large collection of Norwegian arts and crafts, illustrating the history of Norwegians in frontier Iowa. Woodcarving, rosemaling (a decorative art from the 18th century), and other skills are demonstrated. The *Arlington House* is a restored three-story brick, with carved balconies and ornate window arches.

Painter-Bernatz Mill, 200 N. Mill, built in 1851–53, has been restored as a museum. It is the oldest building in town. In 1875 it was converted from stone to roller milling machinery. Until the 1960s it shipped flour to other states. An 1851 building houses industrial exhibits and a restored smithy.

Broadway-Phelps Park Historic District, W. Broadway from Winnebago St. to Park Drive, Upper Broadway, Park St., and Phelps Park, takes in a variety of 19th-century structures. The *Ellsworth-Porter House,* at 401 W. Broadway, and the *Norris Miller House,* 118 N. Mill St., are on the National Register.

HOPKINTON, Delaware County. St. 38, S of US 20.

Delaware County Historical Museum Complex, on and near the former Lenox College campus, St. 38. *Clarke Hall,* formerly part of the college, built in 1890 and used as a girls' dormitory for more than 50 years, is now a museum, with exhibits ranging from college materials and early medical items to a Civil War display and children's toys and furnishings. The *Reformed Presbyterian Church,* dedicated in 1901, now administered by the Historical Society, has a fine arts exhibit as well as natural history and religious exhibits. The *Hopkinton Depot* has been renovated and furnished with wooden tools, a stationmaster's office, and other railroad items. A one-room school has been moved to the museum grounds and furnished. One building displays early farm machinery.

Old Lenox College, a 4-acre campus, on the National Register, has four main brick buildings around

a square with a Civil War monument. The college began as Bowen Collegiate Institute in 1859.

OSKALOOSA, Mahaska County. US 63.

Nelson Pioneer Farm and Craft Museum, Glendale Rd., NE of Penn College campus, has a house, barn, schoolhouse, log cabin, and is still growing. Period furnishings. The farmhouse was built in 1853, the barn in 1856, the school in 1861, the log cabin in 1867; a country store from the late 1880s has been added recently.

PELLA, Marion County. St. 163.

Historical Village and Wyatt Earp Boyhood Home, 507 Franklin, includes 11 buildings which have been restored or refurbished and furnished with period items. There are a pottery and a blacksmith shop, a pioneer log cabin, a Dutch museum with a gristmill in the garden. The town square reflects the Dutch influence but has the look of a half-struck stage set—with old and new, or not-so-new but out-of-style buildings and restored fronts giving it an unusual ap-

West Branch Heritage Museum, West Branch, Iowa. (Drawing by Bill Wagner)

pearance for middle Iowa. Wyatt Earp's boyhood home, for that matter, seems an odd item for mid-Iowa. But it's genuine.

An annual Tulip Festival is a lively scene in May, when citizens dress in Dutch costumes and wooden shoes and scrub the streets.

WEST BRANCH, Cedar County. I-80 E exit 63.

Herbert Hoover National Historic Site is a park containing the Hoover birthplace, a two-room cottage, which has been restored; a replica of his father's blacksmith shop with proper furnishings and tools; the Quaker Meetinghouse, restored, which the future President attended as a boy, and the graves of the Hoovers. The presidential library is in a modern building administered by the National Archives and Records Service. A museum has a film and Hoover memorabilia.

An information center is located just N of a parking lot, on Parkside Drive and Main St.

West Branch Heritage Museum, 109 W. Main St., is free to the public and is maintained by the West Branch Heritage Foundation, which was formed to observe Herbert Hoover's birthday and to preserve local items of pioneer times when many Quakers came to Iowa from Pennsylvania and Ohio. The building was erected in 1884; one room has been furnished as a pioneer dwelling with fireplace, rope bed, and kitchen and dining equipment.

NEBRASKA

...I found the little capital of Nebraska the liveliest city in the United States. The railway company had erected an immense brick car-house, engine-house, and machine shops; and five or six hundred buildings had gone up during the summer. One brick block cost a hundred thousand dollars. Streets were being graded, sidewalks thronged with returned gold-seekers, discharged soldiers, farmers selling produce, speculators, Indians, and other strange characters of border life. The population was eight thousand. Single grocery houses were doing a business of half a million dollars per year; and the pioneer merchants and bankers had accumulated fortunes. The railroad disbursed a quarter of a million dollars per month. Business lots commanded from two to five thousand dollars.
—*Beyond the Mississippi,* by Albert D. Richardson, Hartford, Conn., 1867

BEATRICE, Gage County. St. 4.

Homestead National Monument, 4½ miles NW off St. 4. Daniel Freeman, a farmer from Illinois, filed the first claim when he was on furlough from the Civil War, making this one of the first areas settled under the Homestead Act of 1862, in which a quarter section of Nebraska land went to anyone willing to live on it and farm it for five years. Freeman's Homestead Entry No. 1, entered at the Brownville Land Office early on January 1, 1863, when the Act went into effect, gave him a T-shaped piece of land. The Freemans are buried near the eastern edge of the monument. A restored cabin here is typical of the thousands of sodbuster homes which were scattered on the wide prairie. This cabin was moved from a nearby township and appropriately furnished. There is a self-guiding trail, 1 mile long, beginning at the Visitor Center. The 162-acre site includes the original Freeman cabin, later buildings, and the Freeman graves.

BELLEVUE, Sarpy County. US 73.

Sarpy County Historical Society, 1895 Hancock, has information on the historic old city. The *Old Settlers' Home* is a log cabin believed to have been put up about 1835; it has been moved here from its original site and furnished with pioneer items.

Hamilton House, 2003 Bluff St., was built about 1856, of limestone covered with stucco, two stories, with gabled roof. The Reverend William Hamilton came to Nebraska to direct the Presbyterian Indian Mission at Bellevue.

Bellevue Cemetery, established in 1856, on a hill at the N edge of town, has the grave of Ongpatonga (Big Elk) and 12 of his braves. He was the last full-blooded Omaha chief. The Indians were reburied by the Sarpy County Historical Society in 1954 with a military and Indian funeral.

256

They had first been interred on Elk Hill but were moved when Bellevue College was built in 1883. Indians protested the desecration of their burials, and the bodies were removed to a location near the college entrance. When the college was demolished in 1946, debris covered the graves. They are now in a protected place.

In 1834 a Presbyterian mission was set up at Bellevue, the oldest existing town in Nebraska, a stop on the Lewis and Clark expedition of 1804, and a trading post for the American Fur Company in 1810. The *Presbyterian Church,* 2002 Franklin Ave., was begun in 1856, completed in 1858, with later additions.

Fontanelle Bank, 2212 Main St., was built in 1856. Two-story brick with Italianate elements, it is one of the oldest commercial structures in the state and has served as county courthouse and city hall in times past.

Burlington Depot (Omaha & Southern Railroad Station), Haworth Park, was built about 1869, to serve a railroad built in 1869–70, from Omaha. It is thought to be the oldest depot in the state.

BROWNVILLE, Nemaha County. US 136.

Brownville Historic District includes churches, business structures, and private dwellings from the mid- to late-19th-century. The town, founded as a steamboat stop and freight terminus in the 1850s, rapidly prospered. As elsewhere, railroads eventually took the main line of trade away, river traffic fell off, and Brownville was by-passed.

The *Brownville Historical Society*—(402) 825-6001—has a brochure listing 41 points of historic interest and a marked map for self-guiding. On the walkaround are the *First Telegraph Office West of the Missouri River,* the *Lone Tree Saloon,*

a land office, a *Masonic Building,* and *Carson House,* Main and 3rd Sts., furnished in the 1880s period, originally a one-story brick from 1860 built by Richard Brown, town founder, bought by John L. Carson in 1864, now maintained by the historical society. There is a wheel museum in the same block.

Bailey House, on Main, W of 4th St., was built in 1877 for Benson M. Bailey, a riverboat captain. Now a museum. The *Village Theatre,* on College St. between 2nd and 3rd, may be one of the most unusual you'll find anywhere. It was once the Christian Church and still looks to be. The society owns it; repertory theater is produced by the Nebraska Wesleyan University drama department for eight weeks each summer beginning in July.

Tipton House, S of College on 4th St., built in the late 1860s as a wedding present for the daughter of U.S. Senator T. W. Tipton, is two-story brick, Italianate in style.

Gates House, College and 4th Sts., built in 1859 by Abbott G. Gates, a contractor and mason, may be the oldest brick house in the state. On 4th is the *Pollack House,* built in 1871 by Cyrus Pollack, a grocer. On 4th and Main St. is the *Worthington-Baker House,* a brick residence built about 1863.

Methodist Church, on College, E of 6th, has been in continuous use since 1859, when it was Congregational; it also was used as a medical college for a time.

The *Furnas House,* College and 6th, was built in 1869 for Governor R. W. Furnas, editor, publisher, Civil War veteran, and founder of *The Nebraska Farmer* and other publications.

Muir House, 2nd St., N of Main, a fine example of Italianate, two-story brick, built 1868–72 for Robert V. Muir, is furnished in Victorian style. Another handsome two-story brick residence, the **Minick House,** one block N of Main, between 5th and 6th, was built during the Civil War for George M. Bratton, bought by the Minicks in 1878. Alice Minick was the first woman graduate of the University of Nebraska College of Law. Directly N, facing another street, is the **Hoover House,** a two-story brick, built in the 1870s. The **Christian Church,** due S of the Minick House on Main St., was established in January 1855.

Preservationists and the restoration-minded can take cheer seeing today's Brownville with its well-kept Victorian dwellings. In 1883 J. Sterling Morton, a Nebraska editor as well as politician and the founder of Arbor Day, commented:

"Brownville property was undesirable. No one demanded it. Its value declined with great velocity. The county seat was removed, mercantile houses and banks deserted the town site, until some of the best buildings on the main street were roosting places for bats and owls.

"Grass grew in the streets that had been resonant with the rumble of farm wagons and brisk with the traffic of a rich and prosperous county."

Traffic is relatively busy again, in the streets, and on the river, via the excursion boat, the **Belle of Brownville.**

GRAND ISLAND, Hall County. I-80.

Stuhr Museum of the Prairie Pioneer, 3½ miles N of I-80, Grand Island exit, at the junction of US 34, 281. The main building, designed by Edward Durrell Stone, is on an island reached by a causeway in an 800-foot man-made lake. There are an art gallery and a fine museum with exhibits relating to pioneer times in Nebraska. The Hall County Historical Society was a nonprofit corporation with a long history but a small membership when it initiated and made the first museum collec-

tions. When the present museum board was formed, the Hall County Society turned over its items. Leo B. Stuhr, first president of the museum board, died soon after it was organized but left the bulk of his estate to the museum (around $700,000). Stuhr was the son of pioneer parents; the first museum site was his boyhood home, moved here when more land was needed.

Railroad Town of the Prairie Pioneer, SE of the main building, has 56 original buildings moved to this site, which are typical of Nebraska dwellings and commercial structures along the railroad line of the 19th century. The downtown section has a bank, general store, post office, hotel, barbershop, blacksmith shop, shoe shop, newspaper office, and depot. There are also a school, church, and private homes, including the one in which actor Henry Fonda was born. The depot serves the Nebraska Midland Railroad, an authentic steam train with an 1897 coach and a 1908 Baldwin locomotive. In summer months visitors can ride across 200 acres of prairie. The complex covers some 270 acres, some seeded with Nebraska grasses to create a true prairie background for the outdoor living-history exhibition. There is a farm machinery and antique car exhibit on the museum grounds. The main building is open all year. Outdoor section in season only. Train rides are usually from Memorial Day through Labor Day.

MINDEN, Kearney County. US 6, 34, St. 10, 12 miles S of I-80.

Harold Warp Pioneer Village, on highway, covers three blocks, but a less than a mile walk takes you past everything in "town." The one-room school used by Harold Warp as a child was the nucleus for this longtime re-created village which now covers 20 acres with more than 30,-000 items in 23 buildings. Past the main building with its 10,000 display items are *Elm Creek Fort,* Webster County's first fortification, moved here and furnished, a general store in replica, a land office which is original, a firehouse museum, a depot from Kearney County, a 19th-century school with original furnishings, a sod house in replica, an 1884 church with some original furnishings, Pony Express trappings, a livery stable, farm buildings, and homes and shops. (Years ago when I asked Harold Warp if he had any Civil War items on display, he politely explained that he never displays anything that kills people, at least on purpose.)

OGALLALA, Keith County. US 26.

Front Street, a re-creation of old Nebraska in cow trail days, has a Trails museum, a general store, a Crystal Palace, and other re-created Wild Westery. The *"Hotel"* has a Cowboy's Rest Saloon. There are stagecoach rides to Boot Hill. The *"Mansion on the Hill,"* the oldest brick house in the area, built in 1887, houses the *Keith County Historical Society Museum.*

STEELE CITY, Jefferson County. State 8.

Steele City Historic District includes the livery and blacksmith shop, brick bank building, a small stone church, and an Italianate house, all of the late 19th century. The village was once a trading center on the railroad line. Note: For Old West fans, *Rock Creek Station,* where Wild Bill Hickok shot David McCanles and thus began an endless series of dime novel stories and Old West arguments, is not far away, a few miles to the NW, about 2 miles due E of Quivera Park, SE of Fairbury. (The spelling of McCanles is the subject of one of the endless arguments.)

MISSOURI

St. Louis, on the Mississippi, is the great town of Missouri, and is considered by Missourians to be the star of the West. . . . The town is well built, with good shops, straight streets, never-ending rows of excellent houses, and every sign of commercial wealth and domestic comfort. . . . The new hotel here was to be bigger than all the hotels of all other towns. It is built, and is an enormous pile, and would be handsome but for a terribly ambitious Grecian doorway.

—*North America*, by Anthony Trollope, London, 1862

Crystal City is a stirring village of Jefferson County, Missouri, situated on a small tributary of the Mississippi, about a mile from their junction. It has a population of nearly five hundred, and is engaged chiefly in the manufacture of plate glass. We were much impressed with the enterprise of this place, and trust that as the tide of prosperity rolls on it will feel justified in erecting a commodious hotel, thus sparing future visitors the annoyance to which we were subjected of canvassing the entire village for a night's lodging, which resulted in securing a bed in a room already tenanted by two men and three dogs.

—*Down the Great River*, by Captain Willard Glazier, Philadelphia, 1887

ARROW ROCK, Saline County. St. 14, 13 miles N of I-70.

At this historic town the Santa Fe Trail crossed the Missouri River. *Arrow Rock State Park* preserves the trail and other historical sites. At its busiest, the frontier settlement had about 1,000 inhabitants, and many of them were characters. Lewis and Clark came in June 1804, on their great expedition. On the way back from a later trip William Clark said it was a handsome place for a town. NHL.

Arrow Rock, platted by M. M. Marmaduke in 1829, was first called New Philadelphia. Among early citizens were three who served as governor, though none completed a full term in office: Meredith M. Marmaduke, 1844; Claiborne F. Jackson, in the perilous days of 1860–61; and John S. Marmaduke, 1884–87. Dr. John Sappington, whose office has been restored by the Friends of Arrow Rock, is buried in the family cemetery, 3 miles SW of town on County Road TT, where the *William Sappington House,* built in 1843–45, has been restored. Dr. John had three daughters who became, in turn, the wives of Claiborne Fox Jackson. According to legend, when Jackson asked for the hand of the third daughter, Sappington said, "You can take her but don't come back after the old woman." William Sappington, Dr. John's son, was the physician

The Old Tavern, Arrow Rock, Missouri.
(Courtesy Missouri Division of Tourism)

who discovered the value of quinine in the treatment of malaria.

A walking tour takes in the **Old Tavern,** on Main St., begun in 1834, by Judge Joseph Huston. It is believed to be the county's oldest structure and was the main inn at the start of the Santa Fe Trail.

Old Seminary Building, built in the 1830s, was a dormitory for female students of an early school. It is to be restored. The one-room *Jail* was built in 1871. Legend says that the only prisoner yelled so much he was released. **Dr. Matthew W. Hall House,** built in 1846, has been restored by the state, and furnished by the DAR. The *George Caleb Bingham House,* 1st and High Sts., in the State Park, was built in 1837. NHL.

BETHEL, Shelby County. St. 15.

Bethel Historic District comprises some 50 buildings. Eighteen of these are related to the 19th-century religious communal society founded by Dr. William Keil. (Also see Aurora, Oregon.) **Bethel Colony "Big House,"** on King St., built about 1840, was the home of pioneer settler Samuel Vandiver. It is two-story brick with large fireplaces, walnut woodwork, and a hand-carved rock step at entrance. William Keil lived here in 1844. The building was later adapted

for use as the colony boardinghouse and store. Sons of John C. Bauer (Bower) ran the store; the house is known locally as the Bower house. Restored in 1946, as a residence.

Keil Home (Elim), 1¼ miles E of town on unmarked road, built in the 1840s, was the home of the colony founder, Dr. William Keil; erected by workers from the colony.

BRANSON, Taney County. US 65, St. 76.

Silver Dollar City, 9 miles W on St. 76, is a replica of a pioneer mining village, with a general store, blacksmith shop, newspaper office, stagecoach rides, craft demonstrations, and the 1880-styled Frisco–Silver Dollar steam train. Services are held regularly in the **Wilderness Church,** built by settlers in the 19th century. Its pulpit was carved from a 608-pound piece of oak. In late April and early in May are "Root Digging Days," when the local Ozark householders comb the countryside for medicinal roots and herbs. There are typical Ozark festivities, including square dancing and rolling-pin throwing, and burgoo stew and sassafras tea are served. Unless the price has gone up recently, it's "all you can drink, for 46 cents."

At the **McHaffie Homestead** there is a quilting bee, and many more crafts may be found elsewhere in town in the fall when the annual National Festival of Craftsmen is held. For details write to the **Ozarks Chamber of Commerce,** Dept. C.T., Silver Dollar City, 65616.

FLORISSANT, St. Louis County. See St. Louis, page 267.

HERMANN, Gasconade County. St. 94, W of St. Louis near the Mississippi River.

Hermann Historic District covers about 13 blocks of the 19th-century town, founded by the German Settlement Society of Philadelphia, with many commercial and residential structures in various styles. The *City Hall* is Italianate. The *Dodge House,* Second Empire.

Old Stone Hill Historic District, bounded roughly by W. 12th, Goethe, and Jefferson Sts. and Iron Rd., comprises a wine-producing complex. The *Stone Hill Wine Company* was established in 1847 by Michael Poeschel and became the third-largest in the world until prohibition shut it down. The buildings date from 1869 to 1920. Now back in business with tours and free samples of wine for visitors over 21, grape juice for those younger.

Bottermuller House, 205 E. 8th, at Schiller St., built in 1852, has period furnishings and a stone wine cellar. Open to the public.

Klenk House, 301 Gellert St., built in the mid-1840s, restored and furnished in period. Open daily except Wednesdays, April to November.

Walking tours start in April and continue through the warm months; house tours also begin in April and are sponsored by the *Chamber of Commerce, Historic Hermann, Inc.,* and the *Brush & Palette Club, Inc.*

INDEPENDENCE, Jackson County. I-70, US 24.

Chamber of Commerce, 213 S. Main—(816) 252-4745—and the *City of Independence Department of Tourism,* P.O. Box 1827, Independence, 64050—(816) 836-2150—have literature and maps for self-guiding tours. This was not only the outpost of civilization for the wagon trains of the early pioneering days, but the scene of a number of Civil War conflicts. It is also the last home of the late Harry S Truman, 33rd President of the United States.

Harry S Truman Historic District, on N. Delaware St., is primarily residential and is marked with medallions. The Victorian house and the modern library are within the district. The library is on US 24 and Delaware. The home, at 219 N. Delaware, is not open to the public.

The Reorganized Church of the Latter Day Saints has headquarters in Independence. The Saints and some well-known sinners, the James boys, and Quantrill, have all been part of the town's past.

A *Heritage Trail Tour* begins at the Truman Library and Museum; at Delaware and Waldo, it passes the *Jennings House,* built in 1885 by Aaron F. Sawyer, a banker, with fish-scale shingles, seven working fireplaces, and Tiffany glass transoms. It was designed by Stanford White. An early Truman home, at 909 Waldo, not open, was the family dwelling when Harry Truman was still in school. The *"Summer White House"* (1945–52) and family home, 219 N. Delaware, was built in the 1860s by Mrs. Truman's grandfather; it is near the *First United Presbyterian Church,* on Lexington and Pleasant, built in 1888, which remained open during the Civil War, as others did not. *Overfelt-Johnson House,* on the E side of Pleasant, at Walnut St., dates from 1850, and was built by John Overfelt, a miller, in what is called Missouri River Gothic style. This was one of the roads out of town to Santa Fe. The *Churches of Jesus Christ* are located on more than 60 acres bought in 1831. A *Mormon Visitor Center* has historical exhibits; the *Auditorium* is world headquarters for the Latter Day Saints. The complex is located on both sides of Walnut, E of Grand and on both sides of River St. The *Woodson-Sawyer House,* on the north side of Lexington, at Proctor, is a fine two-story brick dwelling from the 1860s which was the home of Samuel Woodson, a Congressman and circuit court judge, who operated the stage and mail route from here to Salt Lake City. Restored in the 1940s and altered, *Waggoner Home,* on the S side of Pacific, opposite the end of Spring St., was another home of George Caleb Bingham, who had a studio here also. *Jackson Square Courthouse,* in midtown, was first built in 1836 by David F. Wallace and has been remodeled and enlarged several times. It is styled somewhat in the manner of Independence Hall, a look that was created in the last remodeling in 1933. (A master craftsman in carpentry who served as construction superintendent on many fine buildings in Jackson and Johnson counties in the 1930s, including the Auditorium listed above, and—to the best of memory—the remodeling of this Courthouse, was James Hamilton, my father.)

Jackson County Jail and Museum, 217 N. Main St., was the 1859 jail with native limestone walls, which stood less than a block from the square where wagon trains made ready for the arduous journey west to Santa Fe or Oregon. It was restored in 1959 as a museum and serves as headquarters for the Jackson County Historical Society. The marshal's quarters have been authentically furnished in period. Visitors can actually walk into the cells where Frank James and Quantrill, among other 19th-century disturbers of the peace, were locked up for a time. There is an antebellum schoolhouse in the Museum patio which has not been restored, though it looks as good as new. Furnished as it was in the days when it was a private school for the Howard children, built on the family farm in rural Jackson County.

The *William McCoy House,* 410 W. Farmer, was the home of the first mayor of Independence. It was begun by Samuel Owens in 1849, completed in 1856 by William McCoy, who is said to have been locked in his own bank vault by the James boys. It has been authentically restored by Forest and Martha Ingram. The house is not open except on special occasions, but if you linger on the sidewalk looking interested,

there's even a chance Martha Ingram cannot resist inviting you to tour the magnificent rooms, including a master bedroom with most of the original furnishings. McCoy descendants donated these to the house. Ingram, a businessman who became deeply interested in restorations, and his wife, who has long been active in the Jackson County Historical Society, are at home with antiques and historic furnishings and adapting old houses to present-day functions. Ingram also restored one of the oldest antebellum structures in the area near Lee's Summit, *Four Chimneys* (there are five, but the wife of the present owner thinks four is a more romantic number), on Mason School Rd. (Rt. 3). Joseph Janson, a former Chicagoan and advertising man, bought the home and is helping to restore it as a retirement project. Janson, a city man, enjoys the challenge of restoration despite occasional setbacks.

Vaile Mansion, 1400 N. Liberty, is a Charles Addams delight, but not open to sightseers at present. (It has been serving as a nursing home.) It was built in 1871 by Colonel Harvey M. Vaile, who made his fortune operating the onetime famous Star Mail Route. The heavily trimmed brick mansion cost $150,000, from the foundation to the 80-foot turret.

The *Flournoy House,* Lexington and Short, was built of handmade brick in 1826, with period furnishings.

Bullene-Choplin House, 702 N. Delaware, is a restored Victorian home, handsomely furnished. Tours are available.

Webb House, on the NW corner of Mill and Osage, built before 1846. The house, cross wall, and partitions are solid brick with no wood. The iron stairs connect with walnut logs which form the floor joists.

Missouri Town, on the E side of Lake Jacomo, Blue Springs, and Woods Chapel Rd. exits from I-70. The re-created town is open daily and free, administered by the Jackson County Parks. The buildings were moved here and reconstructed in settings as similar to the original as possible. The period is 1855.

Adams House, built in 1845 by Edmund B. Halloway, is Greek Revival in style. *Murphy Barn,* built by William Bowlin, near Lee's Summit dates from 1860. *Bates City House (Sullens-Webb Home),* from the 1840s, is Greek Revival with Steamboat Gothic elements; there are a spiral walnut staircase and two fireplaces. *Woodard Cabin,* about 1837, from the California, Missouri, area, is of log construction. *Salt Box House* came from the Smithville area.

The *Flintlock Church,* built in 1848 by Primitive Baptists 5 miles N of Platte City, was known as the Unity Church. Bee Creek, near the original site, was used for baptisms. The church is of hewn logs with a floor plan in the shape of a cross. The *Samuel-Chevis Tavern,* from the 1820s, originally near Barry, on the county line between Platte and Clay counties, was a stage stop on the roads to Leavenworth, St. Louis, and Weston. Hewn-log construction with a continuous roof covering the dogtrot section; the openings between logs were filled with walnut blocks and lime mortar, a process called chinking.

The *Luttrell Cabin,* from the 1860s, is log construction with a typical loft bedroom. The *Withers House,* built about 1840, was the home of Abjah and Prudence Withers. The wall posts and ceiling beams are hewn basswood. When the house was built near Liberty there were slave cabins and a summer kitchen in the rear.

The *Riffle House,* built about 1858 near Maysville, has pegged post-and-beam construction with hand-hewn ceiling beams. *Blue Springs Law Office* is a quaint one-room building with an entrance that looks almost too grand for the dimensions, but after all it served a lawyer. There are hitching posts at the side, but no clients, and many outbuildings which fit an early community. A young blacksmith and his apprentice are at work and some of their products are in use in the houses; there are farm animals and an herb garden in this growing settlement. Alberta Wilson Constant, the biographer of George Caleb Bingham, has written a fine "history" of Missouri Town as it might have been, though this is unpublished as yet. Mrs. Constant and her husband, Edwin, a retired businessman who serves as curator of the Jackson County Jail Museum, are active in preservation and restoration and the historical society.

ST. CHARLES, St. Charles County. I-70.

St. Charles Historic District, bounded roughly by the Missouri River, Madison, Chauncey, and 2nd Sts., takes in the 19th-century residential and commercial community with many brick, limestone, and hewn-timber structures. The town was founded in 1769 and first settled mostly by French traders, hunters, and later farmers. It was a major river port at the confluence of the Mississippi and the Missouri.

Stone Row, 314–330 S. Main St., dates from the beginning of the community. The houses look much as they did in the early 19th century, with gabled roofs, interior and exterior end chimneys, heavy lintels, and rear wooden galleries.

Newbill-McElhiney House, 625 S. Main, built of brick in 1836. Bays added in 1850s. Franklin S. Newbill was the original builder; Dr. William J. McElhiney, who enlarged the house, was a physician and politician.

First Missouri State Capitol, 208–216 Main, built in the early 19th century, was a meeting place of the state legislature in 1821 when the territory was recognized as a state. In 1826 the capital was moved to Jeffer-

Bolduc House, Sainte Genevieve, Missouri.

son City. Alexander McNair was the first governor. Restored.

St. Charles Tourist Information and Convention Bureau, 205 S. Main, P.O. Box 1176, St. Charles, 63301; phone (314) 946-7776, has printed a fine booklet on the area and has information on local tours. Costumed guides are provided by the St. Charles County Historical Society. The office is just across the street from the old capitol.

Daniel Boone Home, 20 miles SW via St. 94, in Defiance, was built in 1803–10 and is where the great pioneer and woodsman died in 1820. There are many Boone family items among the furnishings.

STE. GENEVIEVE, Ste. Genevieve County. US 61.

(Whether this is pronounced Jen-a-veeve, or Zhonn-uh-vee-ev is beyond me. I once asked a native and he said, "GIN-a-veeve.") The town was the first settlement on the west bank of the Mississippi.

Ste. Genevieve Historic District covers the area founded in 1725; there are about eight remaining early French structures. The settlers prospered after lead deposits were discovered and developed. NHL.

Bolduc House, 123 S. Main, built

about 1777, French colonial, has a large gallery and a massive trussed roof. The furnishings are French-Canadian. The house was owned by Louis Bolduc, a wealthy farmer and miner. NHL.

Guibourd House, NW corner of 4th and Merchant Sts., from the turn of the 19th century, was the home of Jacques Dubreuil Guibourd and is now owned by the Foundation for the Restoration of Ste. Genevieve. It is vertical log construction on a rock foundation, with great Norman beams in the attic, and formal gardens.

The **Chamber of Commerce** has a brochure with map for an easy walking tour of the historic city. Booklets on the history of various houses and the area are on sale at the Museum, on Merchant St. and DuBourg Place, which also has a Civic Tour Service: (314) 883-3461. The **Foundation for the Historic Restoration of Ste. Genevieve** has literature on the town and the rebuilding; the office of the secretary is at 34 S. 3rd St.; call (314) 883-5609.

Among sites on the walking tour: **Ste. Genevieve Catholic Church,** DuBourg at Merchant, built on the site of the first one (1752), was completed in 1880; **Price Brick House,** built in

1790 as a courthouse; later a restaurant and tavern. Furnished in period. **Shaw House–Fur Trading Post,** 2nd and Merchant, adjacent buildings from the 1790s; the house has fittings from an early steamboat. **Jean Baptiste Valle House,** Market and Main, built by the last French commandant in the 1780s; **Bolduc-LeMeilleur House,** from the 1820s, next door to the Bolduc House, was the home of a grandson-in-law of Louis Bolduc. **Beauvais House,** Main and Merchant, from the 1770s, moved from the old village, as was the Bolduc House in the 1780s, has an enormous fireplace which divides the two main rooms. Henry Breckenridge, historian and author, stayed here in the late 18th century and wrote about it. **Green Tree Tavern,** across S. Gabouri St. from the Bolduc House and slightly SW on the road which leads to St. 61, was built in 1790 by Nicolas Janis. His son, François, was a friend of George Rogers Clark. A triangular fireplace opens into three rooms. The roof is supported by 150 stripped walnut saplings.

A **Jour de Fête à Ste. Geneviève,** with tours of historic houses, is held annually in August.

ST. LOUIS, Independent City. Mississippi River, I-70.

The **Convention & Visitors Bureau,** 500 N. Broadway, St. Louis, 63102; phone (314) 421-1023, has literature, advice, and maps for tours of the area. This shipshape bureau even tells you where to yield when driving, how high the Arch is, how much public transportation and car rentals cost, even how much you should be charged for a taxicab, and where to phone for one, what to expect from the climate, where to gamble on the horses (not in St. Louis—across the river in Illinois), how much to tip, and where to find multilingual services if you are tongue-tied in English. Besides that, the bureau people are all good-looking and friendly.

They seem to believe in their motto: "Let the Spirit of St. Louis Smile on You!"

The **Landmarks Association,** Lafayette Sq., also publishes and sells a series of booklets which concern the ethnic heritage of the Soulard, Carondelet, and Hill districts. These are made possible by a grant from the Division of International Education of the U.S. Office of Education. The project was carried out by the Social Science Institute at Washington University, where the booklets, illustrated and with maps, are also for sale. Box 1202, Washington University, 63130.

Carondelet, in the Bellerive Park area, was a French settlement, a "stop-on-the-road between the more prosperous and bustling communities," and had mostly farmers, woodcutters, and some trappers as residents. It was incorporated as a village in 1832.

The Hill, S of I-44 to Columbia, from January Ave. to Kings Highway on the E. Originally, Italians settled the community. The Social Studies booklet says: "The streets are narrow, lined with cars; traffic slow, drivers are courteous," from which one would think the Italians had come and gone, because Italian drivers on Italian roads are all out to win the Grand Prix.

St. John Nepomuck Parish Historic District, 11th and 12th Sts. between Carroll and Lafayette, is a seven-building complex including the 1870 church.

The **Tourist Board,** 911 Locust, has brochures for self-guiding walking tours, too. The **Historic Preservation Pilgrimage** is held annually in the fall. Both bureaus have information on this.

The **St. Louis Chapter of the American Institute of Architects,** 107 N. 7th in the Wainwright Bldg., which was designed by Adler and Sullivan in 1890, has free brochures on historic buildings, and tours.

At the *Jefferson National Expansion Memorial,* with the Gateway Arch, a *Visitor Center,* open daily, has literature on the area; there is also a bookstore. The museum here is one of the most attractively arranged and comprehensive, for its size, in North America. Visitors learn the history of St. Louis and this part of Missouri from wall and floor displays beautifully and chronologically presented, as you walk through the area. This is a National Park Service site.

Lafayette Square, surrounding Lafayette Park, is a residential area with some 400 buildings constructed between 1850 and 1875; many are Italianate and Second Empire and belonged to the wealthier citizens. A tornado in 1896 destroyed many fine homes which were later rebuilt. The annual tour in June takes in 20 homes. An excellent illustrated booklet by John Albury Bryan, published by the *Landmarks Association of St. Louis,* 611 Olive St., Room 2187, zip 63101, gives the story of this historic neighborhood.

Soulard Neighborhood Historic District, roughly bounded by 7th Blvd., Soulard, Lynch, and 12th Sts., is a downtown section of 18th- and 19th-century structures, residential, religious, and commercial, many with Greek Revival and Italianate elements, some Second Empire. The *Soulard Market* is Second Renaissance Revival. The district was settled by French and Americans in the late 18th century. Antoine Soulard was a French immigrant, and the area was platted from his estate.

The *Bremen–Hyde Park Area,* a 19th-century riverfront area, began as an outlying community. The town of Bremen was platted in 1844, and taken into the city in 1855 when it extended from Dock St. N to E. Grand Ave. and from 20th St. to the river. Hyde Park is a green, open space, as it was when the city took over in 1854. "Street Front Heritage," by McCue, Overby, and Way-

man, is a booklet on the architectural history of the area, first published in the July 1976 issue of the *Missouri Historical Society Bulletin.*

Laclede's Landing, bounded by King bridge on the N, Eads bridge on the S, the river on the E, and I-70 on the W, is a nine-block, 22-acre district which is being handsomely restored. There are many cast-iron buildings in the area. The structures are being adapted from warehousing and light industrial uses to offices, shops, entertainment centers, and residences.

Eugene Field House, 634 S. Broadway, is within easy walking distance of most downtown hotels, the Arch area, and Laclede's Landing. It was built in 1845, a Federal-style row house, and was the birthplace of Field. It has an extensive toy museum. Open year round.

Goldenrod Showboat, built in 1909, still offers entertainment at 400 N. Wharf, where it is permanently docked. The largest showboat ever built, it is listed on the National Register.

Old Cathedral and the *Old Courthouse* are also easy to reach from downtown hotels. The 1834 cathedral has been excellently restored; so has the 1839 courthouse. Both are on the National Historic Site of the *Jefferson National Expansion Memorial,* administered by the Park Service.

Florissant, Florissant Rd. NW of downtown, in St. Louis County, is a city with many historic structures which was first settled by the French in 1786. The *Visitors Bureau,* 1060 Rue St., has maps for a self-guiding tour. Green markers on the right side of the pavement also point the way. *Old St. Ferdinand's Shrine,* from the 18th century, and *Taille de Noyer,* once a three-room log cabin, about 1790, rebuilt to a 22-room mansion, are open to visitors. The village was laid out in 16 even squares, with most of the streets named for Catholic saints. Taille de Noyer is headquarters for the Florissant Valley Historical Society, which maintains the richly furnished home.

Note: *St. Louis County Department of Parks and Recreation* has a fine brochure which lists 100 historic buildings (and sells for $1). Write to them at Clayton, 63105, or phone (314) 725-3447.

WESTON, Platte County. St. 45.

Weston Historic District covers 21 blocks.

Weston Historical Museum, Spring and Main Sts., is a good place to be introduced to this onetime steamboat town. Benjamin Holladay of the now historic Butterfield Stage Lines once owned the site. A Tour Committee offers free transportation by bus in the city of Weston. Tour maps are available. There are many fine old structures and historic *Weston Wine Cellars* where visitors are welcome if they have given advance notice. Write to 500 Welt, 64098; or phone (816) 386-5235. The *McCormick Distilling Company* offers tours beginning at their country store, daily from 9 to 4, spring through fall. They also like advance notice: (816) 386-2276.

KANSAS

... we had a large fireplace that made such a big blaze by night we needed no "dips." Coal oil was then unknown, to us at least. I kept my best dresses hanging in the loft. ... One day I went upstairs—by the way, our stairs were hollowed out pieces of wood nailed to the logs; not the hardest way of going upstairs by any means—to see if my dresses were all right. On looking them over I found the best one, a lovely silk and my wedding dress, had two breadths cut to tatters, and all were more or less injured. I put my hand in the pocket of one and felt something warm and soft. I got down the grand stair-case in a hurry, and threw half a dozen young mice in a blazing fire. ... Usually tender-hearted, I had not the least compunction about making a hol-ocaust of those mice. There I was without a dress to wear if a preacher came along and preached somewhere. ...

—"My First Days in Kansas," by Mrs. S. B. White, read at a Home Coming in Junction City, 1909

Of course every one has heard of wicked Dodge; but a great deal has been said and written about it that is not true. Its good side has never been told. ... Many reckless, bad men came to Dodge and many brave men. ... The officers gave them the south side of the railroad-track, but the north side must be kept respectable, and it was. There never was any such thing as shooting at plug hats.

—"Personal Reminiscences of Frontier Life in Southwest Kansas," by R. M. Wright, an address delivered in 1901

ABILENE, Dickinson County. US 40.

"Old Abilene Town," 201 S.E. Sixth at Kuney St., is a replica of Abilene during the peak cattle days with some original buildings. A boulder on the post office lawn marks the end of the Chisholm Trail over which thousands of cattle were driven between the Civil War and the early 1870s. A boulder in the Abilene Cemetery marks the grave of Marshal Tom Smith, a peace officer famous in his day who somehow has escaped the attention of television and movie famemakers.

Joseph G. McCoy in *Historic*

Sketches of the Cattle Trade of the West and Southwest, published in Kansas City in 1874, wrote:

"Abilene became widely known. At a distance one might think it was a city of many thousands instead of a few hundred. The story was told of a newly arrived southern drover who appeared one morning in the midst of the village and asked how far it was to Abilene and in what direction it lay. When told that he was in the place, he could scarcely believe his informer, and broke forth, saying, 'Now look here, stranger, you don't mean this here little scatterin' trick is Abilene!' When assured that it was,

269

he answered, 'Well, I'll swar; I never seed such a little town have such a mighty big name.' "

There were some 40 saloons and many a dance hall. Often cowboys swung off their saddles and rushed in to the dance without bothering to take off their sombreros, pistols, or spurs. An effort was made to establish law and order, but the cowboys shot up the ordinances which were posted around town. A jail was begun, but the cowboys tore it down. When it was rebuilt and guarded around the clock until construction was finished and the roof was bolted on, the cowboys then raided the new building and released the only prisoner. After this, Tom Smith was hired.

Mayor T. C. Henry, speaking at the dedication of a monument to Tom Smith in 1904, said: "It was rumored that Smith had agreed to enforce the law, so a big burly cowboy immediately picked a quarrel with him; but before the aggressor could draw his gun Smith had floored him with a blow from his fist. Another tried the same thing a few days later and Smith leaped on his antagonist, knocking him down, and, taking his own gun, beat him with it and advised him to leave town immediately. After this time Smith had little trouble. The law was upheld to a degree that had never before been known in Abilene. Crime was reduced to a minimum and all was well for one season. After about six months Smith was killed while putting the handcuffs on a murderer. Smith was a man who enforced the law by sheer nerve. He seemed never to think of his gun in time of danger. Only a few times did he use a gun while marshal of Abilene. His successor, "Wild Bill" [William Hickok] was just the opposite. He never forgot that he was armed and could shoot first."

COUNCIL GROVE, Morris County. US 56.

Council Grove Historic District was the last outfitting place on the Santa Fe Trail between the Missouri River and Santa Fe. NHL. *Pioneer Jail,* 502 E. Main St., on US 56, built in 1849, was the only jail on the trail for a time. A shrine now stands at 210 E. Main, the site of the *Council Oak* where in 1825 a treaty was signed between commissioners from Washington and the Osage Indians, gaining a right of way for the trail. At this meeting Council Grove got its name. *Post Office Oak,* on E. Main between Union and Liberty Sts., was a huge tree with a cache at its base which was used as a mail drop by pack trains and other travelers between 1825 and 1847. *Hays Tavern,* 112 West Main, built in 1857 as a trading post and tavern, also served for a courtroom, theatricals, church socials, and other events. Seth Hays was a cousin of Kit Carson, one of the first travelers to use the trail, and a great-grandson of Daniel Boone. *Kaw Methodist Mission,* 500 N. Mission St. at Huffaker St., was built in 1849 of native stone by the Methodist Episcopal Church and used for Indian and white children until 1851, when it became a school for whites only. NHL. An old Indian dwelling of the type the government put up for the Kaw Indians on their reservation has been moved to the mission lawn. The mission building is now a museum.

Last Chance Store, 500 W. Main St., was a place for the Kaws and other Indians to trade animal pelts for supplies, and for those travelers headed west to stock up for the long trip to Santa Fe. Built in 1857 by Tom Hill, it housed a post office, and later served as a government trading house.

Farmers & Drovers Bank, 201 W. Main St., a brick building from 1892, has hand-hewn stone trim, and stained-glass windows. The *Chamber of Commerce* has a brochure for marked historic tours.

Douglas Avenue, Wichita, Kansas. (Drawn by Frenzeny and Tavernier when Wichita was Cow Town. From *The American West,* by Lucius Beebe and Charles Clegg)

DODGE CITY, Ford County. US 56.

Historic Front Street, 500 W. Wyatt Earp Blvd., is an authentic reproduction of the 1870s main street of the once rip-roaring town. The *General Outfitting Store* is two stories high; next to it is the *Long Branch Saloon,* then the *G. M. Hoover Store* for wholesale booze and cigars. A *Dry Goods and Clothing Store* is in the middle of the block, the *Tonsorial Palace* comes next, and the *F. C. Zimmerman Store,* which has firearms, hardware, tinware, lumber, and groceries. *Hardesty House,* a cattle baron's home, moved from the original site, has been restored and furnished. *Beeson Museum* has a large collection of frontier artifacts. The lamp post is original. *Boot Hill,* Spruce St. and Fifth Ave., is a museum on the site of the original burying ground. An old jail, an open grave, and a hangman's tree are part of the décor. Dodge City was the "queen of the cowtowns" from 1872 to 1885. Nearly half a million visitors come each year to see the fake gunfights or watch "Miss Kitty and Her Can-Can Girls" perform on summer nights. *Wells Fargo Concord Stages* are available for short rides.

Wyatt Earp came to Dodge City when he was still a young man and served as marshal three times, during summers when the cattle were being driven from Texas and New Mexico to the railroads here. John "Doc" Holliday was Earp's friend and a dentist when he wasn't too busy as a gunman or gambler. Bat Masterson and Luke Short were other colorful characters in town. Masterson edited a daily paper, the *Vox Populi,* in 1884. It was Republican, and Masterson was appointed a U.S. marshal by President Theodore Roosevelt. He later became a sports reporter for the New York *Morning Telegram*.

R. M. Wright, an early settler at Dodge City, told the Kansas Historical Society about the old days in an address delivered in January 1901. He had been president of the Dodge City Town Company which was organized in 1872. "Dodge was in the very heart of the buffalo country. Hardly had the railroad reached there, long before a depot could be built (they had an office in a box car), business began; and such a business! Dozens of cars a day were loaded with hides and meat, and dozens of car-loads of grain, flour and provisions arrived each day. The streets of Dodge were lined with wagons, bringing in hides and meat and getting supplies from early morning to late at night. . . .

"Our first calaboose in Dodge City was a well fifteen feet deep, into which the drunkards were let down and allowed to remain until they were sober. Sometimes there were several in it at once. It served the purpose well for a time."

WICHITA, Sedgwick County. US 54.

Cow Town, 1717 Sim Park Drive, is a village of some 50 buildings showing life as it might have been here on the banks of the Arkansas River from 1869 to 1880. The reconstruction is by Historic Wichita, Inc. The first log house and hotel, first church, first jail, and other early buildings have been moved to the site. Five of the buildings are more than a century old. Fixtures and furnishings are from original buildings of the period.

ARKANSAS

In building your house, be sure to use a few timbers from an old building. A house composed entirely of new lumber will bring bad luck, usually sickness. If you find your initials in spider webs near the door of your new house, you will be lucky as long as you live there. No furniture or supplies should be carried in until you have put the salt and pepper on the shelf. Never cut a doorway between two rooms after the house is built—that's the worst bad luck of all.

Anonymous, *Ozark Superstitions*

BULL SHOALS, Marion County. St. 178.

Mountain Village, 1 mile S on St. 178. A reconstruction of original pioneer buildings represents the 1890 period in the Ozarks. A yellow railroad depot serves as ticket office and gift shop. The one-room church, built in 1888, stands on a hill; the altar is original, the bell dates back to the 1860s. The rail fence around the church was built by Indians on the Cherokee border in north-central Arkansas in 1828.

The village green has a town pump, wagons, buckboards, and a sorghum mill. Facing the green are an old bank and doctor's office, a blacksmith and coffin shop, early settlers' houses, a slave cabin, and a flying Jenny, which was the merry-go-round of the 19th century. The general store is stocked with the same type of goods that could have been bought nearly a century ago. The one-room schoolhouse, built in 1889, has the old wooden desks with the carved names of long-gone pupils.

The *Martin House*, an 1830 two-story log building, is the oldest in town. The *Jordan House* is a dogtrot

style, 1864. Furnishings include a weaving loom from 1799 and a quilting frame. The *Lynch Flippin House,* 1874, has hand-planed boards, and its furnishings are equally "up to date" for the end of the last century: it has an 1881 phonograph.

EUREKA SPRINGS, Carroll County. US 62.

Indians called this area the "healing place" and camped here to take the water cure. In 1856 Dr. Alvah Jackson discovered the springs, probably accidentally. One story has his hunting dog chasing a panther up the mountain past the spring Dr. Jackson found beneficial. When he brought his son to see the location, the young man found the waters helped his ailing eyes. Dr. Jackson boiled the spring water, bottled it, and sold it as "Magic Eye Water" until the Civil War, when he was too busy caring for wounded soldiers to peddle bottled water. In 1879 Judge J. B. Saunders came from Berryville to see if the wondrous water would help a leg ailment. Apparently the springs worked as well for a leg as an eye; Saunders moved his family to town and word of mouth brought some 400 others soon after. The settlement was incorporated in 1880. Most early-comers arrived by wagon or on horseback and were feeling poorly, but in three years the population had increased to nearly 9,000. Hopeful invalids continued to pour in by stagecoach until a railroad was built. The depot on North Main became busy, as six trains daily unloaded health seekers.

Eureka Springs Historic District comprises about 2 square miles, mostly along Main and Spring Sts., with buildings from the 1880–90 period. Rough-faced stone or pressed brick was usually ornamented with cast- and sheet-iron trimmings. Be sure to get a map from the *Chamber of Commerce,* 5 N. Main St., for two delightful walking tours; the brochures have maps and details for some 37 sites:

One walking tour begins at *Basin Circle Park,* next to the *Basin Park Hotel* in downtown. Free band concerts are given in the park in summer. Take Spring and Main to the *Historical Museum,* restored by the Folk Festival Board. Turn left and go down Armstrong St., noting a Victorian *Cliff Cottage,* with elaborate trim and stained-glass windows. The stone houses have rock retaining walls built after too many fires destroyed the dwellings of the 1880s. There are stopping places for artists or photographers to look out over the picturesque city. You will eventually pass *Hatchet Hall,* the last home of Carry A. Nation, prohibitionist who lived here from 1908 to 1911 and established a girls' school next to her home.

Another walk passes the old *Palace Bath House* and *"Lover's Leap,"* where you don't have to be a lover to sit and rest on the benches. On King St. many houses have stained-glass bay windows, towers, turrets, porches bedecked with Carpenter Gothic, etc. *The Rosalie,* a red-brick structure, open to the public, advertises "interiors unspoiled," possibly an indirect apology for the excess of Carpenter Gothic on its bays, portico, dormers, and eaves.

The stone *Crescent Hotel,* a massive structure known as the "Castle Atop the Ozarks," has 1886 Victorian splendor which has been restored. *"The Castle at Inspiration Point,"* 5½ miles W of town on St. 62, is considerably less luxurious and has a country store, blacksmith shop, and a wooden tower.

FORT SMITH, Sebastian County. I-40.

Fort Smith Chamber of Commerce, 613 Garrison Ave., 72901; phone (501) 783-6118, has an excellent brochure listing historic sites and buildings.

Belle Grove Historic District, N. 5th, 6th, 7th, 8th, from N. C to N. H Sts., has many buildings being restored. Among outstanding sites: *Clayton House,* 514 N. 6th St. (ca. 1882), was the home of William Henry Harrison Clayton, who was U.S. district attorney for the Western District in 1874, making frequent appearances in "Hanging" Judge Isaac Parker's famous court. The elegant mansion is being restored. *McKibben-Bonneville House,* 318 N. 7th (ca. 1871), is Italianate-Victorian, restored; it was the home of Susan Neis Bonneville, widow of General Benjamin Bonneville; shown to groups (minimum ten) by appointment only (782-7854). *Rogers-Tilles House,* 400 N. 8th St. (ca. 1840), believed to have been built by the John Rogers family (he was a city founder); bought by Louis Tilles in 1867. Now houses the *Patent Model Museum,* with 76 original models from 1835 to 1880s. Open weekdays; free.

A complete brochure of Belle Grove restorations is published by the *Belle Fort Smith Tour Incorporated,* P.O. Box 1412, 72902, which sponsors a spring (usually May) event to make a showcase of individual restoration projects, and will be enlarged to include historic Garrison Ave. and other significant neighborhoods.

Old Town, corner of Garrison and 5th, is a reconstruction of late 1800s, now shops and offices, etc., called a tourist "must" by the C. of C.

Free Ferry Rd., which led to the free ferry across the Arkansas River E of town, is lined with "Gilded Age" houses of the turn of the century.

Rogers House, 904 N. 11th St., built by William, son of Captain Rogers, town founder, is Victorian Renaissance.

Miss Laura's House, 123 Front St., is what was known as "a house," often with "of ill repute" added. It was built just before the turn of the century and has been restored by the Donrey Media Group. Miss Laura's "Social Club" was Victorian Baroque and has been mistakenly associated with Pearl Starr, daughter of Belle and possibly Henry Starr, although some accounts give Cole Younger as Pearl's father. Pearl did work in several of the other "social clubs" on Front St. There were half a dozen. The house, now white, was originally forest green with cream trim, which explains how a popular story got started—that Pearl had paid for her mother's headstone at Younger's Bend, Oklahoma, by money earned in the "Pea-Green Bawdy House of Fort Smith."

LITTLE ROCK, Pulaski County. I-40. I-30.

Arkansas Territorial Capitol Restoration, Third, Cumberland, Scott, and Second Sts. Take Markham St. exit off I-30 to the right onto Second St. to parking lot.

This fine restoration of 13 original buildings is set in landscaped grounds with stately trees and trim gardens that allow the visitor to enjoy the best of the Arkansas frontier of 1820–40. Tranquillity is the mood now in the quiet buildings and

surroundings, but in the early years Choctaws, Cherokees, and frontiersmen were arguing over land rights. Boundaries went back and forth like the flag in a game of tug-of-war, until an 1825 treaty with the Choctaws put the present border from Fort Smith to the Red River, and three years later the Cherokees agreed to move west of a line that would extend from Fort Smith to Missouri.

There were hot debates and delay in getting statehood because of the antislavery feeling, but it was gained in June 1836. The panic of 1837 sent hordes of farmers from played-out lands east of the Mississippi into the new state, bringing the usual problems of a fast rise in population. In 1820 there had been less than 15,000 residents in Arkansas; by 1840 the population was more than 97,000.

The restoration opened in 1941, in an area condemned by the city in 1939. Three museum houses are on their original sites; the *Conway House* was moved to a different location and one house was adapted to be used as an office. The *Hinderliter House,* or *The Tavern,* is a two-story clapboard-covered log structure, the oldest house in the city, built between 1826 and 1828. It may have been the last meeting place for the Territorial Legislature in 1835. Jesse Hinderliter operated a grog shop and general store on the main floor and lived upstairs until 1833. One of the upper rooms has wallboards partially removed to show the original construction. Cypress and pine were woods used most often in the Delta and lowlands of the territory; oak and hickory were used in the mountains. When the Hinderliter House was partially remodeled in 1834, the hand-hewn oak logs were covered with hand-beaded red-heart cypress siding. All ceiling beams have the same hand-beaded finish.

The 1840s *Noland House,* in the midblock facing Cumberland, is Georgian red brick. Dwarf English

The Jesse Hinderliter House, Arkansas Territorial Restoration, Little Rock. (Arkansas Department of Parks & Tourism)

boxwood in the back of the house grew from cuttings from Mount Vernon plants, given to the restoration in honor of Mrs. J. Fairfax (Louise) Loughborough, who planned the campaign to create the restoration and was responsible for its success. Lieutenant C. F. M. Noland was a lawyer and journalist who was delegated to deliver the first constitution of the state to Washington. The kitchen and office buildings are on either side of the back court.

Woodruff House, at Second and Cumberland Sts., stands on the grounds where William E. Woodruff built his home and printing office when he followed the seat of government from Arkansas Post to Little Rock in 1821. Woodruff founded the first newspaper in the territory, the *Arkansas Gazette,* in November 1819. He brought its handpress and type from Nashville, Tennessee, to Ar-

kansas Post, traveling by river. The print shop has a working Washington Hand Press and one similar to the one Woodruff used.

The **Conway House** is frame with white oak pegs. Possessions of Elias Conway, fifth governor of Arkansas, are among the furnishings. An original Audubon print, made in Arkansas, is in the house.

The Reception Center has exhibits and an Arkansas Craft Store with handmade items. A pre–Civil War log house of dogtrot style is being moved from Scott, Arkansas, and will be restored to its mid-19th-century appearance. It will reflect a less affluent life style than other buildings of the restoration.

Old State House Square Historic District is roughly bounded by the Arkansas River, Arch, Main, and Second Sts. **Old State House,** 300 W. Markham St., was the capitol from

1836 to 1911 except for two brief periods when trouble temporarily moved the government elsewhere. The Greek Revival structure was designed by Kentuckian Gideon Shryock and was completed in 1840. Additions were made in 1885. The *Old Capitol,* on the site of an Indian burial ground, is being restored; there are state archives, a museum, and a research library in the building. Conducted tours are available.

Walking or driving tours of Little Rock's historic *Quapaw Quarter* take in the general area of MacArthur Park in the downtown section. Among historic buildings: *Frederick Trapnall House,* or *Trapnall Hall,* 423 E. Capitol Ave., built in 1843, has been restored by the Junior League. The Greek Revival house was the home of Trapnall, a lawyer and a political leader. At 615 E. Capitol is the *Walters-Curran-Bell House,* Greek Revival, built in 1842–43.

The restored *Mills House,* 523 E. Sixth St., is Second Empire, built in 1863 by a wealthy planter for his bride. He must have been an optimist. Union forces held the capitol in September 1863. At 503 E. Sixth, the *Absalom Fowler House,* Greek Revival, was built in 1840 by Fowler, a lawyer and land speculator who designed the structure.

Nash House, 601 Rock St., is a Colonial Revival structure built in 1907, now adapted for law offices.

Pike-Fletcher-Terry House, 411 E. Seventh St., was built in 1840 for the controversial explorer, soldier, and author Albert Pike. In an 1872 biographical listing Pike is called a poet born in Boston, but few who knew him thought of his poetry first. As a young man he fought a duel with John Selden Roane, who became governor of Arkansas. Both duelists missed the mark repeatedly, though a disenchanted bystander said he could have hit a squirrel 75 feet away with the same weapons. Pike survived the Mexican War and won a $140,000 suit for the Creek Indians as a lawyer just before the Civil War. In 1861 he organized Cherokees from Indian Territory to fight for the Confederacy and led them into action in the Battle of Pea Ridge, a Confederate loss. He was commissioned a brigadier general, but in the summer of 1862 he resigned, resenting the authority of a fellow general. Both sides regarded him with some suspicion for the duration, but after the war he was again active in Washington and in Memphis as a lawyer and journalist. His home in Little Rock was bought by Captain John Fletcher, whose son John G. grew up to be a poet. Adolphine Fletcher, John's sister, married David D. Terry, who became a U.S. Congressman. The house has been willed to the city. The *Garland-Mitchell House,* 14th and Scott Sts., built in 1873, was the birthplace of John Gould Fletcher, and was the residence of two governors.

Villa Marre, 1321 Scott St., Second Empire, built in 1881, was restored in 1964. Angelo Marre, an Italian immigrant in 1854, became a wealthy saloon owner. It is an imposing dwelling with a fine picket fence. *Rozelle-Murphy House,* at 1301 Scott, built in 1887, and the *Hanger House,* at 1010 Scott, built in 1889, have been restored.

WASHINGTON, Hempstead
County. St. 4, 9 miles NW of Hope.

In the lively days of the frontier many now famous travelers stopped here as they headed down the Southwest Trail. Sam Houston, Albert Pike, James Bowie, David Crockett, and Stephen F. Austin are among the onetime guests of the *Old Tavern.* In 1836 Houston and others were planning the independence of Texas when they stayed here. Albert Pike's desk, which he used when he wrote most of his *Morals and Dogma of Masonry,* is on display and probably gets more attention than the book ever did. The **Washington Historic District** covers the original plat of the city for 1824.

The **Blacksmith Shop** re-creates the site where James Black made the original Bowie knife. He was said to be the only blacksmith in the area who could temper Damascus steel. The knife itself is now owned by Bart Moore, of Tuscaloosa, Alabama, who stores it in a bank vault. In 1890, Moore's grandfather presumably acquired the weapon in payment of a small debt from an elderly Mexican who claimed to have found it next to a dead body after the fall of the Alamo. Bowie, of course, was one of the casualties, and "J. Bowie" is carved into the blade. The Blacksmith Shop, reconstructed in 1960, has three open-hearth furnaces and a blast furnace as well as many old tools.

Block-Catts House, thought to be the oldest two-story dwelling still standing in the state, is a saltbox built in 1828–32, restored. Among its furnishings are a rosewood secretary, a gift from Andrew Jackson, and a blue milk-glass pitcher which once belonged to Jefferson Davis. A 65-foot magnolia tree near the house is a splendid sight in the spring.

The **Gun Museum** has a collection dating back to the 18th century, also historical documents and Indian artifacts.

Sanders-Garland House, 1836, was the home of Augustus H. Garland, a U.S. Senator, Arkansas governor, and Attorney General in President Cleveland's cabinet. A square Chickering piano and a sleighbed are among the period furnishings.

Grandison D. Royston House, Alexander St., is a one-story Greek Revival built in 1845, from heart-of-pine lumber. The outside walls are covered with horizontal beveled siding. The sills are hand-hewn. The house was restored in 1975 by the Pioneer Washington Restoration Foundation, who then gave it to the Arkansas Department of Parks to be included in the Old Washington State Park. Grandison and Mary Royston were married in 1835 and had seven children, four of whom survived early childhood. Royston was a delegate to the first Constitutional Convention in Arkansas and also served as U.S. district attorney for Arkansas, state senator, an adjutant general of militia for the state during the Mexican War, and as representative to the Confederate Congress.

Hempstead County Courthouse, Franklin St. off St. 4 (1833), served as legal headquarters for the state from 1863 to 1865; now restored, with museum. Further restorations will include old streets, picket fences, commercial structures including an opera house, two hotels, a post office, stable, saloon, and jail, lost in a fire in the 1870s.

Texas and Oklahoma

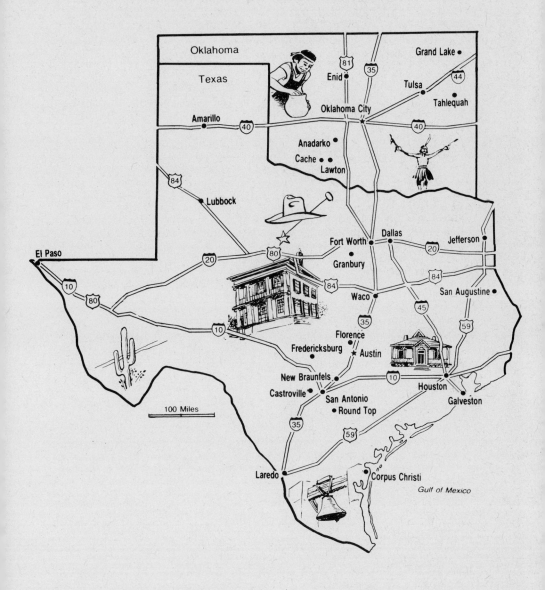

Oklahoma

Texas

Grand Lake

Enid

Tulsa

Tahlequah

Amarillo

Oklahoma City

Anadarko

Cache

Lawton

Lubbock

El Paso

Fort Worth

Dallas

Jefferson

Granbury

Waco

San Augustine

Florence

Fredericksburg

Austin

New Braunfels

Castroville

Houston

San Antonio

Round Top

Galveston

100 Miles

Laredo

Corpus Christi

Gulf of Mexico

TEXAS

For fifty miles away there lay stretched before us a succession of cultivated fields, interspersed with belts of timber, wide expanses of prairie lands with the natural grass, and in the dim horizons, so far off as to be barely distinguished from the clouds themselves, a succession of lofty mountains. The hotel accommodations at Fort Worth need to be greatly enlarged, but there are comfortable private dwellings, and the citizens are kind, courteous, and hospitable.

—*What I Saw in Texas,* by John W. Forney, Philadelphia, 1872

San Antonio is pretty, situated on both banks of the river of the same name. It should contain about 10,000 inhabitants, and is the largest place in Texas, except Galveston.

The houses are well built of stone, and they are generally only one or two stories high. All have verandas in front.

—*Journal of Lt. Col. James Arthur Lyon Fremantle, Coldstream Guards, on His Three Months in the Southern States,* Edinburgh, 1863

CASTROVILLE, Medina County. US 90.

Castroville Historic District takes in the village founded by the Count Henri de Castro, who soon changed his name to plain Henry Castro, and colonists from Alsace. There were more than 700 inhabitants in three years. The only structure listed on the Historic American Buildings Survey, not in the district, is the *Charles de Montel House,* 3 miles NW of town, built in 1846. De Montel (originally Shibenmontel) was a civil engineer who served as guide for the immigrants and later served as a captain in the Confederate Army.

Joe Bendele House, Angelo St. near Florence, is a one-story dwelling moved to this site in 1855. Also on Angelo is the *Joseph Carlé House and Store,* at the corner of Madrid (Houston Square), built by Carlé, who came from Alsace in the mid-19th century. It is two stories with a one-story warehouse at one end. *Louis Haass House,* Florence between Angelo and Amelia Sts., like Carlé's home and many others, is of stone and stucco. Haass built his place sometime before 1850. A few years later John Merian built the one-and-a-half-story dwelling at London and Angelo. The *P. F. Pingenot House,* Petersburg St. between Angelo and Lorenzo Sts., is stuccoed adobe and was sometimes used as a saloon as well as a residence. The *Nicolas Tondre House (Peter Hoog House),* Florence at Amelia Sts., dates from the early 1840s; Tondre's deed to a town lot was made out before the arrival of the settlers.

The *Vance Hotel Complex,* Florence and Florella Sts., includes the *Landmark Inn,* once a stagecoach

280

stop with sections built before 1853, and a separate kitchen and bathhouse. Vance added the inn's second story in 1874. The two-story stone bathhouse is lead-lined, a luxury for tired travelers across Texas in slow-moving days. Guests can still stay at the Landmark. A museum here has Alsatian relics including furniture. The **Vance House** is a two-story dwelling behind the hotel on Florella.

St. Louis Homecoming Day, held annually in August, offers tours of the historic homes and other buildings, including churches. There is also a five-ton beef barbecue in Koenig Park on the banks of the Medina River. About 12,000 visitors enjoy the Alsace-style cooking, and touring the quaint old town with its French-German-Texan mixture of architecture.

DALLAS, Dallas County. I-30.

Dallas Heritage Center, Gano and St. Paul Sts., has a collection of early structures which have been moved here to City Park and restored by the Dallas County Historical Society. The **Morehead-Gano House,** now a house museum, was moved from St. 121, NW of the intersection with Bethel Rd., where it was erected in the mid-19th century. It is one and a half stories of log covered with weatherboarding. The porch, loft, and shed were added in 1858. Restored in 1974 when relocated here. The Greek Revival **Millermore** of cedar and oak is an elegant Victorian house museum, furnished in period. Among other buildings are an 1898 hotel, an 1875 depot, an 1880 section house, and an 1847 Miller log cabin. The park was 100 years old when the nation celebrated its Bicentennial.

Old East Dallas, a onetime area of fine homes from 1890 to the 1930s, is being extensively restored. The **Swiss Avenue Historic District,** on Swiss between Fitzhugh and LaVista, comprises early-20th-century structures,

Vereins-Kirche, Fredericksburg, Texas. (Pen-and-ink drawing by Michael Penick. Courtesy Fredericksburg Chamber of Commerce)

unified by building restrictions and retaining their residential character. It is considered a museum of pre-World War I architecture.

FORT WORTH, Tarrant County. I-20.

Log Cabin Village, in Forest Park, 2121 Colonial Pkwy., has pioneer homes which have been moved here and restored; period furnishings of the 1850s.

FREDERICKSBURG, Gillespie County. US 290.

Fredericksburg Historic District covers the 19th-century settlement which is one of the leading attractions of the Texas "hill country" and is distinguished by its many "Sunday houses"—homes once used by farmers on weekends for socializing and church attendance. Now most of these have been restored and are marked with Texas Medallions.

The **Chamber of Commerce,** with a friendly and helpful staff headed by Bill Chadwick, is located just off Main St. in the **Vereins-Kirche,** a reconstructed octagonal building on the site of the original "coffee mill church." There is a relic display in the lobby; also literature and maps of the historic area for self-guiding tours. Guides are usually available for touring, if desired. The local historical society members are willing volunteers to show off this exceptionally charming town; they maintain the museum in the Vereins-Kirche as well as the *Schandua House,* 111 E. Austin St., an exact restoration with no plumbing or electricity.

The community was settled by emigrants to the Republic of Texas who were financed by the *Adels Verein* (Society of the Nobility) in Prussia. The colonists named their town for Prince Frederick. The original party founded New Braunfels in 1845. In the spring of 1846 when the roads were barely passable a group of 120 took 16 days to reach here by wagon train. They were led by Baron Ottfried Hans van Meusenbach, who—like Castro of Castroville—soon Americanized his name to John O. Meusenbach. He made peace with the Comanche Indians in a treaty signed in May of 1847—a rare agreement in the history of the West, it was never violated by either side. No Indian raids were ever led against Fredericksburg.

The *Heinrich Kammlah House,* 309 W. Main, was built in 1846–50 as a store and residence. The half-timber and stucco building now houses a museum of pioneer items. The *Kiehne-Foerster House,* 405 E. Main, is limestone ashlar with ornamental wooden railings on the outside stair. Erected in 1850, it is probably the first two-story building in town. The exterior has been restored to its original appearance. The *Pape Log Cabin,* 213 W. Creek, at the rear of the *Dangers Stone House,* was the first dwelling and was put up by neighbors for the Widow Pape, who was ill, having never regained her health after the long journey from the homeland. Its

post oak logs have weathered to picturesque variations at the corners of the structure, making almost a foolproof shot for even amateur photographers.

The Reverend Gottlieb Burchard Dangers built the larger house at the front of the lot in 1851. It is typical of the *fachwerk* construction (half masonry and half timber) favored by the settlers until they discovered the native stone was support enough. The furnishings in the Stone House are an excellent example of the German knack for combining practicality and handsomeness. In the kitchen-dining room the meals were prepared in the fireplace and served on a large table nearby which has an iron rod fastened in one end on which hot iron pots could be hung. Transoms, door and window trim, and pegged closets in small spaces in many of the houses also show the German flair for craftsmanship and fine décor made to work for everyday use. Many examples of this are in the *Loeffler-Weber House,* 508 W. Main, which has a log room and loft built by Gerhard Roerig, German immigrant, in the first winter of 1846–47. The rock and half-timber rooms were added in 1867 by Johann Loeffler, a fine cabinetmaker, and the Sunday House was used for 90 years. Now restored, with the wide cypress flooring and oak rafters preserved, it is open on special tours. *John Peter Tatsch House,* 210 N. Bowie St., built by Tatsch in 1852, has a stone fireplace chimney and baking oven big enough to roast a Texas longhorn. The *Krieger-Geyer House,* 512 W. Creek, was built in two stages in 1848 and 1868. It was beautifully restored by the Rodolph Smiths, with the interior of *fachwerk* construction on display in the kitchen and many unusual early furnishings. The cocktail table in the living room was a sauerkraut cutter; the *Kleidershrunk* (wardrobe) has several surprising features including a keyhole made from a deer's skull and an ingenious lock. Mrs. Smith and her daughter, Mrs. Laney Bristol, have been active as tour directors of the Gillespie County Historical Society and are most knowledgeable about Fredericksburg heritage and restorations.

The *White Elephant Saloon* at 242 E. Main is a curiosity not to be missed in passing. Its façade still sports a frisky bas-relief elephant, and whiskey once sold here for 15¢ a quart.

GALVESTON, Galveston County. E end of Galveston Island, connected to the mainland by causeways. Access from the E is via a state-owned and operated ferry which offers a free ride well worth taking if only to see the view and the gulls which compete for food tossed out by passengers.

Strand Historic District comprises more than 45 structures in the commercial area of the 19th century; many have cast-iron features. Nicholas J. Clayton, one of the town's leading architects, was responsible for several brick and marble buildings of great elegance. In early days when the buildings were frame, on pilings which jutted over the bay, merchants could actually receive and ship goods from their back doors and clerks could fish from second-story windows during their lunch hour. Then Ave. A, which had been partially under water, was filled in and the Strand was no longer a waterfront street. The 1900 hurricane changed the scene still further. The Strand has been restored by the Galveston Historical Foundation and the Galveston County Cultural Arts Council, with gas streetlamps and much refurbishing of storefronts long dimmed by the years. Boutiques, galleries, and shops occupy space once devoted to the shipping trade. The *First National Bank,* 1878, now bright red and white, houses the Arts Council. The Junior League has

headquarters in the restored *Truehart-Adriance Bldg.,* 212 22nd St., a real-estate firm in 1881. It is molded pressed brick, stone, cast-iron, and fanciful, if reminiscent of Italian opera settings; or—as described in the National Register—it has a "front parapet with pediment, flanking anthemion ornament, denticulated pressed metal cornice with brackets, terra cotta cartouche in tympanum," etc. Restored. The Register sums it up as High Victorian Italianate. Spruced up for the new boom in Victoriana, it is a building not to be missed. The *Grand Opera House,* 2012–2020 Ave. E (1894), Frank Cox, architect, is Second Renaissance Revival and Richardson Romanesque. It became a movie house, now restored to be used again for the performing arts. It was once one of a chain of seven theaters operated by Henry Greenwall on a loop which included leading Texas cities, as well as Memphis, Louisville, and Little SE Rock. The *Old Customhouse,* SE corner of 20th and Post Office (Ave. E), 1858–61, Ammi B. Young, architect, had its cast-iron trimmings imported from New York. It has been extensively renovated.

At the far end of the Strand, *Ashbel Smith Bldg., "Old Red,"* 914–916 Ave. B, was the first medical college building in Texas and housed the entire medical school. Architect Nicholas Clayton went to Baltimore, Philadelphia, New York, and Boston to study medical schools before completing his plans. Built in 1888–91, Old Red was damaged in the 1900 hurricane and nearly demolished in 1973 but was saved by contributions for its restoration. Unless plans change it will house the first Institute for the Humanities in Medicine.

Ashton Villa, 2328 Broadway, 1858 Italianate, handsomely restored and open for tours, is three-story brick, a Texas palace, once the home of Colonel James M. Brown, master brickmason from the North, who was his own architect and builder and used bricks from his own brickyard. He was also a leading merchant and banker. A memorable slide presentation of the horrendous 1900 hurricane is available as part of the tour, in the *Carriage House,* on the estate.

The Bishop's Palace, 1402 Broadway (Ave. J), is probably the most photographed house in Galveston, though it is far from the most attractive indoors or out. There is plenty of it, and tourists flock to see the many rooms of the three-story structure of rock-faced Texas pink granite with limestone and red sandstone trim. The tile roof has hips, gables, cones, pyramids, and a variety of chimneys. The mansion was the home of Walter Gresham, a lawyer, businessman, and U.S. Congressman; then it became the official residence of the bishop of the Roman Catholic diocese and is now a museum. An interior feature is the octagonal stairwell with stained-glass windows.

Galveston is a paradise for Victorian house fanciers. Days could be well spent on self-guiding walking tours. A *Tourist Information Bureau,* with maps, literature, and guided tours available, is a good place to begin a visit—23rd St. and Seawall Blvd. Much restoration and preservation work is being carried on in various parts of the historic port. *East End Historic District,* Broadway and Market, between 11th and 19th, is a National Historic Landmark, as is the *Strand.*

In 1975, 106 buildings were recorded on the Historic American Buildings Survey Inventory forms. Many have been restored; some are gone. If you buy a local guidebook and look for the buildings which interest you most, chances are you will find most of them looking as fresh as new. One major disappointment is that *Heidenheimer Castle,* 1602 Sealy, is now only a memory. In 1855 its walls were a mixture of mortar and oyster shells. Thirty years later a tower was added and enough additions to make 57 rooms with 27 fireplaces, in a four-story plus basement structure. Now weeds grow on the empty lot.

GRANBURY, Hood County. US 377.

Granbury County Courthouse Historic District, Courthouse Square, comprises a number of two-story limestone Victorian commercial buildings. The *Second Empire Courthouse,* designed by W. C. Dodson, was built in 1890–91. A stairway to the impressive three-story clocktower is trimmed with wrought iron. The building has been restored (the hand-hewn limestone sandblasted white and the trim painted brown); daily tours are conducted by a guide-lecturer.

The *1st National Bank,* NW corner of the Square, began in 1883 when D. C. Cogdell and John H. Traylor opened for business in a 25-foot limestone building. They not only printed but signed their own money. A national charter was granted in 1887 and the structure was enlarged. It now has drive-in windows, but the bankers no longer sign the currency. *Nutt House,* on the Square, was a log grocery store when it was erected in 1880 for owners Jesse and Jacob Nutt, then became a hotel for stagecoach passengers and traveling salesmen in 1893, when the log structure was replaced by a rock building, now marked by a Texas Historical plaque. And a descendant of David Nutt, a town founder, recently came back to Granbury, restored the family home, and bought the Nutt Hotel, reopening the once renowned-for-its-home-style-cooking Nutt House Dining Room and bringing back country flavor to the meals served. (So successfully that customers from Dallas and Fort Worth queue up with Granburyites for Sunday dinner.)

The *Opera House,* also on the

Square, built in 1886, had a grand re-opening in June 1975 following its restoration. **Hood County Jail,** 208 N. Crockett, was built in 1886 to replace an 1873 wooden calaboose.

The **Chamber of Commerce,** 108 W. Pearl St. or Box 277, Granbury, 76048, has information on the area and provides guides. As Texas travel writer Connie Sherley puts it: "What a difference a decade makes. In the 1960s Granbury, which is 35 miles southeast of Fort Worth, was just another Texas town progress had by-passed." Now the town has proven "there's plenty of future in making the most of your past." Among other restorations are a depot, freight store, churches, and a mansion.

HOUSTON, Harris County. I-45.

The Greater Houston Convention & Visitors Council, 1006 Main—(713) 224-5201—has maps, literature, and up-to-the-minute restoration news. The oldest residential section known as the Old Sixth Ward has become a historic district and will be preserved and restored. It is on the N edge of town between Glenwood Cemetery and Houston Ave., Washington Ave., and Memorial Drive, with some houses dating to the 1880s when the railroad developers and the mayor lived here. It should be an interesting area to watch in transition. Many small Victorian cottages were homes of German settlers. In the 1920s through World War II a Jewish colony lived here; later the neighborhood was predominantly Mexican-American, Vietnamese, and home of other ethnic groups.

Chamber of Commerce, 914 Main, has brochures and maps, also.

The **Harris County Heritage Society,** 1100 Bagby, in Sam Houston Park, offers tours of its unusual, privately endowed indoor-outdoor museum in the very heart of town. At present there are seven major buildings and several other structures in the complex. All except the **Kellum-Noble House,** which is on its original site, have been moved here and carefully restored, with heirloom antiques among the well-chosen furnishings. The **Long Row,** a reconstruction of Houston's first shops, now houses a General Store and a replica of Sam Houston's first library, a barbershop, and dressing room. The elegant **Nichols-Rice-Cherry House,** built ca. 1850 by E. B. Nichols, from Cooperstown, New York, later was owned by Nichols's partner, W. M. Rice, founder of Rice University, who lived here until his wife's death then never reentered the house; it was sold for $25 in 1897 to Mrs. E. R. Cherry, who liked the front door. Kellum-Noble House, built by N. K. Kellum, who owned a brickyard, sawmill, lime plant, tannery, and iron foundry, was later the home of the enterprising Zerviah Metcalf Robinson Kelly Noble, who ran one of Houston's first private schools here.

The **San Felipe Cottage,** formerly on the old San Felipe Rd., has been restored to the 1870s period. German immigrants, William and Justine Ruppersburg, built the home in 1868.

St. John Church, built by German farmers in 1891 in NW Harris County, still has the original altar-pulpit and cypress plank pews used by the Evangelical Lutheran congregation.

The **Pillot House,** an 1868 Carpenter Queen Anne cottage, was the home of Eugene Pillot, a Houston landowner. The latticed rear gallery and an inside kitchen believed to have been the first in Houston were restored, but a side porch and bathroom were eliminated because they were not in the original structure.

The **Old Place,** built about 1824, is a cabin from Clear Creek, about 15 miles SE of its present location. The chimney was called "mudcat." Some of the boards covering the cedar frame date to the 1850s, but it is

The House of the Seasons, Jefferson, Texas. (Courtesy Marion County Historical Commission)

likely that moss and bark also were part of the original covering when John R. Williams built his home.

JEFFERSON, Marion County. US 59.

Chamber of Commerce, 108 E. Lafayette—(214) 665-2672—has information on historic sites and the Historical Pilgrimage, first weekend in May.

Jefferson Historic District includes some 56 commercial and residential structures of the onetime steamboat village which was laid out in 1842. Thirteen merit individual listing on the National Register; the Historic American Buildings Survey lists 26 at present. The Texas Medallion has been placed on 47. As if this were not glory enough, the town also claims the first artificial gaslights and gas plant, and the first artificial ice plant, which sold the cold chunks for 10¢ a pound in 1860; also the church bell put up in 1854 (in the Methodist Church) was made from 1,500 Mexican silver dollars. The restored *Excelsior Hotel,* 211 W. Austin, built about 1858, has a museum; the inn has been in continuous operation since its opening. *Jefferson Playhouse,* NW corner of Market and Henderson, built about 1860, has been a Catholic school, a synagogue, more recently a great place to see a melodrama.

Alley-Carlson House, 501 E. Walker St., mid-19th century, has original furnishings. *Beard House,* 212 N. Vale (ca. 1860), was one of few midtown buildings to survive an 1866 fire. *Epperson-McNutt House,* 409 S. Alley, is an elegant Italianate mansion, a style rare in this part of Texas; also known as the *House of the Seasons,* it was the home of B. H. Epperson, lawyer and railroad promoter. *The Magnolias,* 209 E. Broadway, is 1868 Greek Revival, built by Daniel N. Alley, who donated half the land for the city. *Perry House,* Walnut and Clarksville Sts.

(ca. 1858), was the home of Captain William Perry, a maritime officer and owner of the Excelsior Hotel.

Probably the oldest house in town is the *Presbyterian Manse*, Alley and Delta Sts., built in 1853, bought by General James Harrison Rogers in 1856. Museum. *Captain Singleton House*, 204 N. Soda St., is 1870s Greek Revival and was the home of William E. Singleton, who served as sheriff and was also a deputy U.S. marshal, county clerk, and U.S. commissioner.

During the annual pilgrimage many houses are open with southern belles in period dresses as hostesses. *Atalanta*, the Jay Gould private railroad car of the 1890s, is one of the year-round sites in the center of town. The *Jefferson County Historical Society and Museum*, 223 W. Austin, in the onetime U.S. Courthouse and Post Office, built 1888–90, has three floors and a basement of displays. In this historic town where the Big Cypress River flows past the business section, a famous murder trial was held in the 1870s and has not been forgotten. During the pilgrimage, the local 19th-century scandal is reenacted, telling the story of Diamond Bessie (Annie Stone Moore Rothschild), who came to town with her husband Abe, said to be the son of a Cincinnati diamond merchant. Three days after arrival, Bess disappeared; her bullet-ridden body was found in the woods. It took Rothschild seven years and three trials to win an acquittal.

LUBBOCK, Lubbock County. I-27.

Ranching Heritage Center, on campus at Texas Tech University, is a 12-acre site of living history. The outdoor ranching museum has 18 buildings plus windmills, corrals, etc., moved from their original sites and carefully restored and furnished to represent the rancher's life as it was. The Eclipse windmill today pumps well water to a restored meat and milk house. From the 1830s is the one-room pecan and elm cabin, once the headquarters of the Capote Ranch during the Mexican period of Texas history, in the area near San Antonio. The rambling *Barton House* was a rich rancher's home, built about 1909. Among other buildings are a box-and-strip house, which was typical plains style at the turn of the century, a German settler's home from the hill country, blacksmith shop, granary, one-room school, stone bunkhouse, carriage house, and various ranch buildings. The *Visitor Orientation Center* is in the *David M. Devitt and Mallet Ranch Bldg.* There will be more buildings in the expanding project.

ROUND TOP, Fayette County. St. 237.

Henkel Square, Live Oak and First Sts., a restoration area, features the *Edward Henkel House,* NW part of square, built about 1851 by a German settler, now a house museum; *Zapp-Von Rosenberg House,* built on dogtrot plan about 1875, also by a German settler, now a museum.

Carl Wilhelm Rummel House, near NW end of 1st St., built about 1870, also has early furnishings.

Winedale Outdoor Museum, 4 miles E via FM 1457, 2714, is a restored stagecoach stop of the 1830s. There are a number of restored pioneer homes and barns with authentic furnishings; some were moved from original sites.

SAN ANTONIO, Bexar County. I-35.

The Spanish Governor's Palace, opposite Military Plaza, between Dolorosa and W. Commerce, is a single restoration but deserves mention as the only remaining example in Texas of a Spanish colonial dwelling. Built in 1749, when Texas was a wilderness under Spanish control, the historic building is now the property of the city, under the supervision of the San Antonio Conservation Society. Its ten rooms are furnished with priceless antiques and plainer colonial pieces. The walls are about 3 feet thick; the ceiling beams are of hand-hewn timber and many rooms still have native flagstone floors.

The *Alamo,* Alamo Plaza, was established in 1718 by Father Antonio de Oliveras. The present building, begun in 1755, has been restored. It became "The Cradle of Texas Liberty" in 1836 when its outnumbered Texan defenders, facing a trained Mexican army, died to the last man. Museum.

La Villita, Paseo de la Villita in the heart of town, is a re-created and restored adobe village. Casa Villita, an information center for the Conservation Society, hosts an annual fiesta. The building has been restored. *Bolivar Hall,* La Villita, has life-size scenes of old San Antonio and relics, maintained by the Society.

King William Historic District, roughly bounded by Durango, Alamo, and Guenther Sts. and the river, is an area where much restoration is being carried on. In the late 19th century rich Germans built large homes here in a variety of styles. The land was once a mission-owned irrigated farm. Thomas Jefferson Devine and Ernest Altgelt drew up the first plans and laid out streets which still bear the names they chose: Washington, Madison, Beauregard, Sheridan, Johnson, Guenther, and King William. In 1859 Karl Guenther (Americanized to Carl), who'd been successful in milling in the hill country, moved here and built a mill which is still operated by his descendants though it has been greatly expanded. His stone cottage still stands on Guenther St. The *Herman Schuchard House,* 221 E. Guenther, was built about 1892 by Schuchard, a drugstore owner married to Karl's daughter Mathilda. Albert Beckmann was the architect. It was the custom of German families to remain close even after children had married and set up separate homes. So many Germans came to the King William area it was known locally as "Sauerkraut Bend."

Ernest Altgelt House, 226 King William, is limestone ashlar. Altgelt, who developed the fine area which he named for King Wilhelm of Prussia, died before the house was completed in 1878. His home and the *Ball House,* 120 King William, which is stuccoed stone from about 1856, both are listed on the National Register and the Historic American Buildings Survey, as are a number of others in the vicinity. Unfortunately the home of Judge Thomas J. Devine, who helped plan the district and who became a commissioner of the Confederacy, is gone.

In 1870–72 *Anton Fredrich Wulff* built an Italianate home at 107 King William. It was limestone on a plot backing on the river. Wulff, from Hamburg, became San Antonio's first park commissioner. Now headquarters for the Conservation Society. In the 1880s Louis Ogé bought a two-story Greek Revival home at 209 Washington and had it remodeled by Alfred Giles. Ogé, from Alsace, became a Texas Ranger, Indian fighter, and rancher before retiring here.

Giles also designed the *Alex Sartor House,* 217 King William, in 1881. It is Gothic Revival. At 225 King William is the *Robert Hanschke House,* built in 1880 for $1,680 for Hanschke, editor of a German newspaper. The house was altered a number of times but has been restored to its late-19th-century look. The *Alexander Joske House,* 241 King William, was built in 1900 on the site of an earlier building, a cottage which was incorporated into the larger house. Many curbs in the area have an eroded look because they were made of limestone. The Joske curbs are granite.

The *Ike West House,* 422 King William, has a rounded portico that is unusual. It was built about 1888 by Smith M. Ellis. In 1892, Sol West, who was a stockman, paid $8,000 for the place. Ike was his son who inherited the property. It has been restored.

Steves Homestead, Carriage House and River House, 509 King William, built in 1876 for Edward Steves; Alfred Giles, architect. The style is eclectic Gothic Revival in ashlar limestone with a slate-covered mansard roof and iron cresting. Steves owned a large lumberyard and the house has superior millwork. The River House was a natatorium converted into a meeting hall for the San Antonio Conservation Society. Now a house museum, the mansion is open to the public and maintained by the Society.

Edward Steves, Jr., House, 431 King William, is eclectic Gothic Revival and was built in 1884 as a wedding present from Edward Steves, Sr.

Norton House, 401 King William, was begun in 1876—at least the first floor was completed then. Russell Norton, a leading merchant, had bought the property in 1869 for $3,000. In 1882 Edward Polk bought the house; he later added a second floor, three-story tower, and porch. By 1896 Ike T. Pryor, a rancher and cattleman, owned the place. Restored by Walter Nold Mathis in 1967.

"Ladies Boarding School," 419 King William, was built in 1867 with materials which came in an oxcart from Indianola. Mrs. L. N. Edmunds was the Lady who taught school here. Diplomas were given for "literary, classical and scientific knowledge and polite and dignified deportment."

Kalteyer House, 425 King William, was designed by Charles Reilly Gordon, in Romanesque Victorian style in the 1890s, for George Kalteyer. Gordon also drew the plans for the Bexar County Courthouse. A stairwell is three stories with a skylight. A third-floor ballroom and stained-glass windows are part of the luxurious layout. Restored in 1975–76.

Carl Harnisch House, 523 King William, built in the 1880s, is one of the earliest brick houses in town. Designed by Albert F. Beckmann, it has many gables and porches decorated with wooden scrollwork. Harnisch, who owned a fine restaurant, built an ice-cream factory behind his house.

Ed Tewes House, 133 Crofton, was built in 1892. Tewes was a merchant. The date of construction is on the most unusual weathervane.

Hummel House, 309 King William, was designed by Wahrenberger and Beckmann for Charles Hummel, a sporting-goods merchant. There are fireplaces with cast-iron mantels and a fine circular stairway.

The Conservation Society publishes a walking tour of the King William Street area, illustrated, with 26 houses listed.

San Antonio Convention & Visitors Bureau, P.O. Box 2277 (zip 78298), has information on all historic sites and events. Manager Sharon Eason and her friendly staff provide a Texas welcome for one and all.

SAN AUGUSTINE, San Augustine County. US 96 (El Camino Real).

Known as the "Cradle of Texas Liberty," the town has its Main St. following the King's Highway, or Old San Antonio Rd. Founded in 1717, this was the first Anglo settlement in Texas. More than 40 buildings are marked with Texas Medallions, and most of these are open for an annual Tour of Medallion Homes and Places the first weekend each June. Hostesses wearing antebellum hoops and flounces greet visitors at the *Cullen House,* 207 S. Congress, the Greek Revival home built for Ezekiel Cullen, U.S. Congressman and judge in 1839. Now a museum, and headquarters for the

Daughters of the Republic of Texas chapter, which sponsors the tour.

Matthew Cartwright House, 912 E. Main, was built in 1839, Greek Revival, for Cartwright, a leading citizen and landowner. There are a number of outbuildings on the property, including a schoolhouse, office, and wellhouse. The *C. C. Johnson House,* Congress St., was built by Almanzon Houston in 1850.

WACO, McLennan County. I-35.

The *Heritage Society of Waco* has restored and furnished a number of homes; many are open by appointment. The *Brazos River Festival and Pilgrimage,* held annually on the last weekend in April, is supervised by the Society. Tickets are available from P.O. Box 3222, Waco, 76710.

The *Greater Waco Chamber of Commerce,* Civic Center Plaza, Waco, 76703—(817) 752-6551—has tours and also literature and maps. Their *Historic Waco Homes Tour* covers 10 miles and takes one hour; it covers five restored homes, among other sites.

Earle-Napier-Kinnard Museum, 814 S. 4th St. The original part of the house was built in 1858 by John Baylis Earle, who wanted to serve in the Confederate Army but had poor eyesight. Earle made woolen goods for uniforms with machinery that had been smuggled from England by way of Mexico. Captain John Napier, third owner, came to town in 1866, bought the small brick house from Hiram Walker, second owner. Napier made additions. A kitchen was added still later. D. C. Kinnard was Napier's son-in-law, a former chaplain in an Alabama regiment, who became the first pastor of the Cumberland Presbyterian Church. The house has been restored and furnished in the 19th-century period.

Fort House Museum, 503 S. 4th St., built about 1868. Restored and converted to a museum in 1960. Colonel William Aldridge Fort came to Waco before the Civil War. The Junior League bought the building in 1956 and restored the first floor. Cooper Foundation paid for the rest of it.

East Terrace, 100 Mill St., on the Brazos, in Italian villa style, was built about 1872 by John Wesley Mann, whose wife had the remarkable name of Cemira Twaddle. The restoration was given a state award.

Earle-Harrison House, 1901 N. 5th St., is Greek Revival, built in 1858 by Dr. Baylis Wood Earle. It was moved to this site in 1968 and fully restored by the G. H. Pape Foundation. The detached kitchen is a re-created building, now a period museum.

Nell Pape Garden Center, 1705 N. 5th St., was built about 1873 by Sanford Johnson, then sold to P. G. Taylor, who added the two-story north wing. The Waco Council of Garden Clubs received the house by a deed from Mrs. G. H. Pape. A hostess and porter are in residence. There are five giant live oak trees on the grounds. The garden is enclosed.

OKLAHOMA

One man put his stake in the very centre of the lot sites laid out [for the land rush] by the surveyors, and claimed the one hundred and sixty acres around for his homestead holding. They explained to him that he could only have as much land as would make a lot in the town site, and that if he wanted one hundred and sixty acres, must locate it outside of the city limits. He replied that the proclamation said nothing about town sites.

"But, of course," he went on, "if you people want to build a city around my farm, I have no objections. I don't care for city life myself, and I am going to turn this into a vegetable garden. Maybe, though, if you want it very bad, I *might* sell it."

He and the city fought it out for months, and, for all I know, are at it still. At three o'clock, just three hours after the Territory was invaded, the Oklahoma Colony declared the polls open, and voting began for Mayor and City Clerk. About four hundred people voted.

—*The West from a Car-Window,* by Richard Harding Davis, New York, 1892

ANADARKO, Caddo County. US 62.

Indian City—U.S.A., 2½ miles SE of town on St. 8, is an authentic restoration of American Indian dwellings portraying the Plains Tribes cultures from the western part of the state. The seven ancient villages were planned and built under the supervision of the Department of Anthropology at the University of Oklahoma. An *American Indian Exposition* is held annually in mid-August, with a pageant, ceremonial dances, and other attractions. The *Craft Shop* is run by the Indian Arts and Crafts Board. Tours with Indian guides available. In summer months the Indian City dancers perform for the tours.

The villages occupy a hilltop on 160 acres. The houses are individually furnished as well as styled to typify various tribes. Pawnee mud lodges were mound-shaped. The Wichitas had grass-thatched beehive dwellings. The wickiups were the movable "motels" of the Chiricahua Apaches. The Navahos had hogans somewhat like the early settlers' cabins. The Kiowas preferred tepees. All types are here, along with many rare artifacts. There is even a burial platform. Plains Indians wrapped their dead in buffalo robes and placed them on wooden platforms— a way that most claustrophobes would prefer to go.

The site of Indian City is located on a bloody spot where the Tonkawas were massacred by a band of Shawnees and Delawares, October 24, 1862. Thomas C. Battey, a Quaker who went to the Indian territory to teach the Caddo Indians and later went to live with the Kiowas until his health failed, reported that the "Tonqueways" were a tribe from

291

Texas who were said to be cannibals and had eaten a couple of Shawnees in this neighborhood. The Shawnees, with some Creeks and Delawares, pursued the Tonkawas and surprised them in camp, killing more than half of them. Battey's version was something he heard six years after the event. But he was not a man given to repeating what might sound like a tall tale unless he had reason to believe it was true. On the other hand, Bill Burchardt, editor of *Oklahoma Today,* and a longtime western historian, says that the Tonkawas were camped in the draw just below the hill, where these days the Kiowa Veterans "Tonkongo" Ceremony is held each autumn: "Knowing that a powerful alliance of Delawares and Shawnees were after them, the Tonkawas had set out for Fort Arbuckle, seeking the protection of the fort. There was an excellent, year-around spring there in those early days.

"I know Battey's story about the Tonkawas being cannibals. He had the story from the Delawares and Shawnees who had committed the massacre, and I think they made it up to try to justify themselves. They killed 167 Tonkawa men, women, and children in that slaughter.

"There are almost no Tonkawa people left. A very few still live around Tonkawa, Oklahoma, and the old men tell me that their people were never cannibalistic. I believe them."

Note: Also in the Anadarko area are the *Southern Plains Indian Museum,* US 62E, and the *National Hall of Fame for American Indians,* US 62E, an outdoor museum.

CACHE, Comanche County. US 62.
Eagle Park, Cache exit off US 62, is an assembled town with 19 buildings more or less historical. *"Star House,"* once the home of Quanah Parker, was built in the 1890s and has been restored. Quanah was the son of Cynthia Ann Parker, who was captured by Comanches as a child and became the wife of Peta Nokoni, a Quahada Comanche chief. Parker led his people in a luckless stand against the whites. When the Comanches were given land allotments in 1892, he selected 160 acres S of Eagle Mountain to build this house. It was moved from its original site in 1958.

Also here are an 1886 Indian Trading Post, a 1902 Frisco depot, an old newspaper office, and a home that belonged to Frank James.

GRAND LAKE, Ottawa County. S of Miami on US 59.
Har-Ber Village, Lake Rd. 1, 3½ miles W of Grove. A reconstructed pioneer village with the usual general store, barbershop, doctor's office, dentist's office, school, etc. It has some unusual features, not the least of which is the announcement about the conditions of admission: "Admission is free and you are welcome as long as you conduct yourselves as ladies and gentlemen. Please stay on sidewalks. Follow arrows." A self-guided tour brochure is available. The first attraction is the *"Mayor's Home,"* a two-story house moved from Arkansas and rebuilt here. Indeed much of the village seems to have been imported from nearby Arkansas: print shop items are from Winslow, the gallows are a replica of the Fort Smith structure, Judge Parker's picture hangs in the courthouse, and some of the lumber of this building is from a Springdale barn. The post office fixtures are from Huntsville, the foot-operated treadle drill in the dentist's office is from Prairie Grove, the soda fountain and prescription case in the drugstore once saw service in Pettigrew; the bank clock, the church windows, the log cabin, the No. 1 hat and dress shop stock, the one-room school, the doctor's office furnishings, and even the lawyer's shingle all came from the neighboring state. The taped

music at the Stagecoach Inn is by Morris Clarkson, Springdale, Arkansas. By the time the visitor is beginning to wonder if he has accidentally wandered over the state line, he may notice that Har-Ber Village on the Grand Lake of the Cherokees is sponsored by the Jones Truck Lines—of Springdale, Arkansas.

TAHLEQUAH, Cherokee County. US 62, St. 82.

Tsa-La-Gi, 2½ miles SE of town on US 62, St. 10 and 82, then 1 mile E. An authentic replica of an early Cherokee village affords a view of Cherokee life in the 1700s. Indians at work on crafts or playing ancient games speak only their own language as Cherokee guides lead visitors through the village. In an amphitheater adjacent to the village, a drama, *Trail of Tears,* reenacts the tragedy of the forced march during the winter of 1838–39 from Georgia and Tennessee to this area, and depicts Cherokee history to 1907. The musical, written by Kermit Hunter, is performed by a professional cast, nightly except Sunday, from late June through August.

Also in Tahlequah is the old *Cherokee Capitol Building* from 1867 (NHL). It is brick, in Victorian style, on Muskogee Ave. The *Supreme Court Building,* built in 1844, and the *Cherokee National Prison,* built in 1874, are on Water St. The *Cherokee Female Seminary,* 1889, is now part of Northeastern State College. The *Murrell H ne,* 4 miles S of town on St. 82, then 1 mile E at Park Hill, is a restored house with many original antebellum furnishings, built about 1845. George Murrell, a Virginian, followed the Trail of Tears with the Cherokee Indians. The house was robbed during the Civil War, but was the only one in the community which was not destroyed (NHL).

Southwest States

Colorado
Utah
New Mexico
Arizona

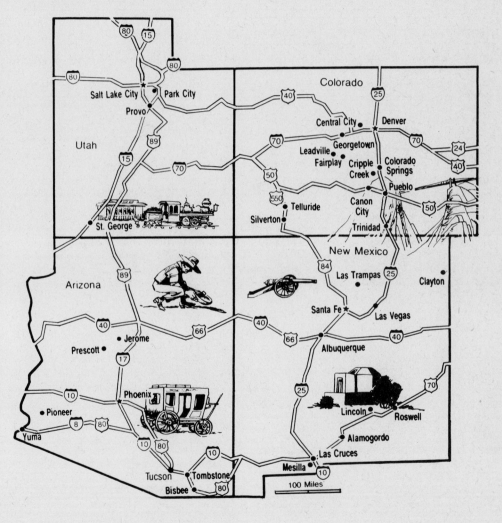

COLORADO

Passing many rude shanties for the sale of whisky and tobacco, along the well-trodden road, soon after noon we galloped into Denver.... Frame and brick edifices were displacing mud-roofed log-cabins. Two theaters were in full blast; and at first glance I could recognize only two buildings. When I left there was no uncoined gold in circulation; now it was the only currency.... Upon every counter stood little scales, and whenever one made a purchase, whether to the amount of ten cents or a thousand dollars, he produced a buck-skin pouch of gold dust and poured out the amount for weighing.
—*Beyond the Mississippi,* by Albert D. Richardson, Hartford, Conn., 1867

OURAY, The Gem of the Rockies.... This is one of the most beautifully situated towns to be found anywhere. Its scenery is idylic....
The town has one hotel of great magnificence worthy of a city ten times its population, besides a good supply of other hostelries of a less splendid character.... The mountain sheep and wapiti have not yet been killed off; deer and trout are abundant. The rides up the roads and trails to neighboring mines and mining camps, through valley and canon, and over mountain and mesa, are not soon exhausted....
—*Over the Range,* by Stanley Wood, Chicago, 1896

CANON CITY, Fremont County. US 50.
Buckskin Joe, 9 miles W on US 50, in Royal Gorge Park. A town made up of log buildings "sought out from remote mountain slopes." To quote the brochure handed visitors to the historic boom town and movie location: "Each authentic structure was selected to match a real building that stood in the original boom town of Buckskin Joe. The town you see was based on an old daguerreotype and the memories of old timers, given new life by Malcolm F. Brown, famed MGM art director."
When the project began, only the Tabor building was standing. Now many log structures will look familiar

to moviegoers. John Wayne used the background for *The Cowboys;* Lee Marvin for *Cat Ballou.* Open mid-April to mid-October.
Canon City Municipal Museum, 6th and Royal Gorge Blvd., has Indian and pioneer artifacts. The *Rudd Cabin* is behind the museum. It was built in 1860; many original furnishings.
Robinson Mansion, S. 1st St. and Riverside Drive (1884), is furnished with antiques and open to the public.

CENTRAL CITY, Gilpin County. St. 119.
Central City Historic District, late-19th-, early-20th-century mining town, with commercial, residential,

public, and some religious structures, almost all erected after a fire in 1874. NHL.

Central City Opera House, Eureka St., 1878, is two stories, rock-faced brick and stone. Eclectic. Altered by repairs and renovations and a wing added, but still the oldest opera house in Colorado.

Central Gold Mine and Museum, 126 Spring St., has relics from the glory days when this area was known as the richest square mile on earth after John Gregory struck it big in 1859 and others arrived quickly to stake their claims. More than $75 million in minerals were produced.

Colorado Central Narrow Gauge Railway, 200 Spring St., above municipal parking lots, re-creates the original 1800s railway and offers a 20-minute ride above the town, pointing out historic landmarks, from June through August.

Teller House, Eureka St., built in 1872, has been restored. Henry M. Teller, U.S. Senator and Secretary of the Interior, and his brother Willard owned this Victorian establishment where the wealthy came. This is the long-famous hotel with the bar where "The Face on the Barroom Floor" was inspired, if that's the word. There were 17 lugubrious verses by H. Antoine D'Arcy, whose name sounds like something he might have written. A painted face is preserved by a brass rail in the barroom. Henry Teller, however, ordered only the genuine best for the establishment: rosewood and walnut furnishings were hauled by oxcart, burro, and narrow-gauge railway to this mountain town after they arrived in Denver. The bedroom where Ulysses Grant stayed in 1873 has been handsomely furnished.

St. James Methodist Church, on Eureka St., organized in July 1859, is said to be the oldest Protestant church in Colorado.

Gilpin County Historical Museum, next to St. Paul's on E. High (Sec-

Mine workings at Cripple Creek, Colorado. (Courtesy Two Mile High Club)

ond) St., is open from Memorial Day through Labor Day. Displays show the old days from 1859, with artifacts and equipment from the mines.

Nevadaville, 2 miles NW of town, once had 13 saloons. Now a ghost town with city hall, fire station, Masonic lodge, and other relics.

CRIPPLE CREEK, Teller County. St. 67.

Cripple Creek Historic District takes in the 1891 boom town, which has only a few of the early buildings remaining: the depot, Imperial Hotel, and jail. William Womack was a homesteader here in 1876 but did not find gold. When the Bennett and Myers Co. bought his land in 1891, they plotted 80 acres, planning to build a town called Fremont. According to legend, one of the company employees was chasing a cow when it fell, tripped the horse and rider, with the two animals and the cowboy all suffering broken bones. Thus Cripple Creek. Gold strikes were made the next spring.

The *Old Homestead Parlour House,* open in summer, is said to have been a pleasure house in the old days. The *District Museum,* E end of Bennett Ave., is housed in a onetime depot. The *Cripple Creek & Victor Narrow Gauge Railroad,* ticket station N of the museum, has been restored. A 4-mile trip is available June to October. The *Mollie Kathleen Gold Mine,* near the top of Tenderfoot Hill, has tours. Melodrama is performed twice daily except Monday in the Gold Bar Room Theatre of the *Imperial Hotel.*

DENVER, Denver County. I-70.

Auraria 9th St. Historic District is a residential area being restored with a park as part of the complex. Brick and frame Victorian structures here were put up in the last part of the 19th century and include Stick style, Italianate, Second Empire, and Victorian.

Larimer Square, 1400 block of Larimer St., is a district of two half-blocks which have been restored, with some modern structures designed to fit the scene. A number of buildings have cast-iron frames and trimmings. The *Gallup-Stanbury Bldg.,* erected in 1873, has High Victorian Italianate elements. The *Clayton Bldg.,* 1882, is eclectic; *Lincoln Hall,* from the 1880s, is Second Empire. The city was founded on this site in the mid-19th century by General William E. Larimer, who put up a cabin at 15th and Larimer. Then came commerce and politics and handsome structures to house the busy men of the era. Here were the first bank, theater, library, post office, and dry goods store. Gaslights, courtyards, shade trees, and London-like buses are part of the renewed scene.

The success of the project begun in 1964 led to the preservation of other Denver landmarks. The *Hospitality Center,* 225 W. Colfax, has information on the many historic sites of the city, maps, brochures. Operated by the *Colorado Visitors Bureau.* Free. *Denver Walking Tours,* from Hampshire House Hotel, 1000 Grant St., offers a two-hour guided tour of the Victorian residential area with talks on the architecture and history.

Heritage Square, just S of US 6 on US 40, in Golden, is a re-creation of an 1880 town. Shops have goods made on the premises. *Heritage Square Opera House* has old-time entertainment year round.

The *Molly Brown House,* 1340 Pennsylvania St., has daily tours. Owned by the *Historic Denver* nonprofit organization, it has been restored and furnished in the 1900s style. Some original items have been found elsewhere and returned. Guides are dressed in the style of the era. Margaret Tobin (Molly) Brown, born in Hannibal, Missouri, in 1867, became rich in Denver, survived the *Titanic* and lived until 1932. *Colorado Governor's Mansion,* 400 E. 8th Ave., is Greek Revival, built in 1908, with an elegant 6-foot iron fence enclosing the grounds. Guided tours on Tuesdays from May to October; free. There are more than two dozen individual listings on the National Register in addition to the above. The *Pioneer Museum,* 911 10th St., has many early items and is open Monday through Friday; free.

FAIRPLAY, Park County. US 285, St. 9.

South Park City Museum, off St. 9. There are 25 authentic buildings and some 40,000 artifacts making up a typical Colorado mining town of the late 19th century. Most of these were moved from other sites, but local boosters say some are on their original sites and in their original condition. A well-done re-creation, in any case. Open mid-May to Memorial Day.

GEORGETOWN, Clear Creek County. I-70.

Georgetown–Silver Plume Historic District comprises parts of two early mining towns of the mid-19th to early 20th century and their vicinity, which grew from the discovery of gold in 1864 until the 1890s. Museums. NHL.

The State Historical Society is developing a complex known as the *Georgetown Loop Railroad and Mining Area* which will feature mines and crushing mills with a historic steam locomotive, already in operation, over a portion of the original loop with Silver Plume. The train now leaves hourly from the Silver Plume Depot, off I-70, built in 1884, from June through August.

Hamill House, Argentine and 3rd Sts., built about 1867 by Joseph Watson, a miner, later expanded by William A. Hamill, Watson's brother-in-law. Museum. The original building was a simple frame; now a Gothic Revival mansion. The Georgetown Historical Society is restoring the building to the look of 1879–85. Hamill, an English mining engineer, spent 13 years and $50,000, in a time when money was money, building the luxurious home.

Hotel de Paris, 409 6th St. Louis DuPuy, a Frenchman, operated the hotel from 1875 to 1900. The building and its furnishings are just as they were—Georgetown was nearly the only mining town never devastated by fire; many luxuries of the Victorian era are on display.

Bowman-White House, 901 Rose St., built in 1893, Victorian Italianate in style, has many original furnishings. Open May to Labor Day.

Grace Episcopal Church, Taos St. between 4th and 5th, dates from 1869–70, refurbished in 1964. The first Episcopal congregation in the territory; the oldest Episcopal church used in the state.

McClellan House, 919 Taos St., built about 1865, by Erskine McClellan, a miner and the owner of a woodworking shop. Eclectic, with some alterations.

Alpine Hose Company No. 2, 507 5th St., was built in 1874, with a bell tower added in 1880. One of four volunteer fire companies in the town. Museum.

Toll House, S side of town adjacent to I-70, is a late-19th-century brick two-story building, with Gothic Revival elements. It was erected near the tollgate of a private road linking Georgetown and Silver Plume with the mines and was owned by Julius G. Poble, superintendent of the Lebanon Mining Company. Museum.

Among other historic structures in town are the old *Missouri Fire House,* the *Star Hook and Ladder Fire House,* the *County Court House,* and the *County Jail.*

LEADVILLE, Lake County. US 24.

Leadville Historic District comprises the late-19th-century mining town with hotel, opera house, bar, church, and homesteads. NHL.

Dexter Cabin, 912 Harrison Ave., built of logs in 1879. This was one of five hunting lodges for James V. Dexter, banker and mining tycoon. The outside fits the onetime boom town, but the inside has furnishings that would not look out of place in Paris, including a crystal chandelier, a Persian rug, etc.

Healy House, at the same location, was built in 1878, also has elaborate interiors with red velvet upholstery, diamond dust mirrors, Victorian settees. The frame building has been restored since it was erected for August R. Meyer, mining engineer. Both house and cabin are maintained by the State Historical Society and are open daily mid-May to October; free.

House with the Eye, 127 W. 4th St. The eye is stained glass. The house is a museum of mining artifacts with 1890 furnishings; a carriage house with early vehicles is also on display. Open daily June to Labor Day.

Tabor Home, 116 E. 5th St., was the 1877 dwelling place for H. A. W. Tabor and his dour wife Augusta. It was moved to this location in 1879 to make room for the *Tabor Opera House.* The house is furnished in period style and open daily.

The *Matchless Mine,* 2 miles E on E. 7th St., was the famous property the dying Tabor told his second wife, Baby Doe, never to give up. In movies, fiction, the *Police Gazette,* and probably in life, the once wealthy and colorful mining magnate said, "Hang on to the Matchless." And Baby Doe held. Augusta, the first wife, meanwhile held on to her savings. Baby Doe Tabor, the onetime beauty who had been married in an expensive ceremony, with President Chester A. Arthur as one of the guests, was found frozen to death in a cabin near the mine where she had struggled to survive for 36 years. The Tabors, all three, are among the most interesting persons of the great mining days in American history. The true history of their lives is dramatic enough without any embellishment by fiction or screen writers. Cabin restored to Baby Doe's era. Open daily, Memorial Day to Labor Day.

Tabor Opera House, 4th St. and US 24, was built and beautifully furnished in 1879. Restored; guided tours daily, Memorial Day to September 9.

The *Chamber of Commerce,* at 9th and Harrison Ave., has maps and brochures on the vivid history of the area. Among the tours suggested is one which follows the "Route of the Silver Kings." Fifteen miles of roadways extend E from Harrison Ave., which is US 24. California, Georgia, and Evans gulches held the mines of the "Silver Kings."

Heritage Museum and Gallery, 9th

and Harrison, has a diorama of the town and its 112 years of mining. Open Memorial Day to Labor Day.

SILVERTON, San Juan County. US 550.

Silverton Historic District covers the silver-mining town of the late 19th century with several early buildings and some operable mines. The *Imperial Hotel* of 1882, the *Congregational Church,* 1881, and the *Courthouse* and *City Hall* built in the early 1900s are within the district. NHL.

Blair St., where hitching posts and kerosene lamps remain, was filled with saloons, dance halls, pleasure houses, and general mischief to such an extent that Bat Masterson was hired to take charge and quiet the rowdies. Half a billion in precious metals were mined since 1880. About $6 million is still mined yearly by a metals corporation.

The *Durango-Silverton Narrow Gauge Train* runs 44 miles between the two towns. The line has been in use since 1882. The ride starts at the *Rio Grande Depot,* 479 Main Ave., in Durango, US 550. Passengers may take a round trip or take the three-hour ride to Silverton and return by motorcoach over US 550, the Million Dollar Highway, during summer season. The route rises from 6,620 to 9,288 feet through the San Juan National Forest and the Animas Valley, so it's little wonder that reservation should be made at least one month in advance: Agent, Rio Grande Depot, Durango, 81301.

TELLURIDE, San Miguel County. St. 145.

Telluride Historic District comprises the late-19th-century mining area, with several original structures: *City Hall, Sheridan Hotel, Miner's Union hall,* and the *opera house.* The settlement began with gold claims in 1875, give or take a year, and became a lively gold camp after the narrow-gauge railroad came this way in 1890. *Chamber of Commerce* has information and maps. Write Telluride, 81435, or phone (303) 728-3614.

The original curtains still hang in the *Sheridan Opera House,* built about 1891, but Sarah Bernhardt and Lillian Russell, who appeared here, are long gone. And so are the nameless girls who worked in the 26 saloons, 12 dance halls, or the cribs, some of which still stand in the Pacific Ave. area, known as Pop Corn Alley. Butch Cassidy is said to have robbed the bank in 1889, making an unexpected $30,000 withdrawal.

The *San Miguel County Historical Museum,* 317 N. First St., is two-story stone, with excellent mining artifacts.

TRINIDAD, Las Animas County. I-25.

The Raton Pass, 15 miles S, was used in the 18th century by Spanish explorers and patrols. It is 7,834 feet high. Trinidad is only 6,025. And Telluride, where Butch Cassidy began his bank-robbing career, is 8,745. Maybe $30,000 is all the cash you can carry at that altitude.

Bloom Mansion and *Old Baca House* are registered historic places, owned by the state and maintained by the State Historical Society. The Victorian home at Walnut and Main and the adobe at 1st and Walnut are open in summer and are furnished in period. Frank G. Bloom, born in Pennsylvania, became a Colorado banker, merchant, and cattleman. Don Felipe Baca, whose home was of mud bricks dried in the sun, was a successful Spanish-American rancher and freighter of the 1860s. There is a Pioneer Museum in the onetime bunkhouse behind the main house, which was occupied by Baca family members until the 1920s. The courtyard has a collection of early vehicles. The first traders in the West passed this way, which was the mountain branch of the Santa Fe Trail. An equestrian statue of Kit Carson stands in Trinidad City Park.

Corazon de Trinidad, roughly bounded by Walnut, 1st, and Animas Sts. and the Purgatoire River, contains many historical structures from 1869–1920, including the 1880 *Columbian Hotel,* which is High Victorian Italianate, and the 1885 *Sherman Bldg.,* with cast-iron pilasters. The area belonged to Mexico until 1848. The town, established in 1861, had a population explosion in the 1880s when the cattle industry was at a peak. *Jaffa Opera House,* 100–116 Main, was built in the boom days of the 1880s and has been restored.

UTAH

This pretty little city [Provo] belongs to the best type of Mormon towns, and a description of it will serve to give the reader a good idea of the characteristics of all the towns built by the Mormons. The dwellings, as a rule, are comfortable, but not imposing in appearance. Many of them are constructed of *adobe* or sun-dried bricks, and all are situated in lots of generous proportions and surrounded by ornamental and fruit trees. Water for irrigating purposes flows down each side of the streets, and shade trees in abundance and of luxuriant growth render the walks cool and inviting. Gardens filled with fruits, flowers and vegetables are the rule, and a quiet, peaceful, industrious semi-rural life is the good fortune of the residents here.
　　—*Over the Range to the Golden Gate,* by Stanley Wood, Chicago, 1896

Brigham Young is 62 years old, of medium height, and with sandy hair and whiskers. An active, iron man, with a clear sharp eye. . . . The gateway of his block is surmounted by a brass American eagle, and they say ("they say" here means anti-Mormons) that he receives his spiritual dispatches through this piece of patriotic poultry. They also say that he receives revelations from a stuffed white calf that is trimmed with red ribbons and kept in an iron box. I don't suppose these things are true. Rumor says that when the Lion House was ready to be shingled, Brigham received a message from the Lord stating that the carpenters must all take hold and shingle it and not charge a red cent for their services. Such carpenters as refused to shingle would go to hell, and no postponement on account of the weather.
　　—*Artemus Ward; His Travels,* by Charles F. Browne, New York, 1865

PARK CITY, Summit County. St. 248.

The onetime mining boom town, which had a population rush when silver, lead, and gold deposits were found toward the end of the 1860s, became a ghost town after the silver crash of 1893. Lately it has been refurbished with shops and "saloons," a *Silver Wheel Theatre,* on Main St., presenting melodramas and other entertainment. The area is thriving as a ski center, and possibly will again equal the heydays when its mines produced more than $250 million in gold, silver, lead, copper, and zinc and no one cared about "powder" or even whether it snowed at all.

Two structures on the Historic American Buildings Survey are the *St. Mary Assumption Church and School,* Park Ave. at Main St. Both are limestone, built in 1883, showing the church and education relationship in the Utah of the 1880s. The church, damaged by fire in 1950, has been repaired.

302

PROVO, Utah County. US 89, 91.

Turbine House, 1620 N., 200 West Sts., was built about 1898 and is recorded in HABS.

Pioneer Museum and Village, 500 N., 500 West Sts., on US 89, 91, has an outstanding collection of pioneer artifacts and is open from June to September 15. Free.

ST. GEORGE, Washington County. US 91.

Chamber of Commerce, in the courthouse at 100 North and 100 East Sts., has brochures on this historic area known as Utah's Dixie, for its balmy winter climate. The yellow brick two-story building, with hipped roof which has a square railing around an octagonal cupola, was constructed in 1867–74. The *Daughters of Utah Pioneers Museum,* 145 N. 100 East, has historical displays open daily except Sundays, June through August, and in winter months by appointment. *Jacob Hamblin Home,* 3 miles W off I-15 in Santa Clara, is an 1862 native sandstone home with period furnishings. It has been restored, and guides are in attendance. Hamblin was a Mormon missionary. Open daily except Thanksgiving and Christmas. Free.

St. George Temple (Church of Jesus Christ of Latter-day Saints) occupies a block bounded by 2nd East, 3rd West, 4th South, and 5th South Sts. It is stuccoed stone with corner turrets and a square entrance tower with an octagonal cupola, built in 1871–77, on a site picked out by Brigham Young, and is the first Mormon temple erected in Utah.

Brigham Young Winter Home, 9 W. 2nd North, is the pleasant dwelling used by the Mormon leader in winter from 1873 until his death in 1877. A front wing was added in 1874. Restored; open six days a week with guides in attendance.

St. George Tabernacle, Main St. at Tabernacle, is red sandstone with a wooden spire, built in 1863–76. Miles Romney, the architect, was also architect for the Young Winter Home. The Historical American Building surveyors took particular interest in the front of the structure, which has tiered platforms filling in a false door which has heavily carved outer architrave topped by vase motifs. The elaborate ceiling ornament also represents an unusual accomplishment under primitive conditions. A *Visitor's Center,* at the east gates, provides guided tours.

SALT LAKE CITY, Salt Lake County. US 40, 89.

Utah Pioneer Village, 2998 S. Connor St., is a collection of some 37 buildings, furnished and restored to their 19th-century look. The earliest structures are from the 1840s. Among exhibits are a meeting house, general store, barbershop, Pony Express station, and depot.

Trolley Square, 5th and 6th South and 6th and 7th East Sts., is a 10-acre complex of shops and entertainment in 1908 trolley barns renovated for today's customers, with an old trolley to clang a welcome.

Temple Square, bounded by North, South, and West Temple and Main St., has a *Visitor Center* at South Temple and Main, with guided tours every half hour, literature, exhibits; open daily and free. Tour takes in the 1867 *Tabernacle,* an *Assembly Hall* of 1882, and the *Old Log House* of 1847, one of the first homes built by a settler, though this is not open to the public, for preservation purposes.

Lion House (1856) and *Beehive House* (1854), 67 E. South Temple at State St., were family residences and were also used by Young for offices and social activities. Beehive House, the first governor's mansion, has been restored. Guided tours.

Daughters of Utah Pioneers Museum, on Capitol Hill, is a replica of the old Salt Lake Theatre and is packed with pioneer relics. Open daily except Sunday; also open Sunday afternoons in summer.

Utah State Historical Society, 603 E. South Temple, is housed in a mansion once the home of the Kearns family, who made millions in mining. Museum. Open daily except Sundays and major holidays. Self-guiding tour.

NEW MEXICO

We are standing, Alex Atcitty and I, on the slope under that great rampart of red rock which runs like a Chinese Wall along the south end of Navajo country. To the east, Mount Taylor rises snowcapped and serene above the blunt shape of Little Haystack Mountain. To the left, eroded sandstone, broken slate, and a half-dead pinon whose branches collect tumbleweeds from the gusty wind. It is November of a year of almost unbroken drought. The air smells of autumn, pine resin, dust, and empty places. The only living things in sight are a sparrow hawk and a disconsolate Hereford. The hawk is scouting the rim of the red mesa for incautious rodents. The cow, resting from its search for something to eat, is staring moodily in the direction of Gallup.

"You know," Atcitty says, "they gave us our choice. A bunch of rich Arkansas River bottomland over in Oklahoma or this." He waves his arm, including erosion, dead brush, cow, and an infinity of gaudy sunset sky in the gestures, and grins at me. "When you understand why we picked this rock pile instead of that thousand-dollar-an-acre cotton land, then you understand Navajos."

—*The Great Taos Bank Robbery; and Other Indian Country Affairs,*
by Tony Hillerman, Albuquerque, 1973

There is some mixture of stone in the structure of the houses; that material being here very convenient and suitable; but the village, with its small fields, scarcely fenced, differed little from those of our Pawnees in appearance; these dwellings are smaller and square instead of round; fine mountain streams are near, and are conducted—as usual—by the main canal of irrigation, through the place.

While my horses were fed, we sat down to a dinner; it was composed of a plate, for each, of poached eggs, and wheaten tortillas; seeing some cheese on a small pine table, I asked for a knife to cut it;—the old man went to a hair trunk, and produced a very common pocket knife. The room had a smooth earthen floor; it was partly covered by a kind of carpeting of primitive manufacture, in white and black—or natural coloring of the wool;—it is called Jerga; around the room, mattresses, doubled pillows, and coverlids, composed a kind of divan; the walls were whitewashed with gypsum,—which rubbing off easily, a breadth of calico was attached to the walls above the divan; there was a doll-like image of the Virgin, and two very rude paintings on boards and some small mirrors; the low room was ceiled with puncheons, supporting earth;—there were several rough board chairs.

—*The Conquest of New Mexico and California,* by P. St. Geo. Cooke,
New York, 1878

ALBUQUERQUE, Bernalillo County. I-40.

Old Town Plaza, 1 block N of Central Ave. at Rio Grande Blvd. *San Felipe de Neri Church,* on the plaza, has been here since 1706. A New York journalist, James Florant Meline, took a long trip on horseback in 1866, and in July reached Albuquerque, but saw it with a dusty eye at best:

"This will never do! Thermometer 70° at six A.M.; 83° in the shade, and 125° in the sun at two P.M. . . . Ungrateful wretch that I am, too. I never once gave thanks, nor even remarked that we had no flies at Santa Fe until they began to torment us here. . . .

"Albuquerque is an uninteresting village of some 1000 inhabitants. A few nice adobe dwellings, and the old church in the Plaza with its modern facade, form the sum total of its architectural interest. This church—above other Mexican churches—is quite aristocratic in having a board floor. Some half-dozen long kneeling benches used for pews at the upper end, show the extent of American innovation. I entered in expectation of hearing a Spanish sermon. The Padre, however, after reading the gospel of the day in Spanish, and making a few remarks upon it, announced there would be no sermon, *'En consideracion del mucho calor.'* "

Today nearly a hundred quaint shops line the plaza and the gaslit streets of Old Town. The bandstand also reflects the Mexican days of the settlement, but four flags flew over Old Town—the Spanish, Mexican, Confederate, and American. The settlement of 1706 was named for the Duke of Albuquerque, viceroy of New Spain. When the railroad came in 1880 the new town developed on the other side of the tracks. Lacy wrought-iron benches, the wrought-iron gazebo bandstand from Mexico, and old trees add to the charm of the

plaza. Within the church a spiral staircase winds around the trunk of a spruce tree. Mass has been held daily since 1706.

Also on the National Register in addition to San Felipe are the *Salvador Armijo House,* 618 Rio Grande Blvd., the *Charles Ilfeld Company Warehouse,* 200 1st St. Northwest, and the *First Methodist Episcopal Church,* 3rd and Lead Ave. When Meline visited in July 1866 he went to a party: "At twelve last night I tore myself away from the gayety of the *baile* given at the handsome residence of Señor Salvador Armijo. . . ."

CLAYTON, Union County. US 56. NE corner of the state.

This was a fairly typical Old West town laid out in the late 19th century as a division point for the Denver, Texas and Fort Worth Railroad. North and west of town *Rabbit Ears (Clayton Complex)* is a National Historic Landmark, on the Cimarron Cutoff of the Santa Fe Trail. The land rises in twin peaks resembling rabbit ears. Because of many springs in the area there were a number of camps when the trail was heavily used.

The historic old *Eklund Hotel* on Main St. has been restored. There are a carriage entrance on the side, and a typical Old West street-overhang on the front. Period antiques furnish the lobby. The ladies' room has a double marble sink and a green velvet "fainting couch." A divider and cabinet in the restaurant came from a Clayton saloon. In the Eklund saloon a fireplace is made of red volcanic rock from Capulin Mountain National Monument. The granddaughter of the sheriff who presided at one of Clayton's biggest events sometimes tends bar here. The happening was the hanging of "Black Jack" Ketchum, who now is buried in Clayton's cemetery. Tom Ketchum (Black Jack) was part of the Hole-in-

The Eklund Hotel, Clayton, New Mexico. (Drawing courtesy Eklund Hotel)

the-Wall Gang and with his brother Sam was a train, bank, and general store robber and cowhand who had gone bad. In July 1899, Black Jack—having had a falling out with his brother—had two other companions when they made a fourth attack on a train in the area of Rabbit Ears. After a chase in which two sheriffs were killed and Ketchum was wounded, Ketchum was arrested, tried, and eventually hanged at Clayton on April 26, 1901. An accident occurred at the hanging because the rope was too long, but the results were the same, although more spectacular than intended—the "most wanted man in the Southwest" was dead. His head had snapped off.

Tony Hillerman, a superb suspense author and tale spinner of southwestern history, in *The Great Taos Bank Robbery,* told of hearing a customer talking to a bartender at Raton: ". . . the fat man was saying, how determined people were, stubborn you might say. Take for example Black Jack Ketchum. Did we know about how Ketchum had found out that climbing the horseshoe curve just southeast of Folsom slowed the Colorado & Southern passenger train down so much that he could step on board right out of his stirrup without even running his horse? That Ketchum now he was one of the most ruthless badmen in the west, but he was also set in his ways, the way people get at Folsom. He robbed exactly that same train at the exact same spot three times running, and the third time, of course, the C&S railroad people had figured out the schedule and put on some guards and they wounded Ketchum and caught him and he was consequently and subsequently hanged over at Clayton with such enthusiasm that his head came off.

"The bartender said he'd heard about that.

"The rest of the gang got away, the fat man said. They drifted over into San Miguel and Santa Fe county and got elected to the legislature."

LAS TRAMPAS, Taos County. St. 76.

Las Trampas Historic District covers the village of Santo Tomas del Rio de Las Trampas, an 18th-century Spanish-American farming community which has preserved its heritage in appearance and culture. The charming town, in the Sangre de Cristo Mountains, was threatened when a modern highway, to cut through the old plaza, was proposed. But preservationists won this battle, and the road passes by.

San Jose de Garcia de Las Trampas, built in 1760–76, is an important example of Spanish Colonial architecture. The bell to the left of the entrance is the one heard by Fray Francisco Dominguez in 1776 when he came to inspect the Spanish borderlands. The same pulpit he saw and described as looking new and badly made is still in use. NHL.

LAS VEGAS, San Miguel County. I-25.

Coronado and his conquistadors were here in 1541, still looking for gold. One soldier was not disappointed in the findings, although many were. Back in Mexico City, he reported: "There we found something we prized more than gold or silver, namely, much maize, beans, and chickens larger than those here of New Spain, and salt better and whiter than I have ever seen in my whole life."

When General Stephen Watts Kearny and his forces arrived, planning to take over the territory for the United States, they thought the settlement looked like brick kilns, but were happy to see irrigation ditches full of muddy water and green fields of corn. (The village described by Cooke in the introduction to this section is Las Vegas.) Kearny made a proclamation from the roof of one of the buildings still standing on the square: he told the Mexicans that their crops would be protected if they remained peaceably at home, and so would their persons and their reli-

gion. It was a popular announcement, and Kearny followed it up by posting sentries to guard the fields, warning his own men with the direst consequences in case of looting. Twenty years later when journalist James Meline came riding along he found everything still peaceful: "Las Vegas (or Begas, as it is pronounced here, the Mexicans not having the fear of the Spanish Academy before their eyes, and calling Vegas, Begas, and Vicente, Bisente), a village of some two thousand souls, is prettily situated on the side of the mountain that rises to the west.

"Here is the distinctly marked termination of the plains, which, as we look north upon them, fall in gentle, green and grassy undulations. . . . Crossing the stony bed of the creek, and passing the alternating fields and adobes, we enter the Plaza. English and Spanish signs intermingled, meet the eye. 'Vienta de las Vegas,' 'Bakery,' 'Effectos,' &c."

The **Old Town Plaza,** laid out in 1835, became an important stop on the Santa Fe Trail. The plaza, bounded by Valencia and Moreno Sts. and roughly by the rear property-line of buildings on Gonzales St. and Hot Springs Blvd., is on the National Register, as are **St. Paul's Memorial Episcopal Church and Guild Hall,** 714–716 National Ave., and **Our Lady of Sorrows Church,** W. National Ave.

The Old Santa Fe Trail ruts can be clearly seen near town.

La Castaneda was once a railroad hotel of red brick, with a tile roof and graceful arched verandas, which flourished when the Santa Fe line replaced the wagon trains. It has been restored, with a plush Victorian interior looking much as it did in 1899 when Teddy Roosevelt and his Rough Riders held their first reunion here after the Cuban war. Their photograph hangs in the refurbished dining room. Twenty men from this community had joined the Rough

Riders. The "reunion" is an annual summer event now.

LINCOLN, Lincoln County. US 380.

Lincoln Historic District includes the whole town. The Murphy-Dolan factions met the Tunstall-McSween forces in a showdown here in 1878 which became known as the Lincoln County War and has been written about and dramatized ever since with many details varying but always with cattle baron John H. Chisum as one of the good guys, and Billy the Kid as one of the losers, although William H. Bonney's fortunes as a romantic character in fiction and film have gone up and down and up again and may never level off to near reality. Even the site of his grave is disputed.

I had no sooner reburied Billy in print, in a previous guidebook, in the cemetery at Fort Sumner than I came across *Pat Garrett: The Biography of a Western Lawman,* by Leon C. Metz, archivist in the University of Texas Library at El Paso, which says:

"Today where muleskinners once cursed and sweated their way across the country, tourists in air-conditioned cars make a quick turn off Highway 60 and drive right up to the grave. Loading their cameras, they snap pictures of the plot and stone, all the while feeling certain that the caliche they stand upon is indeed historic ground. What the tourist sees, of course, is just a concrete tombstone with the names Charles Bowdre, Tom O'Folliard, and Billy the Kid chiseled into it, plus a concrete slab over the graves, all three plots surrounded by a high, heavy wire fence. Underneath that concrete and dirt may lie the remains of a soldier or perhaps some unknown moldering corpse or—perhaps—Billy the Kid. Or there may be nothing. Nobody really knows, and it is not likely that anyone is going to find out."

What happened was partly that no one cared that much about marking the grave, since the Kid's legend had barely got started. The plot was marked only by a small wooden headboard, or cross, which eroded and was eventually swept away in one of the Pecos River floods along with those of soldiers from the fort. When the army removed the bodies to the Santa Fe National Cemetery it's possible Billy went, too.

In any case, the town of Lincoln remains little changed from its famous days. The headquarters of the rivals still are standing. It is a one-street village. The old courthouse, where the Kid was held in 1881 until he escaped, has been restored as a museum of pioneer and Indian history as well as Lincoln County lore. The courthouse, the *Old Tunstall Store,* and other historic buildings are maintained by the Lincoln County Memorial Commission, created in 1949. Descriptive markers tell of the April days in 1881, when good and bad got caught in the crossfire. The *Old Wortley Hotel,* furnished 1880s style, was built in 1872, rebuilt in 1960. This was where Deputy Bob Ollinger was having lunch when Billy the Kid got away. Ollinger ran into the street and was gunned down by the fugitive, who had already killed his jailer. There still are bullet holes in the courthouse to show where the unlucky jailer fell.

MESILLA, Dona Ana County. Off I-10 just SW of Las Cruces.

Mesilla Plaza has a church at one end and adobe buildings on three sides. This was land acquired by the Gadsden Purchase of December 1853. On July 4, 1854, the U.S. flag was raised over the plaza, confirming the treaty. The town became a central point on the Butterfield Overland Mail Route to California. During the Civil War, Mesilla was headquarters for the Confederates, later for the Union. The trial of Billy the Kid was held in an adobe build-

ing at the SE corner of the plaza.
NHL.

Chamber of Commerce, 760 West
Picacho Ave., has tour information
for the old forts and ghost towns of
the area.

SANTA FE, Santa Fe County. US 84, 85.

Santa Fe Plaza is the historic end
of the Santa Fe Trail and a National
Historic Landmark. There were
times when the modern trends en-
croached, but it is now fairly safe
from major change. In the late 1960s
neon signs were removed from storefronts and the Neocolonial portals
were reconstructed to match the Palace of the Governors, which also suffered changes which have been
reversed. In the plaza, a dark gray
obelisk marks the end of the trail. It
wasn't erected until 1910, but it
would have looked at home on any
Civil War battlefield. In the 1830s
Josiah Gregg and some 12 wagoners
had left the main wagon train when
they were past the Colorado River
and ridden ahead to Santa Fe. They
were on hand to witness the arrival of
the caravan. Gregg described the
event in his *Commerce of the Prairies:*
". . . crowds of women and boys
flocked to see the new-comers; while
crowds of *leperos* hung about as usual
to see what they could pilfer. The
wagoners were by no means free from
excitement on this occasion. Informed of the 'ordeal' they had to
pass, they had spent the previous
morning in 'rubbing up;' and now
they were prepared, with clean faces,
sleek combed hair, and their choicest
Sunday suit, to meet the 'fair eyes' of
glistening black that were sure to
stare at them as they passed. There
was yet another preparation to be
made in order to 'show off' to advantage. Each wagoner must tie a bran
new 'cracker' to the lash of his whip;
for, on driving through the streets
and the *plaza publica,* every one strives
to outvie his comrades in the dexter-

ity with which he flourishes this favorite badge of his authority."

The **Palace of Governors (El Pala-
cio Real)** is the oldest public building
in the U.S. It occupies the N side of
the plaza and was built in 1610. It
was erected on a 10-acre tract with a
large courtyard surrounding the
main building. After General Stephen Watts Kearny raised the
American flag for the U.S. and
American governors replaced the
Spanish and Mexican who had gone
before them, the outbuildings which
had fallen into disrepair were torn
down and rebuilt. The east end of the
building, which like the west end had
once contained a massive observation
tower, was reconstructed for the use
of the legislature and a library. The
front portal of peeled logs supporting
a dirt roof was replaced by a balus-
trated Victorian porch in 1878, but
this—fortunately—was removed in
1913 and the original was reproduced. The **Museum of New Mexico** is
here now.

A walking tour of the area should
include the **Fine Arts Museum** on the
NW side of the plaza; although the
building is relatively new, having
opened in 1917, it was erected on the
site of the old Fort Marcy military
headquarters, which had been used
since Spanish days, and is a handsome blend of mission styles.

The **Delgado House,** across from
the Fine Arts building, was built in
1890 of local adobe brick, by Don
Felipe, a leading merchant who was a
grandson of Capitan Manuel Delgado. **Sena Plaza,** one block E of the
place, was the residence of Major
Jose D. Sena, whose 23 children were
born in the 33-room dwelling, now
an office building. **Prince Plaza** was
the home of Governor Bradford
Prince.

St. Francis Cathedral, S of Sena
Plaza, was built under the direction
of Archbishop John Baptist Lamy,
first made famous in Willa Cather's
novel *Death Comes for the Archbishop,*

and more recently the subject of a fine biography, *Lamy of Santa Fe,* by Paul Horgan. The first church was built in 1610; a second one of 1629 was demolished in an Indian uprising in 1680. Rebuilt once more, the church lasted until 1800. Another rebuilding occurred, and in 1869 Lamy began a stone cathedral around the remains of the earlier church, which were removed when the main part of the cathedral was finished.

Loretto Chapel, SW of the cathedral, at 219 Old Santa Fe Trail, was built by the Sisters of Loretto, the first religious group of women to come to the area. "The Miraculous Stairway" is a spiral staircase to the choir loft constructed without visible support and now surrounded by years of legend.

San Miguel Mission, 1½ blocks S from the chapel on the Old Santa Fe Trail, dates from about 1636, is the oldest mission church in the U.S., and has memorabilia on display. NHL. The **Oldest House,** near the mission on De Vargas St., is more than 800 years old with lower walls of "puddled adobe," which is poured mud. The house was part of the Pueblo de Analco. Tree-ring specimens from the ceiling beams indicate they were from the mid-18th century. The **Barrio de Analco Historic District,** De Vargas St. and vicinity, is one of the oldest settled areas in the country. Indians came from Mexico as laborers with the Franciscan missionaries and Spanish leaders who founded the town. "Analco" means "the other side of the water"—the Plaza is across the Santa Fe River. *Santuario de Guadalupe,* 100 Guadalupe St., was renovated in 1976 for the Bicentennial and opened to the public for the first time in years. It is on ground between the old Camino Real, or Chihuahua Trail, and the river. The adobe walls are nearly 3 feet thick. The legions of Americans who have visited the Shrine of Our Lady of Guadalupe in Mexico City will not want to miss the painting of Our Lady which hangs in the sanctuary. Dated 1783, it is signed by Jose de Alzibar, a Mexican colonial artist. For more information, **Chamber of Commerce,** P.O. Box 1928, Santa Fe, 87501—(505) 983-7317— has brochures and maps on this treasured city.

La Cienaga, about 10 miles SW on US 85, is a restored and reconstructed Spanish colonial village of the 18th century. Sponsored by the Colonial New Mexico Historical Foundation, craftsmen come from mountain villages to demonstrate their ancient arts and skills. There are ceremonies and folk dancing. *El Rancho de las Golondrinas,* the village museum, is usually open only once a month. The spring festival takes place late in April. Inquire locally for times.

ARIZONA

Life as we Americans live it was difficult in Ehrenberg.... The Mexicans ... had their fire built between some stones piled up in their yard, a piece of sheet iron laid over the top: this was the cooking-stove. A pot of coffee was made in the morning early, and the family sat on the low porch and drank it, and ate a biscuit. Then a kettle of *frijoles* was put over to boil. These were boiled slowly for some hours, then lard and salt were added, and they simmered down until they were deliciously fit to eat, and had a thick red gravy....

The women ... always wore, when in their *casa*, a low-necked and short-sleeved *camisa*, fitting neatly ... I have always been sorry I did not adopt their house apparel. Instead of that, I yielded to the prejudices ... and sweltered during the day in high-necked and long-sleeved white dresses, kept up the table in American fashion, ate American food in so far as we could get it ... how I wished I had no silver, no table linen, no china, and could revert to the primitive customs of my neighbors!
—*Vanished Arizona*, by Martha Summerhayes, New York, 1908

Prescott, founded in 1864 on Granite Creek, at an altitude of about 5,000 feet, is delightfully situated, and has many fine buildings of wood, brick, and stone. More than others in Arizona, it is described as resembling an eastern town. In 1864–7, Prescott was the temporary seat of government, and since 1877 has been the permanent capital; it has many large mercantile establishments; is well supplied with banks and with public buildings; and has three daily newspapers, including the *Arizona Miner*, the oldest journal of the territory. Its population is about 2,000. Flagstaff, with perhaps 500 inhabitants, is the leading railroad town, and the centre of an active lumbering and mercantile industry....

... [Phoenix] is a thriving town of some 3,000 inhabitants, built largely of adobe, but with many structures of brick and wood, on an open plain formerly classified as desert but now distinguished from Arizona towns for its wealth of shade trees and attractive homes. Excessive heat is the only drawback to comfort in this favored region. The city is reached by a stage route of about 30 miles from Maricopa station on the Southern Pacific....
—*History of Arizona and New Mexico; 1530–1888,* by Hubert Howe Bancroft, San Francisco, 1889

BISBEE, Cochise County. US 80.

The highway runs through **Mule Pass Tunnel,** Arizona's longest, 6,042 feet above sea level. The **Bisbee Restoration Association & Historical Museum,** at Main and Brewery Gulch, has had fine artifacts of Indian and mining days and daily guided tours of the town. Curiously, a new brochure does not list it among the main "Points of Interest," but emphasizes the restored *Copper Queen Hotel,* and the *Copper Queen Mine Tour.* The *Chamber of Commerce* is located near the *Lavender Open Pit Mine,* next door to *Lavender Pit Tours,* on US 80 outside of town. The *Old Jail, Pythian Castle,* once a landmark, now empty, and the *Post-Office-Library* built from native stone, are worth a look.

JEROME, Yavapai County. US 89A.

The lively ghost town is now a historical district. In the hard-scrabble days of the 1880s, mining was the reason for traffic in the settlement on the side of Mingus Mountain. Now it's tourists. The road winds through town for a drop of some 1,500 feet before it reaches the Verde Valley. Like Bisbee, houses are stair-stepped, with roofs often on the same level as another row of basements. The calaboose is known as the *Sliding Jail. Jerome State Historic Park,* off the highway, has the *Douglas Memorial Mining Museum,* open daily except Christmas. James S. Douglas, known as Rawhide Jimmy, was an early mining tycoon and father of Lewis W. Douglas, once ambassador to the Court of St. James.

Al Sieber, a scout for General George Crook, was the first to find copper but failed to develop the claim he staked. Others formed the United Verde Co., which prospered. Mining continued until the 1950s. Main St. is now lined with specialty shops and quaintness, leaving scarcely room for even a skinny miner's ghost.

PHOENIX, Maricopa County. I-17, I-10.

Chamber of Commerce, 805 N. 2nd St., has literature and maps for historical sites.

Pioneer Arizona, 24 miles N off I-17 at Pioneer Rd. exit, is a 550-acre area which re-creates a late-19th-century settlement with dwellings, shops, church, saloon, miner's camp, school, bank, stagecoach stop, an 1860 ranch with real animals, and all the usual trimmings. Write Box 11242, Phoenix, 85061.

TOMBSTONE, Cochise County. US 80.

Tombstone Historic District takes in the "town too tough to die." *Tombstone Courthouse,* 219 E. Toughnut St. (1882), is eclectic; the state's oldest remaining courthouse. *St. Paul's Episcopal Church,* Safford and 3rd Sts. (1882), is adobe with Gothic Revival elements. *City Hall,* 315 E. Fremont (1882), was designed by Frank Walker and is well worth viewing. It has a "front modified false gable with urns at each step . . . the center door providing access for fire equipment . . . segmental arched windows . . . High Victorian Italianate elements." The quotes are from the National Register of Historic Places, not given to overstatement.

Ed Schieffelin was the prospector who was told he would find only his tombstone in Apache country but found silver in 1881. *Schieffelin Hall,* the first major building, housed a theater and a meeting hall for the Masons. More than $37 million in silver had been mined before the shafts were flooded beyond repair and the good times were over—until tourism became the second-biggest business in the world and Tombstone quickly made ready to mine more silver.

The settlement was first a group of miners' shacks on the spot known as Goose Flats; by 1881 the population was 10,000. The *Tombstone Restoration Commission* acquired the courthouse in 1955, after it had stood vacant, and development began which was later taken over by the State Parks Board. There is much memorabilia on display; the second-floor courtroom held many frontier trials. A reconstructed gallows in the rear courtyard shows how some cases ended.

Among the sites: **Tombstone Epitaph Office,** 5th St., where John P. Clum published the paper he had established in a tent-covered shack in May 1880; **Bird Cage Theatre,** Allen and 6th Sts., some original furnishings; **Wyatt Earp Museum,** 5th and Toughnut Sts.; Schieffelin Hall, 4th and Fremont, is adobe, restored, with a historama; **Crystal Palace,** 5th and Allen, restored.

The O.K. Corral, between 3rd and 4th on Allen, is where the most famous private war of the Old West took place. Life-size figures of the Earps, Doc Holliday, the Clantons, and the McLaurys are at permanent stand-off here. The stagecoach office and stables have been restored. **Fly's Photography Gallery,** nearby, has photos of the early days. Camillas Fly took the only known shots of the town in the Earp days. The gallery was an adobe building, with iron covering the Fremont St. entrance to the O.K. Corral, and he was an eyewitness to the fight, as countless others claimed to be but were not. One of his photographs shows the Crystal Bar at what must have been a rare inactive moment: three bartenders in white, one with a bow tie, are standing at attention, as are six customers, foot on rail or elbow on bar-top, waiting for Fly to click the shutter. In 1894 Fly moved to Phoenix with his studio but traded in his equipment to become sheriff of Cochise County. He lived until 1901.

Wells-Fargo Museum, 511 Allen St., has 30 characters in wax; the Earps again, the Clantons, and Doc Holliday, who did all right (or all wrong) without a brother, and other individualists of the 19th century. Also many relics of the Old Southwest.

Boothill Cemetery, at the N city limits off US 80, has restored tombstones for perhaps more colorful persons of the past than actually are buried here.

Underground Mine Tours, Fifth and Toughnut Sts., lead into an old silver shaft, daily at 2 P.M. for nonclaustrophobes.

"Helldorado" is an annual three-day event in which there are reenactments of Tombstone goings-on in the 1880s. "What really happened" seems to be an unending story, and a branch library could be stocked with books dealing only with the Earps, before, during, and after the O.K. Corral. On the afternoon of October 26, 1881, Wyatt and Virgil Earp and Doc Holliday, a friend who was both a gambler and a dentist, shot out a longstanding dispute (and/or feud) with Ike and Bill Clanton, Frank and Tom McLaury (a name that has come out McLowery, McLoury, and other ways), and Billy Claiborne. Who drew first is still a point of argument with some die-hards. The McLaurys and Bill Clanton, indisputably, were dead when it was all over, and Doc Holliday and Virgil Earp were wounded, but survived.

YUMA, Yuma County. I-8.
Yuma County Chamber of Commerce, Convention & Visitors Bureau, 200 First St., P.O. Box 230—(602) 782-2567. An illustrated map with details of the Garces, Cortez, Coronado, Redondo, and Juarez trails and local sites points out some 45 places of interest and gives helpful hints and warnings on how to travel in desert and border areas. The staff is willing and ready to help you with any tour. Among many places of historic interest in town: **Century House,** 240 Madison Ave., now a branch of the Arizona Historical Society, was the home of E. F. Sanguinetti, pioneer merchant. Many relics are on display. Open Tuesday and Saturday.

The Depot, 281 Gila St., now used by the Fine Arts Association, is closed Mondays and holidays.

Southern Pacific Steam Locomotive, on banks of the Colorado River at 2nd Ave. behind City Hall, came from the famous Baldwin Locomotive Works, Schenectady, New York, and was given to the city in 1957. Tours on request at the Customs House.

Customs House (Quartermaster's Residence 1864–83), also on bluff behind City Hall at 2nd, is probably the oldest U.S.-built structure in Yuma. Restored as part of the Yuma Crossing Sites. NHL. Open weekdays: (602) 782-9314.

Yuma Territorial Prison and Museum (1876–1909), E on 1st St. to Gila St., turn S on Gila to Harold C. Giss Pkwy., turn left, go under freeway, and follow signs. Now a state park; the prison housed many famous badmen. Museum open daily except Christmas.

Northwest States

Washington
Oregon
Montana
Wyoming
Idaho
North Dakota
South Dakota

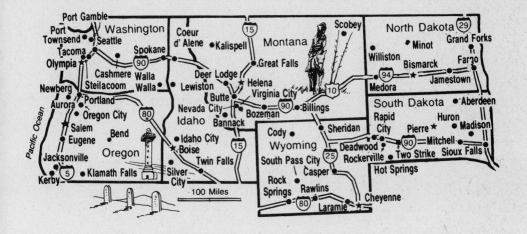

WASHINGTON

The general apprehension . . . that in the West all one need to do is to stake off a few lots, build a cabin or two, select a name, and a city will grow up much after the fashion of vegetables in a garden, is nowise true of Tacoma. When Tacoma was established, other towns on Puget Sound had existed for many years, and naturally they did not extend any encouragement. . . . Tacoma's first breath of life was a battle-cry. . . . Its voice gained in strength. At first Puget Sound only heard it. Then it reached the ears of everybody in Washington Territory, and they were pleased with it. The Pacific Northwest then realized that there was a new voice in the business world and stopped to listen, and soon the entire Pacific Coast was talking about it. . . . [Now] Tacoma helps to feed the world; helps to build the world's houses. . . .
—*Over the Range to the Golden Gate,* by Stanley Wood, Chicago, 1896

CASHMERE, Chelan County. US 97.

Chelan County Historical Society Pioneer Village and Willis Carey Historical Museum, E edge of town, has original buildings moved from other parts of the county. The village is maintained by the nonprofit Society and is dedicated to the pioneers who left homes in the East after the Civil War to risk the perilous crossing to this frontier. The museum, opened in 1959 with the Carey collection of Indian artifacts and relics, has continued to grow. A new wing was added in 1976 and is staffed by volunteer hostesses.

The *Mission* is a replica of the first Christian mission in north-central Washington, which was established by the Oblate Fathers in the mid-19th century. The original stood on the banks of a stream soon christened Mission Creek, just S of today's city limits. The *Richardson Cabin* was a log home at Monitor, built with fir logs cut at Horse Lake, skidded (see Skid Row, Seattle) to the homesite, in 1888. *Buckhorn Saloon* formerly was a home on Badger Mountain; *Weythman Cabin,* of rough sawn lumber cut at the mill up Squilchuck Creek from Wenatchee, is board-and-batten frame, added to an original log cabin, by James Weythman for his bride in 1891.

The *Waterwheel,* built in 1891 by homesteader Andrew S. Burbank, furnished water to irrigate his ranch along the Wenatchee near Cashmere. Rebuilt in 1915 by a captain who used the paddlewheel shaft from a Columbia River sternwheeler, the wheel lifts water from the river for irrigation and is the last survivor of many in use before irrigation canals were created.

Horan Cabin, built in 1872, by Samuel C. Miller, was the Wenatchee River home of the first permanent settler. Miller and Frank Freer operated a trading post. The homestead, bought by Mike Horan in 1896, was rebuilt here and furnished by members of the Horan family.

Among other structures: an assay office of 1879, and a gold mine, with timbers, track, and ore cars from the Blewett Mines; blacksmith shop from 1889, first used as a toolhouse; a post office from Wenatchee which earlier had been a trading post; a doctor-dentist office, once the home of settlers in the Mission Creek Valley, furnished with pioneer equipment; a general store from Dryden, once an 1896 dwelling; a one-room log school, 1886, built by David Treadwell, the first school in Mission (now Cashmere), and a barbershop from Leavenworth. Village and museum are open from April through October.

PORT GAMBLE, Kitsap County. St. 21.

Port Gamble Historic District takes in the town settled in 1853 which became a lumber center. NHL. Lately the old town, which seems like New England in the Pacific Northwest, has been discovered by artists and photographers. It is a company town, owned by the *Pope & Talbot Mill.* More than 60 homes and commercial structures have been restored in New England mill village style. East Machias, Maine, was the home of the company's first partners and town founders, Andrew Pope and William Talbot. The *Masonic Temple* has been here since 1870, and so has the church building which is now *St. Paul's Episcopal* and was originally Congregational.

The *Thomas Driscoll House,* Rainier Ave., has much gingerbread trim and was built about 1887. Now owned by the chief forester at Port Gamble and his busy family, the house is often displayed to touring groups. It has seven fireplaces with the original hearths, but the chimneys were damaged by earthquake, and fires are not built these days.

There is also a secret panel which every resident seems to have found and left a note in. Restorations are planned; inquire locally to find what may be open.

PORT TOWNSEND, Jefferson County. St. 20.

Chamber of Commerce, 2139 Sims Way, has information and a map for tours of historic houses, called the *Sea Gull Tour Guide.*

Port Townsend Historic District extends from the waterfront, covering an area roughly bounded by Scott, Walker, Taft, and Blaine Sts., with many nationally registered commercial, public, and private dwellings. *St. Paul's Episcopal Church,* Jefferson and Tyler Sts., has Stick-style elements, and a bell which twice helped to save ships from running aground in heavy fog. The *Point Wilson Lighthouse,* on land between Juan de Fuca Strait and Admiralty Inlet, has been aiding seamen since 1879.

Among the outstanding residences: *Starrett House,* 444 Clay St. (1889), was called the "House of Four Seasons," because of frescoes on the ceiling of the domed entrance; it is Carpenter Gothic. Starrett was a builder and sawmill operator. The staircase in the front hall is free-hung spiral. There is an indoor widow's walk in the tower; and five kinds of wood in the carved banisters and newel posts.

Frank Bartlett House, 314 Polk St., built in 1883 in Second Empire style. Bartlett, a businessman who had been a stevedore, later served as county treasurer and councilman. Lucile McDonald, Washington historian, relates that the Bartlett custom was to bury a jug in the garden each New Year's Eve; it was dug up and emptied at midnight a year later and then reburied. When hard times came to all of Port Townsend, the Bartletts ran a boardinghouse. Before this happened they had Chinese servants who lived over the carriage house.

Fowler House, Polk and Washington Sts., built before 1865, was the home of Enoch S. Fowler, a builder and captain of a mail and dispatch boat; it is the oldest frame house in town. The captain, from Lubec, Maine, came west with the California gold rush; when he retired from the sea in 1857 he married the widow of another sea captain. Fowler built the first dock in town and the **Leader Building.**

James House, Washington and Harrison Sts. (1889), was the home of Francis Wilcox James, an Englishman, a customs inspector who later ran a trading store. James built the home for his wife, who was still in New England and who died there; then he married his housekeeper. Recently the present owner has been converting the house to an inn.

Tucker House, 706 Franklin, erected by A. Horace Tucker in 1867, has Greek Revival and Italianate elements. Tucker built many houses in town and the first church, St. Paul's Episcopal, and served as mayor. This house was built for his bride. The Tuckers had a bad start on their honeymoon: they had planned a trip to Sequim, but the bride was desperately seasick. The groom left her with friends and came back home in a canoe piloted by an Indian and his seaworthy squaw. Tucker also was the local coffinmaker, had a brickyard and other businesses, and his son inherited this classic little house.

Rothschild House, Taylor and Franklin, the 1868 home of David C. H. Rothschild, a leading merchant, is Greek Revival; now maintained by the Washington Parks and Recreation Commission. Some family possessions, including wedding presents, are among the furnishings.

Old German Consulate, 313 Walker St., was begun in 1890 in Queen Anne style. The interior was not finished for years and the structure was called "Frank's Folly," when builder Frank A. Hastings ran out of funds. The house was bought at a tax sale in 1904, with six lots and a carriage house, for $2,500 (!). But C. A. Olson, who was the buyer, was bidding against a man who wanted to tear the place down for the lumber. August Duddenhausen, a pensioned Civil War veteran who had lost a leg in service, lived with the Olsons, who took care of him during his life and then paid his burial expenses. The house got its name when the custom house was moved to Seattle, and the German consul asked Duddenhausen to handle whatever might come up in Port Townsend. As vice-consul for a time, Duddenhausen carried on consulate business in the Olsons' parlor.

Count Felix von Luckner, who became famous as a sea raider in World War I, was a boy of 16 on a sailing vessel which docked in Port Townsend at a time when Luckner had just heard he was supposed to inherit an estate in Germany. He jumped ship, asking Duddenhausen to lend him $10 to get to the consulate in Seattle. Duddenhausen said no (he probably didn't have 10¢), and Mrs. Olson lent Luckner the money, after hiding him in the cellar until his ship departed. It seems a shame that the National Register lists the house as "Old German Consulate" instead of honoring the long-helpful Olsons.

McIntyre House, 633 Van Buren, was built in the 1870s by Captain James McIntyre, who later was lost at sea when he went down with his ship, the *Bristol*, which struck a rock in Alaskan waters in 1902.

Parrish House, 641 Calhoun, built in 1878 by Hiram Parrish, is the oldest brick house in town.

The **James DeLeo House,** Taylor and Lawrence Sts., built about the end of the 1870s, was the home of a pharmacist, N. D. Hill, who was a member of the town council. The wrought-iron trim is particularly attractive in combination with wooden Gothic details and a rising sun on the front gable.

The **Downs House,** 538 Filmore (1886), was the home of George W. Downs, who ran a sawmill. It has an unusual prism glass window with a bird center, which was added later. The ceilings are 11 feet 9 inches high, and there are four fireplaces.

SEATTLE, King County. I-5.

Pike Place Public Market Historic District is roughly bounded by 1st and Western Aves., Virginia and Pike Sts. The 7-acre area includes brick and frame structures of the early 20th century, with open arcades and ground-floor stalls which formed the early market.

Pioneer Square-Skid Road District comprises an area in the downtown section which was built up in the late 19th century, after a fire in 1889 that destroyed 66 blocks. Elmer H. Fisher was the architect for many of the buildings. Brick, stone, and iron were used. *The Pioneer Building* is Richardson Romanesque.

Newspaperman Bill Speidel's *Underground Tours,* 601 1st Ave., are informative, cover five blocks on foot, take two hours, and are so popular it is advisable to make advance reservations: (206) 682-1511 for information; 682-4646, reservations, tickets. The Pioneer Square Historic District has interesting street-level restaurants, shops, and galleries in the restored old buildings; upper floors house architects, artists, lawyers, and the association headquarters. The Pioneer Square Association met resistance when they started to rebuild the area, but the Grand Central Hotel, which sold several years ago for $90,000, was resold for $155,000 and later for $230,000, all transactions since 1966. When Speidel began his tours he called this "The Forgotten City Which Lies Beneath Seattle's Modern Streets." It is anything but forgotten now.

Skid Road is the original. The name is often thought to be Skid Row and to apply to any area where winos hang out and/or sleep in the streets. Henry Yesler set up a steam sawmill at the bottom of a hill and bought a lot of lumber at the top. Then the city allowed him a 300-foot-wide corridor between the timber and his mill and he skidded the logs downhill.

STEILACOOM, Pierce County. I-5.

Steilacoom Historic District is between Nisqually St. and Puget Sound. The town was first settled in 1851 and is the oldest incorporated American community on Puget Sound. Several of the oldest dwellings in the state are within the district, including ones erected before the establishment of Washington Territory.

Orr House, 1811 Rainier St., was the home of Nathaniel Orr, a nurseryman who came in 1852, bringing orchard stock. Some of the trees he planted are still bearing fruit. The two-story frame home was completed in 1857. Orr was not only a nurseryman but also a wagonmaker, coffinmaker, woodworker, and cabinetmaker.

Steilacoom Catholic Church, 1810 Nisqually, was built in 1855 at Fort Steilacoom and moved here nine years later.

Davidson House, 1802 Commercial St., was built in 1858 by Phillip Keach for his soon-to-be bride, Antoinette Martin. He owned a general store. The dwelling is well preserved, a simple farmhouse with practical architecture, a full-length porch, and five French doors. Keach was also the first town librarian and a county treasurer.

TACOMA, Pierce County. I-5.

Union Passenger Station, 1713 Pacific Ave., is a modified Beaux-Arts

Classical building of 1885–1902. The **Chamber of Commerce** has an information center here in tourist season; also offices at 752 Broadway, with maps and brochures.

Old City Hall, 7th and Commerce (1893), now houses shops and restaurants. The old jail is part of a restaurant and cocktail lounge. A gold-dust safe which once held the city treasury is in the main entryway.

State Historical Society Museum, 315 N. Stadium Way, has photo murals, dioramas, and exhibits.

St. Peter's Chapel-at-Ease, 29090 N. Starr, was built in 1873. The organ and the 965-pound bell were shipped around the Horn. Early manuscripts are on display. The church opened for service in August 1873, after only a week of construction. Services were held here by the Baptists, Congregationalists, Christian Methodists, Presbyterians, Lutherans, and Roman Catholics, and the first organist was of the Jewish faith.

A number of fine homes in the city were built by Ambrose J. Russell and Everette P. Babcock in the late 19th and early 20th centuries. Russell studied at the Beaux Arts in Paris and worked for H. H. Richardson in Boston. Good examples are the **Richard Vaeth House,** 422 North E St.; **Calvin W. Stewart House,** 4305 North 42nd; **George Lewis Gower House,** 417 North E St.; **William R. Rust House,** 1001 North I St.; **F. S. Harmon House,** 4224 North Mason; **William Virges House,** 502 North Tacoma Ave.; **H. F. Alexander House,** 502 North Yakima; **Charles H. Hyde House,** 425 North Tacoma; **Galusha Parson House,** 516 North C St.; **John R. Arkley House,** 602 North E St.; **Henry Rhodes House,** 701 North J; and the **George Dickson House,** 501 Tacoma Ave. North.

Camp Six Logging Museum, in Point Defiance Park, 4 miles N at the end of Pearl St., is a reconstructed logging camp typical of those in the 1880–1900 period, with artifacts, a logging locomotive, and early equipment. Also in the park is the **Job Carr House,** the first home in Tacoma, built in 1865; it also served as post office. Open daily dawn to dark.

At **Old Fort Nisqually,** a reconstruction of the 1833 Hudson's Bay Company outpost, in the park, there is an original structure, the granary, built in 1843; it is the oldest existing building in the state. It was moved to this site from DuPont. NHL.

The **Totem Pole,** 9th and A Sts., was carved by Alaskan Indians, and is the starting point for a marked trail of some 22 points of interest. It is known as the **Kla How Ya Trail,** which means "welcome" in Chinook.

WALLA WALLA, Walla Walla County. US 12.

Whitman Mission National Historic Site, about 7 miles W on US 12, then less than a mile S. The restored mission complex includes a number of houses, mill, and foundations, as well as grave sites, all relating to the mission established by Dr. Marcus and Narcissa Whitman in 1836. They were massacred by Cayuse Indians, with 11 others, in 1847, and are buried in a common grave. The **Visitor Center** has an interpretive museum. There is a self-guiding trail with audio stations.

Fort Walla Walla Museum Complex, Fort Walla Walla Park, has a pioneer village with 14 buildings, most of which are original and have been moved to the site. The **Babcock Railway Depot** was built on the Northern Pacific line NW of town near Eureka about 1880. The **Country Store,** once on the NE corner of the Military Reserve, was built by A. J. Isitt. The **Union School,** built in 1867 near Dixie, is one of the oldest in the area. The **Ransom Clark Cabin** was the home of Clark, who came west with Lieutenant John Frémont in 1843, met Lettice Millican in the Willamette Valley, and married her. They

Pioneer Village, Fort Walla Walla Museum Complex, Walla Walla, Washington. (Courtesy Walla Walla Valley Pioneer & Historical Society)

had one of the first Donation Land Claims and built their cabin just S of Walla Walla in 1859. Also on the grounds are a blacksmith shop, pioneer cabin, blockhouse, and agricultural complex.

The museum is maintained by the **Walla Walla Valley Pioneer and Historical Society,** P.O. Box 616, Walla Walla, 99362. The historical complex is open during summer months, with varying hours: (509) 525-7703. ▪

OREGON

Among the major cities in the United States, none is more blessed in the number and quantity of parks and trails than is the City of Roses. In Portland, it is impossible to live in the city limits and not be within a walking distance of a park. Even the downtown area is rich in parks and squares. A visitor to Portland can come away with a broad view of Portland's past, present and emerging future just by a tour of these "people places."
　　　　　　—The Insider's Guide to Oregon, Vol. IV, Salem, 1977

We arrived at Oregon City situated at the Falls of the Willamette, the place of our destination. This was the 13th of November, 1843, and it was five months and nineteen days after we left Independence, in Missouri. [We] . . . were happy, after a long and tedious tour, over mountains and deserts, through a wild and savage wilderness, to witness . . . the home of civilization, to see houses, farms, mills, storehouses, shops, to hear the busy hum of industry, the noise of the workman's hammer, the sound of the woodman's axe, the crash of falling pines. . . .

Those who intended to cultivate the soil, laid claims, built cabins, and prepared for the coming winter. . . .
　　　　　　—Route Across the Rocky Mountains, by Overton Johnson and William H. Winter, New York, 1846

AURORA, Marion County. US 99.
Aurora Colony Historic District. The colony was settled in 1856 by Germans under the leadership of Dr. William Keil, who had earlier organized a successful Christian communal enterprise in Bethel, Missouri (which see). The colony declined after the leader's death in 1877.

The *Ox Barn Museum and Kraus House,* Second and Liberty Sts., are part of a small complex to preserve the colonial efforts. The barn, built about 1860, served as a station on the stage line which ran between Portland and Sacramento. It is now a museum with furniture and relics of the Aurora Colony. The Kraus House, moved from its original site, has been restored. It was built about 1864. Many original furnishings of the Kraus family are on display. Historian-photographer Lambert Florin, who is a ghost-town specialist, wrote of the Keil wagon train to Oregon:

"If Cheyenne Chief Shot-In-the-Hand saw the desert cavalcade he must have said to his medicine man in whatever way he said things to his medicine man—'Well, old herbs and skulls, I've seen everything now.' Yet whatever the Indians did think of this 'far out' procession on the Oregon Trail, they let it alone. Dr. Wilhelm Keil had a safety factor working for him.

"The outfit would have startled any good honest settler. Leading the string of covered wagons were two mules pulling a hearse, inside it a

324

lead-lined casket filled with alcohol in which was preserved the body of a nineteen-year-old boy. Beside the hearse rode several German band musicians playing doleful Teutonic hymns which were sung by others riding behind. Then followed the wagons with women and children and supplies of a large party heading for the Willamette Valley." Keil, an emigrant from Germany, had been a tailor before he took up religious work full time. The body in the casket was that of Willie, eldest of his five sons, who had died of malaria just before the wagon train was ready to leave Missouri. He had begged not to be left behind and he wasn't. Willie was buried in Willapa, Washington Territory, but the colonists moved on to this area on the west bank of Mill Creek, above its junction with the Pudding River. A number of buildings were still here at least a decade ago, but only lately has the preservation interest developed. Possibly more old structures will be restored.

JACKSONVILLE, Jackson County. St. 238, 5 miles off I-55.

Jacksonville Historic District has a dramatic background. In 1967 the wrecker's ball was poised to swing at the United States Hotel, a once plush hostelry built in 1880, when Dame Fate proved she had an ace up her sleeve, and everything fell into place to save the hotel and the town for today's visitors. What actually happened was that the U.S. National Bank of Portland wanted to open a branch office in Jacksonville. Preservationists got busy and with the help of others in the community talked the bank into using the hotel for its offices. It's fairly safe to say that no U.S. bank today operates out of tumble-down quarters. The great old building was restored even to such small details as its inkwells. NHL.

The town began in 1852 following a gold strike nearby, and became the

The Court House, Jacksonville, Oregon, now a museum. (Courtesy Southern Oregon Historical Society)

main distribution, financial, and trading center in southern Oregon until the Oregon and California Railroad by-passed it. Architectural styles vary. There are Greek Revival, Gothic Revival, and Italianate structures in the basically unaltered commercial and residential sections.

The *Chamber of Commerce,* P.O. Box 33 (zip 97530), has illustrated brochures on the historic sites and urges visitors to feel free to browse in antique stores, art galleries, museums, churches, and even secondhand stores listed. The information center is open from Memorial Day through Labor Day. The *Brunner Building,* the first brick structure in town, erected in 1855 at Main and Oregon Sts., is now the public library. The pioneer *Court House,* 206 N. 5th St., is a free museum with an abundance of early weapons and relics from rocks to fire-fighting equipment.

The *Presbyterian Church,* 6th and California, organized in 1857, was built in 1880 with lumber hauled by wagon from a sugar-pine sawmill more than 125 miles away. Its stained-glass windows came around the Horn. The **Beekman Bank,** 3rd and California, built in 1863, has been restored, with early banking materials on display. In its 27 years of operation, $31 million worth of gold dust was handled. Cornelius C. Beekman was the first successful banker in Oregon. His house of 1876 at 7th and California has original furnishings. **Orth House,** Main and 3rd, was built for an early butcher and city councilman in 1879–80.

McCully House, 5th and California (1861), is a two-story frame dwelling, once the home of Dr. John Wilmer McCully, who arrived here in the 1850s and was the first medical man in the county. In 1862 he left for the gold fields of Idaho and Montana. The house has period furnishings.

The **Methodist Church,** 5th and D Sts., by local legend was erected with funds gathered in one's night's gambling. Every winner is said to have dropped his winnings into a collection plate, and the church was built in 1854. The **Parish House,** 4th and C Sts., was put up six years later.

The **Oddfellows Hall** is still in use from 1860; the **Masonic Temple** was new in 1875. The **Rogue River Valley Railroad Depot,** N. Oregon and C Sts., dates from 1891. It now houses the Chamber of Commerce.

Pioneer Village, 725 N. 5th St., on St. 238 in Jacksonville, has a collection of old buildings in a stockaded settlement which are more than a century old and have been relocated from other Oregon sites and restored. Many still have original furnishings. The first store and post office in the Applegate Valley, built in 1860, and a log smokehouse used for smoking wild hogs are among displays. The smokehouse was built in 1858 by George Meek, whose Uncle Joe was Oregon's first U.S. marshal. A jail, hanging tree, boot hill, barbershop, assay office, saloons, and stagecoach rides are all a part of the village.

KERBY, Josephine County. US 199. 2 miles N of Cave Junction.

Kerbyville Museum is in a house built in 1871, give or take a year, and furnished in period. The outdoor display includes a log schoolhouse, a blacksmith shop, museum, and logging and mining equipment.

The house, two-story frame, was built by Frank Stith for William Naucke, a pioneer merchant. It has been restored. The museum, operated by the county, is well maintained.

NEWBERG, Yamhill County. St. 219.

Champoeg State Park, 7 miles SE of town, off St. 219, comprises 512 acres on the site of the early Willamette River settlement which was lost in a flood in 1861. Here trappers and settlers met in 1843 to accept U.S. jurisdiction rather than that of Britain's Hudson's Bay Company. A new park **Visitor Center** has an interpretive wing, information counter, and viewing deck. Open daily. The **Newell House,** just outside the park entrance, is now a museum. It is a reconstruction with period furnishings. The **Pioneer Mother's Memorial Cabin,** on the river, is a replica of a cabin built before 1861; it is maintained by the DAR. The **Historical Museum** has additional relics of pioneer and river life of the mid-19th century.

In Newberg is the **Minthorn House,** 115 S. River St., which was built in 1881 and was the boyhood home of Herbert Hoover. Dr. Henry Minthorn was superintendent of the Quaker School which Hoover attended as a boy when he lived here with the Minthorns, his foster parents. Their only son had died in 1883. The house, operated by the Herbert Hoover Foundation, has many relics and some original furnishings of the 19th century.

OREGON CITY, Clackamas County. US 99.

McLoughlin House National Historic Site, 713 Center St., preserves the home built for Dr. John McLoughlin, chief factor for the Hudson's Bay Company in the early part of the 19th century. The two-story clapboard house was erected in 1845–46 for his retirement years and has some original furnishings. Oregon City was the first incorporated town west of the Mississippi and the leading community in the Northwest when the Oregon Trail was a busy traffic route.

Also on the National Register: *Dr. Forbes Barclay House,* 719 Center St. (in McLoughlin Park, as is the McLoughlin House). The dwelling was built in 1849–50 for Dr. Barclay, a leading citizen and the former surgeon at Fort Vancouver. It has been moved from its original site. Oriental and western antiques are among the furnishings.

McCarver House (Locust Farm), 554 Warner Parrott Rd., was built in 1850–52 and is considered to be the first "prefab" in Oregon. The lumber was shipped around the Horn from Maine to California and then to Oregon City with General Morton Matthew McCarver when he returned here from California, where he had platted Sacramento for John Sutter and served as a delegate to the first California constitutional convention (Monterey, 1849).

Rose Farm, 534 Holmes Lane (1849); *Captain John C. Ainsworth House,* 19195 S. Leland Rd., an 1851 dwelling, is the only large Greek Revival structure in the Northwest. Furnishings are of the mid-19th century. The collection includes sea chests from the U.S.S. *Constitution.*

PORTLAND, Multnomah County. I-80.

The city is divided into North, Northwest, Northeast, Southeast, and Southwest sections.

Portland Yamhill Historic District is roughly bounded by Taylor, Morrison, both sides of Second Ave., and the Willamette River.

A major urban restoration project begun in 1969 will not be finished until 1980, although several buildings are being opened as completed. This is the *Johns Landing* area. The *Water Tower* was opened in 1973, at 533 S.W. Macadam Ave.

Individual listings on the National Register include: *Bishop's House,* 219–223 S.W. Stark St.; the *Jacob Kamm House,* 1425 S.W. 20th Ave.; the *Morris Marks House,* 1501 S.W. Harrison St.; the *Aubrey R. Watzek House,* 1061 S.W. Skyline Blvd. The *Pittock Mansion,* 3229 N.W. Pittock Drive, off W. Burnside, in Pittock Park; it is French Renaissance in style, stands imposingly about 1,000 feet above the city, and was built in the 1909–14 period by Henry L. Pittock, founder of the *Daily Oregonian.* It has been restored and partially furnished in period.

The *Captain John Andrew Brown House,* N.W. area at 19th Ave. and Hoyt St., was built about 1898 by J. A. Brown, a sea and river-boat captain who began life on the other coast in New England. He helped develop the port here. The house is partially restored.

The *MacKenzie House,* 615 N.W. 20th Ave., is a three-story gabled stone structure built in the 1890s by Dr. K. A. J. MacKenzie, who founded the University of Oregon Medical School and was the owner of the Oregon Railway and Navigation Company. The house was designed by architects Whiddon and Lewis and is said to be "Scotch Baronial" in style. They borrowed from the Henry Hobson Richardson style of architecture. He was the most influential architect in the U.S. following the Civil War for at least a decade. (Trinity Church, Boston, is a good example of his busy look, which ran to towers, arches galore, and lots of exterior trimmings. In his last years he adopted a much simpler style, and one sample of this is Sever Hall at Harvard College.)

Chamber of Commerce Visitors Information Center, 824 S.W. 5th Ave., has information on tours of the area. There are seven commercial or public buildings and six churches on the National Register.

The **Bybee-Howell House,** 12 miles N via US 30 and an unnumbered road, on Howell Park Rd., Sauvie Island, was built in 1856 and was the first dwelling in the state to have plastered interior walls. It is Greek Revival; the first owners were James F. and Julia Ann Bybee. Restored, with period furnishings.

SALEM, Marion County. I-5.

A **Visitor's Information Office** is on the 1st floor of the capitol, just S of the rotunda.

Bush House-Bush Barn, in Bush Park, 600 Mission St. S.E., six blocks S of capitol, is a Victorian mansion of 1877 with period furnishings. Pioneer Asahel Bush was a banker and publisher. The remodeled barn contains an art gallery.

Mission Mill Museum, 260 12th St. S.E., is a complex, comprising the **Thomas Kay Woolen Mill** of 1896; the **Jason Lee House,** built in 1841; the **John D. Boon House,** from 1847; and the **Methodist Mission Parsonage,** of 1841. They are restored and furnished with authentic 19th-cen-

tury pieces. All are on the National Register, as is the **Boon Brick Store,** at 888 Liberty St.

Jason Lee was sent to the Northwest from New England to be a "missionary to the Flatheads." The Flatheads and Nez Perce Indians had sent delegations to St. Louis to ask for missionaries to teach them the white man's religion. Skeptics claimed it was to learn the white man's way with guns. Eventually many missionaries came to the Northwest lands, but Jason Lee's mission was the first Protestant one in this area. He had arrived in the mid-1830s and was advised by Dr. John McLoughlin at Fort Vancouver to avoid the dangerous Flathead country, although it was the Flatheads he was here to help. It was said that McLoughlin, as factor for the British-owned Hudson's Bay Company, wanted to keep American settlers south of the Columbia River. The mission originally was located about 10 miles N of town on the Willamette River. The Lee family is buried in a cemetery at the N end of 25th St. Jason's wife, Anna Pittman Lee, was the first white woman buried in Oregon.

The **Oregon State Highway Division** has a Travel Information Section, 104 Highway Bldg. (zip 97310), with information, maps, and brochures.

MONTANA

The picturesque features of life in a Western Montana town like Missoula are best seen as evening approaches. Crowds of roughly clad men gather around the doors of the drinking-saloons. A group of Indians, who have been squatting on the sidewalk for two hours playing some mysterious game of cards of their own invention breaks up. . . . Some blue-coated soldiers from the neighboring military post, remembering the roll-call at sunset, swing themselves upon their horses and go galloping off. . . . A miner in blue woolen shirt and brown canvas trousers, with a hat of astonishing dimensions and a beard of last year's growth, trots up the street on a mule, and, with droll oaths and shuffling talk, offers the animal for sale to the crowd of loungers on the hotel piazza. No one wants to buy. . . .

Toward nightfall the whole male population seems to be in the street, save the busy Chinamen in the laundries, who keep on sprinkling clothes. . . . More Indians now—a "buck" and two squaws, leading ponies heavily laden with tent, clothes, and buffalo robes. . . .

Now the great event of the day is at hand. The cracking of a whip and a rattle of wheels are heard up the street: the stage is coming. Thirty-six hours ago it left the terminus of the railroad one hundred and fifty miles away. It is the connecting link between the little isolated mountain community and the outside world. . . . The main street of the frontier town, given up at night to drinking and gambling, by no means typifies the whole life of the place. The current of business and society, on the surface of which surges a deal of mud and drift-wood, is steady and decent. There are churches and schools and a wholesome family life.

—*The New North-West,* by E. V. Smalley, New York, 1882

The Bitter-Root Valley is about ninety miles long, and its greatest width is perhaps seven miles. . . . The valley is tolerably well settled for a new country, having about three thousand white inhabitants besides the three hundred stubborn, home-loving Indians who remain with their chief Charlo. The Indian lands are scattered through the valley among the farms of the whites, and their owners occupy log-cabins in winter, but prefer the canvas-covered tepee for their summer dwellings. As a rule, the houses of the white settlers are of hewn logs—a material preferred to sawn lumber because it makes thick walls that are warm in winter and cool in summer. If well built, there is no better dwelling for a mountain country than a log-house, and a little trouble will deck its walls with vines and make it as pretty as it is substantial.

—*The Kalispel Country,* by Eugene V. Smalley, New York, 1885

BANNACK, Beaverhead County. S of St. 278.

Bannack Historic District takes in the old town of 1862, which has been

329

abandoned since 1938. This was the site of the first gold findings in the state, the oldest town, and the first territorial capital. There are frame and log buildings. The *Court House,* built about 1875, was remodeled and became the *Hotel Meade.* When the railroad came to Montana and bypassed this town, Dillon became the county seat.

Skinner's Saloon, owned by Cyrus Skinner, a friend of Henry Plummer, who was an outlaw and a part-time sheriff, was a popular hangout.

Bachelor's Row was lined with wickiups in the busy days of mining. *Yankee Flat* was named by Union sympathizers. Southerners named their part of town Jeff Davis Gulch. Among houses which have been or are being restored is a *"Governor's Mansion,"* a bootlegger's cabin, and other cabins. Other points of interest include an assay office, jail, *Masonic Temple,* the *Apex Mill, First Church, William Roe House,* built about 1866, possibly the first frame house in Montana, and the *First Territorial Meeting Place.*

The miners called the place "Grasshopper Diggings." There was a famous sign on the old trail in the 19th century, which seemed Chaucerian but was merely someone's intention to be helpful. It was nailed on a tree near the confluence of Beaverhead River and Rattlesnake Creek and consisted of a rough board with a message in axle grease:

> *Tu grass Hop Per digins*
> *30 myle*
> *Kepe the trale nex the bluffe*

On the other side it read:

> *To Jonni Grants*
> *One Hundred & twenti myle.*

Jonni Grants is now part of the *Grant-Kohrs Ranch National Historic Site;* see Deer Lodge.

BUTTE, Silver Bow County. US 10, 91.

Butte Historic District comprises the 19th-century mining town. It was first settled in the 1860s by prospectors and their families. Gold placer mining began in 1864; then the town grew during the silver boom of the 1870s and the cooper boom after the Anaconda Copper Co. was founded by Marcus Daly. Butte became a center for the world's copper. There is a 5-square-mile area, known as the Richest Hill on Earth, which has produced more than $2 billion in mineral wealth. NHL.

Copper King Mansion, 219 W. Granite St., is the restored 1884 home built by William Andrews Clark, a copper magnate who was also a U.S. Senator. Among the period furnishings are nine fireplaces which were imported from France.

Chamber of Commerce, Finlen Hotel, 100 E. Broadway, 59701, has information on tours.

World Museum of Mining, W. Park St., is an indoor-outdoor display at the once busy Orphan Girl Mine; there is a reconstructed mining camp with saloon, assay office, mining equipment, and other buildings.

DEER LODGE, Powell County. US 10A.

Grant-Kohrs Ranch National Historic Site, N edge of town on US 10, I-90. John Grant, rancher, was the Jonni Grant of the Chaucerian sign (see Bannack), and was one of the founders of the cattle industry in Montana in the 1850s. In the ranch complex, the two-story frame and brick ranch house from 1863 is still standing; alterations were made in the 1890s. The site is being developed as an interpretive center for Montana ranching days. A number of other buildings from the 1850s and some old corrals exist. The Grant family was filled with individualists. Captain Richard Grant was a factor of the Hudson's Bay Company, supervising trading posts. He lived in a log cabin in Jefferson Valley; his wife was a convent-bred daughter of Red River Indians. Their sons Johnny and James lived in elkskin tepees and their homes became the nucleus of a settlement. The Grants acquired their first herd by trading on the Mormon Trail between Fort Bridger and Salt Lake City, and were said to have been hospitable to most who came their way; the famous sign probably indicated to the trail-weary who must have heard of "Jonni Grant" that food and bed could be found.

In 1866 Conrad Kohrs bought the ranch and enlarged it. He was a cattle baron by the 1880s and was the first to introduce purebred cattle into the state. Kohrs, who started out as a butcher boy in Bannack, became one of the organizers of the Montana Stockgrowers Association.

HELENA, Lewis and Clark County. US 91.

Helena Historic District covers roughly an area from Hauser Rd. to Acropolis, between Garfield and Rodney Sts. This is a two-part district with residential and commercial sections and streetscapes of the late 19th century. There are some large 1890s commercial blocks of rock-faced stone and cast-iron trimmings, Richardson Romanesque in style. The residential section is eclectic with frame, brick, and combinations.

In 1864 four men from Georgia (where a war was still going badly) came to prospect in an area they named "Last Chance Gulch," now Helena's main street after having yielded, with some surrounding land, more than $20 million in gold. Helena has been the state capital since 1875.

Governor's Old Mansion, 304 N. Ewing St., designed by Cass Gilbert, has furnishings of the 19th century.

Completed in 1884, it is brick with terra cotta and stone trim and was the home of a local businessman, William A. Chessman, when the state bought it in 1913 to use as the governor's mansion until 1957. Tours are available through the *Chamber of Commerce,* 201 E. Lyndale, which has information on other historic sites.

Kluge House, 540 W. Main St., was built in the 1880s of hand-hewn logs on the first floor, open timber frame with some brick on second floor. This is considered a rare American example of Prussian 17th- to 19th-century construction; Emil Kluge was a German immigrant. (German construction was considerably more scarce in Montana than in the Texas hill country or parts of the Atlantic seaboard.)

Montana Historical Museum & C. M. Russell Gallery, 225 N. Roberts, should not be missed. It traces the history of the state through dioramas. There is a re-created 1880s street scene, and an excellent collection of Russell's work. In summer the museum is open daily including holidays from Memorial Day through Labor Day. In winter, it is open weekdays; noon to 5 P.M. on weekends and holidays. Closed Thanksgiving, Christmas, and New Year's Day.

Last Chancer Tour Train leaves from the historical museum to major historical sites in summer months.

Pioneer Cabin, 208 S. Park, has authentic furnishings. It was built in 1864. This is one of the sites on a walking tour which begins at the Pedestrian Mall by the Prospectors' Memorial Fountain. Inquire at Chamber of Commerce.

Reeder's Alley, near the S end of Last Chance Gulch, once was a hangout and housing area for muleskinners, miners, and Chinese laundrymen. Now an artists' colony.

Frontier Town, 15 miles W on US 12, is a replica of a pioneer village, hewn out of solid rock and carved from giant trees. The Continental Divide is part of the scenery from here. The museum town is open from April to October.

KALISPELL, Flathead County. US 2.

Fort Kalispell, 3 miles E on US 2, is a replica of a frontier town. There also is a reconstructed Indian village.

NEVADA CITY, Madison County. St. 287.

The old boom town, like nearby Virginia City, has been restored by the Charles A. Bovey family. Some structures have been rebuilt. The two camps in Alder Gulch are surrounded by the Tobacco Root, Ruby, and Gravelly mountain ranges. You can now stroll along a boardwalk past a barbershop with a newly painted pole and old false-front buildings, which have the re-created old-time businesses of dress-making, blacksmithing, general store supplies, etc.

A Montana paper once said of Nevada City that "its turbulent and amazing life, when thousands of seething, struggling and money-mad human beings of every nationality and country on earth, swarmed its single street by day and night, was probably without parallel on the continent."

But even in the 19th century "the media" was not to be trusted entirely. A parallel to Nevada City could be found just down the road at Virginia City.

A number of 1864–1900 buildings have been moved here from other parts of the state. There is a railroad museum in the Depot, nickelodeons in the music hall, and other typical trappings.

SCOBEY, Daniels County. St. 13.

Daniels County Museum & Pioneer Town preserves some 30 buildings from pioneer times, with antique vehicles and farm equipment part of the displays. There are a homesteader's shack, a church, a school, and a number of stores. Open from mid-May to mid-September.

VIRGINIA CITY, Madison County. St. 287.

Virginia City Historic District, Wallace St., takes in the old boom town settled in Alder Gulch with the discovery of the richest placer gold in the country, in 1863. The town became the territorial capital 1865–75. The district contains many restored and reconstructed 19th-century false-front stores and dwellings, the old *Territorial Capitol* building, and the offices of the *Montana Post.* NHL.

The nearby cemetery contains the graves of the notorious Plummer gang, led by Henry Plummer, who worked on both sides of the law in his wayward career. The Charles A. Bovey family have been responsible for the restorations. There are hotels, restaurants, saloons, shops, a Chinatown, a narrow-gauge railroad, gold-panning demonstrations, or opportunities, an opera house with melodramas, and other enticements. Open early June to September. *The Thompson Hickman Memorial Museum,* and the *Virginia City–Madison County Historical Museum,* Wallace St., have many pioneer relics.

WYOMING

Rawlins presents to the curious eye severely utilitarian frame houses, devoid of flowers, turf, or shrub, or even an inclosure where such might be nourished; the invariable fresh paint of the saloons; and the brawny loungers, with a bevy of huge, lumbering Newfoundlands, gaunt hounds, and overgrown curs to bark at the train. . . . The clouds are lowering grimly as we speed on, and fine, sifting snowflakes begin to waver on the gusts of the north wind. Our trail lies over desolate divides, utterly given up to sagebrush and greasewood—a little, low shrub not unlike the sage, with the same gray-green foliage and an intensified unpleasantness of odor. By sunlight it might be less dreary; but now in the cold, colorless twilight, with the fast-thickening snow drawing its pale film over the distances, it is a picture of lifeless desolation. The far-off mountain ranges appear only as ghosts of hills; the Wind River range, away to the north, and south of us the Medicine Bows, gray and spectral through the storm.
—"Out West on the Overland Train," from *Leslie's Magazine* 1877

CHEYENNE, Laramie County. I-25.
Wyoming State Capitol, 24th St. and Capitol Ave., 1886–88, sandstone with stone trim, has second-story balustraded balcony with Corinthian columns and a central octagonal cupola with gold leaf dome. Side wings were added. Beaux-Arts Classicism is a style that went out of style but may be back in these changeable times. (Could be it's already here and I haven't had time to look.)
Governor's Mansion, 300 E. 21st St., is Georgian Revival, built in 1904 and once occupied by the nation's first female governor, Nellie Tayloe Ross (1925–27).
St. Mark's Episcopal Church, 1908 Central Ave., 1886–88, has Early Gothic Revival elements and a projecting square crenelated louvered bell tower with lancet windows added in 1925.
St. Mary's Catholic Cathedral, 2107 Capitol Ave., early 20th-century stone, is "a fine example of Late Gothic Revival," to quote the always-careful National Register editors, who are seldom given to overpraise.
Union Pacific Depot, 121 W. 15th St., 1886–87, is basically Richardson Romanesque. The coming of the railroad was a great event in Cheyenne's history.
Atlas Theatre (Atlas Building), 213 W. 16th St., 1887. Eclectic. The lobby has a tin ceiling, a rare item lately. The structure was put up to house a tea and confectionery shop, later converted.
All these Cheyenne buildings are on the National Register.

CODY, Park County. US 14, 16, 20.
Buffalo Bill (William Frederick Cody) founded the town, which is named for him. It is sometimes called the Eastern Gateway to Yellowstone

National Park, which is 50 miles west, but 50 miles is no distance at all in this part of the world.

Old Trail Town, 3 miles SW on US 14, 16, 20, is a reconstruction. The original wagon trail is still visible in front of the buildings: a trading post, a saloon, a general store, a miner's cabin, a livery barn, a mayor's home, and a blacksmith shop. The *Museum of the Old West* has exhibits of the Plains Indians, some from prehistoric times, frontier guns, carriages, and clothing from early days in Cody.

At the *Buffalo Bill Historical Center,* W of town on US 14, 16, and 20, the Cody boyhood home from near LeClaire, Iowa, has been re-erected. There is a replica of the old Cody ranch. The Center, valued at more than $10 million, contains the *Whitney Gallery,* one of the finest collections of western art in the world, and the *Museum of Northern Plains Indians,* with extremely rare artifacts from ancient times through the beginning of this century.

The *Irma Hotel,* in the heart of town, built by Cody for $80,000, opened in 1902; named for his youngest daughter, it has been in continuous operation.

SOUTH PASS CITY, Fremont County. Off St. 28. About 33 miles S of Lander.

Chief Washakie of the Shoshone Indians called the area the "Valley of the Warm Winds." It lies on the eastern slope of the Wind River Mountains where the Pop Agie River meets with the Little Wind River and flows into the Big Wind. The old Oregon Trail went through Fremont County; in the South Pass City vicinity it crossed St. 28 S of town. The county's west border is the Continental Divide on the crest of the Wind River Mountains. Chief Washakie optimistically asked that this land belong to his people for "as long as the grass shall grow and the rivers shall flow." For a time the land was granted to the Indians as a reservation, but it was "reappropriated."

Virginian John Colter, who was one of the 22 privates first listed as part of the permanent party to accompany Lewis and Clark on their great expedition, is thought to have been the first white man to see this part of the country. On the return journey in 1806 he got permission to leave the main group to explore and try trapping along the Upper Missouri. He is credited with discovering Yellowstone Park. Colter remained in the area for four years, thereby setting a record for staying in the wilderness of the Upper Missouri and the Rocky Mountains longer than any other white man of his time. He eventually married an Indian woman and went back to settle down in Missouri near Daniel Boone, but he died in 1813.

South Pass City became the center of the Sweetwater gold rush. The townsite was laid out in the fall of 1867. The following year Main St. was lined with business buildings and the population had grown to nearly 2,000.

After the Carissa, a hard-rock lode, was found in June of 1867, the rush had begun which led to many new mines with gold-country names: Summit, King Solomon's, Northern Light, Jim Crow, Hoosier Boy, Mohamet, and Lone Star State.

A tablet marks the home and office site of a pioneer heroine to women liberationists. Esther Hobart Morris was the first woman justice of the peace, and some say she co-authored the first Equal Suffrage Law (with W. H. Bright). She came to South Pass City from Illinois in 1869 with her husband and three sons. Mrs. Morris was almost 6 feet tall and weighed nearly 200 pounds; she served for only a few months in 1870, but she handled about 70 cases. Some say that she fined her own husband for assault and battery. A replica of her cabin is being built.

Whether or not Bright had help from the feminine justice of the peace, he was a resident of South Pass City, and the bill became law in 1869. Wyoming thus became the first government in the world to grant equal rights to women.

The town had a district school but no church. Religious citizens depended on sermons from itinerant preachers. The *South Pass News* began as a five-column newspaper in 1869. Two stage lines served the town daily by 1870, running from Point of Rocks, the nearest station on the Union Pacific Railroad. By the mid-1870s the town was on its way to oblivion. Now in the 1970s it is being restored and is a National Historic Landmark. It is administered as a State Historic Site by the Wyoming Recreation Commission.

IDAHO

The first newspaper in our possessions on the Pacific coast, was published in Idaho, nearly fifty years ago, by Spaulding, a missionary among the Piercednose Indians. A log hut still marks his pioneer office; and beside it trees of his own planting flourish and bear fruit.

The crushing mills of Idaho contain between four and five hundred stamps. . . . Idaho, one of our very best mineral States, has little land attractive to the farmer. . . . Yearly, clouds of grasshoppers or "black crickets," covering the ground like a sable mantle, swept over the country in July and August, destroying the crops. The mountains are well timbered and abound in game. . . . The climate is exceedingly healthy.

—*Beyond the Mississippi,* by Albert D. Richardson, Hartford, Conn., 1867

West of Boise the trail and the modern highway run close together along the Boise River to a spot where people now picnic in a pleasant meadow. Grasshoppers jump and zip through the air.

—*Great Trails of the West,* by Richard Dunlop, Nashville, 1971

BOISE, Ada County. I-80.

Julia Davis Park, N of Boise River on the E side of US 30. Original log cabins of pioneer families are on display. I. N. Coston's cabin was made of driftwood and fastened with pegs; Ira B. Pearce's from logs transported by oxen from the mountains. Both have been moved from their original sites. Recently an 1860s adobe house was added. There are stagecoaches, early fire engines, and *"Big Mike,"* a Union Pacific locomotive. The park is named for the wife of pioneer rancher Tom Davis, in whose log cabin the town was platted. Also in the park is the *Idaho State Historical Society Museum,* 610 N. Julia Davis Drive, with pioneer and Indian artifacts.

The *Assay Office,* 210 Main St., is a National Historic Landmark, as a symbol of the importance of mining in the development of the Pacific Northwest. The two-story building of 1870 is made of native sandstone with hipped roof. The first floor, before remodeling, held the assayer's office and equipment including safes and vaults for the storage of the materials he evaluated. The assaying and melting rooms with furnaces and the laboratory were here. The second floor was living quarters for the main assayer. The building is now headquarters for the Boise National Forest.

Department of Commerce & Development, in the Capitol, Room 108, Boise, 83720, has travel information, maps, and tour suggestions.

Moore–De Lamar House, 807 Grove St., was built in 1879 by Christopher W. Moore, a banker and local merchant. Later owner Joseph R. De Lamar was a friend of Presi-

State Capitol, Boise, Idaho. (Idaho Division of Tourism and Industrial Development)

dent Benjamin Harrison and a millionaire. It has been considerably altered in the past century, but the ornately carved interior woodwork remains and the house is listed on the National Register, so it may be restored.

IDAHO CITY, Boise County. St. 21.

Gold was discovered in the Boise Basin in 1862. There were 6,000 inhabitants by 1864 when the county seat changed its name from Bannack City (there is a Bannack, Montana); 250 places of business were doing well until a fire in 1865 destroyed all but the Catholic church, a theater, and the newspaper office (*Idaho World*). Other fires raged in 1867,

1868, and 1871 (the year of the Great Chicago Fire), but each time the town was rebuilt. The Boise Basin had plenty of gold but little water—it was sold by the inch. It is believed that more gold was mined in the 18-square-mile area than in all of Alaska. *Boise National Forest* now surrounds the old town.

Boise Basin Museum, with many relics of the mining era, is at Montgomery and Wall Sts. *Masonic Hall,* on Montgomery, dates from 1865; *Pioneer Lodge No. 1, International Order of Odd Fellows,* was established in 1864. Original furnishings.

St. Joseph's Catholic Church, Wallula St. (1867), was the first parish church in Idaho.

Boot Hill is a restored 40-acre cemetery, with a beautiful wrought-iron gate. *Gold Hill,* 1 mile N of town on Main St., was made of pay dirt.

The *Old Territorial Penitentiary,* built from hand-hewn pine timbers and handmade nails, and the old *Pinney Post Office* (1863), now a museum, are open to the public. The P.O. also served as the Wells-Fargo station. The bricks in this building and others in town were from nearby Elk Creek kiln.

Gold Rush Days are held annually in mid-June.

SILVER CITY, Owyhee County. On local road about 25 miles SW of Murphy (St. 78) and E of De Lamar.

One of the best-preserved of the old mining towns, Silver City is now a historic district. Gold placers were discovered on Jordan Creek in 1863. Rich silver veins were found soon after, and the town grew fast. More than 30 buildings remain from the boom days. The *Idaho Hotel,* built in Ruby City in 1865, was hauled here by oxcart in three sections. It has 50 rooms. The *Masonic Hall,* the newspaper office, several stores, and the schoolhouse are open to visitors. The *Old Schoolhouse Museum* has many mining and pioneer artifacts.

NORTH DAKOTA

From Fargo to Bismarck by rail is a day's journey, the distance being one hundred and ninety-seven miles, and the road running almost as straight as the crow flies. For about forty miles the country is flat, and the landscapes seen from the car-windows would be tame were it not for the vast sweep of vision, which produces upon the mind something of the exhilarating effect of the view from the deck of a ship at sea. All objects on the horizon, the homesteader's shanty, the straw stack, or the plowmen at work with their teams, stand out sharply against the sky and seem magnified to more than twice their real size. Here are no trees save the belts of alders and cottonwoods that fringe the Cheyenne and the Maple rivers, two pretty streams that wander here and there over the plain as if in doubt where to go, and finally, after doubling again and again in their tracks, manage to find the Red River.

—*The New North-West,* by E. V. Smalley, New York, 1882

The claim shanty that John [Dunlava] took his bride to, was roughly built of one thickness of lumber on the framework of two-by-fours. The outside was covered with a building paper that was weather-proofed with tar. The paper was battened on the shanty with lath. The interior of the shanty was unfinished. The two-by-fours were open to view. So far John's homestead had been a gift to him from the government, if he complied with the requirements. Now with Clara's help, he would make it their permanent home. . . . Clara made a paste of flour and pasted newspapers on the walls, over and around the two-by-fours. This helped to keep the wind out, and hold the heat from the stove in. The newspaper on the walls also made the room lighter. The shanty was just one room. It was crowded with two double-beds, a table, cook-stove, and a small heater. . . .

After the first cold spell the frost tightened and sealed the cracks. Frost formed on nail points inside the room as it followed the steel through the walls.

—"Pioneer Days in Cass County," by Mary Dunlava Tellefson, in
Dakota Portraits, Mohall, 1964

FARGO, Cass County. I-94.
Bonanzaville, U.S.A., exit 85, I-94, is a reconstruction of a 19th-century farming town. There are more than 30 buildings, furnished dwellings, a church, school, and general store. A post office, tavern, hotel, theater, bar-bershop, and antique vehicle museum are also part of the re-creation.

JAMESTOWN, Stutsman County. I-94
Frontier Village, E edge of town on I-94, has a 60-ton statue which North

Dakota claims is the world's largest concrete buffalo. (Texas seems to be content with the world's largest jackrabbit, in Odessa, and has not responded to the challenge.) The reconstructed village includes a prairie church, school, general store, craftshop, the first railroad depot, and a caboose once in use in Jamestown; also a land office, jail, and an art gallery re-creating homesteading days in the Dakota Territory.

The land office worked in combination with the railroad. Typical advertisements in the 1880s read: "Northern Pacific Railroad Lands For Sale; The Northern Pacific Railroad Company has a large quantity of very productive and desirable agricultural and grazing lands for sale at low rates and on easy terms." In North Dakota, in 1888, 6,700,000 acres were available. The easy terms were one-tenth cash down for "actual settlers" and the balance in ten equal annual payments at 6 percent interest. Agricultural lands went for $3 to $5 an acre; grazing lands from 75¢ to $3 per acre. Sales in North Dakota between 1888 and 1900 were so great it was possible to retire all of the first-mortgage bonds of the railroad.

MEDORA, Billings County. US 10.

A future President of the United States and a titled Frenchman, married to the beautiful daughter of a millionaire German baron, spent part of their colorful lives in this little North Dakota town. Teddy Roosevelt was then learning how to make a man of himself in the region's rugged Bad Lands. The Marquis de Mores, born Antoine Amédée-Marie-Vincent Manca de Vallombrosa, was only 25 when he arrived in the Bad Lands in 1883. He was handsome, lean, and aristocratic, and recent biographers have been much more lenient with his faults than were observers in his own time. It was said that he was anti-Semitic, and antirepublican, obsessed with his own lineage, rash and money-hungry. But no one ever said he wasn't self-confident, and quick on the draw, whether the weapon drawn was a sword or a pistol.

He had married Medora von Hoffman, whose grandmother was the wife of Governor William Charles Cole Claiborne, of Louisiana, when the pirate Jean Lafitte was having his peak years (1813–14); she interceded in behalf of Lafitte when he asked for pardon for himself and his desperadoes late in 1814. Lafitte's offer was accepted, partially perhaps because of Mrs. Claiborne and partially because he promised to fight for the defense of Louisiana, and in January 1815 did so. When widowed Mrs. Claiborne married a federal judge and moved to Staten Island. Her daughter, Athenais, married another Staten Islander, the German baron Louis von Hoffman, worth $30 million in Wall Street. Their daughter was Medora, for whom the prairie village in North Dakota was named.

De Mores had heard about the money to be made in the cattle business on the free ranges of the Bad Lands and decided to see for himself. He went west with his valet in March 1883. Disappointed at first, he soon made plans to get rich with a packing plant and the real estate he could sell to his hundreds of employees. The town was laid out and named for the marquis's wife. His château was under construction. Marshall Sprague, in his entertaining *A Gallery of Dudes* (Boston, 1966), quotes a Detroit *Free Press* description of the marquis about this time, written by a contemporary:

"He made a picturesque figure in the costume of a plainsman. . . . His figure was set off to advantage by a leather hunting-coat with fringed seams and skirt. It had I know not how many pockets, but each contained some essential—matches, cigars, tobacco, pistol cartridges, a flask, a solar compass of considerable size, a field glass, a 'Multum parvo' knife, very large with blades for every purpose, saws, corkscrews, gimlet, etc. A great white hat with a leather band and an immense brim made a contrast with his black hair. A blue flannel yachting shirt laced at the bosom with yellow silk cord, corduroy trousers, leggings of the same material as the coat, and stout shoes and California spurs completed de Mores' costume. Around his waist was a leather belt filled with gun cartridges; it also held two long-barreled Colt's revolvers of heavy calibre and a bowie knife which would bear inspection even in Arkansas. His gun was double-barreled, made in Paris, a breech loader of plain but accurate finish. . . .

"His own riding pony was short and mettlesome, of a deep cream color. The equipments were a Mexican saddle of uncolored leather, ornamentally stamped; heavy stirrups of a Mexican pattern, a bridle plainly ornamented and Spanish bit, with bridle reins of braided horse hair, knotted and tasseled at short spaces. . . ."

There was drunken talk of killing de Mores in a saloon one night in June 1883, and someone sent an anonymous note to warn the marquis. He first wired the sheriff in Mandan to arrest the three men who had threatened him, but nothing came of it. The marquis and one of his cowboys then went to deal with the rowdies themselves. In a shooting fracas at twilight, one man was wounded and 19-year-old Riley Luffsey was killed. It was ruled an act of self-defense.

The château was finished by August. It was a large farmhouse painted gray with a red roof, shutters, and fireplaces in every room. De Mores had plans to enclose the area with a fence made of elk horns. The marquise arrived with twenty servants. Her square Kurtzmann piano and five tin bathtubs "shaped like seashells" had already arrived by freight car. (A tin bathtub today stands beside the white-painted indoor privy.) De Mores spent $1 million on the model meat-packing plant, which lasted only from 1883 to 1886. He had also built a hotel, a brick church for Medora, and a brick house for his rich father-in-law to summer in. His business began to fail because the cattle were too thin. By the late fall of 1886, the packing plant was closed forever. The family left town on December 2 as if they were only going away for a weekend. De Mores was 37 when in 1896 he was killed on an expedition in North Africa.

In 1903 Medora went back with two of her three children to visit the town named for her and spent six weeks in the château. Caretakers had kept the place ready for them over the years. They returned as if they had indeed been gone only for a fortnight. Everyone welcomed the widow and her children. She gave a party in the town hall to which nearly everyone in Billings County came. The packing plant burned to the ground, for reasons never determined, soon after Medora had gone back to Europe. The children sent a life-size statue of their father to Medora in 1926. Vandals set fire to its wrappings before it could be dedicated, but it was cleaned and the ceremony took place. The sons, who had inherited the property in Medora, kept the caretakers on the job until 1936, when they gave the 28-room château and surrounding grounds, along with the packing-plant site, to the state, with the state historical society as trustee, and with the stipulation that the home become a museum. There are guided tours daily, except in bad weather, as the building is not heated.

Medora Doll House was the summer home de Mores built for Baron von Hoffman. The **De Mores Statue** is in de Mores Memorial Park. As historian Marshall Sprague points out: "And so we have a curious juxtaposition: de Mores, the worshipper of kings, stands in bronze only a few hundred feet from the museum where Theodore Roosevelt, one of the greatest of democrats, is memorialized."

Theodore Roosevelt National Memorial Park, I-94. There is a Visitor Center at Medora with dioramas depicting Roosevelt's life in the Bad Lands. His **Maltese Cross Cabin** is here. When Roosevelt first came to the Dakotas in 1883 to hunt, he bought the Maltese Cross Ranch, 7 miles S of Medora. The following year he established the Elkhorn Ranch, about 35 miles N, which he operated until 1887. He felt that his ranching experiences made him prepared for the vigorous life he led then and later. As a boy he had suffered from chronic asthma, fevers, and other ailments. After he had spent some time in North Dakota he thought of himself as a frontiersman able to handle any challenge, but probably not dreaming that one of them would be a war and another the United States presidency.

Also in the restored town of Medora are an **Indian Artifacts Museum,** the **Roughrider Hotel, St. Mary's Church** of the 1880s, **Joe Ferris General Store,** and a 19th-century-style ice-cream parlor.

SOUTH DAKOTA

There was no plastering, and the house seemed hardly weatherproof. It had a floor, however, and an upper story divided off by beams; over these Mary and I stretched blankets and shawls and so made two rooms. It did not take long to settle our few things, and when wood and water were brought from a distance we were quite ready for house-keeping, except that we lacked a stove and some supplies. . . . and we were in the midst of a Dakota blizzard. The snow was so fine that it penetrated the smallest cracks. . . . Occasionally I melted a little place on the frozen window-pane, and saw that the drifts were almost level with the upper windows on either side, but that the wind had swept a clear space before the door. During the night the sound of the tramping of many feet arose above the roar of the storm. A great drove of mules rushed up to the sheltered side of the house. Their brays had a sound of terror as they pushed, kicked, and crowded themselves against our little cabin. . . .

We did not soon forget our introduction to Dakota. After that we understood why the frontiersman builds his stable near the house . . . that they did not dare to cross in a blizzard from the house to the stable-door without keeping hold of a rope tied fast to the latch as a guide for their safe return when the stock was fed.

> —*Boots and Saddles; or Life in Dakota with General Custer,*
> by Elizabeth B. Custer, New York, 1885

In June, 1879, Prof. Walter T. Jenny and Col. W. J. Thornby left Deadwood on horseback on a mine location trip. They arrived at Buffalo Gap and Colonel Thornby made a dangerous trip through Indian Territory and found and located what are now called the Minnekahta Springs of hot water. . . .

The town has an altitude of 3,260 feet, and is situated in a valley, or canyon, between surrounding hills. When Colonel Thornby located the Minnekahta Springs, he was much attracted by the beautiful Fall river stream, which pursues its course through the town and parallel with the main street. He says that at that time the stream was literally filled with wild geese and ducks, that were in such vast numbers as to be unintimidated by his presence. To-day this river is a glowing mass, winter and summer, of watercress, while tame ducks of varied hue lend a great beauty to its naturally picturesque appearance.

> —*Black Hills Illustrated,* 1904

DEADWOOD, Lawrence County. US 14, 85.

    Deadwood Historic District takes in all of Deadwood Gulch, the site of a rich gold strike in 1875, bringing some 25,000 strangers to the town, which had only one main street; houses were built on both sides of the gulch. NHL. *Lead,* where the **Home-stake,** the largest gold mine in the U.S., was found, is also a historic district. It is about 3 miles to the SW.

Deadwood has been refurbished to have the look of its most historic times. Those in charge of restoration were dismayed with the first set of reconstruction plans, from an out-of-state architectural firm, which would have produced another western TV set or Disneyland attraction. Patty Schaefer, project coordinator, also had regrets about sweet-talking salesmen: "One more aluminum salesman," she remarked, "and the whole town might have taken on the glow of a giant sheet of tin foil."

The buildings have been cleaned, bricks replaced, shutters and other exterior woodwork and decorative ironwork repaired or replaced. Buildings dating back to 1895 on the Ayres block of Main St. now house new shops. Other parts of Main and even Mt. Moriah, the most famous cemetery in this part of the Old West, have been renovated.

Saloon #10, where Wild Bill Hickok drew his last card, was named for a worthless piece of creek bank where it was originally located, called placer claim #10. On August 2, 1876, when Wild Bill was shot in the back by Jack McCall, alias Bill Sutherland, the saloon was a canvas-covered shack, with a few barrels and tables. Today the walls are lined with mementos; the windows are shaped like wheels, and Wild Bill's chair hangs above the door.

Above a long walnut bar are wax replicas of some onetime customers: Calamity Jane, Deadwood Dick, Wild Bill, Potato Creek Johnny, and Preacher Smith. Calamity Jane, born Martha Jane Canary in Missouri, had a wayward career in the West and was often arrested for one thing or another, sometimes drunkenness or what came with it (once in Billing she took an ax to a young woman clerk in a dry goods store for no

A South Dakota General Store. (Courtesy Jim Pollock, South Dakota Division of Tourism)

known reason). But in Deadwood she was remembered as having nursed sick miners.

Potato Creek Johnny reportedly found the biggest nugget discovered in the Black Hills. Potato Creek is near Iron Creek Lake, about 25 miles from town.

Poker Alice was an Englishwoman named Alice Ivers who lived in Deadwood for a time. She operated bawdyhouses and was a faro dealer. The owner of Saloon #10, Lew Keehn, a history lover, is restoring a poker table from Alice's original establishment. She is said to have been one of the many present when Bob Ford, who shot Jesse James, finally got what nearly everyone thought he had coming and was himself shot by Ed O. Kelly in Creede, Colorado. Calamity Jane also was listed as among the bystanders on that not-so-sad occasion. (Ford had shot Jesse James when his back was turned.)

The first Deadwood Dick was Ned Love, a black cowboy who won awards for riding wild horses and as a pistol shot, and roping, during a Deadwood celebration on the 4th of July, 1876. He named himself Deadwood Dick, and a dime novelist who wrote about him made him white. Love was born in Tennessee in a slave cabin in 1854, arrived in Dodge City in 1869, then became a cowpuncher called Red River Dick, taking part in the cattle drives from Texas to Kansas. Bat Masterson was one of his friends and reportedly got him out of trouble when he tried to steal a U.S. Army cannon, for no particular reason. In his autobiography, written in 1907, he had many glorious tales to tell of his adventures, including his having been adopted by an Indian tribe. Sadly, when the railroad took the place of the great trails, Deadwood Dick became a Pullman porter.

The next Deadwood Dick was a man named Brown who stuttered. One of the latest of the line, Richard Clark, is pictured in the portrait gallery of today's Saloon # 10, which is the fourth barroom to have the name and has been in existence since 1890. Two earlier ones burned. Each night except Sunday in summer months *The Trial of Jack McCall* is staged on the streets of town. As the *Black Hills Pioneer* reported the event in August 1876, after McCall shot Hickok in the back of the head while Wild Bill was holding the famous poker hand of aces and eights, he ran down the street and was chased by a number of citizens, caught, taken to a building at the lower end of the town, and put under guard. Then a coroner's jury was summoned and C. H. Sheldon was selected as foreman. After all the evidence was heard, a trial jury was arranged and they also heard that Jack McCall had stood directly behind his victim at a distance of 3 feet and shouted, "Damn you, take that," and fired—the bullet entering the back of the head and coming out the right cheek, rendering instant death. After an hour and thirty minutes, the verdict was: "We, the jury, find Mr. John McCall not guilty."

McCall was later retried and hanged in Yankton.

The renovated *Mt. Moriah Cemetery* stands about 500 feet above the city. Calamity Jane, at her own insistence, is buried beside James Butler Hickok. Preacher Smith is among other old westerners here. The restored town has gained many honors in recent years: the Bicentennial Commission of South Dakota declared it the state's first "Historic City"; it is also an accredited "Flag City," with the Stars and Stripes flying daily.

HOT SPRINGS, Fall River County. US 18.

Hot Springs Historic District takes in River St. in an irregular pattern from Summit Rd. S. to Baltimore St. and includes part of Minnekahta Ave. This is a city of native pink sandstone Victorian buildings in the narrow Fall River Valley. The river never varies in temperature and runs the length of the town, providing trout fishing all winter and fresh watercress.

At the turn of the century 16 excursion trains arrived daily bringing health-seekers to try the waters. The imposing *Evans Hotel* was the 1890s place to be if you were wealthy and feeling poorly and wanted to enjoy it. It was completed in 1892 by Fred T. Evans, who hoped that Hot Springs would be the "Carlsbad of America." The hotel has a castlelike crenelated roofline. Round and flat arches support massive weight above windows.

First named Minnekahta, a Sioux word for "warm waters," the town was renamed in 1886. The railroad came in 1891. Large hotels and bathhouses sprang up soon after, and the Northwestern and Burlington railroads launched a successful advertising campaign to bring the spa-minded to South Dakota for a good soak and a rest. This concept would have surprised the many weary hunters, trappers, traders, explorers, and wagon train households who crossed Sioux land in earlier years.

The pink sandstone, from quarries nearby, was hand-cut and carved by talented stonemasons who also served as architects and builders at times. A number of buildings have been restored with recycled sandstone from others that were out of use or old structures from Cascade Springs, a ghost town not far distant. The community has a full-scale rejuvenation program in progress. The *Fall River Historical Society* and the *Chamber of Commerce* have a walking tour.

The *Heart of Hot Springs Tour* is about eight blocks long. The Chamber of Commerce is in the former terminus of the Fremont, Elkhorn and Missouri Valley and the Chicago, Burlington and Quincy railroads, a Union Depot made of sandstone from the Evans quarry about 6 miles SE of town. Information on the area is available here.

The *Minnekahta Block,* built in 1891, has corner and front trim formed of tooled stone blocks that are actually an integral part of the walls. The checkerboard design was known as "diaper work" by the stonemasons of the era. In *Kidney Spring Park* there is a pavilion for summer band concerts and water that may cure rheumatism and certainly can help quench thirst.

St. Luke's Church, built by Episcopal pioneers in the late 19th century, has been renovated, with the stained-glass windows restored.

Evans Hotel, or *Century House,* has had thousands of guests since 1892 and is still handsome.

Beyond the hotel the *Paint Store* and *Art Gallery* occupy a building once the *Eureka Saloon,* built of Burke quarry stone. A north window provided light for a pioneer photographer as it now serves art students.

All along River St. new businesses take the place of old. *Bessie's Antiques* are in the former *"Fargo Mercantile Cash Store,"* built by Grant Robinson and Fred Berrier in 1910. The *City Hall* was built in 1893 of Burke quarry stone. The *Hot Springs Area Arts Council Art Center* was once the *Opera House,* on the second floor of City Hall. The walls, of stone that weighed 125 pounds per cubic foot, also have provided shelter for a library, post office, fire department, and jail.

Hot Springs was originally divided into upper town and lower town, which was primarily the open flat south end of the valley of the Fall River. A block of Jennings Avenue between River St. and Chicago St., known as *"The Midway,"* has old and new stone buildings.

The *Fall River County Courthouse,* tallest stone structure in the business section, was even taller before it lost its turret. The *Evans Plunge,* at 1145 N. River St., fed by hundreds of warm springs which bubble from a pebble floor, is said to be the largest indoor natural warm-water pool in the world.

MADISON, Lake County. St. 34.

Prairie Village, 3 miles W on US 81, St. 34, is a replica pioneer town with original buildings of the 1890s which have been moved to this site and maintained by the nonprofit Prairie Village Historical Society. On the 110-acre tract are a depot, hotel, jail, bank, sod house, and the *Old Opera House* from Oldham, where Lawrence Welk made his stage debut more than half a century ago. There also are a print shop, dentist's office, and the library from Howard, the first chartered library in Dakota Territory in 1886. The barbershop is from Tolstoy. All buildings are from South Dakota locations.

In the summer there are many attractions which follow the earlier days. The area Ministerial Association holds church services in the *Old Village Church,* which once served Junius, where it was erected in 1906. The *Opera House,* known as the *Social Hall,* was built at Oldham with Socialist funds in 1900. The university repertory theater gives performances in summer.

An unusual feature is the steam-powered carousel, last in service in

Lennox in 1917. It has hand-carved wooden horses from Germany and plays organ music. The popcorn and peanut machine is also steam-powered and once did business on Main St. in Madison, but these days it is run by an electric motor.

An extensive collection of antique steam and gas farm machinery is in action each August (on the last weekend) for the *Annual Steam Threshing Jamboree.* At this busy time, local schoolchildren dressed in the 1890s style attend all-day classes at the old schoolhouse.

ROCKERVILLE, Pennington County. US 16, about 12 miles E of Hill City.

Only Deadwood had richer gold placers in the Dakota Territory than Rockerville when in 1876 the mining stampede got under way. The settlement got its name because of the hundreds of rockers in use along the banks of the gulch. In winter miners had to use handcarts to transport their rockers to the nearest pool or stream to rock out their load. The peak period was in the early 1880s. By 1883 this was nearly a ghost town. It has been rebuilt recently and furnished in the 1870s period. Stores, saloon, and dining rooms are open. The bar fixtures date from 1880. The 1876 cabin, the only original Rockerville building, has served as a store, tavern, gambling hall, and residence and is now restored.

SIOUX FALLS, Minnehaha County. I-90.

Buffalo Ridge, 7 miles W of town off I-90, E of Hartford. A replica Old West town on a 135-acre site on Buffalo Ridge, consisting of the village, an open-air theater, and a buffalo herd. On Main St. are a trading post, shops, a Gold Rush museum, and an authentic jail with gallows.

TWO STRIKE, Jones County. I-90, use exit 40, about halfway between Murdo and Kadoka.

The village, with a land office, saloon, barbershop, general store, blacksmith shop, and marshal's office still is being developed. Some buildings were used for the film *Grasslands.* An entire town will spread over some 80 acres, as the "city" planners feel the old-timers had plenty of land and used it.

California and Nevada

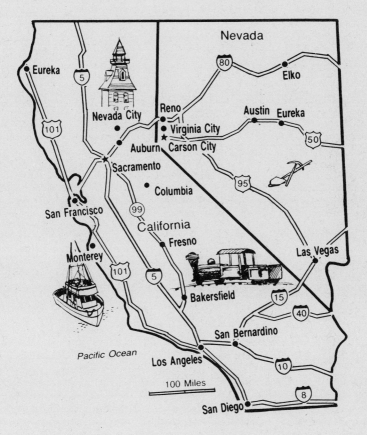

CALIFORNIA

Monterey is composed of houses built of adobe or sun-dried brick, of one or two stories, with a narrow balcony [across] the whole front. About a dozen houses are comfortable and the balance mere hovels. There are some families that style themselves Dons, do nothing but walk the streets with peaked broad-brimmed hats and cloaks or serapas which are brightly colored, checkered ponchoes, a colored shirt, silk or fancy pants slashed down the outside, with fringe and buttons, shoes on their feet and cigar in their mouth.

From a letter by William Tecumseh Sherman, Monterey, March 12, 1847

... he [the miner] turns the river from its ancient bed, and hangs it, for miles together, in wooden flumes upon the mountain's side, or throws it from hill to hill, in aqueducts that tremble at their own airy height; or he pumps a river dry, and takes its golden bottom out.

—*Hutchings' California Magazine,* 1860

AUBURN, Placer County. I-80.

Old Town Auburn was first named North Fork Dry Diggin's. Claude Chana had his second stroke of fortune here when, with three fellow Frenchmen and 25 Indians, he panned for gold and found it. His first break was in deciding to go ahead of the ill-fated Donner Party wagon train which he had joined on the road to California.

On May 16, 1848, Chana and his companions started mining in Auburn Ravine; here and at Rich Flat, on today's Sacramento St., plenty of gold was found. The Auburn '49er Association printed a January 1850 letter Isaac Annis wrote to his daughter which put the scene aptly: "There is so many people here, we are all in a heap. The diggins is full of miners. You have no idea how many there is here." By April he was reporting: "It appears to me there is more men here than there is in the State of New York. You may dig anywhere and you find some gold but some places are richer than others. If it holds on ten years they will dig up all upper California."

Chana's story is a happier one than many of those who struck it rich. He took his fortune to a ranch on Bear River where he could follow the life he really enjoyed, farming. Shortly before his death in 1882 when a friend asked if he had any regrets, Chana said no and then smiled broadly: "I really wish I could die in Auburn. It's so much cooler there in the summertime." Whether or not Chana actually departed with a gentle joke, he went well-off and with a friend at hand. Too many others died forgotten and in abject poverty.

The *Chamber of Commerce,* on Commercial and Maple, has a guide to historic Auburn. There is a 45-ton statue of Claude Chana just off I-80 (at Maple St. turnoff), slightly SW of

City Hall and the Chamber of Commerce. *Old Fire House,* built in 1893, is the home of the *Auburn Hook and Ladder Company,* organized in 1852 and in continuous service since. Auburn's firemen had a lot of practice putting out fires in the early days but not enough in June 1855, when nearly all of the town burned in one hour and 25 minutes. Most Old Town buildings are post-fire. Sites of original *Wells Fargo Office,* the *Orleans Hotel,* and other early buildings are marked.

BAKERSFIELD, Kern County. I-5.
Pioneer Village of the Kern County Museum, 3801 Chester Ave., was begun in 1950 on an 11-acre plot behind the main exhibit building and is aptly named, as it was one of the first of many such reconstructions. Now on 12 acres, it represents a California town of 1860–1910. The *Beale Clock Tower,* a Bakersfield landmark, has been reconstructed at the front of the museum grounds. *Howell House* is an 1891 Victorian mansion, moved to the village as a gift of the Bakersfield *Californian,* with many furnishings given by the Howell family.

The *Souther* (sow-ther) *Ditch Plow* cut a furrow 5 feet wide and 3 feet deep in digging the Kern Island Canal. Forty yoke of oxen pulled it.

The *Sheepherder's Cabin* is a graphic survivor of old times. It had a bed, stove, and other necessities and was moved from place to place by a team of horses—with skids attached to the bottom of the hut.

Among the many unusual exhibits here, in addition to the customary blacksmith shop, jail, school, and church of most reconstructions, are the *Weller Ranch Ensemble,* which seems to include everything down to the hog-scalding kettle; an oil-field central pumping plant, which served in the Kern River Oil Field for 50 years; an oil derrick model with authentic parts gathered from the area, and an oil museum. The village is

open daily; hours vary with the season. Richard C. Bailey, museum director, can furnish details on hours and group rates; zip is 93301; phone (805) 861-2132.

COLUMBIA, Tuolumne County. St. 49.
Columbia State Historic Park, 4 miles N via St. 49 and country road, is a restoration of the 1850 boom town in the heart of the Mother Lode country, first called Hildreth's Diggings, then American Camp, and finally Columbia, the "Gem of the Southern Mines." By 1880 about $87 million in gold had been mined. Water was in short supply. A company, formed in 1851 to build a network of reservoirs, ditches, and flumes, brought water at prices higher than the gold, or so it seemed. In 1854 the miners organized their own Columbia and Stanislaus River Water Company, which built a 60-mile-long aqueduct through the mountains. By the time this was completed in 1858, many miners were moving on and the original water company acquired the new project for a bargain $150,000.

In late 1852 there were more than 150 commercial buildings, and a church, lodge, and a Sons of Temperance society. But in the summer of 1854 fire destroyed nearly everything in the business section except one brick structure. Thirty buildings of brick were put up in the next two years.

Though movies usually show outlaws, dance hall girls, drink, and gambling as the chief problems of the frontier mining towns, often it was fire. Columbia was hit again in August 1857. All frame buildings and several brick ones were demolished. The iron doors and window shutters seen today were part of the rebuilding. The *Wells Fargo Office,* built after 1857, was one of the first to be restored. The large scales on exhibit were used to weigh out gold dust,

Fire House No. 1, El Pueblo de los Angeles State Historic Park, Los Angeles. (Courtesy California Department of State Parks)

more than $55 million in all. The *Schoolhouse,* now with desks, potbellied stove, pump organ, and bell tower, was built in 1860 and used until the late 1930s. *Fallon House Theatre* is used for summer repertory by students of the University of the Pacific. Park headquarters has an illustrated guide with detailed listings of the 42 exhibits now to be visited. The park is open daily.

LOS ANGELES, Los Angeles County. I-5.

El Pueblo de Los Angeles State Historic Park, 420 N. Main, is a restored site in the heart of the city where landmarks have been "revitalized" in a 42-acre area. Free guided walking tours are available, Tuesdays through Saturdays from 10 A.M. to 1 P.M. Call (213) 628-1274 for reservation or information.

Among historic buildings: *The Pico House* (1869), the first elegant hotel with a bathroom on each floor; the *Merced Theatre* (1870), the first theatre building in Los Angeles; the first *Masonic Hall* (1858); the *Avila Adobe,* the oldest residence (1818).

Fire House No. 1 (1884) was home

for a volunteer group, later a paid department, Engine Co. No. 4. Still later a chemical company used the building. The chemical fire fighters used two 50-gallon tanks of bicarbonate of soda, sulfuric acid, and water to control small conflagrations. After 15 years, the firehouse became a warehouse, then a third-rate hotel, and a cheap saloon. Now restored, even to a shining brass pole, it is a popular site for historical fire buffs.

The *Plaza Church, Sepulveda House,* and the *Pelanconi House* are each historical buildings. *Olvera Street* with its scent and look of old Mexico is usually crowded with site-seers and shoppers. A *Visitor Center* has literature on the area, with maps.

Los Angeles Convention & Visitors Bureau, 505 S. Flower St., managed by the efficient and pleasant Christiana Hills, offers all sorts of help, from finding historic sites to how to get around in an often confusing street system, even how to use the telephone in almost any language.

Heritage Square, off York Ave. from the Pasadena Freeway, exit 11, about 3 miles from the Civic Center, is within the original 4 square Spanish leagues or 28 square miles marked off in 1781 and incorporated later as the City of Los Angeles. The *Hale House,* moved to this site, is an interesting example of restoration carried out by thoughtful persons under the handicap of not knowing who the builder or original owner were. The Interiors Committee of the Heritage Square advisory board decided to make the exhibit a period piece of the late 1880s. They are using pieces of this period which are good, adding other pieces which may not have been family possessions but fit the time, and in general are following the recommendations of Charles Locke Eastlake, whose *Hints on Household Taste,* 1872, was popular and vastly influential in the 1880s.

The Interior Committee thinks the

purpose of the restoration is something other than "just doing another Victorian house with antimacassars and bibelots, ad nauseum, exhibiting no definition of aesthetic preference or expertise. Therefore, the Hale House will eventually be a reflection of a very particular taste of the mid to late 19th century; that taste being Queen Anne–Eastlake. . . . The Hale house is what historian Alan Gowans considers 'aesthetic history in its most tangible form.' " The restoration-minded who really want to keep grandpa's ambrotype in the attic can take heart from this positive—if controversial—attitude. By all means visit the Hale House. It is the intent of the Committee "that there be something for everyone . . . for the scholar who wants to study and research . . . for the antiquarian who dwells in nostalgia and loves old things just because they are old . . . for those who would delve into past artistic heritage to adapt for the present . . . cultural historians and sociologists who study and interpret what has been created and abandoned . . . and for all those people who just like to look at old things for a myriad of personal reasons." What could be more fair than that?

Also in Heritage Square are the *Valley Knudsen Garden-Residence,* built between 1877 and 1878, in mansard style, moved here along with a rare coral tree from the original site; *Beaudry St. House,* possibly from the early 1880s, seems to be a combination of Italianate, Eastlake, and Queen Anne styles. The *William Perry Mansion* and the *Palms Railroad Station* will be moved here also. The land, a 10-acre strip, was made available by the City Department of Recreation and Parks to provide a place for historic buildings which could not be preserved at their original sites. The completed project will have a schoolhouse, church, park, a trolley barn, transportation museum, restaurants, and other stores.

Carroll Ave. Restorations, 1300 block between Edgeware and Douglas Sts., comprises nine original Victorian homes, built in 1887–95, in what was the "Angelino Heights" housing development. Two more Victorian houses are to be moved to the block. A walking tour takes in the *Philips House,* 1300, an 1887 Queen Anne–Eastlake structure with stained and painted glass of flower and bird motifs of unusual quality; *Russel House,* 1316, built in 1887–88, Eastlake style, with a beautifully proportioned carriage house in the rear; *Heim House,* 1320, Queen Anne, with two turrets and spindlework; *Scheerer House,* 1324, cottage style typical of the 19th-century *Plan Book*—the carpenter worked from a lithographed picture with changes to suit the owner; in addition to Gothic gingerbread trim, the shingles are diamond-patterned and there is ornamental ironwork. *Newsom House,* 1330, was built by architect Joseph Cather Newsom for Charles Sessions, a dairyman, and is Moorish in style with Chinese guard dogs on either side of the entrance. The main staircase has three panels of leaded glass. *Haskin House,* 1344, was the last of the Victorian structures to be erected on the block and is called the *"Gay Nineties" residence.* There are a number of other notable houses in the area; inquire at the *Carroll Ave. Restoration Foundation,* 1316 Carroll, Los Angeles, 90026.

MONTEREY, Monterey County. St. 1.

Monterey's Path of History is a 3-mile walking tour which takes in some 45 historic sites, many open to the public. A map is available from the *Chamber of Commerce,* 2030 Fremont Ave. or P.O. Box 1770, Monterey, 93940; call (408) 649-3200. A painted red-orange line down the center of the streets leads to historic houses and descriptive plaques mark the area.

Among outstanding places of interest, some of which are national historic or state historical landmarks:

First French Consulate, 404 E. Estero (1830), was occupied by Louis Casquet, first consul from France to California; not open at present.

The **Royal Presidio Chapel,** 550 Church St., founded in 1770 by Junipero Serra and Don Gaspar de Portola. Open daily 7 A.M. to 9 P.M.

Stevenson House, 530 Houston, was home to Robert Louis Stevenson in the fall of 1879 when he rented a room on the second floor to be near Fanny Osbourne, who was married to someone else. Stevenson was 30 years old, with bad lungs, and traveling for his health. He had come to California in 1879 by emigrant ship and train. He and Mrs. Osbourne were married in 1880. After a stay in Calistoga, which he wrote about in *The Silverado Squatters,* he returned to England, very ill with tuberculosis, but still continuing to write. In 1888 he went to Samoa, had an improvement in health for a short time, died suddenly, and is buried there. The house is open daily; a small admission charge also includes the *Pacific Building, First Theatre,* and the *Larkin House.*

Casa Amesti, 516 Polk (1825), a two-story adobe, is an excellent combination of Spanish and American architecture, now known as Monterey style. This was the home of Don Jose Amesti, alcalde of Monterey, and is now the property of the National Trust for Historic Preservation. Open weekends. The Trust has also acquired the **Cooper-Molera Adobe,** next door, built by Juan Bautista Cooper, half-brother of Thomas Larkin.

Larkin House, 510 Calle Principal, the 1830s home of onetime Yankee merchant Thomas Larkin, the only U.S. consul to Mexico in Monterey; this home served as the consulate until 1848. Walter Colton, first American alcalde of Monterey, used one of the rooms as his office. Later it was headquarters for the U.S. military governor of California. Shown by guided tours only. Inquire by calling Department of Parks and Recreation: (408) 373-2103. The 35-minute tours are limited to 15 persons, advance registration required. Daily except Tuesday. NHL.

Sherman's Headquarters, an adobe in the Larkin House Garden, is mentioned in the general's *Memoirs* (1847): "California had settled down to a condition of absolute repose, and we naturally repined at our fate in being so remote from the war in Mexico, where our comrades were reaping large honors.... I had a small adobe-house back of Larkin's. Halleck and Dr. Murray had a small log-house not far off. The company of artillery was still on the hill, under the command of Lieutenant Ord." Ord and Halleck as well as Sherman would become Union generals in the Civil War.

Colton Hall and Old Jail, Pacific St. between Madison and Jefferson, where California's constitution was written in 1849, was put up in 1847–49 by the Reverend Walter Colton, Navy chaplain, the first American alcalde of California in 1846. Open daily.

Casa Serrano, 412 Pacific St., was the bridal home of Florencio Serrano, mayor and schoolteacher, in 1845. The Serranos opened a school. House is open on weekends.

First Theatre, Pacific and Scott Sts., built in 1846 by Jack Swan, a British sailor. Open daily except Tuesdays. Small admission includes other houses.

Casa Del Oro, Scott and Olivier Sts., built in 1843 as a barracks, later a general store, a saloon, and then a residence. Open daily.

Old Whaling Station, on Pacific Ave. at road to Cannery Row, was an 1850s boardinghouse for Portuguese whalers. Sidewalks are of whale bones. The house is not open at present, but visitors may walk inside the gate at the left and see the garden enclosed by a chalk rock wall.

Pacific Bldg. and Memory Garden, Scott and Calle Principal, has an excellent museum with artifacts from the Indian and Spanish eras. Open daily.

Custom House, Fisherman's Wharf, is the oldest government building on the Pacific coast and the only remaining structure in California built by the Mexican government. Open daily. In a letter of March 12, 1847, Sherman wrote: "I, as Quarter Master, occupied with a guard the Custom House, a large building near the wharf and the most conspicuous house in Monterey. In one wing is the hospital, in the centre the stores, and the other wing my office and quarters. All the other officers are under tents on the hill and envy me my papered, comfortable room, where I can write in comfort and sleep without fear of the cold rains that fall here in the rainy or winter season." NHL.

Casa de Castro, Castro Rd., facing the Del Monte Fairways, was the summer home of General Jose Castro and his family. Born in Monterey, Castro served in many civil offices. The home is not open at present. Sherman wrote home of the death of Don Castro's nine-year-old daughter in 1847: "All the girls of the town repaired to the house, and two days were spent in decorating the person of the little girl. A miniature couch with delicate lace curtains, neatly drawn from the decorated canopy, made her bier on which she was borne slowly through the town to the church. A promiscuous company followed, not silently two by two but gaily, without order and with a band of music. I was on the piazza of the Government house, near which it passed and saw the little child lying as though sleeping upon its little bed. Its bearers were women who set their burden down frequently to talk or rest and during this time the band,

consisting of violins, harp and some jingling instruments kept playing Spanish tunes. Guns were fired from the houses which they passed, and upon inquiry, finding that such was the custom of the country, we got out several pistols and fired a perfect salvo of rejoicing that the child had gone to heaven."

Royal Presidio Chapel, 550 Church St., early 1790s stone in Latin cross shape, with 19th-century additions, is the state's only extant presidio chapel and the last remaining 18th-century Spanish structure in the area. NHL.

NEVADA CITY, Nevada County. St. 49.

Chamber of Commerce, 132 Main, has information on a walking tour of town, with a map. The settlement was first called Deer Creek, Dry Diggins, and Caldwell's Upper Store and was settled in 1849. Two years later some 10,000 miners were digging in a 3-mile area. The gold mines closed in 1942, but the boom was long over. At the **Assay Office** here, nuggets from the famous Comstock Lode were first tested.

National Exchange Hotel, Bicknell's Block, 211 Broad St., a three-story brick, built in 1856, has ornamental cast-iron balconies. It has been a hotel continuously.

Firehouse No. 2, 420 Broad St. (1860–61), the town's first permanent firehouse, is the only original one still in use.

Cedar Theater, Broad and Bridge Sts. (1864–65), is the earliest extant theater in the state; it has been modified and still is used.

The Reverend John Steele, author of *Across the Plains in 1850, In Camp and Cabin,* and other books, reached Nevada City in September 1850: "There were a number of good stores, meat shops, bakeries, blacksmith shops, etc., but the gambling saloons were the terror of the town. Their rooms were spacious, supplied with music, and adorned with mirrors,

pictures, and every device to attract the young. . . . There was such a witchery in the music, instrumental and vocal, that the masses were attracted and entranced, and in passing I found it difficult to resist the temptation to go in and listen."

SACRAMENTO, Sacramento County. I-5.

Old Sacramento Historic District, at the junctions of US 40, 50, 99, and St. 16, 24, contains the largest number of 1849 gold rush buildings on the coast.

Brannan Bldgs., at J and Front Sts., were built after the fire of 1852 and remodeled in 1865. On this site Samuel Brannan's store, moved from Sutter's Fort in 1849, was used as an office by James Birch, who operated the first stage line out of town.

Vernon-Brannan Bldg., 112 J St., built in 1853 on the site of the first post office by Henry E. Robinson, postmaster, was later a hotel; the Society of California Pioneers was organized here in 1854.

Sacramento Union Bldg., 121 J St., the newspaper established in 1851 with Dr. J. F. Morse, editor, is said to be the oldest in the West.

B. F. Hastings Bldg., 128–132 J St., was the western terminus of the

Overland Pony Express. At other times the building housed offices of a railroad, the state attorney general, state librarian, and the State Supreme Court.

There are eight more landmark buildings on J St. The *Latham Bldg.,* at 223, 1855 home and office of Milton S. Latham, governor in 1860 and later a U.S. Senator, became a commercial structure after 1864. The *Fashion Saloon,* at 209, was built in 1855 on the site of an earlier saloon destroyed by fire. Nos. 111, 120–124, 200, 208, 224, and 226 are interesting structures from the midcentury.

On K St., *Lady Adams Bldg.,* No. 113, is the only remaining structure not destroyed by the 1852 fire. There are several other 1850s buildings on the street, including the *Ebners Hotel,* No. 116, built in 1856 by Charles and Francis X. Ebner, pioneer hotelmen.

The Embarcadero, on Front St., was the site Sutter chose for a landing on the bank of the Sacramento River for boats from San Francisco to deliver supplies for his fort. After gold was discovered at Coloma, thousands of miners landed here and the business section grew up in this area.

Sutter's Fort (State Historic Park), at 27 and L Sts., was restored in the early 1900s with exhibits including carpenter, blacksmith, and saddle shops. Open daily.

City Hotel, 919 Front St., was built for Brannan & Co. in 1849 with timbers cut for Sutter's gristmill. The *Eagle Theater,* first built for stage performances, was erected at No. 921 Front, in 1849. There are more landmark buildings on Front, Second, and Third Sts. in the Old Sacramento section, and elsewhere in town.

The *California Department of Parks and Recreation,* 1416 9th St., has a library and museum; *Sacramento Museum and History Commission,* 1009 7th St., has collections from 1783. *Friends of Sacramento City and County Museum,* the *Pioneer Association,* and the *Trust for Historic Preservation* also are at this address.

SAN DIEGO, San Diego County. I-15.

Convention & Visitors Bureau, 1200 3rd Ave., Suite 824, has a brochure on historical sections and a tour map for a 52-mile drive marked by blue seagulls. A 24-hour "host" phone helps on holidays when the office is closed by leaving a recorded message on the day's events and tour suggestion: (714) 232-3101; 239-9696.

Old Town San Diego Historic District covers the center of the original settlement, once a Mexican pioneer town, with one-story adobe buildings. After 1846 Americans developed frame structures and hotels. The seat of government was here 1825–31. Now most of the area is the *Old Town San Diego State Historic Park,* 2725 Congress St., representing the 1829–69 period. A green line painted on the streets leads to landmarks. There is a living-history program with home crafts demonstrated at the *Machado-Stewart Adobe* on Congress St. In 1872 a fire destroyed many of the buildings in this area, but two of the four original homes which survived have been restored, the Machado-Stewart Adobe and the *Casa de Estudillo.* The *Machado Adobe* is being completed, and the *Casa Bandini,* once the social center. The *Whaley House,* which may be the oldest brick structure in southern California, with an annex that once served as County Courthouse, and two (of the four) bedrooms upstairs once occupied by the "Tanner Troupe" for theatricals, a landmark hotel, and stables have been restored, reconstructed, and refurnished as needed. Visitors can take guided tours or stroll freely without the worry of cars on the streets. There are

shops and restaurants old and new in style.

Adjacent to the park is another historical area, *Heritage Park,* which is being developed as a regional park to preserve Victorian structures in danger of demolition at their original sites (like Heritage Square in Los Angeles, which see). The *Sherman-Gilbert House* (1887) has a parlor exhibit. *Bushyhead* (1887), *Burton* (1893), and *Christian* (1889) are houses now under restoration.

Villa Montezuma, 1925 K St., built in 1887, is a fine Queen Anne Victorian mansion, maintained by the San Diego Historical Society. Museum.

SAN FRANCISCO, San Francisco County. I-80.

The Convention & Visitors Bureau, 1390 Market St., zip 94102—(415) 626-5500—is one of the busiest and most capable in the U.S., with advice and/or brochures on every aspect of site-seeing in this part of California. With their help you can walk, ride cable cars, transfer to the 697-mile Municipal Railway system, drive, or even eat your way around town in the more than 2,600 restaurants available.

Jackson Square, 400 block, is a reclaimed historic area. The Jackson-Montgomery corner was the site of the city's first bridge in 1844 over the Laguna Salada, a backwater area. To quote the lively brochure written by an anonymous "MB" for the Convention & Visitors Bureau: " 'Jackson sough' was filled in with granite blocks and bricks carried as ballast around the Horn and from China, with the hulks of ships abandoned in the stampede for gold and redwood pilings from the old Montgomery Street waterfront. The area became the heart of the boom town's commercial life. Onto the counters of Gold and Balance Streets miners from the Mother Lode dumped nuggets and gold dust to be weighed and

Pictorial map of Old San Diego, California. (Courtesy of J. W. Parker)

Legend

1. El campo Santo
2. Little Adobe Chapel
3. Whaley House
4. Pendleton House
5. Immaculate Conception
6. Casa de Altamarino
7. Casa de Pedrorena
8. Casa de Estudillo
9. Casa Bandini
10. Seeley Stables "Hazard Collection"
11. Casa de Pío Pico (Bazaar Del Mundo)
12. Old Town Plaza
13. Congress Hall Site
14. Machado Chapel
15. Casa de Stewart
16. Casa de Lopez
17. Fort Stockton
18. Serra Museum
19. Serra Cross
20. Gatewood House
21. Mason Street School
22. Old Town State Park Visitors Center
23. Heritage Park
24. Mormon Visitation, Center
25. Casa de Carrillo
26. Cobblestone Jail Site

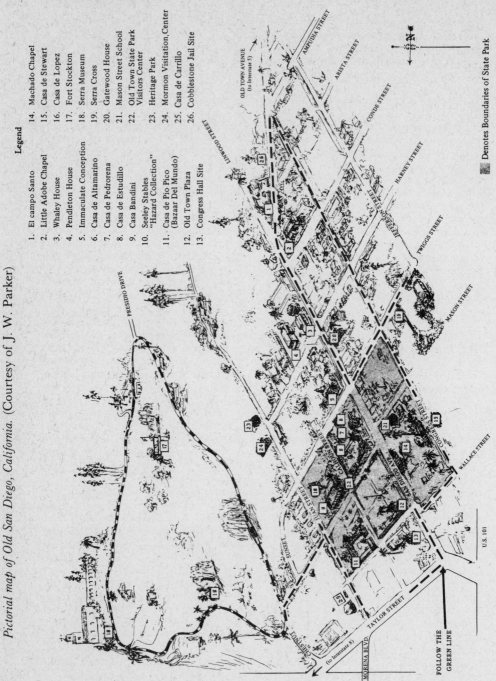

■ Denotes Boundaries of State Park

assayed. Wells Fargo coaches, hansom cabs and drays clattered in and out of the livery stable on Hotaling Place. The buildings which rose along the rutted streets were mostly three-story brick structures. Their doughty walls and vault-like shutters enabled the buildings to withstand the 1864 earthquake and the fire and looting which swept the city in the wake of the 1906 quake."

Restoration began in the 1950s when wholesalers were looking for showrooms. Again to quote "MB": "The lime-encrusted bricks were scraped and sandblasted, the wood painted subtle colors, the fine Federal-style facades enhanced by trees and shrubs." And all this attracted other tradesmen. Today there are 37 buildings in the "Square."

The *S. Harris Company Bldg.*, 451 Jackson, housed a whiskey distillery in 1866. The structure and its iron shutters withstood the 1906 quake and are said to have inspired a jingle by Charles Field:

*If, as they say, God spanked the town
For being over-frisky,*

*Why did He burn His churches down
And spare Hotaling's whiskey?*

Hotaling Place is a refurbished alley. The 500 block on Pacific Ave. has also been "uplifted from raffishness to refinement" in what was once the Barbary Coast.

Ghirardelli Square, along the north waterfront, was once dominated by a woolen mill and a box factory. When Domingo Ghirardelli bought the area in 1893 he had massive red brick buildings erected; in 1915 came the Clock Tower modeled after the Château Blois in the Loire Valley. This area, adjacent to Fisherman's Wharf, has been handsomely restored. The old names of buildings were retained and so were most of the buildings except the old box factory. But new construction was made harmonious with the old **Woolen Mill,** the **Mustard Building,** the **Chocolate Building,** the **Cocoa Building,** and a **Power House.** The complex now houses restaurants, shops, theaters, offices, and galleries.

NEVADA

The Pony Express Trail crossed the mountains over Hastings Pass, through which the modern road from Hobson to Simonsen now runs. It angled southwest to cut across U.S. 50 east of Austin. From this point the trail follows U.S. 50 towards Carson Sink. This is the stretch of the road traversed by Pony Bob Haslam, one of the most famous of the riders. In 1860 he rode 120 miles in eight hours and ten minutes from Smith Creek to Fort Churchill to speed Abraham Lincoln's Inaugural Address toward California.

By the end of that year the Paiute Indians all but stopped the Pony Express. In December, Pony Bob reached Reed's Station on the Carson River, but found no change of horses waiting. He fed the horse he was riding and headed for Fort Churchill, fifteen miles down the trail. At Fort Churchill the next rider, being afraid of the Indians, refused to take the mochila [mail-bag]. Haslam rode on as far as Smiths Creek, for a total ride of 190 miles. He rested and started back with the mail bound for the west. At Cold Springs he discovered the keeper killed by Indians, put spurs to his horse and rode on to the big adobe station at Sand Springs and safety. Pony Bob lived through many such relays to become later in life the manager of the Congress and Auditorium hotels in Chicago.

—Great Trails of the West, by Richard Dunlop, Nashville, 1967

Virginia had grown to be the "livest" town, for its age and population, that America had ever produced. The sidewalks swarmed with people—to such an extent, indeed, that it was generally no easy matter to stem the human tide. The streets themselves were just as crowded with quartz wagons, freight teams and other vehicles. The procession was endless. So great was the pack, that buggies frequently had to wait half an hour for an opportunity to cross the principal street. . . . Money was as plenty as dust; every individual considered himself wealthy, and a melancholy countenance was nowhere to be seen. There were military companies, fire companies, brass bands, banks, hotels, theatres, "hurdy-gurdy houses," wide-open gambling palaces, political pow-wows, civic processions, street fights, murders, inquests, riots, a whiskey mill every fifteen steps, a Board of Aldermen, a Mayor, a City Surveyor, a City Engineer, a Chief of the Fire Department, with First, Second and Third Assistants, a Chief of Police, City Marshal and a large police force, two Boards of Mining Brokers, a dozen breweries and half a dozen jails and station-houses in full operation, and some talk of building a church.

—Roughing It, by Mark Twain, Hartford, Conn., 1872

AUSTIN, Lander County. US 50. *Austin Historic District,* in Pony Canyon at the junction of US 50 and St. 8A. The town had so many brick and adobe buildings, since clay was handier to get than lumber, it suffered less from disastrous fires which leveled or damaged many old settlements. But, spared one disaster, it suffered another—floods, in 1868 and 1874. There still are 13 original brick buildings in two blocks on Main St.

The *Lander County Courthouse,* one street S of Main, was built in 1869 and is the oldest in Nevada.

Stokes Castle, a three-story tower-like structure, was built in 1879 for financier Anson Phelps Stokes. It is 50 feet square at its base, and constructed of hand-hewn granite.

The *Reese River Reveille* was published in the same building on Main St. from May 16, 1863, until 1968, when it moved to Tonopah.

St. George Episcopal Church, N side of Main St., has a pipe organ which was shipped around the Horn and then overland from San Francisco.

The *Gridley Store* at the E end of town on the N side of Main St. was the starting point for the famous Sack-of-Flour Walk. Reuel C. Gridley, pro-southern in feeling, became known from coast to coast when he lost an election bet to Dr. H. S. Herrick, a Unionist. Gridley had to carry a 50-pound sack of flour a mile down the canyon to Clinton. Everyone turned out to watch the goings-on. Later Gridley took the flour on tour and raised more than $175,000 for the aid of the Civil War wounded, by auctioning it off repeatedly.

Chamber of Commerce has self-guiding tour maps: Box 38, zip 89310; phone (702) 964-2692. Today's residents still are fond of a joke. When someone wrote a book called *The Town That Died Laughing,* they admired the title even if they weren't laid away yet. Recently a native artist and his talented wife, who owned an art gallery at Lake Tahoe before coming to Austin, opened a country store. One box in the eclectic collection of old and new reads: "King Tut Cavity Chemical—Best by Test." Mrs. Givens says, "You know what

was carried in that box? Embalming fluid. We sell nuts out of it now."

EUREKA, Eureka County. US 50.

Eureka Historic District, along US 50, looks like a stage setting for a Western. Its mines produced so much lead they broke the world lead market, according to Nevada boosters. Eureka was sometimes called the "Pittsburgh of the West." A number of old buildings remain. The *Chamber of Commerce* has a booklet with the history of the district.

VIRGINIA CITY, Storey County. St. 17, 26 miles SE of Reno.

Virginia City Historic District takes in the whole town. A *Visitors' Bureau* on C St. has a 15-minute film on the history of the town and tours of the district. *Piper's Opera House,* B and Union Sts., had stars such as Edwin Booth, Joseph Jefferson, Julia Dean, Lotta Crabtree, Sarah Bernhardt, and others in its heyday. The Virginia City Restoration Commission has been hard at work to save the city's historic buildings. The *Territorial Enterprise,* where Mark Twain was a reporter, still is in business. Twain's desk is on display. The Virginia City *Times,* on sale at several places in town (the Delta Gift Shop, for one) for a quarter, is packed with information and old photographs of the bonanza town where the Comstock Lode was found, yielding the richest deposits of lode gold and silver ever found.

Mark Twain's *Roughing It* still yields a rich return in laughter and a humorous look at the brawling town of the 1860s. Another journalist jack-of-all-trades was J. Ross Browne, and more than one historian has noted that Twain probably "borrowed" from Browne's writings. Browne is said to have told his wife that he could not compete with "the big gun from Hannibal, Mo." Browne was a globe-trotter in the midcentury, getting around by almost every conveyance possible, ship, boat, horse, mule, stagecoach, and shanks' mare. His observations on "Washoe," as Nevada was called in his time, are, like Twain's, both entertaining and sharp:

"When I was about to start on my trip to Washoe, friends from Virginia [City] assured me I would find hotels there almost, if not quite equal to the best in San Francisco. Now I really don't consider myself fastidious on the subject of hotels. Having traveled in many different countries, I have enjoyed an extensive experience in the way of accommodations, from my mother-earth to the fore-top of a whale-ship, from an Indian wigwam to a Parisian Hotel, from an African palm tree to an Arctic snowbank. . . . I have slept in beds of rivers, and beds of sand, and on the bare bed-rock. . . . with comparative satisfaction. . . .

"Perhaps my experience in Virginia was exceptional; perhaps misfortune was determined to try me to the utmost extremity. I endeavored to find accommodations at a hotel recommended as the best in the place, and was shown a room over the kitchen-stove, in which the thermometer ranged at about 130 to 150 degrees of Fahrenheit. To be lodged and baked at the rate of $2 per night cash, in advance, was more than I could stand.

"The next hotel to which I was recommended was eligibly located on a street composed principally of grogshops and gambling-houses. . . . The walls were constructed of boards fancifully decorated with paper, and affording this facility to a lodger—that he could hear all that was going on in the adjacent room. . . . So much for the famous hotels of Virginia."

Alaska

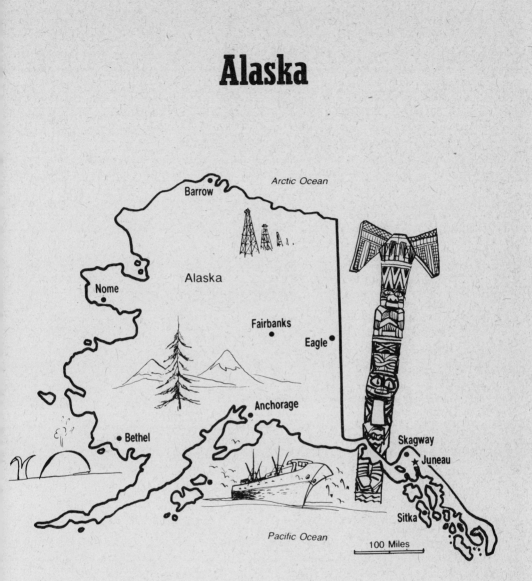

Arctic Ocean

Barrow

Nome

Alaska

Fairbanks

Eagle

Anchorage

Bethel

Skagway

Juneau

Sitka

Pacific Ocean

100 Miles

ALASKA

"Jack Carr," the famous Yukon mail carrier, has given a list for an outfit which, he says, will last one man one year in the Klondike district. This list follows:

Flour, pounds	400
Cornmeal, pounds	50
Rolled oats, pounds	50
Rice, pounds	35
Beans, pounds	100
Candles, pounds	40
Sugar, granulated, pounds	100
Baking powder, pounds	8
Bacon, pounds	200
Soda, pounds	2
Yeast cakes (6 in package) packages	6
Salt, pounds	15
Pepper, pounds	1
Mustard, pounds	½
Ginger, pounds	¼
Apples, evaporated, pounds	25
Peaches, evaporated, pounds	25
Apricots, evaporated, pounds	25
Fish, pounds	25
Pitted plums, pounds	10
Raisins, pounds	10
Onions, evaporated, pounds	50
Potatoes, evaporated, pounds	50
Coffee, pounds	24
Tea, pounds	5
Milk, condensed, dozen	4
Soap, laundry, bars	5[!]
Matches, packages	60
Soup vegetables, pounds	15
Butter, sealed, cans	60[!]
Tobacco, at discretion	....
Stove, steel	1
Gold pan	1
Granite buckets, 1 nest of	3
Cups	1
Plates (tin)	1
Knives and forks, each	1

Spoons—tea, 1; table	2
Whetstones	1
Coffee pot	1
Pick and handle	1
Saw, hand	1
Saw, whip	1
Hatchet	1
Shovels, ½ spring	2
Nails, pounds	20
Files	3
Drawknife	1
Ax and handle	1
Chisels, 3 sizes	3
Butcher knife	1
Hammer	1
Compass	1
Jack plane	1
Square	1
Yukon sleigh	1
Lash rope, ¼-inch, feet	60
Rope, ½-inch, feet	150
Pitch, pounds	15
Oakum, pounds	10
Frying pans	2

> Woolen clothes.
> Boots and shoes.
> Snow-glasses.

If one is not going to build a boat, the oakum, pitch and tools can be dispensed with. In summer a sled is not necessary.
—*Klondike; The Chicago Record's Book for Gold Seekers*, Chicago, 1897

In 1961 the present owners reopened the Golden North Hotel [Skagway], abandoned some time after its heyday in gold rush times. They announced that they would name a room for any family that would swap Victorian stuff in their attics for the modern furnishings being purchased for the hotel. The townfolk were not above taking advantage of such manifest insanity and hustled down with all the cast-offs they could find from grandpa's day.

Sometime during the big swap the scales fell from their eyes as the hotel took shape as a living and loving museum of Skagway's great days. By then, with their names tacked to the doors, they took pride in making their rooms the most authentic of the period. Framed photographs and ancestral portraits came out of broom closets, as did antique crockery of serious market value. Today, the Golden North Hotel is one of the most delightful anachronisms existing in a world of hotel decor that ranges from Hollywood Arabian Nights to Sanitarium Severe."
—*Inside Passage,* by Bern Keating, New York, Doubleday & Co., Inc., 1976

EAGLE, Eastern Alaska. Reached during the summer by Taylor Highway, 64 miles from the junction with Alaska Highway (Mile 904).

Eagle Historic District covers the first incorporated city in Alaska's interior, 1901. This was the main port of entry to the Yukon during the gold rush and sternwheeler days and was a military, judicial, communication, and transportation center. As a stop on the Trans-Alaska Military Rd. and the northern end of the Valdez-Eagle telegraph, it was a busy place until the gold rush headed for Fairbanks and the railroad took much of the traffic. The town dwindled from a population of some 3,000 to only 28 in 1970. The *Old Mule Barn* is now a museum with guided tours by members of the Historical Society daily, June through Labor Day.

Eagle Historical Society, DOT, Eagle, 99738, maintains the *Roald Amundsen Cabin,* where the explorer stayed after his ship the *Gjoa* was frozen in 1905. From here he cabled that he had successfully navigated the Northwest Passage. Daily tours, June to Labor Day.

FAIRBANKS, Interior District. St. 3, the Alaska-Fairbanks Highway.

Fairbanks is the northern end of the line for the Alaska Railroad and the Richardson Highway; it is the southern end of the Elliott Highway to Livengood and Manley Hot Springs and of the Steese Highway, which runs to the Arctic Circle on the Yukon River and provides a fine view of the midnight sun.

Alaskaland, 1st Ave. and the Chena River, is a 40-acre park which re-creates a typical gold rush settlement. Stop first at the *Visitor Information Center.* There are craft demonstrations and a museum. A compound has native wildlife. The *Gold Rush Village* has authentic log cabins, and the *Palace Saloon* has been restored. Live melodramas play at the *Pantages Theater.* The restored riverboat *Nenana* is now used as a night club and also a private club. NHL.

JUNEAU, Southeastern. On the Gastineau channel, reached by the Alaska Marine Highway daily in summer.

For information and reservations, write Pouch R., Juneau, 99801. Air travel year round.

Joe Juneau and Richard Harris discovered gold here in 1880, starting the first rush from parts south. About 100 miners arrived within months. The mining continued until 1944. In 1900 Juneau became the official territorial capital, although the offices remained in Sitka for six more years.

Chamber of Commerce, 200 N. Franklin, has maps, weather advice, and travel suggestions, including an excellent walking tour with historic sites. The *Red Dog Saloon* still looks as it did in its early days and seems just as popular. A melodrama plays nightly in *Last Chance Basin* on the site of a former gold mine. Daily tours are available for the *Governor's Mansion,* 716 Calhoun, and *Wickersham House,* 213 7th St., the home of Judge James Wickersham, historian and pioneer jurist who established the early courts in the interior. Many artifacts are on display.

St. Nicholas Russian Orthodox Church, 326 5th St., is one of the oldest log structures in the area and the first church built in town. Early icons are of particular interest. Guided tours available in summer season. From here photographers will find an excellent view of Juneau harbor.

Alaska State Museum, in the Subport Area; ask locally for directions, or write Pouch FM-DOT, Juneau, 99811. Museum has an expansive collection of Indian and Eskimo artifacts, dioramas, and craft collections. Exhibits range from the Russian days and gold rush period to modern items. Open May through October.

SITKA, Southeastern. Accessible by air and several times weekly by ferry.

Russian Mission Orphanage, Lincoln and Monastery Sts., built 1842–43 for Bishop Innocent Veniaminov, has been a school, seminary, and onetime residence of the Greek Orthodox bishop of Alaska. Now being restored as part of the Sitka National Park, it will show Russian rural architecture as adapted to the New World, and illustrate the mid-19th-century czarist Russian regime here.

When the building was new, the Russian bishop described it as a mansion, having anticipated quarters far less grand. It was two-story, of squared spruce logs, sheathed in siding, with an iron sheeting roof. Chartered by the czar and built by the Russian-American Company for a cost of 25,000 rubles, eventually it became U.S. property and fell into neglect. Congress bought it in 1972 for the national park; preservation work was begun a year later. When fully restored, the main floor will feature exhibits giving the history of the area; the schoolhouse will be stabilized with its exterior restored to the 19th-century look. NHL.

St. Michael's Russian Orthodox Cathedral, Lincoln St., built under the direction of Bishop Veniaminov in the 1840s, destroyed by fire in 1966, now restored to the original design. NHL. The Sitka Madonna Icon is one of its several treasures to be seen during tourist season or by appointment.

The **Sitka National Historical Park,** 6 miles N, has a **Visitor Center,** Metlakahtla and Lincoln Sts., with interpretive displays, an audiovisual program, and a self-guiding walking trail.

SKAGWAY, Southeastern. On the Skagway-Carcross Highway, also on the White Pass & Yukon narrow-gauge railroad. Reached by air from Juneau, Haines, and Whitehorse year round.

Skagway Historic District and White Pass, head of the Taiya Inlet on Lynn Canal, comprises some 100 structures from the late 1890s. When gold was discovered in the Upper Yukon and the Klondike, the town was the last stop to nowhere and called "the jumping-off place." Still to be seen are the depot, hotels, saloon, and lodge halls of the old days. The old **Federal Court** building is a museum; the population reached about 20,000 at its peak but fell to about 700. NHL.

The **Klondike Gold Rush National Park,** new and innovative, follows the "Trail of '98" from Seattle to Skagway to the Chilkoot and White passes. Canada has preserved the city of Dawson and maintains the Yukon Territory part of the trail. The U.S. National Park Service and Parks Canada, with provincial, state, and local agencies have made a joint effort to reestablish this unusual historic trail which thousands trod hopefully in search of gold. The southern end of the park begins in **Pioneer Square Historic District (Visitor Center),** 117 S. Main, which has been partially restored to its appearance in the late 19th century. Now museums along the route tell the story of the Klondike rush. Restored riverboats at **Carcross, Whitehorse,** and **Dawson** reconstruct the paddlewheel days. In traveling through the Canada portion of the trail, the usual customs and immigration laws are followed. Handguns are prohibited in Canada and must be left with the Skagway Police or Royal Canadian Mounted Police at Carcross or Whitehorse; in the U.S. part of the trail, firearms must be broken down and encased. Visitors entering Skagway from Canada report to U.S. Customs and Immigration.

At the **Visitors Center** in Skagway are exhibits and literature on hiking the Chilkoot Trail, also on the restored or preserved old buildings, **Trail of '98 Museum,** and the **Gold Rush Cemetery,** where Soapy Smith and Frank Reid were buried after their shoot-out. Jefferson Randolph Smith (Soapy) was a con artist, gambler, and roughneck who tried to

establish his image as public benefactor, especially kind to elderly
widows and little children, and, of
course, animals. But the town tired of
his double-dealings and gathered a
vigilante commitee to get rid of him.
Soapy attended the meeting carrying
a rifle. Frank Reid, town surveyor,
challenged the intruder with a pistol.
It wasn't high noon or high midnight, as a scriptwriter might have
ordered it, but both fired and both
died as a result, though Soapy went
to his reward at once and Reid took
several days dying. In true melodrama tradition, Soapy is the villain
nearly everyone remembers, not the
law-abiding Reid, although he was
certainly the better shot in this encounter. A drama of the event is performed in old *Eagle's Hall,*
Broadway, during the "Days of '98
Show."

Remember that all artifacts from
the Klondike gold rush are held to be
of international historical importance and valuable property. Souve-
nir hunting, outside of shops, is not
allowed.

For further information write Superintendent, care of P.O. Box 517,
Skagway, 99840.

Hawaii

Niihau
Kauai
Oahu
Pacific Ocean
Honolulu
Molokai
Maui
Lanai
Kahoolawe
Hawaii
Hilo
200 Miles

HAWAII

Housekeeping at last in two little rooms and a chamber. . . . The clapboards are bare and admit quantities of dust which the trade-winds bring in such fearful clouds, as to suggest the fate of Pompeii. We have three chairs, a table, a bedstead, and a nice little secretary. Dr. Judd has converted the round-topped wooden trunk . . . into a safe for our food, by placing it on stilts set in pans of tar water, which keeps out roaches and ants.
—*Life in the Mission,* by Laura F. Judd, Honolulu, 1828

The further I traveled through the town the better I liked it. Every step revealed a new contrast—disclosed something I was unaccustomed to. In place of the grand mud-colored brown fronts of San Francisco, I saw dwellings built of straw, adobes, and cream-colored pebble-and-shell-conglomerated coral, cut into oblong blocks and laid in cement; also a great number of neat white cottages, with green window-shutters; in place of front yards like billiard-tables with iron fences around them, I saw these homes surrounded by ample yards, thickly clad with green grass, and shaded by tall trees, through whose dense foliage the sun could scarcely penetrate; in place of the customary geranium, calla lily, etc., languishing in dust and general debility, I saw luxurious banks and thickets of flowers, fresh as a meadow after a rain, and glowing. . . .
—*Roughing It,* by Mark Twain, Hartford, Conn., 1872

HAWAII COUNTY.

Known as the Big Island, the Volcano Isle, and Orchid Island, Hawaii is the largest and farthest south of the archipelago.

Hilo, county seat and busy harbor town, has an *Information Center* (Wailoa Center), left off Kamehameha Highway onto Pauahi, then 1 block to entrance, for literature, maps, and exhibits. The *Lyman Mission House & Museum,* 276 Haili St., in downtown Hilo, was built in 1839 and has been restored. A museum has Hawaiian historical items and an outstanding volcanic and mineral collection. The Reverend David Lyman and his wife were missionaries to Hawaii in the 1830s. The house is constructed of hand-hewn planks.

City of Refuge National Historic Park, Kailua-Kona vicinity, St. 16, on the SW coast, comprises 180 acres, being restored to the look of the late 18th century. A *Visitor Center* provides a marked walking tour, with taped messages along the way. Take heed of the warnings about loose stones, high waves, and falling coconuts. The park, established in 1961, is open all year. The refuge, built about 1500, is actually located on a 6-acre shelf of ancient lava that dips into the Pacific and is almost square; the ocean forms two sides, and a great wall extends along the other two sides. There were at least five other refuges on the island, but only this one has remained nearly intact. Here those who sought asylum for any reason—lawbreaking or defeat in war— were made welcome. The area including the palace grounds and villages on the inland side of the Great Wall, at the head of Honaunau Bay and to the south, is now administered and protected by the U.S. Department of the Interior. Overnight camping is not allowed, but information on camping elsewhere is available from the *Hawaii Visitors Bureau,* with offices in Hilo, Honolulu, Wailuku, Lihue, and San Francisco, 209 Post St., 94108.

Also in the Kailua-Kona vicinity: *Hulihee Palace,* Alii Drive, St. 182, a beautifully furnished 1838 summer residence for royalty, stuccoed lava rock, two stories, with a rear full-length two-story balustraded gallery. It has been remodeled. *Mokuaikaua Church,* Alii Drive, is the oldest church in the islands and was designed by pioneer missionary Asa Thornton. 1837. Lava Rock and Ohia wood with a New England–style steeple. *King Kamehameha's Residence,* at the water's edge on the grounds of the hotel named for the king, is being restored. Twice daily free walking tours meet on the grounds. Ask at the hotel. The tours include the Ahuena Heiau site where the king spent his last years.

HONOLULU COUNTY, OAHU.

Iolani Palace, 364 S. King St., has been carefully restored over a number of years and is just as carefully furnished with only historically accurate items, following an almost worldwide search for original pieces. It is Italianate villa, Italian Renaissance Revival, and Second Empire. The interior has elegant woodwork in rare woods, including Koa, Kamani, Kou, and Ohia. It was built in 1879–82 and served as the residence of the last two Hawaiian royal rulers, King Kalahaua and his sister who succeeded him, Queen Liliuokalani. She was a poet and composer ("Aloha Oe" was her work) and interested in welfare.

The cornerstone was laid actually on December 31, 1879; the king and future queen moved in, in 1882. And in August 1882, Kalahaua held his first big party in the palace—it was a luncheon for members of the legislature after their 1882 session, and was described as "informal and jolly," as it must have been, inasmuch as the palace furniture had not yet arrived from Boston. When Kalahaua died in 1891, his sister succeeded him but reigned only two years when she was deposed and a provisional government took over. Queen Liliuokalani was imprisoned for some months in the palace before she formally abdicated the throne. (In 1977 I stood in the room where the queen had been imprisoned; workmen were busily restoring it and there was clutter and dust in the air, but the view was magnificent, the chamber was spacious and high-ceilinged, and even a claustrophobe would have chosen this of all possible "prisons.")

The main hallway on the first floor was used as an informal reception room. On the right is the beautifully restored Throne Room. The state dining room across the hallway was used as the Senate Chamber when the building was occupied by the Republic of Hawaii. (The Throne Room was used by the House of Representatives.)

On the second floor, the bedroom of King Kalahaua was used in recent years as the governor's private office and has now been restored. The room, which faces *Kawaiahao Church,* was the queen's "prison," and later served as an office for the lieutenant governor. (In Hawaii the usual directions are seldom used. Mauka means toward the mountain; makai, toward the sea.) The upper hallway served as a sitting room for the royal occupants.

The basement originally held the chamberlain's apartment, a billiard room, servants' quarters, kitchen and pantry, the king's workshop, and recreation quarters where Liliuokalani held a luau shortly before the revolution.

The original woodwork, much of which was white cedar from Port Orford, Oregon, was considerably damaged by time and termites. All of it was removed, stripped, repaired, and restored wherever possible. Herman Bishoff, in charge of the restoration, designed special knives for cutting the many different types of molding. The damaged pieces were so skillfully replaced and blended with the original that it is almost impossible to tell where repairs have been made.

The decorative iron railings of the upper lanais (verandas) were first installed in 1881 at a cost of $5.25 per lineal foot by the Honolulu Iron Works Company. During the recent restorations, broken railing sections were sent to a patternmaker on the mainland, where a mold was made, and new sections welded into place. Then all was sandblasted, primed, and painted so that a perfect railing exists today.

Monarchy Promenade is a walking tour of the once royal area of Honolulu which takes in 18 sites, most of which are fairly near Iolani Palace. A brochure detailing this tour is published by the Department of Land and Natural Resources, Division of State Parks. *Old Honolulu: A Guide to Oahu's Historic Buildings* has been issued by the Historic Buildings Task Force. It is available at the State Archives, near the palace, and elsewhere. Agnes Conrad, one of the editors of *Old Honolulu,* is state archivist.

The Promenade begins at the *Mission Houses Museum* on King St. The original company of missionaries from New England was made up of six young couples, one older couple with five children, and three Hawaiian boys who had attended school in Connecticut. They arrived in 1820. Eleven more companies came in the next 28 years. Twenty-two mission stations were spread throughout the islands. The first stop is at the *Frame House* of 1821 built from precut wooden materials that arrived by sailing ship around the Horn from Boston. In the 1820s the mission families each occupied a room in the mission house, which also served as headquarters for annual meetings. The *Printing House,* 1841, is a two-room coral structure. There was a secondhand Ramage press in the original office. A replica is on display today. *Chamberlain House,* 1831, was the home and storehouse of Levi Chamberlain, business agent for the mission. The *Mission Cemetery* was consecrated in 1823 when the young son of the Reverend and Mrs. Hiram Bingham was buried. Graves of early missionaries and their families are here.

Kawaiahao Church, 957 Punchbowl St., in 1842 replaced four grass houses of worship, each growing larger than the one before. Hiram Bingham designed the New England–style structure. Many national ceremonies have taken place here.

Adobe Schoolhouse, in the back corner of the church grounds, was built by the mission for Hawaiian children, in 1835. *Kawaiahao Cemetery,* near the church, on Punchbowl, has the tomb of William Charles Lunalilo, who reigned as king for a year and more and died in 1874, asking to be buried here rather than at the *Royal Mausoleum* at Nuuanu.

Also on the walking tour are the *Honolulu Hale (City Hall), State Library, State Office Building, statue of Kamehameha I,* the *Royal Tomb* of 1824, on the Diamond Head side of the palace grounds, a pavilion which was the coronation stand in 1883, Iolani Barracks, 1871, built for the

Royal Household Guard, and the Hawaii State Archives: those who are seriously interested in the history of the island and its preservation should step into the modern building behind the enormous banyan tree on the palace grounds and see the old photographs on display in the reception area. If you are lucky enough to catch her at a free moment, say hello to Ms. Conrad, the state archivist. She is in charge of a peerless collection of Hawaiian documents, relics, photographs, and histories which are available to writers, historians, and genealogists. She also has an amazing store of information in her head and if (improbably) she cannot answer your question, she will know who can.

The walking tour continues to the *State Capitol, Our Lady of Peace Cathedral* (1843), the *Fort* of 1817, *St. Andrew's Cathedral* (1867), and *Washington Place* (1846), which is of particular interest to the romantically inclined. This lovely old house with its graceful white columns was built by an American sea captain, John Dominis, who brought his wife and son to settle in the Islands in 1837. They moved into the dwelling in 1846 and Dominis sailed for China on a trading voyage, but the ship was never heard from again. American Commissioner Anthony Ten Eyck rented a suite of rooms in the house and named the place for George Washington, on February 22, 1848. The name was formally proclaimed by the king. In 1862 John Owen Dominis, son of the missing captain, married Lydia K. P. Kapaakea, who became Queen Liliuokalani. After her imprisonment at the palace, the queen was allowed to come here to live and occupied the house until her death in 1917. Not open to the public, but may be viewed through the iron fence.

The last stop on the walking tour is the *Falls of Clyde* at Pier 5 near *Aloha Tower*. This is one of the last surviving square-rigged merchant sailing ships. At the early part of this century she was still engaged in trade in Hawaiian waters. In 1963 the ship was about to be sunk for a breakwater in the Columbia River, when the people of Hawaii came to the rescue, raising enough money to have her towed to Hawaii and restored. The figurehead, a replica, was made in the same shop in Scotland which turned out the original. The ship is now owned by the Bishop Museum and is open as a maritime museum.

Merchant St. Historic District takes in four square blocks in downtown Honolulu's commercial section, with many mid-19th-century structures. The *Bishop Estate Building,* 71–77 Merchant St., is a fine example of Richardson Romanesque. Princess Bernice Pauahi, who inherited the vast estate of the Kamehameha family, married Charles Reed Bishop, a banker, in 1850. When she died in 1884, a trust was set up and a museum erected in her honor. Offices for all this were in the dark gray lava stone building here, which stood next door to the Bishop bank. The lava came from Kamehameha quarries. The estate has long since moved on, but the building still stands. *Bishop Museum Complex,* 1355 Kalihi St., is outstanding. All three buildings are Richardson Romanesque; the collections are worth a lingering visit.

There has seldom been a place where maps and guides are so easy to come by—or sites so easy to reach, and with superb scenery all along the way—as in Honolulu. Chart your own course, but don't miss *Queen Emma's Summer Home,* 2913 Pali Highway, built about 1848, with Greek Revival elements. Owned by Queen Emma, wife of Kamehameha IV, it was used as a summer home until her death in 1888. There is a museum.

Chinatown Historic District is near the downtown waterfront, bounded roughly by Beretania St., Nuuanu Stream, and the harbor.

KAUAI COUNTY.

Waioli Mission District, off St. 56, near the village of Hanalei, is a complex of missionary structures, including old and new Waioli Hu'ia churches, the main mission house, and cottages. This was the religious, educational, social, agricultural, and commercial center of Hanalei from the 19th century into the 20th. The buildings are a mixture of early missionary Hawaiian, Colonial, and even Gothic, but—like nearly everything in Hawaii except the population problem—they come out looking great.

While on Kauai, aptly named the "Garden Island," for its greenery and flowers, don't miss the *Kauai Museum,* in Lihue Shopping Center, which has a historical exhibit and a color film. Another museum is at Hanalei, on the north coast.

MAUI COUNTY.

Lahaina Historic District, W side of the island on St. 30. The seaport contains many frame structures from the mid-19th century when the settlement was developed by missionaries and by those concerned with the whaling industry. The first legislature met here in 1841 when Lahaina was made capital of the island. The *County of Maui Historic Commission* has issued a walking tour brochure which not only tells you where to go but is worth saving for its easy-to-read and comprehensive summary of Mauian history, and old prints. To quote from the introduction:

"A man born in 1800 would have seen the port rise and fall. As a baby, he might have seen the war fleet of the unifying king, Kamehameha I, in Lahaina roads—a mile-long flotilla of platformed double canoes and small schooners. As a young man, he could have watched whalermen come ashore under a black flag, hot to draw missionary blood. In the spring and fall of 1846, he could have counted almost five hundred ships beating their way up the roads to anchor. He would have seen Lahaina challenge the far bigger town of Honolulu for economic leadership, and become at the same time the educational and political capital of the kingdom."

Thus in 1850 Lahaina was the capital, but in the 1860s the Pacific whaling business declined because petroleum was becoming available on the mainland. Again to quote the poet of the Maui Historic Commission, whoever he/she may be: "They are all gone now, the kings and their counselors, the whaling masters and the harpooners and the try-pot men, the ship-chandlers, grogshop keepers, seamen's chaplains, and sharks. Only the whales remain, coming down each mating season to leap and frolic and spout in the roads. It is as if the whaling part of the town is waiting for the time foretold on a stone in the Seamen's Cemetery:

When He who all commands
Shall give to call life's crew together
The words to pipe all hands.

"History has been gentle with Lahaina since the whalers went away. Sugar gave the town a new living. Other men came to plant their faiths and families—Roman Catholics, Episcopalians. Mormons, Buddhists, Westerners of all sorts, Chinese, Japanese, Filipinos. Already some of their story is buried, and archeology will never dig it all up. But enough remains along the streets of Lahaina to give you a sense of two hundred years of history."

Aloha! Now *that's* a brochure! The *Lahaina Restoration Foundation* can be reached for further information at P.O. Box 338, Lahaina, Maui, 96761. Another fine pamphlet, "The Story of Lahaina," is available for a small fee from the **Friends of Lahaina Restoration,** a nonprofit organization.

The walking tour can begin at an ancient banyan tree on Front St., near the harbor. The tree was planted in 1873 to mark the 50th anniversary of Protestant missionary work here and now is more than 60 feet high. The **Pioneer Hotel,** across the street, has been remodeled, but its turn-of-the-century décor has been preserved. Rules for guests, made out in 1901, are still posted in bedchambers.

Maui Visitor Information Center is on Front St., next to the **Baldwin House.** The house, which was the home of Protestant medical missionary Dwight Baldwin and his family from the mid-1830s to the late 1860s, has served as a medical office, missionary center, seamen's chapel, Christian reading rooms, and private dwelling. The Baldwins cultivated not only souls but a garden of native and imported plants: kukui, kou, banana, guava, pomegranate, grapes, and pineapples. House and grounds are restored and open as a museum.

The bark **Carthaginian** has been restored as a maritime museum and is open daily. Called "a floating museum of whaling," it graces the harbor.

Canada

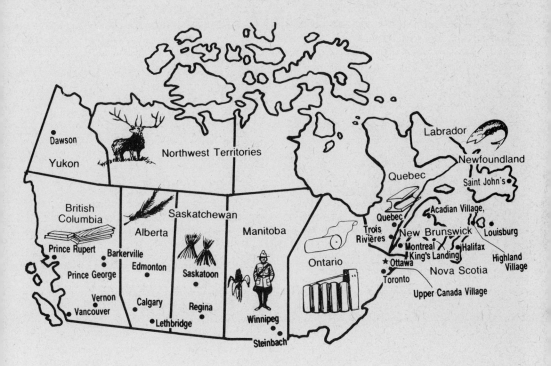

Dawson
Yukon
Northwest Territories
Labrador
Newfoundland
Quebec
Saint John's
British Columbia
Saskatchewan
Alberta
Manitoba
Quebec
Acadian Village,
New Brunswick
Louisburg
Prince Rupert
Barkerville
Trois Rivières
Montreal
Halifax
Prince George
Edmonton
Saskatoon
King's Landing
Highland Village
Ontario
Vernon
Calgary
Regina
Ottawa
Nova Scotia
Vancouver
Lethbridge
Winnipeg
Toronto
Upper Canada Village
Steinbach

CANADA

... The province of Upper Canada is daily receiving a vigorous and healthy population into her bosom.... the fertility of these countries must make a hungry labourer's mouth water,—to think of the plenty of Indian corn, of wheat, oats, barley, &c., all raised on a virgin soil, with no labour but the sowing, after the necessary preliminaries of cutting down the trees or barking them are finished....

The industrious labourer who struggles hard against poverty, the skilful carpenter or shoe-maker, and others of the same class, may, by industry and perseverance, provide for their families in Canada.... But there is *one* condition.... *sobriety;* which everywhere is an essential, but in North America it is all in all. In a country where the cheapness of ardent spirits, the very general want of some comfortable beverage such as beer, and the contagion of bad example, are all combined, it is indispensable that the emigrant arm himself with every possible precaution....
　　　—*The Penny Magazine of the Society for the Diffusion of Useful Knowledge,*
　　　　　　　　　　　　　　　　　　　　　London, 1832

When the sarcastic Voltaire sneered at the New France which was lost to Louis XV through the frivolous influence of a Pompadour and the ignorant indifference of the French court, he thought to gratify the vanity of his monarch by congratulating him upon getting rid of "those 1500 leagues of snow." This seems to have been the text which some modern tourists have taken for their descriptions of Canada; and it would be very amusing to collect such writings of early travelers, and to read them in January in Winnipeg, Toronto, Kingston, Montreal, Quebec, or Halifax, in face of the populations of these cities enjoying the gay delights of the snow in complete unconsciousness of the misery of their existence.
　　　—*Canada as a Winter Resort,* by W. George Beers, New York, 1885

ALBERTA PROVINCE

CALGARY, Primary Highway 2, 1A.

Heritage Park, 1½ miles W off Highway 2, S via Heritage Drive to the Glenmore Reservoir, contains an authentic turn-of-the-century village on a 60-acre site with a general store, pioneer farm machinery, smithy, trading post, a paddlewheel steamer, horse-drawn streetcar, a train, and the 1898 *Canmore Opera House,* built of pine logs, which has variety shows in summer season, daily except Mondays. Park is open daily mid-June through September. On weekends from the end of May to mid-June.

The *Calgary Stampede,* a one-of-a-kind experience no matter how many imitations exist, takes place in July. The *Indian Village* on the Bow River, which has been a permanent part of the Stampede since 1912, has been enlarged. Indians in traditional dress exhibit arts and crafts. The annual stampede is a nine-day affair opening with a parade and with rodeo, chuckwagon races, horse racing, and many other happenings (including a Chicken Dance competition) reviving the cowpunching times. *Victoria Park* and *Confederation Park* are used for various events.

BRITISH COLUMBIA

BARKERVILLE HISTORICAL PARK, Highway 97, 1, or 16.

This historic gold-rush town was once larger than any other city north of San Francisco. Billy Barker was a Cornishman who was thought a fool by the other miners for sinking his shaft below Fraser Canyon and not in the gold-rich fields, actually named Richfield, above the canyon in the summer of 1862. But Barker found what he was looking for at 52 feet below the surface and made $1,000 in 48 hours, soon establishing both the Barker Company and a new site for a gold rush. Like U.S. gold towns, Barkerville, in the Cariboo, was a scattering of log shanties, saloons, and false-front stores, on stilts above one muddy street. Boots cost $50 a pair and a dance with a hurdy-gurdy girl was ten dollars. The town burned in September 1868, but was rebuilt. The price of gold was falling and Barkerville was on the decline. Restoration began in 1958 when only 15 of some 120 original buildings remained. Houses, hotels, saloons, churches, a theater, and shops are being reconstructed to the look of 1869–85.

Ready to visit are *Kelly's Saloon,* *Wellington Moses' Barbershop, Sing Kee's Store,* the *Wake-Up-Jake Cafe,* the *Barkerville Hotel,* the *El Dorado Mine,* and you can ride the *Barkerville Stagecoach.* At *Richfield Courthouse,* a mile up Cariboo Rd., an actor portrays Judge Begbie, who once represented law and order in the area. The *Theatre Royal* puts on melodrama and other shows twice daily except Fridays from the end of June to Labor Day. The park is open all year.

VANCOUVER, Highways 1, 99, 7A.
Gastown, Water St. between Carrall and Abbott Sts., is a restored area of early Vancouver, dating back to the 1880s. Hotels, restaurants, and shops.

VERNON, Highway 97.
O'Keefe Historic Ranch, 8 miles N of town on Highway 97, is a restoration complex of an early ranch settlement with a ranchhouse, general store, post office, blacksmith shop, and *St. Ann's Catholic Church,* the oldest in the interior of British Columbia. Guided tours. Open from spring to early November.

MANITOBA

STEINBACH, Highway 12.

The *Mennonite Village Museum,* just N of town on Highway 12, is a replica of an early Mennonite community with buildings moved to the site and furnished authentically in 18th- and 19th-century articles. A log house built in 1876, a church-school-house, blacksmith shop, and general store are part of the village. There also are outbuildings and equipment displays, and a museum. Open daily in May and June; hours vary in July and August. *Pioneer Days* is an annual event in late July with reenactments and Mennonite food.

NEW BRUNSWICK

ACADIAN VILLAGE, at North River, Rt. 11, between Caraquet and Grand Anse.

The reconstructed village on 3,000 acres opened in May 1977. It reflects the period of 1780 to 1880 when returned Acadians were beginning a new life here. The oldest house dates back to 1797 and comes from Neguac; other houses have been moved from Fredericton and Edmundston and other parts of New Brunswick. The Acadians, who were expelled by the British in 1755 because they refused to swear allegiance to the new government which had taken over Acadie, the name France gave to her Atlantic seaboard possessions, went to Louisiana and other parts of the continent, but some found their way back after a few years. The historical site, open daily during the summer, is a provincial government development, under the jurisdiction of the Historical Resources Administration of the Education Department, and shows how poor but persevering people made a good life with very little. They became experts at reclaiming land from the sea in the swampy lowlands and built a unique canal system that drained the marshes. The old dikes on the Rivière-du-Nord still are in existence. The hay grown in the marshes is kept dry on high platforms. Old time skills are demonstrated, including spinning, weaving, wool-carding, cedar shingle production, soap- and candlemaking, and the drying and barreling of cod. Many of the workers are in costume.

Among the pioneer structures are dwellings, a general store, a tavern, a school, a blacksmith's shop, a reproduced 1827 bridge, and a replica of an 1831 chapel. The *Robin, Jones and Whitman Company Warehouse* here was brought from Caraquet, where it was built about 1855. The company traded food supplies and fishing equipment to the Acadians for their catch and paid with coupons redeemable only at their company store. The *James Blackhall House* (built between 1822 and 1840) was the home of the comparatively well-off Scotsman who served as postmaster, justice of the peace, school trustee, and customs officer. The *Jean-Baltazar Martin House,* built in 1783, is the oldest and has an earthen floor. Ten other homes are named for their builders. *Louis Poirier's* house was a pub where wine and rum were the most popular buys to drink on the premises or take out. The school, moved from Chockpish, in Kent County, had 32 students when it opened in 1879. All furnishings in the village are handmade by the Acadians, collected from various parts of the province and repaired. Over 40 buildings were brought to the site and restored.

The restoration work here was particularly difficult because not a great deal was known about the period represented. Teams of researchers worked on antiques, textiles, archive records, and the skills developed, such as the making of shingles, which helped this deprived group of people not only survive but create a tradition. And it all began when earthbanks and *aboiteaux* were discovered not far from Rt. 11, an ideal location for a restoration based on the people who reclaimed a swamp.

KING'S LANDING, on the Trans-Canada Highway, about 23 miles W of New Brunswick's capital, Fredericton, near Prince William.

The *Historical Settlement* is a village of some 60 restored buildings on the St. John River, a 300-acre site. The 19th-century structures have been authentically furnished for the period; the staff wears period costumes.

The put-together settlement has been assembled to depict life during the 1790–1870 period when the province was prosperous and there was brisk trade on the St. John River. The land was first granted to the King's American Dragoons after the Revolutionary War. Many Loyalists and British settled here. But, as in the western U.S., the arrival of the railroad diminished river traffic and set back the local economy. Although the village is fictional, daily life is enacted as it might have been, with staff members shoeing horses, weaving, quilting, making soap, dipping candles, tilling the land, and taking care of farm animals.

From the *Thomas Jones House* on the hill, the home of one of the mill owners, to the six-sided outhouse with four seats, everything is in keeping with the past: dirt paths and horse-drawn wagons, no telephones, no electric equipment. The *King's Head Inn* is a restoration of an 1855 coaching inn complete to the hot meat pie. Melodrama plays at the *Morehouse Theatre* and the villain gets hit with enough peanuts to satisfy even a visitor from Plains, Georgia. The village is open May to October, 10 A.M. to 7 P.M.

NOVA SCOTIA

HIGHLAND VILLAGE, at Iona, Cape Breton.

This village occupies a 60-acre site, with nine buildings furnished at present, of the 1875–1900 period. The growing collection of restored and staffed structures will depict the history of the Scottish settlers in Nova Scotia. This is one of the few Gaelic-speaking regions remaining in the area; the post office has identifications in English, French, and Gaelic.

Iona was settled in 1802 by the MacNeil family from Barra in the Outer Hebrides and was called Saundrie, but was renamed in 1873 for the Inner Hebrides Island, Iona, where many Scottish chieftains, kings, and a sixth-century monk are buried. The village now has a dwelling, school, forge, carding mill, and store. An annual *Highland Village Day* is held in August with Gaelic songs, piping, Scottish fiddling and dancing, and a stage presentation.

LOUISBURG, on Cape Breton Island.

Originally Louisburg was an enclosed town begun by the French in 1720 to guard their fishing fleets and the mouth of the St. Lawrence River. The *Fortress of Louisburg National Historic Par*k is one of the most ambitious reconstructions in North America; one-fifth of the town of 1745 will be rebuilt as it was in the days when it was twice captured by New Englanders, and then by the British in 1758, and razed in 1760 to prevent its becoming strong again. Although forts are not being considered in this volume, Louisburg was as much a city as a fort. Residents made fine French furniture and hand costumes. In the rich rooms once occupied by the governor and called the *Governor's Wing* of the *King's Bastion Barracks* is the largest collection of period French furniture on this continent. In reconstructing the town, experts had to search several hundred thousand documents for details of architecture, furnishings, and life style.

The residents of Louisburg were experts at masonry, hand-forged hinges and latches, and woodworking as well as clothing production. Today nails are again forged in the Louisburg smithy. To date the project has taken more than 16 years and some $25 million, but even the food made in iron pots in the fireplace is authentic (turnips *can* be tasty). Because chickens of the 18th century (like Americans) were smaller and wirier, the experts at Louisburg are trying to breed a new hybrid to resemble the old. As for the cost of perfection, when the original Louisburg was in production even the usually prodigal Louis XV complained that he expected to see its 10-foot-thick walls looming over the horizon of France.

At one end of the restoration is a reception center with displays interpreting the work of historians, archaeologists, and craftsmen. Open mid-May to mid-October.

ONTARIO

TORONTO, Highways 400, 401.

Black Creek Pioneer Village, 18 miles NW from Toronto City Hall, 1000 Murray Ross Pkwy. in Downsview. This is a re-created town representing rural life in Ontario of the early 19th century. Thirty buildings have been restored, including the usual general store, church, smith, printing office, town hall, and a firehouse. But all have individual touches and furnishings. The living museum depicts how it was in south-central Ontario during three-quarters of a century before the Canadian Confederation in 1867. Homespun-clad villagers perform the old tasks. There are wooden sidewalks on Queen St. The *Laskay Emporium,* in midtown, has all the usual goods from patent medicines to china, along with mouth-watering fudge and an enormous meat cleaver, and fancy parasols hanging in the window to entice customers.

Across the street the *Daniel Stong Farm* is on the original site. Stong was a Pennsylvanian who came to Canada as a boy in 1800. His house of 1816 is a three-room hewn-timber cabin with an open fireplace for heat and cooking. He added the smokehouse, pigsty, chicken house, and barn; and in 1832 he built a two-story, seven-room house with a fancy box-stove imported from Scotland.

Halfway House Inn, a former stagecoach stop, has a licensed dining room with waitresses in homespun costume.

The *Printing Office* and *Weaver's Shop* are lodged in the former *Temperance Hall,* Mill Rd. and Maple Ave. In the printing office are the actual presses that once printed newspapers for many small Ontario towns; two still are used for notices and posters. The weavers produce carpets and bedspreads for village use.

The *Dalziel Earn Log Barn,* like the Stong farm, is an original Black Creek structure. Other buildings were moved to form the village, which opened in 1960.

The *Firehouse* has a hand-pulled and hand-pumped fire wagon from 1837 which used to head for fires with a man on foot and his trumpet heralding the way. The *Gunsmith's Store* has flintlock rifles and powder horns. *Burwick House,* a country gentleman's place, has Chippendale and Spode.

Roblin's Mill, powered by an enormous water wheel, produces whole-wheat flour which is on sale at Laskay's Emporium. The *One-Room Schoolhouse* on Mill Rd. has a cast-iron stove in the rear and a dunce cap at the front where all pupils could see the unfortunate dummy-for-a-day. In *Daniel Flynn's House,* "Mrs. Flynn" dips candles on the iron stove.

The village is open daily, with special weekend events related to the seasons. In May there are sheep shearing, spinning, harrowing, seeding, and gunsmithing. In June there is baking, etc. The *Village Pioneer Program* allows outsiders to learn by taking part in the settlement life and work. For information or reservations called Black Creek Village at 661-6600.

UPPER CANADA VILLAGE, on the banks of the St. Lawrence between Kingston and Cornwall, 7 miles NE of Morrisburg on Highway 2.

There was a decisive battle in the War of 1812 on the site of Crysler Farm where the village now stands. More than 40 buildings have been relocated here and furnished with authentic period items. Costumed workers carry on the old-time crafts, making cabinets, baking bread, dipping candles, spinning, weaving, running a blacksmith shop or an ancient sawmill, or making cheese. Many of the products are for sale.

A log cabin of 1795 houses sheep; an 1800 barn has oxen. *Cook's Tavern* from 1810, used as headquarters by invading American troops, was destroyed during the Battle of Crysler Farm but is rebuilt and serves food and drink as in the beginning. *Willard's Hotel* in midtown is a restored inn which also serves meals. There also are an 1850 tollgate, a stagecoach and an oxcart, and boardwalks for strollers. The St. Lawrence Parks Commission manages the village, which is open daily from mid-May to mid-October.

QUEBEC

MONTREAL, Highways 2, 11. On the St. Lawrence and Ottawa rivers.

Old Montreal, bounded by McGill, Berri, and Notre Dame Sts. and the river. The small settlement of Ville Marie was founded here in 1642; no

The historic section of Trois-Rivières, at the confluence of the St. Maurice and St. Lawrence Rivers, 75 miles from Quebec city. Trois-Rivières, founded in 1634, is one of Canada's oldest cities. (Courtesy of Air Canada)

original buildings remain, but sites are marked by plaques. The old city with its cobblestone streets has been refurbished and preserved. The recommended time for the complete tour is one day; it takes in 2 miles. The *Montreal Convention and Visitors Bureau,* 1270 Sherbrooke St. W. (842-6684), has historical and practical information and illustrated brochures with walking tours. They recommend leaving from the Champ-de-Mars Metro station. There are commemorative plaques all along the way. Group tours are held each Wednesday morning during summer months, weather permitting. For information on these call the *Montreal Museum of Fine Arts,* 866-1505.

Among highlights the *Sulpician Seminary,* on the Place d'Armes, the oldest building in the city, opened in 1685. Its famous wooden clock may be seen through the iron gate and is considered the oldest of its kind in America, although the wooden works stopped long ago and electrical movement was added in 1966. *Notre Dame,* 116 Notre Dame St. W., opened in 1829, to replace a parish church which stood across the street, is considered one of the most beautiful churches in America. The stained-glass windows on the ground floor depict special events of the early days of the colony rather than religious scenes. *Notre-Dame-de-Bonsecours Church,* St. Paul St. (1772), is the oldest church still standing in the city. It is called the "Sailors' Chapel," and many seamen left model ships as tokens of faith. You may climb to a lookout just under the statue of Our Lady for a fine view of the harbor.

QUEBEC, Expressway 440.

Place Royale, Lower Town along the St. Lawrence Riverfront, is a continuing restoration of the 17th- and 18th-century structures. *Information Center* at *Le Picard House,* Saint-Pierre St. During 1970 the Department of Cultural Affairs began the restoration of 15 houses and plans to finish 60 others in this area which is considered the cradle of French civilization in America. In 1608 Samuel de Champlain built his fortified "Habitation" here; it is the oldest French building remaining on its original site in America.

Notre Dame des Victoires was built in 1688 on the site of Champlain's trading post, which was erected 12 years before the Pilgrims set foot on the shores of Massachusetts. *Chevalier House* is furnished in period; it is actually three houses joined: the structure at the corner of Cul-de-Sac and Notre-Dame Sts. was rebuilt in 1959; next to it is one from the 17th century, and altogether the curving building made up the 1752 home for merchant Jean-Baptiste Chevalier. Chevalier died in France about 1763, it is believed, and the house was bought at auction by Jean-Louis Frémont, merchant, who was the grandfather of John Charles Frémont, of pathfinding fame in the U.S., who twice ran unsuccessfully for President. The *Hazeur House,* built in 1684 and 1685, will be restored. It was the finest house in the old town; François Hazeur was a very important merchant who eventually lost his fortune, partially because the sawmill industry and porpoise oil trade in which he invested heavily were unsuccessful for him. He was nearly broke when he died in Quebec in 1708.

There are many other interesting houses open to the public, and guided tours are available. *Le Maison des Vins,* 1 Place Royale, also has guided tours for the underground wine vaults, which date from 1689, and winetasting.

The *Break-neck Stairs* are a challenge, but you can also take a cable car to Place Royale and you can tour it by foot or by calèche. Opposite Sous-le-Fort St., at the foot of the Stairs, is the house built for Louis Joliet in 1684. He was born in Quebec in 1645; in 1672 Governor Frontenac sent Joliet and Father Jacques Marquette on a voyage which resulted in their discovery of the Mississippi River. The restored house has the entrance to the elevator which ascends the cliff to Dufferin Terrace in Upper Town. To descend, catch the elevator in front of the Château Frontenac.

Information centers are at the *Department of Tourism,* 12 Sainte-Anne St., 643-2280; *Urban Community Tourism and Convention Service,* 60 d'Auteuil St., (418) 692-2471; U.S. Consulate, 1 Sainte-Genevieve St., 692-2095.

Chevalier House, Quebec. (Ministère des Affaires Culturelles du Québec)

YUKON TERRITORY

DAWSON

Served by regular air lines and bus from Whitehorse, Dawson is on the Klondike Highway, 330 miles N of Whitehorse and 932 miles N of Vancouver. For details write the *Yukon Department of Tourism and Information,* Box 2703, Whitehorse, Yukon, YIA 2C6. Also recommended is *Milepost,* a travel guide published annually describing in detail the sometime perilous routes in Alaska, the Yukon, British Columbia, the Northwest Territories, and Alberta, by road, ship, and air. Write *Milepost,* Alaska Northwest Publishing Co., Box 4-EEE, Anchorage, Alaska, 99509. National Park Service and Parks Canada brochures also print warnings and advice on hiking the trails, customs, guns, and animals.

But in Dawson the perils and wildlife may all be in the restored saloons, as it is once again becoming a boom town, at least in tourism, as it once was in gold seekers. The *Palace Grand Theatre* has reopened, and you may be lucky enough to get a box seat for *The Gaslight Follies,* a musical based on Klondike days.

The town called "The City of Gold" had its diamond jubilee in 1977, but as an important stop on the new "Trail of '98" it will be lively every summer. Discovery Days is an annual affair with parades, games, and other sports, and with cancan girls high-stepping long into the night with honky-tonk piano players tinnily thumping until dawn. This is in August, midmonth, when the nights are short. Homecoming Weekend is in early September, when former Dawsonites have salmon barbecues (75 years ago most Dawsonites were U.S. citizens), but even if you don't qualify as a homecomer there are many sites to see or try out: *Robert Service's Cabin* is a heritage site, the old sternwheeler *Keno* can be viewed, and *Diamond Tooth Gertie's Gambling Hall* has a roulette wheel still in business. *Minto Park* has old locomotives; *Dawson Museum* has many relics of pioneer times.

Also you can pan for gold and keep any you find; or bus to the Midnight Dome to see the midnight sun in June; or visit nearby Mooseride, by boat, where old river steamers are beached.